T0373222

LOEB CLASSICAL LIBRARY
FOUNDED BY JAMES LOEB 1911

EDITED BY
JEFFREY HENDERSON

PHILOSTRATUS

APOLLONIUS OF TYANA

I

LCL 16

PHILOSTRATUS

THE LIFE OF APOLLONIUS OF TYANA

BOOKS I–IV

EDITED AND TRANSLATED BY
CHRISTOPHER P. JONES

HARVARD UNIVERSITY PRESS
CAMBRIDGE, MASSACHUSETTS
LONDON, ENGLAND
2005

First published 2005
Revised 2012

Library of Congress Control Number 2004060863
CIP data available from the Library of Congress

ISBN 978-0-674-99613-7

Composed in ZephGreek and ZephText by
Technologies 'N Typography, Merrimac, Massachusetts.
Printed on acid-free paper and bound by
The Maple-Vail Book Manufacturing Group

CONTENTS

ACKNOWLEDGMENTS

I have a large debt of thanks. Glen Bowersock, who edited and annotated my Penguin translation of this work thirty-five years ago, has again helped me in many ways with this. Tomas Hägg first told me about John Jackson's marginalia in Conybeare's Loeb translation, and Robert Parker, the owner of Jackson's copy, kindly lent it to me. Peter Grossardt also gave me much useful advice. I also thank my student assistants, Bronwen Everill, Richard Short, and especially Matthew Polk and George Tsiatis. Ivy Livingston has solved many word-processing problems. I am very grateful to the Department of the Classics at Harvard and its Chair, Richard Thomas, for generous financial support.

INTRODUCTION

Philostratus, sometimes called "the Elder" or "of Athens," was born in the later second century and died about the middle of the third. He was of a well connected Athenian family that had particular links with the island of Lemnos, which even at this date still formed part of Athens's possessions. By profession, he was a "sophist" in the sense that this word developed particularly in the Roman period. That is, he was a public speaker of a very special kind, specializing in the type of speech called a "declamation" (*meletē*) that drew its subjects either from imagination or very loosely from history of the classical period. The sophists also employed their skills in real life, on embassies, when delivering speeches to visiting dignitaries, and on other occasions. Some also rose to high positions in the imperial administration. Many, including Philostratus, were active as authors in a variety of genres: poetry, history, handbooks on oratory or on literary subjects such as the art of letter-writing.

Philostratus appears to have received his sophistic education largely or wholly in Athens. Though he is not known to have held a position as a Roman administrator, he was very intimately connected with imperial circles. One of his teachers, Antipater of Hierapolis, became head of the Greek correspondence (*ab epistulis Graecis*) under Septimius Severus (emperor 193–211) and teacher of rhetoric to the two princes, Caracalla and Geta. At some stage Philostratus himself entered the literary circle of the princes' mother, Julia Domna, and from this position was very close to the center of power, especially in the reign of Caracalla (211–217), when Domna traveled with her son on campaign and had general oversight of his correspondence. Then in 217 Caracalla was murdered and Domna took her own life, and the ascendancy of the Severan house seemed at an end. However, it quickly reasserted itself, first under the eccentric Heliogabalus (218–222) and even more under his cousin Alexander Severus (222–235). Almost nothing is known of Philostratus's career in this period, but he had probably moved back to Athens to pursue (or to resume) a career as an author and a professor of rhetoric. These final decades may have seen much, perhaps all, of his literary activity, and according to the Byzantine lexicon called the *Suda* he lived into the reign of Philip the Arab (244–249).

Philostratus is not the only sophist of the period whose writings have survived, but he is one of the best represented both in bulk and variety. It is not certain how many of the works surviving under his name are actually his, but several almost certainly are. The two shortest, *On Athletics* (*Gymnastikos*) and *On Heroes* (*Heroikos*), were probably written in the 220's at the earliest, since they mention a famous athlete of the previous decade, the Phoenician Helix (*Gymnastikos* 46, *Heroes* 15.8). The work in which he celebrates the major figures of his own calling, *The Lives of the Sophists*, must be late, and is usually placed in the 230's, though a case can be made for dating it in the reign of the emperor Gordian (238–244). But his longest work, and also the one that had the greatest resonance, is the *Life of Apollonius of Tyana* in eight books. This is certainly later than the death of Julia Domna in 217, and is earlier than the *Sophists*, though how much earlier cannot be known; a date in the 220's or 230's is likely.

Philostratus's Life of Apollonius

Philostratus may have entitled the work *On Apollonius of Tyana*,[1] but in general form and structure it is a biography, and far the longest that survives from antiquity. It is divided into eight books, with the first and last four forming subunits. The first tetrad is largely taken up with Apollonius's visit to the Wise Men of India, and ends with his visit to Rome and his confrontation with the tyranny of Nero. The second tetrad is more varied. It includes a visit to Ethiopia, where the local sages (whom Philostratus does not call "philosophers" or "sophists" but only "the Naked Ones") prove to be petty and pretentious, the counterpart to the Wise Men of India. The longest episode, however, occupying all of Book VII and most of VIII, is Apollonius's trial before the emperor Domitian, from which he emerges unscathed. This part, too, therefore forms a foil to Apollonius's dealings with the ministers of Nero in Book IV.

It is natural to wonder what materials Philostratus had for so extensive a biography, especially one that took its hero into regions far from the observation of the Roman

[1] There is no need to assume that the preposition *es* implies a favorable account, "in honor of": cf. e.g. I 3.2, where *es Apollonion* surely means no more than "about Apollonius."

Empire. He mentions several sources, only one of which we are able to check against his account. That one is the various letters of Apollonius that have come down in several manuscripts and in excerpts from authors such as John Stobaeus. According to Philostratus, the emperor Hadrian had his own collection of letters, though incomplete (VIII 20), but how far it corresponds to the surviving one cannot be judged. Philostratus also knew other writings of Apollonius, such as his treatise *On Sacrifices*, (almost certainly) a *Life of Pythagoras*, and a will, but these cannot have provided him with much factual information.

However, as a biographer of Apollonius he had at least two predecessors. One of these is a certain Maximus of Aegeae in Cilicia, who seems only to have written about the philosopher's youthful stay in the local sanctuary of Asclepius (I 4). The other, a certain Moeragenes, wrote a biography in four books that Philostratus plainly regards as the chief rival to his own (ibid.), but very little can be deduced about its date or contents. By his own admission, the source that enabled him entirely to surpass his predecessors in depth of characterization and detail of incident is unfortunately one surrounded by problems, Damis of "Nineveh," not the famous Assyrian capital but Hierapolis in Syria, a few miles west of the Euphrates.

Philostratus states that his "more detailed information" comes from the papers of this Damis, which Julia Domna received from a member of Damis's family, before giving them to himself to cast into suitable form. He seems to imply that the extant Life represents this recasting of Damis's notes, though he does not actually say so. It is similarly only an inference from this passage that Domna "commissioned" the *Life of Apollonius* as we now have it.

Apollonius met Damis for the first time in his disciple's city of Hierapolis, and thereafter the two traveled together until very near the end of Apollonius's life. Their conversations take up a large part of the work, especially in the early books, and Philostratus often cites Damis both as an eyewitness to important events in Apollonius's career and in order to correct earlier accounts.

There has long been doubt about these alleged memoirs. Did they come to Philostratus in exactly the way he alleges? Were Domna and he himself taken in by an imposture? Or did he invent Damis from start to finish (with or without the knowledge of Domna, who was dead by the time that he came to write the *Life*)? There can be no certain answer to these questions, but there are some clues. First, Philostratus's account follows a pattern of "self-authentication" that has many parallels in ancient and modern literature. A hitherto unknown witness writes his memoirs, these are mysteriously discovered and given to some authority figure such as the emperor Nero, and thus they acquire a stamp of authenticity.[2] Philostratus himself employs a somewhat similar device in the dialog *On Heroes*. In this an educated rustic, the chief speaker of the dialog, happens to farm land near the tomb of the Greek warrior Protesilaos, who died on the eve of the Trojan War. The hero appears frequently to this rustic, and plies him with much unexpected information about the War, for example that Odysseus arranged with Homer to have his own exploits written up as favorably as possible. In the dialog,

[2] W. Hansen, "Strategies of Authentication in Ancient Popular Literature," in *The Ancient Novel and Beyond*, S. Panayotakis and others, eds. (Leiden, 2003) 301–14.

the rustic conveys this information to the other speaker, a Phoenician merchant who has just landed nearby to pay his respects to the hero's tomb. Philostratus probably expects sophisticated readers to recognize this friendly Protesilaos as a harmless invention of his own, and the same may be assumed to be true of Damis.

A not dissimilar hint to the educated reader occurs in the last book of the *Life of Apollonius*. Here Apollonius, on trial before Domitian, had allegedly written out a full speech of defense, though in the end the emperor gave him only a brief cross-examination. Philostratus is providentially able to give the entire text of the undelivered speech, with much apology for its simple style (which does not in fact differ materially from his own).

As well as his materials for the life of Apollonius, Philostratus incorporates in his biography a variety of other genres and influences. The fully recorded conversations that Apollonius conducts with Damis and other interlocutors have an evident debt to Plato. For the decor of Apollonius's travels across Inner Asia and in India Philostratus must have drawn on travel writers, some of whom he names. These include Ctesias, the Greek doctor at the Persian court in the late fifth century, Nearchus the admiral of Alexander the Great, and Orthagoras, a writer whom Philostratus is one of the very few authors to mention. His account of Apollonius's journey up the Nile to Ethiopia gives the impression of less careful research, but here too he may have drawn on travelers and memoirists. The philosopher's confrontation with Domitian in certain ways recalls the papyrus pamphlets that modern scholars have dubbed the "Acts of the Alexandrian Martyrs." A more likely source is the novel, for example the trial scenes in Books VII and VIII of Achilles Tatius's *Leucippe and Clitophon*.

The "Historical" Apollonius

Given the multiple obscurities surrounding Philostratus's materials and methods, it is not surprising that the "historical" Apollonius is very difficult to recover. A first problem involves the chronology of his life. Damis allegedly did not give his age at death, though "some say it was eighty, some over ninety, and some that he passed a hundred" (VIII 29). Philostratus favors the last alternative (I 14.1). He places the youthful stay of Apollonius in the sanctuary of Asclepius at Aegeae in the reign of Tiberius (reigned 14–37: I 12.2 with note, 15.2), and since his authority here is allegedly Maximus of Aegeae, this information ought to be reliable. He seems to date Apollonius's journey to India to the reign of Claudius (reigned 41–54), to judge from the references to Vardanes, the contemporary king of Parthia (I 21.2 with note; III 58; cf. VIII 7.33). Thereafter, though there are some obscurities, Philostratus makes Apollonius's career unfold in reasonably orderly sequence through the reign of Nero (reigned 54–68), the Year of the Four Emperors (69), and under Vespasian (reigned 69–79) and Domitian (reigned 81–96). He seems to imply that Apollonius's trial before Domitian took place in the year 93, the year in which the emperor banished philosophers from Rome and killed or exiled several senators and their families (VII 4.2 with note). Near the end of the work Apollonius telepathically witnesses the assassination of Domitian in 96 (VIII 25–26), and soon after, writing to Nerva as the reigning emperor (96–98), he hints that neither of them have a long time to live (VIII 27). Philostratus therefore seems to envisage the span of Apollonius's life as stretching from about the beginning of the Christian era to the end of the first century, a coincidence that was not lost on Edward Gibbon (see below).

This chronology, however, does not easily fit the few indications that can be gleaned from the letters. If the letter written by a "Claudius" is not from the emperor but a Greek city magistrate (53), then the first datable ones are from the reign of Nero. The majority are from the Flavian period at the earliest, for instance those to Dio of Prusa (9, 10, etc.) and the doctor Crito of Carian Heraclea (23). However, the longest one in the collection, addressed to a Roman official Valerius who is married to a certain Fabulla (58), is almost certainly from 108/09. Either then Philostratus has placed the birth of Apollonius rather too early (despite the support he seems to derive from Maximus) or the letter to Valerius is not his. The second alternative may be right, since it contains no reference to the doctrine of the transmigration of souls, such as would have been expected in a letter from a Pythagorean philosopher to a bereaved father.[3]

There seems no reason to doubt Philostratus's claim that Apollonius was from a wealthy family and had received an expensive education, though nothing is known of the two teachers the biographer names, Euthydemus "of Phoenicia" at Tarsus (I 7.1) and Euxenus of Heracleia at Aegeae (I 7.2). His adoption of Pythagoreanism is corroborated not only by the letters and the titles of his now lost

[3] For more on the *Letters* see the separate introduction to them in the third volume of this edition.

writings, but also by the indirect testimony of Lucian in his denunciation of Alexander of Abonuteichos, for this self-proclaimed Pythagorean was the pupil of a pupil of Apollonius (Lucian, *Alexander the False Prophet* 5).

It is a feature of Philostratus's text, however, that Apollonius's philosophy is merely sketched in a few superficial strokes: his avoidance of food, clothing, or sacrifice that involves the killing of animals, his reverence for the gods (notably the Sun God), his belief in the transmigration of souls. The "philosophical" Apollonius appears mainly in the conversations that he holds with Damis and a few others, such as Isagoras the Thessalian (VIII 18), on such questions as whether a festival (*panēgyris*) is a material object. Philosophically, these conversations are conducted on a very amateurish level, and serve mainly to show Apollonius as a second Socrates, using dialectic to draw his hearers to an inexorable conclusion. Only rarely (I 16.4) is he represented as giving his pupils instruction in philosophy, and Philostratus does not mention his philosophical writings, not even his *Life of Pythagoras*.

By contrast, Apollonius is made to act very much like the public speakers whom Philostratus was later to describe in his *Lives of the Sophists*. Like Dio of Prusa, he lectures the Alexandrians on their addiction to horse racing. Like Aelius Aristides, he becomes an intimate of the healing god Asclepius and lives in his sanctuary. Like many of the sophists, he travels far and wide, curing cities of their tendency to faction and their neglect of Hellenic values, and counseling emperors. His two longest speeches, his reply to Thespesion in Book VI and his speech of defense in Book VIII, read very much like products of the Second Sophistic, especially those of Dio of Prusa and

Favorinus. It might in fact be wondered whether the historical Apollonius did convey his advice through public speeches, rather than through conversations with individuals (notably those in charge of sanctuaries) and through letters.

Philostratus represents the mature Apollonius, after his return from India, as constantly accompanied by pupils. These pupils are introduced in Book IV, with the sensational story of Menippus of Lycia, the lover of a vampire at Corinth (IV 25), and thereafter they appear throughout the narrative. Apart from Menippus, the only one to be mentioned more than once is Dioscorides of Egypt (IV 38.1, V 43.1). These two may well be real persons, though again they are attested nowhere else.

An aspect of Apollonius that emerges from certain of the letters, though practically invisible in the Life, is his concern for his family and his native city. Several of the letters are addressed to his brother Hestiaeus (Lrs. 35, 44, 55, 72, 73), and yet he appears only in a single chapter of the Life (I 13) as Apollonius's "debauched and drunken brother," never to be mentioned again. Nor does the mature Apollonius as represented by Philostratus ever visit Tyana, or seem to have any connections with it; yet several of the letters are addressed to persons who sound like old acquaintances from there (Lr. 46, Gordius; 48, Diotimus; 49, Ferocianus). Apollonius also writes to the city itself, promising an imminent visit (Lr. 47). Similarly, he writes to cities such as Caesarea of Palestine (Lr. 11) and (probably) Seleuceia Pieria, the port city of Antioch (Lrs. 12–13), and also sends a very friendly letter to Tralles in Caria (Lr. 69). Yet the Philostratean Apollonius rarely visits Greek cities other than those with old Greek credentials, Athens, Corinth, Smyrna, Ephesus, Pergamum, precisely those cities that welcomed the sophists of the Second Sophistic. Cities lacking such a Hellenic pedigree, Alexandria in Egypt, Syrian Antioch, Tarsus, Aspendus, are usually represented as corrupt or ill governed.

In short, Philostratus is not much concerned with Apollonius the Pythagorean philosopher, and his biography can only be read as an approximate guide to the historical Apollonius. This Apollonius, if his letters can be trusted, did claim to have crossed Mesopotamia and to have visited India in his youth, and also to have visited Ethiopia.[4] Such a journey is not inconceivable for a philosopher of the imperial period, or even before. In Apollonius's lifetime, Plutarch depicts a contemporary who had traveled beyond the borders of Egypt and into the Indian Ocean, collecting materials for a work of theology. The Neoplatonist Plotinus, a younger contemporary of Philostratus, joined the Persian expedition of Gordian III "in order to compare the wisdom of the Persians and the Indians," but was forced to turn back.[5] There is no reason to doubt that the historical Apollonius was an itinerant Pythagorean philosopher, traveling mainly in the eastern part of the Roman empire. He was a religious and moral preacher, with a predilection for staying in temples and issuing advice to the personnel; an advisor to cities, who received honorific testimonials from several of them; a teacher with numerous pupils; and a spiritual counselor to at least a few highly placed Romans. These Romans perhaps included the em-

[4] India: I 23.3, cf. Lr. 78. Ethiopia: lost letter cited in VI 27.4.

[5] Friend of Plutarch: *De def. or.* 410 A-B. Plotinus: Porphyry *Plot*. 3.

perors Vespasian and Titus, though Philostratus may have invented the story of Apollonius's persecution by Domitian. Some of the letters are certainly spurious, however, and much of the detail given in the *Life*, particularly Apollonius's travels to exotic parts and his confrontations with Nero and Domitian, is also fiction.

At the same time, the difficulty, or rather impossibility, that modern scholarship confronts in trying to reconstruct the "historical" Apollonius, as also the "historical" Jesus, need not detract from our appreciation of Philostratus's imaginary Apollonius. Late antique readers from Eusebius on were fully prepared to distinguish the improbability of the narrative from the charm of the text. It was not for nothing that a reader like Photius in the ninth century singled out certain passages of the work for their special beauty.[6] A similar judgment on the work is implied by the large number of surviving manuscripts. By artfully combining Platonic dialog, travel literature, romance, and other genres, Philostratus built up a picture of an ascetic holy man that was to resonate both with committed pagans like Hierocles, and (more important for the survival of the work) with devout ecclesiastics such as Photius. The resurgence of Late Antiquity as a period having its own distinct preoccupations and art forms has made recent generations better able to overlook those features of the *Life* that dissatisfied scholars of the nineteenth and twentieth centuries. It is now possible to see the work as something that has its own special kind of truth: a prophetic portrait of a new kind of person, a holy man who placed his trust in contact with the gods rather than in received doctrine, and for

[6] *Bibliotheca* 331 A (V 191 Henry).

whom religious observance and self-denial were the essential prerequisites of wisdom.[7]

The Travels of Apollonius

Much of the *Life* concerns Apollonius's travels, which take him to the furthest east and west of the known world, and also far up the Nile, though he travels no farther north than Etruria. His various journeys are best considered together here, partly because doing so helps to illuminate Philostratus's methods, but also in order to collect information that would otherwise be dispersed among footnotes.

The first and most important of these journeys is the eastern one, to visit the Wise Ones of India.[8] These live beyond the farthest point of Alexander's advance into India, the river Hyphasis (Beas: II 43), and in his account of Apollonius's outward journey Philostratus follows closely that of Alexander, just as Apollonius on his return journey follows the route of Alexander's admiral Nearchus.

After crossing the Euphrates at Zeugma (I 20.1) Apollonius passes Ctesiphon (I 21.1) and meets the "Median"

[7] Cf. M. Frede in R. Sorabji, ed., *Aristotle and After, Bulletin of the Institute of Classical Studies, London*, Suppl. 68 (London 1997) 5, "Apollonius may be the earliest Greek philosopher we can identify who claims that philosophical understanding ultimately requires divine inspiration, an inspiration to be attained by an ascetic life and, perhaps, by certain ritual practices."

[8] For full discussion of the various places and their real locations, see the Loeb edition of Arrian's *Anabasis* and *Indica* by P. A. Brunt (2 vols., 1976–1983) and A. B. Bosworth's *A Historical Commentary on Arrian's* History of Alexander, 2 (Oxford, 1995).

king in Babylon (I 25.1), though in fact the Parthian kings resided not in Babylon but in Ctesiphon. Next the narrative brings the party to the Caucasus, that is, the Hindu Kush over which Alexander had also marched (II 2.1). They thus arrive at the Cophen (modern Kabul, II 8), a tributary of the Indus, the chief river of the modern Punjab. The next feature mentioned is the mountain of Nysa (II 8), also associated with Alexander, of which the actual site is uncertain. Philostratus is correct in observing that the citadel of Aornos ("Birdless"), associated with one of Alexander's greatest successes in India, lay too far out of their way to visit (II 10): this would have involved a long detour up the valley of the Indus. The party then reaches the Indus (II 12.1), and proceeds to Taxila (Takshashila, northwest of modern Rawalpindi), the capital of the Indian king Phraotes. Philostratus seems to think that Porus, the great adversary of Alexander, also ruled in Taxila, though his kingdom really lay farther south, between the Hydaspes (Jhelum) and the Acesines (Chenab). Though Philostratus mentions the Acesines later in the text (II 17.1), he does not mention Apollonius's crossing of it, but only his crossing of the Hydraotes (Ravi) and his arrival at the Hyphasis (Beas; II 43). Here he ends Book II, with an emphatic reminder that Alexander had advanced no further.

From this point on Philostratus's geography becomes increasingly difficult to reconcile with actuality, and he may well be working largely from fantastic reports, such as those of the historian Ctesias, or his own imagination. The chief feature is "the arm of the Caucasus that extends to the Red Sea" (III 4.1), that is, the Indian Ocean, but this is a geographical impossibility. From the top of this mountain the party sees a plain divided by irrigation canals derived from the Ganges, which is said to be a further fifteen days away (5.1). At the foot of the mountain they come to a large city called Parax or Paraka (9), four days' journey away from the Wise Men's hill (10.1). The city cannot be identified, though Philostratus might have found it in one of his sources.

After leaving the Wise Men, Apollonius travels for ten days down to the Red Sea "keeping the Ganges on his right and the Hyphasis on his left" (50.2) and then takes a ship down the last part of the Hyphasis to the sea. This too is a geographical absurdity, since the two rivers flow in opposite directions, but there is no point in emending the text to save Philostratus. Sailing along the coast, they pass the mouth of the Indus and the city called Patala (near modern Hyderabad), to which "Alexander's fleet came under the command of Nearchus" (53): this is a fairly clear signal that he is now using the account of Nearchus, which can be followed through its adaptation in Arrian's Indica. Patala is in fact near the mouth of the Indus, if not by the sea, and the last places mentioned in Book III, the island of Biblus (53; off modern Karachi), Pagala in the land of the Oreitae (54; coastal Baluchistan), Stobera (55; possibly Arrian's "Calyba") in the land of the Fish Eaters, and the island of Selera (56; possibly Arrian's "Nosala"), agree reasonably closely with Nearchus. But whereas Nearchus ended his voyage at Babylon, Apollonius disembarks there and proceeds by land to Ninos (Hierapolis-Bambyke) and to Syrian Antioch, from where he sails to Paphos and Ionia (58).

His next long journey, to Gadeira (Cádiz), is very sketchily described, and Philostratus's main purpose may have been to take him to the western limit of the known world, which Alexander had allegedly aspired to reach. Book V, which describes this journey, begins with a brief but tolerably accurate account of the northwest African coast, going from Abinna, the southern "Pillar" of Hercules (near modern Ceuta), through the Tingae (Tangier) down to the river Salex (Salé, near Rabat; V 1). What Philostratus says about the Greek culture of Gadeira is also correct, and in Apollonius's lifetime the city produced a celebrated Pythagorean called Moderatus. A city called Hispola, described as so backward as never to have seen a tragic actor, is perhaps Seville (V 9). Apollonius returns from Spain by way of "Africa and Etruria" before reaching western Sicily (VI 11), and this route too seems so odd that editors have suspected the text.

His last major journey takes him to the counterparts and rivals of the Indian Wise Men, the Naked Ones of Ethiopia. Here his travels bear even less relation to actuality than in India, even when he is inside Roman Egypt. The excursus that opens Book VI alleges that Ethiopia joins Egypt at Meroe (1.1: north of modern Khartoum); just below, however, Philostratus puts the boundary at "Sykaminos" (2.1), which must be the site usually called Hierasykaminos, the modern Muharraka some eighty miles south of Assouan. Apollonius then proceeds towards "Memnon," the celebrated statue of Amenhotep III at Thebes, to which he is guided by a youth who plies a boat out of Memphis (3.1). This is doubly impossible, since Thebes is some two hundred and fifty miles north of Sykaminos, and Memphis some three hundred miles north of Thebes. Philostratus appears to place the Naked Ones close to Memnon (6.1), and after leaving them Apollonius proceeds up the Nile, eventually reaching "the last [cataract] for those descending the river," which in reality is just above Assouan (26.1). They then pass three further cataracts before they decide against seeking the sources of the Nile (VI 26.2). After stopping in an Ethiopian village (VI 27.1), they turn back, and Apollonius is next found conversing with Titus in Tarsus of Cilicia (VI 30.1).

The Afterlife of the Story

The impact of Apollonius's life and example seems to have been considerable even before Philostratus's lengthy treatment. Apart from the shorter works by Maximus and Moeragenes, Lucian's pamphlet on Alexander of Abonuteichos is eloquent testimony to Apollonius's influence. This miracle worker had allegedly been the youthful lover of a sorcerer (*goēs*) "of the kind who promise spells and heavenly incantations"; this man in turn was from Tyana and "a follower of the famous Apollonius and familiar with all his flummery (*tragōdia*)."[9] Alexander too was to be a religious innovator of the century after Apollonius, a professed Pythagorean and at the same time the self-appointed high priest of Glycon, a reincarnation of Asclepius.

It is not known how Julia Domna become interested in Apollonius, but other empresses before and after her showed an interest in philosophy and exotic religions. In addition, as a native of Emesa in the province of Syria, she was from a region where Apollonius's influence was partic-

[9] Lucian, *Alex*. 5.

ularly strong;[10] her son Caracalla dedicated a shrine to Apollonius in Tyana (VIII 31.3 and note); and her great-nephew Alexander Severus is said to have had an image of Apollonius among his household gods (*Historia Augusta: Alexander* 29.2). Once Philostratus's biography became known, the philosopher's reputation was assured. There is no reason to doubt the report that the emperor Aurelian (270–275), an ardent devotee of the Sun god, also revered him (*Historia Augusta: Aurelian* 24). In the early fourth century, the Diocletianic official Sossianus Hierocles used Philostratus's portrait for an attack on Christianity in his *Lover of Truth*, and about the same time the poet Soterichos of Oasis wrote the life of Apollonius in verse (*Suda* Σ 877). From this time on, he becomes an icon of paganism, and conversely a target of Christians. An inscription from Mopsouhestia in Cilicia, approximately of the fourth century, celebrates him for "shining forth from Tyana [and] extinguishing the errors of men."[11] The ardent polytheist Nicomachus Flavianus, consul in 394, either copied Philostratus's *Life* or translated it into Latin; his approximate contemporaries, Ammianus Marcellinus and the unknown author of the *Historia Augusta*, are other admirers of Apollonius; and his portrait appears in a gallery of Neoplatonic heroes found at Aphrodisias in Caria.[12]

[10] Tarsus and Aegeae lie in the neighboring province of Cilicia, as does Mopsouheștia, where an inscription honoring Apollonius has been found.

[11] *SEG* 28, 1251.

[12] Nicomachus: Sidonius Apollinaris, *Ep*. 8.3.1. Gallery: R. R. R. Smith, *Journal of Roman Studies* 80 (1990) 127–55, especially 141–44.

Hierocles's pamphlet initiated a controversy that lasted well into modern times. The first known response came from Eusebius of Caesarea, the church historian and biographer of Constantine, who in his *Reply to Hierocles* (included in this Loeb Philostratus edition) managed at one and the same time to charge Philostratus with credulity and Apollonius with sorcery. By a curious twist of intellectual history, Eusebius both confirmed Philostratus as the authoritative source on Apollonius (Origen in the previous century appears not to have known the *Life*), and also served as a kind of antidote against the possibly harmful effects of Philostratus's work.

In the eastern empire, Apollonius continued to be both feared as an emissary of the Evil One and admired as a magician until the fall of Constantinople, and his fame spread to the Islamic world, where he enjoyed a new life as the sorcerer Balinas.[13] The preservation of the *Life of Apollonius* in over twenty manuscripts, stretching in time from the eleventh to the sixteenth centuries, testifies both to the power of the hero's reputation and to the art of his biographer.

In western Christianity, there is a similar ambiguity about Apollonius, though his memory died out sooner. Jerome and Augustine, for example, are far from condemnatory in their observations about him. Later in the fifth century, the ex-bishop of Clermont, Sidonius Apollinaris, copied Nicomachus's translation or made a new version, and sent it to an official of the Visigothic king Euric with extravagant praise of its hero: "With all due deference to

[13] *Encyclopedia of Islam* I 994–95; *Oxford Dictionary of Byzantium* I 137–38.

the Catholic faith, read of someone similar to yourself in many respects: sought by riches, but never seeking them; eager for knowledge, moderate towards money; abstemious in feasts, wearing linen among those in purple, severe among vases of alabaster."[14] After Sidonius, however, Apollonius appears to fade from the western consciousness until the revival of learning.

The rediscovery of Greek literature in the Renaissance renewed Apollonius's western fortunes, though now the disputes were less between Christians and pagans than between the various branches of Christianity that developed in and after the Reformation. The *editio princeps* did not appear until 1502, when Aldus Manutius included Eusebius's pamphlet in the same volume "so that the antidote may accompany the poison"; this practice has continued until the present day, though not always from the same motive, and was followed in the previous Loeb translation. In the seventeenth century, torn as it was by wars of religion, Apollonius again became a lightning rod for defenders and critics of Christianity. While Le Nain de Tillemont denounced him as an agent of the Devil, in 1680 Charles Blount published a translation of the first two books (the first in English), amply supplied with notes that scandalized the faithful.[15]

In a notorious footnote, Gibbon observed:[16] "Apollonius of Tyana was born about the same time as Jesus

[14] Sidonius Apollinaris, *Ep*. 8.3.5.

[15] On Blount see further below, section on Editions and Translations.

[16] *Decline and Fall* ch. XI, I 328 n. 71 in the edition of J. B. Bury (New York, 1914).

Christ. His life (that of the former) is related in so fabulous a manner by his disciples, that we are at a loss to discover whether he was a sage, an impostor, or a fanatic." Gibbon's "expression of ludicrous scorn" had the unexpected effect of provoking the first complete English translation of the *Life*, that of the Irish divine Edward Berwick (see below). The debates about Apollonius, the reality of Damis, and the motives of Julia Domna and Philostratus, continued to rage during the rest of nineteenth century and well into the twentieth. Those intervening included the celebrated Tübingen theologian Ferdinand Christian Baur, John Henry Newman, and the theosophist G. R. S. Mead.

As a work of literature, by contrast, the afterlife of the *Life of Apollonius* has not received much attention, and any sketch can only be impressionistic. In this aspect it does not seem to have had much success, at least in western Europe. The exception is the episode of Apollonius's confrontation with the vampire or "Lamia" (IV 25). Robert Burton retold this story in the *Anatomy of Melancholy* (1621), whence it formed the basis of Keats's narrative poem *Lamia*, and Goethe based his *Braut von Corinth* very loosely on the same incident. The same poet's *Erlkönig*, wonderfully set to music by Schubert, also recalls an incident in the *Life* (III 38). By contrast with this neglect in western Europe, Constantin Cavafy made the *Life* a source for no less than four of his poems; in one of these a nostalgic polytheist of sixth-century Alexandria muses on Philostratus's phrase, "If he did die" (VIII 29).[17]

[17] "If actually dead," no. 103 in *C. P. Cavafy, Collected Poems*, translated by E. Keeley and P. Sherrard (Princeton, 1992). Other poems involving Apollonius are nos. 53, "But the wise per-

Manuscripts

All manuscripts, at least as reported, share a large number of errors. Some of these may go back to Philostratus's own manuscript, but there are too many to be explained except by the assumption of a common archetype (which may of course have been supplied with variants). One of the shared errors is the absurd ἐπ᾽ Ἄργους at VI 30.1, corrected to ἐς Ταρσοὺς by Cobet. Since this error must be due to copying from uncial (ΕСΤΑΡСΟΥС > επαργους), a late antique exemplar had probably survived centuries of neglect and been recopied at some date prior to the first extant witness, the 11th century Laurentianus LXIX 33 (Kayser's f). About twenty-five witnesses are known, though some are incomplete or contain only excerpts. After the Laurentianus, the next oldest is Escorialensis Gr. 227 (Kayser's E) of the 12th,[18] and all the rest are of the 14th century or later, including Kayser's pet, Parisinus 1801 (his p). Without fresh collation of the manuscripts it is impossible to eliminate any witnesses, and in making an interim text I have treated any variant transmitted by the manuscripts as possibly correct.

ceive things about to happen" and 137, "Apollonios of Tyana in Rhodes"; also "In the groves of Ephesos" in R. Lavagnini, ed., Ἀτελῆ Ποιήματα (Athens, 1994), 187–94. See G. W. Bowersock, "Cavafy and Apollonius," *Grand Street* 2 no. 3 (Spring 1983) 180–89.

[18] On this manuscript, collated for Kayser by E. Miller, see Gr. de Andrés, *Catálogo de los codices griegos de la Real Biblioteca de El Escorial* (Escorial, 1965) II 58. Miller's dating to the 10th century, followed by Kayser, persists in modern editions.

Editions and Translations

The neglect of the work as literature is reflected in the neglect of the text. The first major step forward, after Aldus's *editio princeps*, was the edition of F. Morel (Morellus) in 1608. Richard Bentley contemplated an ambitious edition that was to include the *Life* and much else, but this came to nothing, though he left valuable notes in his margin of Morel. He also passed some of his notes and emendations to the young German scholar Gottfried Olearius, and Olearius's edition of 1709, defective though it was, provided the first solid basis for further research. In the eighteenth century, some fine philologists undertook to improve and elucidate the text, notably J. J. Reiske and L. C. Valckenaer. In the early nineteenth, Friedrich Jacobs contributed greatly to the improvement of the text, and translated the whole work into German.

So far the nearest approach to a proper edition is that of C. L. Kayser in 1844.[19] Not long after, Anton Westermann published a text largely derived from Kayser, and yet with a number of excellent suggestions and observations; he also performed the service of dividing the chapters up into sections. Kayser returned to the Life in his *editio minor*, published by Teubner in 1870. This has often been reprinted, but in several ways it represented a step backwards from his earlier one. Despite the many criticisms of his methods expressed by Cobet and others, Kayser appears not to have done much more work on the *Life* after 1844, and he puts into his text of 1870 a number of conjectures that he had

[19] Kayser's edition of 1853, also published in Zurich, is an unaltered reprint of the 1844 one.

previously relegated to the apparatus. He also missed the opportunity to subdivide the chapters as Westermann had done. The Greek text of Conybeare in his Loeb translation of 1912 closely followed Kayser's of 1870.[20] By contrast, the *Letters* and the *Contra Hieroclem* have recently received excellent editions.

Translations of the *Life* have been many. A Latin one, by Alamanno Rinuccini, accompanied Aldus's *editio princeps*. The first English one was begun by the eccentric and polemical deist Charles Blount, but he published only the first two books, supplying them with a commentary that often strayed far from the subject under discussion, for example: "I have my self been sometimes Master of a Pack of Hounds, and although I must acknowledge that [it] had its inconveniences, (which all other things have) yet the good doth far exceed the evil of it; and the only thing which makes this exercise so little esteem'd of in Books, is, for that the Learned (who are the chief Authors of our publick Writings) have seldom had leisure to be acquainted with this Recreation."[21] This work is said to have been suppressed in 1693 for its attacks on established religion, and in the same year Blount committed suicide, allegedly after falling desperately in love with the sister of his late wife. The first full English translation is due to the Reverend Edward Berwick, vicar of Leixlip near Dublin, Ireland. He claimed to have translated the work only in order "to set in its true light the character of Apollonius and to wipe away

[20] V. Mumprecht's Greek text of 1983 is an unacknowledged reprint of Conybeare's, with the addition of an apparatus borrowed from Kayser.

[21] Blount (1680) 89.

an uncandid insinuation of Mr Gibbon, who seems glad (as he does on every occasion) to fix a stigma on the Divine Author of our religion."[22] In the last century, the year 1912 saw no less than two simultaneous translations of the *Life*, by J. S. Phillimore and F. C. Conybeare, whose Loeb translation has long been standard. Eleven years later there appeared an often overlooked American translation by Charles P. Eells. In recent years translations have multiplied, and even since my own abridged version in the Penguin Classics series (1970), there have been others in German, Russian, Italian, and Spanish.

The Present Text and Translation

Given the lack of a proper edition of the *Life*, I have tried to produce an interim text by taking Kayser's of 1870 as a point of departure, and improving it in various ways: (1) by purging it of Kayser's overly bold emendations; (2) by taking account of conjectures made both before and after Kayser's first edition, and rejected by him in the second (for example Valckenaer's brilliant Αἰνίῳ in VII 2.2), and also of ones that became known after 1870, notably those of J. J. Reiske published by K. Schenkl in 1893 (see Bibliography); (3) by subdividing Kayser's chapters into shorter sections, in which I have often followed Westermann. Here and there I also have slightly altered the boundaries between chapters observed by previous editors.

Most entries in the *apparatus criticus* take a form such as this: " Νινίῳ Bentl.: Νίνῳ." By this I indicate that I have adopted the conjecture of a modern scholar such as

[22] Cited by G. W. Bowersock in Jones (1970) 20.

Bentley, and rejected the reading of most or all of the manuscripts, which I give after the colon. I have cited individual manuscripts only where the scribe or his exemplar appears to have made a correct conjecture. I have sometimes cited readings of authors such as Eusebius where they diverge from the manuscripts of Philostratus. I have marked excisions with square brackets followed by "secl(usit)" and the name of the scholar to whom the excision is due, and I have marked additions by putting the added word or words in angle brackets followed simply by the name of the relevant scholar. Thus "‹τοῦ› Rsk." indicates that I have followed Reiske in adding τοῦ, while "[ἀπ'] secl. Headlam" indicates that I have followed Headlam in excising ἀπ(ὸ). I have occasionally referred to conjectures of others than those named in the Bibliography, usually ones made *en passant* in editions or commentaries and cited by an earlier editor such as Kayser, and in such cases have cited the source from which I have drawn the reference. Following is a listing of the sources mentioned in the apparatus; an asterisk indicates those noted more fully in the Bibliography.

Bentl(ey): conjectures of Richard Bentley preserved in his copy of Morel's edition in the British Library, and reported by Kayser, mainly in his 1844 edition.[23]

*Cob(et)

*Conyb(eare)

Euseb(ius, *Reply to Hierocles*)

*Headlam

*Jac(obs)

[23] For Bentley's projected edition, Hägg (1982).

Jackson: John Jackson's marginalia in his copy of Conybeare's Loeb translation; these go up to V 21.
Jon(es): the present editor
*Kay(ser)
*Lucarini
*Morel
*Ol(earius)
Phot.: Photius, *Bibliotheca*
*Radermacher
*Richards
*R(ei)sk(e): see in Bibliography Schenkl, 1893
Suda: *Suidae Lexicon*
*Valck(enaer): see in Bibliography Schenkl, 1892
*West(ermann)

Other citations employ the commonly used abbreviations listed in the *Oxford Classical Dictionary*.

For the purpose of the present translation I have started from my own of 1970, though making many alterations in the interest of style and accuracy. I have added those chapters (about a quarter of the whole) not translated in the first version.

BIBLIOGRAPHY

The bibliography on Apollonius and on Philostratus's *Life* has grown tremendously in recent years. Very full bibliographies will be found in the items cited below under the names Bowie, Dzielska, Flinterman, Mumprecht, and Schirren in the section "Studies."

Editions and Text of the Life

Cobet, C. G. "Miscellanea Critica: Vita Apollonii Tyanensis," *Mnemosyne* 8 (1859) 77–80, 117–81.

Headlam, W. "Various Conjectures III: Philostratus," *Journal of Philology* 23 (1895) 260–263.

Jacobs, Fr. *Observationes in Aeliani Historiam Animalium et Philostrati Vitam Apollonii*. Jena 1804.

Kayser, C. L. *Flavii Philostrati quae supersunt*. Zurich, 1844.

——— *Flavii Philostrati Opera auctiora* I. Leipzig, 1870.

Lucarini, C. M. "Ad Philostrati Vitam Apollonii," *Hermes* 132 (2004) 253–54.

Manutius, A. *Philostrati de uita Apollonii Tyanei octo. Iidem libri Latini interprete Alemano Rinuccino. Eusebius contra Hieroclem qui Tyaneum Christo conferre conatus fuerit. Idem Latinus interprete Zenobio Acciolo*. Venice, 1501–1502.

Morel, F. *Philostrati Lemnii opera quae exstant. Philostrati imagines et Callistrati ecphrases. Item Eusebii Cæsariensis episcopi liber contra Hieroclem*. Paris, 1608.

Olearius, G. *Philostratorum quae supersunt omnia*. Leipzig, 1709.

Platt, A. "Miscellanea," *Classical Quarterly* 5 (1911) 256–57.

Radermacher, L. "Observationum et Lectionum variarum Specimen," *Jahrbücher für classische Philologie* 41 (1895) 253–56.

Richards, H. "Notes on the Philostrati," *Classical Quarterly* 3 (1909) 104–09.

Schenkl, K. "Valckenarii Animadversiones in Philostratos," *Wiener Studien* 14 (1892) 267–77.

——— "Ioannis Iacobi Reiskii Animadversiones in Philostratos," *Wiener Studien* 15 (1893) 116–127.

Westermann, A. *Philostratorum et Callistrati Opera*. Paris, 1849.

Translations into English

Berwick, E. *The Life of Apollonius of Tyana*. London, 1809.

Blount, C. *The Two First Books of Philostratus, Concerning the Life of Apollonius Tyaneus*. London, 1680.

Conybeare, F. C. *The* Life of Apollonius of Tyana, *the* Epistles of Apollonius *and the Treatise of Eusebius*. Loeb Classical Library, 1912.

Eells, Charles P. *Life and Times of Apollonius of Tyana*. Stanford, Calif., 1923.

Jones, C. P. *Philostratus*: Life of Apollonius. Edited, abridged, and introduced by G. W. Bowersock. Harmondsworth, Middlesex, 1970.

Phillimore, J. S. *In Honour of Apollonius of Tyana*. Oxford, 1912.

Studies and Discussions

Anderson, G. *Philostratus: Biography and Belles-lettres in the Third Century A.D.* London and Dover, New Hampshire, 1986.

——— *Sage, Saint, and Sophist: Holy Men and Their Associates in the Early Roman Empire*. London and New York, 1994.

Bowie, E. L. "Apollonius of Tyana: Tradition and Reality," in *Aufstieg und Niedergang der römischen Welt* II 16.2, 1652–99. Berlin and New York, 1978.

——— "Philostratus: Writer of Fiction," in John R. Morgan and R. Stoneman, *Greek Fiction* 181–99. London 1994.

Dzielska, M. *Apollonius of Tyana in Legend and History*. Rome, 1986.

Flinterman, J.-J. *Power*, Paideia *and Pythagoreanism*. Amsterdam, 1995.

Francis, J. A. "Truthful Fiction: New Questions to Old Answers on Philostratus's *Life of Apollonius*," *American Journal of Philology* 119 (1998) 419–41.

Grosso, F. "La *Vita di Apollonio di Tiana* come Fonte storica," *Acme* 7 (1954) 333–532.

Hägg, T. "Bentley, Philostratus, and the German Printers," *Journal of Hellenic Studies* 102 (1982) 214–216.

Jones, C. P. "Apollonius of Tyana's Passage to India," *Greek, Roman and Byzantine Studies* 42 (2001) 185–99.

——— "Philostratus and the Gordiani," *Mediterraneo Antico* 5 (2002) 759–67.

Meyer, E. "Apollonios von Tyana und die Biographie des Philostratos," *Hermes* 52 (1917) 371–424 = (with revisions) *Kleine Schriften* 2, 131–91. Halle, 1924.

Mumprecht, V. *Philostratos: Apollonios*. Munich and Zurich, 1983.

Raynor, D. H. "Moeragenes and Philostratus: Two Views of Apollonius of Tyana," *Classical Quarterly* 34 (1984), 222–26.

Schirren, T. ΦΙΛΟΣΟΦΟΣ ΒΙΟΣ: *Philostrats* Vita Apollonii *als symbolische Form*. Tübingen, 2003.

THE LIFE OF APOLLONIUS OF TYANA

Α´

1. Οἱ τὸν Σάμιον Πυθαγόραν ἐπαινοῦντες τάδε ἐπ' αὐτῷ φασιν· ὡς Ἴων μὲν οὔπω εἴη, γένοιτο δὲ ἐν Τροίᾳ ποτὲ Εὔφορβος, ἀναβιοίη τε ἀποθανών, ἀποθάνοι δέ, ὡς ᾠδαὶ Ὁμήρου, ἐσθῆτά τε τὴν ἀπὸ θνησειδίων παραιτοῖτο καὶ καθαρεύοι βρώσεως, ὁπόση ἐμψύχων, καὶ τοῦ θῦσαι· μὴ γὰρ αἱμάττειν τοὺς βωμούς, ἀλλὰ ἡ μελιττοῦτα καὶ ὁ λιβανωτὸς καὶ τὸ ἐφυμνῆσαι, φοιτᾶν ταῦτα τοῖς θεοῖς παρὰ τοῦ ἀνδρὸς τούτου, γιγνώσκειν τε, ὡς ἀσπάζοιντο τὰ τοιαῦτα οἱ θεοὶ μᾶλλον ἢ τὰς ἑκατόμβας καὶ τὴν μάχαιραν ἐπὶ τοῦ κανοῦ.

2 Ξυνεῖναι γὰρ δὴ τοῖς θεοῖς καὶ μανθάνειν παρ' αὐτῶν, ὅπῃ τοῖς ἀνθρώποις χαίρουσι καὶ ὅπῃ ἄχθονται, περί τε φύσεως ἐκεῖθεν λέγειν· τοὺς μὲν γὰρ ἄλλους τεκμαίρεσθαι τοῦ θείου καὶ δόξας ἀνομοίους ἀλλήλαις περὶ αὐτοῦ δοξάζειν, ἑαυτῷ δὲ τόν τε Ἀπόλλω ἥκειν ὁμολογοῦντα, ὡς αὐτὸς εἴη, ξυνεῖναι δὲ καὶ μὴ ὁμολογοῦντας τὴν Ἀθηνᾶν καὶ τὰς Μούσας καὶ θεοὺς ἑτέρους, ὧν τὰ εἴδη καὶ τὰ ὀνόματα οὔπω τοὺς ἀνθρώπους γιγνώσκειν.

3 Καὶ ὅ τι ἀποφήναιτο ὁ Πυθαγόρας, νόμον τοῦτο οἱ

BOOK I

1. According to his admirers, Pythagoras of Samos was not really an Ionian, but was born as Euphorbus at Troy, and after dying as the poems of Homer relate came to life again. He shunned clothing made from animal skins, and abstained from all food or sacrifices of living creatures, since he never defiled altars with blood; instead honey cakes, frankincense, and hymns were this Master's offerings to the gods. He knew that such things were more welcome to them than hecatombs and the basket surmounted by the knife.[1]

2 Being conversant with the gods, he had learned what makes them angry or pleased with mankind, and on this he based his teachings about nature. Others, he said, merely guessed about the divine and had contradictory views about it, whereas he had been visited by Apollo, who fully admitted his identity, and also (though they did not confess it) by Athena, the Muses, and other gods, whose shapes and names were quite unknown to humanity.

3 All Pythagoras's revelations his disciples considered

[1] Baskets, sometimes made of silver or gold, were used in Greek ritual to hold the sacrificial knife.

ὁμιληταὶ ἡγοῦντο καὶ ἐτίμων αὐτὸν ὡς ἐκ Διὸς ἥκοντα, καὶ ἡ σιωπὴ δὲ ὑπὲρ τοῦ θείου σφίσιν ἐπησκεῖτο·[1] πολλὰ γὰρ θεῖά τε καὶ ἀπόρρητα ἤκουον, ὧν κρατεῖν χαλεπὸν ἦν μὴ πρῶτον μαθοῦσιν, ὅτι καὶ τὸ σιωπᾶν λόγος. καὶ μὴν καὶ τὸν Ἀκραγαντῖνον Ἐμπεδοκλέα βαδίσαι φασὶ τὴν σοφίαν ταύτην. τὸ γὰρ "χαίρετ', ἐγὼ δ' ὔμμιν θεὸς ἄμβροτος, οὐκέτι θνητός," καὶ "ἤδη γάρ ποτ' ἐγὼ γενόμην κούρη τε κόρος τε," καὶ ὁ ἐν Ὀλυμπίᾳ βοῦς, ὃν λέγεται πέμμα ποιησάμενος θῦσαι, τὰ Πυθαγόρου ἐπαινοῦντος εἴη ἄν. καὶ πλείω ἕτερα περὶ τῶν τὸν Πυθαγόρου τρόπον φιλοσοφησάντων ἱστοροῦσιν, ὧν οὐ προσήκει με νῦν ἅπτεσθαι σπεύδοντα ἐπὶ τὸν λόγον, ὃν ἀποτελέσαι προὐθέμην.

2. Ἀδελφὰ γὰρ τούτοις ἐπιτηδεύσαντα Ἀπολλώνιον, καὶ θειότερον ἢ ὁ Πυθαγόρας τῇ σοφίᾳ προσελθόντα, τυραννίδων τε ὑπεράραντα καὶ γενόμενον κατὰ χρόνους οὔτ' ἀρχαίους οὔτ' αὖ νέους, οὔπω οἱ ἄνθρωποι γιγνώσκουσιν ἀπὸ τῆς ἀληθινῆς σοφίας, ἣν φιλοσόφως τε καὶ ὑγιῶς ἐπήσκησεν, ἀλλ' ὁ μὲν τό, ὁ δὲ τὸ ἐπαινεῖ τοῦ ἀνδρός, οἱ δέ, ἐπειδὴ μάγοις Βαβυλωνίων καὶ Ἰνδῶν Βραχμᾶσι καὶ τοῖς ἐν Αἰγύπτῳ Γυμνοῖς συνεγένετο, μάγον ἡγοῦνται αὐτὸν καὶ διαβάλλουσιν ὡς βιαίως σοφόν, κακῶς γιγνώσκοντες· Ἐμπεδοκλῆς τε γὰρ καὶ Πυθαγόρας αὐτὸς καὶ Δημόκριτος ὁμιλήσαντες μάγοις καὶ πολλὰ δαιμόνια εἰπόντες οὔπω ὑπήχθησαν τῇ τέχνῃ, Πλάτων τε βαδίσας ἐς Αἴγυ-

[1] ἐπησκεῖτο Richards: ἐπήσκητο

law, and they honored him as an envoy from Zeus. Hence they practiced silence on celestial subjects, having heard many sacred secrets which it would have been difficult to keep, except that they had learned first that even silence is a form of discourse. They say that Empedocles of Acragas[2] followed the same school of wisdom. His verses, "Farewell, I am an immortal god to you and no longer a mortal" and "Once I was both girl and boy," and the ox which he is said to have made out of pastry and sacrificed at Olympia, are perhaps marks of one who followed Pythagoras's doctrines. Many more stories are told about philosophers of Pythagoras's kind, but it is not appropriate for me to start on them here, being eager for the account that I have set myself to complete.

2. The practices of Apollonius were very much like this, and he approached wisdom and overcame tyrannies in a more inspired way than Pythagoras. Yet though he lived in times that were neither ancient nor modern, people do not know him for the genuine wisdom which he practiced philosophically and sincerely. Instead, they single out only this or that of his deeds, while because of his association with Babylonian magicians, Indian Brahmans, and the Naked Ones of Egypt, some think him a sorcerer and misrepresent him as a philosophic impostor, but in this they are wrong. Empedocles, Pythagoras himself, and Democritus[3] associated with magicians, and said many inspired things without being seduced by the art. Plato too went to Egypt,

[2] Fifth-century Sicilian philosopher (ca. 492–432 BCE), noted for his writings on natural philosophy and religion.

[3] Fifth-century philosopher from Abdera in Thrace.

πτον, καὶ πολλὰ τῶν ἐκεῖ προφητῶν τε καὶ ἱερέων ἐγκαταμίξας τοῖς ἑαυτοῦ λόγοις, καὶ καθάπερ ζωγράφος ἐσκιαγραφημένοις ἐπιβαλὼν χρώματα, οὔπω μαγεύειν ἔδοξε, καίτοι πλεῖστα ἀνθρώπων φθονηθεὶς ἐπὶ σοφίᾳ.

2 Οὐδὲ γὰρ τὸ προαισθέσθαι πολλὰ καὶ προγνῶναι διαβάλλοι ἂν τὸν Ἀπολλώνιον ἐς τὴν σοφίαν ταύτην, ἢ διαβεβλήσεταί γε καὶ Σωκράτης ἐφ᾿ οἷς παρὰ τοῦ δαιμονίου προεγίγνωσκε, καὶ Ἀναξαγόρας ἐφ᾿ οἷς προὔλεγε· καίτοι τίς οὐκ οἶδε τὸν Ἀναξαγόραν Ὀλυμπίασι μέν, ὁπότε ἥκιστα ὗε, παρελθόντα ὑπὸ κωδίῳ ἐς τὸ στάδιον ἐπὶ προρρήσει ὄμβρου, οἰκίαν τε ὡς πεσεῖται προειπόντα μὴ ψεύσασθαι, πεσεῖν γάρ, νύκτα τε ὡς ἐξ ἡμέρας ἔσται, καὶ ὡς λίθοι περὶ Αἰγὸς ποταμοὺς τοῦ οὐρανοῦ ἐκδοθήσονται, προαναφωνήσαντα ἀληθεῦσαι; καὶ σοφίᾳ ταῦτα τοῦ Ἀναξαγόρου προστιθέντες ἀφαιροῦνται τὸν Ἀπολλώνιον τὸ κατὰ σοφίαν προγιγνώσκειν, καί φασιν ὡς μάγῳ τέχνῃ ταῦτ᾿ ἔπραττεν.

3 Δοκεῖ οὖν μοι μὴ περιϊδεῖν τὴν τῶν πολλῶν ἄγνοιαν, ἀλλ᾿ ἐξακριβῶσαι τὸν ἄνδρα τοῖς τε χρόνοις, καθ᾿ οὓς εἶπέ τι ἢ ἔπραξε, τοῖς τε τῆς σοφίας τρόποις, ὑφ᾿ ὧν ἔψαυσε τοῦ δαιμόνιός τε καὶ θεῖος νομισθῆναι. ξυνείλεκται δέ μοι τὰ μὲν ἐκ πόλεων, ὁπόσαι αὐτοῦ ἤρων, τὰ δὲ ἐξ ἱερῶν, ὁπόσα ὑπ᾿ αὐτοῦ ἐπανήχθη παραλελυμένα τοὺς θεσμοὺς ἤδη, τὰ δὲ ἐξ ὧν εἶπον ἕτεροι περὶ αὐτοῦ, τὰ δὲ ἐκ τῶν ἐκείνου ἐπιστολῶν.

where he picked up much from the local prophets and priests, and mixed it into his own doctrines like a painter adding color to a sketch. Yet he was never thought a magician, even though no one attracted more jealousy because of their wisdom.

Nor can Apollonius's frequent presentiments and prophecies disqualify him in relation to such wisdom, or else Socrates will get the same reputation because of the foreknowledge granted by his guardian spirit, and so will Anaxagoras[4] because of his predictions. Who does not know that once at Olympia during a drought, Anaxagoras came into the stadium wearing a sheepskin, thus prophesying rain; and that when he predicted that a certain house would collapse, it did and he was proved right? Similarly, when he proclaimed that the day would turn into night and that stones would fall out of the sky at Aegospotamoi, his words came true. Yet people ascribe all this to wisdom in Anaxagoras, while refusing to credit Apollonius with the foreknowledge of wisdom, and saying that these deeds were done by magic art. 2

I have therefore decided to remedy the general ignorance and to give an accurate account of the Master, observing the chronology of his words and acts, and the special character of the wisdom by which he came close to being thought possessed and inspired. I have gathered my materials from the many cities that were devoted to him, from the shrines that he set right when their rules had fallen into neglect, from other people's reports about him, 3

[4] Fifth-century philosopher from Clazomenae in Ionia, later resident in Athens; said to have predicted an eclipse of the sun and the fall of a meteorite at Aegospotamoi in Thrace.

ἐπέστελλε δὲ βασιλεῦσι, σοφισταῖς, φιλοσόφοις, Ἠλείοις, Δελφοῖς, Ἰνδοῖς, Αἰγυπτίοις ὑπὲρ θεῶν, ὑπὲρ ἐθῶν, ὑπὲρ ἠθῶν, ὑπὲρ νόμων, παρ᾽ οἷς ὅ τι ἀνατράποιτο,[2] ἐπηνώρθου.

3. Τὰ δὲ ἀκριβέστερα ὧδε συνελεξάμην. ἐγένετο Δάμις ἀνὴρ οὐκ ἄσοφος τὴν ἀρχαίαν ποτὲ οἰκῶν Νίνον. οὗτος τῷ Ἀπολλωνίῳ προσφιλοσοφήσας ἀποδημίας τε αὐτοῦ ἀναγέγραφεν, ὧν κοινωνῆσαι καὶ αὐτός φησι, καὶ γνώμας καὶ λόγους καὶ ὁπόσα ἐς πρόγνωσιν εἶπε. καὶ προσήκων τις τῷ Δάμιδι τὰς δέλτους τῶν ὑπομνημάτων τούτων οὔπω γιγνωσκομένας ἐς γνῶσιν ἤγαγεν Ἰουλίᾳ τῇ βασιλίδι. μετέχοντι δέ μοι τοῦ περὶ αὐτὴν κύκλου, καὶ γὰρ τοὺς ῥητορικοὺς πάντας λόγους ἐπῄνει καὶ ἠσπάζετο, μεταγράψαι τε προσέταξε τὰς διατριβὰς ταύτας καὶ τῆς ἀπαγγελίας αὐτῶν ἐπιμεληθῆναι, τῷ γὰρ Νινίῳ[3] σαφῶς μέν, οὐ μὴν δεξιῶς γε ἀπηγγέλλετο.

2 Ἐνέτυχον δὲ καὶ Μαξίμου τοῦ Αἰγιέως βιβλίῳ ξυνειληφότι τὰ ἐν Αἰγαῖς Ἀπολλωνίου πάντα, καὶ διαθῆκαι δὲ τῷ Ἀπολλωνίῳ γεγράφαται, παρ᾽ ὧν ὑπάρχει μαθεῖν, ὡς ὑποθειάζων τὴν φιλοσοφίαν ἐγένετο. οὐ γὰρ Μοιραγένει γε προσεκτέον βιβλία μὲν ξυνθέντι ἐς Ἀπολλώνιον τέτταρα, πολλὰ δὲ τῶν περὶ

[2] ἀνατράποιτο Jackson: ἂν πράττοιτο
[3] Νινίῳ Bentl.: Νίνῳ

[5] On Damis, see Introduction. “Old Ninos” was another name for Hierapolis in Syria, not far from the Euphrates.

and from his own letters. These he wrote to kings, sophists, philosophers, Eleans, Delphians, Indians, and Egyptians, on the subject of gods, about customs, morals, and laws, setting upright whatever had been overturned among such people.

3. But my more detailed information I have gathered as follows. There was a certain Damis, not devoid of wisdom, who once lived in Old Ninos.[5] This man became a disciple of Apollonius and wrote up not only his journeys, on which he claims to have been his companion, but also his sayings, speeches, and predictions. The notebooks containing the memoirs of Damis were unknown until a member of his family brought them to the attention of the empress Julia.[6] Since I was a member of her salon (for she admired and encouraged all rhetorical discourse), she set me to transcribe these works of Damis and to take care over their style, since the style of the man from Ninos was clear but rather unskillful.

I have also read the book of Maximus of Aegeae, which 2
contains all that Apollonius did there,[7] and the will written by Apollonius himself, which gives an idea of how inspired he was in his philosophy. Moeragenes does not deserve attention: he wrote four books about Apollonius and yet was greatly ignorant about the Master. So much for the way I

[6] Julia Domna, wife of Septimius Severus and mother of Caracalla, had a circle of literary men of which Philostratus was a member. She committed suicide in 217.

[7] Maximus is otherwise unknown, but probably a writer of the second century who held the position of imperial secretary (*ab epistulis*). Aegeae was an important port on the Cilician coast, with a sanctuary of the god Asclepius.

τὸν ἄνδρα ἀγνοήσαντι. ὡς μὲν οὖν ξυνήγαγον ταῦτα διεσπαρμένα[4] καὶ ὡς ἐπεμελήθην τοῦ ξυνθεῖναι αὐτά, εἴρηκα, ἐχέτω δὲ ὁ λόγος τῷ τε ἀνδρὶ τιμήν, ἐς ὃν ξυγγέγραπται, τοῖς τε φιλομαθεστέροις ὠφέλειαν· ἦ γὰρ ἂν μάθοιεν, ἃ μήπω γιγνώσκουσιν.

4. Ἀπολλωνίῳ τοίνυν πατρὶς μὲν ἦν Τύανα, πόλις Ἑλλὰς ἐν τῷ Καππαδοκῶν ἔθνει, πατὴρ δὲ ὁμώνυμος, γένος ἀρχαῖον καὶ τῶν οἰκιστῶν ἀνημμένον, πλοῦτος ὑπὲρ τοὺς ἐκεῖ, τὸ δὲ ἔθνος βαθύ. κυούσῃ δὲ αὐτὸν τῇ μητρὶ φάσμα ἦλθεν Αἰγυπτίου δαίμονος ὁ Πρωτεὺς ὁ παρὰ τῷ Ὁμήρῳ ἐξαλλάττων· ἡ δὲ οὐδὲν δείσασα ἤρετο αὐτόν, τί ἀποκυήσοι· ὁ δὲ "ἐμέ" εἶπε. "σὺ δὲ τίς;" εἰπούσης "Πρωτεὺς" ἔφη "ὁ Αἰγύπτιος θεός." ὅστις μὲν δὴ τὴν σοφίαν ὁ Πρωτεὺς ἐγένετο, τί ἂν ἐξηγοίμην τοῖς γε ἀκούουσι τῶν ποιητῶν, ὡς ποικίλος τε ἦν καὶ ἄλλοτε ἄλλος καὶ κρείττων τοῦ ἁλῶναι, γιγνώσκειν τε ὡς ἐδόκει καὶ προγιγνώσκειν πάντα; καὶ μεμνῆσθαι χρὴ τοῦ Πρωτέως, μάλιστα ἐπειδὰν προϊὼν ὁ λόγος δεικνύῃ τὸν ἄνδρα πλείω μὲν ἢ ὁ Πρωτεὺς προγνόντα, πολλῶν δὲ ἀπόρων τε καὶ ἀμηχάνων κρείττω γενόμενον ἐν αὐτῷ μάλιστα τῷ ἀπειλῆφθαι.

5. Τεχθῆναι δὲ ἐν λειμῶνι λέγεται, πρὸς ᾧ νῦν τὸ ἱερὸν αὐτῷ ἐκπεπόνηται. καὶ μηδὲ ὁ τρόπος ἀγνοείσθω, ὃν ἀπετέχθη· ἀγούσῃ γὰρ τῇ μητρὶ τόκου ὥραν ὄναρ ἐγένετο βαδίσαι ἐς τὸν λειμῶνα καὶ ἄνθη κεῖραι.

[4] διεσπαρμένα Jackson: διεσπασμένα

gathered these scattered materials and for my care in assembling them. May my work bring honor to the Master who is its subject, and profit to those with an inclination to learning, for they really might learn things quite new to them.

4. By origin Apollonius came from Tyana, a Greek city in the region of Cappadocia.[8] He was the son of a man with the same name, and descended from an old family that went back to the founders. Its wealth was exceptional there, even though the region is rich. When his mother was still carrying him, she had a vision of an Egyptian divinity, Proteus who changes shape in Homer. She was not at all frightened, but asked him who her child would be. He replied: "Myself." When she asked "Who are you?" he said, "Proteus, the Egyptian god." Now for those who know the poets why should I describe how wise Proteus was, how shifting, multiform, and impossible to catch, and how he seemed to have all knowledge and foreknowledge? But the reader must bear Proteus in mind, especially when the course of my story shows that my hero had the greater prescience of the two, and rose above many difficult and baffling situations just when he was cornered.

5. Apollonius's birth is said to have occurred in a meadow, near which the elaborate temple to him now stands. The manner of his delivery is worth knowing. His mother was near her time when she was told in a dream to go to the meadow and gather flowers. When she got there,

[8] Tyana was a prosperous city situated at an important junction on the Cappadocian (northwestern) side of the Taurus range. Cappadocia was normally thought rather backward, and hence Philostratus's insistence on Tyana's "Greek" culture.

καὶ δῆτα ἀφικομένη αἱ μὲν δμωαὶ προσεῖχον τοῖς ἄνθεσιν ἐσκεδασμέναι κατὰ τὸν λειμῶνα, αὐτὴ δὲ ἐς ὕπνον ἀπήχθη κλιθεῖσα ἐν τῇ πόᾳ. κύκνοι τοίνυν, οὓς ὁ λειμὼν ἔβοσκε, χορὸν ἐστήσαντο περὶ αὐτὴν καθεύδουσαν, καὶ τὰς πτέρυγας, ὥσπερ εἰώθασιν, ἄραντες ἀθρόον ἤχησαν, καὶ γάρ τι καὶ ζεφύρου ἦν ἐν τῷ λειμῶνι, ἡ δὲ ἐξέθορέ τε ὑπὸ τῆς ᾠδῆς καὶ ἀπέτεκεν, ἱκανὴ δὲ πᾶσα ἔκπληξις μαιεύσασθαι καὶ πρὸ τῆς ὥρας. οἱ δὲ ἐγχώριοί φασιν ὡς ὁμοῦ τε τίκτοιτο καὶ σκηπτὸς ἐν τῇ γῇ πεσεῖσθαι δοκῶν ἐμμετεωρισθείη τῷ αἰθέρι, καὶ ἀφανισθείη ἄνω, τό, οἶμαι, ἐκφανὲς καὶ ὑπὲρ πάντα τὰ ἐν τῇ γῇ καὶ τὸ ἀγχοῦ θεῶν καὶ ὁπόσα ὅδε ὁ ἀνὴρ ἐγένετο, φαίνοντες οἱ θεοὶ καὶ προσημαίνοντες.

6. Ἔστι δέ τι περὶ Τύανα ὕδωρ Ὁρκίου Διός, ὥς φασι, καλοῦσι δὲ αὐτὸ Ἀσβαμαῖον, οὗ πηγὴ ἀναδίδοται ψυχρά, παφλάζει δέ, ὥσπερ ὁ θερμαινόμενος λέβης. τοῦτο εὐόρκοις μὲν ἵλεών τε καὶ ἡδὺ ὕδωρ, ἐπιόρκοις δὲ παρὰ πόδας ἡ δίκη· ἀποσκήπτει γὰρ καὶ ἐς ὀφθαλμοὺς καὶ ἐς χεῖρας καὶ ἐς πόδας, καὶ ὑδέροις ἁλίσκονται καὶ φθόαις, καὶ οὐδ᾽ ἀπελθεῖν δυνατόν, ἀλλ᾽ αὐτόθι ἔχονται καὶ ὀλοφύρονται πρὸς τῷ ὕδατι ὁμολογοῦντες ἃ ἐπιώρκησαν· οἱ μὲν δὴ ἐγχώριοί φασι παῖδα τοῦ Διὸς τὸν Ἀπολλώνιον γεγονέναι, ὁ δ᾽ ἀνὴρ Ἀπολλωνίου ἑαυτὸν καλεῖ.

7. Προϊὼν δὲ ἐς ἡλικίαν, ἐν ᾗ γράμματα, μνήμης τε ἰσχὺν ἐδήλου καὶ μελέτης κράτος, καὶ ἡ γλῶττα Ἀττικῶς εἶχεν, οὐδ᾽ ἀπήχθη τὴν φωνὴν ὑπὸ τοῦ

her servant girls wandered over the meadow busying themselves with the flowers, while she lay down in the grass and fell asleep. Some swans feeding there formed a circle around her as she slept, and raising their wings in their characteristic way made a sudden noise, for there was a slight breeze in the meadow. The musical sound made her jump up and give birth, any alarm being enough to cause birth even before the due time. The locals also say that as Apollonius was born a bolt of lightning, which seemed just about to strike the earth, hung poised in the air and then disappeared upwards. No doubt the gods were giving a signal and an omen of his brilliance, his exaltation above earthly things, his closeness to heaven, and all the Master's other qualities.

6. There is a pool near Tyana allegedly sacred to Zeus the Guardian of Oaths, though they call it "Asbamaean." A spring of cold water rises there which bubbles like a cauldron on the fire. For those who keep their word the water is propitious and sweet, but for those who break it punishment is at hand, for the water attacks their eyes, their hands, and their feet, and they catch dropsy or consumption. Unable even to leave the place, they are caught there, groaning by the fountain and confessing their perjuries. Now the locals say that Apollonius was the son of Zeus, but the Master calls himself "son of Apollonius."

7. When he reached an age to study literature, he showed a retentive memory and a power of application; his Greek was of the Attic kind and his accent unaffected by

ἔθνους, ὀφθαλμοί τε πάντες ἐς αὐτὸν ἐφέροντο, καὶ γὰρ περίβλεπτος ἦν τὴν ὥραν. γεγονότα δὲ αὐτὸν ἔτη τεσσαρακαίδεκα ἄγει ἐς Ταρσοὺς ὁ πατὴρ παρ᾽ Εὐθύδημον τὸν ἐκ Φοινίκης. ὁ δὲ Εὐθύδημος ῥήτωρ τε ἀγαθὸς ἦν καὶ ἐπαίδευε τοῦτον, ὁ δὲ τοῦ μὲν διδασκάλου εἴχετο, τὸ δὲ τῆς πόλεως ἦθος ἄτοπόν τε ἡγεῖτο καὶ οὐ χρηστὸν ἐμφιλοσοφῆσαι, τρυφῆς τε γὰρ οὐδαμοῦ μᾶλλον ἅπτονται, σκωπτόλαι τε καὶ ὑβρισταὶ πάντες, καὶ δεδώκασι τῇ ὀθόνῃ μᾶλλον ἢ τῇ σοφίᾳ Ἀθηναῖοι, ποταμός τε αὐτοὺς διαρρεῖ Κύδνος, ᾧ παρακάθηνται, καθάπερ τῶν ὀρνίθων οἱ ὑγροί. τό τοι "παύσασθε μεθύοντες τῷ ὕδατι" Ἀπολλωνίῳ πρὸς αὐτοὺς ἐν ἐπιστολῇ εἴρηται.

2 Μεθίστησιν οὖν τὸν διδάσκαλον δεηθεὶς τοῦ πατρὸς ἐς Αἰγὰς τὰς πλησίον, ἐν αἷς ἡσυχία τε πρόσφορος τῷ φιλοσοφήσοντι καὶ σπουδαὶ νεανικώτεραι, καὶ ἱερὸν Ἀσκληπιοῦ καὶ ὁ Ἀσκληπιὸς αὐτὸς ἐπίδηλος τοῖς ἀνθρώποις. ἐνταῦθα ξυνεφιλοσόφουν μὲν αὐτῷ Πλατώνειοί τε καὶ Χρυσίππειοι καὶ οἱ ἀπὸ τοῦ περιπάτου, διήκουε δὲ καὶ τῶν Ἐπικούρου λόγων, οὐδὲ γὰρ τούτους ἀπεσπούδαζε, τοὺς δέ γε Πυθαγορείους ἀρρήτῳ τινὶ σοφίᾳ ξυνέλαβε· διδάσκαλος μὲν γὰρ ἦν αὐτῷ τῶν Πυθαγόρου λόγων οὐ πάνυ σπουδαῖος, οὐδὲ ἐνεργῷ τῇ φιλοσοφίᾳ χρώμενος, γαστρός τε γὰρ ἥττων ἦν καὶ ἀφροδισίων καὶ κατὰ τὸν Ἐπίκουρον ἐσχημάτιστο· ἦν δὲ οὗτος Εὔξενος ὁ ἐξ Ἡρακλείας τοῦ Πόντου, τὰς δὲ Πυθαγόρου δόξας ἐγίγνωσκεν, ὥσπερ οἱ ὄρνιθες ἃ μανθάνουσι παρὰ τῶν ἀνθρώπων,

the region. All eyes were turned to him, so conspicuous was his youthful bloom. When he reached fourteen his father took him to Tarsus to study with Euthydemus of Phoenicia. Euthydemus was a good orator and began to teach him, but he, though devoted to his teacher, considered the manners of the city corrupt and hostile to philosophy. The Tarsians are exceptionally given to luxury, all of them frivolous and insulting, and more devoted to fine linen than the Athenians are to philosophy. The river Cydnus runs through their city, and they sit beside it like water fowl. This is why Apollonius says to them in a letter, "Stop getting drunk on water."

So with his father's permission he got his teacher to 2
move to Aegeae nearby, where there was quiet suitable for a lover of wisdom, and activity of a more vigorous kind. There was also a sanctuary of Asclepius, where Asclepius himself appeared to humans. There his fellow pupils included followers of Plato, Chrysippus, and the Peripatos,[9] and he also heard the doctrines of Epicurus, considering not even these unworthy of his attention. The Pythagorean ones, however, he absorbed by some mysterious faculty. His teacher in the doctrines of Pythagoras was not a very good man or one who put his philosophy into practice, being devoted to gluttony and sex, and patterned after Epicurus. This man, Euxenus from Heracleia on the Pontus,[10] knew the beliefs of Pythagoras as birds know what they learn from humans. Birds express wishes like

[9] Chrysippus: Stoic of the third century BCE. The Peripatos ("Walkway") refers to the school of Aristotle.

[10] Euxenus is otherwise unknown.

τὸ γὰρ "χαῖρε" καὶ τὸ "εὖ πρᾶττε" καὶ τὸ "Ζεὺς ἵλεως" καὶ τὰ τοιαῦτα οἱ ὄρνιθες εὔχονται, οὔτε εἰδότες ὅ τι λέγουσιν οὔτε <εὖ>[5] διακείμενοι πρὸς τοὺς ἀνθρώπους, ἀλλὰ ἐρρυθμισμένοι τὴν γλῶτταν.

3 Ὁ δέ, ὥσπερ οἱ νέοι τῶν ἀετῶν ἐν ἁπαλῷ μὲν τῷ πτερῷ παραπέτονται τοῖς γειναμένοις αὐτοὺς μελετώμενοι ὑπ' αὐτῶν τὴν πτῆσιν, ἐπειδὰν δὲ αἴρεσθαι δυνηθῶσιν, ὑπερπέτονται τοὺς γονέας ἄλλως τε κἂν λίχνους αἴσθωνται καὶ κνίσης ἕνεκα πρὸς τῇ γῇ πετομένους, οὕτω καὶ ὁ Ἀπολλώνιος προσεῖχέ τε τῷ Εὐξένῳ παῖς ἔτι, καὶ ἤγετο ὑπ' αὐτοῦ βαίνων ἐπὶ τοῦ λόγου, προελθὼν δὲ ἐς ἔτος δέκατον καὶ ἕκτον ὥρμησεν ἐπὶ τὸν τοῦ Πυθαγόρου βίον, πτερωθεὶς ἐπ' αὐτὸν ὑπό τινος κρείττονος. οὐ μὴν τόν γε Εὔξενον ἐπαύσατο ἀγαπῶν, ἀλλ' ἐξαιτήσας αὐτῷ προάστειον παρὰ τοῦ πατρός, ἐν ᾧ κῆποί τε ἁπαλοὶ ἦσαν καὶ πηγαί, "σὺ μὲν ζῆθι τὸν σεαυτοῦ τρόπον" ἔφη "ἐγὼ δὲ τὸν Πυθαγόρου ζήσομαι."

8. Ἡγουμένου δὲ αὐτὸν τοῦ Εὐξένου μεγάλης διανοίας ἅπτεσθαι καὶ ἐρομένου, ὁπόθεν ἄρξοιτο "ὅθεν περ οἱ ἰατροί," ἔφη, "καὶ γὰρ ἐκεῖνοι καθαίροντες τὰς γαστέρας τοὺς μὲν οὐδὲ νοσεῖν ἐῶσι, τοὺς δὲ ἰῶνται." καὶ εἰπὼν τοῦτο τὰς μὲν ἐμψύχους βρώσεις ὡς οὔτε καθαρὰς καὶ τὸν νοῦν παχυνούσας παρῃτήσατο, τραγήματα δὲ καὶ λάχανα ἐσιτεῖτο, καθαρὰ εἶναι φάσκων, ὁπόσα ἡ γῆ αὐτὴ δίδωσι, καὶ τὸν οἶνον καθαρὸν μὲν ἔφασκεν εἶναι πῶμα ἐκ φυτοῦ οὕτως ἡμέρου τοῖς ἀνθρώποις ἥκοντα, ἐναντιοῦσθαι δὲ τῇ

"Good day," "All the best," and "God bless you," without knowing what they mean or feeling any goodwill for humans, but simply because their tongues have been trained.

But Apollonius was like those young eagles with wings 3
still undeveloped that fly beside their parents as they practice flight under their guidance; when they are able to soar they rise higher than their parents, especially if they see them to be gluttons that keep near the ground to gorge themselves. Similarly Apollonius in his boyhood attended to Euxenus and was led by him along the path of reason, but when he reached fifteen he aspired to Pythagoras's way of life, to which some higher power gave him wings to climb. Yet he continued to love Euxenus, and persuaded his father to give him a suburban estate with charming gardens and fountains. "You live your own way," he said, "and I will live Pythagoras's way."

8. Euxenus thought he was undertaking an ambitious scheme, and asked him where he would start. "As doctors do," he replied; "they too purge their patients' stomachs and either prevent them falling ill, or cure them." And after saying this he refused the meat of animals as impure and dulling the mind, and lived off dried fruit and vegetables, saying that everything was pure which the earth produced unaided. Wine, he said, was a pure drink, since it came from a plant so beneficial to humans, but it ob-

[5] <εὖ> Jon.

τοῦ νοῦ συστάσει, διαθολοῦντα τὸν ἐν τῇ ψυχῇ αἰθέρα.

2 Μετὰ δὲ τὴν κάθαρσιν τῆς γαστρὸς τοιαύτην γενομένην, ἀνυποδησίαν τε ποιεῖται κόσμημα καὶ λίνου ἐσθῆτα ἀμπίσχεται. παραιτησάμενος τὴν ἀπὸ τῶν ζῴων, ἀνῆκέ τε τὴν κόμην καὶ ἐν τῷ ἱερῷ ἔζη. ἐκπεπληγμένων δὲ αὐτὸν τῶν περὶ τὸ ἱερὸν καὶ τοῦ Ἀσκληπιοῦ ποτε πρὸς τὸν ἱερέα φήσαντος, ὡς χαίροι θεραπεύων τοὺς νοσοῦντας ὑπὸ Ἀπολλωνίῳ μάρτυρι, ξυνῄεσαν ἐς τὰς Αἰγὰς ἐφ᾿ ἱστορίᾳ Κίλικές τε αὐτοὶ καὶ οἱ πέριξ, ὅ τε Κιλίκιος λόγος "ποῖ τρέχεις; ἦ ἐπὶ τὸν ἔφηβον;" ἐπ᾿ ἐκείνῳ τε ἐλέγετο καὶ παροιμιώδη τιμὴν ἔσχεν.

9. Ἄξιον δὲ μηδὲ τὰ ἐν τῷ ἱερῷ παρελθεῖν βίον γε ἀφηγούμενον ἀνδρός, ὃς καὶ τοῖς θεοῖς ἦν ἐν λόγῳ. μειράκιον γὰρ δὴ Ἀσσύριον παρὰ τὸν Ἀσκληπιὸν ἧκον ἐτρύφα νοσοῦν καὶ ἐν πότοις ἔζη, μᾶλλον δὲ ἀπέθνησκεν· ὑδέρῳ δὲ ἄρα εἴχετο καὶ μέθῃ χαῖρον αὐχμοῦ ἠμέλει. ἠμελεῖτο δὴ ὑπὸ τοῦ Ἀσκληπιοῦ διὰ ταῦτα, καὶ οὐδὲ ὄναρ αὐτῷ ἐφοίτα. ἐπιμεμφομένῳ δὲ ταῦτα ἐπιστὰς ὁ θεὸς "εἰ Ἀπολλωνίῳ" ἔφη "διαλέγοιο, ῥᾴων ἔσῃ." προσελθὼν οὖν τῷ Ἀπολλωνίῳ "τί ἂν" ἔφη "τῆς σῆς σοφίας ἐγὼ ἀπολαύσαιμι; κελεύει γάρ με ὁ Ἀσκληπιὸς συνεῖναί σοι." "ὃ" ἦ δ᾿ ὃς "ἔσται σοι πρὸς τὰ παρόντα πολλοῦ ἄξιον· ὑγιείας γάρ που δέῃ;" "νὴ Δί'" εἶπεν "ἥν γε ὁ Ἀσκληπιὸς ἐπαγγέλλεται μέν, οὐ δίδωσι δέ."

2 "Εὐφήμει," ἔφη "τοῖς γὰρ βουλομένοις δίδωσι, σὺ

structed mental balance by confusing the ether in the soul.

After purging his stomach in this way, he made going 2
barefoot his way of dressing up, and wore linen clothes, refusing those made from animals. He also grew his hair long, and lived in the sanctuary. The personnel of the sanctuary were awed by him, and Asclepius told the priests that he was glad to cure the sick with Apollonius as his witness, and so people came to Aegeae both from Cilicia and from the neighboring regions to satisfy their curiosity. The Cilician saying, "Where are you running? To see the young boy?" became applied to Apollonius and acquired the status of a proverb.

9. It would not be right to pass over his way of life in the sanctuary when I am recounting the life of a Master held in esteem even by the gods. An Assyrian[11] youth had come to visit Asclepius, but indulged himself even on his sickbed. Drink was his life, or rather his death, for in fact he had dropsy and from love of wine neglected a dry diet. So Asclepius neglected him and did not even visit him in sleep. But when the youth reproached him for this, the god appeared to him and said, "If you talk with Apollonius, you will get relief." So going to Apollonius he said, "What profit can I get from your philosophy, since Asclepius has told me to converse with you?" "Profit very valuable in your present condition," was the reply, "for I suppose you want health?" "Indeed I do," he said; "Asclepius promises it to me, but does not give it."

"Do not blaspheme," Apollonius said; "he gives it to 2

[11] Throughout the *Life* Philostratus uses "Assyrian" rather than "Syrian" as the more literary and archaic term.

δὲ ἐναντία τῇ νόσῳ πράττεις, τρυφῇ γὰρ διδοὺς ὀψοφαγίαν ἐπεσάγεις ὑγροῖς καὶ διεφθορόσι τοῖς σπλάγχνοις, καὶ ὕδατι ἐπαντλεῖς πηλόν." ταυτὶ μὲν σαφέστερα, οἶμαι, τῆς Ἡρακλείτου σοφίας ἐχρησμῴδει· ὁ μὲν γὰρ δεῖσθαι ἔφη τοῦ ποιήσοντος ἐξ ἐπομβρίας αὐχμόν, ἐσελθόντος αὐτὸν τουτουὶ τοῦ πάθους, οὐκ εὐξύνετά που λέγων, οὐδὲ δῆλα, ὁ δ' ἤγαγεν ἐς ὑγίειαν τὸ μειράκιον τὰ σοφὰ σαφῶς ἑρμηνεύσας.

10. Ἰδὼν δὲ ἀθρόον ποτὲ ἐν τῷ βωμῷ αἷμα καὶ διακείμενα ἐπὶ τοῦ βωμοῦ τὰ ἱερά, τεθυμένους τε βοῦς Αἰγυπτίους καὶ σῦς μεγάλους, καὶ τὰ μὲν δέροντας αὐτούς, τὰ δὲ κόπτοντας, χρυσίδας τε ἀνακειμένας δύο καὶ λίθους ἐν αὐταῖς τῶν Ἰνδικωτάτων καὶ θαυμασίων, προσελθὼν τῷ ἱερεῖ "τί ταῦτα;" ἔφη "λαμπρῶς γάρ τις χαρίζεται τῷ θεῷ." ὁ δὲ "θαυμάσῃ" ἔφη "μᾶλλον, ὅτι μήτε ἱκετεύσας ποτὲ ἐνταῦθα μήτε διατρίψας, ὃν οἱ ἄλλοι χρόνον, μήτε ὑγιάνας πω παρὰ τοῦ θεοῦ, μηδ' ἅπερ αἰτήσων ἦλθεν ἔχων (χθὲς γὰρ δὴ ἀφιγμένῳ ἔοικεν) ὁ δ' οὕτως ἀφθόνως θύει. φησὶ δὲ πλείω μὲν θύσειν, πλείω δὲ ἀναθήσειν, εἰ πρόσοιτο αὐτὸν ὁ Ἀσκληπιός. ἔστι δὲ τῶν πλουσιωτάτων· κέκτηται γοῦν ἐν Κιλικίᾳ βίον πλείω ἢ Κίλικες ὁμοῦ πάντες· ἱκετεύει δὲ τὸν θεὸν ἀποδοῦναί οἱ τὸν ἕτερον τῶν ὀφθαλμῶν ἐξερρυηκότα."

2 Ὁ δὲ Ἀπολλώνιος, ὥσπερ γεγηρακὼς εἰώθει, τοὺς ὀφθαλμοὺς ἐς τὴν γῆν στήσας "τί δὲ ὄνομα αὐτῷ;" ἤρετο. ἐπεὶ δὲ ἤκουσε, "δοκεῖ μοι," ἔφη "ὦ ἱερεῦ, τὸν ἄνθρωπον τοῦτον μὴ προσδέχεσθαι τῷ ἱερῷ, μιαρὸς

those who want it, but you are acting contrary to your illness. In your self-indulgence you are burdening your intestines with rich food when they are soft and bloated, and pouring water on mud." These prescriptions were clearer, I think, than the wisdom of Heraclitus,[12] who, when he was afflicted by the same condition, said he needed something to bring drought after a deluge, a remark not at all comprehensible and clear. Yet Apollonius restored the youth to health by expressing wise counsels in simple form.

10. Once he saw the altar covered with blood and the victims lying beside it. Egyptian oxen and large pigs had been sacrificed, some were being flayed and others cut up. Two gold vessels had been dedicated, inset with marvelous stones of the finest Indian kind. Going up to the priest, Apollonius asked, "What is all this? Someone is giving the god sumptuous gifts." "You will be even more amazed," said the other, "to hear that he has not been a suppliant here, or passed as much time here as the others, or been given health by the god, or received what he came to ask for (for I think he arrived yesterday), and yet he is sacrificing so generously. He says he will offer more sacrifices and more dedications if Asclepius admits him. He is extremely rich, for he possesses a larger fortune in Cilicia than all the other Cilicians combined, and he is begging the god to give him back the eye that he has lost."

Apollonius fixed his glance on the ground, as he used to 2
in his old age too, and asked, "What is his name?" On hearing it he said, "It seems to me best, your reverence, not to admit this man to the sanctuary. Somebody unclean

[12] Philosopher who lived about 500 BCE, noted for the obscurity of his sayings.

γάρ τις ἥκει καὶ κεχρημένος οὐκ ἐπὶ χρηστοῖς τῷ πάθει, καὶ αὐτὸ δὲ τὸ πρὶν εὑρέσθαι τι παρὰ τοῦ θεοῦ πολυτελῶς θύειν οὐ θύοντός ἐστιν, ἀλλ' ἑαυτὸν παραιτουμένου σχετλίων τε καὶ χαλεπῶν ἔργων." ταῦτα μὲν ὁ Ἀπολλώνιος. ὁ δ' Ἀσκληπιὸς ἐπιστὰς νύκτωρ τῷ ἱερεῖ "ἀπίτω" ἔφη "ὁ δεῖνα τὰ ἑαυτοῦ ἔχων, ἄξιος γὰρ μηδὲ τὸν ἕτερον τῶν ὀφθαλμῶν ἔχειν." ἀναμανθάνων οὖν ὁ ἱερεὺς τὸν ἄνθρωπον, γυνὴ μὲν τῷ Κίλικι τούτῳ ἐγεγόνει θυγατέρα ἔχουσα προτέρων γάμων, ὁ δὲ ἤρα τῆς κόρης καὶ ἀκολάστως εἶχε, ξυνῆν τε οὐδ' ὡς λαθεῖν· ἐπιστᾶσα γὰρ ἡ μήτηρ τῇ εὐνῇ τῆς μὲν ἄμφω, τοῦ δὲ τὸν ἕτερον τῶν ὀφθαλμῶν ἐξέκοψεν ἐναράξασα τὰς περόνας.

11. Τό γε μὴν θύοντας ἢ ἀνατιθέντας μὴ ὑπερβάλλειν τὸ μέτριον ὧδε αὐτῷ ἐφιλοσοφεῖτο· πλειόνων γάρ ποτε ξυνεληλυθότων ἐς τὸ ἱερὸν ἄρτι ἐξεληλαμένου τοῦ Κίλικος, ἤρετο τὸν ἱερέα οὑτωσί· "ἆρα" ἔφη "οἱ θεοὶ δίκαιοι;" "δικαιότατοι μὲν οὖν" εἶπε. "τί δέ· ξυνετοί;" "καὶ τί" ἔφη "ξυνετώτερον τοῦ θείου;" "τὰ δὲ τῶν ἀνθρώπων ἴσασιν, ἢ ἄπειροι αὐτῶν εἰσι;" "καὶ μὴν τοῦτ'" ἔφη "πλεονεκτοῦσι μάλιστα οἱ θεοὶ τῶν ἀνθρώπων, ὅτι οἱ μὲν ὑπ' ἀσθενείας οὐδὲ τὰ ἑαυτῶν ἴσασι, τοῖς δὲ γιγνώσκειν ὑπάρχει τὰ ἐκείνων τε καὶ τὰ αὑτῶν."

2 "Πάντα" ἔφη "ἄριστα, ὦ ἱερεῦ, καὶ ἀληθέστατα. ἐπεὶ τοίνυν πάντα γιγνώσκουσι, δοκεῖ μοι τὸν ἥκοντα ἐς θεοῦ καὶ χρηστὰ ἑαυτῷ ξυνειδότα τοιάνδε εὐχὴν εὔχεσθαι· 'ὦ θεοί, δοίητέ μοι τὰ ὀφειλόμενα.' ὀφείλε-

has come, who met his affliction in inauspicious circumstances. Extravagant sacrifices offered when a man has not yet obtained anything from the god are not sacrifices, but excuses offered for shocking and wicked deeds." Apollonius said no more, but Asclepius appeared to the priest by night and said, "Let So-and-So keep his goods and go; he does not deserve even to have one eye." The priest made inquiries about the man, and this Cilician had a wife with a daughter by a previous marriage, and he had fallen in love with the girl, behaved outrageously and slept with her. But they were found out, since the mother caught them in bed, and with a thrust of her brooch pins put out both of the girl's eyes and one of the man's.

11. In fact Apollonius gave a discourse about not going to excess when we make a sacrifice or dedication. Many people had gathered at the shrine soon after the expulsion of the Cilician, and he questioned the priest thus. "Are the gods just?" he asked. "Of course, entirely just," was the reply. "Are they intelligent too?" "Why," was the reply, "what is more intelligent than divinity?" "Do they know about human affairs, or are they ignorant of them?" "That is the greatest advantage of gods over humans," said the priest. "Humans in their frailty do not even understand their own affairs, but the gods understand the business of humans as well as their own."

"Very good answers, your reverence," said Apollonius, 2
"and very true. Well, since they understand everything, I think that someone coming to a god's abode with a clear conscience should pray, 'O gods, give me what I deserve.'

ται γάρ που, ὦ ἱερεῦ, τοῖς μὲν ὁσίοις τὰ ἀγαθά, τοῖς δὲ φαύλοις τἀναντία, καὶ οἱ θεοὶ οὖν εὖ ποιοῦντες ὃν μὲν ἂν ὑγιᾶ τε καὶ ἄτρωτον κακίας εὕρωσι, πέμπουσι δήπου στεφανώσαντες οὐ χρυσοῖς στεφάνοις, ἀλλ' ἀγαθοῖς πᾶσιν, ὃν δ' ἂν κατεστιγμένον ἴδωσι καὶ διεφθορότα, καταλείπουσι τῇ δίκῃ, τοσοῦτον αὐτοῖς ἐπιμηνίσαντες, ὅσον ἐτόλμησαν καὶ ἱερὰ ἐσφοιτᾶν μὴ καθαροὶ ὄντες." καὶ ἅμα ἐς τὸν Ἀσκληπιὸν βλέψας "φιλοσοφεῖς," ἔφη "ὦ Ἀσκληπιέ, τὴν ἄρρητόν τε καὶ συγγενῆ σαυτῷ φιλοσοφίαν μὴ συγχωρῶν τοῖς φαύλοις δεῦρο ἥκειν, μηδ' ἂν πάντα σοι τὰ ἀπὸ Ἰνδῶν καὶ Σαρδῴων ξυμφέρωσιν. οὐ γὰρ τιμῶντες τὸ θεῖον θύουσι ταῦτα καὶ ἀνάπτουσιν, ἀλλ' ὠνούμενοι τὴν δίκην, ἣν οὐ ξυγχωρεῖτε αὐτοῖς δικαιότατοι ὄντες." πολλὰ τοιαῦτα ἐν τῷ ἱερῷ ἐφιλοσόφει ἐν ἐφήβῳ ἔτι.

12. Κἀκεῖνα τῆς ἐν Αἰγαῖς διατριβῆς· Κιλίκων ἦρχεν ὑβριστὴς ἄνθρωπος καὶ κακὸς τὰ ἐρωτικά· ἐς τοῦτον ἦλθε λόγος τῆς τοῦ Ἀπολλωνίου ὥρας, ὁ δὲ ἐρρῶσθαι φράσας οἷς ἔπραττεν, ἐν Ταρσοῖς δὲ ἄρα ἀγορὰν ἦγεν, ἐξωρμήθη ἐς τὰς Αἰγὰς νοσεῖν τε ἑαυτὸν φήσας καὶ τοῦ Ἀσκληπιοῦ δεῖσθαι, καὶ προσελθὼν τῷ Ἀπολλωνίῳ βαδίζοντι ἰδίᾳ "σύστησόν με" ἔφη "τῷ θεῷ." ὁ δὲ ὑπολαβὼν "καὶ τί σοι δεῖ τοῦ συστήσοντος," εἶπεν "εἰ χρηστὸς εἶ; τοὺς γὰρ σπουδαίους οἱ θεοὶ καὶ ἄνευ τῶν προξενούντων ἀσπάζονται." "ὅτι νὴ Δί'," ἔφη "Ἀπολλώνιε, σὲ μὲν ὁ θεὸς πεποίηται ξένον, ἐμὲ δὲ οὔπω." "ἀλλὰ κἀμοῦ" ἔφη "καλοκαγαθία προὔ-

The devout surely deserve good, your reverence, and the wicked the opposite. Hence, if the gods in their kindness find a man to be sincere and free from sin, they send him on his way crowned not with mere crowns of gold, but with every blessing. But if they see a man to be besmirched and corrupt, they leave him to receive his retribution, showing their anger with him only insofar as he dared to enter a holy place when not in a state of purity." At the same time, turning his eyes to the statue of Asclepius he said, "It is your ineffable and native wisdom you practice, Asclepius, when you forbid the wicked to come here, even if they amass all the wealth of India and Sardinia for you.[13] They do not make these sacrifices and dedications to honor divinity, but to buy a favorable judgment, which you gods in your great justice do not grant." And he gave many such philosophic disquisitions in the sanctuary while still in his early youth.

12. The following story also concerns his stay in Aegeae. The ruler of Cilicia was a bully and a lecher. When he heard talk of Apollonius's youthful beauty he dropped what was doing—in fact he was holding court in Tarsus—and dashed off to Aegeae, saying he was ill and needed Asclepius. He came up to Apollonius when he was walking alone, and said, "Introduce me to the god." "Why do you need an introduction," said he, "if you are good? The gods welcome virtuous men without any go-betweens." "Because, by Zeus," said the man, "the god has made you his guest, Apollonius, but not me." "It was my virtue that rec-

[13] Sardinia does not produce precious stones, but Philostratus may have thought that stones such as sard (carnelian) and sardonyx came from there.

ξένησεν, ᾗ χρώμενος, ὡς δυνατὸν νέῳ, θεράπων τέ εἰμι τοῦ Ἀσκληπιοῦ καὶ ἑταῖρος· εἰ δὲ καὶ σοὶ καλοκαγαθίας μέλει, χώρει θαρρῶν παρὰ τὸν θεὸν καὶ εὔχου, ὅ τι ἐθέλεις." "νὴ Δί'," εἶπεν "ἤν σοί γε προτέρῳ εὔξωμαι." "καὶ τί" ἔφη "ἐμοὶ εὔξῃ;" "ὃ" ἦ δ' ὃς "εὔχεσθαι δεῖ τοῖς καλοῖς· εὐχόμεθα δὲ αὐτοῖς κοινωνεῖν τοῦ κάλλους καὶ μὴ φθονεῖν τῆς ὥρας."

2 Ἔλεγε δὲ ταῦτα ὑποθρύπτων ἑαυτὸν καὶ τοὺς ὀφθαλμοὺς ὑγραίνων καὶ τί γὰρ οὐχ ἑλίττων τῶν οὕτως ἀσελγῶν τε καὶ ἐπιρρήτων. ὁ δὲ ταυρηδὸν ὑποβλέψας ‹ἐς›[6] αὐτὸν "μαίνῃ," ἔφη, "ὦ κάθαρμα." τοῦ δ' οὐ μόνον πρὸς ὀργὴν ταῦτα ἀκούσαντος, ἀλλὰ καὶ ἀπειλήσαντος, ὡς ἀποκόψοι αὐτοῦ τὴν κεφαλήν, καταγελάσας ὁ Ἀπολλώνιος "ὦ ἡ δεῖνα ἡμέρα" ἀνεβόησε· τρίτη δὲ ἄρα ἦν ἀπ' ἐκείνης, ἐν ᾗ δήμιοι κατὰ τὴν ὁδὸν ἀπέκτειναν τὸν ὑβριστὴν ἐκεῖνον, ὡς ξὺν Ἀρχελάῳ τῷ Καππαδοκίας βασιλεῖ νεώτερα ἐπὶ Ῥωμαίους πράττοντα. ταῦτα καὶ πολλὰ τοιαῦτα Μαξίμῳ τῷ Αἰγιεῖ ξυγγέγραπται, ἠξιώθη δὲ καὶ βασιλείων ἐπιστολῶν οὗτος εὐδοκιμῶν τὴν φωνήν.

13. Ἐπεὶ δὲ τεθνεῶτα τὸν πατέρα ἤκουσεν, ἔδραμεν ἐς τὰ Τύανα, κἀκεῖνον μὲν ταῖς ἑαυτοῦ χερσὶν ἔθαψε πρὸς τῷ τῆς μητρὸς σήματι, ἐτεθνήκει δὲ κἀκείνη οὐ πάλαι, τὴν δὲ οὐσίαν λαμπρὰν οὖσαν διέλαχε πρὸς τὸν ἀδελφὸν, ἀκόλαστόν τε καὶ φιλοπότην ὄντα. καὶ τῷ μὲν τρίτον τε καὶ εἰκοστὸν ἦν ἔτος καὶ ἡλικία οἵα μὴ ἐπιτροπεύεσθαι, ὁ δ' αὖ εἴκοσι γεγόνει καὶ οἱ νόμοι αὐτὸν ὑπεῖχον τοῖς ἐπιτρόποις. διατρίψας οὖν ἐν

ommended me," he replied, "and because I practice it as far as a young man can, I am Asclepius's servant and companion. If you too care for virtue, go before the god without fear and make what prayer you want." "I will," he replied, "if I can pray to you first." "What are you going to pray to me for?" Apollonius asked. "What one must pray for from the beautiful," said the man. "We pray them to share their beauty and not be miserly with their young bloom."

He said this with a limp posture and moist eyes and all 2
the insinuating movements of such unspeakable lechers. Scowling at him beneath his brows, Apollonius said, "You are mad, you trash." The man was not only furious at these words, but threatened to cut off Apollonius's head, at which Apollonius laughed and shouted, "Ah for the day." That was the day after next, and on it public slaves executed the tyrant in the highway for conspiring with Archelaus, the king of Cappadocia, against Rome.[14] This and much else of the kind has been recorded by Maximus of Aegeae, who as an admired speaker was put in charge of the imperial correspondence.

13. When Apollonius heard that his father had died, he hurried to Tyana and with his own hands laid him to rest near the tomb of his mother, since she too had died not long before. The estate, a wealthy one, he divided with his debauched and drunken brother, who at twenty-two was over the age for a guardian, while Apollonius at twenty was subjected to guardians by the laws. After a further stay in

[14] The last king of Cappadocia, deposed by Tiberius in 17 CE.

---

6 <ἐς> Cob.

Αἰγαῖς πάλιν, καὶ τὸ ἱερὸν Λύκειόν τε ἀποφήνας καὶ Ἀκαδημίαν, φιλοσοφίας γὰρ ἠχὼ πάσης ἐν αὐτῷ ἦν, ἐπανῆλθεν ἐς τὰ Τύανα ἀνὴρ ἤδη καὶ κύριος τῶν ἑαυτοῦ. εἰπόντος δὲ πρὸς αὐτόν τινος, ὡς σωφρονίσαι τὸν ἀδελφὸν προσήκοι αὐτῷ καὶ μεταβαλεῖν τοῦ τρόπου, "τουτὶ μὲν θρασὺ" ἔφη "δόξει, πρεσβύτερον γὰρ νέος πῶς ἂν σωφρονίζοιμι; ὡς δέ μοι δυνατόν, ἰάσομαι αὐτὸν τουτωνὶ τῶν παθῶν·" δίδωσι δὴ αὐτῷ τὴν ἡμίσειαν τῆς ἑαυτοῦ μοίρας, τὸν μὲν πλειόνων δεῖσθαι φήσας, ἑαυτὸν δὲ ὀλίγων,

2 Ἐφιστὰς δὲ αὐτὸν καὶ σοφῶς ὑπαγόμενος ἐς τὸ σωφρονίζοντι πείθεσθαι "ὁ μὲν πατὴρ" ἔφη "μεθέστηκεν, ὃς ἐπαίδευέ τε ἡμᾶς καὶ ἐνουθέτει, λοιπὸς δὲ σὺ ἐμοὶ καὶ σοὶ δήπου ἐγώ. εἴτ᾽ οὖν ἐγώ τι ἁμαρτάνοιμι, σύμβουλος γίγνου καὶ ἰῶ τἀμά, εἴτ᾽ αὐτός τι ἁμαρτάνοις, ἀνέχου διδάσκοντος." κἀκεῖνον μέν, ὥσπερ οἱ καταψῶντες τοὺς δυσηνίους τε καὶ μὴ εὐαγώγους τῶν ἵππων, ἐς πειθὼ ἤγαγε καὶ μετερρύθμισε τῶν ἁμαρτημάτων πολλῶν ὄντων, καὶ γὰρ κύβων ἥττητο καὶ οἴνου, καὶ ἐφ᾽ ἑταίρας[7] ἐκώμαζεν ἐπαιρούσης αὐτὸν κόμης, ἣν καὶ βαφαῖς ἤσκει, σοβῶν τε καὶ ἄνω βαίνων. ἐπεὶ δὲ καὶ τὰ πρὸς τὸν ἀδελφὸν αὐτῷ εὖ εἶχεν, ἐπὶ τοὺς ἄλλους ἤδη συγγενεῖς ἐτράπετο, καὶ τοὺς δεομένους σφῶν ἀνεκτήσατο τῇ λοιπῇ οὐσίᾳ μικρὰ ἑαυτῷ ὑπολιπόμενος. ὅτε δὴ τὸν μὲν Κλαζομένιον Ἀναξαγόραν ἀγέλαις τε καὶ μήλοις[8] τὰ ἑαυτοῦ ἀνέντα προβάτοις ἔφη μᾶλλον ἢ ἀνθρώποις φιλοσο-

Aegeae, in which he made the shrine a Lyceum and an Academy, since it rang entirely with philosophy, he returned to Tyana after reaching manhood and coming into his own estate. When somebody told him that it was his duty to correct his brother and make him change his ways, he replied, "That will look arrogant, for how can a young man like me correct someone my senior? But I will do my best to cure him of these afflictions." And so he gave him half of his own inheritance, saying that his brother needed much and himself little.

After getting his attention and wisely inducing him to respond to correction, he said, "Father is no longer here to educate us and give us advice; you are all my family now, and of course I am yours. So if I do wrong, advise me and save me from error, and if you do wrong, bear with me when I instruct you." Thus, as people stroke restive and disobedient horses, he made his brother listen to persuasion and cured him of all his many faults. Previously he had been devoted to dice and drink, and had run after mistresses, priding himself on his hair, on which he even used dyes, and strutting about in his vanity. Now that Apollonius and his brother were on good terms, he started on his other relatives, and won over the impecunious among them with the rest of his estate. He left only a little for himself, saying that when Anaxagoras of Clazomenae let cattle and sheep have his land he was acting like a philosopher towards 2

---

[7] *ἑταίρας* Valck.: *ἑταιραῖς*
[8] *καὶ μήλοις* M. Casaubon (Kay.): *καμήλοις*

φῆσαι, τὸν δὲ Θηβαῖον Κράτητα καταποντώσαντα τὴν οὐσίαν οὔτε ἀνθρώποις γενέσθαι ἐπιτήδειον οὔτε προβάτοις.

3 Εὐδοκιμήσαντος δὲ τοῦ Πυθαγόρου ἐπὶ τῷ λόγῳ, ὃν ἔλεγε περὶ τοῦ μὴ δεῖν παρ' ἄλλην ἰέναι γυναῖκα ἢ τὴν ἑαυτοῦ, τουτὶ μὲν ἑτέροις ἔφη ὑπὸ Πυθαγόρου προειρῆσθαι, αὐτὸς δὲ μήτ' ἂν γῆμαι μήτ' ἂν ἐς ὁμιλίαν ἀφικέσθαι ποτὲ ἀφροδισίων, ὑπερβαλλόμενος καὶ τὸ τοῦ Σοφοκλέους. ὁ μὲν γὰρ λυττῶντα ἔφη καὶ ἄγριον δεσπότην ἀποφυγεῖν ἐς γῆρας ἐλθών, ὁ δ' ὑπ' ἀρετῆς τε καὶ σωφροσύνης οὐδ' ἐν μειρακίῳ ἡττήθη τούτου, ἀλλὰ καὶ νέος ὢν καὶ τὸ σῶμα ἐρρωμένος ἐκράτει τε καὶ λυττῶντος ἐδέσποζεν. ἀλλ' ὅμως συκοφαντοῦσί τινες ἐπὶ ἀφροδισίοις αὐτόν, ὡς διαμαρτίᾳ ἐρωτικῇ χρησάμενον καὶ διὰ τοῦτο ἀπενιαυτίσαντα ἐς τὸ Σκυθῶν ἔθνος, ὃς οὔτε ἐφοίτησέ ποτε ἐς Σκύθας οὔτε ἐς ἐρωτικὰ πάθη ἀπηνέχθη· οὔκουν οὐδὲ Εὐφράτης ποτὲ ἐσυκοφάντησεν ἐπὶ ἀφροδισίοις τὸν ἄνδρα, καίτοι ψευδῆ γράμματα κατ' αὐτοῦ ξυνθείς, ὡς ἐν τοῖς περὶ Εὐφράτου λόγοις δείξομεν, διεφέρετο δὲ πρὸς τὸν Ἀπολλώνιον, ἐπειδὴ πάνθ' ὑπὲρ χρημάτων αὐτὸν πράττοντα ἐπέκοπτεν[9] οὗτος καὶ ἀπῆγε τοῦ χρηματίζεσθαί τε καὶ τὴν σοφίαν καπηλεύειν. ἀλλὰ ταῦτα μὲν ἐς τοὺς αὐτῶν χρόνους ἀναβεβλήσθω μοι.

14. Ἐρομένου δέ ποτε τὸν Ἀπολλώνιον τοῦ Εὐξένου, τί δῆτα οὐ ξυγγράφοι καίτοι γενναίως δοξάζων

[9] ἐπέκοπτεν Rsk.: ἐπέσκωπτεν

animals rather than humans, and when Crates of Thebes[15] threw his inheritance into the sea he had benefited neither humans nor animals.

Now Pythagoras was praised for saying that a man should not approach any woman except his wife, but according to Apollonius Pythagoras had prescribed that for others, but he himself was not going to marry or even have sexual intercourse. In this he surpassed the famous saying of Sophocles, who claimed that he had escaped from a raging, wild master when he reached old age.[16] Thanks to his virtue and self-mastery, Apollonius was not subject to it even as an adolescent, but despite his youth and physical strength he overcame and "mastered" its rage. Even so some people slander him on sexual grounds, claiming that he had an illicit affair and consequently went into banishment in the Scythian region, though he never once visited Scythia or fell prey to sexual passion. Even Euphrates[17] does not slander the Master on sexual grounds in the mendacious attack that he wrote against him, as I will show when my account comes to Euphrates. Their quarrel came about because Apollonius rebuked him for doing anything for money, and tried to dissuade him from money-grubbing and selling wisdom at a discount. But I should defer these details to their proper time. 3

14. Euxenus once asked Apollonius why he did not become a writer when his ideas were noble and his diction

[15] Cynic philosopher of the late fourth and early third centuries. [16] An often quoted remark of the fifth-century tragedian, first appearing in Plato's *Republic* (329 C).

[17] Stoic philosopher, contemporary and persistent enemy of Apollonius.

καὶ ἀπαγγελίᾳ χρώμενος δοκίμῳ καὶ ἐγηγερμένῃ, "ὅτι" ἔφη "οὔπω ἐσιώπησα." καὶ ἐνθένδε ἀρξάμενος σιωπᾶν ᾠήθη δεῖν, καὶ τὴν μὲν φωνὴν κατεῖχεν, οἱ δ' ὀφθαλμοὶ καὶ ὁ νοῦς πλεῖστα μὲν ἀνεγίγνωσκον, πλεῖστα δὲ ἐς μνήμην ἀνελέγοντο. τό τοι μνημονικὸν ἑκατοντούτης γενόμενος καὶ ὑπὲρ τὸν Σιμωνίδην ἔρρωτο, καὶ ὕμνος αὐτῷ τις ἐς τὴν μνημοσύνην ᾔδετο, ἐν ᾧ πάντα μὲν ὑπὸ τοῦ χρόνου μαραίνεσθαί φησιν, αὐτόν γε μὴν τὸν χρόνον ἀγήρω τε καὶ ἀθάνατον παρὰ τὴν μνημοσύνην[10] εἶναι.

2 Οὐ μὴν ἄχαρις τά γε ἐς ξυνουσίας ἦν παρ' ὃν ἐσιώπα χρόνον, ἀλλὰ πρὸς τὰ λεγόμενα καὶ οἱ ὀφθαλμοί τι ἐπεσήμαινον καὶ ἡ χεὶρ καὶ τὸ τῆς κεφαλῆς νεῦμα, οὐδὲ ἀμειδὴς ἢ σκυθρωπὸς ἐφαίνετο, τὸ γὰρ φιλέταιρόν τε καὶ τὸ εὐμενὲς εἶχε. τοῦτον ἐπιπονώτατον αὐτῷ φησι γενέσθαι τὸν βίον ὅλων πέντε ἐτῶν ἀσκηθέντα, πολλὰ μὲν γὰρ εἰπεῖν ἔχοντα μὴ εἰπεῖν, πολλὰ δὲ πρὸς ὀργὴν ἀκούσαντα μὴ ἀκοῦσαι, πολλοῖς δ' ἐπιπλῆξαι προαχθέντα "'τέτλαθι δὴ κραδίη' τε καὶ γλῶττα" πρὸς ἑαυτὸν φάναι, λόγων τε προσκρουσάντων αὐτῷ παρεῖναι τὰς ἐλέγξεις τότε.

15. Διέτριψέ τε τοὺς τῆς σιωπῆς χρόνους τὸν μὲν ἐν Παμφύλοις, τὸν δὲ ἐν Κιλικίᾳ, καὶ βαδίζων δι' οὕτω τρυφώντων ἐθνῶν οὐδαμοῦ ἐφθέγξατο, οὐδ' ὑπήχθη γρύξαι. ὁπότε μὴν στασιαζούσῃ πόλει ἐντύχοι, πολλαὶ δὲ ἐστασίαζον ὑπὲρ θεαμάτων οὐ σπουδαίων, παρελθὼν ἂν καὶ δείξας ἑαυτόν, καί τι καὶ μελλούσης

pure and alert. "Because I have not yet fallen silent," he answered. From then on he considered himself bound to silence, though while he held his tongue, his eyes and mind read and stored away very many things in his memory. In fact even when he was a hundred he surpassed Simonides himself in power of recollection.[18] He used to sing a hymn in honor of Memory, in which he says that all things wither in time, but time itself is ageless and immortal thanks to memory.

He was not however socially unattractive during the time of his silence, but when spoken to he replied with his eyes, his hands, or by motions of his head; and he did not seem unsmiling or gloomy, but retained his love of society and his kindness. He says that this way of life, which he practiced for five whole years, was extremely difficult. He could not speak when he had much to say, and could not hear when he heard much to make him angry. He was impelled to correct many people, but said to himself, "'Bear up, my heart,'[19] and my tongue too," and when remarks offended him he deferred refuting them for a time. 2

15. He spent the time of his silence partly in Pamphylia and partly in Cilicia, and though he traveled among such pleasure-loving regions he never uttered a sound or was induced even to murmur. Whenever a city he visited was in turmoil, as many were because of their worthless amusements, he would enter, show himself, and give some hint of

[18] Poet of the late sixth and early fifth centuries from the Aegean island of Ceos, believed to have invented the art of memorization. [19] Homer, *Odyssey* 20.18.

---

[10] τὴν μνημοσύνην Richards: τῆς μνημοσύνης

ἐπιπλήξεως τῇ χειρὶ καὶ τῷ προσώπῳ ἐνδειξάμενος, ἐξῄρητ᾽ ἂν ἀταξία πᾶσα καὶ ὥσπερ ἐν μυστηρίοις ἐσιώπων. καὶ τὸ μὲν τοὺς ὀρχηστῶν τε καὶ ἵππων ἕνεκα στασιάζειν ὡρμηκότας ἀνασχεῖν οὔπω μέγα, οἱ γὰρ ὑπὲρ τοιούτων ἀτακτοῦντες, ἂν πρὸς ἄνδρα ἴδωσιν, ἐρυθριῶσί τε καὶ αὑτῶν ἐπιλαμβάνονται καὶ ῥᾷστα δὴ ἐς νοῦν ἥκουσι.

2 Λιμῷ δὲ πεπιεσμένην πόλιν οὐ ῥᾴδιον εὐηνίῳ καὶ πιθανῷ λόγῳ μεταδιδάξαι καὶ ὀργῆς παῦσαι, ἀλλ᾽ Ἀπολλωνίῳ καὶ ἡ σιωπὴ πρὸς τοὺς οὕτω διακειμένους ἤρκει. ἀφίκετο μὲν γὰρ ἐς Ἄσπενδον τὴν Παμφύλων (πρὸς Εὐρυμέδοντι δὲ οἰκεῖται ποταμῷ ἡ πόλις αὕτη, τρίτη τῶν ἐκεῖ), ὄροβοι δ᾽ ὤνιοι καὶ τὰ ἐς βρῶσιν ἀναγκαῖα διέβοσκεν αὐτούς, τὸν γὰρ σῖτον οἱ δυνατοὶ ξυγκλείσαντες εἶχον, ἵν᾽ ἐκκαπηλευθείη τῆς χώρας. ἀνηρέθιστο δὴ ἐπὶ τὸν ἄρχοντα ἡλικία πᾶσα καὶ πυρὸς ἐπ᾽ αὐτὸν ἥπτοντο, καίτοι προσκείμενον τοῖς βασιλείοις ἀνδριᾶσιν, οἳ καὶ τοῦ Διὸς τοῦ ἐν Ὀλυμπίᾳ φοβερώτεροι ἦσαν τότε καὶ ἀσυλότεροι, Τιβερίου γε ὄντες, ἐφ᾽ οὗ λέγεταί τις ἀσεβῆσαι δόξαι, τυπτήσας τὸν ἑαυτοῦ δοῦλον φέροντα δραχμὴν ἀργυρᾶν νενομισμένην ἐς Τιβέριον. προσελθὼν οὖν τῷ ἄρχοντι ἤρετο αὐτὸν τῇ χειρί, ὅ τι εἴη τοῦτο, τοῦ δὲ ἀδικεῖν μὲν

---

[20] Dancers, also called "pantomimes," performed mythological ballets, and were a popular type of entertainment in the Roman empire.

his intended rebuke by his hand and his expression. That would end all disturbance, and silence fell as if at the Mysteries. But there is nothing wonderful about restraining people beginning to fight over dancers[20] or horses, since those misbehaving over such matters will blush, recover themselves, and return to their senses at the sight of a true man.

When a city is gnawed by famine, however, it is no easy 2
matter to win it over with calm and persuasive words and to check its fury, though with Apollonius even silence was enough to control those in such a condition. He once came to Aspendus in Pamphylia, a city situated on the river Eurymedon, and the third in importance of the province. Vetch was on sale, and people lived off anything that gave sustenance, as the upper classes were keeping the grain stored up to create a shortage in the territory.[21] People of every age were infuriated with the chief magistrate, and had begun to light torches to burn him alive, even though he clung to the statues of the emperor. At that time these were more feared and sacrosanct than the Zeus at Olympia, since they represented Tiberius. (In his reign, they say, a man was convicted for treason simply for beating his own slave when the slave was carrying a silver drachma with Tiberius's image.)[22] So Apollonius went to the magistrate and by means of a gesture asked him the matter. The man said he had done no wrong, but was being wronged to-

[21] Bitter vetch was mainly used as animal fodder.

[22] Tiberius was highly suspicious of treason (*maiestas*). Cf. the story of Jesus shown a Roman *denarius* with the "image and circumscription of Caesar," probably Tiberius (Luke 20.24).

οὐδὲν φήσαντος, ἀδικεῖσθαι δὲ μετὰ τοῦ δήμου, λόγου δ᾽ εἰ μὴ τύχοι, ξυναπολεῖσθαι τῷ δήμῳ,

3 Μετεστράφη τε εἰς τοὺς περιεστηκότας ὁ Ἀπολλώνιος καὶ ἔνευσεν ὡς χρὴ ἀκοῦσαι, οἱ δὲ οὐ μόνον ἐσιώπησαν ὑπ᾽ ἐκπλήξεως τῆς πρὸς αὐτόν, ἀλλὰ καὶ τὸ πῦρ ἔθεντο ἐπὶ τῶν βωμῶν τῶν αὐτόθι. ἀναθαρρήσας οὖν ὁ ἄρχων "ὁ δεῖνα" ἔφη "καὶ ὁ δεῖνα" πλείους εἰπὼν "τοῦ λιμοῦ τοῦ καθεστηκότος αἴτιοι, τὸν γὰρ σῖτον ἀπολαβόντες φυλάττουσι κατ᾽ ἄλλος ἄλλο τῆς χώρας." διακελευομένων δὲ τῶν Ἀσπενδίων ἀλλήλοις ἐπὶ τοὺς ἀγροὺς φοιτᾶν, ἀνένευσεν ὁ Ἀπολλώνιος μὴ πράττειν τοῦτο, μετακαλεῖν δὲ μᾶλλον τοὺς ἐν τῇ αἰτίᾳ καὶ παρ᾽ ἑκόντων εὑρέσθαι τὸν σῖτον. ἀφικομένων δὲ μικροῦ μὲν ἐδέησε καὶ φωνὴν ἐπ᾽ αὐτοὺς ῥῆξαι, παθών τι πρὸς τὰ τῶν πολλῶν δάκρυα, καὶ γὰρ παιδία ξυνερρυήκει καὶ γύναια, καὶ ὠλοφύροντο οἱ γεγηρακότες, ὡς αὐτίκα δὴ ἀποθανούμενοι λιμῷ. τιμῶν δὲ τὸ τῆς σιωπῆς δόγμα, γράφει ἐς γραμματεῖον ἐπίπληξιν καὶ δίδωσιν ἀναγνῶναι τῷ ἄρχοντι· ἡ δὲ ἐπίπληξις ὧδε εἶχεν· "Ἀπολλώνιος σιτοκαπήλοις Ἀσπενδίων. ἡ γῆ πάντων μήτηρ, δικαία γάρ, ὑμεῖς δὲ ἄδικοι ὄντες πεποίησθε αὐτὴν αὑτῶν μόνων μητέρα. καὶ εἰ μὴ παύσεσθε, οὐκ ἐάσω ὑμᾶς ἐπ᾽ αὐτῆς ἑστάναι." ταῦτα δείσαντες ἐνέπλησαν τὴν ἀγορὰν σίτου, καὶ ἀνεβίω ἡ πόλις.

16. Ἐπεφοίτησε καὶ Ἀντιοχείᾳ τῇ μεγάλῃ πεπαυμένος τοῦ σιωπᾶν, καὶ παρῆλθεν ἐς τὸ ἱερὸν τοῦ Δαφναίου Ἀπόλλωνος, ᾧ περιάπτουσιν Ἀσσύριοι τὸν

gether with the people, and if he could not get a hearing, he and they would perish together.

Turning to the bystanders, Apollonius nodded to them 3
to listen, and out of reverence for him they not only fell silent, but also put their torches on the nearby altars. Recovering his courage, the magistrate said, "so-and-so and so-and-so" (naming several people) "are responsible for the present famine. They are holding back the grain and storing it in different parts of the territory." The Aspendians began to urge each other to go to these estates, but Apollonius shook his head to show that they should not do this, but instead summon the accused and recover the grain from them voluntarily. On their arrival, he could scarcely help breaking into speech against them, being rather moved by the tears of the people, for women and children had gathered, and the aged were groaning as if about to die of starvation on the spot. Yet he obeyed his vow of silence, writing his reproach on a writing tablet and giving it to the magistrate to read. This was his reproach: "Apollonius to the corn merchants of Aspendus. The earth in her justice is the mother of all, but you in your injustice have made her mother to yourselves alone. If you do not stop I will not even let you stand on the earth's face." Frightened by his words, they flooded the market with grain, and the city revived.

16. Visiting Antioch the Great when his silence was over, he went to the sanctuary of Apollo at Daphne.[23] The Assyrians connect a well known Arcadian myth with this

[23] Daphne ("Laurel") was a suburb of Antioch with a celebrated temple of Apollo.

μῦθον τὸν Ἀρκάδα· τὴν γὰρ τοῦ Λάδωνος Δάφνην ἐκεῖ μεταφῦναι λέγουσι καὶ ποταμὸς αὐτοῖς ῥεῖ Λάδων, καὶ φυτὸν τιμᾶται παρ' αὐτοῖς δάφνης, τοῦτο δὴ τὸ ἀντὶ τῆς παρθένου. κυπαρίττων τε ὕψη ἀμήχανα περιέστηκε κύκλῳ τὸ ἱερόν, καὶ πηγὰς ἐκδίδωσιν ὁ χῶρος ἀφθόνους τε καὶ ἠρεμούσας, αἷς τὸν Ἀπόλλω φασὶ ῥαίνεσθαι. ἐνταῦθα κυπαρίττου τι ἔρνος ἡ γῆ ἀναδέδωκεν ἐπὶ Κυπαρίττῳ φασὶν ἐφήβῳ Ἀσσυρίῳ, καὶ πιστοῦται τὴν μεταβολὴν ἡ ὥρα τοῦ φυτοῦ.

2 Καὶ ἴσως νεανικώτερον ἅπτεσθαι δοκῶ τοῦ λόγου διαμυθολογῶν τὰ τοιαῦτα· ἀλλ' οὐχ ὑπὲρ μυθολογίας ταῦτα. τί δέ μοι ὁ λόγος βούλεται; ὁ Ἀπολλώνιος ἰδὼν τὸ ἱερὸν χαρίεν μέν, σπουδὴν δ' ἐν αὐτῷ οὐδεμίαν, ἀλλ' ἀνθρώπους ἡμιβαρβάρους καὶ ἀμούσους, "Ἄπολλον," ἔφη "μετάβαλε τοὺς ἀφώνους ἐς δένδρα, ἵνα κἂν ὡς κυπάριττοι ἠχῶσιν." τὰς δὲ πηγὰς ἐπισκεψάμενος, ὡς γαλήνην ἄγουσι καὶ κελαρύζει σφῶν οὐδεμία, "ἡ ἀφωνία" εἶπεν "ἡ ἐνταῦθα οὐδὲ ταῖς πηγαῖς ξυγχωρεῖ φθέγγεσθαι." πρὸς δὲ τὸν Λάδωνα ἰδὼν "οὐχ ἡ θυγάτηρ" ἔφη "σοὶ μόνη μετέβαλεν, ἀλλὰ καὶ σὺ τῷ δόξαι βάρβαρος ἐξ Ἕλληνός τε καὶ Ἀρκάδος."

3 Ἐπεὶ δὲ ἔγνω διαλέγεσθαι, τὰ μὲν ὁμιλούμενα τῶν χωρίων καὶ ἀτακτοῦντα παρῃτεῖτο, φήσας οὐκ ἀνθρώπων ἑαυτῷ δεῖν ἀλλ' ἀνδρῶν, τὰ δὲ σεμνότερα ἐσεφοίτα καὶ ᾤκει τῶν ἱερῶν τὰ μὴ κληιστά. ἡλίου μὲν δὴ ἀνίσχοντος ἐφ' ἑαυτοῦ τινα ἔπραττεν, ἃ μόνοις ἐποίει δῆλα τοῖς ἐτῶν τεττάρων σιωπᾶν γεγυμνασμέ-

place, saying that Daphne the daughter of Ladon was transformed there, and they have a flowing river Ladon, and honor a laurel tree as the transfiguration of the girl. Cypresses of enormous height surround the sanctuary, and the place produces plentiful, gentle springs, in which Apollo is said to dip. The soil has yielded a slender cypress tree, named after an Assyrian youth called Cypress, they say, and the tree's beauty corroborates the transformation.

Perhaps I seem to be beginning my story in a rather ju- 2
venile way, inserting such tales, but they are not here simply as tales. What then does my account mean? Apollonius saw that the sanctuary was pleasant, but it contained no serious pursuit, but instead some semi-barbarous and uncultured folk. "Apollo," he said, "change these dumb creatures into trees so that they can at least make a sound as cypresses." After observing how calm the springs were, and how none of them splashed, he said, "The silence here even prevents the fountains from making a sound." And looking at the Ladon he said, "Not only was your daughter transformed, but you were too, since you seem to have become a barbarian after being a Greek and an Arcadian."

When he decided to converse, he avoided crowded and 3
unruly places, saying that he needed the company of true men, and not mere humans. Instead he visited the holiest places and lived in any sanctuary that was not closed. At sunrise he used to perform certain rites by himself, which he revealed only to those who had kept silence for four

νοις. τὸν δὲ μετὰ ταῦτα καιρόν, εἰ μὲν Ἑλλὰς ἡ πόλις εἴη καὶ τὰ ἱερὰ γνώριμα, ξυγκαλῶν ἂν τοὺς ἱερέας ἐφιλοσόφει περὶ τῶν θεῶν καὶ διωρθοῦτο αὐτούς, εἴ που τῶν νομιζομένων ἐξαλλάττοιεν, εἰ δὲ βάρβαρά τε καὶ ἰδιότροπα εἴη, διεμάνθανε τοὺς ἱδρυσαμένους αὐτὰ καὶ ἐφ' ὅτῳ ἱδρύθη, πυθόμενός τε, ὅπῃ θεραπεύεται ταῦτα καὶ ὑποθέμενος, εἴ τι σοφώτερον τοῦ δρωμένου ἐνθυμηθείη, μετῄει ἐπὶ τοὺς ὁμιλητὰς καὶ ἐκέλευεν ἐρωτᾶν, ἃ βούλονται. ἔφασκε γὰρ χρῆναι τοὺς οὕτω φιλοσοφοῦντας ἠοῦς μὲν ἀρχομένης ξυνεῖναι θεοῖς, προϊούσης δὲ περὶ θεῶν, τὸν δὲ μετὰ ταῦτα καιρὸν ἀνθρωπείων πέρι τὰς ξυνουσίας ποιεῖσθαι.

4 Εἰπὼν δ' ἂν πρὸς τοὺς ἑταίρους, ὁπόσα ἠρώτων, καὶ ἱκανῶς τῆς τοιαύτης ξυνουσίας ἔχων, ἐπὶ τὴν διάλεξιν ἀνίστατο λοιπὸν τὴν ἐς πάντας, οὐ πρὸ μεσημβρίας, ἀλλ' ὁπότε μάλιστα ἡ ἡμέρα ἑστήκοι. καὶ διαλεχθεὶς ἂν ὡς ἀπαρκεῖν ᾤετο, ἠλείφετό τε καὶ τριψάμενος ἵει ἑαυτὸν ἐς ὕδωρ ψυχρόν, γῆρας ἀνθρώπων καλῶν τὰ βαλανεῖα. τῆς γοῦν Ἀντιοχείας ἀποκλεισθείσης ἐς αὐτὰ ἐπὶ μεγάλοις ἁμαρτήμασιν, "ἔδωκεν ὑμῖν" ἔφη "ὁ βασιλεὺς κακοῖς οὖσι βιῶναι πλείονα ἔτη." Ἐφεσίων δὲ βουλομένων καταλιθῶσαι τὸν ἄρχοντα ἐπὶ τῷ μὴ ἐκπυροῦν τὰ βαλανεῖα, "ὑμεῖς μὲν τὸν ἄρχοντα" ἔφη "αἰτιᾶσθε ἐπειδὴ πονηρῶς λοῦσθε, ἐγὼ δὲ ὑμᾶς ὅτι λοῦσθε."

17. Λόγων δὲ ἰδέαν ἐπήσκησεν οὐ διθυραμβώδη καὶ φλεγμαίνουσαν ποιητικοῖς ὀνόμασιν, οὐδ' αὖ κατεγλωττισμένην καὶ ὑπεραττικίζουσαν, ἀηδὲς γὰρ τὸ

years. In the following hours, if the city was Greek and its cult was famous, he would call the priests together for a lecture about the gods, setting them right if they had deviated from any tradition. If the cult was exotic and peculiar, he would make inquiries about the founders and the purpose of the foundation. Then, after finding out the reason for the customs and suggesting any way that occurred to him of making the ritual more philosophic, he would go to his disciples and tell them to put any questions they liked. For he held that those of his philosophy should converse with the gods as day broke, but about them as it advanced, and thereafter they should talk about human affairs.

When he had answered all his disciples' questions and 4
had had enough of such conversation, he would next get up and give his general lecture, not before noon but when the day was turning. After conversing as much as he thought enough, he would anoint and rub himself down, and then take a cold dip. Public bathhouses he called "men's senility," and when Antioch had been shut out of its baths as punishment for grave misconduct, he said, "The emperor has given you more years of life despite your errors." And when the Ephesians wanted to stone the chief magistrate for not heating the baths, he said, "You blame the magistrate because you bathe in discomfort, but I blame you for bathing."

17. The style of speech he adopted was not rhapsodic and turgid with poetic vocabulary, and yet not pedantic or overly Attic, since he considered unpleasant a style that

ὑπὲρ τὴν μετρίαν Ἀτθίδα ἡγεῖτο, οὐδὲ λεπτολογίᾳ ἐδίδου, οὐδὲ διῆγε τοὺς λόγους, οὐδὲ εἰρωνευομένου τις ἤκουσεν ἢ περιπατοῦντος ἐς τοὺς ἀκροωμένους, ἀλλ' ὥσπερ ἐκ τρίποδος ὅτε διαλέγοιτο "οἶδα" ἔλεγε καὶ "δοκεῖ μοι" καὶ "ποῖ φέρεσθε;" καὶ "χρὴ εἰδέναι." καὶ αἱ δόξαι βραχεῖαι καὶ ἀδαμάντινοι κύριά τε ὀνόματα καὶ προσπεφυκότα τοῖς πράγμασι, καὶ τὰ λεγόμενα ἠχὼ εἶχεν, ὥσπερ ἀπὸ σκήπτρου θεμιστευόμενα. ἐρομένου δὲ αὐτὸν τῶν στενολεσχούντων τινός, ὅτου ἕνεκα οὐ ζητοίη, "ὅτι" ἔφη "μειράκιον ὢν ἐζήτησα, νῦν δὲ οὐ χρὴ ζητεῖν, ἀλλὰ διδάσκειν ἃ εὕρηκα." "πῶς οὖν, Ἀπολλώνιε, διαλέξεται ὁ σοφός;" πάλιν ἐπερομένου αὐτὸν "ὡς νομοθέτης," ἔφη "δεῖ γὰρ τὸν νομοθέτην, ἃ πέπεικεν ἑαυτόν, ταῦτα ἐπιτάγματα ἐς τοὺς πολλοὺς ποιεῖσθαι." ὧδε αὐτῷ τὰ ἐν Ἀντιοχείᾳ ἐσπουδάζετο, καὶ ἐπέστρεφεν ἐς ἑαυτὸν ἀνθρώπους ἀμουσοτάτους.

18. Μετὰ δὲ ταῦτα λογισμὸν ἑαυτῷ διδοὺς ἀποδημίας μείζονος, ἐνθυμεῖται τὸ Ἰνδικὸν ἔθνος καὶ τοὺς ἐν αὐτῷ σοφούς, οἳ λέγονται Βραχμᾶνές τε καὶ Ὑρκάνιοι εἶναι, προσήκειν φήσας νέῳ ἀνδρὶ ἀποδημεῖν τε καὶ ὑπερορίῳ αἴρεσθαι. εὕρημα δὲ τοὺς μάγους ἐποιεῖτο, οἳ Βαβυλῶνα καὶ Σοῦσα οἰκοῦσι, καὶ γὰρ ἂν καὶ τὰ ἐκείνων διαμαθεῖν ὁδῷ χρώμενος. καὶ πρὸς τοὺς ὁμιλητὰς ἑπτὰ ὄντας ἀνέφηνε τὴν γνώμην. πειρωμένων δὲ αὐτῶν ξυμβουλεύειν ἕτερα, εἴ πῃ ἀφελχθείη τῆς ὁρμῆς ταύτης, "ἐγὼ μὲν θεοὺς" ἔφη "συμ-

was more than moderately Attic. He was not given to logic-chopping or to long discourses, and he was never heard being ironic or argumentative with his listeners. In answering he spoke as if *ex cathedra*, saying "I know," "I believe," "Where are you off to?" "You ought to know." His sentences were short and lapidary, his vocabulary correct and fitted to the circumstances, and his sayings had the ring of commandments issued from a throne. When some quibbler asked him why he did not engage in inquiry, he replied, "Because I inquired in my youth; now it is my duty not to inquire but to teach what I have found." And when the man asked him next, "How will a wise man converse?" he replied, "Like a lawgiver: for a lawgiver must make his own convictions into ordinances for the many." This is how he conversed in Antioch, winning the admiration of people completely without culture.

18. After this he pondered making a greater journey, and decided on the country of India and the wise men there called Brahmans and Hyrcanians.[24] He said that a young man ought to travel and be off to foreign parts. He considered the Magi that live in Babylon and Susa an extra dividend,[25] for he would learn their ways too in the course of his journey. When he revealed his decision to his disciples, who were seven in number, they tried to urge some other plan in the hope of diverting him from this resolution. "I," he replied, "have taken advice from the gods, and

[24] The Brahmans were the priestly caste of the Hindus, known to the Greeks since Alexander the Great. Hyrcania is the region southeast of the Caspian, and thus far from India, so that the text may be corrupt.

[25] Wise men and advisers of the Persian kings. Babylon was by now a ghost city, but Susa was still important under the Parthians.

βούλους πεποίημαι καὶ τὰ δεδογμένα εἴρηκα, ὑμῶν δὲ βάσανον ἐποιούμην, εἰ πρὸς ἅπερ ἐγὼ ἔρρωσθε. ἐπεὶ τοίνυν μαλακῶς ἔχετε, ὑμεῖς μὲν ὑγιαίνετε" ἔφη "καὶ φιλοσοφεῖτε· ἐμοὶ δὲ βαδιστέα, οἷ σοφία τε καὶ δαίμων με ἄγει." ταῦτα εἰπὼν ἐξελαύνει τῆς Ἀντιοχείας μετὰ δυοῖν θεραπόντοιν, ὥπερ[11] αὐτῷ πατρικὼ ἤστην, ὁ μὲν ἐς τάχος γράφων, ὁ δὲ ἐς κάλλος.

19. Καὶ ἀφικνεῖται ἐς τὴν ἀρχαίαν Νίνον, ἐν ᾗ ἄγαλμα ἵδρυται τρόπον βάρβαρον, ἔστι δὲ ἄρα Ἰὼ ἡ Ἰνάχου, καὶ κέρατα τῶν κροτάφων ἐκκρούει μικρὰ καὶ οἷον μέλλοντα. ἐνταῦθα διατρίβοντι καὶ πλείω ξυνιέντι περὶ τοῦ ἀγάλματος ἢ οἱ ἱερεῖς καὶ προφῆται, προσεφοίτησε Δάμις ὁ Νίνιος, ὃν κατ᾽ ἀρχὰς ἔφην ξυναποδημῆσαί οἱ, καὶ ξυνέμπορον γενέσθαι τῆς σοφίας πάσης καὶ πολλὰ τοῦ ἀνδρὸς διασώσασθαι. ὃς ἀγασθεὶς αὐτὸν καὶ ζηλώσας τῆς ὁδοῦ "ἴωμεν," ἔφη "Ἀπολλώνιε, σὺ μὲν θεῷ ἑπόμενος, ἐγὼ δὲ σοί, καὶ γάρ με καὶ πολλοῦ ἄξιον εὕροις ἄν· εἰ μὲν ἄλλο τι οὐκ οἶδα, τὸ δ᾽ οὖν ἐς Βαβυλῶνα ἧκον,[12] πόλεις τε, ὁπόσαι εἰσίν, οἶδα ἀνελθὼν οὐ πάλαι καὶ κώμας, ἐν αἷς πολλὰ ἀγαθά, καὶ μὴν καὶ τὰς φωνὰς τῶν βαρβάρων, ὁπόσαι εἰσίν, εἰσὶ δὲ ἄλλη μὲν Ἀρμενίων, ἄλλη δὲ Μήδων τε καὶ Περσῶν, ἄλλη δὲ Καδουσίων, καταλαμβάνω[13] δὲ πάσας." "ἐγὼ δέ," εἶπεν "ὦ ἑταῖρε, πασῶν ξυνίημι, μαθὼν μηδεμίαν."

[11] ὥπερ Cob.: οἵπερ [12] ἧκον Kay.: ἄγον
[13] καταλαμβάνω Jackson: μεταλαμβάνω

have told you my decision. I was testing you to see if you had the same strength as I do. But since you are weak, I wish you health and love of knowledge, but I must go where wisdom and my guardian spirit lead me." So saying, he left Antioch with two family servants, of whom one was a shorthand writer and the other a calligrapher.

19. And so he arrived in Old Ninos, where there is an idol of barbarian type in the shape of Io the daughter of Inachus, with little horns projecting from her temples and just breaking through.[26] Since Apollonius during his stay showed more knowledge about the idol than the priests and the prophets, Damis of Ninos came to hear him. This is the man whom I mentioned at the beginning as Apollonius's companion, who shared in all his wisdom and preserved many details about the Master. Struck with admiration and eager to share his journey, he said, "Let us go, Apollonius, you following God and I following you, for you might find me very valuable. I may not know anything else, but I have been to Babylon; and, having returned from there recently, I know all the cities there are and the villages, in which there are many good things, and moreover I know every one of the barbarian languages. The Armenians have one, the Medes and Persians another, the Cadusians another,[27] and I understand them all." "But I, my friend," replied Apollonius, "know them all, and have learned none."

[26] Syrian Hierapolis ("Old Ninos") had a famous cult of the goddess Atargatis. Io was a heroine of Argos whom Hera out of jealousy turned into a cow.

[27] Nomadic tribe living southwest of the Caspian.

2 Θαυμάσαντος δὲ τοῦ Νινίου "μὴ θαυμάσῃς," εἶπεν "εἰ πάσας οἶδα φωνὰς ἀνθρώπων· οἶδα γὰρ δὴ καὶ ὅσα σιωπῶσιν ἄνθρωποι." ὁ μὲν δὴ Ἀσσύριος προσηύξατο αὐτόν, ὡς ταῦτα ἤκουσε, καὶ ὥσπερ δαίμονα ἔβλεπε, συνῆν τε αὐτῷ ἐπιδιδοὺς τὴν σοφίαν καὶ ὅ τι μάθοι μνημονεύων. φωνὴ δὲ ἦν τῷ Ἀσσυρίῳ ξυμμέτρως πράττουσα, τὸ γὰρ λογοειδὲς οὐκ εἶχεν, ἅτε παιδευθεὶς ἐν βαρβάροις, διατριβὴν δὲ ἀναγράψαι καὶ συνουσίαν, καὶ ὅ τι ἤκουσεν ἢ εἶδεν ἀνατυπῶσαι, καὶ ὑπόμνημα τῶν τοιούτων ξυνθεῖναι σφόδρα ἱκανὸς ἦν, καὶ ἐπετήδευε τοῦτο ἄριστα ἀνθρώπων.

3 Ἡ γοῦν δέλτος ἡ τῶν ἐκφατνισμάτων τοιοῦτον τῷ Δάμιδι νοῦν εἶχεν· ὁ Δάμις ἐβούλετο μηδὲν τῶν Ἀπολλωνίου ἀγνοεῖσθαι, ἀλλ᾽ εἴ τι καὶ παρεφθέγξατο ἢ εἶπεν, ἀναγεγράφθαι καὶ τοῦτο. καὶ ἄξιόν γε εἰπεῖν, ἃ καὶ πρὸς τὸν μεμψάμενον τὴν διατριβὴν ταύτην ἀπεφθέγξατο. διασύροντος γὰρ αὐτὸν ἀνθρώπου ῥᾳθύμου τε καὶ βασκάνου, καὶ τὰ μὲν ἄλλα ὀρθῶς ἀναγράφειν φήσαντος, ὁπόσαι γνῶμαί τέ εἰσι καὶ δόξαι τοῦ ἀνδρός, ταυτὶ δὲ τὰ οὕτω μικρὰ ξυλλεγόμενον παραπλήσιόν που τοῖς κυσὶ πράττειν τοῖς σιτουμένοις τὰ ἐκπίπτοντα τῆς δαιτός, ὑπολαβὼν ὁ Δάμις "εἰ δαῖτες" ἔφη "θεῶν εἰσι καὶ σιτοῦνται θεοί, πάντως που καὶ θεράποντες αὐτοῖς εἰσιν, οἷς μέλει τοῦ μηδὲ τὰ πίπτοντα τῆς ἀμβροσίας ἀπόλλυσθαι." τοιοῦδε μὲν ἑταίρου καὶ ἐραστοῦ ἔτυχεν, ᾧ τὸ πολὺ τοῦ βίου συνεπορεύθη.

20. Παριόντας δὲ αὐτοὺς ἐς τὴν μέσην τῶν ποτα-

The man from Ninos was amazed, but Apollonius said, "Do not be surprised if I know all human languages: I also know all that humans keep unspoken." The Assyrian worshiped him when he said this, regarding him as a supernatural being, and he became his companion, growing in wisdom and remembering everything he learned. The Assyrian's Greek was mediocre, for he lacked elegance of style, having been educated among barbarians. Yet he was very well able to record a discourse or a conversation, describing what he had heard or seen and making an account of such experiences, and he was better fitted to do this than anybody. 2

Damis's *Scrap Book* was composed for this purpose, that he wished nothing about Apollonius to go unknown, but even his asides and random remarks to be recorded. It is worth noting the retort he made to a man who criticized this pursuit. Some lazy and malevolent creature ridiculed him, saying that he was right to put down everything that constituted the sayings and opinions of the Master, but in collecting such trifling things he was acting like a dog that feeds on the scraps fallen from a dinner. Damis replied, "If the gods have dinners and the gods take food, they must certainly have attendants to make sure that even the scraps of ambrosia do not go to waste." This was the kind of companion and admirer that Apollonius found as a traveling companion for most of his life. 3

20. When they were about to cross to Mesopotamia, the

μῶν ὁ τελώνης ὁ ἐπιβεβλημένος τῷ Ζεύγματι πρὸς τὸ πινάκιον ἦγε καὶ ἠρώτα, ὅ τι ἀπάγοιεν, ὁ δὲ Ἀπολλώνιος "ἀπάγω" ἔφη "σωφροσύνην, δικαιοσύνην, ἀρετήν, ἐγκράτειαν, ἀνδρείαν, ἄσκησιν," πολλὰ οὕτω καὶ[14] θήλεα εἴρας ὀνόματα. ὁ δ' ἤδη βλέπων τὸ ἑαυτοῦ κέρδος "ἀπόγραψαι[15] οὖν" ἔφη "τὰς δούλας." ὁ δὲ "οὐκ ἔξεστιν," εἶπεν "οὐ γὰρ δούλας ἀπάγω ταύτας, ἀλλὰ δεσποίνας."

2 Τὴν δὲ τῶν ποταμῶν μέσην ὁ Τίγρις ἀποφαίνει καὶ ὁ Εὐφράτης ῥέοντες μὲν ἐξ Ἀρμενίας καὶ Ταύρου λήγοντος, περιβάλλοντες δὲ ἤπειρον, ἐν ᾗ καὶ πόλεις μέν, τὸ δὲ πλεῖστον κῶμαι, ἔθνη τε Ἀρμένια καὶ Ἀράβια, ἃ ξυγκλείσαντες οἱ ποταμοὶ ἔχουσιν, ὧν καὶ νομάδες οἱ πολλοὶ στείχουσιν, οὕτω τι νησιώτας ἑαυτοὺς νομίζοντες, ὡς ἐπὶ θάλαττάν τε καταβαίνειν φάσκειν, ὅτ' ἐπὶ τοὺς ποταμοὺς βαδίζοιεν, ὅρον τε ποιεῖσθαι τῆς γῆς τὸν τῶν ποταμῶν κύκλον· ἀποτορνεύσαντες γὰρ τὴν προειρημένην ἤπειρον ἐπὶ τὴν αὐτὴν ἴενται θάλατταν. εἰσὶ δ', οἵ φασιν ἐς ἕλος ἀφανίζεσθαι τὸ πολὺ τοῦ Εὐφράτου καὶ τελευτᾶν τὸν ποταμὸν τοῦτον ἐν τῇ γῇ. λόγου δ' ἔνιοι θρασυτέρου ἐφάπτονται, φάσκοντες αὐτὸν ὑπὸ τῇ γῇ ῥέοντα ἐς Αἴγυπτον ἀναφαίνεσθαι καὶ Νείλῳ συγκεράννυσθαι.

3 Ἀκριβολογίας μὲν δὴ ἕνεκα καὶ τοῦ μηδὲν παραλελεῖφθαί μοι τῶν γεγραμμένων ὑπὸ τοῦ Δάμιδος, ἐβουλόμην ἂν καὶ τὰ διὰ τῶν βαρβάρων τούτων

tax collector in charge of Zeugma took them to the notice board and asked them what they were exporting.[28] "Prudence," replied Apollonius, "Justice, Virtue, Temperance, Courage, Perseverance," thus stringing out many nouns in the feminine. The official, immediately thinking of his own profit, said, "Well then, register your servants." "I cannot," retorted Apollonius, "since it is not my servants I am exporting, but my governesses."

Mesopotamia is created by the Tigris and the Euphrates flowing from Armenia and the foothills of the Taurus, since they define a landmass that contains some cities but mostly villages. The Armenian and Arabian tribes that are included by these rivers mostly travel as nomads. Yet they consider themselves to be island dwellers, and say they are going down to the sea when they approach the rivers, and they believe the circuit of the rivers, which after circumscribing this landmass enter the same sea, to be the limit of the world. Some say that most of the Euphrates disappears into a marsh and that this river ends in the earth, while others, venturing an even bolder account, say that after flowing underground it reappears in Egypt, mingling with the Nile. 2

To be precise and to leave out nothing that Damis wrote, I would have liked to tell of their conversations as they traveled among these barbarians. But my narrative 3

[28] Zeugma ("Junction") was a major crossing point of the Euphrates between Roman and Parthian territory; the "notice board" must have contained a list of dutiable items.

---

14 *οὕτω καὶ* Jackson: *καὶ οὕτω*
15 *ἀπόγραψαι* Rsk.: *ἀπογράψαι*

πορευομένοις[16] σπουδασθέντα εἰπεῖν, ξυνελαύνει δὲ ἡμᾶς ὁ λόγος ἐς τὰ μείζω τε καὶ θαυμασιώτερα, οὐ μὴν ὡς δυοῖν γε ἀμελῆσαι τούτοιν, τῆς τε ἀνδρείας, ᾗ χρώμενος ὁ Ἀπολλώνιος διεπορεύθη βάρβαρα ἔθνη καὶ λῃστρικά, οὐδ᾽ ὑπὸ Ῥωμαίοις πω ὄντα, τῆς τε σοφίας, ᾗ τὸν Ἀράβιον τρόπον ἐς ξύνεσιν τῆς τῶν ζῴων φωνῆς ἦλθεν. ἔμαθε δὲ τοῦτο διὰ τουτωνὶ τῶν Ἀραβίων πορευόμενος, ἄριστα γιγνωσκόντων τε αὐτὸ καὶ πραττόντων. ἔστι γὰρ τῶν Ἀραβίων ἤδη κοινὸν καὶ τῶν ὀρνίθων ἀκούειν μαντευομένων, ὁπόσα οἱ χρησμοί, ξυμβάλλονται δὲ τῶν ἀλόγων, σιτούμενοι τῶν δρακόντων οἱ μὲν καρδίαν φασίν, οἱ δὲ ἧπαρ.

21. Κτησιφῶντα δὲ ὑπερβαλὼν καὶ παριὼν ἐς τὰ Βαβυλῶνος ὅρια, φρουρὰ μὲν αὐτόθι ἦν ἐκ βασιλέως, ἣν οὐκ ἂν παρῆλθέ τις μὴ οὐκ ἐρωτηθεὶς ἑαυτόν τε καὶ πόλιν καὶ ἐφ᾽ ὅ τι ἥκοι. σατράπης δὲ τῇ φρουρᾷ ταύτῃ ἐπετέτακτο, βασιλέως τις, οἶμαι, ὀφθαλμός, ὁ γὰρ Μῆδος ἄρτι ἐς τὸ ἄρχειν ἥκων οὐ ξυνεχώρει ἑαυτῷ ἀδεῶς ζῆν, ἀλλὰ ὄντα τε καὶ οὐκ ὄντα δεδιὼς ἐς φόβους κατεπεπτώκει καὶ πτοίας. ἄγονται τοίνυν παρὰ τὸν σατράπην Ἀπολλώνιός τε καὶ οἱ ἀμφ᾽ αὐτόν, ὁ δὲ ἔτυχε μὲν σκηνὴν ἐφ᾽ ἁρμαμάξης πεποιημένος καὶ ἐξελαύνων ποι, ἰδὼν δὲ ἄνδρα αὐχμοῦ πλέων, ἀνέκραγέ τε ὥσπερ τὰ δειλὰ τῶν γυναίων καὶ ξυνεκαλύψατο, μόγις τε ἀναβλέψας ἐς αὐτόν, "πόθεν ἡμῖν

16 ‹πορευομένοις› Kay.

urges me on to greater and more extraordinary subjects, though I cannot neglect these two points: the courage that Apollonius showed in travelling among barbarous and rapacious tribes, not yet subject even to Rome,[29] and the wisdom whereby he attained understanding of the language of animals, in the Arabian way. He learned this too while traveling among these Arabs, who are excellent in the knowledge and practice of this science. For indeed all Arabs share the ability to hear birds predicting everything that oracles do, and they understand dumb animals by eating the hearts of snakes, or by another account the livers.

21. After he had passed Ctesiphon and was crossing the borders of Babylon, he found there a royal guardpost.[30] This you could not pass without being asked your identity, your city, and the purpose of your voyage. A governor had been made responsible for this guardpost, a sort of "King's Eye," I suppose, for having just come to power the Mede did not allow himself to live in security, but feared everything, real or unreal, and had fallen into terrors and tremblings.[31] So Apollonius and his group were led before the governor, who just at that moment had set up his tent on a wagon and was driving somewhere. Seeing a man completely unkempt, he shouted out like a frightened woman and covered his face. Then, making an effort to look at Apollonius, he said to him, "What place has sent

[29] Northern Mesopotamia, with a predominantly Arabian population, was made into a Roman province by Septimius Severus (193–211), and thus in Philostratus's lifetime.

[30] In fact Ctesiphon on the Tigris was the Parthian capital, not Babylon.

[31] The "King's Eyes" and "Ears" were secret agents of the Achaemenid kings of Persia. Philostratus consistently calls the Parthian king a "Mede."

ἐπιπεμφθεὶς ἥκεις;" οἷον δαίμονα ἠρώτα. ὁ δὲ "ὑπ' ἐμαυτοῦ," ἔφη "εἴ πῃ καὶ ἄκοντες ἄνδρες γένοισθε."

2 Πάλιν ἤρετο, ὅστις ὢν ἐσφοιτᾷ τὴν βασιλέως χώραν, ὁ δὲ "ἐμὴ" ἔφη "πᾶσα ἡ γῆ, καὶ ἀνεῖταί μοι δι' αὐτῆς πορεύεσθαι." τοῦ δὲ "βασανιῶ σε," εἰπόντος "εἰ μὴ λέγοις," "εἰ γὰρ ταῖς σαυτοῦ χερσίν," εἶπεν "ὡσαύτως[17] βασανισθείης, θιγὼν ἀνδρός." ἐκπλαγεὶς δὲ αὐτὸν ὁ εὐνοῦχος, ἐπεὶ μηδὲ ἑρμηνέως ἑώρα δεόμενον, ἀλλ' ὑπολαμβάνοντα τὴν φωνὴν ἀλύπως τε καὶ εὐκόλως "πρὸς θεῶν" εἶπε "τίς εἶ;" λιπαρῶν ἤδη καὶ μεταβαλὼν τοῦ τόνου. ὑπολαβὼν δὲ ὁ Ἀπολλώνιος "ἐπειδὴ μετρίως" ἔφη "ταῦτα καὶ οὐκ ἀπανθρώπως ἤρου, ἄκουε, ὅς εἰμι. εἰμὶ μὲν ὁ Τυανεὺς Ἀπολλώνιος, ἡ δὲ ὁδὸς παρὰ τὸν Ἰνδῶν βασιλέα καθ' ἱστορίαν τῶν ἐκεῖ, βουλοίμην δ' ἂν καὶ τῷ σῷ βασιλεῖ ἐντυχεῖν, φασὶ γὰρ αὐτὸν οἱ ξυγγεγονότες οὐ τῶν φαύλων εἶναι, εἰ δὴ Οὐαρδάνης οὗτος, ὁ τὴν ἀρχὴν ἀπολωλυῖάν ποτ' αὐτῷ νῦν ἀνακεκτημένος." "ἐκεῖνος," ἔφη "θεῖε Ἀπολλώνιε· πάλαι γάρ σε ἀκούομεν.[18] σοφῷ δὲ ἀνδρὶ κἂν αὐτοῦ παραχωρήσειε τοῦ χρυσοῦ θρόνου, καὶ πέμποι δ' ἂν ὑμᾶς ἐς Ἰνδοὺς ἐπὶ καμήλου ἕκαστον. ἐγὼ δὲ καὶ ξένον ἐμαυτοῦ ποιοῦμαί σε, καὶ δίδωμί σοι τούτων τῶν χρημάτων," ἅμα θησαυρὸν χρυσοῦ δείξας "ὁπόσα βούλει δράττεσθαι, καὶ μὴ ἐς ἅπαξ, ἀλλὰ δεκάκις."

3 Παραιτησαμένου δὲ αὐτοῦ τὰ χρήματα "σὺ δ' ἀλλὰ

[17] ὡσαύτως Jon.: ὡς αὐτὸς

[18] ἀκούομεν Richards: ἠκούομεν

you to visit us?" as if questioning a spirit. "I sent myself," said Apollonius, "in case you might become true men, even against your will."

Next the governor asked him who he was, coming as a visitor to the king's country. "All the world is mine," Apollonius replied, "and it is open to me to voyage through it all." The governor said, "I will torture you if you do not tell me." "If only you yourself," said Apollonius, "might be tortured in the same way after laying hands on a real man." The eunuch was amazed at him, since he saw that he did not even need an interpreter, but understood the language effortlessly and easily. "For heaven's sake, who are you?" he said, this time pleading and changing his tone. In reply, Apollonius said, "Since you asked this modestly and not rudely, I will tell you who I am. I am Apollonius of Tyana, and my journey takes me to the king of India in order to learn about matters there. Your king too I would like to meet, since those who have met him say he is quite respectable, at least if he is Vardanes, who has now restored his kingdom after it had previously been lost to him."[32] "He is indeed, godly Apollonius," said the eunuch. "We have been hearing about you for a long time. To a wise man he would yield his golden throne itself, and he would provide each of you with a camel on your way to India. As for me, I make you my guest, and I permit you to clutch as much of this money as you wish" (at the same time showing him a treasure of gold) "and not just once, but ten times over." 2

When Apollonius declined the money, the eunuch said, 3

[32] Vardanes II, king of Parthia ca. 40–45. He had succeeded his father Artabanus only after a struggle with his brother Gotarzes.

οἴνου" ἔφη "Βαβυλωνίου, προπίνει δὲ αὐτοῦ βασιλεὺς δέκα ἡμῖν σατράπαις, ἀμφορέα ἔχε, συῶν τε καὶ δορκάδων τεμάχη, ὀπτὰ ἄλευρά τε καὶ ἄρτους, καὶ ὅ τι ἐθέλεις. ἡ γὰρ μετὰ ταῦτα ὁδὸς ἐπὶ πολλὰ στάδια κῶμαί εἰσιν οὐ πάνυ εὔσιτοι." καὶ λαβόμενος ἑαυτοῦ ὁ εὐνοῦχος, "οἷον," ἔφη "ὦ θεοί, ἔπαθον· ἀκούων γὰρ τὸν ἄνδρα μήτ' ἀπὸ ζῴων σιτεῖσθαι μήτε οἴνου πίνειν, παχέως αὐτὸν καὶ ἀμαθῶς ἑστιῶ." "ἀλλ' ἔστι σοι" ἔφη "καὶ λεπτῶς με ἑστιᾶν, ἢν ἄρτους τε δῷς καὶ τραγήματα." "δώσω" ἔφη "ζυμίτας τε ἄρτους, καὶ φοίνικος βαλάνους ἠλεκτρώδεις τε καὶ μεγάλας. δώσω καὶ λάχανα, ὁπόσα ὁ Τίγρις κηπεύει." "ἀλλ' ἡδίω" εἶπεν ὁ Ἀπολλώνιος "τὰ ἄγρια καὶ αὐτόματα λάχανα τῶν ἠναγκασμένων καὶ τεχνητῶν." "ἡδίω μέν," ἔφη ὁ σατράπης "ἡ χώρα δὲ ἡμῖν ἡ ἐπὶ Βαβυλῶνος ἀψινθίου πλήρης οὖσα ἀηδῆ αὐτὰ φύει καὶ πικρά." πλὴν ἀλλὰ τοῦ σατράπου γε ἀπεδέξατο, καὶ ἀπιὼν ἤδη "ὦ λῷστε," ἔφη "μὴ λῆγε μόνον καλῶς, ἀλλὰ καὶ ἄρχου," νουθετῶν που αὐτὸν ἐπὶ τῷ "βασανιῶ σε," καὶ οἷς ἐν ἀρχῇ βαρβαρίζοντος ἤκουσε.

22. Προελθόντες δὲ εἴκοσι στάδια λεαίνῃ ἐντυγχάνουσιν ἀπεσφαγμένῃ ἐν θήρᾳ, καὶ ἦν τὸ θηρίον μέγα καὶ ὅσον οὔπω εἶδον, ἐβόων τε οἱ ἐκ τῆς κώμης συνερρυηκότες, καί, νὴ Δί', οἱ τεθηρακότες, ὥς τι μέγα θαῦμα ἐν αὐτῷ ὁρῶντες. καὶ ἦν ἀτεχνῶς θαῦμα, σκύμνους γὰρ ἀνατμηθεῖσα ὀκτὼ εἶχεν. ὁ δὲ τῆς λεαίνης τόκος, αἱ λέαιναι μηνῶν μὲν κυΐσκουσιν ἕξ, τρὶς δὲ ἀποτίκτουσιν, ἀριθμὸς δὲ τῶν σκύμνων παρὰ

"Well, at least take a jar of Babylonian wine, which the king drinks when toasting us ten governors. And in addition take roast slices of pork and venison, flour, loaves of bread, and whatever you like. From here on, your way lies for many stades through villages that are not very well supplied." Then, recovering himself, he said, "Ye gods, what has come over me? I have heard that the Master eats no animals and drinks no wine, and I am giving him a heavy, boorish dinner." Apollonius replied, "Well, you can give me a light dinner, if you give me wheat loaves and dried fruits." "I will give you unleavened bread," was the answer, "and great amber-colored dates. I will also give you every kind of vegetable that the market gardens of the Tigris afford." "But wild and natural vegetables are sweeter than forced, artificial ones," replied Apollonius. "Sweeter, certainly," said the governor, "but our soil around Babylon is full of wormwood, so that they grow unpleasant and bitter." Still, Apollonius approved of the governor, and on his departure said, "My excellent friend, do not just make a fine ending, but a fine start too," rebuking him for his words, "I will torture you," and the other barbarous things he had heard from him at first.

22. After proceeding for twenty stades, they came across a lioness that had been slaughtered in a hunt. It was a big animal, larger than they had ever seen, and people from the village had run together and were shouting, and so indeed were the hunters, as if they saw some great miracle in it. In fact, it really was a miracle, since when it was cut open it had eight cubs. This is how the lioness breeds. Lionesses are pregnant for six months, and give birth three times, the number of their cubs being three at the first

μὲν τὴν πρώτην τρεῖς, ἐπὶ δὲ τῆς δευτέρας δύο, τρίτου δὲ ἁπτομένη τόκου μονήρη σκύμνον ἀποτίκτει μέγαν, οἶμαι, καὶ ἀγριώτερον τῆς φύσεως. οὐ γὰρ προσεκτέα τοῖς λέγουσιν, ὡς ξήναντες οἱ σκύμνοι τὰς τῶν λεαινῶν μήτρας ἐκδίδονται τοῦ σπλάγχνου. δοκεῖ γὰρ τῇ φύσει τὸ τικτόμενον καὶ τὸ τίκτον ἐπιτήδεια εἶναι ἀλληλοῖς ὑπὲρ σωτηρίας τοῦ γένους.

2 Ἐνιδὼν οὖν ὁ Ἀπολλώνιος τῷ θηρίῳ καὶ πολὺν χρόνον ἐπισχὼν "ὦ Δάμι," ἔφη "ὁ χρόνος τῆς παρὰ βασιλέα ἀποδημίας ἐνιαυτοῦ ἔσται καὶ μηνῶν ὀκτώ, οὔτε γὰρ ἐκεῖνος ἀνήσει θᾶττον, οὔτε ὑμῖν λῷον ἀπελθεῖν πρὸ τούτου. τεκμαίρεσθαι δὲ χρὴ τῶν μὲν σκύμνων ἐς μῆνας, τῆς λεαίνης δὲ ἐς ἐνιαυτόν, τέλεια γὰρ τελείοις παραβλητέα." "οἱ δὲ δὴ στρουθοὶ" ἔφη ὁ Δάμις "οἱ παρὰ τῷ Ὁμήρῳ τί φήσουσιν, οὓς ὁ δράκων μὲν ἐν τῇ Αὐλίδι ἐδαίσατο ὀκτὼ ὄντας ἐννάτην ἐπ' αὐτοῖς τὴν μητέρα ἑλών; Κάλχας δ' ἐξηγούμενος ταῦτα ἐννέα ἐνιαυτοῖς ἀνεῖπε καταπολεμήσεσθαι τὴν Τροίαν. καὶ ὅρα μὴ καθ' Ὅμηρόν τε καὶ Κάλχαντα ἐς ἐννέα ἡμῖν ἔτη ἡ ἀποδημία τείνῃ." "καὶ εἰκότως," ἔφη "ὦ Δάμι, καὶ τοὺς νεοττοὺς Ὅμηρος ἐνιαυτοῖς εἰκάζει, γεγόνασι γὰρ ἤδη καί εἰσιν. ἐγὼ δὲ ἀτελῆ θηρία καὶ μήπω γεγονότα, ἴσως δὲ μηδ' ἂν γενόμενα, πῶς ἂν ἐνιαυτοῖς εἰκάζοιμι; τὰ γὰρ παρὰ φύσιν οὔτ' ἂν γένοιτο, ταχεῖάν τε ἴσχει διαφθοράν, κἂν γένηται. ἀλλ' ἕπου δὴ τῷ λόγῳ, καὶ ἴωμεν εὐξάμενοι[19] τοῖς θεοῖς, οἳ ταῦτα φαίνουσι."

birth, two at the second. When they undertake a third pregnancy they produce a single cub, a large one, so I understand, and more savage than lions naturally are. (We should not pay attention to people who say that cubs scratch lionesses' innards before emerging from the womb, for parent and offspring have a natural affinity for each other that ensures the preservation of the species.)

Well, Apollonius looked into the animal, and after pon- 2
dering a long time said: "Damis, the duration of our journey to the king will be one year and eight months. He will not release us sooner, and it will not be propitious for us to leave before then. We must infer the months from the cubs, and the year from the lioness, for you have to compare units with units." "Well," said Damis, "what will we infer from Homer's sparrows, which the snake at Aulis devoured? They were eight, and the snake also caught the mother, making nine. When Calchas interpreted all that, he foretold that Troy would be taken in nine years; so maybe according to Homer and Calchas our absence will last for nine years?"[33] "It is reasonable," Apollonius replied, "for Homer to equate the chicks with years, since they have birth and existence. But how could I equate unformed animals that have not yet been born, and perhaps might not even have survived to birth, with years? For unnatural things cannot come about, and if they do, they are subject to swift decay. So follow my reasoning, and let us depart after praying to the gods who reveal all this."

[33] An incident at Aulis narrated by Odysseus in the *Iliad* (2.301–20).

---

[19] *εὐξάμενοι* Cob.: *εὐξόμενοι*

23. Προελθόντι δὲ αὐτῷ ἐς τὴν Κισσίαν χώραν καὶ πρὸς Βαβυλῶνι ἤδη ὄντι δόξα ἐνυπνίου ἐφοίτησεν, ὧδε τῷ φήναντι θεῷ ξυντεθεῖσα. ἰχθῦς ἐκπεπτωκότες τῆς θαλάττης ἐν τῇ γῇ ἤσπαιρον, θρῆνον ἀνθρώπων ἱέντες καὶ ὀλοφυρόμενοι τὸ ἐκβεβηκέναι τῶν ἠθῶν.[20] δελφῖνά τε τῇ γῇ παρανέοντα ἱκέτευον ἀμῦναί σφισιν ἐλεεινοὶ ὄντες, ὥσπερ τῶν ἀνθρώπων οἱ ἐν τῇ ξένῃ κλαίοντες. ἐκπλαγεὶς δὲ οὐδὲν ὑπὸ τοῦ ἐνυπνίου, ξυμβάλλεται μὲν αὐτοῦ ὅπως καὶ ὅπῃ εἶχε, διαταράττειν δὲ βουλόμενος τὸν Δάμιν, καὶ γὰρ τῶν εὐλαβεστέρων αὐτὸν ἐγίγνωσκεν, ἀπαγγέλλει πρὸς αὐτὸν τὴν ὄψιν, δέος πλασάμενος ὡς ἐπὶ πονηροῖς, οἷς εἶδεν, ὁ δὲ ἀνεβόησέ τε ὡς αὐτὸς ἰδὼν ταὐτά,[21] καὶ ἀπῆγε τὸν Ἀπολλώνιον τοῦ πρόσω "μή πῃ" ἔφη "καὶ ἡμεῖς ὥσπερ ἰχθύες ἐκπεσόντες τῶν ἠθῶν ἀπολώμεθα, καὶ πολλὰ ἐλεεινὰ ἐν τῇ ἀλλοδαπῇ εἴπωμεν, καί που καὶ ἐς ἀμήχανον ἐμπεσόντες ἱκετεύσωμεν δυνάστην τινὰ ἢ βασιλέα, ὁ δὲ ἡμᾶς ἀτιμάσῃ, καθάπερ τοὺς ἰχθῦς οἱ δελφῖνες."

2 Γελάσας δὲ ὁ Ἀπολλώνιος "σὺ μὲν οὔπω φιλοσοφεῖς," εἶπεν "εἰ δέδιας ταῦτα, ἐγὼ δὲ οἷ τὸ ἐνύπνιον τείνει δηλώσω. Ἐρετριεῖς γὰρ τὴν Κισσίαν ταύτην χώραν οἰκοῦσιν οἱ ἐξ Εὐβοίας ποτὲ Δαρείῳ ἀναχθέντες ἔτη ταῦτα πεντακόσια, καὶ λέγονται, ὥσπερ ἡ ὄψις ἐφάνη, ἰχθύων πάθει περὶ τὴν ἅλωσιν χρήσασθαι, σαγηνευθῆναι γὰρ δὴ καὶ ἁλῶναι πάντας. ἐοίκασιν

[20] τῶν ἠθῶν Cob.: τοῦ ἤθους [21] ταὐτά Jackson: ταῦτα

23. He proceeded into the territory of Cissia,[34] and was nearly at Babylon when he received a vision in a dream. This is how the god who granted the vision arranged it. Fish had been cast up from the sea and were gasping on land, wailing like humans, and grieving at being exiled from their element. They begged a dolphin that was swimming close to land to help them in their piteous state, like humans weeping in a foreign land. Apollonius was not at all dismayed by the dream, but realized its meaning and tendency. But wanting to scare Damis, whom he saw to be overly pious, he reported the vision to him, pretending that what he had seen foreboded ill. Damis shouted out as if having had the same vision, and tried to prevent Apollonius from going further, "in case" he said, "somehow we too perish in exile from our domain like fish, and say many piteous things in a foreign land. Perhaps we may get into a hopeless situation and entreat some ruler or king, and he may dishonor us as the dolphins did the fish."

At this Apollonius said laughing, "You are not yet a lover 2
of wisdom if you fear that. I will show you what the dream portends. In this territory of Cissia there live Eretrians whom Darius transported here from Euboea five hundred years ago. Just as the vision revealed, they are said to have suffered the fate of the fish, being all taken in a dragnet and captured.[35] It seems therefore as if the gods are telling me

[34] In Susiana or Elymais, north of the Persian Gulf.

[35] Darius I (522–486) punished the Eretrians of Euboea for their support of the Ionian revolt by transplanting them to Cissia in 490. Cf. Herodotus 6.99–101.

οὖν οἱ θεοὶ κελεύειν με ἐς αὐτοὺς παρελθόντα ἐπιμεληθῆναι σφῶν, εἴ τι δυναίμην. ἴσως δὲ καὶ αἱ ψυχαὶ τῶν Ἑλλήνων, οἵπερ ἔλαχον τὴν ἐνταῦθα μοῖραν, ἐπάγονταί με ἐπ᾿ ὠφελείᾳ τῆς γῆς. ἴωμεν οὖν ἐξαλλάξαντες τῆς ὁδοῦ, περὶ μόνου ἐρωτῶντες τοῦ φρέατος πρὸς ᾧ οἰκοῦσι. λέγεται δὲ τοῦτο κεκρᾶσθαι μὲν ἀσφάλτου καὶ ἐλαίου καὶ ἅλατος,[22] ἐκχέαντος δὲ τοῦ ἀνιμήσαντος ἀποχωρεῖν ταῦτα καὶ ἀπ᾿ ἀλλήλων κρίνεσθαι."

3 Παρελθεῖν μὲν δὴ ἐς τὴν Κισσίαν καὶ αὐτὸς ὡμολόγηκεν ἐν οἷς πρὸς τὸν Κλαζομένιον σοφιστὴν γράφει, χρηστὸς γὰρ οὕτω τι καὶ φιλότιμος ἦν, ὡς ἐπειδὴ Ἐρετριέας εἶδε, <τοῦ>[23] σοφιστοῦ τε ἀναμνησθῆναι καὶ γράψαι πρὸς αὐτὸν ἅ τε εἶδεν ἅ τε ὑπὲρ αὐτῶν ἔπραξεν· καὶ παρακελεύεταί οἱ παρὰ τὴν ἐπιστολὴν πᾶσαν ἐλεεῖν τοὺς Ἐρετριέας, καὶ ὁπότε μελετῴη τὸν περὶ αὐτῶν λόγον, μηδὲ τὸ κλάειν ἐπ᾿ αὐτοῖς παραιτεῖσθαι.

24. Ξυνῳδὰ δὲ τούτοις καὶ ὁ Δάμις περὶ τῶν Ἐρετριέων ἀναγέγραφεν· οἰκοῦσι γὰρ ἐν τῇ Μηδικῇ, Βαβυλῶνος οὐ πολὺ ἀπέχοντες, ἡμέρας <τεττάρας>[24] δρομικῷ ἀνδρί, ἡ χώρα δὲ ἄπολις, ἡ γὰρ Κισσία κῶμαι πᾶσα, καί τι καὶ νομάδων ἐν αὐτῇ γένος μικρὰ τῶν ἵππων ἀποβαίνοντες. ἡ δὲ τῶν Ἐρετριέων οἰκεῖται μὲν τῶν ἄλλων μέση, περιβέβληται δὲ ποταμοῦ τάφρον, ἣν αὐτοὶ βαλέσθαι περὶ τῇ κώμῃ λέγονται, τεῖχος αὐτὴν ποιούμενοι πρὸς τοὺς ἐν τῇ Κισσίᾳ

[22] ἅλατος Jackson: ὕδατος

to come to them, and to assist them in any way I can. Perhaps also the souls of those Greeks whose fate it was to come here are leading me on to help their land. So let us leave our route, and ask only about the well near which they live. It is said that this well is a mixture of pitch, oil, and salt, but when you draw it up and pour it out, these elements divide and separate from one another."[36]

He himself has confessed that he entered Cissia in his letter to the sophist of Clazomenae,[37] since he was so kind and generous that on seeing the Eretrians, he remembered the sophist and wrote to him about what he had seen and what he had done for them. Throughout the letter he urges him to show them pity, and be ready even to shed tears whenever he improvises a speech on that subject. 3

24. Damis's account of the Eretrians agrees with this. They live in Media, not far from Babylon, four days away for a fast traveler.[38] Their land has no cities, since Cissia is all villages, and there is also a race of nomads there who rarely dismount from their horses. The part inhabited by the Eretrians is in the middle of the general area, and is surrounded by a river channel, which they themselves are said to have put around their village as a defense against

[36] This well is also mentioned by Herodotus (6.119). It is unclear whether the sentence "It is said. . ." is spoken by Apollonius or the author.

[37] Scopelian of Clazomenae in Ionia, younger contemporary of Apollonius.

[38] An error, since Cissia is in the region of Susa.

---

23 ‹τοῦ› Rsk.

24 ‹τεττάρας› (i.e. δʹ) Rsk.

βαρβάρους. ὕπομβρος δὲ ἀσφάλτῳ ἡ χώρα καὶ πικρὰ ἐμφυτεῦσαι, βραχυβιώτατοί τε οἱ ἐκείνῃ ἄνθρωποι, τὸ γὰρ ἀσφαλτῶδες ποτὸν ἐς πολλὰ τῶν σπλάγχνων ἱζάνει. τρέφει δ' αὐτοὺς λόφος ἐν ὁρίοις τῆς κώμης, ὃν ὑπεραίροντα τοῦ παρεφθορότος χωρίου σπείρουσί τε καὶ ἡγοῦνται γῆν.

2 Φασὶ δὲ ἀκοῦσαι τῶν ἐγχωρίων, ὡς ἑπτακόσιοι μὲν τῶν Ἐρετριέων πρὸς τοῖς ὀγδοήκοντα ἥλωσαν, οὔτι που μάχιμοι πάντες, ἦν γάρ τι καὶ θῆλυ ἐν αὐτοῖς γένος καὶ γεγηρακός, ἦν δ', οἶμαί, τι καὶ παιδία, τὸ γὰρ πολὺ τῆς Ἐρετρίας τὸν Καφηρέα ἀνέφυγε καὶ ὅ τι ἀκρότατον τῆς Εὐβοίας. ἀνήχθησαν δὲ ἄνδρες μὲν ἀμφὶ τοὺς τετρακοσίους, γύναια δὲ ἴσως δέκα, οἱ δὲ λοιποὶ ἀπ' Ἰωνίας τε καὶ Λυδίας ἀρξάμενοι διεφθάρησαν ἐλαυνόμενοι ἄνω. λιθοτομίαν δὲ αὐτοῖς παρεχομένου τοῦ λόφου, καί τινες καὶ λιθουργοὺς εἰδότες τέχνας, ἱερά τε ἐδείμαντο Ἑλληνικὰ καὶ ἀγοράν, ὁπόσην εἰκὸς ἦν, βωμούς τε ἱδρύσαντο Δαρείῳ μὲν δύο, Ξέρξῃ δὲ ἕνα, Δαριδαίῳ δὲ πλείους. διετέλεσαν δὲ ἐς Δαριδαῖον ἔτη μετὰ τὴν ἅλωσιν ὀκτὼ καὶ ὀγδοήκοντα, γράφοντες τὸν Ἑλλήνων τρόπον, καὶ οἱ τάφοι δὲ οἱ ἀρχαῖοι σφῶν "ὁ δεῖνα τοῦ δεῖνος" γεγράφαται, καὶ τὰ γράμματα Ἑλλήνων μέν, ἀλλ' οὔπω ταὐτά.[25] ἰδεῖν φασι καὶ ναῦς ἐγκεχαραγμένας τοῖς τάφοις, ὡς ἕκαστος ἐν Εὐβοίᾳ ἔζη [πορθμεύων ἢ πορφυρεύων][26] ἢ θαλάττιον ἢ καὶ ἁλουργὸν πράττων,

[25] ταὐτά Jackson: ταῦτα [26] secl. Ol.

the barbarians in Cissia. The soil is impregnated with asphalt and hard to plant, and the people there live very short lives, since bituminous liquid settles in the stomachs of many of them. They get their living from a hill on the edge of the village, which rises above the polluted land, and they sow it and consider it true soil.

The travelers claim to have heard from the locals that 2
the Eretrians who were caught numbered seven hundred and eighty, not all of them fighters, since there were some women among them and some old people. (I suppose there were children too, since most of the Eretrians had fled to Caphereus[39] and the mountainous parts of Euboea.) Those that were transported inland included about four hundred men and perhaps ten women, but the others died as they were driven inland, starting from Ionia and Lydia. The hill provided them with a quarry, and since some of them knew the art of stone-working, they built Greek sanctuaries and a reasonably large agora, and they set up altars, two to Darius, one to Xerxes, but several to Daridaeus.[40] They lasted for eighty-eight years down to the time of Daridaeus, writing in the Greek way, and their ancient tombs are inscribed, "so-and-so, son of so-and-so." Their script is that of Greeks, though not identical. The travelers also say they also saw ships carved on the tombstones, showing how each man lived in Euboea either as a

39 Cape of southeastern Euboea.

40 Darius I (522–486), Xerxes I (486–465), Darius II Ochus (424–404). The form "Dariaeus" is found in the late fifth-century historian Ctesias.

καί τι καὶ ἐλεγεῖον ἀναγνῶναι γεγραμμένον ἐπὶ ναυτῶν τε καὶ ναυκλήρων σήματι·

Οἵδε ποτ᾽ Αἰγαίοιο βαθύρροον οἶδμα πλέοντες
  Ἐκβατάνων πεδίῳ κείμεθ᾽ ἐνὶ μεσάτῳ.
χαῖρε κλυτή ποτε πατρὶς Ἐρέτρια, χαίρετ᾽
  Ἀθῆναι,
  γείτονες Εὐβοίης, χαῖρε θάλασσα φίλη.

3 Τοὺς μὲν δὴ τάφους διεφθορότας ἀναλαβεῖν τε αὐτὸν ὁ Δάμις φησὶ καὶ ξυγκλεῖσαι, χέασθαί τε καὶ ἐπενεγκεῖν σφισιν, ὁπόσα νόμιμα, πλὴν τοῦ τεμεῖν τι ἢ καθαγίσαι, δακρύσαντά τε καὶ ὑποπλησθέντα ὁρμῆς τάδε ἐν μέσοις ἀναφθέγξασθαι· "Ἐρετριεῖς οἱ κλήρῳ τύχης δεῦρ᾽ ἀπενεχθέντες, ὑμεῖς μέν, εἰ καὶ πόρρω τῆς αὐτῶν, τέθαφθε γοῦν, οἱ δ᾽ ὑμᾶς ἐνταῦθα ῥίψαντες ἀπώλοντο περὶ τὴν ὑμετέραν νῆσον ἄταφοι δεκάτῳ μεθ᾽ ὑμᾶς ἔτει· τὸ γὰρ ἐν κοίλῃ Εὐβοίᾳ πάθος θεοὶ φαίνουσιν." Ἀπολλώνιος δὲ πρὸς τὸν σοφιστὴν ἐπὶ τέλει τῆς ἐπιστολῆς "καὶ ἐπεμελήθην," φησὶν "ὦ Σκοπελιανέ, τῶν σῶν Ἐρετριέων νέος ὢν ἔτι, καὶ ὠφέλησα ὅ τι ἐδυνάμην, καὶ τοὺς τεθνεῶτας αὐτῶν καὶ τοὺς ζῶντας." τί δῆτα ἐπεμελήθη τῶν ζώντων; οἱ πρόσοικοι τῷ λόφῳ βάρβαροι σπειρόντων τῶν Ἐρετριέων αὐτὸν ἐληίζοντο τὰ φυόμενα περὶ τὸ θέρος ἥκοντες, καὶ πεινῆν ἔδει γεωργοῦντας ἑτέροις. ὁπότ᾽ οὖν παρὰ βασιλέα ἀφίκετο, εὕρετο αὐτοῖς τὸ χρῆσθαι μόνους τῷ λόφῳ.

sailor or a purple-fisher.[41] They also made out an elegy written on a grave of sailors and shipowners:[42]

Here now we lie on Ecbatana's plain,[43]
But once we sailed the deep Aegaean's swell.
Farewell, Eretrian homeland, old in fame,
And nearby Athens, and dear sea, farewell.

According to Damis, Apollonius restored the tombs 3
that had fallen into disrepair, closed them up, and made libations and offerings to them, all of the customary kind except that he did not perform slaughter or heroic rites. He wept and said the following as he stood filled with emotion among the tombs: "You Eretrians who were carried here by the decision of fate, at least you have received burial, though far from your homeland. But those who dumped you here perished unburied off your island ten years after you, since the gods make manifest the disaster in the Hollows of Euboea."[44] Apollonius also says to the sophist at the end of his letter, "I assisted your Eretrians when I was still young, Scopelian, and gave them what help I could, both their dead and those that were living." In what way did he "assist" the living? When the Eretrians had sown, the barbarians living near their hill used to come and plunder their crops in summer, and they had to go hungry while farming for others. On meeting the king, Apollonius had the use of the hill reserved for them alone.

41 Fishers of the shellfish (*murex*) from which purple was made. 42 This poem recurs in the *Greek Anthology* (VII 256). 43 Ecbatana was in fact on the Iranian plateau, far from Babylon. 44 In 480 part of the Persian fleet was wrecked in the Hollows of Euboea (Herodotus 8.13).

25. Τὰ δὲ ἐν Βαβυλῶνι τοῦ ἀνδρὸς τούτου, καὶ ὁπόσα Βαβυλῶνος πέρι προσήκει γιγνώσκειν, τοιάδε εὗρον. ἡ Βαβυλὼν τετείχισται μὲν ὀγδοήκοντα καὶ τετρακόσια στάδια, τοσαύτη κύκλῳ, τεῖχος δὲ αὐτῆς τρία μὲν τὸ ὕψος ἡμίπλεθρα, πλέθρου δὲ μεῖον τὸ εὗρος, ποταμῷ δὲ Εὐφράτῃ τέμνεται ξὺν ὁμοιότητι τοῦ εἴδους, ὃν ἀπόρρητος ὑποστείχει γέφυρα τὰ βασίλεια τὰ ἐπὶ ταῖς ὄχθαις ἀφανῶς ξυνάπτουσα. γυνὴ γὰρ λέγεται Μήδεια τῶν ἐκείνῃ ποτὲ ἄρχουσα τὸν ποταμὸν ὑποζεῦξαι τρόπον, ὃν μήπω τις ποταμὸς ἐζεύχθη. λίθους γὰρ δὴ, καὶ χάλικα,[27] καὶ ἄσφαλτον, καὶ ὁπόσα ἐς ὕφυδρον[28] ξύνδεσιν ἀνθρώποις εὕρηται, παρὰ τὰς ὄχθας τοῦ ποταμοῦ νήσασα τὸ ῥεῦμα ἐς λίμνας ἔτρεψε. ξηρόν τε ἤδη τὸν ποταμὸν ᾤρυγεν ὀργυιὰς ἐς δύο σήραγγα ἐργαζομένη κοίλην, ἵν᾿ ἐς τὰ βασίλεια τὰ παρὰ ταῖς ὄχθαις ὥσπερ ἐκ γῆς ἀναφαίνοιτο, καὶ ἤρεψεν αὐτὴν ἴσως τῷ τοῦ ῥεύματος δαπέδῳ. οἱ μὲν δὴ θεμέλιοι ἐβεβήκεσαν καὶ οἱ τοῖχοι τῆς σήραγγος, ἅτε δὲ τῆς ἀσφάλτου δεομένης τοῦ ὕδατος ἐς τὸ λιθοῦσθαί τε καὶ πήγνυσθαι, ὁ Εὐφράτης ἐπαφείθη ὑγρῷ τῷ ὀρόφῳ, καὶ ὧδε ἔστη τὸ ζεῦγμα.

2 Τὰ δὲ βασίλεια χαλκῷ μὲν ἤρεπται καὶ ἀπ᾿ αὐτῶν ἀστράπτει, θάλαμοι δὲ καὶ ἀνδρῶνες καὶ στοαί, τὰ μὲν ἀργύρῳ, τὰ δὲ χρυσοῖς ὑφάσμασι, τὰ δὲ χρυσῷ αὐτῷ καθάπερ γραφαῖς ἠγλάισται, τὰ δὲ ποικίλματα τῶν πέπλων ἐκ τῶν Ἑλληνικῶν σφίσιν ἥκει λόγων, Ἀν-

25. The following is roughly what I have found about the activities of the Master in Babylon, and what is worth knowing about the place. Babylon has a wall of four hundred and eighty stades, so large is its extent, and a wall one and a half plethra high but less than one plethron thick.[45] It is divided into two similar-looking sections by the river Euphrates, under which there runs a secret tunnel that invisibly joins the palaces on the two banks. They say that a Median woman who once ruled there spanned the river in a way that no river was spanned before. Using stones, gravel, bitumen, everything that humans have devised as underwater sealants, and piling these up along the banks of the river, she diverted the stream into pools. When the river was empty, she dug to a depth of two fathoms, making a hollow channel that was to emerge out of the earth, as it were, into the palaces on the banks. Over this she placed a roof at the level of the riverbed. As soon as the floors and the walls of the tunnel were firm, but the pitch needed water to become solid and fixed, the Euphrates was brought in over the roof while it was still moist, and thus the connection stood firm.

The palaces have roofs of bronze that produce a dazzling effect. The bedchambers, men's quarters and colonnades are adorned either with silver or tapestries of gold, but some with pure gold formed into pictures. The subjects portrayed on their tapestries come from Greek tales, 2

[45] A plethron = about 100 feet. Philostratus's description very closely follows that of Herodotus, 1.179–86.

---

[27] χάλικα Jackson: χαλκὸν
[28] ὕφυδρον Jackson: ἔφυδρον

δρομέδαι καὶ Ἀμυμῶναι καὶ Ὀρφεὺς πολλαχοῦ. χαίρουσι δὲ τῷ Ὀρφεῖ, τιάραν ἴσως καὶ ἀναξυρίδα τιμῶντες, οὐ γὰρ μουσικήν γε, οὐδὲ ᾠδάς, αἷς ἔθελγεν. ἐνύφανταί που καὶ ὁ Δᾶτις τὴν Νάξον ἐκ τῆς θαλάττης ἀνασπῶν, καὶ Ἀρταφέρνης περιεστηκὼς τὴν Ἐρέτριαν, καὶ τῶν ἀμφὶ Ξέρξην ἃ νικᾶν ἔφασκεν· Ἀθῆναι γὰρ δὴ ἐχόμεναί εἰσι καὶ Θερμοπύλαι καὶ τὰ Μηδικώτερα ἔτι, ποταμοὶ ἐξαιρούμενοι τῆς γῆς, καὶ θαλάττης ζεῦγμα, καὶ ὁ Ἄθως ὡς ἐτμήθη.

3 Φασὶ δὲ καὶ ἀνδρῶνι ἐντυχεῖν, οὗ τὸν ὄροφον ἐς θόλου ἀνῆχθαι σχῆμα οὐρανῷ τινι εἰκασμένον, σαπφειρίνῃ δὲ αὐτὸν κατηρέφθαι λίθῳ (κυανωτάτη δὲ ἡ λίθος καὶ οὐρανία ἰδεῖν), καὶ θεῶν ἀγάλματα, οὓς νομίζουσιν, ἵδρυται ἄνω καὶ χρυσᾶ φαίνεται, καθάπερ ἐξ αἰθέρος. δικάζει μὲν δὴ ὁ βασιλεὺς ἐνταῦθα, χρυσαῖ δὲ ἴυγγες ἀποκρέμανται τοῦ ὀρόφου τέτταρες, τὴν Ἀδράστειαν αὐτῷ παρεγγυῶσαι καὶ τὸ μὴ ὑπὲρ τοὺς ἀνθρώπους αἴρεσθαι. ταύτας οἱ μάγοι αὐτοί φασιν ἁρμόττεσθαι φοιτῶντες ἐς τὰ βασίλεια, καλοῦσι δὲ αὐτὰς θεῶν γλώττας.

26. Περὶ δὲ τῶν μάγων Ἀπολλώνιος μὲν τὸ ἀποχρῶν εἴρηκε, συγγενέσθαι γὰρ αὐτοῖς καὶ τὰ μὲν μαθεῖν, τὰ δὲ ἀπελθεῖν διδάξας, Δάμις δὲ τοὺς μὲν λόγους, οἷοι ἐγένοντο τῷ ἀνδρὶ πρὸς τοὺς μάγους, οὐκ οἶδεν, ἀπαγορεῦσαι γὰρ αὐτῷ μὴ συμφοιτᾶν παρ᾽ αὐτοὺς ἰόντι, λέγει δ᾽ οὖν φοιτᾶν αὐτὸν τοῖς μάγοις μεσημβρίας τε καὶ ἀμφὶ μέσας νύκτας, καὶ ἐρέσθαι

with figures of Andromeda, Amymone, and Orpheus in many places. (The Persians like Orpheus, perhaps because they honor his headband and trousers, since they do not honor his music or the songs that were his charm.) Also woven into the tapestries are Datis drawing up Naxos from the sea, Artaphernes encircling Eretria, and the alleged victories of Xerxes. The occupation of Athens is there, Thermopylae, and things even more typically Median—the rivers of the earth drained dry, a bridge over the sea, and the cutting of Athos.[46]

They say that they also visited men's quarters with a 3
domed roof imitating a kind of sky, roofed with sapphire (this stone is very blue and heavenly to look at). Images of the gods whom the Persians worship were set up on high and looked golden, as if they were in the upper air. This is where the king sits in judgment, and four golden fetishes[47] hang from the ceiling, reminding him of Adrasteia[48] and that he must not elevate himself above the human. The Magi say that they themselves hang these up when they visit the palace, calling them "the tongues of the gods."

26. About the Magi Apollonius has said enough, to the effect that he met with them and got some instruction from them, but gave them some too before his departure. Damis does not know what kind of conversation the Master had with the Magi, since he himself was forbidden to follow when he went to them. But he does say that Apollonius visited the Magi at noon and about midnight, and

[46] These are all events of Xerxes's invasion of Greece in 480.

[47] Literally "wrynecks," but apparently used to denote some kind of idol.

[48] Nemesis, the goddess of retribution.

ποτε "τί οἱ μάγοι;" τὸν δὲ ἀποκρίνασθαι "σοφοὶ μέν, ἀλλ᾽ οὐ πάντα." ταυτὶ μὲν ὕστερον.

27. Ἀφικομένῳ δὲ αὐτῷ ἐς Βαβυλῶνα ὁ σατράπης ὁ ἐπὶ τῶν μεγάλων πυλῶν, μαθὼν ὅτι ὑπὲρ ἱστορίας ἥκοι, ὀρέγει χρυσῆν εἰκόνα τοῦ βασιλέως, ἣν εἰ μὴ προσκυνήσειέ τις, οὐ θεμιτὸν ἦν ἐσφοιτᾶν ἔσω. πρεσβεύοντι μὲν οὖν παρὰ τοῦ Ῥωμαίων ἄρχοντος οὐδεμία ἀνάγκη τούτου, παρὰ βαρβάρων δὲ ἥκοντι ἢ ἀφιστοροῦντι τὴν χώραν, εἰ μὴ τὴν εἰκόνα προθεραπεύσειεν, ἄτιμον διειλῆφθαι. καὶ σατραπεύεται παρὰ τοῖς βαρβάροις τὰ οὕτως εὐήθη. ἐπεὶ τοίνυν τὴν εἰκόνα εἶδε, "τίς" ἔφη "οὗτος;" ἀκούσας δὲ ὅτι ὁ βασιλεύς "οὗτος," εἶπεν "ὃν ὑμεῖς προσκυνεῖτε, εἰ ἐπαινεθείη ὑπ᾽ ἐμοῦ καλὸς κἀγαθὸς δόξας, μεγάλων τεύξεται·" καὶ εἰπὼν ταῦτα διὰ πυλῶν ᾔει. θαυμάσας δὲ ὁ σατράπης αὐτόν, ἐπηκολούθησέ τε καὶ κατασχὼν τὴν χεῖρα τοῦ Ἀπολλωνίου δι᾽ ἑρμηνέως ἤρετο ὄνομά τε αὐτοῦ καὶ οἶκον, καὶ ὅ τι ἐπιτηδεύοι, καὶ ἐφ᾽ ὅ τι φοιτῴη. καὶ ἀπογραψάμενος ταῦτα ἐς γραμματεῖον στολήν τε αὐτοῦ καὶ εἶδος, ἐκεῖνον μὲν περιμεῖναι κελεύει,

28. Δραμὼν δὲ αὐτὸς παρὰ τοὺς ἄνδρας, οἳ δὴ νομίζονται βασιλέως ὦτα, ἀνατυποῖ τὸν Ἀπολλώνιον προειπών, ὅτι μήτε προσκυνεῖν βούλεται μήτε τι ἀνθρώπῳ ἔοικεν· οἱ δὲ ἄγειν[29] κελεύουσι τιμῶντά τε καὶ μηδὲν ὕβρει πράττοντα, ἐπεὶ δὲ ἦλθεν, ἤρετο αὐτὸν ὁ πρεσβύτατος ὅ τι μαθὼν καταφρονήσειε τοῦ βασιλέως, ὁ δὲ "οὔπω" ἔφη "κατεφρόνησα." "κατα-

that he himself once asked him, "What are the Magi like?" and he replied, "Wise, but not in every respect." But that was later.

27. When he arrived at Babylon, the official in charge of the great gates, learning that he had come as a sightseer, held out to him a golden statue of the king before which one had to do obeisance, or he was forbidden to enter. An ambassador from the Roman governor was not compelled to do this, but anyone coming from a barbarian land, or touring the country, was led away in disgrace if he did not worship the statue first. Such are the pointless duties the barbarians give to their officials. When Apollonius saw the statue, he asked, "Who is this?" Hearing it was the king, he said, "This man you bow down to will be well rewarded if I praise him for showing himself good and honest." So saying he passed through the gates. The official followed him in amazement, and taking hold of Apollonius's arm asked him through an interpreter his name, his family, his profession, and his purpose in coming, and after registering all this in a notebook, as well as his dress and appearance, he told Apollonius to wait.

28. Then he himself rushed off to the potentates they consider to be the King's Ears, and described Apollonius to them, warning them that he refused to bow down and was nothing like an ordinary human. They told him to bring Apollonius with respect and no roughness of any sort, and when he had come, the oldest of them asked him what had induced him to disrespect the king. "I have not disres-

---

29 δὲ ἄγειν Bentl.: δὴ ἄγειν or διάγειν

φρονήσειας δ' ἄν;" πάλιν ἐρομένου, "νὴ Δί'" εἶπεν "ἤν γε ξυγγενόμενος μὴ καλόν τε καὶ ἀγαθὸν εὕρω αὐτόν." "ἀπάγεις δὲ δὴ τίνα αὐτῷ δῶρα;" τοῦ δὲ αὖ τήν τε ἀνδρείαν καὶ δικαιοσύνην καὶ τὰ τοιαῦτα φήσαντος "πότερον," ἔφη, "ὡς οὐκ ἔχοντι;" "μὰ Δί'," εἶπεν "ἀλλ' ὡς μαθησομένῳ χρῆσθαι, ἢν ἔχῃ αὐτάς." "καὶ μὴν χρώμενος τούτοις" ἔφη "τήν τε βασιλείαν, ἣν ὁρᾷς, ἀπολωλυῖαν αὐτῷ ἀνέλαβε, τόν τε οἶκον ἐπανήγαγε τοῦτον οὐκ ἀπόνως, οὐδὲ ῥᾳθύμως." "ποστὸν δὲ δὴ τοῦτο ἔτος τῇ ἀνακτηθείσῃ ἀρχῇ;" "τρίτου" ἔφη "ἀρχόμεθα, δύο ἤδη που μῆνες."

2 Ἀναστήσας οὖν, ὥσπερ εἰώθει, τὴν γνώμην, "ὦ σωματοφύλαξ," εἶπεν "ἢ ὅ τί σε προσήκει καλεῖν, Δαρεῖος ὁ Κύρου καὶ Ἀρταξέρξου πατήρ, τὰ βασίλεια ταῦτα κατασχὼν ἑξήκοντα, οἶμαι, ἔτη, λέγεται τελευτὴν ὑποπτεύσας τοῦ βίου τῇ δικαιοσύνῃ θῦσαι, καὶ 'ὦ δέσποινα,' εἰπεῖν, 'ἥ τίς ποτε εἶ,' ὥσπερ ἐπιθυμήσας μὲν πάλαι τῆς δικαιοσύνης, οὔπω δὲ αὐτὴν γιγνώσκων, οὐδὲ δοκῶν κεκτῆσθαι, τὼ παῖδέ τε οὕτως ἀμαθῶς ἐπαίδευσεν, ὡς ὅπλα ἐπ' ἀλλήλους ἄρασθαι, καὶ ὁ μὲν τρωθῆναι, ὁ δὲ ἀποθανεῖν ὑπὸ τοῦ ἑτέρου, σὺ δ' ἤδη τοῦτον, ἴσως οὐδ' ἐν τῷ βασιλείῳ θρόνῳ καθῆσθαι εἰδότα, ξυνειληφέναι ὁμοῦ πάσας[30] ἀρετὰς βούλει καὶ ἐπαίρεις αὐτόν, σοὶ φέρων, οὐκ ἐμοί, κέρδος, εἰ βελτίων γένοιτο."

3 Βλέψας οὖν ὁ βάρβαρος ἐς τὸν πλησίον "ἕρμαιον" ἔφη "θεῶν τις ἄγει τουτονὶ τὸν ἄνδρα ἐνταῦθα, ἀγαθὸς

pected him," said Apollonius, "yet." "Might you?" asked the other. "Yes indeed," he replied, "if on meeting him I find he is not good and honest." "What are the gifts you are bringing him?" Apollonius again named Courage and Justice and so on, and the other said, "Because he does not have them?" "Certainly not," replied Apollonius, "but because he will learn to exercise them if he has them." "Why," came the reply, "it was by the exercise of them that he recovered this kingdom you see after it had been lost to him, and restored this house of his with much effort and energy." "How many years is it since the recovery of his power?" said Apollonius. "It is two months since the third year began," was the reply.

Apollonius then said with his usual elevation of mind, 2
"Bodyguard, or whatever your title is, Darius the father of Cyrus and Artaxerxes, they say, ruled this kingdom for sixty years or so, I think.[49] Then, suspecting that his end was near, he sacrificed to Justice saying, 'O my lady, whoever you are,' as if he had long desired Justice but even then did not know who she was, or think that he possessed her. And he educated his two sons so foolishly that they made war on each other, and the one was wounded and the other killed by his rival. But this king, who probably does not even know how to sit on his royal throne, you claim to be a model of all the virtues. You extol him, even though you, not I, would be the gainer if he increased in virtue."

Looking at his neighbor, the barbarian said, "The Mas- 3
ter is a miracle that some god has brought here. As one

[49] Darius II Ochus in fact ruled for twenty years.

---

30 πάσας Boissevain (Kay.): τὰς

γὰρ ξυγγενόμενος ἀγαθῷ πολλῷ βελτίω τὸν βασιλέα ἡμῖν ἀποφανεῖ καὶ σωφρονέστερον καὶ ἡδίω, ταυτὶ γὰρ διαφαίνεται τοῦ ἀνδρός." ἐσέθεον οὖν εὐαγγελιζόμενοι πᾶσιν, ὅτι ἀνὴρ ἐπὶ ταῖς βασιλέως θύραις ἑστήκοι σοφός τε καὶ Ἕλλην καὶ ξύμβουλος ἀγαθός.

29. Ἐπεὶ δὲ τῷ βασιλεῖ ἀνηγγέλη ταῦτα, ἔτυχε μὲν θύων παρόντων αὐτῷ τῶν μάγων, τὰ γὰρ ἱερὰ ὑπ' ἐκείνοις δρᾶται, καλέσας δὲ αὐτῶν ἕνα "ἥκει" ἔφη "τὸ ἐνύπνιον, ὃ διηγούμην σοι τήμερον ἐπισκοπουμένῳ με ἐν τῇ εὐνῇ." ὄναρ δὲ ἄρα τῷ βασιλεῖ τοιοῦτον ἀφῖκτο. ἐδόκει Ἀρταξέρξης εἶναι ὁ τοῦ Ξέρξου καὶ μεθεστηκέναι ἐς ἐκεῖνον τὸ εἶδος, περιδεῶς τε εἶχε, μὴ ἐς μεταβολὴν ἤδη τὰ πράγματα ἥκῃ αὐτῷ, ἐς τοῦτο ἐξηγουμένῳ τὴν μεταβολὴν τοῦ εἴδους. ἐπεὶ δὲ ἤκουσεν Ἕλληνά τε καὶ σοφὸν εἶναι τὸν ἥκοντα, ἐσῆλθεν αὐτὸν Θεμιστοκλῆς ὁ Ἀθηναῖος, ὃς ἀπὸ Ἑλλήνων ποτὲ ἥκων ξυνεγένετο τῷ Ἀρταξέρξῃ, καὶ πολλοῦ ἄξιον ἐκεῖνόν τε ἐποίησεν ἑαυτόν τε παρέσχετο. καὶ προτείνας τὴν δεξιὰν "κάλει," ἔφη "καὶ γὰρ ἂν καὶ ἀπὸ τοῦ καλλίστου ἄρξαιτο ξυνθύσας τε καὶ ξυνευξάμενος."

30. Εἰσῄει μὲν δὴ παραπεμπόμενος ὑπὸ πλειόνων, τουτὶ γὰρ ᾤοντο καὶ τῷ βασιλεῖ χαρίζεσθαι, μαθόντες ὡς χαίροι ἀφιγμένῳ, διϊὼν δὲ ἐς τὰ βασίλεια οὐ διέβλεψεν ἐς οὐδὲν τῶν θαυμαζομένων, ἀλλ' ὥσπερ ὁδοιπορῶν διῄει αὐτά, καὶ καλέσας τὸν Δάμιν "ἤρου με" ἔφη "πρώην, ὅ τι ὄνομα ἦν τῇ Παμφύλῳ[31] γυναικί, ἣ δὴ Σαπφοῖ τε ὁμιλῆσαι λέγεται καὶ τοὺς ὕμνους, οὓς

good man consorting with another, he will make our king much better, much more moderate and gentle, for the man clearly has these qualities." So they ran to spread the good news everywhere that there was a Master standing at the king's doors who was wise, a Greek, and an excellent adviser.

29. When the king received this message, he was just in the middle of sacrificing in the presence of the Magi, who superintend the performance of sacred rites. He called one of them and said, "This is the dream that I described to you today when you attended my levee." In fact the king had had this dream. He dreamt he was Artaxerxes the son of Xerxes, and had changed into his shape, and he was now in terror lest his fortunes might undergo alteration, since that was how he interpreted the alteration of shape. But hearing that the visitor was a Greek and a wise man, he was reminded of Themistocles of Athens, who had once come from the Greeks and resided with Artaxerxes, giving him importance and gaining importance for himself. So stretching out his right hand the king said, "Call him, for he can make an excellent start by joining me in sacrifice and prayer."

30. Thus Apollonius was escorted in by a crowd, who thought this would please the king, having heard of his joy at Apollonius's arrival. He while passing through the palace did not glance at any of the famous sights, but went by them as if he were travelling a highway. Addressing Damis, he said, "The other day you were asking me the name of the Pamphylian woman who was allegedly a companion of Sappho, and composed the hymns they sing to Artemis of

---

31 Παμφύλῳ Bentl.: Παμφύλου

ἐς τὴν Ἄρτεμιν τὴν Περγαίαν ᾄδουσι, ξυνθεῖναι τὸν Αἰολέων τε καὶ Παμφύλων τρόπον." "ἠρόμην," ἔφη "τὸ δὲ ὄνομα οὐκ εἶπας." "οὐκ, ὦ χρηστέ, εἶπον, ἀλλ' ἐξηγούμην σοι τοὺς νόμους τῶν ὕμνων καὶ τὰ ὀνόματα, καὶ ὅπῃ τὰ Αἰολέων ἐς τὸ ἀκρότατόν τε καὶ τὸ ἴδιον Παμφύλων παρήλλαξε. πρὸς ἄλλῳ μετὰ ταῦτα ἐγενόμεθα, καὶ οὐκέτ' ἤρου με περὶ τοῦ ὀνόματος. καλεῖται τοίνυν ἡ σοφὴ αὕτη Δαμοφύλη, καὶ λέγεται τὸν Σαπφοῦς τρόπον παρθένους τε ὁμιλητρίας κτήσασθαι ποιήματά τε ξυνθεῖναι τὰ μὲν ἐρωτικά, τὰ δὲ ὕμνους. τά τοι ἐς τὴν Ἄρτεμιν καὶ παρῴδηται αὐτῇ καὶ ἀπὸ τῶν Σαπφοῦς ᾖσται." ὅσον μὲν δὴ ἀπεῖχε τοῦ ἐκπεπλῆχθαι βασίλεια[32] τε καὶ ὄγκον, ἐδήλου τῷ μηδὲ ὀφθαλμῶν ἄξια ἡγεῖσθαι τὰ τοιαῦτα, ἀλλὰ ἑτέρων πέρι διαλέγεσθαι κἀκεῖνα δήπου ἡγεῖσθαι ὁρᾶν.

31. Προϊδὼν δὲ ὁ βασιλεὺς προσιόντα, καὶ γάρ τι καὶ μῆκος ἡ τοῦ ἱεροῦ αὐλὴ εἶχε, διελάλησέ τε πρὸς τοὺς ἐγγύς, οἷον ἀναγιγνώσκων τὸν ἄνδρα, πλησίον τε ἤδη γιγνομένου μέγα ἀναβοήσας "οὗτος" ἔφη "ὁ Ἀπολλώνιος, ὃν Μεγαβάτης ὁ ἐμὸς ἀδελφὸς ἰδεῖν ἐν Ἀντιοχείᾳ φησὶ θαυμαζόμενόν τε καὶ προσκυνούμενον ὑπὸ τῶν σπουδαίων, καὶ ἀπεζωγράφησέ μοι τότε τοιοῦτον αὐτόν, ὁποῖος ἥκει."

2 Προσελθόντα δὲ καὶ ἀσπασάμενον προσεῖπέ τε ὁ βασιλεὺς φωνῇ Ἑλλάδι, καὶ δὴ ἐκέλευσε[33] θύειν μετ' αὐτοῦ· λευκὸν δὲ ἄρα ἵππον τῶν σφόδρα Νισαίων

[32] βασίλεια Lucarini: βασιλέα

Perge in a combination of Aeolian and Pamphylian styles." "I did ask you," he replied, "but you did not tell me her name." "No, my friend, but I explained to you the melodies of the hymns and the references in them, and how she transposed the Aeolian style into something truly exquisite and peculiarly Pamphylian. After that we went on to another subject, and you no longer asked me her name. Well, this skilful woman's name was Damophyle, and they say that like Sappho she gathered a group of girls around her and composed poems, some of them love poems and others hymns. The hymn to Artemis is a derivative work of hers, taken from Sappho's poems."[50] How far he was from being daunted by the palace and the pomp he revealed by not even thinking such things worth a glance, but instead he talked about other things, and no doubt considered them to be what he was looking at.

31. The forecourt of the sanctuary being rather long, the king saw him coming, and spoke to his retinue as if he recognized the Master. When Apollonius got near, he said in a loud voice, "This is the Apollonius whom my brother Megabates says he saw in Antioch, the object of admiration and obeisance from virtuous people. He gave a sketch of him at that time which agrees with the man approaching."

As Apollonius came up and offered a greeting, the king 2
addressed him in the Greek tongue, and invited him to join him in making sacrifice. He was just about to sacrifice a horse of the finest Nisaean kind to the Sun, and had

[50] This Damophyle is otherwise unknown, and is probably Philostratus's invention.

33 δὴ ἐκέλευσε Kay.: διεκέλευσε

καταθύσειν ἔμελλε τῷ Ἡλίῳ φαλάροις κοσμήσας ὥσπερ ἐς πομπήν, ὁ δ᾽ ὑπολαβὼν "σὺ μέν, ὦ βασιλεῦ, θῦε," ἔφη, "τὸν σαυτοῦ τρόπον, ἐμοὶ δὲ ξυγχώρησον θῦσαι τὸν ἐμαυτοῦ." καὶ δραξάμενος τοῦ λιβανωτοῦ, "Ἥλιε," ἔφη, "πέμπε με ἐφ᾽ ὅσον τῆς γῆς ἐμοί τε καὶ σοὶ δοκεῖ, καὶ γιγνώσκοιμι ἄνδρας ἀγαθούς, φαύλους δὲ μήτε ἐγὼ μάθοιμι μήτε ἐμὲ φαῦλοι." καὶ εἰπὼν ταῦτα τὸν λιβανωτὸν ἐς τὸ πῦρ ἧκεν, ἐπισκεψάμενος δὲ αὐτὸ ὅπῃ διανίσταται, καὶ ὅπῃ θολοῦται, καὶ ὁπόσαις κορυφαῖς ᾄττει, καί που[34] καὶ ἐφαπτόμενος τοῦ πυρός, ὅπῃ εὔσημόν τε καὶ καθαρὸν φαίνοιτο, "θῦε," ἔφη, "λοιπόν, ὦ βασιλεῦ, κατὰ τὰ σαυτοῦ πάτρια, τὰ γὰρ πάτρια τἀμὰ τοιαῦτα."

32. Καὶ ἀνεχώρησε τῆς θυσίας, ὡς μὴ κοινωνοίη τοῦ αἵματος. μετὰ δὲ τὴν θυσίαν προσῆλθε καὶ "ὦ βασιλεῦ," ἔφη "τὴν φωνὴν τὴν Ἑλλάδα πᾶσαν γιγνώσκεις, ἢ σμικρὰ αὐτῆς ὑπὲρ τοῦ εὐξυμβόλου ἴσως καὶ τοῦ μὴ ἀηδὴς δοκεῖν, εἴ τις ἀφίκοιτο Ἕλλην;" "πᾶσαν" εἶπεν "ἴσα τῇ ἐγχωρίῳ ταύτῃ, καὶ λέγε ὅ τι βούλει, διὰ τοῦτο γάρ που ἐρωτᾷς." "διὰ τοῦτο," ἔφη "καὶ ἄκουε. ἡ μὲν ὁρμή μοι τῆς ἀποδημίας Ἰνδοί εἰσι, παρελθεῖν δὲ οὐδ᾽ ὑμᾶς ἐβουλήθην, σέ τε ἀκούων ἄνδρα, οἷον ἐξ ὄνυχος ἤδη ὁρῶ, σοφίαν τε, ἥπερ ὑμῖν ἐστιν ἐπιχώριος μελετωμένη μάγοις ἀνδράσι, κατιδεῖν δεόμενος, εἰ τὰ θεῖα, ὡς λέγονται, σοφοί εἰσι.

2 "Σοφία δὲ ἐμοὶ Πυθαγόρου Σαμίου ἀνδρός, ὃς

[34] που Kay.: ὅπου

adorned it with metal disks as if for a procession. But Apollonius replied, "You may sacrifice your own way, Majesty, but allow me to sacrifice in mine." He took a handful of frankincense and said, "Sun, send me as far across the world as seems good to you and to me. Let me come to know good men, but let me not hear of bad ones, or they of me." So saying he dropped the frankincense into the flames, and observed how they divided, where they were smoky, how many tongues they flickered with, and he also touched the fire wherever it seemed auspicious and pure. He then said, "Now, Majesty, sacrifice according to your ancestral customs, because mine are as you see."[51]

32. He then left the sacrifice in order not to participate in bloodshed. After it, he approached the king and said, "Majesty, do you know Greek perfectly, or just a smattering for the sake of politeness, and in order not to seem rude if any Greek arrives?" "I know it perfectly," was the reply, "as well as I know the local language here. So say whatever you please, since that is the point of your question, surely." "It is," said Apollonius, "so listen. India is the object of my journey, but I did not want to pass by your country too, since I had heard you were a true man such as I now see on close inspection. I also needed to observe the wisdom that is your specialty, the kind that the revered Magi pursue, to see if they are as wise in spiritual matters as their reputation makes out.

"My own wisdom, however, comes from a Samian Mas- 2

[51] Divination by means of flames arising from incense ("libanomancy") was a Pythagorean specialty.

θεούς τε θεραπεύειν ὧδέ με ἐδιδάξατο, καὶ ξυνιέναι σφῶν ὁρωμένων τε καὶ οὐχ ὁρωμένων, φοιτᾶν τε ἐς διάλεξιν θεῶν, καὶ γηίνῳ τούτῳ ἐρίῳ ἐστάλθαι, οὐ γὰρ προβάτου ἐπέχθη, ἀλλ᾽ ἀκήρατος ἀκηράτων φύεται ὕδατός τε καὶ γῆς δῶρα ὀθόνη. καὶ αὐτὸ δὲ τὸ ἄνετον τῆς κόμης ἐκ Πυθαγόρου ἐπήσκησα, καὶ τὸ καθαρεύειν ζῴου βορᾶς ἐκ τῆς ἐκείνου μοι σοφίας ἥκει. ξυμπότης μὲν δὴ καὶ κοινωνὸς ῥᾳστώνης ἢ τρυφῆς οὔτ᾽ ἂν σοὶ γενοίμην οὔτ᾽ ἂν ἑτέρῳ οὐδενί, φροντίδων δὲ ἀπόρων τε καὶ δυσευρέτων δοίην ἂν λύσεις, οὐ γιγνώσκων τὰ πρακτέα μόνον, ἀλλὰ καὶ προγιγνώσκων." ταῦτα ὁ Δάμις μὲν διαλεχθῆναί φησι τὸν ἄνδρα, Ἀπολλώνιος δὲ ἐπιστολὴν αὐτὰ πεποίηται, πολλὰ δὲ καὶ ἄλλα τῶν ἑαυτῷ ἐς διάλεξιν εἰρημένων ἐς ἐπιστολὰς ἀνετυπώσατο.

33. Ἐπεὶ δὲ χαίρειν ὁ βασιλεὺς ἔφη καὶ ἀγάλλεσθαι ἥκοντι μᾶλλον ἢ εἰ τὰ Περσῶν καὶ Ἰνδῶν πρὸς τοῖς οὖσιν αὐτῷ ἐκτήσατο, ξένον τε ποιεῖσθαι καὶ κοινωνὸν τῆς βασιλείου στέγης, "εἰ ἐγώ σε, ὦ βασιλεῦ," εἶπεν "ἐς πατρίδα τὴν ἐμὴν Τύανα ἥκοντα ἠξίουν οἰκεῖν οὗ ἐγώ, ᾤκήσας ἂν ἄρα;" "μὰ Δί'" εἶπεν "εἰ μὴ τοσαύτην γε οἰκίαν οἰκήσειν ἔμελλον, ὁπόσην δορυφόρους τε καὶ σωματοφύλακας ἐμοὺς αὐτόν τε ἐμὲ λαμπρῶς δέξασθαι." "ὁ αὐτὸς οὖν" ἔφη "καὶ παρ᾽ ἐμοῦ λόγος. εἰ γὰρ ὑπὲρ ἐμαυτὸν οἰκήσω, πονηρῶς διαιτήσομαι, τὸ γὰρ ὑπερβάλλον λυπεῖ τοὺς σοφοὺς μᾶλλον ἢ ὑμᾶς τὸ ἐλλεῖπον. ξενιζέτω με οὖν ἰδιώτης ἔχων ὁπόσα ἐγώ, σοὶ δὲ ἐγὼ ξυνέσομαι ὁπόσα

ter called Pythagoras. He taught me to reverence the gods as I do, to understand them whether or not I saw them, to enter into conversation with them, and to use this natural fabric. It is not woven from sheep's wool, but is unadulterated linen, which grows as the gift of unadulterated water and earth. My neglect of my hair is also something I practice after Pythagoras's example, and my abstention from animal food comes to me from his wisdom. I can never be your boon companion or join you or anyone else in idleness or luxury, but I can give you solutions to intractable and insoluble problems, for I am able not only to tell the right course of action, but to foretell it." This is the conversation that Damis says the Master had, but Apollonius has put it into a letter, and he expressed many things in letters that he had said in conversation.

33. The king said he was more pleased and delighted by Apollonius's arrival than if he had added Persia and India to his present realm, and he declared him a guest and a sharer of the royal roof. But Apollonius said, "If you had come to my city of Tyana, Majesty, and I was asking you to live where I did, would you do so?" "Certainly not," replied the king, "unless I was going to occupy a house large enough to accommodate my spearmen, my bodyguards, and myself in style." "The same argument holds on my side," said Apollonius. "If my quarters are too good for me, I will be uncomfortably situated, because excess vexes the wise more than deficiency vexes people like you. So let an ordinary person be my host, and have the same things as I do, and I will join you as often as you wish." The king

βούλει." ξυνεχώρει ὁ βασιλεύς, ὡς μὴ ἀηδές τι αὐτῷ λάθοι πράξας, καὶ ᾤκησε παρ' ἀνδρὶ Βαβυλωνίῳ χρηστῷ τε καὶ ἄλλως γενναίῳ.

2 Δειπνοῦντι δὲ ἤδη εὐνοῦχος ἐφίσταται τῶν τὰς ἀγγελίας διαφερόντων, καὶ προσειπὼν τὸν ἄνδρα "βασιλεὺς" ἔφη "δωρεῖταί σε δέκα δωρεαῖς, καὶ ποιεῖται κύριον τοῦ ἐπαγγεῖλαι αὐτάς, δεῖται δέ σου μὴ μικρὰ αἰτῆσαι, μεγαλοφροσύνην γὰρ ἐνδείξασθαι σοί τε καὶ ἡμῖν βούλεται." ἐπαινέσας δὲ τὴν ἐπαγγελίαν, "πότε οὖν χρὴ αἰτεῖν;" ἤρετο, ὁ δὲ "αὔριον" ἔφη, καὶ ἅμα ἐφοίτησε παρὰ πάντας τοὺς βασιλέως φίλους τε καὶ ξυγγενεῖς, παρεῖναι κελεύων αἰτοῦντι καὶ τιμωμένῳ τῷ ἀνδρί. φησὶ δὲ ὁ Δάμις ξυνιέναι μέν, ὅτι μηδὲν αἰτήσοι, τόν τε τρόπον αὐτοῦ καθεωρακώς, καὶ εἰδὼς εὐχόμενον τοῖς θεοῖς εὐχὴν τοιαύτην, "ὦ θεοί, δοίητε μοι μικρὰ ἔχειν καὶ δεῖσθαι μηδενός," ἐφεστηκότα μέντοι ὁρῶν καὶ ἐνθυμουμένῳ ὅμοιον, οἴεσθαι ὡς αἰτήσοι μέν, βασανίζοι δέ, ὅ τι μέλλει αἰτήσειν.

34. Ὁ δὲ ἑσπέρας ἤδη "ὦ Δάμι," ἔφη "θεωρῶ πρὸς ἐμαυτόν, ἐξ ὅτου ποτὲ οἱ βάρβαροι τοὺς εὐνούχους σώφρονας ἡγοῦνται, καὶ ἐς τὰς γυναικωνίτιδας ἐσάγονται." "ἀλλὰ τοῦτο," ἔφη "ὦ Ἀπολλώνιε, καὶ παιδὶ δῆλον. ἐπειδὴ γὰρ ἡ τομὴ τὸ ἀφροδισιάζειν ἀφαιρεῖται σφᾶς, ἀνεῖνταί σφισιν αἱ γυναικωνίτιδες, κἂν ξυγκαθεύδειν ταῖς γυναιξὶ βούλωνται." "τὸ δὲ ἐρᾶν" εἶπεν "ἢ τὸ ξυγγίγνεσθαι γυναιξὶν ἐκτετμῆσθαι αὐτοὺς οἴει;" "ἄμφω," ἔφη "εἰ γὰρ σβεσθείη τὸ μόριον ὑφ' οὗ διοιστρεῖται τὸ σῶμα, οὐδ' ἂν τὸ ἐρᾶν ἐπέλθοι

granted this in order not to cause him any unintended discomfort, and he moved in with a kindly and generally well bred Babylonian gentleman.

He was just having dinner when a eunuch came up 2
from the messenger service. Addressing the Master, he said, "The king presents you with ten presents, and gives you the choice of naming them. He asks you not to make a trifling request, since he wants to display his generosity before you and before us." Thanking him for the announcement, Apollonius asked, "When must I make my request?" "Tomorrow," he said, and immediately went round all the friends and relatives of the king, inviting them to be present when the Master made his request and was honored. Damis claims to have guessed that Apollonius was not going to make any request, since he had observed his ways, and knew that the prayer he offered to the gods was this: "Gods, grant that I have little and need nothing." However, when he saw Apollonius silent as if in meditation, he inferred that he was about to ask for something, and was considering what it would be.

34. In the evening, Apollonius said, "Damis, I am pondering within myself why barbarians think eunuchs chaste, and admit them into their women's quarters." "Why, a child can see that," said Damis. "Castration takes away their ability to have sex, and that is why they have access to harems, even if they want to sleep with the women." "What then do you think has been excised from them, erotic feelings or the ability to sleep with women?" "Both, since if the member which throws the body into frenzy has been done away with, no one can have sexual passion." After a

οὐδενί.” ὁ δὲ βραχὺ ἐπισχὼν “αὔριον,” ἔφη “ὦ Δάμι, μάθοις ἄν, ὅτι καὶ εὐνοῦχοι ἐρῶσι καὶ τὸ ἐπιθυμητικόν, ὅπερ ἐσάγονται διὰ τῶν ὀφθαλμῶν, οὐκ ἀπομαραίνεται σφῶν, ἀλλ᾽ ἐμμένει θερμόν τε καὶ ζώπυρον, δεῖ γάρ τι περιπεσεῖν, ὃ τὸν σὸν ἐλέγξει λόγον. εἰ δὲ καὶ τέχνη τις ἦν ἀνθρωπεία τύραννός τε καὶ δυνατὴ τὰ τοιαῦτα ἐξωθεῖν τῆς γνώμης, οὐκ ἄν μοι δοκῶ τοὺς εὐνούχους ποτὲ ἐς τὰ τῶν σωφρονούντων ἤθη προσγράψαι κατηναγκασμένους τὴν σωφροσύνην, καὶ βιαίῳ τέχνῃ ἐς τὸ μὴ ἐρᾶν ἠγμένους. σωφροσύνη γὰρ τὸ ὀρεγόμενόν τε καὶ ὀργῶντα[35] μὴ ἡττᾶσθαι ἀφροδισίων, ἀλλ᾽ ἀπέχεσθαι καὶ κρείττω φαίνεσθαι τῆς λύττης ταύτης.”

2 Ὑπολαβὼν οὖν ὁ Δάμις “ταῦτα μὲν καὶ αὖθις ἐπισκεψόμεθα,” ἔφη “ὦ Ἀπολλώνιε, ἃ δὲ χρὴ ἀποκρίνασθαι αὔριον πρὸς τὴν τοῦ βασιλέως ἐπαγγελίαν λαμπρὰν οὖσαν διεσκέφθαι προσήκει. αἰτήσεις μὲν γὰρ ἴσως οὐδέν, τὸ δ᾽ ὅπως ἂν μὴ ἄλλῳ, φασί, τύφῳ παραιτεῖσθαι δοκοίης, ἅπερ ἂν ὁ βασιλεὺς διδῷ, τοῦτο ὅρα καὶ φυλάττου αὐτό, ὁρῶν οἶ τῆς γῆς εἶ καὶ ὅτι ἐπ᾽ αὐτῷ κείμεθα. δεῖ δὲ φυλάττεσθαι διαβολάς, ὡς ὑπεροψίᾳ χρώμενον, γιγνώσκειν τε ὡς νῦν μὲν ἐφόδιά ἐστιν ἡμῖν ὁπόσα ἐς Ἰνδοὺς πέμψαι, ἐπανιοῦσι δὲ ἐκεῖθεν οὔτ᾽ ἂν ἀποχρῆσαι[36] ταῦτα, γένοιτό τε[37] οὐκ ἂν ἕτερα.”

35. Καὶ τοιᾷδε ὑπέθαλπεν αὐτὸν τέχνῃ, μὴ ἀπαξιῶσαι λαβεῖν, ὅ τι διδοίη, ὁ δὲ Ἀπολλώνιος ὥσπερ ξυλλαμβάνων αὐτῷ τοῦ λόγου “παραδειγμάτων δέ,”

short pause, Apollonius said, "You will find out tomorrow, Damis, that eunuchs too have sexual passion, and that their capacity for desire, absorbed through the eyes, does not wither away, but remains hot and glowing. Something is fated to occur that will refute your argument. In fact, even if human beings had some supreme skill that was able to expel such things from the mind, I do not think it could lead eunuchs into habits of self-control, making them self-controlled by compulsion, or depriving them of sexual passion by some drastic method. Self-control means that someone in a state of desire and excitement is not overcome by the sexual urge, but instead uses restraint, and shows himself to be master of this madness."

In reply Damis said, "We will discuss this matter another time, Apollonius, but we ought to consider what answer to make to the king's generous offer tomorrow. You will not ask for anything, perhaps, but you should make sure not to seem to refuse out of the proverbial 'pride of another kind.'[52] You must avoid that, considering where in the world you are and our dependence on the king. You must also guard against accusations that you are acting with contempt, and remember that we have enough provisions to get us to India, but these will not be enough for the return journey, and we will have no other resource." 2

35. Damis tried by this kind of device to induce Apollonius not to refuse any gift from the king, and Apollonius,

[52] When Diogenes the Cynic mocked Plato for having carpets by saying, "I walk on Plato's pride," Plato replied, "With pride of another kind, Diogenes" (Diog. Laert. 6.26). Cf. VI 11.19.

---

35 ὀργῶντα Bentl.: ὁρμῶντα
36 ἀποχρήσαι Kay.: ἀποχρῆσαι
37 τε Jackson: δὲ

εἶπεν "ὦ Δάμι, ἀμελήσεις; ἐν οἷς ἐστιν, ὡς Αἰσχίνης μὲν ὁ τοῦ Λυσανίου παρὰ Διονύσιον ἐς Σικελίαν ὑπὲρ χρημάτων ᾤχετο, Πλάτων δὲ τρὶς ἀναμετρῆσαι λέγεται τὴν Χάρυβδιν ὑπὲρ πλούτου Σικελικοῦ, Ἀρίστιππος δὲ ὁ Κυρηναῖος καὶ Ἑλίκων ὁ ἐκ Κυζίκου καὶ Φύτων, ὅτ' ἔφευγε Ῥηγίον, οὕτω τι ἐς τοὺς Διονυσίου κατέδυσαν θησαυρούς, ὡς μόγις ἀνασχεῖν ἐκεῖθεν. καὶ μὴν καὶ τὸν Κνίδιόν φασιν Εὔδοξον ἐς Αἴγυπτόν ποτε ἀφικόμενον, ὑπὲρ χρημάτων τε ὁμολογεῖν ἥκειν, καὶ διαλέγεσθαι τῷ βασιλεῖ ὑπὲρ τούτου. καὶ ἵνα μὴ πλείους διαβάλλω, Σπεύσιππον τὸν Ἀθηναῖον οὕτω τι ἐρασιχρήματον γενέσθαι φασίν, ὡς ἐπὶ τὸν Κασσάνδρου γάμον ἐς Μακεδονίαν κωμάσαι ποιήματα ψυχρὰ ξυνθέντα, καὶ δημοσίᾳ ταῦθ' ὑπὲρ χρημάτων ᾆσαι.

2 "'Εγὼ δὲ ἡγοῦμαι, ὦ Δάμι, τὸν ἄνδρα τὸν σοφὸν πλείω κινδυνεύειν ἢ οἱ πλέοντές τε καὶ ξὺν ὅπλοις μαχόμενοι, φθόνος γὰρ ἐπ' αὐτὸν στείχει καὶ σιωπῶντα, καὶ φθεγγόμενον, καὶ ξυντείνοντα, καὶ ἀνιέντα, κἂν παρέλθῃ τινά,[38] κἂν προσέλθῃ τῳ, κἂν προσείπῃ κἂν μὴ προσείπῃ. δεῖ δὲ πεφράχθαι τὸν ἄνδρα, γιγνώσκειν τε ὡς ἀργίας μὲν ἡττηθεὶς ὁ σοφὸς ἢ χολῆς, ἢ ἔρωτος, ἢ φιλοποσίας, ἢ ἑτοιμότερόν τι τοῦ καιροῦ πράξας ἴσως ἂν καὶ ξυγγνώμην φέροιτο, χρήμασι δὲ

[38] τινά Jackson: τι

[53] Dionysius II, king of Sicily, attracted many philosophers to his court. Of those mentioned here, Aeschines (not the famous orator), Plato, and Aristippus were all pupils of Socrates, and

as if pursuing his line of argument, said, "Are you not going to provide precedents, Damis? For example, Aeschines the son of Lysanias went off to Dionysius in Sicily to get money; Plato is said to have passed Charybdis three times in pursuit of Sicilian wealth; Aristippus of Cyrene, Helicon from Cyzicus, and Phyton when he was in exile from Rhegium, all these plunged so deeply into Dionysius's treasures that they only just emerged from them.[53] They also say that Eudoxus of Cnidus[54] once arrived in Egypt admitting that he had come for money, and spoke with the king on the subject. Not to speak ill of others too, they say Speusippus the Athenian[55] was so money-mad that he burst into the wedding of Cassander in Macedonia after composing some bombastic poems, and sang them in public for a fee.

2 "In my opinion, Damis, the wise man runs more dangers than sailors and armored fighters, for envy dogs him whether silent or speaking, in toil or relaxation, whether he passes a man by or accosts him, or addresses someone or fails to. The man must be well armed, and recognize that if a sage is overcome by anger, sexual desire, or alcohol, or acts somewhat more eagerly than the occasion demands, he might perhaps be forgiven. But if he degrades himself

Helicon a pupil of Plato. Phyton of Rhegium, mentioned here as a courtier of Dionysius II, is said in VII 2.2 to have died at the hands of Dionysius I.

[54] Celebrated mathematician and astronomer, said to have visited King Nectanebos of Egypt (ruled 382–364).

[55] Nephew of Plato and his successor as head of the Academy. Cassander, regent and later king of Macedon, married a half-sister of Alexander the Great in 316.

ὑποθεὶς ἑαυτὸν οὔτ᾽ ἂν ξυγγινώσκοιτο καὶ μισοῖτ᾽ ἄν, ὡς ὁμοῦ πάσας κακίας συνειληφώς. μὴ γὰρ ἂν ἡττηθῆναι χρημάτων αὐτόν, εἰ μὴ γαστρὸς ἥττητο καὶ ἀμπεχόνης, καὶ οἴνου, καὶ τοῦ ἐς ἑταίρας φέρεσθαι. σὺ δ᾽ ἴσως ἡγῇ τὸ ἐν Βαβυλῶνι ἁμαρτεῖν ἧττον εἶναι τοῦ Ἀθήνησιν ἢ Ὀλυμπίασιν ἢ Πυθοῖ, καὶ οὐκ ἐνθυμῇ ὅτι σοφῷ ἀνδρὶ Ἑλλὰς πάντα, καὶ οὐδὲν ἔρημον ἢ βάρβαρον χωρίον οὔτε ἡγήσεται ὁ σοφὸς οὔτε νομιεῖ, ζῶν γε ὑπὸ τοῖς τῆς ἀρετῆς ὀφθαλμοῖς, καὶ βλέπει μὲν ὀλίγους τῶν ἀνθρώπων, μυρίοις δ᾽ ὄμμασιν αὐτὸς ὁρᾶται.

3 "Εἰ δὲ καὶ ἀθλητῇ ξυνῆσθα τούτων τινί, ὦ Δάμι, οἳ παλαίειν τε καὶ παγκρατιάζειν ἀσκοῦσιν, ἆρα ἂν ἠξίους αὐτόν, εἰ μὲν Ὀλύμπια ἀγωνίζοιτο καὶ ἐς Ἀρκαδίαν ἴοι, γενναῖόν τε καὶ ἀγαθὸν εἶναι, καὶ νὴ Δί᾽, εἰ Πύθια ἄγοιτο ἢ Νέμεα, ἐπιμελεῖσθαι τοῦ σώματος, ἐπειδὴ φανεροὶ οἱ ἀγῶνες καὶ τὰ στάδια ἐν σπουδαίῳ τῆς Ἑλλάδος, εἰ δὲ θύοι Φίλιππος Ὀλύμπια πόλεις ᾑρηκώς, ἢ ὁ τούτου παῖς Ἀλέξανδρος ἐπὶ ταῖς ἑαυτοῦ νίκαις ἀγῶνα ἄγοι, χεῖρον ἤδη παρασκευάζειν τὸ σῶμα καὶ μὴ φιλονίκως ἔχειν, ἐπειδὴ ἐν Ὀλύνθῳ ἀγωνιεῖται ἢ Μακεδονίᾳ ἢ Αἰγύπτῳ, ἀλλὰ μὴ ἐν Ἕλλησι καὶ σταδίοις τοῖς ἐκεῖ;" ὑπὸ μὲν δὴ τῶν λόγων τούτων ὁ Δάμις οὕτω διατεθῆναί φησιν, ὡς ξυγκαλύψασθαί τε ἐφ᾽ οἷς αὐτὸς εἰρηκὼς ἔτυχε, παραιτεῖσθαί τε τὸν Ἀπολλώνιον ξυγγνώμην αὐτῷ ἔχειν,

---

[56] A brutal combination of wrestling and boxing.

for money he cannot be forgiven, but will be detested as the embodiment of all the vices at once. He would not have fallen victim to money, it will seem, if he had not also fallen victim to gluttony, fine clothing, wine and the company of prostitutes. You perhaps think that doing wrong in Babylon matters less than doing so in Athens, Olympia, or Delphi. You do not take into account that to a wise man Greece is everywhere, and he will not consider or believe any place to be deserted or uncivilized. He lives in the sight of virtue, and though he sees few people he himself is observed with a thousand eyes.

"Suppose, Damis, you were the associate of one of 3
those athletes who practice wrestling and the pancration.[56] If he was competing at Olympia and going to Arcadia, you would surely expect him to be noble and bold, or indeed to look after his physique if the Pythian or the Nemean games were on, since those contests are public and their stadia are in the authentic Greece. But suppose Philip was making an Olympic sacrifice to celebrate his capture of cities, or his son Alexander were holding a contest to celebrate his own victories. Would you expect the athlete to train his body less well then, and not desire victory just because he would be competing in Olynthus, Macedonia, or Egypt, rather than in Greece and the stadia there?"[57] So affected was Damis by these arguments that he says his own previous remarks made him hide his face, and he begged Apollonius's pardon for his failure to understand him, and

[57] After capturing Olynthus in 348, Philip held games on the model of the Olympics in Dium, Macedonia. Alexander celebrated games in Tyre and elsewhere, but not (so far as is known) in Egypt.

εἰ μήπω κατανενοηκὼς αὐτὸν ἐς ξυμβουλίαν τε καὶ πειθὼ τοιαύτην ὥρμησεν. ὁ δὲ ἀναλαμβάνων αὐτὸν "θάρρει," ἔφη "οὐ γὰρ ἐπίπληξιν ποιούμενος, ἀλλὰ τοὐμὸν ὑπογράφων σοι, ταῦτα εἶπον."

36. Ἀφικομένου δὲ τοῦ εὐνούχου καὶ καλοῦντος αὐτὸν παρὰ τὸν βασιλέα "ἀφίξομαι," εἶπεν "ἐπειδὰν τὰ πρὸς τοὺς θεοὺς εὖ μοι ἔχῃ." θύσας οὖν καὶ εὐξάμενος ἀπῄει, περιβλεπόμενός τε καὶ θαυμαζόμενος τοῦ σχήματος. ὡς δὲ ἔσω παρῆλθε, "δίδωμί σοι" ἔφη ὁ βασιλεὺς "δέκα δωρεὰς ἄνδρα σε ἡγούμενος, οἷος οὔπω τις ἀπὸ Ἑλλήνων δεῦρ' ἦλθεν." ὁ δὲ ὑπολαβὼν "οὐ πάσας," εἶπεν "ὦ βασιλεῦ, παραιτήσομαι, μίαν δέ, ἣν ἀντὶ πολλῶν δεκάδων αἱροῦμαι, προθύμως αἰτήσω." καὶ ἅμα τὸν περὶ τῶν Ἐρετριέων διῆλθε λόγον ἀναλαβὼν ἀπὸ τοῦ Δάτιδος. "αἰτῶ οὖν" ἔφη "μὴ περικόπτεσθαι τοὺς ἀθλίους τούτους τῶν ὁρίων τε καὶ τοῦ λόφου, ἀλλὰ νέμεσθαι σφᾶς μέτρον τῆς γῆς, ὃ Δαρεῖος ἐνόμισε, δεινὸν γάρ, εἰ τῆς αὑτῶν ἐκπεσόντες μηδ' ἣν ἀντ' ἐκείνης ἔχουσιν ἕξουσιν."

2 Ξυντιθέμενος οὖν ὁ βασιλεὺς "Ἐρετριεῖς" εἶπεν "ἐς μὲν τὴν χθὲς ἡμέραν ἐμοῦ τε πολέμιοι καὶ πατέρων ἐμῶν ἦσαν, ἐπειδὴ ὅπλων ποτὲ ἐφ' ἡμᾶς ἦρξαν, καὶ παρεωρῶντο, ὡς τὸ γένος αὐτῶν ἀφανισθείη. λοιπὸν δὲ φίλοι τε ἀναγεγράψονται καὶ σατραπεύσει αὐτῶν ἀνὴρ ἀγαθός, ὃς δικαιώσει τὴν χώραν. τὰς δὲ ἐννέα δωρεὰς" ἔφη "διὰ τί οὐ λήψῃ;" "ὅτι, ὦ βασιλεῦ" εἶπεν "οὔπω φίλους ἐνταῦθα ἐκτησάμην." "αὐτὸς δὲ οὐδενὸς δέῃ;" φήσαντος "τῶν γε τραγημάτων" ἔφη "καὶ τῶν

for unthinkingly offering him such advice and arguments. Apollonius cheered him up by saying, "Never mind. I said all this not to rebuke you, but to give you an impression of myself."

36. The eunuch arrived with an invitation to the king, but Apollonius said, "I will come when I am on good terms with the gods." So after offering sacrifice and prayer he went off, with his appearance causing admiration and wonder. On his entrance, the king said, "I give you ten gifts, since I consider you a man whose equal has never yet come here from Greece." Apollonius replied, "I will not decline them all, Majesty, but there is one which I prefer to many tens of gifts, and I will ask it eagerly," whereupon he gave his account of the Eretrians, beginning with Datis.[58] "So I ask," he said, "that these poor people not be cut off from their frontiers and their hill, but should work the amount of land that Darius allotted for them. It is shameful that after exile from their own land they should not have the land they were given in its stead."

The king consented, saying, "Until yesterday the Ere- 2
trians were enemies to me and my ancestors, since they once took up arms against us, and we neglected them in hopes that that their tribe might disappear. But from now on they will be inscribed as my friends, and a good man will govern them, and determine their territory. But why will you not accept the nine gifts?" he said. "Because, Majesty," replied Apollonius, "I have not yet made friends here." "But do you not need anything yourself?" "Yes, the dried fruits," said Apollonius, "and the loaves; they make a de-

[58] Datis, admiral of Darius in 490, besieged and sacked Eretria (cf. 23.2).

ἄρτων, ἅ με ἡδέως τε καὶ λαμπρῶς ἑστιᾷ."

37. Τοιαῦτα δὴ λαλούντων πρὸς ἀλλήλους, κραυγὴ τῶν βασιλείων ἐξεφοίτησεν εὐνούχων καὶ γυναικῶν ἅμα· εἴληπτο δὲ ἄρα εὐνοῦχός τις ἐπὶ μιᾷ τῶν τοῦ βασιλέως παλλακῶν ξυγκατακείμενός τε καὶ ὁπόσα οἱ μοιχοὶ πράττων, καὶ ἦγον αὐτὸν οἱ ἀμφὶ τὴν γυναικωνῖτιν ἐπισπῶντες τῆς κόμης, ὃν δὴ ἄγονται τρόπον οἱ βασιλέως δοῦλοι. ἐπεὶ δὲ ὁ πρεσβύτατος τῶν εὐνούχων ἐρῶντα μὲν τῆς γυναικὸς πάλαι ᾐσθῆσθαι ἔφη, καὶ προειρηκέναι οἱ μὴ προσδιαλέγεσθαι αὐτῇ, μηδὲ ἅπτεσθαι δέρης ἢ χειρός, μηδὲ κοσμεῖν ταύτην μόνην τῶν ἔνδον, νῦν δὲ καὶ ξυγκατακείμενον εὑρηκέναι καὶ ἀνδριζόμενον ἐπὶ τὴν γυναῖκα, ὁ μὲν Ἀπολλώνιος ἐς τὸν Δάμιν εἶδεν, ὡς δὴ τοῦ λόγου ἀποδεδειγμένου, ὃς ἐφιλοσοφεῖτο αὐτοῖς περὶ τοῦ καὶ εὐνούχων τὸ ἐρᾶν εἶναι,

2 Ὁ δὲ βασιλεὺς πρὸς τοὺς παρόντας "ἀλλ' αἰσχρόν γε" εἶπεν "ὦ ἄνδρες, παρόντος ἡμῖν Ἀπολλωνίου περὶ σωφροσύνης ἡμᾶς, ἀλλὰ μὴ τοῦτον, ἀποφαίνεσθαι· τί οὖν κελεύεις, Ἀπολλώνιε, παθεῖν αὐτόν;" "τί δὲ ἄλλο ἢ ζῆν;" εἶπε, παρὰ τὴν πάντων ἀποκρινάμενος δόξαν. ἀνερυθριάσας οὖν ὁ βασιλεὺς "εἶτα οὐ πολλῶν" ἔφη "θανάτων ἄξιος, ὑφέρπων οὕτως τὴν εὐνὴν τὴν ἐμήν;" "ἀλλ' οὐχ ὑπὲρ ξυγγνώμης" ἔφη "βασιλεῦ, ταῦτα εἶπον, ἀλλ' ὑπὲρ τιμωρίας, ἣ ἀποκναίσει αὐτόν. εἰ γὰρ ζήσεται νοσῶν καὶ ἀδυνάτων ἁπτόμενος, καὶ μήτε σῖτα μήτε ποτὰ ἥσει αὐτὸν μήτε θεάματα, ἃ σέ τε καὶ τούς σοι συνόντας εὐφρανεῖ, πηδήσεταί τε ἡ καρδία

lightful and plentiful dinner for me."

37. They were conversing among themselves in this way when a shout of eunuchs and of women together rose from the royal quarters. A eunuch had in fact been caught in bed with one of the king's wives, doing everything seducers do. The guardians of the harem were dragging him along by the hair, which is how the king's slaves are summoned. The senior eunuch said he had long since noticed that this one was in love with the woman. He had warned him not to talk to her, or to touch her neck or her hand, and among all the women inside he was forbidden to dress only this one. Apollonius looked at Damis at this confirmation of their learned discussion about the capacity of eunuchs for sexual passion.

The king said to his attendants, "In the presence of 2
Apollonius, gentlemen, it is wrong for us rather than him to give an opinion about chastity. So what sentence do you order for him, Apollonius?" "There is only one: life," said Apollonius, giving a completely unexpected answer. Flushing, the king said, "So you do not think he deserves to die many times over for creeping into my bed?" "I spoke as I did," Apollonius replied, "not to get him a pardon, but a sentence that will waste him away. If he lives diseased and grasping at impossibilities, neither food nor drink will please him, nor the sights that cheer you and your atten-

θαμὰ ἐκθρώσκοντος τοῦ ὕπνου, ὃ δὴ μάλιστα περὶ τοὺς ἐρῶντάς φασι γίγνεσθαι, καὶ τίς μὲν οὕτω φθόη τήξει αὐτόν, τίς δὲ οὕτω λιμὸς ἐπιθρύψει τὰ σπλάγχνα; εἰ δὲ μὴ τῶν φιλοψύχων εἴη τις, αὐτός, ὦ βασιλεῦ, δεήσεταί σού ποτε καὶ ἀποκτεῖναι αὐτὸν ἢ ἑαυτόν γε ἀποκτενεῖ, πολλὰ ὀλοφυρόμενος τὴν παροῦσαν ταύτην ἡμέραν, ἐν ᾗ μὴ εὐθὺς ἀπέθανε." τοῦτο μὲν δὴ τοιοῦτον τοῦ Ἀπολλωνίου καὶ οὕτω σοφόν τε καὶ ἥμερον, ἐφ᾽ ᾧ ὁ βασιλεὺς ἀνῆκε τὸν θάνατον τῷ εὐνούχῳ.

38. Μέλλων δέ ποτε πρὸς θήρᾳ γίγνεσθαι τῶν ἐν τοῖς παραδείσοις θηρίων, ἐς οὓς λέοντές τε ἀπόκεινται τοῖς βαρβάροις καὶ ἄρκτοι καὶ παρδάλεις, ἠξίου τὸν Ἀπολλώνιον παρατυχεῖν οἱ θηρῶντι, ὁ δὲ "ἐκλέλησαι, ὦ βασιλεῦ," ἔφη "ὅτι μηδὲ θύοντί σοι παρατυγχάνω; καὶ ἄλλως οὐχ ἡδὺ θηρίοις βεβασανισμένοις καὶ παρὰ τὴν φύσιν τὴν ἑαυτῶν δεδουλωμένοις ἐπιτίθεσθαι." ἐρομένου δὲ αὐτὸν τοῦ βασιλέως, πῶς ἂν βεβαίως καὶ ἀσφαλῶς ἄρχοι, "πολλοὺς" ἔφη "τιμῶν, πιστεύων δὲ ὀλίγοις." πρεσβευομένου δέ ποτε τοῦ τῆς Συρίας ἄρχοντος περὶ κωμῶν, οἶμαι, δύο προσοίκων τῷ Ζεύγματι, καὶ φάσκοντος ὑπακηκοέναι μὲν αὐτὰς Ἀντιόχῳ καὶ Σελεύκῳ πάλαι, νῦν δὲ ὑπ᾽ αὐτῷ εἶναι Ῥωμαίοις προσηκούσας, καὶ τοὺς μὲν Ἀραβίους τε καὶ Ἀρμενίους μὴ ἐνοχλεῖν τὰς κώμας, αὐτὸν δὲ ὑπερβαίνοντα τοσαύτην γῆν καρποῦσθαι σφᾶς, ὡς αὐτοῦ μᾶλλον ἢ Ῥωμαίων οὔσας,

2 Μεταστησάμενος ὁ βασιλεὺς τοὺς πρέσβεις "τὰς

dants. His heart will pound, he will often start from sleep (that is said to be the most frequent symptom of sexual passion), and no consumption will waste him so much, no hunger will so gnaw his stomach. But if he is not the sort of man that clings to life, Majesty, he himself will one day beg you to kill him, or he will kill himself, bitterly regretting this present day in which he did not suffer instant death." That was Apollonius's advice, so wise and mild, which led the king to spare the eunuch's life.

38. Once the king was about to go off to hunt the animals in the parks, in which the barbarians keep lions, bears, and leopards. He asked Apollonius to join him in the hunt, but he replied, "Have you forgotten, Majesty, that I do not even join you when you sacrifice?[59] Besides, it is no pleasure to attack animals that are tortured and enslaved against their natures." When the king asked him how to rule firmly and safely, Apollonius replied, "By honoring many and trusting few." The governor of Syria once sent him an embassy concerning two or more villages near Zeugma, I think, alleging that they had been subject to Antiochus and Seleucus long ago, but were now under his command and belonged to the Romans.[60] The Arabians and Armenians, he said, did not harass the villages, but the king had crossed such a great distance in order to exploit them, as if they were his property rather than the Romans'.

Dismissing the ambassadors, the king said, "Apollo- 2

[59] See 31.2.

[60] On Zeugma, see 20.1.

μὲν κώμας ταύτας," ἔφη "Ἀπολλώνιε, ξυνεχώρησαν τοῖς ἐμοῖς προγόνοις οἱ βασιλεῖς, οὓς εἶπον, τροφῆς ἕνεκα τῶν θηρίων, ἃ παρ' ἡμῖν ἁλισκόμενα φοιτᾷ ἐς τὴν ἐκείνων διὰ τοῦ Εὐφράτου, οἱ δ' ὥσπερ ἐκλαθόμενοι τούτου καινῶν τε καὶ ἀδίκων ἅπτονται. τίς οὖν φαίνεταί σοι τῆς πρεσβείας ὁ νοῦς;" "μέτριος, ὦ βασιλεῦ," ἔφη "καὶ ἐπιεικής, εἰ, ἃ δύνανται καὶ ἄκοντος ἔχειν ἐν τῇ ἑαυτῶν ὄντα, βούλονται παρ' ἑκόντος εὑρίσκεσθαι μᾶλλον." προσετίθει δὲ καὶ τὸ μὴ δεῖν ὑπὲρ κωμῶν, ὧν μείζους κέκτηνται τάχα καὶ ἰδιῶται, διαφέρεσθαι πρὸς Ῥωμαίους καὶ πόλεμον οὐδ' ὑπὲρ μεγάλων αἴρεσθαι.

3 Νοσοῦντι δὲ τῷ βασιλεῖ παρών, τοσαῦτά τε καὶ οὕτω θεῖα περὶ ψυχῆς διεξῆλθεν, ὡς τὸν βασιλέα ἀναπνεῦσαι καὶ πρὸς τοὺς παρόντας εἰπεῖν, ὅτι "Ἀπολλώνιος οὐχ ὑπὲρ τῆς βασιλείας μόνης ἀφροντιστεῖν εἴργασταί με, ἀλλὰ καὶ ὑπὲρ τοῦ θανάτου."

39. Τὴν δὲ σήραγγα τὴν ὑπὸ τῷ Εὐφράτῃ δεικνύντος αὐτῷ ποτε τοῦ βασιλέως καὶ "τί σοι φαίνεται τὸ θαῦμα;" εἰπόντος, καταβάλλων τὴν τερατουργίαν ὁ Ἀπολλώνιος "θαῦμα ἂν ἦν, ὦ βασιλεῦ," ἔφη, "εἰ διὰ τοῦ ποταμοῦ βαθέος οὕτω καὶ ἀπόρου ὄντος πεζῇ ἐβαδίζετε." δείξαντος δὲ καὶ τὰ ἐν Ἐκβατάνοις τείχη καὶ θεῶν φάσκοντος ταῦτα εἶναι οἴκησιν, "θεῶν μὲν οὐκ ἔστιν ὅλως οἴκησις," εἶπεν "εἰ δὲ ἀνδρῶν οὐκ οἶδα· ἡ γὰρ Λακεδαιμονίων, ὦ βασιλεῦ, πόλις ἀτείχιστος ᾤκισται."

2 Καὶ μὴν καὶ δίκην τινὰ δικάσαντος αὐτοῦ κώμαις,

nius, these villages were granted to my ancestors by the kings they mentioned, to maintain the animals that are caught in our country and exported across the Euphrates to their territory. Under a pretense of forgetting this, they are preparing some new injustice. What do you think the purpose of this embassy is?" "It is moderate and reasonable, Majesty," he replied, "since they prefer to obtain with your consent what they might take without it, the places being in their territory." In addition, he said, the king should not quarrel with the Romans over villages that were probably smaller than some owned by private citizens, or start a war with them even over large ones.

Attending the king in an illness, Apollonius gave so 3
many inspired discourses on the soul that after his recovery the king said to those present, "Apollonius has made me indifferent not only to my kingdom but even to death."

39. The king once showed him the tunnel under the Euphrates,[61] asking, "What do you think of this miracle?" To belittle the artificiality, Apollonius said, "It would be a real miracle, Majesty, if you people could wade through such a deep and turbulent river." When the king showed him the walls of Ecbatana and claimed they were the home of gods, Apollonius said, "They are certainly not the home of gods, and perhaps not of heroes either, since the city in which the Spartans live, Majesty, has no walls."

Moreover, when the king had judged a dispute between 2

[61] Cf. 25.1.

καὶ μεγαλοφρονουμένου πρὸς τὸν Ἀπολλώνιον, ὡς δυοῖν ἡμερῶν ἠκροαμένος εἴη τῆς δίκης, "βραδέως γ'" ἔφη "τὸ δίκαιον εὗρες." χρημάτων δὲ ἐκ τῆς ὑπηκόου φοιτησάντων ποτὲ ἀθρόων, ἀνοίξας τοὺς θησαυροὺς ἐδείκνυ τῷ ἀνδρὶ τὰ χρήματα, ὑπαγόμενος αὐτὸν ἐς ἐπιθυμίαν πλούτου. ὁ δὲ οὐδὲν ὧν εἶδε θαυμάσας "σοὶ ταῦτα," ἔφη "ὦ βασιλεῦ, χρήματα, ἐμοὶ δὲ ἄχυρα." "τί ἂν οὖν" ἔφη "πράττων καλῶς αὐτοῖς χρησαίμην;" "χρώμενος," ἔφη, "βασιλεὺς γὰρ εἶ."

40. Πολλὰ τοιαῦτα πρὸς τὸν βασιλέα εἰπὼν, καὶ τυχὼν αὐτοῦ προθύμου πράττειν ἃ ξυνεβούλευεν, ἔτι καὶ τῆς πρὸς τοὺς μάγους ξυνουσίας ἱκανῶς ἔχων "ἄγε, ὦ Δάμι," ἔφη "ἐς Ἰνδοὺς ἴωμεν. οἱ μὲν γὰρ τοῖς Λωτοφάγοις προσπλεύσαντες ἀπήγοντο τῶν οἰκείων ἠθῶν ὑπὸ τοῦ βρώματος, ἡμεῖς δὲ μὴ γευόμενοί τινος τῶν ἐνταῦθα καθήμεθα πλείω χρόνον τοῦ εἰκότος τε καὶ ξυμμέτρου." "κἀμοὶ" ἔφη ὁ Δάμις "ὑπερδοκεῖ ταῦτα. ἐπεὶ δὲ ἐνεθυμούμην τὸν χρόνον, ὃν ἐν τῇ λεαίνῃ διεσκέψω, περιέμενον ἀνυσθῆναι αὐτόν. οὔπω μὲν οὖν ἐξήκει πᾶς, ἐνιαυτὸς γὰρ ἡμῖν ἤδη καὶ μῆνες τέτταρες. εἰ δὲ ἤδη κομιζοίμεθα, εὖ ἂν ἔχοι;" "οὐδὲ ἀνήσει ἡμᾶς," ἔφη "ὦ Δάμι, ὁ βασιλεὺς πρότερον ἢ τὸν ὄγδοον τελευτῆσαι μῆνα· χρηστὸν γάρ που ὁρᾷς αὐτὸν καὶ κρείττω ἢ βαρβάρων ἄρχειν."

41. Ἐπεὶ δὲ ἀπαλλάττεσθαι λοιπὸν ἐδόκει, καὶ ξυνεχώρησέ ποτε ὁ βασιλεὺς ἀπιέναι, ἀνεμνήσθη τῶν δωρεῶν ὁ Ἀπολλώνιος, ἃς ἀνεβάλλετο ἔς τ' ἂν φίλοι αὐτῷ γένωνται, καὶ "ὦ βέλτιστε" ἔφη "βασιλεῦ, τὸν

some villages and was boasting to Apollonius that he had taken two days to hear the case, he said, "You took a long time to find where justice was." When much money had once come to the king from his subjects, he opened his treasury to show the Master his money and to tempt him with love of wealth. But he admired nothing he was shown, saying only, "This is money to you, Majesty, but rubbish to me." "Well, what is the best way for me to use it?" "Make use of it," was the reply, "for you are a king."

40. When he had said many such things to the king, whom he found eager to take his advice, and when he had had enough of the company of the Magi, "Come, Damis," he said, "let us set out for India. Those who landed among the Lotus Eaters were led by the food to forget their native ways, but we have not tasted any of the local products, and yet we are loitering for a longer time than is right and proper." "I fully agree," said Damis, "but thinking of the time that you saw the lioness to predict,[62] I have been waiting for its completion. But it is not all up yet, since we have been here a year and four months, and would it be well for us to set out now?" "The king will not let us go, Damis," he replied, "before the eighth month is past. He is a kindly man, as you see, and too good to be a ruler of barbarians."

41. But when it finally seemed time to be off, and the king had given permission for their departure, Apollonius remembered the gifts that he had asked leave to defer until he had made some friends there. "Excellent Majesty," he

[62] See 22.2.

ξένον οὐδὲν εὖ πεποίηκα καὶ μισθὸν ὀφείλω τοῖς μάγοις. σὺ οὖν ἐπιμελήθητι αὐτῶν καὶ τοὐμὸν προθυμήθητι περὶ ἄνδρας σοφούς τε καὶ σοὶ σφόδρα εὔνους." ὑπερησθεὶς οὖν ὁ βασιλεὺς "τούτους μὲν αὔριον ζηλωτοὺς" ἔφη "καὶ μεγάλων ἠξιωμένους ἀποδείξω σοι, σὺ δ' ἐπεὶ μηδενὸς δέῃ τῶν ἐμῶν, ἀλλὰ τούτοις γε ξυγχώρησον χρήματα παρ' ἐμοῦ λαβεῖν καὶ ὅ τι βούλονται," τοὺς ἀμφὶ τὸν Δάμιν δείξας. ἀποστραφέντων οὖν κἀκείνων τὸν λόγον τοῦτον, "ὁρᾷς," ἔφη "ὦ βασιλεῦ, τὰς ἐμὰς χεῖρας, ὡς πολλαί τέ εἰσι καὶ ἀλλήλαις ὅμοιαι;"

2 "Σὺ δὲ ἀλλὰ ἡγεμόνα ἄγου" ὁ βασιλεὺς ἔφη "καὶ καμήλους, ἐφ' ὧν ὀχήσεσθε, τὸ γὰρ μῆκος τῆς ὁδοῦ κρεῖττον ἢ βαδίσαι πᾶσαν." "γιγνέσθω," ἔφη "ὦ βασιλεῦ, τοῦτο, φασὶ γὰρ τὴν ὁδὸν ἄπορον εἶναι μὴ οὕτως ὀχουμένῳ, καὶ ἄλλως τὸ ζῷον εὔσιτόν τε καὶ ῥᾴδιον βόσκειν, ὅπου μὴ χιλὸς εἴη. καὶ ὕδωρ δέ, οἶμαι, χρὴ ἐπισιτίσασθαι καὶ ἀπάγειν αὐτὸ ἐν ἀσκοῖς, ὥσπερ τὸν οἶνον." "τριῶν ἡμερῶν" ἔφη ὁ βασιλεὺς "ἄνυδρος ἡ χώρα, μετὰ ταῦτα δὲ πολλὴ ἀφθονία ποταμῶν τε καὶ πηγῶν, βαδίζειν δὲ <δεῖ>[39] τὴν ἐπὶ Καυκάσου, τὰ γὰρ ἐπιτήδεια ἄφθονα καὶ φίλη ἡ χώρα." ἐρομένου δὲ αὐτὸν τοῦ βασιλέως ὅ τι αὐτῷ ἀπάξει ἐκεῖθεν, "χαρίεν," ἔφη "ὦ βασιλεῦ, δῶρον· ἢν γὰρ ἡ συνουσία τῶν ἀνδρῶν σοφώτερόν με ἀποφήνῃ, βελτίων ἀφίξομαί σοι ἢ νῦν εἰμι." περιέβαλεν ὁ βασιλεὺς ταῦτα εἰπόντα καὶ "ἀφίκοιο," εἶπε "τὸ γὰρ δῶρον μέγα."

said, "I have not yet done my host a favor, and I owe the Magi a fee. Please take care of them, and for my sake show them kindness as your wise and very loyal subjects." Overjoyed, the king replied, "I will make them envied and highly honored for your sake tomorrow. But since you want none of my possessions, at least let these" (pointing to Damis and the others) "receive money from me, and whatever else they like." But when they too declined this offer, Apollonius said, "You see, Majesty, how many hands I have, and how they resemble one another."

"Well, take a guide anyhow," said the king, "and cam- 2
els to ride on. The distance is too great for you to walk the whole way." "As you wish, Majesty," he said. "The journey is apparently impossible without such transport, and moreover they are animals easy to feed, even where there is no fodder. We must also provide ourselves with water, I think, carrying it in skins like wine." "The land is waterless for three days," said the king, "but after that there are plenty of rivers and springs. You must take the Caucasus road, on which supplies are abundant and the country is friendly." When the king asked him what he would bring back to him from there, he replied, "A fine gift, king. If their company makes me wiser, I will come back to you a better man than I am now." The king embraced him at these words, and said, "Come back: that will be a great gift."

---

39 <δεῖ> Kay.

Β´

1. Ἐντεῦθεν ἐξελαύνουσι περὶ τὸ θέρος αὐτοί τε ὀχούμενοι καὶ ὁ ἡγεμών, ἱπποκόμος δὲ ἦν τῶν καμήλων καὶ τὰ ἐπιτήδεια, ὁπόσων ἐδέοντο, ἦν ἄφθονα βασιλέως δόντος, ἥ τε χώρα, δι' ἧς ἐπορεύοντο, εὖ ἔπραττεν, ἐδέχοντο δὲ αὐτοὺς αἱ κῶμαι θεραπεύουσαι· χρυσοῦ γὰρ ψάλιον ἡ πρώτη κάμηλος ἐπὶ τοῦ μετώπου ἔφερε, γιγνώσκειν τοῖς ἐντυγχάνουσιν, ὡς πέμποι τινὰ ὁ βασιλεὺς τῶν ἑαυτοῦ φίλων.

2. Προσιόντες δὲ τῷ Καυκάσῳ φασὶν εὐωδεστέρας τῆς γῆς αἰσθέσθαι· τὸ δὲ ὄρος τοῦτο ἀρχὴν ποιώμεθα Ταύρου τοῦ δι' Ἀρμενίας τε καὶ Κιλίκων ἐπὶ Παμφύλους καὶ Μυκάλην στείχοντος, ἣ τελευτῶσα ἐς θάλατταν, ἣν Κᾶρες οἰκοῦσι, τέρμα τοῦ Καυκάσου νομίζοιτ' ἄν, ἀλλ' οὐχ, ὥς ἔνιοί φασιν, ἀρχή, τό τε γὰρ τῆς Μυκάλης ὕψος οὔπω μέγα καὶ αἱ ὑπερβολαὶ τοῦ Καυκάσου τοσοῦτον ἀνεστᾶσιν, ὡς σχίζεσθαι περὶ αὐτὰς τὸν ἥλιον. περιβάλλει δὲ Ταύρῳ ἑτέρῳ καὶ τὴν ὅμορον τῇ Ἰνδικῇ Σκυθίαν πᾶσαν κατὰ Μαιῶτίν τε καὶ ἀριστερὸν Πόντον, σταδίων μάλιστα δισμυρίων μῆκος, τοσοῦτον γὰρ ἐπέχει μέτρον τῆς γῆς ὁ ἀγκὼν τοῦ Καυκάσου. τὸ δὲ περὶ τοῦ ἐν τῇ ἡμεδαπῇ Ταύρου

BOOK II

1. They set out from there in the summer, riding with their guide, who served as groom for the camels. They had abundant provisions, and as much as they needed, by the gift of the king; the territory through which they traveled was prosperous; and the villages received them with attention, as the leading camel had a gold chain on its brow to tell those they met that the king was sending one of his friends on their way.

2. As they approached the Caucasus,[1] they say that they noticed the soil smelling sweeter. This range can be considered as the origin of the Taurus that runs through Armenia and Cilicia to Pamphylia and Mycale.[2] Here it terminates at the sea that borders on Caria, and should be considered the end of the Caucasus, and not its beginning, as some say. The height of Mycale is not very great, while the passes of the Caucasus are so elevated that they say the sun grazes against them. By means of a second Taurus, the Caucasus surrounds all of Scythia bordering on India, and is about twenty thousand stadia in length: that is the extent of the land enclosed within its angle. As for what is said about the Taurus in our region, that it stretches beyond

[1] On the geographical references to India in this book, see Introduction.

[2] Mount Mycale, north of the Meander.

λεγόμενον, ὡς ὑπὲρ τὴν Ἀρμενίαν πορεύοιτο, χρόνῳ ἀπιστηθὲν πιστοῦνται λοιπὸν αἱ παρδάλεις, ἃς οἶδα ἁλισκομένας ἐν τῇ Παμφύλων ἀρωματοφόρῳ. χαίρουσι γὰρ τοῖς ἀρώμασι κἀκ πολλοῦ τὰς ὀσμὰς ἕλκουσαι φοιτῶσιν ἐξ Ἀρμενίας διὰ τῶν ὀρῶν πρὸς τὸ δάκρυον τοῦ στύρακος, ἐπειδὰν οἵ τε ἄνεμοι ἀπ᾽ αὐτοῦ πνεύσωσι καὶ τὰ δένδρα ὀπώδη γένηται.

2 Καὶ ἁλῶναί ποτέ φασιν ἐν τῇ Παμφυλίᾳ πάρδαλιν στρεπτῷ ἅμα, ὃν περὶ τῇ δέρῃ ἔφερε, χρυσοῦς δὲ ἦν καὶ ἐπεγέγραπτο Ἀρμενίοις γράμμασι· "βασιλεὺς Ἀρσάκης θεῷ Νυσίῳ." βασιλεὺς μὲν δὴ Ἀρμενίας τότε ἦν Ἀρσάκης, καὶ αὐτός, οἶμαι, ἑλὼν[1] τὴν πάρδαλιν ἀνῆκε τῷ Διονύσῳ διὰ μέγεθος τοῦ θηρίου. Νύσιος γὰρ ὁ Διόνυσος ἀπὸ τῆς ἐν Ἰνδοῖς Νύσης Ἰνδοῖς τε ὀνομάζεται καὶ πᾶσι τοῖς πρὸς ἀκτῖνα ἔθνεσιν. ἡ δὲ χρόνον μέν τινα ὑπεζεύχθη ἀνθρώπῳ καὶ χεῖρα ἠνέσχετο ἐπαφωμένην τε καὶ καταψῶσαν, ἐπεὶ δὲ ἀνοίστρησεν αὐτὴν ἔαρ, ὅτε δὴ ἀφροδισίων ἥττους καὶ παρδάλεις, ἀνέθορεν ἐς τὰ ὄρη πόθῳ ἀρσένων ὡς εἶχε τοῦ κόσμου, καὶ ἥλω περὶ τὸν κάτω Ταῦρον ὑπὸ τοῦ ἀρώματος ἑλχθεῖσα. ὁ δὲ Καύκασος ὁρίζει μὲν τὴν Ἰνδικήν τε καὶ Μηδικήν, καθήκει δὲ ἐπὶ τὴν Ἐρυθρὰν θάλατταν ἑτέρῳ ἀγκῶνι.

3. Μυθολογεῖται δὲ ὑπὸ τῶν βαρβάρων τὸ ὄρος, ἃ καὶ Ἕλληνες ἐπ᾽ αὐτῷ ᾄδουσιν, ὡς Προμηθεὺς μὲν ἐπὶ φιλανθρωπίᾳ δεθείη ἐκεῖ, Ἡρακλῆς δὲ ἕτερος, οὐ γὰρ

[1] ἑλὼν Schenkl 1892: ἰδὼν

Armenia, that was disbelieved for a long time, but now is confirmed by the fact that leopards, as I know, are trapped in the spice-bearing part of Pamphylia. They love these spices, and inhaling their perfumes from far away they migrate from Armenia through the mountains to the gum of the storax tree, when the winds blow from that direction and the trees produce their gum.[3]

They say that a female leopard was once captured in 2
Pamphylia with a collar around its neck, and this collar was of gold and had written on it in gold letters, "King Arsaces to the Nysian God." Arsaces was king of Armenia at the time,[4] and after capturing the leopard, I believe, he dedicated it to Dionysus because of the beast's size. (Dionysus is called "the Nysian" after Nysa in India, both by the Indians and all the nations of the Orient.) For a while, this animal could be yoked by humans, and allowed itself to be touched and stroked by hand. When spring, however, threw it into a frenzy (a time when leopards too are subject to sexual urges) it bounded off to the mountains lusting for a male, still wearing its decoration, and was caught in the lower Taurus, to which it been attracted by the spice. The Caucasus is the limit of the Indian and Median territories, but extends to the Red Sea by another arm.

3. The barbarians tell the same myths about the mountain as the Greeks do in their poetry, that Prometheus was bound there because of his kindness to man. Heracles (a

[3] Storax (*styrax officinalis*) was valued both for its wood and its resin, and was used mainly as incense. Galen (XIV 79) praises the storax of Pamphylia for its medicinal qualities.

[4] An Arsaces ruled Armenia briefly about the year 35 CE.

τὸν Θηβαῖόν γε βούλονται, μὴ ἀνάσχοιτο τοῦτο, ἀλλὰ τοξεύσειε τὸν ὄρνιν, ὃν ἔβοσκεν ὁ Προμηθεὺς τοῖς σπλάγχνοις· δεθῆναι δὲ αὐτὸν οἱ μὲν ἐν ἄντρῳ φασίν, ὃ δὴ ἐν πρόποδι τοῦ ὄρους δείκνυται, καὶ δεσμὰ ὁ Δάμις ἀνῆφθαι τῶν πετρῶν λέγει οὐ ῥᾴδια ξυμβαλεῖν τὴν ὕλην, οἱ δ᾽ ἐν κορυφῇ τοῦ ὄρους· δικόρυμβος δὲ ἡ κορυφή, καί φασιν ὡς τὰς χεῖρας ἀπ᾽ αὐτῶν ἐδέθη διαλειπουσῶν οὐ μεῖον ἢ στάδιον, τοσοῦτος γὰρ εἶναι. τὸν δὲ ὄρνιν τὸν ἀετὸν οἱ τῷ Καυκάσῳ προσοικοῦντες ἐχθρὸν ἡγοῦνται καὶ καλιάς γε, ὁπόσας ἐν τοῖς πάγοις οἱ ἀετοὶ ποιοῦνται, καταπιμπρᾶσιν ἱέντες βέλη πυρφόρα, θήρατρά τε ἐπ᾽ αὐτοὺς ἵστανται τιμωρεῖν τῷ Προμηθεῖ φάσκοντες· ὧδε γὰρ τοῦ μύθου ἥττηνται.

4. Παραμείψαντες δὲ τὸν Καύκασον τετραπήχεις ἀνθρώπους ἰδεῖν φασιν, οὓς ἤδη μελαίνεσθαι, καὶ πεντεπήχεις δὲ ἑτέρους ὑπὲρ τὸν Ἰνδὸν ποταμὸν ἐλθόντες. ἐν δὲ τῇ μέχρι τοῦ ποταμοῦ τούτου ὁδοιπορίᾳ τάδε εὗρον ἀφηγήσεως ἄξια· ἐπορεύοντο μὲν γὰρ ἐν σελήνῃ λαμπρᾷ, φάσμα δὲ αὐτοῖς ἐμπούσης ἐνέπεσε τὸ δεῖνα γινομένη καὶ τὸ δεῖνα αὖ καὶ οὐδὲν εἶναι, ὁ δὲ Ἀπολλώνιος ξυνῆκεν, ὅ τι εἴη, καὶ αὐτός τε ἐλοιδορεῖτο τῇ ἐμπούσῃ, τοῖς τε ἀμφ᾽ αὐτὸν προσέταξε ταὐτὸ πράττειν, τουτὶ γὰρ ἄκος εἶναι τῆς προσβολῆς ταύτης· καὶ τὸ φάσμα φυγῇ ᾤχετο τετριγός ὥσπερ τὰ εἴδωλα.

5. Κορυφὴν δ᾽ ὑπερβάλλοντες τοῦ ὄρους καὶ βαδίζοντες αὐτήν, ἐπειδὴ ἀποτόμως εἶχεν, ἤρετο οὑτωσὶ τὸν Δάμιν· "εἰπέ μοι," ἔφη "ποῦ χθὲς ἦμεν;" ὁ δὲ "ἐν τῷ

different one, since they do not mean the Theban) was outraged, and shot the bird that was feeding on Prometheus's entrails. A cave is pointed out at the foot of the mountain that they say is the one he was imprisoned in, and according to Damis, the chains are attached to the rocks, and are of a material not easy to make out. Others, however, say that Prometheus was bound on the mountain's summit. This summit has two peaks, no less than a stade apart, and he was allegedly tied with each of his hands on one of them, so great was his size. The bird in question, the eagle, is considered an enemy by those bordering the Caucasus, and they set fire to any nests that the eagles make in the crags by shooting fire-bearing arrows into them. They also lay traps for them, claiming to avenge Prometheus, such a hold does the myth have over them.

4. After crossing the Caucasus they say they saw people four cubits tall, who were already rather black, and once they had crossed the river Indus they saw others of five cubits. As for the journey as far as this river, this is what I have found worth noting. They were traveling in full moonlight when they encountered a phantom, a vampire that changed into this and that and yet was nonexistent. Apollonius realized what it was, and himself rebuked the vampire and told the others to do the same, since that was the way to counter this attack. The vampire went off gibbering like a ghost.

5. To cross the highest part of the mountain, they went on foot, since it was precipitous. Apollonius put this question to Damis. "Tell me, where were we yesterday?" "In

πεδίῳ" ἔφη. "τήμερον δέ, ὦ Δάμι, ποῦ;" "ἐν τῷ Καυκάσῳ," εἶπεν "εἰ μὴ ἐμαυτοῦ ἐκλέλησμαι." "πότε οὖν κάτω μᾶλλον ἦσθα;" πάλιν ἤρετο, ὁ δὲ "τουτὶ μὲν" ἔφη "οὐδὲ ἐπερωτᾶν ἄξιον· χθὲς μὲν γὰρ διὰ κοίλης τῆς γῆς ἐπορευόμεθα, τήμερον δὲ πρὸς τῷ οὐρανῷ ἐσμέν." "οἴει οὖν," ἔφη "ὦ Δάμι, τὴν μὲν χθὲς ὁδοιπορίαν κάτω εἶναι, τὴν δὲ τήμερον ἄνω;" "νὴ Δί'," εἶπεν "εἰ μὴ μαίνομαί γε." "τί οὖν ἡγῇ" ἔφη "παραλλάττειν τὰς ὁδοὺς ἀλλήλων ἢ τί τήμερον πλέον εἶναί σοι τοῦ χθές;" "ὅτι χθὲς" ἔφη "ἐβάδιζον οὗπερ πολλοί, σήμερον δέ, οὗπερ ὀλίγοι." "τί γάρ," ἔφη, "ὦ Δάμι, οὐ καὶ τὰς ἐν ἄστει λεωφόρους ἐκτρεπομένῳ βαδίζειν ἐστὶν ἐν ὀλίγοις τῶν ἀνθρώπων;" "οὐ τοῦτο" ἔφη "εἶπον, ἀλλ' ὅτι χθὲς μὲν διὰ κωμῶν ἐκομιζόμεθα καὶ ἀνθρώπων, σήμερον δὲ ἀστιβές τι ἀναβαίνομεν χωρίον καὶ θεῖον, ἀκούεις γὰρ τοῦ ἡγεμόνος, ὅτι οἱ βάρβαροι θεῶν αὐτὸ ποιοῦνται οἶκον" καὶ ἅμα ἀνέβλεπεν ἐς τὴν κορυφὴν τοῦ ὄρους.

2 Ὁ δὲ ἐμβιβάζων αὐτὸν ἐς ὃ ἐξ ἀρχῆς ἠρώτα, "ἔχεις οὖν εἰπεῖν, ὦ Δάμι, ὅ τι ξυνῆκας τοῦ θείου βαδίζων ἀγχοῦ τοῦ οὐρανοῦ;" "οὐδὲν" ἔφη. "καὶ μὴν ἐχρῆν γε," εἶπεν, "ἐπὶ μηχανῆς τηλικαύτης καὶ θείας οὕτως ἑστηκότα, περί τε τοῦ οὐρανοῦ σαφεστέρας ἤδη ἐκφέρειν δόξας περί τε τοῦ ἡλίου καὶ τῆς σελήνης, ὧν γε καὶ ῥάβδῳ ἴσως ἡγῇ ψαύσειν προσεστηκὼς τῷ οὐρανῷ τούτῳ." "ἃ χθὲς" ἔφη "περὶ τοῦ θείου ἐγίγνωσκον, γιγνώσκω καὶ τήμερον καὶ οὔπω μοι ἑτέρα προσέπεσε περὶ αὐτοῦ δόξα." "οὐκοῦν," ἔφη "ὦ Δάμι, κάτω τυγ-

the plain," he replied. "And where are we today, Damis?" "In the Caucasus," he said, "unless I have forgotten who I am." "When were you lower down, then?" Apollonius asked next, and the other said, "This question is not even worth asking, since yesterday we were traveling through a cleft of the earth, but today we are near heaven." "You think, then," said Apollonius, "that yesterday's journey was below and today's above?" "Of course," replied Damis, "unless I have gone mad." "In what way," said Apollonius, "do you think our two paths differ from one another, then? What is better for you yesterday than today?" "Yesterday," said Damis, "we were traveling where there were many people, but today where there are few." "Why, Damis," said Apollonius, "can you not turn out of the thoroughfares in the city and walk where there are few people?" "I did not mean that," said Damis, "but rather that yesterday we were traveling through villages and human habitation, while today we are climbing some untrodden and sacred region. You have heard our guide say that the barbarians consider it the home of the gods." As he said this, he looked up at the peak of the mountain.

Bringing him back to the original question, Apollonius 2
said, "Is there anything, Damis, that you can claim to have realized about the divine as you walk near heaven?" "Nothing," he replied. "Well," said Apollonius, "when you are standing on so large and sacred a platform, you should express clearer notions about the heaven, the sun and the moon. Perhaps you think you can touch them with a rod, standing close to heaven here." "What I knew about divinity yesterday," said Damis, "I know today too, and no new belief about it has occurred to me yet." "In that case, Damis," said Apollonius, "you are still below, and have got

χάνεις ὢν ἔτι καὶ οὐδὲν παρὰ τοῦ ὕψους εἴληφας, ἀπέχεις τε τοῦ οὐρανοῦ ὁπόσον χθές· καὶ εἰκότως σε ἠρόμην, ἃ ἐν ἀρχῇ· σὺ γὰρ ᾤου γελοίως ἐρωτᾶσθαι."

3 "Καὶ μὴν" ἔφη "καταβήσεσθαί γε σοφώτερος ᾤμην ἀκούων, Ἀπολλώνιε, τὸν μὲν Κλαζομένιον Ἀναξαγόραν ἀπὸ τοῦ κατὰ Ἰωνίαν Μίμαντος ἐπεσκέφθαι τὰ ἐν τῷ οὐρανῷ, Θαλῆν τε τὸν Μιλήσιον ἀπὸ τῆς προσοίκου Μυκάλης, λέγονται δὲ καὶ τῷ Παγγαίῳ ἔνιοι φροντιστηρίῳ χρήσασθαι καὶ ἕτεροι τῷ Ἄθῳ. ἐγὼ δὲ μέγιστον τούτων ἀνελθὼν ὕψος οὐδὲν σοφώτερος ἐμαυτοῦ καταβήσομαι." "οὐδὲ γὰρ ἐκεῖνοι," ἔφη "αἱ γὰρ τοιαίδε περιωπαὶ γλαυκότερον μὲν τὸν οὐρανὸν ἀποφαίνουσι καὶ μείζους τοὺς ἀστέρας καὶ τὸν ἥλιον ἀνίσχοντα ἐκ νυκτός, ἃ καὶ ποιμέσιν ἤδη καὶ αἰπόλοις ἐστὶ δῆλα, ὅπῃ δὲ τὸ θεῖον ἐπιμελεῖται τοῦ ἀνθρωπείου γένους, καὶ ὅπῃ χαίρει ὑπ᾽ αὐτοῦ θεραπευόμενον, ὅ τί τε ἀρετὴ καὶ ὅ τι δικαιοσύνη τε καὶ σωφροσύνη, οὔτε Ἄθως ἐκδείξει τοῖς ἀνελθοῦσιν οὔτε ὁ θαυμαζόμενος ὑπὸ τῶν ποιητῶν Ὄλυμπος, εἰ μὴ διορῴη αὐτὰ ἡ ψυχή, ἥν, εἰ καθαρὰ καὶ ἀκήρατος αὐτῶν ἅπτοιτο, πολλῷ μεῖζον ἔγωγ᾽ ἂν φαίην ᾄττειν τουτουὶ τοῦ Καυκάσου."

6. Ὑπερβάντες δὲ τὸ ὄρος ἐντυγχάνουσιν ἐπ᾽ ἐλεφάντων ἤδη ὀχουμένοις ἀνδράσιν, εἰσὶ δ᾽ οὗτοι μέσοι Καυκάσου καὶ ποταμοῦ Κωφῆνος ἄβιοί τε καὶ ἱππόται τῆς ἀγέλης ταύτης, καὶ κάμηλοι δὲ ἐνίους ἦγον, αἷς χρῶνται Ἰνδοὶ ἐς τὰ δρομικά, πορεύονται δὲ χίλια στάδια τῆς ἡμέρας γόνυ οὐδαμοῦ κάμψασαι. προσ-

nothing from being up high, but are as far from heaven as you were yesterday. So the question I put to you at first was a reasonable one, though it seemed a ridiculous one to you."

"And yet," said Damis, "I thought that I would be wiser 3
when I descended, Apollonius, having heard that Anaxagoras of Clazomenae observed the heavenly bodies from Mimas in Ionia, as Thales of Miletus did from nearby Mycale. Some people, they say, have used Pangaeus for advanced study, and others Athos.[5] But though I have climbed this mountain that is the highest of all, I shall come down it none the wiser." "Nor did they," said Apollonius. "Such vantage points show the heaven more brilliant, the stars bigger, and the sun rising during the night, but such things are evident to shepherds and goatherds too. But how the Deity cares about the human race, and how it loves to receive worship from it, what virtue is and justice and chastity, all this Athos will not reveal to those who climb it, nor will the famous Olympus so admired by the poets, unless the soul discerns them. If it is pure and unblemished when it apprehends them, in my opinion it soars much higher than the Caucasus here."

6. Once they had crossed the mountain, they began to encounter men riding on elephants. These live between the Caucasus and the river Cophen, destitutes who drive this kind of herd. Some, however, rode on camels that are used by the Indians for speed, and can go a thousand stades a day without once bending their knees to rest. One

[5] Mimas is a mountain enclosing the gulf of Smyrna, and Pangaeus a mountain of Thrace.

ελάσας οὖν τῶν Ἰνδῶν εἷς ἐπὶ καμήλου τοιαύτης ἠρώτα τὸν ἡγεμόνα οἷ[2] στείχοιεν, ἐπεὶ δὲ τὸν νοῦν τῆς ἀποδημίας ἤκουσεν, ἀπήγγειλε τοῖς νομάσιν, οἱ δὲ ἀνεβόησαν ὥσπερ ἡσθέντες ἐκέλευόν τε πλησίον ἥκειν καὶ ἀφικομένοις οἶνόν τε ᾤρεγον, ὃν ἀπὸ τῶν φοινίκων σοφίζονται καὶ μέλι ἀπὸ ταὐτοῦ φυτοῦ καὶ τεμάχη λεόντων καὶ παρδάλεων, ὧν καὶ τὰ δέρματα νεόδαρτα ἦν, δεξάμενοι δὲ πλὴν τῶν κρεῶν πάντα ἀπήλασαν <ἐς>[3] τοὺς Ἰνδοὺς καὶ ἐχώρουν πρὸς ἕω.

7. Ἀριστοποιουμένων δὲ αὐτῶν πρὸς πηγῇ ὕδατος, ἐγχέας ὁ Δάμις τοῦ παρὰ τῶν Ἰνδῶν οἴνου "Διὸς" ἔφη "Σωτῆρος ἥδε σοι, Ἀπολλώνιε, διὰ πολλοῦ γε πίνοντι. οὐ γὰρ, οἶμαι, παραιτήσῃ καὶ τοῦτον, ὥσπερ τὸν ἀπὸ τῶν ἀμπέλων" καὶ ἅμα ἔσπεισεν, ἐπειδὴ τοῦ Διὸς ἐπεμνήσθη. γελάσας οὖν ὁ Ἀπολλώνιος "οὐ καὶ χρημάτων" ἔφη "ἀπεχόμεθα, ὦ Δάμι;" "νὴ Δί'" εἶπεν "ὡς πολλαχοῦ ἐπεδείξω." "ἆρ' οὖν" ἔφη "χρυσῆς μὲν δραχμῆς καὶ ἀργυρᾶς ἀφεξόμεθα, καὶ οὐχ ἡττησόμεθα τοιούτου νομίσματος καίτοι κεχηνότας ἐς αὐτὸ ὁρῶντες οὐκ ἰδιώτας μόνον, ἀλλὰ καὶ βασιλέας, εἰ δὲ χαλκοῦν τις ὡς ἀργυροῦν ἢ ὑπόχρυσόν τε καὶ κεκιβδηλευμένον ἡμῖν διδοίη, ληψόμεθα τοῦτο, ἐπεὶ μὴ ἐκεῖνό ἐστιν, οὗ οἱ πολλοὶ γλίχονται;

2 "Καὶ μὴν καὶ νομίσματά ἐστιν Ἰνδοῖς ὀρειχάλκου τε καὶ χαλκοῦ μέλανος, ὧν δεῖ δήπου πάντα ὠνεῖσθαι πάντας ἥκοντας ἐς τὰ Ἰνδῶν ἤθη. τί οὖν; εἰ χρήματα ἡμῖν ᾤρεγον οἱ χρηστοὶ νομάδες, ἆρ' ἄν, ὦ Δάμι, παραιτούμενόν με ὁρῶν ἐνουθέτεις τε καὶ ἐδίδασκες,

of the Indians rode up to them on such a camel, and asked their guide where they were headed. When he heard the purpose of their journey, he reported it to the herdsmen, and with a shout of joy they invited the party to approach. On their arrival, they offered them wine which they contrive to make from dates, honey from the same tree, and steaks cut from lions and leopards that they had just flayed. After accepting everything except the meat, the party started off for India in an easterly direction.

7. They were having breakfast by a source of water, into which Damis mixed some of the Indians' wine, saying, "This is your libation to Zeus the Savior, Apollonius, since you have not drunk for a long time. I do not think you will refuse this wine, as you do wine made from grapes." So saying he poured a libation, since he had mentioned Zeus. Apollonius laughed and said, "We shun money too, do we not, Damis?" "Yes indeed," was the reply, "as you have often demonstrated." "Well," said Apollonius, "let us agree that we shun a gold or silver drachma, and are not tempted by such a coin, although we see not just private citizens gaping after it, but kings too. Suppose then that someone gave us a bronze coin as if it were silver, or a gold-plated and counterfeit coin: are we going to accept that, when it is not of the kind which most people are greedy for?

"Why, the Indians have coins of brass and black bronze, 2
with which all who come to the Indian region doubtless have to buy everything. Well then, suppose these good herdsmen offered us money, and you saw me refuse it: surely you would not blame me, pointing out that the other

---

[2] *οἱ* Cob.: *οὗ*

[3] <*ἐς*> Conyb.

ὅτι χρήματα μὲν ἐκεῖνά ἐστιν, ἃ Ῥωμαῖοι χαράττουσιν ἢ ὁ Μήδων βασιλεύς, ταυτὶ δὲ ὕλη τις ἑτέρα κεκομψευμένη τοῖς Ἰνδοῖς; καὶ ταῦτα πείσας τίνα ἂν ἡγήσω με; ἆρ' οὐ κίβδηλόν τε καὶ τὴν φιλοσοφίαν ἀποβεβληκότα μᾶλλον ἢ οἱ πονηροὶ στρατιῶται τὰς ἀσπίδας; καίτοι ἀσπίδος μὲν ἀποβληθείσης ἑτέρα γένοιτ' ἂν τῷ ἀποβαλόντι κακίων οὐδὲν τῆς προτέρας, ὡς Ἀρχιλόχῳ δοκεῖ, φιλοσοφία δὲ πῶς ἀνακτητέα τῷ γε ἀτιμάσαντι αὐτὴν καὶ ῥίψαντι; καὶ νῦν μὲν ἂν ξυγγιγνώσκοι ὁ Διόνυσος οὐδενὸς οἴνου ἡττημένῳ, τὸν δὲ ἀπὸ τῶν φοινίκων εἰ πρὸ τοῦ ἀμπελίνου αἱροίμην, ἀχθέσεται, εὖ οἶδα, καὶ περιυβρίσθαι φήσει τὸ ἑαυτοῦ δῶρον. ἐσμὲν δὲ οὐ πόρρω τοῦ θεοῦ, καὶ γὰρ τοῦ ἡγεμόνος ἀκούεις, ὡς πλησίον ἡ Νῦσα τὸ ὄρος, ἐφ' οὗ ὁ Διόνυσος πολλά, οἶμαι, καὶ θαυμαστὰ πράττει.

3 "Καὶ μὴν καὶ τὸ μεθύειν, ὦ Δάμι, οὐκ ἐκ βοτρύων μόνων ἐσφοιτᾷ τοὺς ἀνθρώπους, ἀλλὰ καὶ ἀπὸ τῶν φοινίκων παραπλησίως ἐκβακχεύει· πολλοῖς γοῦν ἤδη τῶν Ἰνδῶν ἐνετύχομεν κατεσχημένοις τῷ οἴνῳ τούτῳ, καὶ οἱ μὲν ὀρχοῦνται πίπτοντες, οἱ δὲ ᾄδουσιν ὑπονυστάζοντες, ὥσπερ οἱ παρ' ἡμῖν ἐκ πότου νύκτωρ τε καὶ οὐκ ἐν ὥρᾳ ἀναλύοντες. ὅτι δὲ οἶνον ἡγῇ καὶ τοῦτο τὸ πῶμα, δηλοῖς τῷ σπένδειν τε [ἀπ'][4] αὐτοῦ τῷ Διὶ καὶ ὁπόσα ἐπ' οἴνῳ εὔχεσθαι. καὶ εἴρηταί μοι, ὦ

[4] [ἀπ'] secl. Headlam.

is money of the kind which Rome or the Median king strikes, but this is some different substance devised by the Indians? And if you persuaded me in this case,[6] what would you think I was? Would you not think me an impostor, who had abandoned philosophy more than cowardly soldiers abandon their shields? However, if someone abandons his shield, he can get another one not at all inferior to the previous, so Archilochus thinks,[7] but there is no way you can recover philosophy once you have dishonored and jettisoned it. Moreover, Dionysus might pardon someone for not being partial to any wine, but I am quite sure he will be angry with me for preferring date wine to the kind made from grapes, and will say I am insulting his own gift. We are not far from the god, since you have heard our guide saying that we are near Mount Nysa,[8] where I believe Dionysus performs many miracles.

"In addition, drunkenness does not come to people only from grapes, but is intoxicating when derived from dates too. We have met many Indians under the influence of this wine, some dancing when they have fallen over, others singing when they are nodding off, like those at home who leave off drinking not when they should, but at night. You show that you consider this liquid too to be wine when you pour a libation of it to Zeus, and make all the prayers that are proper over wine. Well, this is what I have to say in 3

[6] I.e., if you persuaded me to drink date wine.

[7] Poet of the mid-sixth century from Paros, later colonist on Thasos. He lost his shield fighting barbarians on the mainland opposite, and wrote a much-quoted poem which ended, "I'll get one just as good right away."

[8] Usually referred to as a city, not a mountain.

Δάμι, πρὸς σὲ ὑπὲρ ἐμαυτοῦ ταῦτα· οὔτε γὰρ σὲ τοῦ πίνειν ἀπάγοιμ᾽ ἂν οὔτε τοὺς ὀπαδοὺς τούτους, ξυγχωροίην δ᾽ ἂν ὑμῖν καὶ κρεῶν σιτεῖσθαι, τὸ γὰρ ἀπέχεσθαι τούτων ὑμῖν μὲν ἐς οὐδὲν ὁρῶ προβαῖνον, ἐμαυτῷ δὲ ἐς ἃ ὡμολόγηταί μοι πρὸς φιλοσοφίαν ἐκ παιδός." ἐδέξαντο τὸν λόγον τοῦτον οἱ περὶ τὸν Δάμιν καὶ ἠσπάσαντο εὐωχεῖσθαι, ῥᾷον ἡγούμενοι πορεύσεσθαι, ἢν ἀφθονώτερον διαιτῶνται.

8. Διαβάντες δὲ τὸν Κωφῆνα ποταμὸν αὐτοὶ μὲν ἐπὶ νεῶν, κάμηλοι δὲ πεζῇ τὸ ὕδωρ, ὁ γὰρ ποταμὸς οὔπω μέγας, ἐγένοντο ἐν τῇ βασιλευομένῃ ἠπείρῳ, ἐν ᾗ ἀνατεῖνον πεφύτευται Νῦσα ὄρος ἐς κορυφὴν ἄκραν, ὥσπερ ὁ ἐν Λυδίᾳ Τμῶλος, ἀναβαίνειν δ᾽ αὐτὸ ἔξεστιν, ὡδοποίηται γὰρ ὑπὸ τοῦ γεωργεῖσθαι. ἀνελθόντες οὖν ἱερῷ Διονύσου ἐντυχεῖν φασιν, ὃ δὴ Διόνυσον ἑαυτῷ φυτεῦσαι δάφναις περιεστηκυίαις κύκλῳ, τοσοῦτον περιεχούσαις τῆς γῆς, ὅσον ἀπόχρη νεῷ ξυμμέτρῳ, κιττόν τε περιβαλεῖν αὐτὸν καὶ ἀμπέλους ταῖς δάφναις, ἄγαλμά τε ἑαυτοῦ ἔνδον στήσασθαι γιγνώσκοντα ὡς ξυμφύσει τὰ δένδρα ὁ χρόνος καὶ δώσει τινὰ ἀπ᾽ αὐτῶν ὄροφον, ὃς οὕτω ξυμβέβληται νῦν, ὡς μήτε ὕεσθαι τὸ ἱερὸν μήτ᾽ ἀνέμῳ ἐσπνεῖσθαι. δρέπανα δὲ καὶ ἄρριχοι καὶ ληνοὶ καὶ τὰ ἀμφὶ ληνοὺς ἀνάκειται τῷ Διονύσῳ χρυσᾶ καὶ ἀργυρᾶ καθάπερ τρυγῶντι. τὸ δὲ ἄγαλμα εἴκασται μὲν ἐφήβῳ Ἰνδῷ, λίθου δὲ ἔξεσται λευκοῦ. ὀργιάζοντος δὲ αὐτοῦ καὶ σείοντος τὴν Νῦσαν ἀκούουσιν αἱ πόλεις αἱ ὑπὸ τῷ ὄρει καὶ ξυνεξαίρονται.

my own defense, Damis. I do not want to keep you or these companions of ours from drinking, and I do not mind you all eating meat as well, since I see that avoidance of such things is of no advantage to you, while for me it leads to the philosophic goal I have set myself from boyhood." Damis and the others accepted this argument and were glad to eat their fill, thinking that more plentiful nourishment would make their journey easier.

8. They themselves crossed the river Cophen in boats, while the camels forded the water since the river is not at all deep, and thus they arrived in the region ruled by the king. Here Mount Nysa rises up, planted to its very peak like Tmolos in Lydia, and since paths have been made for the purpose of cultivation it can be climbed. After doing so, they say they found a sanctuary of Dionysus, which the god is said to have planted for himself with laurel trees growing all around it. These take up enough ground to be sufficient for a modest temple. He also trained ivy and vines around the laurels, and among them he set up a statue of himself, knowing that time would cause the trees to grow together and make a kind of natural roof. This is now so densely woven that no rain falls on the sanctuary and no wind blows into it. There are pruning hooks, baskets, and wine presses with their equipment in gold and silver, all dedicated to Dionysus as if he was harvesting the grapes. The statue looks like a youthful Indian, and is of polished marble. When the god revels and shakes Nysa, the cities beneath the mountain hear him and join in his ecstasy.

9. Διαφέρονται δὲ περὶ τοῦ Διονύσου τούτου καὶ Ἕλληνες Ἰνδοῖς καὶ Ἰνδοὶ ἀλλήλοις· ἡμεῖς μὲν γὰρ τὸν Θηβαῖον ἐπ᾽ Ἰνδοὺς ἐλάσαι φαμὲν στρατεύοντά τε καὶ βακχεύοντα, τεκμηρίοις χρώμενοι τοῖς τε ἄλλοις καὶ τῷ Πυθοῖ ἀναθήματι, ὃ δὴ ἀπόθετον οἱ ἐκεῖ θησαυροὶ ἴσχουσιν· ἔστι δὲ ἀργύρου Ἰνδικοῦ δίσκος, ᾧ ἐπιγέγραπται "Διόνυσος ὁ Σεμέλης καὶ Διὸς ἀπὸ Ἰνδῶν Ἀπόλλωνι Δελφῷ."

2 Ἰνδῶν δὲ οἱ περὶ Καύκασον καὶ Κωφῆνα ποταμὸν ἐπηλύτην Ἀσσύριον αὐτόν φασιν ἐλθεῖν τὰ τοῦ Θηβαίου εἰδότα· οἱ δὲ τὴν Ἰνδοῦ τε καὶ Ὑδραώτου μέσην νεμόμενοι καὶ τὴν μετὰ ταῦτα ἤπειρον, ἣ δὴ ἐς ποταμὸν Γάγγην τελευτᾷ, Διόνυσον γενέσθαι ποταμοῦ παῖδα Ἰνδοῦ λέγουσιν, ᾧ φοιτήσαντα τὸν ἐκ Θηβῶν ἐκεῖνον θύρσου τε ἅψασθαι καὶ δοῦναι ὀργίοις, εἰπόντα δέ, ὡς εἴη Διὸς καὶ τῷ τοῦ πατρὸς ἐμβιῴη μηρῷ τόκου ἕνεκα, Μηρόν τε εὑρέσθαι παρ᾽ αὐτοῦ ὄρος, ᾧ προσβέβηκεν ἡ Νῦσα, καὶ τὴν Νῦσαν τῷ Διονύσῳ ἐκφυτεῦσαι ἀπάγοντα ἐκ Θηβῶν τὸ γόνυ τῆς ἀμπέλου, οὗ καὶ Ἀλέξανδρος ὀργιάσαι.

3 Οἱ δὲ τὴν Νῦσαν οἰκοῦντες οὔ φασι τὸν Ἀλέξανδρον ἀνελθεῖν ἐς τὸ ὄρος, ἀλλ᾽ ὁρμῆσαι μέν, ἐπειδὴ φιλότιμός τε ἦν καὶ ἀρχαιολογίας ἥττων, δείσαντα δὲ μὴ ἐς ἀμπέλους παρελθόντες οἱ Μακεδόνες, ἃς χρόνου ἤδη οὐχ ἑωράκεσαν, ἐς πόθον τῶν οἴκοι ἀπενεχθῶσιν ἢ ἐπιθυμίαν τινὰ οἴνου ἀναλάβωσιν εἰθισμένοι ἤδη

9. The Greeks have a different opinion from the Indians about this Dionysus, as the Indians do with each other. We say that the Theban Dionysus traveled to India as a general and an ecstatic, and our evidence includes the dedication at Delphi, which is kept locked away in the storehouses there. It is a disc of Indian silver with this inscription: "Dionysus the son of Semele and Zeus after his Indian victory to Apollo of Delphi."

Among the Indians, those near the Caucasus and the river Cophen say that this person was a visitor from Assyria who knew about the deeds of the Theban. Those who live in the region between the Indus and the Hydraotes and in the land beyond, which extends as far as the river Ganges, say that Dionysus was born the son of the river Indus. The famous Theban, after paying him a visit, took up the thyrsus and went in for ecstatic rites. Claiming he was the son of Zeus and had lived in his father's thigh in order to reach birth, the Theban discovered a mountain called Meros (Thigh),[9] to which Nysa is adjacent and he planted it for Dionysus with a slip of the vine he had brought from Thebes. Here, they say, Alexander reveled. 2

But the inhabitants of Nysa deny that Alexander climbed the mountain. He desired to, since he was ambitious and devoted to antiquity, but was afraid that the Macedonians, not having seen vines for a long time, once they had come across them would be overcome by regret for those of their native land, and would feel a desire for wine after getting used to water. So he skirted Nysa after 3

[9] An unidentified mountain near Nysa, on which Alexander the Great had held a bacchic revel, according to some accounts. Greek legend said that Zeus had kept the embryonic Dionysus in his thigh.

τῷ ὕδατι, παρελάσαι τὴν Νῦσαν, εὐξάμενον τῷ Διονύσῳ καὶ θύσαντα ἐν τῇ ὑπωρείᾳ. καὶ γιγνώσκω μὲν οὐκ ἐς χάριν ταῦτα ἐνίοις γράφων, ἐπειδὴ οἱ ξὺν Ἀλεξάνδρῳ στρατεύσαντες οὐδὲ ταῦτα ἐς τὸ ἀληθὲς ἀνέγραψαν, δεῖ δὲ ἀληθείας ἐμοὶ γοῦν, ἣν εἰ κἀκεῖνοι ἐπῄνεσαν, οὐκ ἂν ἀφείλοντο καὶ τοῦδε τοῦ ἐγκωμίου τὸν Ἀλέξανδρον· τοῦ γὰρ ἀνελθεῖν ἐς τὸ ὄρος καὶ βακχεῦσαι αὐτόν, ἃ ἐκεῖνοι λέγουσι, μεῖζον, οἶμαι, τὸ ὑπὲρ καρτερίας τοῦ στρατοῦ μηδὲ ἀναβῆναι.

10. Τὴν δὲ Ἄορνον πέτραν οὐ πολὺ ἀπέχουσαν τῆς Νύσης ἰδεῖν μὲν οὔ φησιν ὁ Δάμις, ἐν ἐκβολῇ γὰρ κεῖσθαι τῆς ὁδοῦ καὶ δεδιέναι τὸν ἡγεμόνα ἐκτρέπεσθαί ποι παρὰ τὸ εὐθύ, ἀκοῦσαι δέ, ὡς ἁλωτὸς μὲν Ἀλεξάνδρῳ γένοιτο, Ἄορνος δὲ ὀνομάζοιτο οὐκ ἐπειδὴ στάδια πεντεκαίδεκα ἀνέστηκε, πέτονται γὰρ καὶ ὑπὲρ τοῦτο οἱ ἱεροὶ ὄρνιθες, ἀλλ᾿ ἐν κορυφῇ τῆς πέτρας ῥῆγμα εἶναί φασι τοὺς ὑπερπετομένους τῶν ὀρνίθων ἐπισπώμενον, ὡς Ἀθήνησί τε ἰδεῖν ἐστιν ἐν προδόμῳ τοῦ Παρθενῶνος καὶ πολλαχοῦ τῆς Φρυγῶν καὶ Λυδῶν γῆς, ἀφ᾿[5] οὗ τὴν πέτραν Ἄορνον κεκλῆσθαί τε καὶ εἶναι.

11. Ἐλαύνοντες δὲ ἐπὶ τὸν Ἰνδὸν παιδὶ ἐντυγχάνουσι τρισκαίδεκά που ἔτη γεγονότι ἐπ᾿ ἐλέφαντος ὀχουμένῳ, καὶ παίοντι τὸ θηρίον. ἐπεὶ δὲ ἐθαύμασαν ὁρῶντες "τί ἔργον," ἔφη "ὦ Δάμι, ἀγαθοῦ ἱππέως;" "τί δ᾿ ἄλλο γε," εἶπεν, "ἢ ἱζήσαντα ἐπὶ τοῦ ἵππου

[5] ἀφ᾿ Rsk.: ὑφ᾿

praying to Dionysus and sacrificing in the foothills. I am aware that this account of mine will displease some people, but those who were on Alexander's campaign falsified this part of it too. I by contrast am bound to the truth, and if those historians too had honored it, they would not have deprived Alexander of this additional praise. For rather than climbing the mountain and holding revel, as they assert, it was a nobler act to ensure the endurance of his army by not climbing it.

10. The crag called Aornos[10] is not far from Nysa, but Damis claims not to have seen it, since it lay off their route and their guide was afraid of diverging anywhere from their forward path. He apparently heard, however, that Alexander managed to take it, and it was so called not because it rises fifteen stades, since sacred birds can fly above that level, but because there is a cleft at the summit of the rock, and this sucks in the birds that fly over it. You can see the same thing at Athens in the forecourt of the Parthenon,[11] and in many parts of Phrygia and Lydia. This is the feature which causes the crag both to be called and to be "birdless."

11. As they were approaching the Indus, they met a boy about thirteen years old riding an elephant and beating the animal. When they had got over their surprise at the sight, Apollonius said, "What is the function of a good horse rider, Damis?" "What else," he replied, "than to sit on the

[10] Aornos = "birdless," the modern Pir-sar on the upper Indus, taken by Alexander after fierce fighting.

[11] Untrue: there was however a cleft under the Erechtheion, and also a legend that Athena had banned crows from the Acropolis.

ἄρχειν τε αὐτοῦ καὶ τῷ χαλινῷ στρέφειν καὶ κολάζειν ἀτακτοῦντα καὶ προορᾶν, ὡς μὴ ἐς βόθρον ἢ τάφρον ἢ χάσμα κατενεχθείη ὁ ἵππος, ὅτε γε δι' ἕλους ἢ πηλοῦ χωροίη;" "ἄλλο δὲ οὐδέν, ὦ Δάμι, ἀπαιτήσομεν" ἔφη "τὸν ἀγαθὸν ἱππέα;" "νὴ Δί'," εἶπε "τό τε ἀναπηδῶντι μὲν τῷ ἵππῳ πρὸς τὸ σιμὸν ἐφεῖναι τὸν χαλινόν, κατὰ πρανοῦς δὲ ἰόντι οἱ μὴ ξυγχωρεῖν, ἀλλ' ἀνθέλκειν, καὶ τὸ καταψῆσαι δὲ τὰ ὦτα ἢ τὴν χαίτην, καὶ μὴ ἀεὶ ἡ μάστιξ σοφοῦ ἔμοιγε δοκεῖ ἱππέως, καὶ ἐπαινοίην ἂν τὸν ὧδε ὀχούμενον." "τῷ δὲ δὴ μαχίμῳ τε καὶ πολεμιστηρίῳ τίνων δεῖ;" "τῶν γε αὐτῶν," ἔφη "ὦ Ἀπολλώνιε, καὶ πρός γε τούτοις τοῦ βάλλειν τε καὶ φυλάττεσθαι, καὶ τὸ ἐπελάσαι δὲ καὶ τὸ ἀπελάσαι καὶ τὸ ἀνειλῆσαι πολεμίους καὶ μὴ ἐᾶν ἐκπλήττεσθαι τὸν ἵππον, ὅτε δουπήσειεν ἀσπὶς ἢ ἀστράψειαν αἱ κόρυθες ἢ παιανιζόντων τε καὶ ἀλαλαζόντων βοὴ γένοιτο, σοφίᾳ, οἶμαι, ἱππικῇ πρόσκειται."

2 "Τοῦτον οὖν" ἔφη "τὸν ἐπὶ τοῦ ἐλέφαντος ἱππέα τί φήσεις;" "πολλῷ" ἔφη "θαυμασιώτερον, Ἀπολλώνιε, τὸ γὰρ θηρίῳ τηλικούτῳ ἐπιτετάχθαι τηλικόνδε ὄντα καὶ εὐθύνειν αὐτὸ καλαύροπι, ἣν ὁρᾷς αὐτὸν ἐμβαλόντα τῷ ἐλέφαντι, ὥσπερ ἄγκυραν, καὶ μήτε τὴν ὄψιν τοῦ θηρίου δεδιέναι μήτε τὸ ὕψος μήτε τὴν ῥώμην τοσαύτην οὖσαν, δαιμόνιον ἔμοιγε δοκεῖ, καὶ οὐδ' ἂν ἐπίστευσα, μὰ τὴν Ἀθηνᾶν, εἰ ἑτέρου ἤκουσα." "τί οὖν," ἔφη "εἰ ἀποδόσθαι τις ἡμῖν τὸν παῖδα βούλοιτο, ὠνήσῃ αὐτόν, ὦ Δάμι;" "νὴ Δί'," εἶπε "τῶν γε ἐμαυτοῦ πάντων. τὸ γὰρ ὥσπερ ἀκρόπολιν κατειληφότα δε-

horse, govern it, turn it with the bit, punish it when it is unruly, and watch out so that the horse does not fall into a hole, a ditch, or a cleft, when it is going through marshes or mud." "And shall we expect nothing more from a good rider?" said Apollonius. "Oh yes," replied Damis, "when the horse is galloping uphill he must relax the bit, but when it is going downhill he must not indulge it but hold it in. He must stroke its ears or its mane, since the constant use of the whip does not seem to me the mark of a good rider, but I would praise him for riding as I have said." "Well," said Apollonius, "what skills does a fierce, warlike rider need?" "The same ones, Apollonius," replied Damis, "and in addition he must strike blows and avoid them, advance and retreat, press the enemy and not let the horse shy at the clang of a shield, the flash of plumes, or the noise of men chanting in victory or giving a war whoop—this is part of a rider's skill."

"Well," said Apollonius, "how will you describe this 2
elephant rider?" "As someone much more amazing, Apollonius," said Damis. "For someone of that size to be in charge of an elephant, to drive it with a stick such as you see him sticking into the elephant like an anchor, not to fear the sight of the animal or its height or its colossal strength, that seems superhuman to me. By Athena, I would not have believed it if I had heard it from someone else." "Well, then," said Apollonius, "suppose someone were willing to sell us the boy, would you buy him, Damis?" "Yes indeed," said Damis, "with everything I own. For to be master of the largest animal on the face of the

σπόζειν θηρίου μεγίστου ὧν ἡ γῆ βόσκει, ἐλευθέρας ἔμοιγε δοκεῖ φύσεως καὶ λαμπρᾶς εἶναι." "τί οὖν χρήσῃ τῷ παιδί," ἔφη "εἰ μὴ καὶ τὸν ἐλέφαντα ὠνήσῃ;" "τῇ τε οἰκίᾳ" ἔφη "ἐπιστήσω τῇ ἐμαυτοῦ καὶ τοῖς οἰκέταις καὶ πολλῷ βέλτιον τούτων ἢ ἐγὼ ἄρξει." "σὺ δὲ οὐχ ἱκανὸς" ἔφη "τῶν σεαυτοῦ ἄρχειν;" "ὅν γε" εἶπε "καὶ σὺ τρόπον, ὦ Ἀπολλώνιε· καταλιπὼν γὰρ τἀμὰ περίειμι, ὥσπερ σύ, φιλομαθῶν καὶ περιφρονῶν τὰ ἐν τῇ ξένῃ."

3 "Εἰ δὲ δὴ πρίαιο τὸν παῖδα, καὶ ἵππω σοι γενοίσθην ὁ μὲν ἁμιλλητήριος, ὁ δὲ πολεμικός, ἀναθήσῃ αὐτόν, ὦ Δάμι, ἐπὶ τοὺς ἵππους;" "ἐπὶ μὲν τὸν ἁμιλλητήριον" εἶπεν "ἴσως ἄν, ἐπειδὴ καὶ ἑτέρους ὁρῶ, τὸν δὲ μάχιμόν τε καὶ ὁπλιτεύοντα πῶς ἂν ἀναβαίνοι οὗτος; οὔτε γὰρ ἀσπίδα δύναιτ' ἂν φέρειν, ἧς δεῖ τοῖς ἱππεύουσιν, οὔτ' ἂν θώρακα ἢ κράνος, αἰχμὴν δὲ πῶς οὗτος, ὃς οὐδὲ ἄτρακτον βέλους ἢ τοξεύματος κραδαίνοι ἄν, ψελλίζομενος ὡς τὸ εἰκὸς ἔτι;" "ἕτερον οὖν τι," ἔφη "ὦ Δάμι, ἐστίν, ὃ τὸν ἐλέφαντα τοῦτον ἡνιοχεῖ καὶ πέμπει, καὶ οὐχ ὁ ἡνίοχος οὗτος, ὃν σὺ μονονοὺ προσκυνεῖς ὑπὸ θαύματος." τοῦ δὲ εἰπόντος "τί ἂν εἴη τοῦτο, Ἀπολλώνιε; ὁρῶ γὰρ ἐπὶ τοῦ θηρίου πλὴν τοῦ παιδὸς οὐδὲν ἕτερον,"

4 "Τὸ θηρίον" ἔφη "τοῦτο εὐπαίδευτόν τε παρὰ πάντα ἐστί, κἀπειδὰν ἅπαξ ἀναγκασθῇ ὑπὸ ἀνθρώπῳ[6] ζῆν, ἀνέχεται τὰ ἐκ τοῦ ἀνθρώπου πάντα καὶ ὁμοήθειαν ἐπιτηδεύει τὴν πρὸς αὐτόν, χαίρει τε σιτούμενον ἀπὸ τῆς χειρός, ὥσπερ οἱ μικροὶ τῶν κυνῶν, προσιόντα τε

earth would be like occupying a citadel, and in my opinion the mark of a free and exalted nature." "Well," said Apollonius, "what use will you have for the boy if you do not buy the elephant too?" "I will put him in charge of my own household and of the servants," said Damis, "and he will govern them much better than I do." "Why, are you not able to control your own servants?" asked Apollonius. "As much as you are, Apollonius," said Damis, "for like you I go around in search of knowledge and studying foreign cultures."

3 "Well, suppose you bought the boy and you had two horses, one a race horse and one a war horse, would you put him up on these horses?" "Perhaps on the race-horse," was the reply, "since I see other people too doing that, but how could this boy ride a horse trained for battles and armor? He could not carry a shield, which cavalrymen need, nor a breastplate or a helmet, and how could he carry a spear? He could not even manage the shaft of a missile or an arrow, when he is probably still lisping." "Well then, Damis," said Apollonius, "it is something else that rides and accompanies this elephant, not the driver, whom you are practically worshiping in your admiration." Damis replied, "And what can that be, Apollonius? Because I do not see anything on the animal except this boy."

4 "This animal," said Apollonius, "is easier to train than any other, and once it has been forced to live under a human's control, it puts up with anything from the human and adapts its habits to him. It likes to eat from his hand, as little dogs do; it fondles him with its trunk when he comes

[6] ἀνθρώπῳ Kay.: ἀνθρώπων

τῇ προνομαίᾳ αἰκάλλει, καὶ τὴν κεφαλὴν ἐς τὴν φάρυγγα ἐσωθοῦντα ἀνέχεται, καὶ κέχηνεν ἐφ᾿ ὅσον τῷ ἀνθρώπῳ δοκεῖ, καθάπερ ἐν τοῖς νομάσιν ἑωρῶμεν. νύκτωρ δὲ λέγεται τὴν δουλείαν ὀλοφύρεσθαι, μὰ Δί᾿, οὐ τετριγός, ὁποῖον εἴωθεν, ἀλλ᾿ οἰκτρόν τε καὶ ἐλεεινὸν ἀνακλαῖον,[7] εἰ δὲ ἄνθρωπος ἐπισταίη ὀδυρομένῳ ταῦτα, ἴσχει τὸν θρῆνον ὁ ἐλέφας, ὥσπερ αἰδούμενος. αὐτὸς δὴ ἑαυτοῦ, ὦ Δάμι, ἄρχει καὶ ἡ πειθὼ αὐτὸν ἡ τῆς φύσεως ἄγει μᾶλλον ἢ ὁ ἐπικείμενός τε καὶ ἀπευθύνων."

12. Ἐπὶ δὲ τὸν Ἰνδὸν ἐλθόντες ἀγέλην ἐλεφάντων ἰδεῖν φασι περαιουμένους τὸν ποταμὸν καὶ τάδε ἀκοῦσαι περὶ τοῦ θηρίου· ὡς οἱ μὲν αὐτῶν ἕλειοι, οἱ δ᾿ αὖ ὄρειοι, καὶ τρίτον ἤδη γένος πεδινοί εἰσιν, ἁλίσκονταί τε ἐς τὴν τῶν πολεμικῶν χρείαν. μάχονται γὰρ δὴ ἐπεσκευασμένοι πύργους οἵους κατὰ δέκα καὶ πεντεκαίδεκα ὁμοῦ τῶν Ἰνδῶν δέξασθαι, ἀφ᾿ ὧν τοξεύουσί τε καὶ ἀκοντίζουσιν οἱ Ἰνδοί, καθάπερ ἐκ πυλῶν βάλλοντες. καὶ αὐτὸ δὲ τὸ θηρίον χεῖρα τὴν προνομαίαν ἡγεῖται καὶ χρῆται αὐτῇ ἐς τὸ ἀκοντίζειν. ὅσον δὲ ἵππου Νισαίου μείζων ὁ Λιβυκὸς ἐλέφας, τοσοῦτον τῶν ἐκ Λιβύης οἱ Ἰνδοὶ μείζους.

2 Περὶ δὲ ἡλικίας τοῦ ζῴου καὶ ὡς μακροβιώτατον, εἴρηται μὲν καὶ ἑτέροις, ἐντυχεῖν δὲ καὶ οὗτοί φασιν ἐλέφαντι περὶ Τάξιλα μεγίστην τῶν ἐν Ἰνδοῖς πόλιν, ὃν μυρίζειν τε οἱ ἐπιχώριοι καὶ ταινιοῦν· εἶναι γὰρ δὴ τῶν πρὸς Ἀλέξανδρον ὑπὲρ Πώρου μεμαχημένων εἷς οὗτος, ὅν, ἐπειδὴ προθύμως ἐμεμάχητο, ἀνῆκεν ὁ Ἀλέ-

near, allows him to thrust his head down its throat, and opens its mouth as wide as the man wishes, as we saw among the nomads. But they say that at night it grieves over its state of slavery, not indeed with its usual trumpeting, but with sad, pitiful moans, and if a human comes up when it is mourning like this, the elephant checks its grief as if from shame. It governs itself therefore, Damis, and is led more by the prompting of its own nature than by the driver who directs it."

12. When they reached the Indus, they say they saw a herd of elephants crossing the river, and were told the following about the animal. Some of them live in marshes, others in mountains, and a third type on the plain, and they are caught for use in warfare. When they fight, they are equipped with towers made so as to hold up to ten or fifteen Indians simultaneously. The Indians fire arrows and lances from these towers, as if shooting from gates. The animal itself considers its trunk a hand and uses it for hurling lances. The Indian elephants exceed those from Libya in size to the same extent as those exceed a Nisaean horse.

The age of the animal and its great length of life have 2
been discussed by others, but these two say that they encountered in Taxila, the largest city in India, an elephant which the natives perfumed and bedecked with ribbons. This indeed was one of these that had fought on the side of Porus[12] against Alexander, and because it had fought val-

[12] King of a territory in the modern Punjab, whom Alexander first defeated, and then set up as a dependent ruler.

---

[7] ἀνακλαῖον Huetius (Kay.): ἀνακλᾶον

ξανδρος τῷ Ἡλίῳ. εἶναι δὲ αὐτῷ καὶ χρυσοῦ ἕλικας περὶ τοῖς εἴτ᾿ ὀδοῦσιν εἴτε κέρασι καὶ γράμματα ἐπ᾿ αὐτῶν Ἑλληνικὰ λέγοντα "Ἀλέξανδρος ὁ Διὸς τὸν Αἴαντα τῷ Ἡλίῳ," ὄνομα γὰρ τοῦτο τῷ ἐλέφαντι ἔθετο μεγάλου ἀξιώσας μέγαν. ξυνεβάλοντο δὲ οἱ ἐπιχώριοι πεντήκοντα εἶναι καὶ τριακόσια ἔτη μετὰ τὴν μάχην, οὔπω λέγοντες καὶ ὁπόσα γεγονὼς ἐμάχετο.

13. Ἰόβας δέ, ὃς ἦρξέ ποτε τοῦ Λιβυκοῦ ἔθνους, φησὶ μὲν ξυμπεσεῖν ἀλλήλοις ἐπ᾿ ἐλεφάντων πάλαι Λιβυκοὺς ἱππέας, εἶναι δὲ τοῖς μὲν πύργον ἐς τοὺς ὀδόντας κεχαραγμένον, τοῖς δὲ οὐδέν, νυκτὸς δὲ ἐπιλαβούσης τὴν μάχην ἡττηθῆναι μὲν τοὺς ἐπισήμους φησί, φυγεῖν δὲ ἐς τὸν Ἄτλαντα τὸ ὄρος, αὐτὸς δὲ ἑλεῖν τετρακοσίων μήκει ἐτῶν ὕστερον τῶν διαφυγόντων ἕνα, καὶ τοὐπίσημον εἶναι αὐτῷ κοῖλον καὶ οὔπω περιτετριμμένον ὑπὸ τοῦ χρόνου. οὗτος ὁ Ἰόβας τοὺς ὀδόντας κέρατα ἡγεῖται τῷ φύεσθαι μὲν αὐτοὺς ὅθεν περ οἱ κρόταφοι, παραθήγεσθαι δὲ μηδενὶ ἑτέρῳ, μένειν δ᾿ ὡς ἔφυσαν καὶ μή, ὅπερ οἱ ὀδόντες, ἐκπίπτειν εἶτ᾿ ἀναφύεσθαι.

2 Ἐγὼ δ᾿ οὐ προσδέχομαι τὸν λόγον· κέρατά τε γὰρ εἰ μὴ πάντα, τά γε τῶν ἐλάφων ἐκπίπτει καὶ ἀναφύεται, ὀδόντες δὲ οἱ μὲν τῶν ἀνθρώπων ἐκπεσοῦνται καὶ ἀναφύσονται πάντες, ζῴων δ᾿ ἂν οὐδενὶ ἑτέρῳ χαυλιόδους ἢ κυνόδους αὐτομάτως ἐκπέσοι, οὐδ᾿ ἂν ἐπανέλθοι ἐκπεσών, ὅπλου γὰρ ἕνεκα ἡ φύσις ἐμβιβάζει αὐτοὺς ἐς τὰς γένυς. καὶ ἄλλως τὰ κέρατα γραμμὴν ἀποτορνεύει κύκλῳ πρὸς τῇ ῥίζῃ κατ᾿ ἐνιαυτὸν ἑκα-

iantly Alexander dedicated it to Helios. It had gold bangles on its teeth or (if you prefer) tusks, and on these were Greek inscriptions saying "Alexander the son of Zeus dedicates Ajax to the Sun." "Ajax" was what he called the elephant, thinking a great creature deserved a great name.[13] The natives reckoned that the battle had occurred three hundred and fifty years before, but did not say how old the animal was when it fought.

13. Juba, however, the former ruler of the African people,[14] says that long ago African riders fought a battle on elephants. The animals on one side had a tower engraved on their tusks, while those on the other had nothing. When night ended the battle, the marked animals were defeated and ran away to Mount Atlas. He personally captured one of the runaways four hundred long years later, and its mark was still deep and not yet worn away by time. This Juba believes that the tusks are horns, since they grow out of the place of the temples, and are not sharpened by anything external, but remain in their natural state, and do not fall out and grow back again like teeth.

I do not accept this reasoning. Even if not all horns fall 2
out and grow back, those of deer do. As for humans, all their teeth fall out and grow back, but in no other animals do the teeth or the tusks fall out naturally, nor can they be restored when they do, since nature implants them into the jaws as a weapon. In addition, horns produce a circular ridge at their base every year, as can be seen in goats,

[13] Ajax the son of Telamon is called "great" in Homer, to distinguish him from his namesake, Ajax son of Oileus.

[14] King of Mauretania from 25 BCE to ca. 23 CE, a prolific writer on history, ethnography, and other topics.

στον, ὡς αἶγές τε δηλοῦσι καὶ ποῖμναι καὶ βόες, ὀδοὺς δὲ λεῖος ἐκφύεται καὶ ἢν μὴ πηρώσῃ τι αὐτόν, τοιόσδε ἀεὶ μένει, μετέχει γὰρ τῆς λιθώδους ὕλης τε καὶ οὐσίας. καὶ μὴν καὶ τὸ κερασφορεῖν περὶ τὰ δίχηλα τῶν ζῴων μόνα ἕστηκε, τὸ δὲ ζῷον τοῦτο πεντώνυχον καὶ πολυσχιδὲς τὴν βάσιν, ἣ διὰ τὸ μὴ ἐσφίγχθαι χηλαῖς ὥσπερ ἐν ὑγρῷ ἕστηκε. καὶ τοῖς μὲν κερασφόροις ἅπασιν ὑποβάλλουσα ἡ φύσις ὀστᾶ σηραγγώδη περιφύει τὸ κέρας ἔξωθεν, τὸ δὲ τῶν ἐλεφάντων πλῆρες ἀποφαίνει καὶ ὅμοιον, ἀναπτύξαντι δὲ σύριγξ αὐτὸ λεπτὴ διέρπει μέσον, ὥσπερ τοὺς ὀδόντας.

3 Εἰσὶ δὲ οἱ μὲν τῶν ἑλείων ὀδόντες πελιδνοὶ καὶ μανοὶ μεταχειρίσασθαί τε ἄτοποι, πολλαχοῦ γὰρ αὐτῶν ὑποδεδύκασι σήραγγες, πολλαχοῦ δὲ ἀνεστᾶσι χάλαζαι μὴ ξυγχωροῦσαι τῇ τέχνῃ, οἱ δὲ τῶν ὀρείων μείους μὲν ἢ οὗτοι, λευκοὶ δὲ ἱκανῶς καὶ δύσεργον περὶ αὐτοὺς οὐδέν, ἄριστοι δὲ οἱ τῶν πεδινῶν ὀδόντες, μέγιστοί τε γὰρ καὶ λευκότατοι καὶ ἀναπτύξαι ἡδεῖς καὶ γίγνονται πᾶν ὅ τι θέλει ἡ χείρ. εἰ δὲ καὶ ἤθη ἐλεφάντων χρὴ ἀναγράφειν, τοὺς μὲν ἐκ τῶν ἑλῶν ἁλισκομένους ἀνοήτους ἡγοῦνται καὶ κώφους[8] Ἰνδοί, τοὺς δὲ ἐκ τῶν ὀρῶν κακοήθεις τε καὶ ἐπιβουλευτὰς καὶ ἢν μὴ δέωνταί τινος, οὐ βεβαίους τοῖς ἀνθρώποις, οἱ πεδινοὶ δὲ χρηστοί τε εἶναι λέγονται καὶ εὐάγωγοι καὶ μιμήσεως ἐρασταί· γράφουσι γοῦν καὶ ὀρχοῦνται καὶ παρενσαλεύουσι πρὸς αὐλὸν καὶ πηδῶσιν ἀπὸ τῆς γῆς ἐκεῖνοι.

14. Ἰδὼν δὲ τοὺς ἐλέφαντας ὁ Ἀπολλώνιος τὸν

sheep, and oxen, but a tooth grows smooth, and always retains its original shape unless harmed by something, since it partakes of the material and nature of stone. Moreover, having horns is a property only of cloven-footed animals, while the elephant has five nails and several clefts in its foot, which has a soft cushion, as it were, and lacks hooves to make it firm. Since nature supplies all horned animals with porous bones, it puts a covering on the outside of their horns, but it makes the elephant's tusk full and even, though if you split it you find a narrow channel running through the middle, as in teeth.

The tusks of the marsh elephants are dark, fibrous, and 3
difficult to work, since in many places they have sunken cavities, in many others knots that resist fashioning, while the tusks of the mountain kind are smaller than those but very white and not at all difficult to work. But the tusk of the plains elephant is the best, largest, and whitest, easy to split and capable of anything the hand desires. If I must describe the elephants' natures, the marsh kind are considered by the Indians to be stupid and deaf; the mountain kind to be malevolent, crafty, and only loyal to human beings when they need something; while they say the plains kind are good, tractable, and fond of mimicry. These ones write, dance, sway to the music of the pipe, and jump in the air.

14. Apollonius saw the elephants crossing the Indus,

---

[8] κώφους Jac.: κούφους

Ἰνδὸν περαιουμένους, ἦσαν δέ, οἶμαι, τριάκοντα, καὶ χρωμένους ἡγεμόνι τῷ σμικροτάτῳ σφῶν, καὶ τοὺς μείζους αὐτῶν ἀνειληφότας τοὺς αὑτῶν πώλους ἐπὶ τὰς τῶν ὀδόντων προβολάς, τάς τε προνομαίας ἐπεζευχότας δεσμοῦ ἕνεκα, "ταῦτα μέν," ἔφη "ὦ Δάμι, οὐδὲ ἐπιτάττοντος οὐδενὸς αὐτοῖς ἀφ᾿ ἑαυτῶν οὗτοι διὰ ξύνεσίν τε καὶ σοφίαν πράττουσι, καὶ ὁρᾷς, ὡς παραπλησίως τοῖς σκευαγωγοῦσιν ἀνειλήφασι τοὺς πώλους, καὶ καταδησάμενοι αὐτοὺς ἄγουσιν;" "ὁρῶ," ἔφη "ὦ Ἀπολλώνιε, ὡς σοφῶς τε αὐτὸ καὶ ξυνετῶς πράττουσι. τί οὖν βούλεται τὸ εὔηθες ἐκεῖνο φρόντισμα, τοῖς ἐρεσχελοῦσι φυσικὴν ἢ μὴ τὴν πρὸς τὰ τέκνα εἶναι εὔνοιαν; τουτὶ γὰρ καὶ ἐλέφαντες ἤδη βοῶσιν, ὡς παρὰ τῆς φύσεως αὐτοῖς ἥκει· οὐ γὰρ δὴ παρὰ ἀνθρώπων γε μεμαθήκασιν αὐτό, ὥσπερ τὰ ἄλλα, οἵ γε μηδὲ ξυμβεβιώκασί πω ἀνθρώποις, ἀλλὰ φύσει κεκτημένοι τὸ φιλεῖν, ἃ ἔτεκον, προκήδονταί τε αὐτῶν καὶ παιδοτροφοῦσι."

2 "Καὶ μὴ τοὺς ἐλέφαντας εἴπῃς, ὦ Δάμι· τοῦτο γὰρ τὸ ζῷον δεύτερον ἀνθρώπου τάττω κατὰ ξύνεσίν τε καὶ βουλάς, ἀλλὰ τάς τε ἄρκτους ἐνθυμοῦμαι μᾶλλον, ὡς ἀγριώταται θηρίων οὖσαι πάνθ᾿ ὑπὲρ τῶν σκύμνων πράττουσι, τούς τε λύκους, ὡς ἀεὶ προσκείμενοι τῷ ἁρπάζειν ἡ μὲν θήλεια φυλάττει, ἃ ἔτεκεν, ὁ δὲ ἄρρην ὑπὲρ σωτηρίας τῶν σκυλάκων ἀπάγει αὐτῇ σῖτον, τάς τε παρδάλεις ὡσαύτως, αἳ διὰ θερμότητα χαίρουσι τῷ γίγνεσθαι μητέρες, δεσπόζειν γὰρ δὴ τότε βούλονται τῶν ἀρρένων καὶ τοῦ οἴκου ἄρχειν, οἱ δὲ ἀνέχονται τὸ

about thirty of them, I think, and using the smallest of their number as leader, while the larger ones carried their own young on their projecting tusks, fastening their trunks around them for security. "This, Damis," he said, "they do not because anyone has told them, but because of their understanding and intelligence. You see the way in which they carry their young like porters, and tie them on to transport them?" "Yes, Apollonius," said Damis, "I see how cleverly and intelligently they do it. What is the point of that silly problem which people toy with as to whether it is natural to feel goodwill for offspring? Even elephants are enough to proclaim that it comes to them from nature. They certainly have not acquired it from humans as they have other things, since they have not yet lived together with humans. It is because they have acquired their love of offspring by nature that they care for them and feed their young."

"Do not only mention elephants, Damis," said Apollo- 2
nius, "since I consider them an animal second to humans in intelligence and rational capacity. I am thinking rather of bears. They are the most savage of animals, and yet they do anything for their cubs. Or wolves: they are always occupied in plunder, and yet the she wolf guards her young, and the male preserves the cubs by bringing her food. So also leopards: because of their hot temperaments, they love motherhood, since then they want to lord it over the males and rule the household, and the males allow them to do

ἐξ αὐτῶν πᾶν ἡττώμενοι τοῦ τόκου. λέγεται δέ τις καὶ περὶ τῶν λεαινῶν λόγος, ὡς ἐραστὰς μὲν ποιοῦνται τοὺς παρδάλεις καὶ δέχονται αὐτοὺς ἐπὶ τὰς εὐνὰς τῶν λεόντων ἐς τὰ πεδία, τῆς δὲ γαστρὸς ὥραν ἀγούσης ἀναφεύγουσιν ἐς τὰ ὄρη καὶ τὰ τῶν παρδάλεων ἤθη, στικτὰ γὰρ τίκτουσιν, ὅθεν κρύπτουσιν αὐτὰ καὶ θηλάζουσιν ἐν σκολιαῖς λόχμαις, πλασάμεναι ἀφημερεύειν πρὸς θήραν. εἰ γὰρ φωράσειαν τουτὶ οἱ λέοντες, διασπῶνται τοὺς σκύμνους καὶ ξαίνουσι τὴν σπορὰν ὡς νόθον.

3 "Ἐνέτυχες δήπου καὶ τῶν Ὁμηρείων λεόντων ἑνί, ὡς ὑπὲρ τῶν ἑαυτοῦ σκύμνων δεινὸν βλέπει καὶ ῥώννυσιν ἑαυτὸν μάχης ἅπτεσθαι. καὶ τὴν τίγριν δὲ χαλεπωτάτην οὖσάν φασιν ἐν τῇδε τῇ χώρᾳ καὶ περὶ τὴν θάλατταν τὴν Ἐρυθρὰν ἐπὶ τὰς ναῦς ἵεσθαι, τοὺς σκύμνους ἀπαιτοῦσαν, καὶ ἀπολαβοῦσαν μὲν ἀπιέναι χαίρουσαν, εἰ δὲ ἀποπλεύσαιεν, ὠρύεσθαι αὐτὴν πρὸς τῇ θαλάττῃ καὶ ἀποθνήσκειν ἐνίοτε. τὰ δὲ τῶν ὀρνίθων τίς οὐκ οἶδεν; ὡς ἀετοὶ μὲν καὶ πελαργοὶ καλιὰς οὐκ ἂν πήξαιντο μὴ πρότερον αὐταῖς ἐναρμόσαντες ὁ μὲν τὸν ἀετίτην λίθον, ὁ δὲ τὸν λυχνίτην ὑπὲρ τῆς ᾠογονίας καὶ τοῦ μὴ πελάζειν σφίσι τοὺς ὄφεις.

4 "Κἂν τὰ ἐν τῇ θαλάττῃ σκοπῶμεν, τοὺς μὲν δελφῖνας οὐκ ἂν θαυμάσαιμεν, εἰ χρηστοὶ ὄντες φιλοτεκνοῦσι, φαλαίνας δὲ καὶ φώκας καὶ τὰ ζῳοτόκα ἔθνη πῶς οὐ θαυμασόμεθα, εἰ φώκη μέν, ἣν εἶδον ἐγὼ ἐν Αἰγαῖς καθειργμένην ἐς κυνήγια, οὕτως ἐπένθησεν ἀποθανόντα τὸν σκύμνον, ὃν ἐν τῷ οἰκίσκῳ ἀπεκύη-

anything out of devotion to their offspring. And there is a story told about lionesses, that they take leopards as lovers, and receive them into the lions' beds in the plains, but when their wombs reach their time they retreat to the mountains and the haunts of the leopards. Their offspring are spotted, so they conceal them and suckle them in dense thickets, pretending that they are away hunting. If ever the lions find this out, they tear the pups to pieces and mangle the brood as bastards.

"No doubt you have come across one of the Homeric 3
lions, and how it looks fierce in defense of its own cubs, and summons up its strength in order to do battle.[15] The tigress is the most savage of animals in this region, and yet they say it will go even to the ships on the Red Sea and beg for the return of its cubs. If it recovers them, it goes away happy, but if the ships sail away, it howls on the shore and some of them even die. As for birds, everyone knows about them. Eagles and storks cannot make their nests without first incorporating in them an eagle stone or a lamp stone,[16] in order to ensure that the eggs will hatch and that snakes will not approach them.

"Suppose we consider sea creatures. We cannot won- 4
der at dolphins loving their young out of kindness, but how can we not wonder at whales, seals, and sea mammals? I once saw a seal caged for the purpose of a wild-beast show at Aegeae, and it so mourned for the dead pup that it had

[15] *Iliad* 17.133–36.

[16] Eagle stone: lump of clay ironstone. Lamp stone: red-colored precious stone.

σεν, ὡς μὴ προσδέξασθαι τριῶν ἡμερῶν σῖτον, καίτοι βορωτάτη θηρίων οὖσα, φάλαινα δὲ ἐς τοὺς χηραμοὺς τῆς φάρυγγος ἀναλαμβάνει τοὺς σκύμνους, ἐπειδὰν φεύγῃ τι ἑαυτῆς μεῖζον; καὶ ἔχιδνα ὤφθη ποτὲ τοὺς ὄφεις, οὓς ἀπέτεκε, λιχμωμένη καὶ θεραπεύουσα ἐκείνῃ τῇ γλώττῃ. μὴ γὰρ δεχώμεθα, ὦ Δάμι, τὸν εὐήθη λόγον, ὡς ἀμήτορες οἱ τῶν ἐχιδνῶν τίκτονται, τουτὶ γὰρ οὐδὲ ἡ φύσις ξυγκεχώρηκεν, οὔτε ἡ πεῖρα." ὑπολαβὼν οὖν ὁ Δάμις "ξυγχωρεῖς οὖν" ἔφη "τὸν Εὐριπίδην ἐπαινεῖν ἐπὶ τῷ ἰαμβείῳ τούτῳ, ᾧ πεποίηται αὐτῷ ἡ Ἀνδρομάχη λέγουσα 'ἅπασι δ' ἀνθρώποις ἄρ' ἦν ψυχὴ τέκνα.'" "ξυγχωρῶ," ἔφη "σοφῶς γὰρ καὶ δαιμονίως εἴρηται, πολλῷ δ' ἂν σοφώτερον καὶ ἀληθέστερον εἶχεν, εἰ περὶ πάντων ζῴων ὕμνητο." "ἔοικας," ἔφη "Ἀπολλώνιε, μεταγράφειν τὸ ἰαμβεῖον, ἵν' οὕτως ᾄδοιμεν 'ἅπασι δὲ ζῴοις ἄρ' ἦν ψυχὴ τέκνα.' καὶ ἕπομαί σοι, βέλτιον γάρ.

15. "Ἀλλ' ἐκεῖνό μοι εἰπέ· οὐκ ἐν ἀρχῇ τῶν λόγων ἔφαμεν σοφίαν εἶναι περὶ τοὺς ἐλέφαντας καὶ νοῦν περὶ ἃ πράττουσι;" "καὶ εἰκότως," εἶπεν "ὦ Δάμι, ἔφαμεν, εἰ γὰρ μὴ νοῦς ἐκυβέρνα τόδε τὸ θηρίον, οὔτ' ἂν αὐτὸ διεγίγνετο οὔτ' ἂν τὰ ἔθνη, ἐν οἷς γίγνεται." "τί οὖν" ἔφη "οὕτως ἀμαθῶς καὶ οὐ πρὸς τὸ χρήσιμον ἑαυτοῖς τὴν διάβασιν ποιοῦνται; ἡγεῖται μὲν γάρ, ὡς ὁρᾷς, ὁ μικρότατος, ἕπεται δὲ αὐτῷ τις ὀλίγῳ μείζων, εἶτα ὑπὲρ τοῦτον ἕτερος, καὶ οἱ μέγιστοι κατόπιν πάντες. ἔδει δέ που τὸν ἐναντίον τρόπον αὐτοὺς πορεύ-

given birth to in its cage that it did not accept food for three days, though seals are the most voracious of animals. A whale takes its young into the hollows of its gullet when it is running from something larger than itself. And a viper has been observed to lick the snakes it had borne, and fondle them with that well known tongue. For let us not accept, Damis, that ignorant fable about the young of vipers having no mothers, since that is something which neither nature nor experience has confirmed." In reply Damis said, "So you are willing to praise Euripides and that verse in which he makes Andromache say, 'So for all humans children are their life'?"[17] "I am," said Apollonius, "because it is a wise and inspired remark, and would be wiser and truer if the praise concerned all living things." "You seem, Apollonius," said Damis, "to rewrite the verse, so that we should recite it thus: 'So for all creatures children are their life.' I agree with you, it is better that way.

15. "But tell me this. Did we not say at the beginning of our discussion that elephants possessed wisdom and sense in their actions?" "And quite plausibly, Damis," said Apollonius, "since if this animal did not have sense to govern it, neither it, nor the peoples among whom it exists, would survive." "Well then," said Damis, "why do they make their crossing in a way so stupid and disadvantageous to themselves? As you see, the smallest one leads, and he is followed by one slightly bigger, then by one bigger than him, while all the largest are in the rear. Surely they should cross

[17] *Andromache* 418–19.

εσθαι καὶ τοὺς μεγίστους τείχη καὶ προβλήματα ἑαυτῶν ποιεῖσθαι."

2 "Ἀλλ', ὦ Δάμι," ἔφη "πρῶτον μὲν ὑποφεύγειν ἐοίκασι δίωξιν ἀνθρώπων, οἷς που καὶ ἐντευξόμεθα ἑπομένοις τῷ ἴχνει, πρὸς δὲ τοὺς ἐπικειμένους δεῖ[9] τὰ κατὰ νώτου πεφράχθαι μᾶλλον, ὥσπερ ἐν τοῖς πολέμοις, καὶ τοῦτο τακτικώτατον ἡγοῦ τῶν θηρίων, ἔπειτα ἡ διάβασις, εἰ μὲν προδιέβαινον οἱ μέγιστοι σφῶν, οὔπω τεκμαίρεσθαι παρεῖχον ἂν τοῦ ὕδατος εἰ διαβήσονται πάντες, τοῖς μὲν γὰρ εὔπορός τε καὶ ῥᾳδία ἡ περαίωσις ὑψηλοτάτοις οὖσι, τοῖς δὲ χαλεπή τε καὶ ἄπορος, μὴ ὑπεραίρουσι τοῦ ῥεύματος, διελθὼν δὲ ὁ σμικρότατος τὸ ἄλυπον ἤδη καὶ τοῖς λοιποῖς ἑρμηνεύει, καὶ ἄλλως οἱ μὲν μείζους προεμβαίνοντες κοιλότερον ἂν τὸν ποταμὸν ἀποφαίνοιεν τοῖς σμικροῖς, ἀνάγκη γὰρ συνιζάνειν τὴν ἰλὺν ἐς βόθρους διά τε βαρύτητα τοῦ θηρίου διά τε παχύτητα τῶν ποδῶν, οἱ δ' ἐλάττους οὐδὲν ἂν βλάπτοιεν τὴν τῶν μειζόνων διαπορείαν ἧττον ἐμβοθρεύοντες."

16. Ἐγὼ δὲ εὗρον ἐν τοῖς Ἰόβα λόγοις, ὡς καὶ ξυλλαμβάνουσιν ἀλλήλοις ἐν τῇ θήρᾳ καὶ προΐστανται τοῦ ἀπειπόντος, κἂν ἐξέλωνται αὐτόν, τὸ δάκρυον τῆς ἀλόης ἐπαλείφουσι τοῖς τραύμασι περιεστῶτες ὥσπερ ἰατροί. πολλὰ τοιαῦτα ἐφιλοσοφεῖτο αὐτοῖς ἀφορμὰς ποιουμένοις τὰ λόγου ἄξια.

17. Τὰ δὲ Νεάρχῳ τε καὶ Ὀρθαγόρᾳ[10] περὶ τοῦ

just the opposite way, and make the largest ones their walls and ramparts?"

"No, Damis," said Apollonius. "First, they seem to be 2
evading pursuit from humans following their tracks, whom we shall perhaps meet. When under attack, it is the rear that needs protection above all, just as in war, and you should consider this animal a more skilful tactician than any. Second, as to the crossing, if the largest of them went first, they could not form an estimate about the water and whether they could all cross it, since for these it is readily and easily crossed, being the tallest, but for the others it is difficult and tricky, as they do not exceed the level of the stream. But if the smallest crosses, that tells the rest to expect no harm. In addition, if the larger went first, they would make the river deeper for the small ones. The mud would inevitably form trenches because of the animal's weight and the thickness of its feet, whereas the smaller ones cannot impede the crossing of the larger, since they tread less deeply."

16. Now I myself have found in the accounts of Juba that elephants collaborate when hunting and defend an injured comrade, and if they carry him away they smear aloe gum on his wounds, standing around him like doctors. The two had many such learned discussions, taking whatever was noteworthy as their starting point.

17. Now what Nearchus and Orthagoras have said

---

9 δεῖ Kay.: ἔδει

10 Ὀρθαγόρᾳ F. Jacoby on *FGrHist* 713: Πυθαγόρᾳ

Ἀκεσίνου ποταμοῦ εἰρημένα, ὡς ἐσβάλλει μὲν ἐς τὸν Ἰνδὸν οὗτος, τρέφει δὲ ὄφεις ἑβδομήκοντα πηχῶν μῆκος, τοιαῦτα εἶναί φασιν, ὁποῖα εἴρηται, καὶ ἀνακείσθω μοι ὁ λόγος ἐς τοὺς δράκοντας, ὧν ὁ Δάμις ἀφηγεῖται τὴν θήραν. ἀφικόμενοι δὲ ἐπὶ τὸν Ἰνδὸν καὶ πρὸς διαβάσει τοῦ ποταμοῦ ὄντες ἤροντο τὸν Βαβυλώνιον, εἴ τι τοῦ ποταμοῦ οἶδε, διαβάσεως πέρι ἐρωτῶντες, ὁ δὲ οὔπω ἔφη πεπλευκέναι αὐτόν, οὐδὲ γιγνώσκειν, ὁπόθεν πλεῖται.

2 "Τί οὖν" ἔφασαν "οὐκ ἐμισθώσω ἡγεμόνα;" "ὅτι ἔστιν" ἔφη "ὁ ἡγησόμενος" καὶ ἅμα ἐδείκνυ τινὰ ἐπιστολὴν ὡς τοῦτο πράξουσαν, ὅτε δὴ καὶ τὸν Οὐαρδάνην τῆς τε φιλανθρωπίας καὶ τῆς ἐπιμελείας ἀγασθῆναί φασι· πρὸς γὰρ τὸν ἐπὶ τοῦ Ἰνδοῦ σατράπην ἔπεμψε τὴν ἐπιστολὴν ταύτην, καίτοι μὴ ὑποκείμενον τῇ ἑαυτοῦ ἀρχῇ, εὐεργεσίας ἀναμιμνήσκων αὐτόν, καὶ χάριν μὲν οὐκ ἂν ἐπ' ἐκείνῃ ἀπαιτῆσαι φάσκων, οὐ γὰρ εἶναι πρὸς τοῦ ἑαυτοῦ τρόπου τὸ ἀνταπαιτεῖν, Ἀπολλώνιον δὲ ὑποδεξαμένῳ καὶ πέμψαντι οἷ βούλεται χάριν ἂν γνῶναι. χρυσίον δὲ τῷ ἡγεμόνι ἔδωκεν, ἵν' εἰ δεηθέντα τὸν Ἀπολλώνιον αἴσθοιτο, δοίη τοῦτο καὶ μὴ ἐς ἄλλου χεῖρα βλέψειεν.

3 Ἐπεὶ δὲ τὴν ἐπιστολὴν ὁ Ἰνδὸς ἔλαβε, μεγάλων τε ἀξιοῦσθαι ἔφη καὶ φιλοτιμήσεσθαι περὶ τὸν ἄνδρα μεῖον οὐδὲν ἢ εἰ ὁ βασιλεὺς τῶν Ἰνδῶν ὑπὲρ αὐτοῦ ἔγραφε, καὶ τήν τε ναῦν τὴν σατραπίδα ἔδωκεν αὐτῷ ἐμβῆναι πλοῖά τε ἕτερα, ἐφ' ὧν αἱ κάμηλοι ἐκομίζοντο, ἡγεμόνα τε τῆς γῆς πάσης, ἣν ὁ Ὑδραώτης

about the Acesines,[18] that it joins with the Indus and contains snakes seventy cubits long, all this they say corresponds to the facts, and I will reserve my account of the dragons, since Damis has described how they are hunted.[19] When they had reached the Indus and were preparing to cross it, they asked their Babylonian guide if he had any experience of the river, questioning him about the crossing. He said that he had never sailed on it before, and in fact did not know at what point the crossing was made.

"Why did you not hire a guide, then?" they asked. "We 2
have a guide," he answered, revealing a letter designed for the purpose. This, it seems, really made them admire the courtesy and thoughtfulness of Vardanes, as he had sent this letter to the viceroy of the Indus despite not having him as a subject. He reminded him of a benefit, but said he would not ask a return for that, it not being in his nature to ask a return for favors; but he would be grateful if the viceroy welcomed Apollonius and looked after him. He had also given money to the guide to give to Apollonius if he noticed him in need of anything, so that he would not have to depend on another's generosity.

When the Indian received the letter, he said that he felt 3
greatly honored, and would be as attentive to Apollonius as if the king of India had written on his behalf. He gave him the vice-regal ship to cross in and other boats in which the camels were ferried over, as well as a guide for the whole region bordered by the Hydraotes. He also wrote to his

[18] Nearchus: companion and admiral of Alexander, who wrote an account of the campaign in India and of his own return by sea with Alexander's fleet. Orthagoras: historian of uncertain date who wrote about India.

[19] III 6–8.

ὁρίζει, πρός τε τὸν βασιλέα τὸν ἑαυτοῦ ἔγραψε μὴ χείρω αὐτοῦ Οὐαρδάνου γενέσθαι περὶ ἄνδρα Ἕλληνά τε καὶ θεῖον.

18. Τὸν μὲν δὴ Ἰνδὸν ὧδε ἐπεραιώθησαν σταδίους μάλιστα τεσσαράκοντα, τὸ γὰρ πλόιμον αὐτοῦ τοσοῦτον, περὶ δὲ τοῦ ποταμοῦ τούτου τάδε γράφουσι· τὸν Ἰνδὸν ἄρχεσθαι μὲν ἐκ τοῦ Καυκάσου μείζω αὐτόθεν ἢ οἱ κατὰ τὴν Ἀσίαν ποταμοὶ πάντες, προχωρεῖν δὲ πολλοὺς τῶν ναυσιπόρων ἑαυτοῦ ποιούμενον, ἀδελφὰ δὲ τῷ Νείλῳ πράττοντα τῇ τε Ἰνδικῇ ἐπιχεῖσθαι γῆν τε ἐπάγειν τῇ γῇ καὶ παρέχειν Ἰνδοῖς τὸν Αἰγυπτίων τρόπον σπείρειν.

2 Χιόσι δ' Αἰθιόπων τε καὶ Καταδούπων ὀρῶν ἀντιλέγειν μὲν οὐκ ἀξιῶ διὰ τοὺς εἰπόντας, οὐ μὴν ξυντίθεμαί γε λογιζόμενος τὸν Ἰνδόν, ὡς ταὐτὸν τῷ Νείλῳ ἐργάζεται μὴ νιφομένης τῆς ὑπὲρ αὐτὸν χώρας, καὶ ἄλλως τὸν θεὸν οἶδα κέρατα τῆς γῆς ξυμπάσης Αἰθίοπάς τε καὶ Ἰνδοὺς ἀποφαίνοντα μελαίνοντά τε τοὺς μὲν ἀρχομένου ἡλίου, τοὺς δὲ λήγοντος, ὃ πῶς ἂν ξυνέβαινε περὶ τοὺς ἀνθρώπους, εἰ μὴ καὶ τὸν χειμῶνα ἐθέροντο; ἣν δὲ ἀνὰ πᾶν ἔτος θάλπει γῆν ἥλιος, πῶς ἄν τις ἡγοῖτο νίφεσθαι, πῶς δ' ἂν τὴν χιόνα χορηγὸν τοῖς ἐκείνῃ ποταμοῖς γίγνεσθαι τοῦ ὑπεραίρειν τὰ σφῶν αὐτῶν μέτρα; εἰ δὲ καὶ φοιτᾶν χιόνα ἐς τὰ οὕτω πρόσειλα, πῶς ἂν αὐτὴν ἐς τοσόνδε ἀναχυθῆναι πέλαγος; πῶς δ' ἂν ἀποχρῆσαι ποταμῷ βυθίζοντι Αἴγυπτον;

19. Κομιζόμενοι δὲ διὰ τοῦ Ἰνδοῦ πολλοῖς μὲν

own king, advising him to prove as good as Vardanes to a man who was both a Greek and divine.

18. Thus they crossed the Indus at a width of about forty stades, so great is its navigable size. In their account of this river, they relate that it rises in the Caucasus, already larger at its source than any single river in Asia, and as it progresses it absorbs other navigable rivers. Acting like the Nile, it floods India, covering the soil with soil and allowing the Indians to sow in the Egyptian way.

I hardly dare deny the snows of Ethiopia and the moun- 2
tains of the Cataract, considering those who have spoken about them, but when I contemplate the Indus I cannot agree. This behaves as the Nile does without snow falling in the region above it. Besides, I know that god has made Ethiopia and India the limits of the entire earth, and causes those in the farthest east and the farthest west to be black: and how could that happen to those peoples unless they were sunburned even in winter? And if a land is warmed by the sun throughout the year, how could it conceivably have snow? And how could the snow be sufficient to make the rivers there rise above their usual levels? And even if snow fell in such tropical regions, how could it create such a flood when it melted? And how could it be enough for a river that floods all of Egypt?

19. As they crossed the Indus, they say, they observed

ποταμίοις ἵπποις ἐντυχεῖν φασι, πολλοῖς δὲ κροκοδείλοις, ὥσπερ οἱ τὸν Νεῖλον πλέοντες, λέγουσι δὲ καὶ ἄνθη τῷ Ἰνδῷ εἶναι, οἷα τοῦ Νείλου ἀναφύεται, καὶ τὰς ὥρας, αἳ περὶ τὴν Ἰνδικήν εἰσι, χειμῶνος μὲν ἀλεεινὰς εἶναι, θέρους δὲ πνιγηράς, πρὸς δὲ τοῦτο ἄριστα μεμηχανῆσθαι τῷ δαίμονι, τὴν γὰρ χώραν αὐτοῖς θαμὰ ὕεσθαι.

2 Φασὶ δὲ καὶ ἀκοῦσαι τῶν Ἰνδῶν, ὡς ἀφικνοῖτο μὲν ὁ βασιλεὺς ἐπὶ τὸν ποταμὸν τοῦτον, ὅτε ἀναβιβάζοιεν αὐτὸν αἱ ὧραι, θύοι δὲ αὐτῷ ταύρους τε καὶ ἵππους μέλανας (τὸ γὰρ λευκὸν ἀτιμότερον Ἰνδοὶ τίθενται τοῦ μέλανος δι', οἶμαι, τὸ ἑαυτῶν χρῶμα), θύσαντα δὲ καταποντοῦν φασι τῷ ποταμῷ χρυσοῦν μέτρον, εἰκασμένον τῷ ἀπομετροῦντι τὸν σῖτον, καὶ ἐφ' ὅτῳ μὲν τοῦτο πράττει ὁ βασιλεύς, οὐ ξυμβάλλεσθαι τοὺς Ἰνδούς, αὐτοὶ δὲ τεκμαίρεσθαι τὸ μέτρον καταποντοῦσθαι τοῦτο ἢ ὑπὲρ ἀφθονίας καρπῶν, οὓς γεωργοὶ ἀπομετροῦσιν, ἢ ὑπὲρ ξυμμετρίας τοῦ ῥεύματος, ὡς μὴ κατακλύσειε τὴν γῆν πολὺς ἀφικόμενος.

20. Πορευθέντας δὲ αὐτοὺς ὑπὲρ τὸν ποταμὸν ἦγεν ὁ παρὰ τοῦ σατράπου ἡγεμὼν εὐθὺ τῶν Ταξίλων, οὗ τὰ βασίλεια ἦν τῷ Ἰνδῷ. στολὴν δὲ εἶναι τοῖς μετὰ τὸν Ἰνδὸν λίνου φασὶν ἐγχωρίου καὶ ὑποδήματα βύβλου καὶ κυνῆν, ὅτε ὕοι, καὶ βύσσῳ δὲ τοὺς φανερωτέρους αὐτῶν φασιν ἐστάλθαι, τὴν δὲ βύσσον φύεσθαι δένδρου φασὶν ὁμοίου μὲν τῇ λεύκῃ τὴν βάσιν, παραπλησίου δὲ τῇ ἰτέᾳ τὰ πέταλα. καὶ ἡσθῆναι τῇ βύσσῳ φησὶν ὁ Ἀπολλώνιος, ἐπειδὴ ἔοικε φαιῷ τρί-

many hippopotamuses and many crocodiles, as those who sail the Nile do. They say also that there are flowers in the Indus similar to those that grow in the Nile, that the climate in India is warm in winter and stifling in summer, and that it has been excellently constituted by fortune so that the soil has continual rain.

They also claim to have heard from the Indians that the 2
king visited this river when the season caused it to rise, and sacrificed black bulls and horses to it, white being held in less regard by the Indians than black because of their own color, I suppose. After his sacrifice he throws into the river a golden measure, resembling those used for measuring grain. The Indians could not make out why the king did this; but our travelers inferred that the reason for throwing in this measure was either to ensure either a plentiful harvest, which farmers "measure" out, or else a "measured" flow, so that the river should not flood the land by coming down too full.

20. When they had crossed the river, the guide from the viceroy led them straight to Taxila where the Indian had his palace. They say that those on the other side of the Indus wore the local linen, shoes of bark, and hats for the rain, while the upper class dressed in cotton. This, they relate, grows on a tree with a trunk like a poplar and with leaves like a willow. Apollonius says he was pleased by the cotton, since it looked like a gray philosopher's cloak. In

βωνι. καὶ ἐς Αἴγυπτον δὲ ἐξ Ἰνδῶν ἐς πολλὰ τῶν ἱερῶν φοιτᾷ ἡ βύσσος.

2 Τὰ δὲ Τάξιλα μέγεθος μὲν εἶναι κατὰ τὴν Νίνον, τετειχίσθαι δὲ ξυμμέτρως, ὥσπερ αἱ Ἑλλάδες, βασίλεια δὲ εἶναι ἀνδρὸς τὴν Πώρου τότε ἀρχὴν ἄρχοντος, νεὼν δὲ πρὸ τοῦ τείχους ἰδεῖν φασιν οὐ παρὰ πολὺ τῶν ἑκατομπόδων[11] λίθου κογχυλιάτου, καὶ κατεσκευάσθαι τι ἱερὸν ἐν αὐτῷ ἧττον μὲν ἢ κατὰ τὸν νεὼν τοσοῦτόν τε ὄντα καὶ περικίονα, θαυμάσαι δὲ ἄξιον· χαλκοῖ γὰρ πίνακες ἐγκεκρότηνται τοίχῳ ἑκάστῳ, γεγραμμένοι τὰ Πώρου τε καὶ Ἀλεξάνδρου ἔργα· γεγράφαται δὲ ὀρειχάλκῳ, καὶ ἀργύρῳ, καὶ χρυσῷ, καὶ χαλκῷ μέλανι ἐλέφαντες, ἵπποι, στρατιῶται, κράνη, ἀσπίδες, λόγχαι δὲ καὶ βέλη, καὶ ξίφη σιδήρου πάντα, καὶ ὥσπερ λόγος εὐδοκίμου γραφῆς, οἷον εἰ Ζεύξιδος εἴη τι ἢ Πολυγνώτου τε καὶ Εὐφράνορος, οἳ τὸ εὔσκιον ἠσπάσαντο καὶ τὸ ἔμπνουν[12] καὶ τὸ ἐσέχον τε καὶ ἐξέχον, οὕτως, φασί, κἀκεῖ διαφαίνεται, καὶ ξυντετήκασιν αἱ ὗλαι καθάπερ χρώματα.

3 Ἡδὺ δὲ καὶ αὐτὸ τὸ ἦθος τῆς γραφῆς· ἀναθεὶς γὰρ ταῦτα μετὰ τὴν τοῦ Μακεδόνος τελευτὴν ὁ Πῶρος νικᾷ ἐν αὐτοῖς ὁ Μακεδὼν, καὶ τὸν Πῶρον ἀνακτᾶται τετρωμένον, καὶ δωρεῖται τὴν Ἰνδικὴν ἑαυτοῦ λοιπὸν οὖσαν. λέγεται δὲ καὶ πενθῆσαι τὸν Ἀλέξανδρον ἀποθανόντα ὁ Πῶρος, ὀλοφύρασθαί τε ὡς γενναῖον καὶ

11 ἑκατομπόδων Kay.: ἑκατὸν ποδῶν
12 ἔμπνουν Jac.: εὔπνουν

fact, cotton comes from India to many of the sanctuaries in Egypt.

Taxila, they said, was similar to Ninos in size,[20] symmetrically fortified like a Greek city, and was the seat of the king then ruling Porus's domain. They say they saw a temple in front of the walls a little less than hundred-foot ones in length and built with shell stone.[21] Inside it there was a shrine comparatively small for such a large, many-columned temple, but worth admiring. Into every wall there are nailed bronze panels illustrating the deeds of Alexander and Porus. On them, in brass, silver, gold, and dark bronze, there are depicted elephants, horses, soldiers, helmets and shields, with spears, javelins, and swords all in iron. Just as they say of a famous painting, for example one by Zeuxis, Polygnotus, or Euphranor,[22] that the artists liked shadow, verisimilitude, and perspective, the same effects, so they say, are visible here too, and the materials are blended like colors. 2

The moral of the pictures was also pleasing. Though Porus had dedicated them after the death of the Macedonian, the Macedonian is shown as the victor, winning the wounded Porus over, and giving him India though it was now his own. They say too that Porus mourned Alexander at his death, and grieved for him as a good and noble king, 3

[20] That is, Syrian Hierapolis, the birthplace of Damis; see I 3.1.

[21] Certain temples were known as "hundred-footers" (*hekatompeda*). "Shell stone" is a kind of limestone found in the Mediterranean with embedded shells or shell fragments. There is no evidence that it was used at Taxila.

[22] Classic Greek painters of the fifth and fourth centuries BCE.

χρηστὸν βασιλέα, ζῶντός τε Ἀλεξάνδρου μετὰ τὴν ἐκ τῆς Ἰνδικῆς ἀναχώρησιν μήτε εἰπεῖν τι ὡς βασιλεὺς καίτοι ξυγχωροῦντος, μήτε προστάξαι τοῖς Ἰνδοῖς, ἀλλ᾽ ὥσπερ σατράπης σωφροσύνης μεστὸς εἶναι, καὶ πράττειν ἐς χάριν τὴν ἐκείνου πάντα.

21. Οὐ ξυγχωρεῖ μοι ὁ λόγος παρελθεῖν, ἃ περὶ τοῦ Πώρου τούτου ἀναγράφουσι· πρὸς διαβάσει γὰρ τοῦ Μακεδόνος ὄντος καὶ ξυμβουλευόντων αὐτῷ ἐνίων τοὺς ὑπὲρ τὸν Ὕφασίν τε καὶ τὸν Γάγγην ποταμὸν ποιεῖσθαι ξυμμάχους, οὐ γὰρ ἂν πρὸς τὴν Ἰνδικὴν πᾶσαν ξυμφρονοῦσαν παρατάξεσθαί ποτε αὐτόν, "εἰ τοιοῦτόν ἐστί μοι" ἔφη "τὸ ὑπήκοον, ὡς μὴ σώζεσθαι ἄνευ ξυμμάχων, ἐμοὶ βέλτιον τὸ μὴ ἄρχειν." ἀπαγγείλαντος δὲ αὐτῷ τινος, ὅτι Δαρεῖον ᾕρηκε "βασιλέα," ἔφη "ἄνδρα δὲ οὔ." τὸν δὲ ἐλέφαντα, ἐφ᾽ οὗ μάχεσθαι ἔμελλε, κοσμήσαντος τοῦ ὀρεωκόμου καὶ εἰπόντος "οὗτος σέ, ὦ βασιλεῦ, σώσει,"[13] "ἐγὼ μὲν οὖν" ἔφη "τοῦτον, ἤν γε ἀνὴρ ἐμαυτῷ ὅμοιος γένωμαι." γνώμην δὲ ποιουμένων θῦσαι αὐτὸν τῷ ποταμῷ ὡς μὴ δέξαιτο τὰς Μακεδόνων σχεδίας, μηδὲ εὔπορος τῷ Ἀλεξάνδρῳ γένοιτο, "οὐκ ἔστιν" ἔφη "τῶν ὅπλα ἐχόντων τὸ καταρᾶσθαι."

2 Μετὰ δὲ τὴν μάχην, ὅτε καὶ τῷ Ἀλεξάνδρῳ θεῖός τε καὶ ὑπὲρ τὴν φύσιν τὴν ἀνθρωπείαν ἔδοξεν, εἰπόντος τῶν ξυγγενῶν τινος, "εἰ δὲ προσεκύνησας διαβάντα, ὦ Πῶρε, οὔτ᾽ ἂν ἡττήθης μαχόμενος οὔτ᾽ ἂν τοσοῦτοι Ἰνδῶν ἀπώλοντο, οὔτ᾽ ἂν αὐτὸς ἐτέτρωσο," "ἐγὼ τὸν Ἀλέξανδρον" εἶπε "φιλοτιμότατον ἀκούων ξυνῆκα, ὅτι

and that while Alexander lived he never spoke like a king, though Alexander allowed him to, or ordered the Indians around. Like a viceroy, he was full of modesty, and did everything to please his friend.

21. My account forbids me to omit the records of this Porus. When the Macedonian was about to cross, some were advising Porus to make allies of those beyond the Hyphasis and the Ganges, saying that Alexander would not dare to confront an entirely united India. Porus however replied: "If my realm is of such a kind that it cannot be saved without allies, it would be better for me not to be king." When the news came of the capture of Darius,[23] he called him "a king, but no man." When the groom had prepared the elephant on which he was to fight, and said to him, "This will keep you safe, Majesty," he replied, "No, I will keep it safe, if I prove a man worthy of myself." When some people advised him to sacrifice to the river so that it should not bear the Macedonians' rafts or be passable for Alexander, he said, "It is not for those in arms to curse."

And after the battle, when Alexander had seen how 2
godlike he was and superhuman in nature, one of his relatives said to him, "Porus, if you had done obeisance when he crossed, you would not have been defeated in battle, or lost so many Indians, or received a wound yourself." He replied: "Having heard of Alexander's great ambition, I knew

[23] Darius III, last Achaemenid king of Persia, killed by some of his followers after the battle of Gaugamela (331 BCE).

---

13 σώσει Cob.: οἴσει

προσκυνήσαντα μὲν δοῦλόν με ἡγήσεται, πολεμήσαντα δὲ βασιλέα, καὶ θαυμάζεσθαι μᾶλλον ἠξίουν ἢ ἐλεεῖσθαι, καὶ οὐκ ἐψεύσθην· παρασχὼν γὰρ ἐμαυτόν, οἷον Ἀλέξανδρος εἶδε, πάντα ἐν ἡμέρᾳ μιᾷ καὶ ἀπώλεσα καὶ ἀνεκτησάμην."[14] τοιοῦτον μὲν τὸν Ἰνδὸν τοῦτον ἐξιστοροῦσι, γενέσθαι δέ φασιν αὐτὸν κάλλιστον Ἰνδῶν καὶ μῆκος, ὅσον οὔπω τινὰ ἀνθρώπων τῶν μετὰ τοὺς Τρωϊκοὺς ἄνδρας, εἶναι δὲ κομιδῇ νέον, ὅτε τῷ Ἀλεξάνδρῳ ἐπολέμει.

22. Ὃν δὲ διέτριβεν ἐν τῷ ἱερῷ χρόνον, πολὺς δὲ οὗτος ἐγένετο, ἔστ' ἀναγγελθείη[15] τῷ βασιλεῖ ξένους ἥκειν, "ὦ Δάμι" ἔφη ὁ Ἀπολλώνιος, "ἔστι τι γραφική;" "εἴ γε" εἶπε "καὶ ἀλήθεια." "πράττει δὲ τί ἡ τέχνη αὕτη;" "τὰ χρώματα" ἔφη "ξυγκεράννυσιν, ὁπόσα ἐστί, τὰ κυανᾶ τοῖς βατραχείοις, καὶ τὰ λευκὰ τοῖς μέλασι, καὶ τὰ πυρσὰ τοῖς ὠχροῖς." "ταυτὶ δὲ" ἦ δ' ὃς "ὑπὲρ τίνος μίγνυσιν; οὐ γὰρ ὑπὲρ μόνου τοῦ ἄνθους, ὥσπερ αἱ κήριναι."[16] "ὑπὲρ μιμήσεως" ἔφη "καὶ τοῦ κύνα τε ἐξεικάσαι, καὶ ἵππον, καὶ ἄνθρωπον, καὶ ναῦν, καὶ ὁπόσα ὁρᾷ ὁ ἥλιος. ἤδη δὲ καὶ τὸν ἥλιον αὐτὸν ἐξεικάζει τοτὲ μὲν ἐπὶ τεττάρων ἵππων, οἷος ἐνταῦθα λέγεται φαίνεσθαι, τοτὲ δ' αὖ καὶ διαπυρσεύοντα τοῦ οὐρανοῦ, ἐπειδὰν αἰθέρα ὑπογράφῃ καὶ θεῶν οἶκον." "μίμησις οὖν ἡ γραφική, ὦ Δάμι;" "τί δὲ ἄλλο;" εἶπεν "εἰ γὰρ μὴ τοῦτο πράττοι, γελοία δόξει χρώματα ποιοῦσα εὐήθως."

2 "Τὰ δ' ἐν τῷ οὐρανῷ" ἔφη "βλεπόμενα, ἐπειδὰν αἱ νεφέλαι διασπασθῶσιν ἀπ' ἀλλήλων, τοὺς κενταύρους

that if I made obeisance, he would think me a slave, but if war, a king. I preferred to be admired rather than pitied, and I was not disappointed. I proved myself the man Alexander saw me to be, and so in a single day I lost everything and regained it." This is the character which they attribute to the Indian, and they also say that he was the handsomest man in India and taller than any man since the heroes at Troy, and was very young when he warred with Alexander.

22. Apollonius spent what turned out to be a long time in this temple until the king could be informed that visitors had arrived. "Damis," he said, "is there such a thing as painting?" "Yes," said Damis, "if there is such a thing as truth." "What does this art do?" "It blends all the colors there are," said Damis, "blue with green, white with black, red with yellow." "What does it blend them for?" asked Apollonius, "since it is not simply for superficial color, like made-up women." "For imitation," Damis replied, "in order to reproduce dogs, horses, humans, ships, everything under the sun. In fact art sometimes represents the sun himself with his four horses, which is the way they say he appears in these regions; and sometimes again blazing in heaven, when art represents the heavens and the home of the gods." "So painting is imitation, Damis?" "Of course," was the reply; "if that was not its business, it would be considered absurd, a pointless mixing of colors."

"Now," said Apollonius, "the things we see in the sky, 2
when the clouds are separated from one another, centaurs

---

14 ἀνεκτησάμην Lucarini: ἐκτησάμην

15 ἀναγγελθείη Platt: ἂν ἀγγελθῇ

16 κήριναι J. Toup (Kay.): κορῖναι

καὶ τραγελάφους καὶ, νὴ Δί', οἱ λύκοι τε καὶ οἱ ἵπποι, τί φήσεις; ἆρ' οὐ μιμητικῆς εἶναι ἔργα;" "ἔοικεν," ἔφη. "ζωγράφος οὖν ὁ θεός, ὦ Δάμι, καὶ καταλιπὼν τὸ πτηνὸν ἅρμα, ἐφ' οὗ πορεύεται διακοσμῶν τὰ θεῖά τε καὶ ἀνθρώπεια, κάθηται τότε ἀθύρων τε καὶ γράφων ταῦτα, ὥσπερ οἱ παῖδες ἐν τῇ ψάμμῳ;" ἠρυθρίασεν ὁ Δάμις ἐς οὕτως ἄτοπον ἐκπεσεῖν δόξαντος τοῦ λόγου. οὐχ ὑπεριδὼν οὖν αὐτὸν ὁ Ἀπολλώνιος, οὐδὲ γὰρ πικρὸς πρὸς τὰς ἐλέγξεις ἦν, "ἀλλὰ μὴ τοῦτο" ἔφη "βούλει λέγειν, ὦ Δάμι, τὸ ταῦτα μὲν ἄσημά τε καὶ ὡς ἔτυχε διὰ τοῦ οὐρανοῦ φέρεσθαι τό γε ἐπὶ τῷ θεῷ, ἡμᾶς δὲ φύσει τὸ μιμητικὸν ἔχοντας ἀναρρυθμίζειν τε αὐτὰ καὶ ποιεῖν;" "μᾶλλον" ἔφη "τοῦτο ἡγώμεθα, ὦ Ἀπολλώνιε, πιθανώτερον γὰρ καὶ πολλῷ βέλτιον."

3 "Διττὴ ἄρα ἡ μιμητική, ὦ Δάμι, καὶ τὴν μὲν ἡγώμεθα οἵαν τῇ χειρὶ ἀπομιμεῖσθαι καὶ τῷ νῷ, γραφικὴν δὲ εἶναι ταύτην, τὴν δ' αὖ μόνῳ τῷ νῷ εἰκάζειν." "οὐ διττήν," ἔφη ὁ Δάμις "ἀλλὰ τὴν μὲν τελεωτέραν ἡγεῖσθαι προσήκει γραφικήν γε οὖσαν, ἣ δύναται καὶ τῷ νῷ καὶ τῇ χειρὶ ἐξεικάσαι, τὴν δὲ ἑτέραν ἐκείνης μόριον, ἐπειδὴ ξυνίησι μὲν καὶ μιμεῖται τῷ νῷ καὶ μὴ γραφικός τις ὤν, τῇ χειρὶ δὲ οὐκ ἂν ἐς τὸ γράφειν αὐτὰ χρήσαιτο." "ἆρα," ἔφη "ὦ Δάμι, πεπηρωμένος τὴν χεῖρα ὑπὸ πληγῆς τινος ἢ νόσου;" "μὰ Δί'" εἶπεν "ἀλλ' ὑπὸ τοῦ μήτε γραφίδος τινὸς ἧφθαι, μήτε[17] ὀργάνου τινὸς ἢ χρώματος, ἀλλ' ἀμαθῶς ἔχειν τοῦ γράφειν."

4 "Οὐκοῦν," ἔφη "ὦ Δάμι, ἄμφω ὁμολογοῦμεν μι-

and goat-deer, and wolves and horses for that matter—how do you account for them? As the results of imitation, surely?" "I suppose so," Damis said. "Then does god seem to be an artist, Damis? Does he leave the winged chariot in which he travels setting the affairs of gods and men to right, and does he then sit drawing these things for fun, as boys do in sand?" Damis blushed at the absurd conclusion to which his argument seemed to come, but Apollonius did not humiliate him, for he was not harsh in refutation, but said, "Surely what you mean, Damis, is that the things passing through the sky are shapeless and haphazard as far as god is concerned, but we, because imitation is in our nature, rearrange and create them?" "Yes," said Damis, "let us rather think that, Apollonius, as it is more plausible and far better."

"Well then, imitation is of two kinds, Damis. Let us 3
hold that one kind is imitation of both the hand and the mind, and this is painting, and the other is imagination of the mind alone." "It is not of two kinds," said Damis. "The one kind we should consider more perfect, since it is painting, which can depict both with the mind and the hand, whereas the other is a part of the first, since one can comprehend and copy things in the mind without being a painter, but he cannot use his hand to represent them." "Because his hand is maimed by an injury or by disease, Damis?" asked Apollonius. "Of course not," said Damis, "but because he has never handled any kind of brush, tool, or color, and is ignorant of painting."

"Well then, Damis," said Apollonius, "we are both 4

---

[17] μήτε West.: μηδὲ

μητικὴν μὲν ἐκ φύσεως τοῖς ἀνθρώποις ἥκειν, τὴν γραφικὴν δὲ ἐκ τέχνης. τουτὶ δ᾽ ἂν καὶ περὶ τὴν πλαστικὴν φαίνοιτο. τὴν δὲ δὴ ζωγραφίαν αὐτὴν οὔ μοι δοκεῖς μόνον τὴν διὰ τῶν χρωμάτων ἡγεῖσθαι, καὶ γὰρ ἓν χρῶμα ἐς αὐτὴν ἤρκεσε τοῖς γε ἀρχαιοτέροις τῶν γραφέων, καὶ προϊοῦσα τεττάρων εἶτα πλειόνων ἥψατο, ἀλλὰ καὶ γραμμὴν καὶ τὸ ἄνευ χρώματος, ὃ δὴ σκιᾶς τε ξύγκειται καὶ φωτός, ζωγραφίαν προσήκει καλεῖν. καὶ γὰρ ἐν αὐτοῖς ὁμοιότης τε ὁρᾶται εἶδός τε καὶ νοῦς καὶ αἰδὼς καὶ θρασύτης, καίτοι χηρεύει χρωμάτων ταῦτα, καὶ οὔτε αἷμα ἐνσημαίνει οὔτε κόμης τινὸς ἢ ὑπήνης ἄνθος, ἀλλὰ μονοτρόπως ξυντιθέμενα τῷ τε ξανθῷ ἀνθρώπῳ ἔοικε καὶ τῷ λευκῷ. κἂν τούτων τινὰ τῶν Ἰνδῶν λευκῇ τῇ γραμμῇ γράψωμεν, μέλας δήπου δόξει, τὸ γὰρ ὑπόσιμον τῆς ῥινὸς καὶ οἱ ὀρθοὶ βόστρυχοι καὶ ἡ περιττὴ γένυς καὶ ἡ περὶ τοῖς ὀφθαλμοῖς οἷον ἔκπληξις μελαίνει τὰ ὁρώμενα, καὶ Ἰνδὸν ὑπογράφει τοῖς γε μὴ ἀνοήτως ὁρῶσιν.

5 "Ὅθεν εἴποιμ᾽ ἂν καὶ τοὺς ὁρῶντας τὰ τῆς γραφικῆς ἔργα μιμητικῆς δεῖσθαι. οὐ γὰρ ἂν ἐπαινέσειέ τις τὸν γεγραμμένον ἵππον ἢ ταῦρον μὴ τὸ ζῷον ἐνθυμηθείς, ᾧ εἴκασται, οὐδ᾽ ἂν τὸν Αἴαντά τις τὸν Τιμομάχου ἀγασθείη, ὃς δὴ ἀναγέγραπται αὐτῷ μεμηνώς, εἰ μὴ ἀναλάβοι τι ἐς τὸν νοῦν Αἴαντος εἴδωλον καὶ ὡς εἰκὸς αὐτὸν ἀπεκτονότα τὰ ἐν τῇ Τροίᾳ βουκόλια καθῆσθαι ἀπειρηκότα, βουλὴν ποιούμενον καὶ

agreed that the art of imitation comes to humans from nature, but that of painting from skill, and the same would appear to be true of sculpture. But, to take portraiture, I do not think you consider it merely the art of using colors, since painters of earlier times were content with only one color, and as portraiture advanced it involved four and then more colors. Line-drawing and monochrome, involving only light and shade, deserve to be called portraiture too, since in them too we can see similarity, shape, intelligence, modesty, boldness, although they are devoid of color and do not indicate blood or the color of a person's hair or beard, but being composed in one color, they convey a fair-haired man and a white-haired one. And if we draw one of these Indians with a white line, he will surely seem black; the snub nose, fuzzy hair, prominent jaws, and a look of surprise, as it were, in the eyes lend blackness to the picture, and convey an Indian at least to an educated observer.[24]

"I would say, then, that those who view the works of 5
painters need the imitative faculty, since no one will praise the picture of a horse or bull if he has no idea of the creature represented. No one is likely to admire Timomachus's Ajax, when the artist represents him as insane, if he does not call to mind the image of Ajax and how he is likely to have looked after killing the cattle at Troy, sitting in despair and turning over the thought of suicide.[25] But these reliefs

[24] The meaning seems to be that drawing with black on a white surface is enough to convey the impression of a white man, and drawing with white on a black surface that of a black one.

[25] Timomachus is a painter of disputed date from Byzantium. His *Mad Ajax* was purchased by Julius Caesar and displayed at Rome.

ἑαυτὸν κτεῖναι. ταυτὶ δέ, ὦ Δάμι, τὰ τοῦ Πώρου δαίδαλα μήτε χαλκευτικῆς μόνον ἀποφαινώμεθα, γεγραμμένοις γὰρ εἴκασται, μήτε γραφικῆς, ἐπειδὴ ἐχαλκεύθη, ἀλλ᾽ ἡγώμεθα σοφίσασθαι αὐτὰ γραφικόν τε καὶ χαλκευτικὸν ἕνα ἄνδρα, οἷον δή τι παρ᾽ Ὁμήρῳ τὸ τοῦ Ἡφαίστου περὶ τὴν τοῦ Ἀχιλλέως ἀσπίδα ἀναφαίνεται. μεστὰ γὰρ καὶ ταῦτα 'ὀλλύντων τε καὶ ὀλλυμένων,' καὶ τὴν γῆν ᾑματῶσθαι φήσεις χαλκῆν οὖσαν."

23. Τοιαῦτα σπουδάζοντι τῷ ἀνδρὶ ἐφίστανται παρὰ τοῦ βασιλέως ἄγγελοι καὶ ἑρμηνεύς, ὡς ποιοῖτο αὐτὸν ὁ βασιλεὺς ξένον ἐς τρεῖς ἡμέρας, μὴ γὰρ πλειόνων νενομίσθαι τοὺς ξένους ἐνομιλεῖν τῇ πόλει, καὶ ἡγοῦντο αὐτῷ ἐς τὰ βασίλεια. ἡ πόλις δ᾽ ὡς μὲν ἔχει τοῦ τείχους, εἴρηκα, φασὶ δ᾽ ὡς εὐτάκτως τε καὶ Ἀττικῶς τοὺς στενωποὺς τέτμηται κατεσκεύασταί τε οἰκίαις, εἰ μὲν ἔξωθεν ὁρῴη τις αὐτάς, ἕνα ἐχούσαις ὄροφον, εἰ δ᾽ ἔσω παρέλθοι τις, ὑπογείοις ἤδη καὶ παρεχομέναις ἴσα τοῖς ἄνω τὰ ὑπὸ τῇ γῇ.

24. Ἱερὸν δὲ ἰδεῖν Ἡλίου φασίν, ᾧ ἀνεῖτο Αἴας ἐλέφας, καὶ ἀγάλματα Ἀλεξάνδρου χρυσᾶ καὶ Πώρου ἕτερα, χαλκοῦ δ᾽ ἦν ταῦτα μέλανος. οἱ δὲ τοῦ ἱεροῦ τοῖχοι, πυρσαῖς λίθοις ὑπαστράπτει χρυσὸς αὐγὴν ἐκδιδοὺς ἐοικυῖαν ἀκτῖνι. τὸ δὲ ἕδος αὐτὸ μαργαρίτιδος ξύγκειται ξυμβολικὸν τρόπον, ᾧ βάρβαροι πάντες ἐς τὰ ἱερὰ χρῶνται.

---

[26] Homer, *Iliad* 18.483–608.

of Porus, Damis, we should not define merely as the work of bronze-casters since they look like pictures, or as the work of painters, since they are cast in bronze. Let us rather think them the creations of a single man who combined the arts of painting and bronze-casting, just as Hephaestus is represented in Homer doing with the shield of Achilles.[26] Those pictures too are full of men 'killing and being killed,'[27] and one can say that the ground is smeared with blood, even though it is of bronze."

23. As the Master was giving this discourse, messengers arrived from the king with an interpreter, announcing that he would have Apollonius as his guest for three days, since it was not lawful for strangers to stay in the city longer, and they led the way to the palace. I have mentioned what the walls of the city were like. The party says that it was divided into orderly rows of houses like Athens,[28] and the houses were so built that from the outside they appeared to be of only one story, but when you went inside they proved to be subterranean, and of the same height below ground as above.

24. They say there was also a shrine of the Sun, to whom Ajax the elephant had been consecrated,[29] and statues of Alexander in gold and others of Porus which were of dark bronze. The walls of the shrine were of red stone that had a golden sheen, giving off a light like the sun's rays. The image itself was of mother-of-pearl, made in the symbolic shape that all barbarians use for their holy objects.

27 Homer, *Iliad* 4.451, 8.65.

28 Some of the excavated streets of Taxila are in fact laid out in rectangles. Some manuscripts have "disorderly" (*ataktōs*).

29 See 12.2.

25. Περὶ δὲ τὰ βασίλεια οὔτε ὄγκον ἰδεῖν φασιν οἰκοδομημάτων, οὔτε δορυφόρους ἢ φύλακας, ἀλλ᾽ οἷα περὶ τὰς τῶν λαμπρῶν οἰκίας, ὀλίγους οἰκέτας καὶ διαλεχθῆναι τῷ βασιλεῖ δεομένους τρεῖς, οἶμαι, ἢ τέτταρας, καὶ τὸν κόσμον τοῦτον ἀγασθῆναι μᾶλλον ἢ τὰ ἐν Βαβυλῶνι φλεγμαίνοντα, καὶ πολλῷ πλέον ἔσω παρελθόντες· καὶ γὰρ τοὺς ἀνδρῶνας καὶ τὰς στοὰς καὶ τὴν αὐλὴν πᾶσαν κεκολάσθαι φασίν.

26. Ἔδοξεν οὖν τῷ Ἀπολλωνίῳ φιλοσοφεῖν ὁ Ἰνδὸς καὶ παραστησάμενος τὸν ἑρμηνέα "χαίρω," εἶπεν "ὦ βασιλεῦ, φιλοσοφοῦντά σε ὁρῶν." "ἐγὼ δὲ ὑπερχαίρω," ἔφη, "ἐπειδὴ οὕτω περὶ ἐμοῦ οἴει." "τουτὶ δὲ νενόμισται παρ᾽ ὑμῖν," εἶπεν, "ἢ σὺ πρὸς τὸ ἐπιεικὲς τοῦτο τὴν ἀρχὴν κατεστήσω;" "σωφρόνως" ἔφη "νενομισμένῳ σωφρονέστερον χρῶμαι, καὶ πλεῖστα μὲν ἔχω ἀνθρώπων, δέομαι δὲ ὀλίγων, τὰ γὰρ πολλὰ τῶν φίλων τῶν ἐμαυτοῦ ἡγοῦμαι." "μακάριε τοῦ θησαυροῦ," εἶπεν, "εἰ χρυσοῦ τε καὶ ἀργύρου ἀντερύῃ τοὺς φίλους, ἐξ ὧν ἀναφύεταί σοι πολλά τε καὶ ἀγαθά." "καὶ μὴν καὶ τοῖς ἐχθροῖς" ἔφη, "κοινωνῶ τοῦ πλούτου. τοὺς γὰρ ἀεί ποτε διαφόρους τῇ χώρᾳ ταύτῃ βαρβάρους προσοικοῦντας, καὶ καταδρομαῖς χρωμένους ἐς τἀμὰ ὅρια, ὑποποιοῦμαι τουτοισὶ τοῖς χρήμασι καὶ δορυφορεῖταί μοι ὑπ᾽ αὐτῶν ἡ χώρα, καὶ οὔτε αὐτοὶ ἐπὶ τἀμὰ φοιτῶσι τούς τε ὁμόρους αὐτοῖς βαρβάρους ἀνείργουσι, χαλεποὺς ὄντας." ἐρομένου δὲ αὐτὸν τοῦ Ἀπολλωνίου, εἰ καὶ Πῶρος αὐτοῖς ἐτέλει

25. In the palace they say that they saw no elaborate rooms, no bodyguards or watchmen, but just as in the houses of the upper class a few slaves and three or four people awaiting an audience with the king. They say they admired this simplicity more than the splendor of Babylon, and even more so when they went inside, since they say that the men's quarters and the colonnades and the whole forecourt were plain.

26. Apollonius concluded that the Indian was a philosopher and, keeping the interpreter beside him, he said, "I am glad, king, to see that you are a philosopher." "I am very glad," he replied, "that you think me so." "Is this the custom with you," said Apollonius, "or did you introduce this moderation into your kingdom?" "Our customs are modest, and I observe them even more modestly," he replied. "I have more than any human, but need little, considering most things to belong to my own friends." "Congratulations on your treasure," said Apollonius, "if you value your friends above gold and silver, and many advantages accrue to you from them." "Why," he said, "I give a share of my riches to my enemies too. There once were barbarians constantly hostile to my country, who made incursions across my borders, but I win them over with this money and they patrol my realm. They do not encroach on my possessions, but keep out their barbarian neighbors, who are fierce." Apollonius asked him if Porus too had paid

χρήματα, "Πῶρος" εἶπε "πολέμου ἤρα, ἐγὼ δὲ εἰρήνης."

2 Πάνυ τοῖς λόγοις τούτοις ἐχειροῦτο τὸν Ἀπολλώνιον, καὶ οὕτως αὐτοῦ ἡττήθη, ὡς Εὐφράτῃ ποτὲ ἐπιπλήττων μὴ φιλοσοφοῦντι "ἡμεῖς δὲ ἀλλὰ τὸν Ἰνδὸν Φραώτην αἰδώμεθα," φάναι, ὄνομα γὰρ τῷ Ἰνδῷ τοῦτο ἦν. σατράπου δέ, ἐπειδὴ μεγάλων παρ᾽ αὐτοῦ ἠξιώθη, βουληθέντος αὐτὸν ἀναδῆσαι μίτρᾳ χρυσῇ κεκοσμημένῃ λίθοις ποικίλοις, "ἐγώ," ἔφη, "εἰ καὶ τῶν ζηλούντων τὰ τοιαῦτα ἦν, παρῃτησάμην ἂν αὐτὰ νῦν καὶ ἀπέρριψα τῆς κεφαλῆς Ἀπολλωνίῳ ἐντυχών, οἷς δὲ μήπω πρότερον ἀναδεῖσθαι ἠξίωσα, πῶς ἂν νῦν κοσμοίμην τὸν μὲν ξένον ἀγνοήσας, ἐμαυτοῦ δὲ ἐκλαθόμενος;"

3 Ἤρετο αὐτὸν καὶ περὶ διαίτης ὁ Ἀπολλώνιος, ὁ δὲ "οἴνου μὲν" ἔφη "πίνω τοσοῦτον, ὅσον τῷ Ἡλίῳ σπένδω, ἃ δ᾽ ἂν ἐν θήρᾳ λάβω, ταῦτα σιτοῦνται ἕτεροι, ἐμοὶ δ᾽ ἀπόχρη τὸ γεγυμνάσθαι. τὰ δὲ ἐμὰ σιτία λάχανα καὶ φοινίκων ἐγκέφαλοι καὶ ὁ καρπὸς τῶν φοινίκων καὶ ὁπόσα ὁ ποταμὸς κηπεύει. πολλὰ δέ μοι καὶ ἀπὸ δένδρων φύεται, ὧν γεωργοὶ αἵδε αἱ χεῖρες." ταῦτα ἀκούων ὁ Ἀπολλώνιος ὑπερήδετό τε καὶ ἐς τὸν Δάμιν θαμὰ ἑώρα.

27. Ἐπεὶ δὲ ἱκανῶς διελέχθησαν περὶ τῆς ὁδοῦ τῆς παρὰ τοὺς Βραχμᾶνας, τὸν μὲν παρὰ τοῦ Βαβυλωνίου ἡγεμόνα ἐκέλευσε ξενίζειν, ὥσπερ εἰώθει τοὺς ἐκ Βαβυλῶνος ἥκοντας, τὸν δὲ παρὰ τοῦ σατράπου ἀπιέναι λαβόντα ἐφόδια. αὐτὸς δὲ λαβόμενος τῆς τοῦ Ἀπολ-

them money. "Porus loved war," he replied, "but I love peace."

Apollonius was quite won over by these remarks, and 2
was so struck by him that once, when he was rebuking Euphrates for not being a philosopher, he said, "But let us at least respect the Indian Phraotes" (since that was the Indian's name).[30] A viceroy who had been greatly favored by him wanted to crown him with a golden diadem studded with multicolored stones, but he said, "Even if I were the kind of man to covet such things, I would have declined them now and torn them from my head on meeting Apollonius. But since I never saw fit to wear such crowns before, how could I use ornaments now, mistaking my guest and forgetting myself?"

Apollonius also asked him about his diet and he said, 3
"Of wine I drink as much as I pour out to the Sun, and others eat the spoils of my hunting, since the exercise is enough for me. My food consists of vegetables, the pith and fruit of date palms, and everything that the river nourishes. I also eat many things from trees cultivated by these hands of mine." Apollonius was delighted when he heard this, and kept glancing at Damis.

27. When they had conversed enough about the journey to the Brahmans, the king gave orders for the guide from the king of Babylon to be entertained, as was his custom with visitors from Babylon, and dismissed the guide from the viceroy with provisions for the road. Then, taking

30 No king of this name is known among the rulers of Taxila.

λωνίου χειρός, καὶ κελεύσας ἀπελθεῖν τὸν ἑρμηνέα "ἆρ' ἂν" ἔφη "ποιήσαιό με συμπότην;" ἤρετο δ' αὐτὸν φωνῇ Ἑλλάδι. ἐκπλαγέντος δὲ τοῦ Ἀπολλωνίου, καὶ "τοῦ χάριν οὐκ ἐξ ἀρχῆς οὕτω διελέγου;" φήσαντος, "ἔδεισα" ἔφη "θρασὺς δόξαι μὴ γιγνώσκων ἐμαυτόν, μηδ' ὅτι βάρβαρον εἶναί με δοκεῖ τῇ τύχῃ, σοῦ δὲ ἡττηθείς, ἐπειδὴ καὶ σὲ ὁρῶ ἐμοὶ χαίροντα, οὐκ ἠδυνήθην ἐμαυτὸν κρύπτειν, ὡς δὲ μεστός εἰμι τῆς Ἑλλήνων φωνῆς, ἐν πολλοῖς δηλώσω."

2 "Τί οὖν" εἶπεν "οὐκ αὐτὸς ἐπήγγειλας ἐμοὶ τὸ συμπόσιον, ἀλλ' ἐμέ σοι κελεύεις ἐπαγγέλλειν;" "ὅτι σε" ἔφη "βελτίω ἐμαυτοῦ ἡγοῦμαι, τὸ γὰρ βασιλικώτερον σοφία ἔχει." καὶ ἅμα ἦγεν αὐτόν τε καὶ τοὺς ἀμφ' αὐτόν, οὗπερ εἰώθει λοῦσθαι. τὸ δὲ βαλανεῖον παράδεισος ἦν σταδίου μῆκος, ᾧ μέση κολυμβήθρα ἐνωρώρυκτο πηγὰς ἐκδεχομένη ποτίμου τε καὶ ψυχροῦ ὕδατος, τὰ δὲ ἐφ' ἑκάτερα δρόμοι ἦσαν, ἐν οἷς ἀκοντίῳ τε καὶ δίσκῳ τὸν Ἑλληνικὸν τρόπον ἑαυτὸν ἐξήσκει, καὶ γὰρ τὸ σῶμα ἔρρωτο ὑπό τε ἡλικίας, ἑπτὰ γὰρ καὶ εἴκοσιν ἔτη γεγονὼς ἦν, ὑπό τε τοῦ ὧδε γυμνάζεσθαι. ἐπεὶ δὲ ἱκανῶς ἔχοι, ἐπήδα ἐς τὸ ὕδωρ καὶ ἐγύμναζεν ἑαυτὸν τῷ νεῖν. ὡς δὲ ἐλούσαντο, ἐβάδιζον ἐς τὸ συσσίτιον ἐστεφανωμένοι, τουτὶ δὲ νενόμισται Ἰνδοῖς, ἐπειδὰν ἐν[18] τοῦ βασιλέως πίνωσιν.

28. Ἄξιον δὲ μηδὲ τὸ σχῆμα παραλιπεῖν τοῦ πότου σαφῶς γε ἀναγεγραμμένον ὑπὸ τοῦ Δάμιδος· εὐωχεῖ-

[18] ἐν Richards: ἐς

Apollonius's hand, and ordering the interpreter to leave, he said, "Will you make me your drinking-companion?" asking him in the Greek language. In amazement Apollonius asked, "Why did you not talk this way from the beginning?" "I was afraid," said the king, "to appear forward and not 'to know myself,'[31] or that it pleases fate to make me a barbarian. But overcome by you, and seeing that you are pleased with me, I could not conceal my true self, and will fully satisfy you that I am thoroughly grounded in the Greek language."

"Well then," said Apollonius, "why did not you invite 2
me to dinner yourself instead of asking me to invite you?" "Because I think you are superior to me," he said, "since wisdom is more kingly." So saying, he led Apollonius and his party to the place where he usually bathed. His bathing place was a park about a stade long. In the middle a pool had been dug so that springs of cold, drinkable water flowed into it, and on either side there were tracks in which the king practiced the javelin and the discus in the Greek way, for he was strong in body both because of his age (since he was twenty-seven) and because of this exercise. Whenever he had had enough, he would jump into the water and exercise himself by swimming. When they had bathed, they proceeded to the dining room wearing wreaths, since that is the custom of the Indians when they drink in the king's presence.

28. It would not be right to omit the arrangement of the feast either, since Damis has described it in detail. The

[31] Alluding to the Delphic maxim "Know thyself."

ται μὲν γὰρ ἐπὶ στιβάδος ὁ βασιλεὺς καὶ τῶν ξυγγενῶν μέχρι πέντε οἱ ἐγγύς, οἱ δὲ λοιποὶ πάντες ἐν θάκοις συσσιτοῦσι. τράπεζα δέ, ὥσπερ βωμὸς ὕψος ἐς γόνυ ἀνδρὸς ἐξῳκοδόμηται μέση, κύκλον ἐπέχουσα χοροῦ ξυμβεβλημένου ἀνδρῶν τριάκοντα, ἐφ᾿ ἧς δάφναι τε διαστρώννυνται καὶ κλῶνες ἕτεροι παραπλήσιοι μὲν τῇ μυρρίνῃ, φέροντες δὲ Ἰνδοῖς μύρον. ἐνταῦθα διάκεινται ἰχθῦς μὲν καὶ ὄρνιθες, διάκεινται δὲ λέοντές τε ὅλοι καὶ δορκάδες καὶ σύες καὶ τίγρεων ὀσφύες (τὰ γὰρ λοιπὰ τοῦ θηρίου παραιτοῦνται ἐσθίειν, ἐπειδὴ τὸ ζῷον τοῦτό φασιν, ὅταν πρῶτον γένηται, τοὺς ἐμπροσθίους τῶν ποδῶν ἀνίσχοντι αἴρειν τῷ Ἡλίῳ). καὶ ἀνιστάμενος ὁ δαιτυμὼν φοιτᾷ πρὸς τὴν τράπεζαν καὶ τὰ μὲν ἀνελόμενος τούτων, τὰ δὲ ἀποτεμὼν ἀπελθὼν ἐς τὸν ἑαυτοῦ θᾶκον ἐμπίπλαται, θαμινὰ ἐπεσθίων τοῦ ἄρτου.

2 Ἐπειδὰν δὲ ἱκανῶς ἔχωσιν, ἐσφέρονται κρατῆρες ἀργυροῖ τε καὶ χρυσοῖ, δέκα συμπόταις ἀποχρῶν εἷς, ἀφ᾿ ὧν πίνουσι κύψαντες, ὥσπερ ποτιζόμενοι. μεταξὺ δὲ πίνοντες ἐπεσάγονται ἀγερωχίας ἐπικινδύνους καὶ οὐκ ἔξω τοῦ σπουδάζειν· παῖς γάρ τις, ὥσπερ ὁ τῶν ὀρχηστρίδων, ἀνερριπτεῖτο κούφως συναφιεμένου αὐτῷ βέλους ἐς τὸ ἄνω, καὶ ἐπειδὴ πολὺ ἀπὸ τῆς γῆς γένοιτο, ἐκυβίστα ὁ παῖς ὑπεραίρων ἑαυτὸν τοῦ βέλους, καὶ ἁμαρτόντι τοῦ κυβιστᾶν ἕτοιμα ἦν βεβλῆσθαι· ὁ γὰρ τοξότης πρὶν ἀφιέναι περιῄει τοὺς ξυμπότας ἐπιδεικνὺς τὴν ἀκίδα καὶ διδοὺς ἔλεγχον τοῦ βέλους. καὶ τὸ διὰ σφενδόνης δὲ τοξεῦσαι,

king dines on a couch with no more than five of his close kin, while all the rest sit on chairs to share the meal. There is a table built in the middle like an pedestal about the height of a man's knee, and with a circumference as large as a circle of thirty people close together. On it they strew branches of laurel and of other plants that resemble laurel, but in India produce perfume, and they set out fish, fowl, whole lions, venison, boar, and loins of tiger (they avoid eating the other parts of this animal, since they say that immediately after birth it raises its front paws to the rising sun). The guest gets up, goes to the table, and taking or carving what he likes, goes back to his chair and takes his fill, eating a lot of bread as well.

When they are satisfied, bowls of silver and gold are 2
carried in, each one enough for ten guests, and they bend over to drink from them like animals being watered. As they drink, they exhibit shows of skill that are dangerous and quite worth attention. A boy, like the ones that accompany dancing girls, was tossed high while an arrow was shot at the same time into the air, and when the boy was high above the ground he twisted himself, lifting himself over the arrow, sure of being hit if he twisted wrongly, since before shooting the archer went round the diners showing the point and letting them test the arrow. Shooting through

καὶ τὸ ἐς τρίχα ἰέναι, καὶ τὸν υἱὸν τὸν ἑαυτοῦ σκιαγραφῆσαι βέλεσιν ἀνεστῶτα πρὸς σανίδα, σπουδάζουσιν ἐν τοῖς πότοις, καὶ κατορθοῦσιν αὐτὰ μεθύοντες.

29. Οἱ μὲν δὴ περὶ τὸν Δάμιν ἐξεπλήττοντο αὐτὰ ὡς εὔσκοπα καὶ τὴν ξυμμετρίαν τῆς τοξείας ἐθαύμαζον, ὁ δὲ Ἀπολλώνιος, ξυνεσίτει γὰρ τῷ βασιλεῖ ὁμοδιαίτῳ ὄντι, τούτοις μὲν ἧττον προσεῖχε, πρὸς δὲ τὸν βασιλέα "εἰπέ μοι, ὦ βασιλεῦ," ἔφη "πόθεν οὕτως ἔχεις φωνῆς Ἑλλάδος φιλοσοφία τε ἡ περὶ σὲ πόθεν ἐνταῦθα; οὐ γὰρ ἐς διδασκάλους γε οἶμαι ἀναφέρειν, ἐπεὶ μηδὲ εἶναί τινας ἐν Ἰνδοῖς εἰκὸς διδασκάλους τούτου."

2 Γελάσας οὖν ὁ βασιλεὺς "οἱ μὲν παλαιοὶ" ἔφη "τὰς ἐρωτήσεις τῶν καταπλεόντων ἐποιοῦντο, εἰ λησταί εἰσιν, οὕτως αὐτὸ καίτοι χαλεπὸν ὂν κοινὸν ἡγοῦντο, ὑμεῖς δέ μοι δοκεῖτε τοὺς ἐπιφοιτῶντας ὑμῖν ἐρωτᾶν, μὴ φιλόσοφοί εἰσιν, οὕτως αὐτὸ καίτοι θειότατον τῶν κατ' ἀνθρώπους ὂν καὶ τοῖς ἐπιτυχοῦσιν ὑπάρχειν οἴεσθε. καὶ ὅτι μὲν παρ' ὑμῖν ταὐτὸν τῷ λῃστεύειν ἐστίν, οἶδα, ὁμοίῳ μὲν γὰρ σοὶ ἀνδρὶ οὔ φασιν εἶναι ἐντυχεῖν, τοὺς δὲ πολλοὺς ὥσπερ σκυλεύσαντας αὐτὸ ἑτέρων περιβεβλῆσθαί τε ἀναρμόστως καὶ σοβεῖν ἀλλοτρίαν ἐσθῆτα ἐπισύροντας· καὶ νὴ Δί', ὥσπερ οἱ λῃσταὶ τρυφῶσιν εἰδότες ὅτι ὑπὸ τῇ δίκῃ κεῖνται, οὕτω κἀκείνους φασὶ γαστρί τε διδόναι, καὶ ἀφροδισίοις, καὶ ἀμπεχόνῃ λεπτῇ. τὸ δὲ αἴτιον· νόμοι ὑμῖν, οἶμαι, εἰσίν, εἰ μὲν τὸ νόμισμα παραφθείροι τις,

a hoop, aiming at a hair, and outlining one's own son with arrows while he stands against a board, these constitute their pursuits as they drink, and they succeed in doing them even when drunk.

29. Damis and the others were amazed by this sharpness of eye, and admired the accuracy of the shooting, but Apollonius, who was eating with the king at the same table, was not so interested in such things, and said to the king: "Tell me, king, how it is that you have such command of Greek, and where did you get your philosophy from in these parts? I do not think you will ascribe it to teachers, since there is not likely to be anybody to teach this subject in India."

The king said with a laugh, "Men of old had this question about those arriving by sea, whether they were pirates, so common did they consider piracy to be, despite its cruelty. But you people seem to me to ask your visitors whether they are philosophers, so much do you consider this within the competence even of ordinary people, though it is the most divine of human possessions. Among you, I know, it is no different from piracy, since I hear that it is impossible to meet men of your own type. With most of you, philosophy is something filched from others, which people wear like an ill-fitting garment, prancing around dressed in other people's clothes. Indeed, just as pirates indulge themselves, knowing that they are liable to the law, so they say those types are devoted to gluttony, sex, and fine haberdashery. The reason is that you have laws to put 2

ἀποθνήσκειν αὐτόν, καὶ παιδίον εἴ τις παρεγγράφοι,[19] ἢ οὐκ οἶδ' ὅ τι ἐπὶ τούτῳ, τοὺς δὲ τὴν φιλοσοφίαν ὑποβαλλομένους ἢ παραφθείροντας οὐδείς, οἶμαι, νόμος παρ' ὑμῖν ἴσχει, οὐδὲ ἀρχή τις ἐπ' αὐτοὺς τέτακται.

30. "Παρ' ἡμῖν δὲ ὀλίγοι μὲν τοῦ φιλοσοφεῖν ἅπτονται, δοκιμάζονται δὲ ὧδε· χρὴ τὸν νέον, ἐπειδὰν ὀκτωκαίδεκα ἔτη γεγονὼς τύχῃ, τουτὶ δ', οἶμαι, καὶ παρ' ὑμῖν ἐφήβου μέτρον, ὑπὲρ τὸν Ὕφασιν ποταμὸν ἐλθεῖν παρὰ τοὺς ἄνδρας, <ἐς>[20] οὓς σὺ ὥρμηκας, εἰπόντα δημοσίᾳ πρότερον ὅτι φιλοσοφήσοι, ἵν' ᾖ τοῖς βουλομένοις ἐξείργειν αὐτόν, εἰ μὴ καθαρὸς φοιτῴη. καθαρὸν δὲ λέγω πρῶτον μὲν τὸ ἐς πατέρα καὶ μητέρα ἧκον, μὴ περὶ αὐτοὺς ὄνειδός τι ἀναφαίνοιτο, εἶθ' οἱ τούτων γονεῖς καὶ τρίτον γένος ἐς ἄνω, μὴ ὑβριστής τις ἢ ἀκρατὴς ἢ χρηματιστὴς ἄδικος. ὅταν δὲ μηδεμία οὐλὴ περὶ τούτους ἀναφαίνηται, μηδὲ στίγμα ὅλως μηδέν, αὐτὸν ἤδη διορᾶν τὸν νέον καὶ βασανίζειν, πρῶτον μέν, εἰ μνημονικός, εἶτα, εἰ κατὰ φύσιν αἰδήμων, ἀλλὰ μὴ πλαττόμενος τοῦτο, μὴ μεθυστικός, μὴ λίχνος, μὴ ἀλαζών, μὴ φιλόγελως, μὴ θρασύς, μὴ φιλολοίδορος, εἰ πατρὸς ὑπήκοος, εἰ μητρός, εἰ διδασκάλων, εἰ παιδαγωγῶν, ἐπὶ πᾶσιν, εἰ μὴ κακὸς περὶ τὴν ἑαυτοῦ ὥραν.

2 "Τὰ μὲν δὴ τῶν γειναμένων αὐτὸν καὶ οἳ ἐκείνους ἐγείναντο, ἐκ μαρτύρων ἀναλέγονται καὶ γραμμάτων, ἃ δημοσίᾳ κεῖται. ἐπειδὰν γὰρ τελευτήσῃ ὁ Ἰνδός, φοιτᾷ ἐπὶ θύρας αὐτοῦ μία ἀρχὴ τεταγμένη ὑπὸ τῶν

someone to death for counterfeiting money, or entering a son illegally as a citizen, and whatever you like in addition, but you have no law restraining those who falsely claim or corrupt philosophy, and there is no magistrate appointed against such people.

30. "With us, however, few people aim to be philosophers, and they are examined as follows. The young man who has attained the age of eighteen (which I think is also your criterion for an ephebe) goes across the river Hyphasis to the Masters whom you are seeking, after first making an open profession of his intention to be a philosopher, so that anyone who wishes can exclude him if he is not a pure student. By 'pure' I mean first as regards his father and mother, in whom nothing disgraceful must appear, and then his parents up to the third generation; none of them must be violent, or dissolute, or dishonest in making money. If no such defect appears in them, and no blemish of any kind, then they inspect and test the young man. First, has he a good memory? Then, is he self-respecting by nature and not by pretence, not a drunkard, a glutton, a boaster or a prankster, not rash or argumentative? Is he obedient to his father, mother, teachers, guides, above all, does he use his young looks for vice?

"Information about his parents and their parents they 2
collect from witnesses and from documents that are publicly available. For when an Indian dies, there goes to his house a special magistrate appointed by the laws to record

---

19 παρεγγράφοι Kay.: παρεγγράψαιτο or παραγράψαιτο
20 <ἐς> Jon.

νόμων ἀναγράφειν αὐτόν, ὡς ἐβίω, καὶ ψευσαμένῳ τι ἢ ψευσθέντι τῷ ἄρχοντι ἐπιτιμῶσιν οἱ νόμοι μὴ ἄρξαι αὐτὸν ἔτι ἀρχὴν μηδεμίαν, ὡς παραποιήσαντα βίον ἀνθρώπου. τὰ δὲ τῶν ἐφήβων ἐς αὐτοὺς ὁρῶντες ἀναμανθάνουσι· πολλὰ μὲν γὰρ ὀφθαλμοὶ τῶν ἀνθρωπείων ἠθῶν ἑρμηνεύουσι, πολλὰ δ' ἐν ὀφρύσι καὶ παρειαῖς κεῖται γνωματεύειν τε καὶ θεωρεῖν, ἀφ' ὧν σοφοί τε καὶ φυσικοὶ ἄνδρες, ὥσπερ ἐν κατόπτρῳ εἴδωλα, τοὺς νοῦς τῶν ἀνθρώπων διαθεῶνται. μεγάλων γὰρ δὴ ἀξιουμένης φιλοσοφίας ἐνταῦθα, καὶ τιμὴν τούτου παρ' Ἰνδοῖς ἔχοντος, ἀνάγκη πᾶσα ἐκβασανίζεσθαί τε τοὺς ἐπ' αὐτὴν ἰόντας ἐλέγχοις τε ὑποβεβλῆσθαι μυρίοις. ὡς μὲν δὴ ἐπὶ διδασκάλοις αὐτὸ ποιούμεθα καὶ ἐς δοκιμασίαν ἡμῖν τὸ φιλοσοφεῖν ἥκει, σαφῶς εἴρηκα, τοὐμὸν δὲ ὧδε ἔχει·

31. "Ἐγὼ μὲν πάππου βασιλέως ἐγενόμην, ὃς ἦν μοι ὁμώνυμος, πατρὸς δὲ ἰδιώτου. καταλειφθεὶς γὰρ κομιδῇ νέος ἐπίτροποι μὲν αὐτῷ ἐγένοντο δύο τῶν ξυγγενῶν κατὰ τοὺς τῶν Ἰνδῶν νόμους, ἔπραττον δὲ ὑπὲρ αὐτοῦ τὰ βασιλικὰ οὐ χρηστῶς, μὰ τὸν Ἥλιον, οὐδὲ ξυμμέτρως, ὅθεν βαρεῖς τοῖς ὑπηκόοις ἐφαίνοντο καὶ ἡ ἀρχὴ κακῶς ἤκουε. ξυστάντες οὖν ἐπ' αὐτοὺς τῶν δυνατῶν τινες ἐπιτίθενταί σφισιν ἐν ἑορτῇ καὶ κτείνουσι τῷ Ἰνδῷ θύοντας, αὐτοί τε ἐπεσπηδήσαντες τῷ ἄρχειν ξυνέσχον τὰ κοινά. δείσαντες οὖν οἱ ξυγγενεῖς περὶ τῷ πατρὶ μήπω ἑκκαίδεκα ἔτη γεγονότι πέμπουσιν αὐτὸν ὑπὲρ τὸν Ὕφασιν παρὰ τὸν ἐκεῖ

how he lived. If the official is at all deceitful or deceived, the laws forbid him to hold any further office for having falsified a human life. Information about the young men they gather by looking at them directly. Many human characteristics are conveyed by the eyes and many await interpretation and observation in the brows and the cheeks, and by means of them skilled students of nature inspect human minds, like images in a mirror. Philosophy is highly valued here, and the pursuit enjoys honor among the Indians, so that it is absolutely essential for candidates in philosophy to undergo scrutiny and face countless tests. Well, the fact that we study it with teachers, and that it involves examination, all this I have clearly explained. However, my own story is as follows.

31. "My grandfather was a king, and had the same name as myself, but my father was a commoner. He was orphaned very young, and two relatives became his guardians, as the laws of the Indians require. They managed the affairs of the kingdom on his behalf neither with virtue, I swear by the Sun, nor with moderation, so that their subjects thought them oppressive, and their rule fell into disrepute. Certain of the barons, therefore, formed a conspiracy and attacked them at a festival, killing them as they sacrificed to the Indus, and then usurped power for themselves and governed the state. So my father's relatives were afraid for him, since he was not yet eleven years old, and sent him across the Hyphasis to the king there, since he has

βασιλέα. πλειόνων δὲ ἢ ἐγὼ ἄρχει καὶ εὐδαίμων ἡ χώρα παρὰ πολὺ τῆς ἐνταῦθα.

2 "Βουλομένου δ' αὐτὸν τοῦ βασιλέως παῖδα ποιεῖσθαι, τουτὶ μὲν παρῃτήσατο φήσας μὴ φιλονεικεῖν τῇ τύχῃ ἀφῃρημένῃ αὐτὸν τὸ ἄρχειν, ἐδεήθη δ' αὐτοῦ ξυγχωρῆσαί οἱ φιλοσοφῆσαι βαδίσαντι παρὰ τοὺς σοφούς, καὶ γὰρ ἂν καὶ ῥᾷον καρτερῆσαι τὰ οἴκοι κακά. βουλομένου δὲ τοῦ βασιλέως καὶ κατάγειν αὐτὸν ἐπὶ τὴν πατρῴαν ἀρχήν 'εἰ γνησίως' ἔφη 'φιλοσοφοῦντα αἴσθοιο, κάταγε, εἰ δὲ μή, ἔα με οὕτως ἔχειν.' αὐτὸς οὖν ὁ βασιλεὺς ἥκων παρὰ τοὺς σοφοὺς μεγάλων ἂν ἔφη παρ' αὐτῶν τυχεῖν, εἰ τοῦ παιδὸς ἐπιμεληθεῖεν γενναίου τὴν φύσιν ἤδη ὄντος. οἱ δὲ κατιδόντες τι ἐν αὐτῷ πλέον ἠσπάσαντο προσδοῦναί οἱ τῆς αὑτῶν σοφίας, καὶ προθύμως ἐπαίδευον προσκείμενον πάνυ τῷ μανθάνειν. ἑβδόμῳ δὲ ἔτει νοσῶν ὁ βασιλεύς, ὅτε δὴ καὶ ἐτελεύτα, μεταπέμπεται αὐτὸν καὶ κοινωνὸν τῆς ἀρχῆς ἀποφαίνει τῷ υἱῷ τήν τε θυγατέρα ὁμολογεῖ πρὸς ὥραν οὖσαν.

3 "Ὁ δέ, ἐπειδὴ τὸν τοῦ βασιλέως υἱὸν εἶδε κολάκων καὶ οἴνου καὶ τῶν τοιούτων κακῶν ἥττω μεστόν τε ὑποψιῶν πρὸς αὐτόν, 'σὺ μὲν' ἔφη 'ταῦτ' ἔχε καὶ τῆς ἀρχῆς ἁπάσης ἐμφοροῦ, καὶ γὰρ εὔηθες μηδὲ τὴν προσήκουσαν ἑαυτῷ βασιλείαν ἀνακτήσασθαι[21] δυνηθέντα θρασέως δοκεῖν ἐπὶ τὴν μὴ προσήκουσαν ἥκειν. ἐμοὶ δὲ τὴν ἀδελφὴν δίδου, τουτὶ γὰρ μόνον ἀπόχρη μοι τῶν σῶν.' καὶ λαβὼν τὸν γάμον ἔζη πλησίον τῶν σοφῶν ἐν κώμαις ἑπτὰ εὐδαίμοσιν, ἃς

more subjects than I do, and his territory is far more fertile than this one.

"The king wanted to adopt my father as his son, but he 2
declined. He said he did not want to quarrel with fortune which had taken away his kingdom, but he asked the king to allow him to go to the Wise Men and study philosophy, since that way he would more easily endure his domestic misfortunes. When the king actually wanted to restore him to his father's rule, he said, 'Restore me if you find me studying philosophy sincerely, but otherwise leave me as I am.' The king went in person to the Wise Men, and said they would be doing him a great favor by looking after the boy, who was already of noble nature. But they saw something more in him, and seized the opportunity to give him a share of their own wisdom, and were glad to educate him, while he followed their lessons very attentively. After six years had passed, the king had an illness which was eventually fatal, so that he sent for my father and made him a co-ruler of his kingdom with his own son. He also gave him the hand of his daughter, who was just entering maturity.

"Now my father observed that the king's son was a prey 3
to flatterers, wine, and suchlike evils, and full of suspicion towards himself, so he said to him: 'You may keep these things, and enjoy all your power to the full. I was not even able to recover a throne that was mine, and it would be stupid to seem to have rash ambitions for one that belonged to another. However, grant me your sister; that alone of your possessions is enough for me.' He received permission to marry her, and lived near the Wise Men in

---

21 *ἀνακτήσασθαι* Jackson: *κτήσασθαι*

ἐπέδωκε τῇ ἀδελφῇ ὁ βασιλεὺς ἐς ζώνην. γίγνομαι τοίνυν ἐγὼ τοῦ γάμου τούτου καί με ὁ πατὴρ τὰ Ἑλλήνων παιδεύσας ἄγει παρὰ τοὺς σοφοὺς πρὸ ἡλικίας ἴσως, δώδεκα γάρ μοι τότε ἦν ἔτη, οἱ δὲ ἔτρεφον ἴσα καὶ ἑαυτῶν παῖδα, οὓς γὰρ ἂν ὑποδέξωνται τὴν Ἑλλήνων φωνὴν εἰδότας, ἀγαπῶσι μᾶλλον, ὡς ἐς τὸ ὁμόηθες αὐτοῖς ἤδη προσήκοντας.

32. "Ἀποθανόντων δέ μοι καὶ τῶν γονέων οὐ μετὰ πολὺ ἀλλήλων, αὐτοί με βαδίσαντα ἐπὶ τὰς κώμας ἐκέλευσαν ἐπιμεληθῆναι τῶν ἐμαυτοῦ, γεγονότα ἐννεακαίδεκα ἔτη. τὰς μὲν οὖν κώμας ἀφῄρητό με ἤδη ὁ χρηστὸς θεῖος καὶ οὐδὲ τὰ γῄδιά μοι ὑπέλιπε τὰ κεκτημένα τῷ πατρί, πάντα γὰρ τῇ ἑαυτοῦ ἀρχῇ προσήκειν αὐτά, ἐμὲ δ' ἂν μεγάλων παρ' αὐτοῦ τυχεῖν, εἴ με ἐῴη ζῆν. ἔρανον οὖν ξυλλεξάμενος παρὰ τῶν τῆς μητρὸς ἀπελευθέρων ἀκολούθους εἶχον τέτταρας. καί μοι ἀναγιγνώσκοντι τοὺς Ἡρακλείδας τὸ δρᾶμα ἐπέστη τις ἐντεῦθεν ἐπιστολὴν φέρων παρὰ ἀνδρὸς ἐπιτηδείου τῷ πατρί, ὅς με ἐκέλευσε διαβάντα τὸν Ὑδραώτην ποταμὸν ξυγγίγνεσθαί οἱ περὶ τῆς ἀρχῆς τῆς ἐνταῦθα, πολλὰς γὰρ ἐλπίδας εἶναί μοι ἀνακτήσασθαι αὐτὴν μὴ ἐλινύοντι.

2 "Τὸ μὲν δὴ δρᾶμα θεῶν τις οἶμαι ἐπὶ νοῦν ἤγαγε καὶ εἰπόμην τῇ φήμῃ, διαβὰς δὲ τὸν ποταμὸν τὸν μὲν ἕτερον τῶν βεβιασμένων ἐς τὴν ἀρχὴν τεθνάναι ἤκουσα, τὸν δὲ ἕτερον ἐν τοῖς βασιλείοις πολιορκεῖσθαι τούτοις. ἐχώρουν δὴ ξυντείνων καὶ βοῶν πρὸς τοὺς ἐν ταῖς κώμαις, δι' ὧν ἔστειχον, ὡς ὁ τοῦ δεῖνος εἴην υἱὸς

seven rich villages which the king gave to his sister for her dowry. I am the child of this marriage, and my father after giving me a Greek education took me to the Wise Men, perhaps prematurely, because I was then twelve years old. But they brought me up like their own son, since they are especially fond of those they accept who know the Greek language, thinking them already akin to themselves in manners.

32. "But when my parents also died at no great interval of time, the Wise Men told me to go to the villages and look after my own affairs, being now nineteen. Well, I had already been deprived of the villages by my kind uncle, who had not even left me the estates acquired by my father; he said they all belonged to his kingdom, and he was doing me a great favor by leaving me my life. Well, after taking up a collection from my mother's freedmen, I had four servants. I was reading the play *The Children of Heracles*[32] when someone arrived from here, bringing a letter from a close friend of my father. He urged me to cross the river Hydraotes and to confer with him about the kingdom here, for he had great hopes that I could win it back if I showed some energy.

"Well, I think one of the gods put the play into my mind, 2
so in obedience to the omen I crossed the river. I learned that one of the usurpers of the kingdom had died, and the other was under siege in this very palace. I hastened my advance, shouting to those living in the villages through which I passed that I was the son of so-and-so, and was go-

[32] Extant play of Euripides involving the punishment of Eurystheus, the king of Argos, for his persecution of Heracles's children.

καὶ ἐπὶ τὴν ἀρχὴν τὴν ἐμαυτοῦ ἴοιμι, οἱ δὲ χαίροντές τε καὶ ἀσπαζόμενοί με προὔπεμπον παραπλήσιον ἡγούμενοι τῷ πάππῳ, ἐγχειρίδιά τε ἦν αὐτοῖς καὶ τόξα καὶ πλείους ἀεὶ ἐγιγνόμεθα, καὶ προσελθόντα ταῖς πύλαις οὕτω τι ἄσμενοι ἐδέξαντο οἱ ἐνταῦθα, ὡς ἀπὸ τοῦ βωμοῦ τοῦ Ἡλίου δᾷδας ἁψάμενοι πρὸ πυλῶν τε ἥκειν καὶ ἡγεῖσθαι δεῦρο, ἐφυμνοῦντες πολλὰ τῷ πατρὶ καὶ τῷ πάππῳ, τὸν δὲ ἔσω κηφῆνα περιτειχισάμενοι[22] εἶρξαν, καίτοι ἐμοῦ παραιτουμένου μὴ τοιῷδε τρόπῳ ἀποθανεῖν αὐτόν."

33. Ὑπολαβὼν οὖν ὁ Ἀπολλώνιος "Ἡρακλειδῶν" ἔφη "κάθοδον ἀτεχνῶς διελήλυθας, καὶ ἐπαινετέοι οἱ θεοὶ τῆς διανοίας, ὅτι γενναίῳ ἀνδρὶ ἐπὶ τὰ ἑαυτοῦ στείχοντι ξυνήραντο τῆς καθόδου. ἀλλ' ἐκεῖνό μοι περὶ τῶν σοφῶν εἰπέ· οὐ καὶ ὑπὸ Ἀλεξάνδρῳ ποτὲ ἐγένοντο οὗτοι καὶ ἀναχθέντες αὐτῷ περὶ τοῦ οὐρανοῦ ἐφιλοσόφησαν;" "Ὀξυδράκαι" ἔφη "ἐκεῖνοι ἦσαν, τὸ δὲ ἔθνος τοῦτο ἐλευθεριάζει τε ἀεὶ καὶ πολεμικῶς ἐξήρτυται, σοφίαν τε μεταχειρίζεσθαί φασιν οὐδὲν χρηστὸν εἰδότες· οἱ δὲ ἀτεχνῶς σοφοὶ κεῖνται μὲν[23] τοῦ Ὑφάσιδος καὶ τοῦ Γάγγου μέσοι, τὴν δὲ χώραν ταύτην οὐδὲ ἐπῆλθεν ὁ Ἀλέξανδρος, οὔτι που τὰ ἐν αὐτῇ δείσας, ἀλλ', οἶμαι, τὰ ἱερὰ ἀπεσήμηνεν αὐτῷ. εἰ δὲ καὶ διέβη τὸν Ὕφασιν καὶ τὴν περὶ αὐτοὺς γῆν ἠδυνήθη ἑλεῖν, ἀλλὰ τήν γε τύρσιν, ἣν ἐκεῖνοι κατοικοῦσιν, οὐδ' ἂν μυρίους μὲν Ἀχιλλέας, τρισμυρίους δὲ

[22] περιτειχισάμενοι Scheibe (Kay.): πέριξ τὸ τεῖχος

ing in quest of my own kingdom. Giving me a joyful welcome, they followed me in the belief that I resembled my grandfather, arming themselves with daggers and bows, and our numbers kept growing. As I approached the gates, the inhabitants welcomed me so happily that they lit firebrands from the altar of the Sun, came out before the gates, and led me here, singing many praises of my father and grandfather. As for the drone inside, they imprisoned him and walled him in, though I begged that he should not die in this way."

33. Apollonius said in reply, "You have narrated a real *Return of the Children of Heracles*. The gods be praised for their scheme in helping a virtuous man to return when he went in pursuit of his own. But tell me this about the Wise Men: did these same men not once fall into Alexander's power, and on being brought before him give a discourse about heaven?" "Those were Oxydrakae,"[33] said the other, "and that tribe is always claiming its freedom and preparing for war. They say they are conversant with philosophy, but they know nothing about virtue. The true Wise Men are situated half way between the Hyphasis and the Ganges, in territory which Alexander did not even approach, not because he was afraid of what it contained, presumably, but I suppose because he had received contrary signals from sacrifices. Even if he had crossed the Hyphasis, and been able to seize the land around the Wise Men, he could have brought ten thousand Achilleses and thirty

[33] People situated between the rivers Akesines (Chenab) and Hydraotes (Ravi).

---

[23] μὲν West.: μέντοι

Αἴαντας ἄγων ποτὲ ἐχειρώσατο. οὐ γὰρ μάχονται τοῖς προσελθοῦσιν, ἀλλὰ διοσημίαις τε καὶ σκηπτοῖς βάλλοντες ἀποκρούονται σφᾶς ἱεροὶ καὶ θεοφιλεῖς ὄντες.

2 "Τὸν γοῦν Ἡρακλέα τὸν Αἰγύπτιον καὶ τὸν Διόνυσον ξὺν ὅπλοις διαδραμόντας τὸ Ἰνδῶν ἔθνος φασὶ μέν ποτε ἐλάσαι ἐπ' αὐτοὺς ἅμα, μηχανάς τε παλαμήσασθαι καὶ τοῦ χωρίου ἀποπειρᾶσθαι, οἱ δὲ ἀντιπράττειν οὐδέν, ἀλλ' ἀτρεμεῖν, ὡς ἐκείνοις ἐφαίνοντο, ἐπεὶ δ' αὐτοὶ προσῄεσαν, πρηστῆρες αὐτοὺς ἀπεώσαντο καὶ βρονταὶ κάτω στρεφόμεναι καὶ ἐμπίπτουσαι τοῖς ὅπλοις, τήν τε ἀσπίδα χρυσῆν οὖσαν ἀποβαλεῖν ἐκεῖ λέγεται ὁ Ἡρακλῆς, καὶ πεποίηνται αὐτὴν ἀνάθημα οἱ σοφοὶ διά τε τὴν τοῦ Ἡρακλέους δόξαν, διά τε τὸ ἐκτύπωμα τῆς ἀσπίδος· αὐτὸς γὰρ πεποίηται ὁ Ἡρακλῆς ὁρίζων τὰ Γάδειρα, καὶ τὰ ὄρη στήλας ποιούμενος, τόν τε Ὠκεανὸν ἐς τὰ ἔσω[24] ἐπισπώμενος. ὅθεν δηλοῦται μὴ τὸν Θηβαῖον Ἡρακλέα, τὸν δὲ Αἰγύπτιον ἐπὶ τὰ Γάδειρα ἐλθεῖν καὶ ὁριστὴν γενέσθαι τῆς γῆς."

34. Τοιαῦτα διαλεγομένων αὐτῶν ἐπῆλθεν [ὁ][25] ὕμνος αὐλῷ ἅμα, ἐρομένου δὲ τοῦ Ἀπολλωνίου τὸν βασιλέα, ὅ τι ἐθέλοι ὁ κῶμος, "Ἰνδοὶ" ἔφη "παραινέσεις τῷ βασιλεῖ ᾄδουσιν, ἐπειδὰν πρὸς τῷ καθεύδειν γίγνηται, ὀνείρασί τε ἀγαθοῖς χρῆσθαι χρηστόν τε ἀνίστασθαι καὶ εὐξύμβολον τοῖς ὑπηκόοις." "πῶς οὖν," ἔφη "ὦ βασιλεῦ, διάκεισαι πρὸς ταῦτα; σὲ γάρ που αὐλοῦσιν." "οὐ καταγελῶ," ἔφη "δεῖ γὰρ προσίεσθαι αὐτὰ τοῦ νόμου ἕνεκεν, παραινέσεως μέντοι

thousand Ajaxes without ever subduing them. They do not fight their attackers, but fend them off by hurling thunder and lightning at them, being holy and beloved of the gods.

"Indeed, it is said that once upon a time the Egyptian 2
Heracles and Dionysus, after invading the land of India with an army, made a concerted campaign against them, devising siege engines and trying to take their citadel. The Wise Men took no countermeasures and stayed quiet, so it appeared to their assailants, but when these approached, they were driven off by whirlwinds and thunderbolts that hurtled down and struck their weapons, so that they say Heracles lost his shield, which was of gold, on that occasion. The Wise Men made a dedication of it, both because of Heracles's fame and because of the relief on the shield; for it shows Heracles himself limiting the earth at Gadeira,[34] turning the mountains into boundary stones, and admitting the Ocean between them. This shows that it was not the Theban but the Egyptian Heracles that reached Gadeira, and was the surveyor of the earth."

34. They were conversing in this way when the sound reached them of a hymn accompanied by the pipe. Apollonius asked the king what this revelry meant, and he replied: "The Indians sing words of advice to their king when he is ready for sleep, in order that he should enjoy happy dreams, and be kind when he gets up and approachable towards his subjects." "And how do you take all this, king," said Apollonius, "since clearly they are serenading you?" "I do not laugh at it," he replied, "since one must allow it for

[34] Modern Cádiz.

---

[24] ἔσω Bentl.: ἔξω [25] secl. Kay.

μηδεμιᾶς δεῖσθαι, ὅσα γὰρ ἂν ὁ βασιλεὺς μετρίως τε καὶ χρηστῶς πράττῃ, ταῦτα ἑαυτῷ δήπου χαριεῖται μᾶλλον ἢ τοῖς ὑπηκόοις."

35. Τοιαῦτα διαλεχθέντες ἀνεπαύσαντο, ἐπεὶ δὲ ἡμέρα ὑπεφαίνετο, αὐτὸς ὁ βασιλεὺς ἀφίκετο ἐς τὸ δωμάτιον, <ἐν>[26] ᾧ ἐκάθευδον οἱ περὶ τὸν Ἀπολλώνιον, καὶ τὸν σκίμποδα ἐπιψηλαφήσας προσεῖπέ τε τὸν ἄνδρα, καὶ ἤρετο αὐτόν, ὅ τι ἐνεθυμεῖτο, "οὐ γάρ που καθεύδεις" εἶπεν "ὕδωρ πίνων καὶ καταγελῶν τοῦ οἴνου." "οὐ γὰρ καθεύδειν ἡγῇ" ἔφη "τοὺς τὸ ὕδωρ πίνοντας;" "καθεύδειν μέν," ἔφη "λεπτὸν δὲ ὕπνον, ὅνπερ ἄκροις αὐτῶν τοῖς ὀφθαλμοῖς ἐφιζάνειν φῶμεν, οὐ τῷ νῷ." "ἀμφοτέροις" εἶπε, "καὶ ἴσως τῷ νῷ μᾶλλον· εἰ γὰρ μὴ ἀτρεμήσει ὁ νοῦς, οὐδὲ ὑποδέξονται οἱ ὀφθαλμοὶ τὸν ὕπνον. οἱ γοῦν μεμηνότες οὐδὲ καθεύδειν δύνανται διὰ τὴν τοῦ νοῦ πήδησιν, ἀλλ' ἐς ἄλλα καὶ ἄλλα ἀπιούσης τῆς ἐννοίας γοργότερόν τε ἀναβλέπουσι καὶ ἀναιδέστερον, ὥσπερ οἱ ἄυπνοι τῶν δρακόντων.

2 "Ἐπεὶ τοίνυν, ὦ βασιλεῦ," εἶπε "σαφῶς ἡρμήνευται τὸ τοῦ ὕπνου ἔργον καὶ ἅττα δηλοῦται τοῖς ἀνθρώποις, σκεψώμεθα, τί μειονεκτήσει ἐν τῷ ὕπνῳ τοῦ μεθύοντος ὁ τὸ ὕδωρ πίνων." "μὴ σοφίζου," ἔφη ὁ βασιλεὺς "εἰ γὰρ μεθύοντα ὑποθήσῃ, οὐ καθευδήσει γ' οὗτος,[27] βακχεύουσα γὰρ ἡ γνώμη στροβήσει τε αὐτὸν καὶ ταραχῆς ἐμπλήσει· δοκοῦσί τοι πάντες οἱ ἐκ μέθης καταδαρθεῖν πειρώμενοι ἀναπέμπεσθαί τε ἐς τὸν ὄροφον, καὶ αὖ ὑπόγειοι εἶναι δίνην τε ἐμ-

custom's sake. But one should not need any advice, for any things that a king does with moderation and kindness will doubtless give more pleasure to him than to his subjects."

35. After this conversation, they went to bed, but at daybreak the king himself came into the room where Apollonius and his companions were sleeping. After groping for the bunk he addressed the Master, and asked him what he was thinking about, "since no doubt you are not sleeping," he said, "being a teetotaler who laughs at wine." "Why," said Apollonius, "do you not think teetotalers sleep?" "They do," the other replied, "but it is a light sleep, the kind which we say settles on the surface of their eyes, not on the mind." "On both," said Apollonius, "and perhaps more on the mind, since if the mind cannot rest, the eyes too will receive no sleep. Madmen cannot go to sleep at all because of the throbbing of their minds; their thoughts rove from one subject to another, and so their glances get fiercer and bolder, like those of unsleeping snakes.

"Well, Majesty," he continued, "since we have clearly 2
explained the effect of sleep and what things are revealed to humans, let us consider how a teetotaler fares worse than a drunkard in the matter of sleep." "Do not confuse the issue," said the king, "for if you are talking about a drunkard, he at least will not sleep; his raging thoughts will spin him around and fill him with turmoil. Why, everyone who tries to sleep after being drunk feels that he is being raised to the roof and then is below ground, and a whirling

---

26 <ἐν> Jon. (ᾧ ἐνεκάθευδον Rsk.)
27 γ᾽ οὗτος Rsk.: τοῦτο

πεπτωκέναι σφίσιν, οἷα δὴ περὶ τὸν Ἰξίονα λέγεται ξυμβαίνειν. οὔκουν ἀξιῶ τὸν μεθύοντα, ἀλλὰ τὸν πεπωκότα μὲν τοῦ οἴνου, νήφοντα δὲ θεωρεῖν, ὡς καθευδήσει, καὶ ὡς πολλῷ βέλτιον τοῦ ἀοίνου."

36. Καλέσας οὖν ὁ Ἀπολλώνιος τὸν Δάμιν "πρὸς δεινὸν ἄνδρα" ἔφη "ὁ λόγος καὶ σφόδρα γεγυμνασμένον τοῦ διαλέγεσθαι." "ὁρῶ," ἔφη "καὶ τοῦτ' ἴσως ἦν τὸ μελαμπύγου τυχεῖν. κἀμὲ δὲ πάνυ αἱρεῖ ὁ λόγος, ὃν εἴρηκεν· ὥρα οὖν σοι ἀφυπνίσαντι ἀποτελεῖν αὐτόν." ἀνακουφίσας οὖν τὴν κεφαλὴν ὁ Ἀπολλώνιος "καὶ μὴν ὅσον" ἔφη "πλεονεκτοῦμεν οἱ τὸ ὕδωρ πίνοντες πρὸς τὸ καθεύδειν ἥδιον, ἐγὼ δηλώσω τοῦ γε σοῦ λόγου ἐχόμενος· ὡς μὲν γὰρ τετάρακται ἡ γνώμη τοῖς μεθύουσι καὶ μανικώτερον διάκεινται, σαφῶς εἴρηκας, ὁρῶμεν γὰρ τοὺς μέθῃ κατεσχημένους διττὰς μὲν σελήνας δοκοῦντας βλέπειν, διττοὺς δὲ ἡλίους, τοὺς δὲ ἧττον πεπωκότας, κἂν πάνυ νήφωσιν, οὐδὲν μὲν τούτων ἡγουμένους, μεστοὺς δὲ εὐφροσύνης καὶ ἡδονῆς, ἣ δὴ προσπίπτει σφίσιν οὐδὲ ἐξ εὐπραγίας πολλάκις, καὶ μελετῶσι δὲ οἱ τοιοῦτοι δίκας οὐδὲ φθεγξάμενοί πω ἐν δικαστηρίῳ, καὶ πλουτεῖν φασιν οὐδὲ δραχμῆς αὐτοῖς ἔνδον οὔσης.

2 "Ταῦτα δέ, ὦ βασιλεῦ, μανικὰ πάθη· καὶ γὰρ αὐτὸ τὸ ἥδεσθαι διακινεῖ τὴν γνώμην, καὶ πολλοὺς οἶδα τῶν σφόδρα ἡγουμένων εὖ πράττειν οὐδὲ καθεύδειν δυναμένους, ἀλλ' ἐκπηδῶντας τοῦ ὕπνου, καὶ τοῦτ' ἂν εἴη τὸ παρέχειν φροντίδας καὶ τἀγαθά. ἔστι δὲ καὶ φάρμακα ὕπνου μεμηχανημένα τοῖς ἀνθρώποις, ὧν

seizes him such as they say happens to Ixion. It is not therefore with reference to the drunkard, but to the man who remains sober even when drinking wine, that I think we should be discussing the nature of his sleep, and how it will be much better than a teetotaler's."

36. Addressing Damis, Apollonius said, "My discussion is with a clever man, and one well practiced in dialectic." "So I see," said Damis, "and this is perhaps what the proverb means about catching a Tartar. I too am very taken with the discourse he has given, so it is high time you woke up and finished it off." So raising his head Apollonius said, "Yet I will prove the advantage which we teetotalers have in the matter of sleeping soundly, using your own arguments. You clearly said that drunkards are confused in their minds and rather inclined to madness. We see those prey to drunkenness thinking that they see two moons and two suns,[35] while those who have drunk less, even if they are fully sober, have no such thoughts as that, but are full of cheerfulness and pleasure. This often comes over them without being the result of any success, and people like that rehearse legal speeches when they have never even been in a courtroom, and say they are rich when they have not got a drachma in the house.

"These are manic tendencies, Majesty, for pleasure it- 2
self disturbs the mind. I know many people who thought themselves very well off and yet had insomnia, starting up from their sleep, and this is what the saying means that 'even good fortune breeds cares.' People have devised sleeping drugs, which they drink or rub on, and then they

[35] Allusion to Euripides, *Bacchae* 918–19.

πιόντες τε καὶ ἀλειψάμενοι καθεύδουσιν, ἐκτείναντες αὑτοὺς ὥσπερ ἀποθανόντες, ὅθεν μετά τινος λήθης ἀνίστανται καὶ ἄλλοσέ ποι μᾶλλον εἶναι ἢ οὗπέρ εἰσι[28] δοκοῦσιν. ὅτι μὲν δὴ τὰ πινόμενα, μᾶλλον δὲ τὰ ἐπαντλούμενα τῇ ψυχῇ καὶ τῷ σώματι οὐ γνήσιον οὐδὲ οἰκεῖον ἐπεσάγεται τὸν ὕπνον, ἀλλ' ἢ βαθὺν καὶ ἡμιθνῆτα, ἢ βραχὺν καὶ διασπώμενον ὑπὸ τῶν ἐντρεχόντων, κἂν χρηστὰ ᾖ, ξυνθήσῃ τάχα, εἰ μὴ τὸ δύσερι μᾶλλον ἢ τὸ ἐριστικὸν σπουδάζεις.

3 "Οἱ δὲ ἐμοὶ ξυμπόται τὰ μὲν ὄντα ὁρῶσιν ὡς ὄντα, τὰ δὲ οὐκ ὄντα οὔτ' ἀναγράφουσιν αὑτοῖς οὔθ' ὑποτυποῦνται, κοῦφοί τε οὔπω ἔδοξαν, οὐδὲ μεστοὶ βλακείας οὐδὲ εὐηθείας, ἢ ἱλαρώτεροι τοῦ προσήκοντος, ἀλλ' ἐφεστηκότες εἰσὶ καὶ λογισμοῦ πλέῳ, παραπλήσιοι δείλης τε καὶ ὁπότε ἀγορὰ πλήθει, οὐ γὰρ νυστάζουσιν οὗτοι, κἂν πόρρω τῶν νυκτῶν σπουδάζωσιν. οὐ γὰρ ἐξωθεῖ αὐτοὺς ὁ ὕπνος ὥσπερ δεσπότης βρίσας ἐς τὸν αὐχένα δεδουλωμένον ὑπὸ τοῦ οἴνου, ἀλλ' ἐλεύθεροί τε καὶ ὀρθοὶ φαίνονται, καταδαρθόντες[29] δὲ καθαρᾷ τῇ ψυχῇ δέχονται τὸν ὕπνον, οὔτε ὑπὸ τῶν εὐπραγιῶν ἀνακουφιζόμενοι αὑτοῦ,[30] οὔτε ὑπὸ κακοπραγίας τινὸς ἐκθρώσκοντες. ξύμμετρος γὰρ πρὸς ἄμφω ταῦτα ψυχὴ νήφουσα καὶ οὐδετέρου τῶν παθῶν ἥττων, ὅθεν καθεύδει ἥδιστα καὶ ἀλυπότατα μὴ ἐξισταμένη τοῦ ὕπνου.

37. "Καὶ μὴν καὶ τὸ μαντικὸν τὸ ἐκ τῶν ὀνειράτων, ὃ θειότατον τῶν ἀνθρωπίνων δοκεῖ, ῥᾷον διορᾷ μὴ ξυντεθολωμένη ὑπὸ τοῦ οἴνου, ἀλλ' ἀκήρατος δεχο-

sleep stretched out as if they were dead. After that, they get up in a kind of amnesia, and think they are somewhere other than they really are. Things that people drink, or more precisely drown body and soul with, do not produce a true or proper sleep, but rather one that is deep and deathlike, or brief and disturbed by random thoughts, even if they are pleasant ones. You will perhaps agree to that, unless you are more interested in argument than in debate.

"But my fellow drinkers see things as they really are, 3
and do not conceive or imagine what is unreal. Never have they seemed lightheaded or full of exaggeration and folly, or unduly cheerful, but are attentive, full of reason, unaltered both at evening and at noon, because they never nod, even when they study far into the night. Sleep does not overpower them like a slave driver, treading on necks that are subjugated by wine. They are visibly free and upright, and when they drift off, they receive sleep with an untainted soul, not suspended over it by good fortune, or starting out of it from misfortune. For a sober soul is equally immune to both of these, and subject to neither of the two emotions, and hence it enjoys the soundest and most untroubled rest, and is not woken from sleep.

37. "Moreover, prophecy arising from dreams, which is agreed to be the most heavenly of all human gifts, is more easily visible to a soul that is not obfuscated by wine, but in

---

[28] *εἶναι . . . εἰσι* Jackson: *εἰσιν . . . εἶναι*
[29] *καταδαρθόντες* Cob.: *καταδαρθέντες*
[30] *αὐτοῦ* Kay.: *αὐτοὶ*

μένη αὐτὸ καὶ περιαθροῦσα. οἱ γοῦν ἐξηγηταὶ τῶν ὄψεων, οὓς ὀνειροπόλους οἱ ποιηταὶ καλοῦσιν, οὐδ᾽[31] ἂν ὑποκρίναιντο ὄψιν οὐδεμίαν μὴ πρότερον ἐρόμενοι τὸν καιρόν, ἐν ᾧ εἶδεν. ἂν μὲν γὰρ ἑῷος ᾖ καὶ τοῦ περὶ τὸν ὄρθρον ὕπνου, ξυμβάλλονται αὐτὴν ὡς ὑγιῶς μαντευομένης τῆς ψυχῆς, ἐπειδὰν ἀπορρύψηται τὸν οἶνον, εἰ δ᾽ ἀμφὶ πρῶτον ὕπνον ἢ μέσας νύκτας, ὅτε βεβύθισταί τε καὶ ξυντεθόλωται ἔτι ὑπὸ τοῦ οἴνου, παραιτοῦνται τὴν ὑπόκρισιν σοφοὶ ὄντες. ὡς δὲ καὶ τοῖς θεοῖς δοκεῖ ταῦτα καὶ τὸ χρησμῶδες ἐν ταῖς νηφούσαις ψυχαῖς τίθενται, σαφῶς δηλώσω.

2 "'Εγένετο, ὦ βασιλεῦ, παρ᾽ Ἕλλησιν Ἀμφιάρεως ἀνὴρ μάντις." "οἶδα," εἶπε "λέγεις γάρ που τὸν τοῦ Οἰκλέους, ὃν ἐκ Θηβῶν ἐπανιόντα ἐπεσπάσατο ἡ γῆ ζῶντα." "οὗτος, ὦ βασιλεῦ," ἔφη "μαντευόμενος ἐν τῇ Ἀττικῇ νῦν ὀνείρατα ἐπάγει τοῖς χρωμένοις, καὶ λαβόντες οἱ ἱερεῖς τὸν χρησόμενον σίτου τε εἴργουσι μίαν ἡμέραν καὶ οἴνου τρεῖς, ἵνα διαλαμπούσῃ τῇ ψυχῇ τῶν λογίων σπάσῃ. εἰ δὲ ὁ οἶνος ἀγαθὸν ἦν τοῦ ὕπνου φάρμακον, ἐκέλευσεν ἂν ὁ σοφὸς Ἀμφιάρεως τοὺς θεωροὺς τὸν ἐναντίον ἐσκευασμένους τρόπον καὶ οἴνου μεστούς, ὥσπερ ἀμφορέας, ἐς τὸ ἄδυτον αὐτὸ φέρεσθαι.

3 "Πολλὰ δὲ καὶ μαντεῖα λέγοιμ᾽ ἂν εὐδόκιμα παρ᾽ Ἕλλησί τε καὶ βαρβάροις, ἐν οἷς ὁ ἱερεὺς ὕδατος, ἀλλ᾽ οὐχὶ οἴνου σπάσας ἀποφθέγγεται τὰ ἐκ τοῦ

[31] οὐδ᾽ West.: οὐκ

a pure and impressionable state for receiving it. Interpreters of visions, 'dream dealers' as poets call them, cannot interpret any vision without first ascertaining the time when the soul perceived it. If it comes in the early morning from dawntime sleep, they interpret it in the belief that the soul prophesies correctly when it is purged of wine; but if it comes in the first sleep or the small hours, when the soul is still weighed down and obfuscated by wine, they withhold interpretation, and wisely too. That the gods are also of this opinion, and implant the prophetic power in souls that are sober, I will clearly prove.

"There once existed among the Greeks, Majesty, a prophet 2
called Amphiaraus."[36] "I know"; he replied, "you mean the son of Oicles, whom the earth swallowed up alive as he was returning from Thebes." "Yes, Majesty," Apollonius replied, "though now he prophesies in Attica. He sends dreams to his inquirers, so that the priests take the would-be inquirer, and deprive him of food for one day and of wine for three, so that he can absorb the messages with his soul in a state of illumination. If wine were a good sleeping draught, the wise Amphiaraus would have told sacred visitors to prepare themselves in the opposite way, and to be carried into the very shrine full up with wine, like casks.[37]

"I could name many oracles highly reputed among 3
Greeks and barbarians in which the priest partakes of water, not wine, before pronouncing from the tripod. So you

[36] Legendary Argive prophet, with an oracle on the territory of Oropus between Boeotia and Attica.

[37] Pun on the word for "cask," *amphoreus*.

τρίποδος. θεοφόρητον δὴ κἀμὲ ἡγοῦ καὶ πάντας, ὦ βασιλεῦ, τοὺς τὸ ὕδωρ πίνοντας· νυμφόληπτοι γὰρ ἡμεῖς καὶ βάκχοι τοῦ νήφειν." "ποιήσῃ οὖν," ἔφη "ὦ Ἀπολλώνιε, κἀμὲ θιασώτην;" "εἴπερ μὴ φορτικὸς" εἶπε "τοῖς ὑπηκόοις δόξεις· φιλοσοφία γὰρ περὶ βασιλεῖ ἀνδρὶ ξύμμετρος μὲν καὶ ὑπανειμένη θαυμαστὴν ἐργάζεται κρᾶσιν, ὥσπερ ἐν σοὶ διαφαίνεται, ἡ δ' ἀκριβὴς καὶ ὑπερτείνουσα φορτική τε, ὦ βασιλεῦ, καὶ ταπεινοτέρα τῆς ὑμετέρας σκηνῆς φαίνεται, καὶ τύφου δὲ αὐτό τι ἂν <ἔχειν>[32] ἡγοῖντο βάσκανοι."

38. Ταῦτα διαλεχθέντες, καὶ γὰρ ἡμέρα ἤδη ἐτύγχανεν, ἐς τὸ ἔξω προῆλθον. καὶ ξυνεὶς ὁ Ἀπολλώνιος, ὡς χρηματίζειν δέοι τὸν βασιλέα πρεσβείαις τε καὶ τοῖς τοιούτοις, "σὺ μέν," ἔφη "ὦ βασιλεῦ, τὰ προσήκοντα τῇ ἀρχῇ πρᾶττε, ἐμὲ δὲ τὸν καιρὸν τοῦτον ἄνες τῷ Ἡλίῳ, δεῖ γάρ με τὴν εἰθισμένην εὐχὴν εὔξασθαι." "καὶ ἀκούοι γε εὐχομένου," ἔφη "χαριεῖται γὰρ πᾶσιν, ὁπόσοι τῇ σοφίᾳ τῇ σῇ χαίρουσιν. ἐγὼ δὲ περιμενῶ σε ἐπανιόντα, καὶ γὰρ δικάσαι τινὰς χρὴ δίκας, αἷς παρατυχὼν τὰ μέγιστά με ὀνήσεις."

39. Ἐπανελθὼν οὖν προκεχωρηκυίας ἤδη τῆς ἡμέρας ἠρώτα περὶ ὧν ἐδίκασεν, ὁ δὲ "τήμερον" ἔφη "οὐκ ἐδίκασα, τὰ γὰρ ἱερὰ οὐ ξυνεχώρει μοι." ὑπολαβὼν οὖν ὁ Ἀπολλώνιος "ἐφ' ἱεροῖς οὖν" ἔφη "ποιεῖσθε καὶ ταύτας, ὥσπερ τὰς ἐξόδους τε καὶ τὰς στρατείας;" "νὴ Δί'" εἶπε "καὶ γὰρ ἐνταῦθα κίνδυνος, εἰ ὁ δικάζων ἀπενεχθείη τοῦ εὐθέος." εὖ λέγειν τῷ Ἀπολλωνίῳ ἔδοξε, καὶ ἤρετο αὐτὸν πάλιν, τίς εἴη, ἣν δικάσοι

should consider myself and all teetotalers, Majesty, to be divinely inspired; we are mediums, and fanatics of sobriety." "Well then, Apollonius," said the king, "will you make me a member of your conclave?" "I will," said Apollonius, "unless that makes your subjects think you irksome. Philosophy in a royal personage forms a wonderful blend when it is measured and moderate, as it appears to be in you, but if it is harsh and concentrated it seems irksome, Majesty, and too humble for the state of such as you, and envious people would say that it has an element of pride."

38. During this conversation daylight had come, and they went outdoors. Realizing that the king had to deal with embassies and so on, Apollonius said, "You must perform the duties of your position, Majesty, but during this interval leave me free to worship the Sun god, since I have to offer him my usual prayer." "May he hear your prayer," said the king, "for he will be generous to all that favor your wisdom. I will await your return, since I must judge some cases in which your presence will be very useful to me."

39. Returning when the day was now far along, Apollonius asked the king about the cases he had judged. He replied, "I did not dispense justice today, since the omens prevented me." Apollonius said in answer, "Why, do your lawsuits depend on omens, as your departures and your campaigns do?" "Certainly," he replied, "since here too there is danger if the judge strays from what is right." The answer seemed good to Apollonius, and he asked him again what case it was that he was going to judge, "since I

---

32 ‹ἔχειν› Kay.

δίκην, "ὁρῶ γὰρ" εἶπεν "ἐφεστηκότα σε καὶ ἀποροῦντα, ὅπῃ ψηφίσαιο."

2 "Ὁμολογῶ" ἔφη "ἀπορεῖν, ὅθεν ξύμβουλον ποιοῦμαί σε· ἀπέδοτο μὲν γάρ τις ἑτέρῳ γῆν, ἐν ᾗ θησαυρὸς ἀπέκειτό τις οὔπω δῆλος, χρόνῳ δὲ ὕστερον ἡ γῆ ῥαγεῖσα χρυσοῦ τινα ἀνέδειξε θήκην, ἥν φησι μὲν ἑαυτῷ προσήκειν μᾶλλον ὁ τὴν γῆν ἀποδόμενος, καὶ γὰρ οὐδ' ἂν ἀποδόσθαι τὴν γῆν, εἰ προὔμαθεν, ὅτι βίον ὑπ'[33] αὐτῇ ἔχοι. ὁ πριάμενος δὲ αὐτὸς ἀξιοῖ πεπᾶσθαι, ἃ ἐν τῇ λοιπὸν ἑαυτοῦ γῇ εὗρε. καὶ δίκαιος μὲν ὁ ἀμφοῖν λόγος, εὐήθης δ' ἂν ἐγὼ φαινοίμην, εἰ κελεύσαιμι ἄμφω νείμασθαι τὸ χρυσίον, τουτὶ γὰρ ἂν καὶ γραῦς διαιτῴη."

3 Ὑπολαβὼν οὖν ὁ Ἀπολλώνιος "ὡς μὲν οὐ φιλοσόφω" ἔφη "τὼ ἄνδρε, δηλοῖ τὸ περὶ χρυσίου διαφέρεσθαι σφᾶς, ἄριστα δ' ἄν μοι δικάσαι δόξεις ὧδε ἐνθυμηθείς, ὡς οἱ θεοὶ πρῶτον μὲν ἐπιμέλειαν ποιοῦνται τῶν ξὺν ἀρετῇ φιλοσοφούντων, δεύτερον δὲ τῶν ἀναμαρτήτων τε καὶ μηδὲν πώποτε ἀδικεῖν δοξάντων. διδόασι δὲ τοῖς μὲν φιλοσοφοῦσι διαγιγνώσκειν εὖ τὰ θεῖά τε καὶ τὰ ἀνθρώπεια, τοῖς δ' ἄλλως χρηστοῖς βίον ἀποχρῶντα, ὡς μὴ χήτει ποτὲ τῶν ἀναγκαίων ἄδικοι γένωνται. δοκεῖ δή μοι, βασιλεῦ, καθάπερ ἐπὶ τρυτάνης ἀντικρῖναι τούτους καὶ τὸν ἀμφοῖν ἀναθεωρῆσαι βίον, οὐ γὰρ ἄν μοι δοκοῦσιν οἱ θεοὶ τὸν μὲν ἀφελέσθαι καὶ τὴν γῆν, εἰ μὴ φαῦλος ἦν, τῷ δ' αὖ καὶ τὰ ὑπὸ τῇ γῇ δοῦναι, εἰ μὴ βελτίων ἦν τοῦ ἀποδομένου."

see," he said, "that you are hesitating and uncertain on which side your verdict will be."

"I am uncertain, I admit," he said, "and that is why I 2
am making you my counselor. One man sold another some land that contained a hidden treasure. Some time later, a fissure in the earth revealed a jar of gold. The seller of the land says that the jar properly belongs to him, and that he would not have sold the land had he known in advance that it contained his fortune, while the buyer for his part claims to be the possessor of what he found in land now belonging to him. The arguments of both are just, but I would seem a simpleton if I ordered both to share the gold, since even an old woman could decide that."

Apollonius said in reply, "That the two men are not 3
philosophers follows from their quarrelling about gold, but it seems to me that you will judge best if you take the following into consideration. The gods provide first of all for those who are virtuous students of wisdom, and secondly for innocent people who have never been seen to do wrong. They grant philosophers the ability to distinguish correctly between things divine and human, but to all other good people they grant enough to live on, so that they may not become unjust for lack of necessities. It seems to me, therefore, Majesty, that you should weigh these two as in a balance, and examine the lives of them both. The gods would not have deprived one of them of his land as well, it seems to me, unless he was bad, nor would they have given the other what was actually below ground, unless he was better than the seller."

---

[33] ὑπ' Jackson: ἐπ'

4 Ἀφίκοντο ἐς τὴν ὑστεραίαν δικασόμενοι ἄμφω, καὶ ὁ μὲν ἀποδόμενος ὑβριστής τε ἠλέγχετο καὶ θυσίας ἐκλελοιπώς, ἃς ἔδει τοῖς ἐν τῇ γῇ θεοῖς θύειν, ὁ δὲ ἐπιεικής τε ἐφαίνετο καὶ ὁσιώτατα θεραπεύων τοὺς θεούς. ἐκράτησεν οὖν ἡ τοῦ Ἀπολλωνίου γνώμη, καὶ ἀπῆλθεν ὁ χρηστὸς ὡς παρὰ τῶν θεῶν ταῦτα ἔχων.

40. Ἐπεὶ δὲ τὰ τῆς δίκης ὧδε ἔσχε, προσελθὼν ὁ Ἀπολλώνιος τῷ Ἰνδῷ "τήμερον" εἶπεν "ἡ τρίτη τῶν ἡμερῶν, ἐν αἷς ἐποιοῦ με, ὦ βασιλεῦ, ξένον, τῆς δ' ἐπιούσης ἕω χρὴ ἐξελαύνειν ἑπόμενον τῷ νόμῳ." "ἀλλ' οὐδὲ ὁ νόμος" εἶπεν "ἤδη διαλέγεταί σοι, καὶ γὰρ τῇ αὔριον μένειν ἔξεστιν, ἐπειδὴ μετὰ μεσημβρίαν ἀφίκου." "χαίρω" ἔφη "τῷ ξενίῳ, καὶ γάρ μοι δοκεῖς κατασοφίζεσθαι[34] τὸν νόμον δι' ἐμέ." "εἰ γὰρ καὶ λῦσαι αὐτὸν ἠδυνάμην" εἶπε "τό γε ὑπὲρ σοῦ. ἀλλ' ἐκεῖνό μοι εἰπέ, Ἀπολλώνιε, αἱ κάμηλοι, ἐφ' ὧν ὀχεῖσθαί σέ φασιν, οὐκ ἐκ Βαβυλῶνος ἄγουσιν ὑμᾶς;" "ἐκεῖθεν" ἔφη "δόντος γε αὐτὰς Οὐαρδάνου." "ἔτ' οὖν ὑμᾶς ἀπάγειν δυνήσονται, τοσαῦτα ἤδη στάδια ἐκ Βαβυλῶνος ἥκουσαι;"

2 Ἐσιώπησε μὲν ὁ Ἀπολλώνιος, ὁ δὲ Δάμις "οὔπω συνίησιν," ἔφη "ὦ βασιλεῦ, τῆς ἀποδημίας ὁ ἀνὴρ οὗτος, οὐδὲ τῶν ἐθνῶν, ἐν οἷς λοιπόν ἐσμεν, ἀλλ' ὡς πανταχοῦ σέ τε καὶ Οὐαρδάνην ἕξων παιδιὰν ἡγεῖται τὸ ἐς Ἰνδοὺς παρελθεῖν. τό τοι τῶν καμήλων οὐ διομολογεῖται πρὸς σέ, ὃν ἔχει τρόπον· διάκεινται γὰρ οὕτω κακῶς, ὡς αὐταὶ μᾶλλον ὑφ' ἡμῶν φέρεσθαι, καὶ δεῖ ἑτέρων. ἂν γὰρ ὀκλάσωσιν ἐν ἐρήμῳ που τῆς

On the next day the two parties came to argue their case, and the seller turned out to be a scofflaw who had omitted the customary sacrifices to the gods below earth, while the other appeared to be virtuous and their very reverent worshiper. Apollonius's opinion therefore prevailed, and the good man left as if he had got his rewards from the gods. 4

40. When the dispute had been settled in this way, Apollonius approached the Indian and said, "This is the third of the days, Majesty, in which you were to make me your guest. At dawn tomorrow I must leave as the law commands." "No," he said, "not even the law requires this of you, but you can stay tomorrow too, since you arrived in the afternoon." "I appreciate your present," said Apollonius, "as you seem to be stretching the law for my benefit." "I only wish," he replied, "that for you I could break it. But tell me, Apollonius, the camels which I hear you are riding, they have brought you from Babylon, have they not?" "Yes," said Apollonius, "Vardanes gave them to us." "Will they be able to carry you on again, then, when they have already come so many stades from Babylon?"

Apollonius did not answer, but Damis said, "The Master here has no conception of this journey, or of the tribes among which we are going to be. He supposes we will find others like you and Vardanes everywhere, and that reaching India is child's play. As for the camels, he does not admit to you what state they are in; they are in such bad shape that on the contrary we are carrying them, not they us, and we need others. If they collapse in some deserted part of 2

[34] καταςοφίζεσθαι Valck.: καὶ σοφίζεσθαι

Ἰνδικῆς, ἡμεῖς μὲν" ἔφη "καθεδούμεθα τοὺς γῦπάς τε καὶ τοὺς λύκους ἀποσοβοῦντες τῶν καμήλων, ἡμῶν δὲ οὐδεὶς ἀποσοβήσει, προσαπολούμεθα γάρ." ὑπολαβὼν οὖν ὁ βασιλεὺς "ἐγὼ" ἔφη "τοῦτο ἰάσομαι, ὑμῖν τε γὰρ ἑτέρας δώσω (τεττάρων, οἶμαι, δεῖσθε) καὶ ὁ σατράπης δὲ ὁ ἐπὶ τοῦ Ἰνδοῦ πέμψει ἐς Βαβυλῶνα ἑτέρας τέτταρας. ἔστι δέ μοι ἀγέλη καμήλων ἐπὶ τῷ Ἰνδῷ, λευκαὶ πᾶσαι."

3 "Ἡγεμόνα δὲ" εἶπεν ὁ Δάμις "οὐκ ἄν, ὦ βασιλεῦ, δοίης;" "καὶ κάμηλόν γε" ἔφη "τῷ ἡγεμόνι δώσω καὶ ἐφόδια, ἐπιστελῶ δὲ καὶ Ἰάρχᾳ τῷ πρεσβυτάτῳ τῶν σοφῶν, ἵν' Ἀπολλώνιον μὲν ὡς μηδὲν κακίω ἐμαυτοῦ δέξηται, ὑμᾶς δὲ ὡς φιλοσόφους τε καὶ ὀπαδοὺς ἀνδρὸς θείου." καὶ χρυσίον δὲ ἐδίδου ὁ Ἰνδὸς καὶ ψήφους καὶ ὀθόνας καὶ μυρία τοιαῦτα· ὁ δὲ Ἀπολλώνιος χρυσίον μὲν ἔφη ἱκανὸν ἑαυτῷ εἶναι δόντος γε Οὐαρδάνου τῷ ἡγεμόνι ἀφανῶς αὐτό, τὰς δὲ ὀθόνας λαμβάνειν, ἐπειδὴ ἐοίκασι τρίβωνι τῶν ἀρχαίων τε καὶ πάνυ Ἀττικῶν. μίαν δέ τινα τῶν ψήφων ἀνελόμενος "ὦ βελτίστη" εἶπεν "ὡς ἐς καιρόν σε καὶ οὐκ ἀθεεὶ εὕρηκα," ἰσχύν, οἶμαί, τινα ἐν αὐτῇ καθεωρακὼς ἀπόρρητόν τε καὶ θείαν. οἱ δὲ ἀμφὶ τὸν Δάμιν χρυσίον μὲν οὐδ' αὐτοὶ προσίεντο, τῶν ψήφων δὲ ἱκανῶς ἐδράττοντο, ὡς θεοῖς ἀναθήσοντες, ὅτε ἐπανέλθοιεν ἐς τὰ ἑαυτῶν ἤθη.

41. Καταμείνασι δὲ αὐτοῖς καὶ τὴν ἐπιοῦσαν, οὐ γὰρ μεθίετο σφῶν ὁ Ἰνδός, δίδωσι τὴν πρὸς τὸν Ἰάρχαν ἐπιστολὴν γεγραμμένην ὧδε· "Βασιλεὺς Φρα-

India, we will sit fending vultures and wolves away from the camels, but no one will fend them away from us, because we will be dead too." So the king answered, "I will remedy that, and give you new ones. You need four, I believe, and the viceroy guarding the Indus will send four others to Babylon, since I have a herd of pure white camels by the Indus."

"Will you not also give us a guide, Majesty?" said 3
Damis. "Of course," he replied, "and I will give the guide a camel and provisions, and I will write to Iarchas, the senior philosopher, so that he will welcome Apollonius as a man not inferior to myself, and welcome you as lovers of wisdom and as the companions of a holy man." The Indian also offered them money, precious stones, linen, and countless similar things. But Apollonius said that he had enough money, since Vardanes had given some secretly to the guide; but he would take the linen, since it resembled a philosopher's cloak of the old-fashioned, genuine Attic kind. He also took one of the stones and said, "You excellent stone, I have found you at the right time and not without divine assistance." I suppose he had discerned some mysterious, divine power in it. Damis and the others refused gold, but helped themselves to plenty of the precious stones, planning to dedicate them to the gods after returning to their own countries.

41. When they had stayed there the next day too, since the Indian did not want to part with them, he gave them his letter to Iarchas, which ran as follows: "King Phraotes

ώτης Ἰάρχᾳ διδασκάλῳ καὶ τοῖς περὶ αὐτὸν χαίρειν. Ἀπολλώνιος ἀνὴρ σοφώτατος σοφωτέρους ὑμᾶς ἑαυτοῦ ἡγεῖται καὶ μαθησόμενος ἥκει τὰ ὑμέτερα. πέμπετε οὖν αὐτὸν εἰδότα ὁπόσα ἴστε· ὡς ἀπολεῖται οὐδὲν τῶν μαθημάτων ὑμῖν, καὶ γὰρ λέγει ἄριστα ἀνθρώπων καὶ μέμνηται. ἰδέτω δὲ καὶ τὸν θρόνον, ἐφ᾽ οὗ καθίσαντί μοι τὴν βασιλείαν ἔδωκας, Ἰάρχα πάτερ. καὶ οἱ ἑπόμενοι δὲ αὐτῷ ἄξιοι ἐπαίνου, ὅτι τοιοῦδε ἀνδρὸς ἥττηνται. εὐτύχει καὶ εὐτυχεῖτε."

42. Ἐξελάσαντες δὲ τῶν Ταξίλων καὶ δύο ἡμερῶν ὁδὸν διελθόντες, ἀφίκοντο ἐς τὸ πεδίον, ἐν ᾧ λέγεται πρὸς Ἀλέξανδρον ἀγωνίσασθαι Πῶρος, καὶ πύλας ἐν αὐτῷ ἰδεῖν φασι ξυγκλειούσας οὐδέν, ἀλλὰ τροπαίων ἕνεκα ᾠκοδομημένας. ἀνακεῖσθαι γὰρ ἐπ᾽ αὐτῶν τὸν Ἀλέξανδρον ἐφεστηκότα τετραρρύμοις ἅρμασιν, οἷος ἐπὶ τοῖς Δαρείου σατράπαις ἐν Ἰσσοῖς ἕστηκε. διαλείπουσαι δ᾽ οὐ πολὺ ἀλλήλων δύο ἐξῳκοδομῆσθαι λέγονται πύλαι, καὶ φέρειν ἡ μὲν Πῶρον, ἡ δὲ Ἀλέξανδρον, ξυμβεβηκότε, οἶμαι, μετὰ τὴν μάχην, ὁ μὲν γὰρ ἀσπαζομένῳ ἔοικεν, ὁ δὲ προσκυνοῦντι.

43. Ποταμὸν δὲ Ὑδραώτην ὑπερβάντες καὶ πλείω ἔθνη ἀμείψαντες, ἐγένοντο πρὸς τῷ Ὑφάσιδι, στάδια δὲ ἀπέχοντες τούτου τριάκοντα βωμοῖς τε ἐνέτυχον, οἷς ἐπεγέγραπτο "Πατρὶ Ἄμμωνι, καὶ Ἡρακλει ἀδελφῷ, καὶ Ἀθηνᾷ Προνοίᾳ, καὶ Διὶ Ὀλυμπίῳ, καὶ Σαμόθρᾳξι Καβείροις, καὶ Ἰνδῷ Ἡλίῳ, καὶ Δελφῷ Ἀπόλλωνι." φασὶ δὲ καὶ στήλην ἀνακεῖσθαι χαλκῆν, ᾗ

greets his teacher Iarchas and his companions. Apollonius, a very wise man, thinks you wiser than himself, and is coming to learn your lore. When he leaves you, make sure he knows all that you do. He will not forget any of your lessons, since he is the most eloquent of humans and the most retentive. Let him see the throne on which I sat when you gave me my kingdom, father Iarchas. His companions also deserve praise for their devotion to such a Master. Goodbye to yourself and your followers."

42. When they had left Taxila and gone two days' journey, they came to the plain on which the battle of Alexander and Porus is reported to have occurred, and they say they saw gates there which did not enclose anything, but were built as a trophy. On top of them there was dedicated a statue of Alexander riding an eight-horse chariot, the way he stood when he conquered the viceroys of Darius at Issus.[38] In fact there are said to be two sets of gates, not far from one another, one bearing Porus and the other Alexander, represented as they met after the battle, I suppose, since one of them appears in a pose of greeting, and the other in a pose of obeisance.

43. When they had crossed the Hydraotes and passed several tribes, they came to the Hyphasis. About thirty stades further on they found altars with this inscription: "To my father Ammon, my brother Heracles, Athena of Forethought, Olympian Zeus, the Cabiri of Samothrace, the Sun of India, and Apollo of Delphi." They say there was also a bronze tablet dedicated there with the legend "Alex-

[38] City of eastern Cilicia near which Alexander won a great victory over Darius III (and not only over his satraps) in 333 BCE.

ἐπιγεγράφθαι "Ἀλέξανδρος ἐνταῦθα ἔστη." τοὺς μὲν δὴ βωμοὺς Ἀλεξάνδρου ἡγώμεθα τὸ τῆς ἑαυτοῦ ἀρχῆς τέρμα τιμῶντος, τὴν δὲ στήλην τοὺς μετὰ τὸν Ὕφασιν Ἰνδοὺς ἀναθεῖναι, δοκῶ μοι λαμπρυνομένους ἐπὶ τῷ Ἀλέξανδρον μὴ προελθεῖν πρόσω.

ander stopped here." We must suppose that the altars were set up by Alexander to honor the limit of his empire, while the Indians across the Hyphasis dedicated the tablet, presumably in order to boast that Alexander had advanced no further.

Γ´

1. Περὶ δὲ τοῦ Ὑφάσιδος καὶ ὁπόσος τὴν Ἰνδικὴν διαστείχει καὶ ὅ τι περὶ αὐτὸν θαῦμα, τάδε χρὴ γιγνώσκειν. αἱ πηγαὶ τοῦ ποταμοῦ τούτου βλύζουσι μὲν ἐκ πεδίου ναυσίποροι αὐτόθεν, προϊοῦσαι δὲ καὶ ναυσὶν ἤδη ἄποροί εἰσιν. ἀκρωνυχίαι γὰρ πετρῶν παραλλὰξ ὑπανίσχουσι τοῦ ὕδατος, περὶ ἃς ἀνάγκη τὸ ῥεῦμα ἑλίττεσθαι καὶ ποιεῖν τὸν ποταμὸν ἄπλουν. εὖρος δὲ αὐτῷ κατὰ τὸν Ἴστρον, ποταμῶν δὲ οὗτος δοκεῖ μέγιστος, ὁπόσοι δι᾽ Εὐρώπης ῥέουσι. δένδρα δέ οἱ προσόμοια φύει παρὰ τὰς ὄχθας, καί τι καὶ μύρον ἐκδίδοται τῶν δένδρων, ὃ ποιοῦνται Ἰνδοὶ γαμικὸν χρίσμα, καὶ εἰ μὴ τῷ μύρῳ τούτῳ ῥάνωσι τοὺς νυμφίους οἱ ξυνιόντες ἐς τὸν γάμον, ἀτελὴς δοκεῖ καὶ οὐκ ἐς χάριν τῇ Ἀφροδίτῃ ξυναρμοσθείς.

2 Ἀνεῖσθαι δὲ τῇ θεῷ ταύτῃ λέγουσιν αὐτό τε τὸ περὶ τῷ ποταμῷ νέμος καὶ τοὺς ἰχθῦς τοὺς ταώς, οὓς οὗτος μόνος ποταμῶν τρέφει. πεποίηνται δὲ αὐτοὺς ὁμωνύμους τοῦ ὄρνιθος, ἐπεὶ κυάνεοι μὲν αὐτοῖς οἱ λόφοι, στικταὶ δὲ αἱ φολίδες, χρυσᾶ δὲ τὰ οὐραῖα καί, ὁπότε βούλοιντο, ἀνακλώμενα. ἔστι δέ τι θηρίον ἐν τῷ ποταμῷ τούτῳ σκώληκι εἰκασμένον λευκῷ. τοῦτο οἱ τήκον-

BOOK III

1. About the Hyphasis,[1] its size as it crosses India and its remarkable features, one should know the following. The headwaters of this river emerge from a level plain and are navigable from their source, though as they proceed they become impassible for boats. Jagged rocks rise out of the water on each side in turn, and the current as it twists around them necessarily makes the river unnavigable. In breadth it equals the Danube, which is considered the largest river to traverse Europe. Trees of a corresponding size grow along the banks, giving off a kind of balm which the Indians use as a marriage perfume, and if those invited to the wedding omit to sprinkle this perfume on the couple, the ceremony is considered to be invalid and contracted without the favor of Aphrodite.

They say that the woods on the banks of the river are 2
dedicated to this goddess, as are the famous peacock fish, which breed only in this river. These have received the same name as the bird because of their blue dorsal fins, spotted scales, and golden tail fins which they can spread at will. There is another creature in this river that resembles a white worm, and is melted down to produce an oil. This oil

[1] On the geographical references in this book, and Apollonius's supposed route, see Introduction.

τες ἔλαιον ποιοῦνται, πῦρ δὲ ἄρα τοῦ ἐλαίου τούτου ἐκδίδοται καὶ στέγει αὐτὸ πλὴν ὑελοῦ οὐδέν. ἁλίσκεται δὲ τῷ βασιλεῖ μόνῳ τὸ θηρίον τοῦτο πρὸς τειχῶν ἅλωσιν. ἐπειδὰν γὰρ θίγῃ τῶν ἐπάλξεων ἡ πιμελή, πῦρ ἐκκαλεῖται κρεῖττον σβεστηρίων, ὁπόσα ἀνθρώποις πρὸς τὰ πυρφόρα εὕρηται.

2. Καὶ τοὺς ὄνους δὲ τοὺς ἀγρίους ἐν τοῖς ἕλεσι τούτοις ἁλίσκεσθαί φασιν, εἶναι δὲ τοῖς θηρίοις τούτοις ἐπὶ μετώπου κέρας, ᾧ ταυρηδόν τε καὶ οὐκ ἀγεννῶς μάχονται, καὶ ἀποφαίνειν τοὺς Ἰνδοὺς ἔκπωμα τὸ κέρας τοῦτο, οὐ γὰρ οὔτε νοσῆσαι τὴν ἡμέραν ἐκείνην ὁ ἀπ᾽ αὐτοῦ πιὼν οὔτε ἂν τρωθεὶς ἀλγῆσαι, πυρός τε διεξελθεῖν ἂν καὶ μηδ᾽ ἂν φαρμάκοις ἁλῶναι ὁπόσα ἐπὶ κακῷ πίνεται, βασιλέων δὲ τὸ ἔκπωμα εἶναι καὶ βασιλεῖ μόνῳ ἀνεῖσθαι τὴν θήραν.

2 Ἀπολλώνιος δὲ τὸ μὲν θηρίον ἑωρακέναι φησὶ καὶ ἄγασθαι αὐτὸ τῆς φύσεως, ἐρομένου δὲ αὐτὸν τοῦ Δάμιδος, εἰ τὸν λόγον τὸν περὶ τοῦ ἐκπώματος προσδέχοιτο, "προσδέξομαι" εἶπεν "ἢν ἀθάνατον μάθω τὸν βασιλέα τῶν δεῦρο Ἰνδῶν ὄντα, τὸν γὰρ ἐμοί τε καὶ τῷ δεῖνι ὀρέγοντα πῶμα ἄνοσόν τε καὶ οὕτως ὑγιὲς πῶς οὐχὶ μᾶλλον εἰκὸς αὐτὸν ἐπεγχεῖν ἑαυτῷ τούτου, καὶ ὁσημέραι πίνειν ἀπὸ τοῦ κέρατος τούτου μέχρι κραιπάλης; οὐ γὰρ διαβαλεῖ τις, οἶμαι, <τὸ>[1] τούτῳ μεθύειν."

3. Ἐνταῦθα καὶ γυναίῳ φασὶν ἐντετυχηκέναι τὰ μὲν ἐκ κεφαλῆς ἐς μαζοὺς μέλανι, τὰ δὲ ἐκ μαζῶν ἐς πόδας λευκῷ[2] πάντα, καὶ αὐτοὶ μὲν ὡς δεῖμα φυγεῖν,

produces a flame and can only be contained in glass. The king alone may catch the animal for the purpose of taking cities, for as soon as its fat touches the parapets it produces a flame that overcomes any of the fire-extinguishing devices which humans have devised against incendiary missiles.

2. The famous wild asses[2] are apparently also caught in the marshes here. These creatures have a horn on their foreheads with which they fight lowering their heads, and not without courage. The Indians make a cup out of this horn, and whoever drinks from it cannot fall ill that day or feel pain if he is wounded; he can pass through fire and is immune against drugs that are usually fatal if drunk. These cups are the king's private property and he alone is free to hunt the animal.

Apollonius says he saw the creature and admired its 2
qualities, but when Damis asked him if he believed the story about the cup, he replied, "I will believe it, if I hear that the king of the Indians in these parts is immortal. The man who can offer so medicinal and healthy a drink to me or to anybody must surely serve himself with it too, and drink from this horn every day to the point of intoxication. No one will condemn getting drunk on this, I imagine."

3. They also say they met a woman there who was black from the top of her head to her breasts, and completely white from her breasts to her feet. The others thought she

[2] Not a true onager, but a unicorn, a creature first mentioned by the historian Ctesias.

---

[1] ⟨τὸ⟩ Kay.

[2] λευκῷ Kay.: λευκὰ

τὸν δὲ Ἀπολλώνιον ξυνάψαι τε τῷ γυναίῳ τὴν χεῖρα καὶ ξυνεῖναι ὅ τι εἴη· ἱεροῦται δὲ ἄρα τῇ Ἀφροδίτῃ Ἰνδῇ τοιαύτη, καὶ τίκτεται τῇ θεῷ γυνὴ ποικίλη, καθάπερ ὁ Ἆπις Αἰγυπτίοις.

4. *Ἐντεῦθέν φασιν ὑπερβαλεῖν τοῦ Καυκάσου τὸ κατατεῖνον ἐς τὴν Ἐρυθρὰν θάλασσαν, εἶναι δὲ αὐτὸ ξυνηρεφὲς ἴδαις ἀρωμάτων. τοὺς μὲν δὴ πρῶνας τοῦ ὄρους τὸ κιννάμωμον φέρειν, προσεοικέναι δὲ αὐτὸ νέοις κλήμασι, βάσανον δὲ τοῦ ἀρώματος τὴν αἶγα εἶναι· κινναμώμου γὰρ εἴ τις αἰγὶ ὀρέξειε, κνυζήσεται πρὸς τὴν χεῖρα, καθάπερ κύων, ἀπιόντι τε ὁμαρτήσει τὴν ῥῖνα ἐς αὐτὸ ἐρείσασα, κἂν ὁ αἰπόλος ἀπάγῃ, θρηνήσει καθάπερ λωτοῦ ἀποσπωμένη.*

2 *Ἐν δὲ τοῖς κρημνοῖς τοῦ ὄρους λίβανοί τε ὑψηλοὶ πεφύκασι καὶ πολλὰ εἴδη ἕτερα καὶ τὰ δένδρα αἱ πεπερίδες, ὧν γεωργοὶ πίθηκοι. καὶ οὐδὲ ᾧ εἴκασται τοῦτο, παρεῖταί σφισιν, ὃν δὲ εἴρηται τρόπον, ἐγὼ δηλώσω. τὸ δένδρον ἡ πεπερὶς εἴκασται μὲν τῷ παρ᾽ Ἕλλησιν ἄγνῳ τά τε ἄλλα καὶ τὸν κόρυμβον τοῦ καρποῦ, φύεται δὲ ἐν τοῖς ἀποτόμοις οὐκ ἐφικτὸς τοῖς ἀνθρώποις, οὗ λέγεται πιθήκων οἰκεῖν δῆμος ἐν μυχοῖς τοῦ ὄρους καὶ ὅ τι αὐτοῦ κοῖλον, οὓς πολλοῦ ἀξίους οἱ Ἰνδοὶ νομίζοντες, ἐπειδὴ τὸ πέπερι ἀποτρυγῶσι, τοὺς λέοντας ἀπ᾽ αὐτῶν ἐρύκουσι κυσί τε καὶ ὅπλοις. ἐπιτίθεται δὲ πιθήκῳ λέων νοσῶν μὲν ὑπὲρ φαρμάκου, τὴν γὰρ νόσον αὐτῷ τὰ κρέα ἴσχει ταῦτα, γεγηρακὼς δὲ ὑπὲρ σίτου, τῆς γὰρ τῶν ἐλάφων καὶ συῶν θήρας ἔξωροι γεγονότες τοὺς πιθήκους λαφύσ-*

was a freak and ran away, but Apollonius took the woman by the hand, realizing what she was: for in fact such women in India are considered sacred to Aphrodite, and bicolored women are born to serve the goddess, like Apis in Egypt.[3]

4. From there they record that they crossed the arm of the Caucasus that extends to the Red Sea, and that it is covered with spice-bearing shrubs. The foothills produce cinnamon, which looks like the tendrils of a vine but is identified by means of nanny goats. If you offer cinnamon to a goat, it will nuzzle your hand like a dog, and as you go away it will follow, burying its nose in the shrub; if the goatherd leads it off it will wail as if dragged away from a lotus plant.

In the folds of the mountain, however, grow tall frank- 2
incense trees and many other kinds too, including pepper-bearing trees that are harvested by monkeys. Since the party did not fail to note what the tree looked like, I shall describe it. The pepper tree looks like the Greek willow in every respect, down to the clusters of fruit, except that it grows on precipices where it is inaccessible to humans. But they say that a tribe of monkeys lives there in the clefts and hollows of the mountain, and the Indians value them so highly that, when the animals are harvesting the peppers, they use dogs and weapons to keep lions away from them. A lion will attack a monkey either to get a cure when it is ill, for this meat arrests its diseases, or to get food when it is old. When lions are past the age for hunting deer and boar,

[3] The Egyptian Apis bull, an incarnation of Ptah, was black with white patches.

σουσιν ἐς τοῦτο χρώμενοι τῇ λοιπῇ ῥώμῃ. οὐ μὴν οἱ ἄνθρωποι περιορῶσιν, ἀλλ᾽ εὐεργέτας ἡγούμενοι τὰ θηρία ταῦτα πρὸς τοὺς λέοντας ὑπὲρ αὐτῶν αἰχμὴν αἴρονται.

3 Τὰ γὰρ πραττόμενα περὶ τὰς πεπερίδας ὧδε ἔχει· προσελθόντες οἱ Ἰνδοὶ τοῖς κάτω δένδρεσι, τὸν καρπὸν ἀποθερίσαντες ἅλως ποιοῦνται μικρὰς περὶ τὰ δένδρα καὶ τὸ πέπερι περὶ αὐτὰς ξυμφοροῦσιν οἷον ῥιπτοῦντες, ὡς ἄτιμόν τι καὶ μὴ ἐν σπουδῇ τοῖς ἀνθρώποις, οἱ δὲ ἄνωθεν καὶ ἐκ τῶν ἀβάτων ἀφεωρακότες ταῦτα, νυκτὸς γενομένης ὑποκρίνονται τὸ τῶν Ἰνδῶν ἔργον καὶ τοὺς βοστρύχους τῶν δένδρων περισπῶντες ῥιπτοῦσι φέροντες ἐς τὰς ἅλως. οἱ Ἰνδοὶ δὲ ἅμα ἡμέρᾳ σωροὺς ἀναιροῦνται τοῦ ἀρώματος οὐδὲ πονήσαντες οὐδέν, ἀλλὰ ῥᾴθυμοί τε καὶ καθεύδοντες.

5. Ὑπεράραντες δὲ τοῦ ὄρους πεδίον ἰδεῖν φασι λεῖον κατατετμημένον ἐς τάφρους πλήρεις ὕδατος, εἶναι δὲ αὐτῶν τὰς μὲν ἐπικαρσίους, τὰς δὲ ὀρθάς, διηγμένας ἐκ τοῦ ποταμοῦ τοῦ Γάγγου τῆς τε χώρας ὅρια οὔσας τοῖς τε πεδίοις ἐπαγομένας, ὁπότε ἡ γῆ διψῴη. τὴν δὲ γῆν ταύτην ἀρίστην φασὶ τῆς Ἰνδικῆς εἶναι καὶ μεγίστην τῶν ἐκεῖ λήξεων, πεντεκαίδεκα ἡμερῶν ὁδοῦ μῆκος ἐπὶ τὸν Γάγγην, ὀκτωκαίδεκα δὲ ἀπὸ θαλάσσης ἐπὶ τὸ τῶν πιθήκων ὄρος, ᾧ ξυμπαρατείνει[3] πεδιὰς πᾶσα ἡ χώρα μέλαινά τε καὶ πάντων εὔφορος. ἰδεῖν μὲν γὰρ ἐν αὐτῇ στάχυας ἀνεστῶτας, ὅσον οἱ δόνακες, ἰδεῖν δὲ κυάμους τριπλασίους τῶν

they use their remaining strength to gobble up the monkeys. The humans, however, feeling the monkeys to be their benefactors, intervene by taking up arms to defend them against the lions.

But the method used for the peppers is this. The Indi- 3
ans make their way to the trees lower down, pick the fruit, and after making little clearings around the trees collect the peppers in them, as if they were dumping it as garbage of no use to humans. The monkeys watch from their inaccessible places above, and when night comes they imitate the actions of the Indians by tearing the clusters of fruit from the trees and bringing them to be dumped in the clearings. At dawn the Indians carry off the piles of spice that they have gotten with no effort at all, in fact at their ease and during sleep.

5. After crossing the mountain, they say they saw a smooth plain divided up by ditches full of water, some of them running diagonally and others straight, and brought from the Ganges. These serve as boundaries for the land, and also irrigate the plain when the soil is dry. The land here they say is the best in India and forms the largest of its regions, requiring a fifteen days' journey to the Ganges, and one of eighteen days between the sea and the mountain of the monkeys. The land alongside the mountain is level, with dark soil that can grow anything. They say they saw wheat standing as tall as bulrushes on it, beans three

---

3 ᾧ. . . . εὔφορος coniunxit Radermacher

Αἰγυπτίων τὸ μέγεθος σήσαμόν τε καὶ κέγχρον ὑπερφυᾶ πάντα.

2 Ἐνταῦθα καὶ τὰ κάρυα φύεσθαί φασιν, ὧν πολλὰ πρὸς ἱεροῖς ἀνακεῖσθαι τοῖς δεῦρο θαύματος ἕνεκα. τὰς δὲ ἀμπέλους φύεσθαι μὲν μικράς, καθάπερ αἱ Λυδῶν τε καὶ Μαιόνων, ποτίμους δὲ εἶναι καὶ ἀνθοσμίας ὁμοῦ τῷ ἀποτρυγᾶν. ἐνταῦθα καὶ δένδρῳ φασὶν ἐντετυχηκέναι προσεοικότι τῇ δάφνῃ, φύεσθαι δὲ αὐτοῦ κάλυκα εἰκασμένην τῇ μεγίστῃ ῥόᾳ, καὶ μῆλον ἐγκεῖσθαι τῇ κάλυκι κυάνεον μέν, ὥσπερ τῶν ὑακίνθων αἱ κάλυκες, πάντων δὲ ἥδιστον, ὁπόσα ἐξ ὡρῶν ἥκει.

6. Καταβαίνοντες δὲ τὸ ὄρος δρακόντων θήρᾳ περιτυχεῖν φασι, περὶ ἧς ἀνάγκη λέξαι· καὶ γὰρ σφόδρα εὔηθες ὑπὲρ μὲν τοῦ λαγὼ καὶ ὅπως ἁλίσκεται καὶ ἁλώσεται, πολλὰ εἰρῆσθαι τοῖς ἐς φροντίδα βαλλομένοις ταῦτα, ἡμᾶς δὲ παρελθεῖν λόγον γενναίας τε καὶ δαιμονίου θήρας μηδὲ τῷ ἀνδρὶ παραλειφθέντα, ἐς ὃν ταῦτα ἔγραψα.

2 Δρακόντων μὲν γὰρ δὴ ἀπείροις μήκεσι κατέζωσται πᾶσα ἡ Ἰνδικὴ χώρα καὶ μεστὰ μὲν αὐτῶν ἕλη, μεστὰ δὲ ὄρη, κενὸς δὲ οὐδεὶς λόφος. οἱ μὲν δὴ ἕλειοι νωθροί τέ εἰσι καὶ τριακοντάπηχυ μῆκος ἔχουσι καὶ κράνος αὐτοῖς οὐκ ἀνέστηκεν, ἀλλ᾿ εἰσὶ ταῖς δρακαίναις ὅμοιοι, μέλανες δὲ ἱκανῶς τὸν νῶτον καὶ ἧττον φολιδωτοὶ τῶν ἄλλων. καὶ σοφώτερον ἧπται τοῦ λόγου περὶ αὐτῶν Ὅμηρος ἢ οἱ πολλοὶ ποιηταί, τὸν γὰρ δράκοντα τὸν ἐν Αὐλίδι τὸν πρὸς τῇ πηγῇ

times larger than the Egyptian kind, and sesame and millet, all of it enormous.

They also say that those nuts grow here that are often 2
dedicated in our sanctuaries as curiosities. The vines, however, are small in size, like those in Lydia and Maeonia,[4] but the wine they produce is drinkable and of a fine bouquet from the time of vintage. They also came across a tree there like a laurel, bearing a fruit resembling the largest pomegranate, and the center inside the husk was as blue as the flowers of the bluebell, and sweeter than any other thing the seasons produce.

6. Coming down the mountain, they say they chanced on a snake hunt, which I must describe. Those who are concerned about such things have written much about the hare, and how it is caught and can be caught. It would be extremely foolish of me, therefore, to omit an account of a fine, extraordinary hunt, when it was included by the Master about whom I am writing.

All the countryside of India is infested by snakes of 2
enormous length. The marshes are full of them, and the mountains too, and no hill is free from them. The marsh ones are sluggish, with a length of thirty cubits, and have no crest that stands up. They resemble female snakes, having very dark backs and fewer scales than other varieties. Homer gives a more expert account of them than most poets when he describes the snake living near the fountain

[4] Maeonia is the region around Sardis in Asia Minor.

οἰκοῦντα περὶ νῶτα "δαφοινὸν" εἴρηκεν, οἱ δὲ ἄλλοι ποιηταὶ τὸν ὁμοήθη τούτῳ τὸν ἐν τῷ τῆς Νεμέας ἄλσει φασὶ καὶ λοφιὰν ἔχειν, ὅπερ οὐκ ἂν περὶ τοὺς ἑλείους εὕροιμεν.

7. Οἱ δὲ[4] ὑπὸ τὰς ὑπωρείας τε καὶ τοὺς λόφους ἵενται μὲν[5] ἐς τὰ πεδία ἐπὶ θήρᾳ, πλεονεκτοῦσι δὲ τῶν ἑλείων πάντα, καὶ γὰρ ἐς πλέον τοῦ μήκους ἐλαύνουσι καὶ ταχύτεροι τῶν ὀξυτάτων ποταμῶν φέρονται, καὶ διαφεύγει αὐτοὺς οὐδέν. τούτοις καὶ λοφιὰ φύεται νέοις μὲν ὑπανίσχουσα τὸ μέτριον, τελειουμένοις δὲ συναυξανομένη τε καὶ συνανιοῦσα ἐς πολύ, ὅτε δὴ πυρσοί τε καὶ πριόνωτοι γίγνονται.

2 Οὗτοι καὶ γενειάσκουσι καὶ τὸν αὐχένα ὑψοῦ αἴρουσι καὶ τὴν φολίδα στίλβουσι δίκην ἀργύρου, αἱ δὲ τῶν ὀφθαλμῶν κόραι λίθος ἐστὶ διάπυρος, ἰσχὺν δ' αὐτῶν ἀμήχανον εἶναί φασιν ἐς πολλὰ τῶν ἀποθέτων. γίγνεται δὲ τοῖς θηρῶσιν ὁ πεδινὸς εὕρημα, ἐπειδὰν τῶν ἐλεφάντων τινὰ ἐπισπάσηται, τουτὶ γὰρ ἀπόλλυσιν ἄμφω τὰ θηρία. καὶ κέρδος τοῖς ἑλοῦσι δράκοντας ὀφθαλμοί τε γίγνονται καὶ δορὰ καὶ ὀδόντες. εἰσὶ δὲ τὰ μὲν ἄλλα ὅμοιοι τοῖς τῶν μεγίστων συῶν, λεπτότεροι δὲ καὶ διάστροφοι καὶ τὴν αἰχμὴν ἄτριπτοι, καθάπερ οἱ τῶν μεγάλων ἰχθύων.

8. Οἱ δὲ ὄρειοι δράκοντες τὴν μὲν φολίδα χρυσοῖ φαίνονται, τὸ δὲ μῆκος ὑπὲρ τοὺς πεδινούς, γένεια δὲ αὐτοῖς βοστρυχώδη, χρυσᾶ κἀκεῖνα, καὶ κατωφρύωνται μᾶλλον ἢ οἱ πεδινοί, ὄμμα τε ὑποκάθηται τῇ ὀφρύι

at Aulis as "of russet back,"[5] while other poets describe the related snake in the Nemean wood[6] as having a crest, something not to be found in marsh snakes.

7. The snakes of the foothills and the ridges come to the plain to hunt. They are in every way superior to the marsh variety; they grow to greater length, move faster than the swiftest rivers, and nothing escapes them. These do have a crest, which is of moderate height when they are young, but grows commensurately as they reach maturity until it gets very tall, while the snakes turn crimson and develop serrated backs.

These ones also grow beards and raise their necks high, 2
and glitter like silver with their scales. Their eyeballs are flashing stones that are said to have an irresistible power to do many mysterious things. The plains snake is a boon for hunters when it is dragging off an elephant, because that is ruinous for both animals, and those who capture snakes also get possession of the eyes, skin, and teeth. These last are in every respect like the tusks of the largest boars, except that they are lighter, spiral in shape, and permanently sharp like those of large fish.

8. The mountain snakes have scales of golden appearance, and they are of greater length than the plains variety, and have bushy beards, which are also golden. They have more prominent eyebrows than the plains variety, and under the eyebrow an eye with a terrible, insolent look.

[5] *Iliad* 2.308. [6] According to legend, a snake killed the baby Opheltes in the grove of Nemea, and the Seven against Thebes founded the Nemean games in his memory.

---

[4] οἱ δὲ Kay.: καὶ τοὺς [5] μὲν Kay.: δὲ

δεινὸν καὶ ἀναιδὲς δεδορκός, ὑπόχαλκόν τε ἠχὼ φέρουσιν, ἐπειδὰν τῇ γῇ ὑποκυμαίνωσιν, ἀπὸ δὲ τῶν λόφων πυρσῶν ὄντων πῦρ αὐτοῖς ἄττει λαμπαδίου πλέον. οὗτοι καὶ τοὺς ἐλέφαντας αἱροῦσιν, αὐτοὶ δὲ ὑπὸ τῶν Ἰνδῶν οὕτως ἁλίσκονται.

2 Κοκκοβαφεῖ πέπλῳ χρυσᾶ ἐνείραντες γράμματα τίθενται πρὸ τῆς χειᾶς ὕπνον ἐγγοητεύσαντες τοῖς γράμμασιν, ὑφ' οὗ νικᾶται τοὺς ὀφθαλμοὺς ὁ δράκων ἀτρέπτους ὄντας, καὶ πολλὰ τῆς ἀπορρήτου σοφίας ἐπ' αὐτὸν ᾄδουσιν, οἷς ἄγεταί τε καὶ τὸν αὐχένα ὑπεκβαλὼν[6] τῆς χειᾶς ἐπικαθεύδει τοῖς γράμμασι. προσπεσόντες οὖν οἱ Ἰνδοὶ κειμένῳ πελέκεις ἐναράττουσι, καὶ τὴν κεφαλὴν ἀποτεμόντες λῄζονται τὰς ἐν αὐτῇ λίθους. ἀποκεῖσθαι δέ φασιν ἐν ταῖς τῶν ὀρείων δρακόντων κεφαλαῖς λίθους τὸ μὲν εἶδος ἀνθηρὰς καὶ πάντα ἀπαυγαζούσας χρώματα, τὴν δὲ ἰσχὺν ἀρρήτους <καὶ>[7] κατὰ τὸν δακτύλιον, ὃν γενέσθαι φασὶ τῷ Γύγῃ.

3 Πολλάκις δὲ καὶ τὸν Ἰνδὸν αὐτῷ πελέκει καὶ αὐτῇ τέχνῃ συλλαβὼν ἐς τὴν αὑτοῦ χειὰν φέρων ᾤχετο, μονονοὺ σείων τὸ ὄρος. οὗτοι καὶ τὰ ὄρη τὰ περὶ τὴν Ἐρυθρὰν οἰκεῖν λέγονται, σύριγμα δὲ δεινόν φασιν ἀκούεσθαι τούτων καὶ κατιόντας αὐτοὺς ἐπὶ τὴν θάλατταν πλεῖν ἐπὶ πολὺ τοῦ πελάγους. περὶ δὲ ἐτῶν μήκους τοῦ θηρίου τούτου γνῶναί τε ἄπορον καὶ εἰπεῖν

6 ὑπεκβαλὼν J. Toup (Jac.): ὑπερβαλὼν
7 <καὶ> Radermacher

They also make a sound rather like clashing bronze when they burrow underground, and from their crests, which are crimson, there gleams a fire brighter than a torch. These also catch elephants, and they in turn are caught by the Indians in the following way.

The Indians weave golden letters into a crimson cloth, 2
and put it in front of the snake's hole, after casting a soporific spell on the letters. This cloth captivates the unwavering eye of the snake, and the Indians also recite many secret spells against it, so that it is charmed into poking its head out of the hole and falling asleep over the letters. Then the Indians attack it where it lies with axe blows, cut off the head, and steal the stones contained within it. In the head of the mountain snake, they say, there are hidden stones of variegated colors giving off every hue, and having a magic power like the supposed ring of Gyges.[7]

But often the snake seizes the Indian despite his axe 3
and his magic, and carries him off into its hole, almost making the mountain shake. It is also said that these snakes inhabit the mountains around the Red Sea,[8] where their fearful hissing can be heard, and that they come down to the shore and swim far out into the deep. This creature's length of life defies discovery, and if stated would defy

[7] Gyges, a seventh-century king of Lydia, was supposed to have had a ring that made the wearer invisible.

[8] The ancients used the term Red Sea for the Indian Ocean between Africa and India and also for its two great arms, the western one (the modern "Red Sea") and the eastern (the modern "Arabian" or "Persian" gulf). Here the Indian Ocean is meant.

ἄπιστον. τοσαῦτα περὶ δρακόντων οἶδα.

9. Τὴν δὲ πόλιν τὴν ὑπὸ τῷ ὄρει μεγίστην οὖσαν φασὶ μὲν καλεῖσθαι Πάρακα, δρακόντων δὲ ἀνακεῖσθαι κεφαλὰς ἐν μέσῃ πλείστας, γυμναζομένων τῶν ἐν ἐκείνῃ Ἰνδῶν τὴν θήραν ταύτην ἐκ νέων. λέγονται δὲ καὶ ζῴων ξυνιέναι φθεγγομένων τε καὶ βουλευομένων σιτούμενοι δράκοντος οἱ μὲν καρδίαν, οἱ δὲ ἧπαρ. προϊόντες δὲ αὐλοῦ μὲν ἀκοῦσαι δόξαι νομέως δή τινος ἀγέλην τάττοντος, ἐλάφους δὲ ἄρα βουκολεῖσθαι λευκάς, ἀμέλγουσι δὲ Ἰνδοὶ ταύτας εὐτραφὲς ἡγούμενοι τὸ ἀπ᾽ αὐτῶν γάλα.

10. Ἐντεῦθεν ἡμερῶν τεττάρων ὁδὸν πορευόμενοι δι᾽ εὐδαίμονος καὶ ἐνεργοῦ τῆς χώρας προσελθεῖν φασι τῇ τῶν σοφῶν τύρσει. τὸν δὲ ἡγεμόνα κελεύσαντα συνοκλάσαι τὴν κάμηλον ἀποπηδῆσαι αὐτῆς περιδεᾶ καὶ ἱδρῶτος πλέων. τὸν δὲ Ἀπολλώνιον ξυνεῖναι μὲν οὗ ἥκοι, γελάσαντα δὲ ἐπὶ τῷ τοῦ Ἰνδοῦ δέει "δοκεῖ μοι" φάναι "οὗτος, εἰ καὶ κατέπλευσεν ἐς λιμένα μακρόν τι ἀναμετρήσας πέλαγος, ἀχθεσθῆναι ἂν τῇ γῇ καὶ δεῖσαι τὸ ἐν ὅρμῳ εἶναι." καὶ ἅμα εἰπὼν ταῦτα προσέταξε τῇ καμήλῳ συνιζῆσαι, καὶ γὰρ δὴ καὶ ἐθὰς λοιπὸν ἦν τῶν τοιούτων,

2 Περίφοβον δὲ ἄρα ἐποίει τὸν ἡγεμόνα τὸ πλησίον τῶν σοφῶν ἥκειν, Ἰνδοὶ γὰρ δεδίασι τούτους μᾶλλον ἢ τὸν σφῶν αὐτῶν βασιλέα, ὅτι καὶ βασιλεὺς αὐτός, ὑφ᾽ ᾧ ἔστιν ἡ χώρα, περὶ πάντων, ἃ λεκτέα τε αὐτῷ καὶ πρακτέα, ἐρωτᾷ τούσδε τοὺς ἄνδρας, ὥσπερ οἱ ἐς θεοῦ πέμποντες, οἱ δὲ σημαίνουσι μέν, ὅ τι λῷον αὐτῷ

belief. So much for my knowledge of snakes.

9. The city below the mountain is very large, and by their account is called Paraka. In the center of it there are dedicated many snake heads, since the Indians of that region practice this kind of hunting from an early age. They are said also to understand the speech and advice of animals by eating either the heart or the liver of a snake.[9] As the party proceeded they thought they heard the pipe of some herdsman herding his flock, but it was a flock of white deer, which the Indians milk, believing their milk to be nutritious.

10. From there they traveled for four days through rich, well tilled country before nearing the Wise Men's citadel. Ordering his camel to kneel, their guide jumped off it, terrified and dripping with sweat. Apollonius however realized where he had arrived, and laughing at the Indian's fear said, "Even if this man had sailed into harbor after crossing some wide sea, I think, he would be distressed by land, and fear being in port." So saying he made his camel crouch, being by now used to such things.

What caused the guide such terror was the proximity of 2
the Wise Men, since the Indians fear them even more than their own king. In fact the king himself who rules the country asks the advice of these notables on every subject, what to say and what to do, like those who send to a god for advice; and they signify what it would be good for him to

[9] Compare I 20.3, on the Arabs' understanding of birds.

πράττειν, ὅ τι δὲ μὴ λῷον, ἀπαγορεύουσί τε καὶ ἀποσημαίνουσι.

11. Καταλύσειν δὲ μέλλοντες ἐν τῇ κώμῃ τῇ πλησίον (ἀπέχει δὲ τοῦ ὄχθου τῶν σοφῶν οὔπω στάδιον), ἰδεῖν φασι νεανίαν δρόμῳ ἥκοντα μελάντατον Ἰνδῶν πάντων, ὑποστίλβειν δὲ αὐτῷ μηνοειδῶς τὸ μεσόφρυον. τουτὶ δὲ ἀκούω χρόνοις ὕστερον καὶ περὶ Μέμνονα[8] τὸν Ἡρώδου τοῦ σοφιστοῦ τρόφιμον (ἀπ' Αἰθιόπων δὲ ἦν) ἐν μειρακίῳ δόξαι, προϊόντος δὲ ἐς ἄνδρας ἐκλιπεῖν τὴν αὐγὴν ταύτην καὶ συναφανισθῆναι τῇ ὥρᾳ, τὸν δὲ Ἰνδὸν χρυσῆν μὲν φέρειν φασὶν ἄγκυραν, ἣν νομίζουσιν Ἰνδοὶ κηρύκειον ἐπὶ τῷ πάντα ἴσχειν.

12. Προσδραμόντα δὲ τῷ Ἀπολλωνίῳ φωνῇ Ἑλλάδι προσειπεῖν αὐτόν, καὶ τοῦτο μὲν οὔπω θαυμαστὸν δόξαι διὰ τὸ καὶ τοὺς ἐν τῇ κώμῃ πάντας ἀφ' Ἑλλήνων φθέγγεσθαι,[9] τὸ δὲ "ὁ δεῖνα χαῖρε" τοῖς μὲν ἄλλοις παρασχεῖν ἔκπληξιν, τῷ δὲ ἀνδρὶ θάρσος ὑπὲρ ὧν ἀφῖκτο, βλέψας γὰρ ἐς τὸν Δάμιν, "παρὰ ἄνδρας" ἔφη "σοφοὺς ἀτεχνῶς ἥκομεν, ἐοίκασι γὰρ προγιγνώσκειν." καὶ ἅμα ἤρετο τὸν Ἰνδόν, ὅ τι χρὴ πράττειν, ποθῶν ἤδη τὴν ξυνουσίαν, ὁ δὲ Ἰνδὸς "τούτους μὲν" ἔφη "καταλύειν χρὴ ἐνταῦθα, σὲ δὲ ἥκειν ὡς ἔχεις, κελεύουσι γὰρ αὐτοί." Τὸ μὲν δὴ "αὐτοὶ" Πυθαγόρειον ἤδη τῷ Ἀπολλωνίῳ ἐφάνη, καὶ ἠκολούθει χαίρων.

[8] Μέμνονα Ol.: Μένωνα [9] ἀφ' Ἑλλ. φθ. *suspectum*

do, and forbid and warn him against what it would not be.

11. They were about to put up in the nearby village, which is less than a stade from the Wise Men's hill, when they say they saw a young man running towards them, blacker than any Indian, but with a crescent-shaped mark gleaming on his forehead. I gather that the same thing appeared long afterwards in Memnon, the foster son (though he was Ethiopian) of the sophist Herodes,[10] when he was still a youth, but as he entered manhood this white mark faded and vanished along with his prime. The Indian also carried a golden anchor, they say, which is a customary symbol of messengers in India since it "secures" everything.

12. He ran up to Apollonius and greeted him in Greek, which was not in itself surprising since everybody in the village talked Greek. But while his saying "Greetings" with the appropriate name amazed the others, it assured the Master of his mission, since he looked at Damis and said, "We have come to men of true wisdom, since they seem to have foreknowledge." Immediately he asked the Indian what he had to do, being now eager to meet them, and the Indian said, "These must stay here, but you must come as you are, because they themselves invite you." The word "themselves" in itself seemed Pythagorean to Apollonius, and he followed gladly.[11]

[10] Herodes Atticus, the great Athenian sophist of the mid-second century, had several such foster sons, including the African Memnon.

[11] "He himself said" was the way Pythagoreans quoted the sayings of the founder.

13. Τὸν δὲ ὄχθον, ἐφ᾽ οὗ οἱ σοφοὶ ἀνῳκισμένοι εἰσίν, ὕψος μὲν εἶναι κατὰ τὴν Ἀθηναίων φασὶν ἀκρόπολιν, ἀνίστασθαι δὲ ἐκ πεδίου ἄνω, εὐφυᾶ δὲ ὁμοίως πέτραν ὀχυροῦν αὐτὸν κύκλῳ περιήκουσαν, ἧς πολλαχοῦ δίχηλα ὁρᾶσθαι ἴχνη, καὶ γενειάδων τύπους καὶ προσώπων, καί που καὶ νῶτα ἰδεῖν ἀπωλισθηκόσιν ὅμοια. τὸν γὰρ Διόνυσον, ὅτε ξὺν Ἡρακλεῖ ἀπεπειρᾶτο τοῦ χωρίου, προσβαλεῖν μὲν αὐτῷ φασι κελεῦσαι τοὺς Πᾶνας, ὡς πρὸς τὸ σιμὸν[10] ἱκανούς, ἐμβροντηθέντας δὲ αὐτοὺς ὑπὸ τῶν σοφῶν πεσεῖν ἄλλον ἄλλως, καὶ τὰς πέτρας οἷον ἐντυπωθῆναι τὰ τῆς διαμαρτίας σχήματα. περὶ δὲ τῷ ὄχθῳ νεφέλην ἰδεῖν φασιν, ἐν ᾗ τοὺς Ἰνδοὺς οἰκεῖν φανερούς τε καὶ ἀφανεῖς καθ᾽[11] ὅ τι βούλονται. πύλας δὲ εἰ μὲν καὶ ἄλλας εἶναι τῷ ὄχθῳ, οὐκ εἰδέναι. τὸ γὰρ περὶ αὐτὸν νέφος οὔτε ἀκλείστῳ ξυγχωρεῖν οὔτ᾽ αὖ ξυγκεκλεισμένῳ φαίνεσθαι.

14. Αὐτὸς δὲ ἀναβῆναι μὲν κατὰ τὸ νότιον μάλιστα τοῦ ὄχθου τῷ Ἰνδῷ ἑπόμενος, ἰδεῖν δὲ πρῶτον μὲν φρέαρ ὀργυιῶν τεττάρων, οὗ τὴν αὐγὴν ἐπὶ τὸ στόμιον ἀναπέμπεσθαι κυανωτάτην οὖσαν, καὶ ὁπότε ἡ μεσημβρία τοῦ ἡλίου σταίη περὶ αὐτό, ἀνιμᾶσθαι τὴν αὐγὴν ὑπὸ[12] τῆς ἀκτῖνος καὶ χωρεῖν ἄνω, παρεχομένην εἶδος θερμῆς ἴριδος. μαθεῖν δὲ ὕστερον περὶ τοῦ φρέατος, ὡς σανδαρακίνη μὲν εἴη ἡ ὑπ᾽ αὐτῷ γῆ, ἀπόρρητον δὲ τὸ ὕδωρ ἡγοῖντο καὶ οὔτε πίνοι τις αὐτὸ οὔτε ἀνασπῴη, ὅρκιον δὲ νομίζοιτο τῇ πέριξ Ἰνδικῇ πάσῃ.

13. They say that the hill where the Wise Men have their settlement is about the height of the Acropolis at Athens, though it rises sheer from a plain, and it is similarly defended by natural rock on every side. In many parts of this rock there could be seen prints of cloven hooves and impressions of beards, faces, and also backs as if people had slid down. It seems that when Dionysus in alliance with Heracles tried to take the place, he asked the Pans to attack it, thinking they would be good on sloping ground. They, however, were crazed by the Wise Men and fell everywhere, and the rocks had as it were been imprinted with the traces of their impiety. Around the hill they say they saw a cloud, and inside it the Indians live, visible or invisible as they please. They did not know if the hill had any other kind of gate, since the surrounding cloud prevented your seeing whether it was open or closed.

14. Apollonius says that he went up the hill roughly from the south, following the Indian. The first thing he saw was a well four fathoms deep, from which a deep blue light rose to the surface, and whenever the sun at its zenith stood above it, this light was drawn up by the sun's ray and rose upwards looking like a rainbow of fire. He later learned that the soil at the bottom of the well was realgar,[12] and that the Indians considered the water magical, and so neither drew nor drank from it; the whole region of India round about considered it a pledge of oaths.

[12] A red mineral containing arsenic and sulfur.

---

[10] τὸ σιμὸν Valck.: τὸν σεισμὸν
[11] καθ' West.: καὶ
[12] ὑπὸ Jackson: ἀπὸ

2 Πλησίον δὲ τούτου κρατῆρα εἶναι πυρός, οὗ φλόγα ἀναπέμπεσθαι μολυβδώδη, καπνὸν δὲ οὐδένα ἀπ᾿ αὐτῆς ἄττειν, οὐδὲ ὀσμὴν οὐδεμίαν, οὐδὲ ὑπερχυθῆναί ποτε ὁ κρατὴρ οὗτος, ἀλλ᾿ ἀναδίδοσθαι τοσοῦτος, ὡς μὴ ὑπερβλύσαι τοῦ βόθρου. ἐνταῦθα Ἰνδοὶ καθαίρονται τῶν ἀκουσίων, ὅθεν οἱ σοφοὶ τὸ μὲν φρέαρ ἐλέγχου καλοῦσι, τὸ δὲ πῦρ ξυγγνώμης. καὶ διττὼ ἑωρακέναι φασὶ πίθω λίθου μέλανος ὄμβρων τε καὶ ἀνέμων ὄντε. ὁ μὲν δὴ τῶν ὄμβρων, εἰ αὐχμῷ ἡ Ἰνδικὴ πιέζοιτο, ἀνοιχθεὶς νεφέλας ἀναπέμπει καὶ ὑγραίνει τὴν γῆν πᾶσαν, εἰ δὲ ὄμβροι πλεονεκτοῖεν, ἴσχει αὐτοὺς ξυγκλειόμενος, ὁ δὲ τῶν ἀνέμων πίθος ταὐτόν, οἶμαι, τῷ τοῦ Αἰόλου ἀσκῷ πράττει, παρανοιγνύντες γὰρ τὸν πίθον ἕνα τῶν ἀνέμων ἀνιᾶσιν ἐμπνεῖν ὥρᾳ, κἀντεῦθεν ἡ γῆ ἔρρωται.

3 Θεῶν δὲ ἀγάλμασιν ἐντυχεῖν φασιν, εἰ μὲν Ἰνδοῖς ἢ Αἰγυπτίοις, θαῦμα οὐδέν, τὰ δέ γε ἀρχαιότατα τῶν παρ᾿ Ἕλλησι, τό τε τῆς Ἀθηνᾶς τῆς Πολιάδος, καὶ τὸ τοῦ Ἀπόλλωνος τοῦ Δηλίου, καὶ τὸ τοῦ Διονύσου τοῦ Λιμναίου, καὶ τὸ τοῦ Ἀμυκλαίου καὶ ὁπόσα ὧδε ἀρχαῖα, ταῦτα ἱδρύεσθαί τε τοὺς Ἰνδοὺς τούτους καὶ νομίζειν Ἑλληνικοῖς ἤθεσι. φασὶ δ᾿ οἰκεῖν τὰ μέσα τῆς Ἰνδικῆς, καὶ τὸν ὄχθον ὀμφαλὸν ποιοῦνται τοῦ λόφου τούτου, πῦρ τε ἐπ᾿ αὐτοῦ ὀργιάζουσιν, ὅ φασιν ἐκ τῶν τοῦ ἡλίου ἀκτίνων αὐτοὶ ἕλκειν· τούτῳ καὶ τὸν ὕμνον ἡμέραν ἅπασαν ἐς μεσημβρίαν ᾄδουσιν.

15. Ὁποῖοι μὲν δὴ οἱ ἄνδρες καὶ ὅπως οἰκοῦντες τὸν ὄχθον, αὐτὸς ὁ ἀνὴρ δίεισιν· ἐν μιᾷ γὰρ τῶν

Near this, he says, there was a fiery crater, which gave off a lead-colored flame, but no smoke came from it or even an odor, and this crater never overflowed, but rose in such a way as never to spill out of its hollow. There the Indians purify themselves from accidental crimes, and for that reason the Wise Men call the well "the Well of Proof" and the fire "the Fire of Forgiveness." They also say they saw two jars of black stone, one of Winds and the other of Rains. The Jar of Rains is opened whenever India is afflicted with drought, and releases clouds, thus watering the whole land; but if there is too much rain, it is closed and so checks it. The Jar of Winds has the same effect as Aeolus's bag,[13] I suppose, because by opening it slightly they release one of the winds to blow in due season and thus the land prospers. 2

They say they also came across idols of gods, some, not surprisingly, Indian or Egyptian, but also the earliest of Greek statues, those of Athena Polias, Delian Apollo, Dionysus of the Marshes, and Apollo of Amyclae,[14] and others of similar antiquity, which these Indians set up and worship with Greek rites. They claim to inhabit the center of India, and regard the peak of this hill as its navel. On it they worship a mystic fire that they claim personally to light from the sun's rays. They sing their hymn to this fire every day about noon. 3

15. Now the Wise Men's nature and their way of life on the hill are described by the Master himself, since in one of

[13] In Homer, *Odyssey* 10.19–27, Aeolus gives Odysseus a bag containing the winds in order to speed his voyage.

[14] These statues are all of the archaic period, from the eighth century to the sixth.

πρὸς Αἰγυπτίους ὁμιλιῶν "εἶδον" φησὶν "Ἰνδοὺς Βραχμᾶνας οἰκοῦντας ἐπὶ τῆς γῆς καὶ οὐκ ἐπ' αὐτῆς, καὶ ἀτειχίστως τετειχισμένους, καὶ οὐδὲν κεκτημένους καὶ[13] τὰ πάντων." ταυτὶ δὲ ἐκεῖνος μὲν σοφώτερον ἔγραψεν, ὁ δέ γε Δάμις φησὶ χαμευνίᾳ μὲν αὐτοὺς χρῆσθαι, τὴν γῆν δὲ ὑποστρωννύναι πόας, ἃς ἂν αὐτοὶ αἱρῶνται, καὶ μετεωροποροῦντας δὴ ἰδεῖν ἀπὸ τῆς γῆς ἐς πήχεις δύο, οὐ θαυματοποιίας ἕνεκα, τὸ γὰρ φιλότιμον τοῦτο παραιτεῖσθαι τοὺς ἄνδρας, ἀλλ' ὁπόσα τῷ Ἡλίῳ ξυναποβαίνοντες τῆς γῆς δρῶσιν, ὡς πρόσφορα τῷ θεῷ πράττοντας.[14]

2 Τό τοι πῦρ, ὃ ἀπὸ τῆς ἀκτῖνος ἐπισπῶνται καίτοι σωματοειδὲς ὂν οὔτε ἐπὶ βωμοῦ καίειν αὐτοὺς οὔτε ἐν ἰπνοῖς φυλάττειν, ἀλλ' ὥσπερ τὰς αὐγάς, αἳ ἐξ ἡλίου τε ἀνακλῶνται καὶ ὕδατος, οὕτω μετέωρόν τε ὁρᾶσθαι αὐτὸ καὶ σαλεῦον ἐν τῷ αἰθέρι. τὸν μὲν οὖν δὴ Ἥλιον ὑπὲρ τῶν ὡρῶν, ἃς ἐπιτροπεύει αὐτός, ἵν' ἐς καιρὸν τῇ γῇ ἴωσι[15] καὶ ἡ Ἰνδικὴ εὖ πράττῃ, νύκτωρ δὲ λιπαροῦσι τὴν ἀκτῖνα μὴ ἄχθεσθαι τῇ νυκτί, μένειν δέ, ὡς ὑπ' αὐτῶν ἤχθη. τοιοῦτον μὲν δὴ τοῦ Ἀπολλωνίου τὸ "ἐν τῇ γῇ τε εἶναι τοὺς Βραχμᾶνας καὶ οὐκ ἐν τῇ γῇ."

3 Τὸ δὲ "ἀτειχίστως τετειχισμένους" δηλοῖ τὸν ἀέρα, ὑφ' ᾧ ζῶσιν, ὑπαίθριοι γὰρ δοκοῦντες αὐλίζεσθαι σκιάν τε ὑπεραίρουσιν αὐτῶν, καὶ ὕοντος οὐ ψεκάζονται καὶ ὑπὸ τῷ ἡλίῳ εἰσίν, ἐπειδὰν αὐτοὶ βούλωνται. τὸ δὲ "μηδὲν κεκτημένους τὰ πάντων ἔχειν" ὧδε ὁ Δάμις ἐξηγεῖται· πηγαί, ὁπόσαι τοῖς βάκχοις παρὰ τῆς γῆς ἀναθρώσκουσιν, ἐπειδὰν ὁ Διόνυσος αὐτούς

his addresses to the Egyptians he says, "I saw the Indian Brahmans living on the earth and not on it, walled without walls, owning nothing and owning everything." This is his rather philosophical account, while Damis says that they sleep on the ground, and the earth makes a bed for them of any grass they choose. He also says he saw them levitating as much as two cubits from the ground, not for ostentation, since their Eminences deplore that kind of vanity, but because all the rites they perform to the Sun they do above the earth like him, considering this practice appropriate for the god.

The fire they draw from the sun's ray looks substantial, 2
but they do not light it on an altar or keep it in lanterns. Instead it is like rays of the sun reflected off water, and appears suspended and shimmering in the sky. They pray to the Sun on behalf of the seasons which it dispenses, asking for them to come at the right time for the land and for India to prosper, and at night they implore the sunbeam not to be hostile to the dark, but remain as it was when they drew it down. That is the meaning of Apollonius's saying, "The Brahmans are on the earth and not on the earth."

But "walled without walls" refers to the climate in 3
which they live, since although they appear to camp out in the open air, they bring shade to cover themselves, they are not wetted when it rains, and have sunshine whenever they want. The words, "with no possessions except the whole world's," are interpreted by Damis in this way. Just as streams of water burst from the ground for worshipers of Bacchus when the god sets both them and the earth quak-

---

13 καὶ Ol.: ἢ 14 πράττοντας Kay.: πράττοντες
15 ἴωσι Cob.: ὦσι

τε καὶ τὴν γῆν σείσῃ, φοιτῶσι καὶ τοῖς Ἰνδοῖς τούτοις ἑστιωμένοις τε καὶ ἑστιῶσιν. εἰκότως οὖν ὁ Ἀπολλώνιος τοὺς μηδὲν μὲν ἐκ παρασκευῆς, αὐτοσχεδίως δὲ ἃ βούλονταιποριζομένους, ἔχειν φησὶν ἃ μὴ ἔχουσιν.

4 Κομᾶν δὲ ἐπιτηδεύουσιν, ὥσπερ Λακεδαιμόνιοι πάλαι, καὶ Θούριοι, Ταραντῖνοί τε καὶ Μήλιοι, καὶ ὁπόσοις τὰ Λακωνικὰ ἦν ἐν λόγῳ, μίτραν τε ἀναδοῦνται λευκήν, καὶ γυμνὸν αὐτοῖς βάδισμα, καὶ τὴν ἐσθῆτα ἐσχηματίζοντο παραπλησίως ταῖς ἐξωμίσιν. ἡ δὲ ὕλη τῆς ἐσθῆτος ἔριον αὐτοφυὲς ἡ γῆ φύει, λευκὸν μὲν ὥσπερ τὸ Παμφύλων, μαλακώτερον δὲ τίκτει, ἡ <δὲ>[16] πιμελὴ οἷα ἔλαιον ἀπ᾽ αὐτοῦ λείβεται.[17] τοῦτο ἱερὰν ἐσθῆτα ποιοῦνται καὶ εἴ τις ἕτερος παρὰ τοὺς Ἰνδοὺς τούτους ἀνασπῴη αὐτό, οὐ μεθίεται ἡ γῆ τοῦ ἐρίου. τὴν δὲ ἰσχὺν τοῦ δακτυλίου καὶ τῆς ῥάβδου, ἃ φορεῖν αὐτοὺς ἄμφω, δύνασθαι μὲν πάντα, δύω δὲ ἀρρήτω τετιμῆσθαι.

16. Προσιόντα δὲ τὸν Ἀπολλώνιον οἱ μὲν ἄλλοι σοφοὶ προσήγοντο ἀσπαζόμενοι ταῖς χερσίν, ὁ δὲ Ἰάρχας ἐκάθητο μὲν ἐπὶ δίφρου ὑψηλοῦ, χαλκοῦ δὲ μέλανος ἦν καὶ πεποίκιλτο χρυσοῖς ἀγάλμασιν, οἱ δὲ τῶν ἄλλων δίφροι χαλκοῖ μέν, ἄσημοι δὲ ἦσαν, ὑψηλοὶ δὲ ἧττον, ὑπεκάθηντο γὰρ τῷ Ἰάρχᾳ. τὸν δὲ Ἀπολλώνιον ἰδὼν φωνῇ τε ἠσπάσατο Ἑλλάδι καὶ τὰ τοῦ Ἰνδοῦ γράμματα ἀπῄτει. θαυμάσαντος δὲ τοῦ Ἀπολλωνίου τὴν πρόγνωσιν, καὶ γράμμα γε ἓν ἔφη λείπειν τῇ ἐπιστολῇ, δέλτα εἰπών, παρῆλθε γὰρ αὐτὸν

ing, so they appear for the benefit of those Indians when the Indians are guests or hosts at dinner. Apollonius therefore rightly says that they have what they do not have, since they make no preparations in advance, but obtain everything they want on the spot.

They wear their hair long as used to be done by the Spartans, the Thurians of Tarentum, the Melians, and all the peoples that valued Spartan ways, and they bind it with a white ribbon. Their feet are bare, and they dressed in something like our one-sleeved tunic. The material for their clothing is wool that grows naturally from the earth, white like Pamphylian wool but softer, and exuding a grease like oil.[15] They make this into their sacred cloth, and if anybody except these Indians tries to pluck this wool, the earth will not release it. The ring and the rod, both of which they carry, have a power which is capable of anything, and both are valued for their mysterious powers. 4

16. As Apollonius approached, the other Wise Men went up to him and greeted him with embraces, but Iarchas remained seated on a high chair. This was of dark bronze ornamented with golden images, while the others sat on chairs also of bronze, but with no images and less high, since they sat below Iarchas. On seeing Apollonius, Iarchas greeted him in Greek and asked for the Indian's letter. When Apollonius marveled at his clairvoyance, Iarchas added that there was one letter missing in the docu-

[15] Apparently cotton. Philostratus refers to cotton by a different name, *byssos*, in II 20.1.

---

[16] <δὲ> Jac.

[17] λείβεται Kay.: λείβεσθαι

γράφοντα, καὶ ἐφάνη τοῦτο ὧδε ἔχον.

2 Ἀναγνοὺς δὲ τὴν ἐπιστολήν, "πῶς," ἔφη "ὦ Ἀπολλώνιε, περὶ ἡμῶν φρονεῖτε;" "πῶς" εἶπεν "ἢ ὡς δηλοῖ τὸ ὑμῶν ἕνεκα ἥκειν με ὁδόν, ἣν μήπω τις τῶν ὅθενπερ ἐγὼ ἀνθρώπων;" "τί δὲ ἡμᾶς πλέον οἴει σαυτοῦ γιγνώσκειν;" "ἐγὼ μὲν" εἶπε "σοφώτερά τε ἡγοῦμαι τὰ ὑμέτερα καὶ πολλῷ θειότερα. εἰ δὲ μηδὲν πλέον ὧν οἶδα παρ' ὑμῖν εὕροιμι, μεμαθηκὼς ἂν εἴην καὶ τὸ μηκέτ' ἔχειν[18] ὅ τι μάθοιμι."

3 Ὑπολαβὼν οὖν ὁ Ἰνδὸς "οἱ μὲν ἄλλοι" ἔφη "τοὺς ἀφικνουμένους ἐρωτῶσι, ποταποί τε ἥκουσι καὶ ἐφ' ὅ τι, ἡμῖν δὲ σοφίας ἐπίδειξιν πρώτην ἔχει τὸ μὴ ἀγνοῆσαι τὸν ἥκοντα. ἔλεγχε δὲ πρῶτον τοῦτο." καὶ εἰπὼν ταῦτα πατρόθεν τε διῄει τὸν Ἀπολλώνιον καὶ μητρόθεν, καὶ τὰ ἐν Αἰγαῖς πάντα, καὶ ὡς προσῆλθεν αὐτῷ ὁ Δάμις, καὶ εἰ δή τι ἐσπούδασαν ὁδοιποροῦντες ἢ σπουδάζοντος ἑτέρου εἶδον, πάντα ταῦθ' ὥσπερ κοινωνήσας αὐτοῖς τῆς ἀποδημίας ὁ Ἰνδὸς ἀπνευστί τε καὶ σαφῶς εἶρεν.[19]

4 Ἐκπλαγέντος δὲ τοῦ Ἀπολλωνίου καὶ ὁπόθεν εἰδείη[20] ἐπερομένου, "καὶ σὺ μέτοχος" ἔφη "τῆς σοφίας ταύτης ἥκεις, ἀλλ' οὔπω πάσης." "διδάξῃ οὖν με" ἔφη "τὴν σοφίαν πᾶσαν;" "καὶ ἀφθόνως γε," εἶπε "τουτὶ γὰρ σοφώτερον τοῦ βασκαίνειν τε καὶ κρύπτειν τὰ σπουδῆς ἄξια. καὶ ἄλλως, Ἀπολλώνιε, μεστόν σε ὁρῶ τῆς Μνημοσύνης, ἣν ἡμεῖς μάλιστα θεῶν ἀγαπῶμεν." "ἦ γὰρ καθεώρακας," εἶπεν "ὅπως πέφυκα;" "ἡμεῖς,"

ment, a D that the writer had left out, and this proved to be true.

2 After reading the letter, he said, "Apollonius, what is your opinion of us?" "Why," said Apollonius, "it is shown by my taking a journey for your sake such as no one among those I come from has ever taken." "What knowledge do you think we have that you lack?" "It is my opinion," he replied, "that your ways are wiser and much more inspired. But if I were to find nothing among you that I do not know, I would also have learned that there is nothing further for me to learn."

3 So the Indian replied, "Other people ask newcomers where they come from and what their mission is, but for us it is the first proof of our wisdom that we are not ignorant about our visitors. Let me prove this first." Whereupon he recounted Apollonius's ancestry on his father's and his mother's side, all his experiences in Aegeae, how Damis joined him, all the things that they had discussed on the journey or had learned from the discussions of others. All this the Indian reeled off fluently and clearly, just as if he had shared their journey.

4 In amazement Apollonius asked him how he knew, and he replied, "You have come with a part of this wisdom, but not of all." "Will you let me learn it all, then?" Apollonius asked. "Unstintingly," Iarchas replied; "that is more philosophical than grudging and concealing what is important. Besides, Apollonius, I see that you are well endowed with Memory, the god whom we honor most." "What?" said Apollonius, "Have you already made out my nature?" "We,

---

18 μηκέτ᾽ ἔχειν Bentl.: μὴ κατέχειν

19 εἶρεν Cob.: εἴρηκεν 20 εἰδείη Cob.: ᾔδει

ἔφη "ὦ Ἀπολλώνιε, πάντα ὁρῶμεν τὰ τῆς ψυχῆς εἴδη ξυμβόλοις αὐτὰ μυρίοις ἐξιχνεύοντες. ἀλλ' ἐπεὶ μεσημβρία πλησίον, καὶ τὰ πρόσφορα τοῖς θεοῖς χρὴ παρασκευάσαι, νῦν μὲν ταῦτ' ἐκπονῶμεν, μετὰ ταῦτα δέ, ὁπόσα βούλει, διαλεγώμεθα, παρατύγχανε δὲ πᾶσι τοῖς δρωμένοις." "νὴ Δί'," εἶπεν "ἀδικοίην ἂν τὸν Καύκασον καὶ τὸν Ἰνδόν, οὓς ὑπερβὰς δι' ὑμᾶς ἥκω, εἰ μὴ πάντων ἐμφοροίμην ὧν δρῴητε." "ἐμφοροῦ" ἔφη "καὶ ἴωμεν."

17. Ἐλθόντες οὖν ἐπὶ πηγήν τινα ὕδατος, ἥν φησιν ὁ Δάμις ἰδὼν ὕστερον ἐοικέναι τῇ ἐν Βοιωτοῖς Δίρκῃ, πρῶτα μὲν ἐγυμνώθησαν, εἶτα ἐχρίσαντο τὰς κεφαλὰς ἠλεκτρώδει φαρμάκῳ, τὸ δὲ οὕτω τι τοὺς Ἰνδοὺς ἔθαλπεν, ὡς ἀτμίζειν τὸ σῶμα καὶ τὸν ἱδρῶτα χωρεῖν ἀστακτί, καθάπερ τῶν πυρὶ λουομένων, εἶτα ἔρριψαν ἑαυτοὺς ἐς τὸ ὕδωρ καὶ λουσάμενοι ὧδε πρὸς τὸ ἱερὸν ἐβάδιζον ἐστεφανωμένοι καὶ μεστοὶ τοῦ ὕμνου.

2 Περιστάντες δὲ ἐν χοροῦ σχήματι καὶ κορυφαῖον ποιησάμενοι τὸν Ἰάρχαν ὀρθαῖς ταῖς ῥάβδοις τὴν γῆν ἔπληξαν, ἡ δὲ κυρτωθεῖσα δίκην κύματος ἀνέπεμψεν αὐτοὺς ἐς δίπηχυ τοῦ ἀέρος. οἱ δὲ ᾖδον ᾠδήν, ὁποῖος ὁ παιὰν ὁ τοῦ Σοφοκλέους, ὃν Ἀθήνησι τῷ Ἀσκληπιῷ ᾄδουσιν. ἐπεὶ δὲ ἐς τὴν γῆν κατῆραν, καλέσας ὁ Ἰάρχας τὸ μειράκιον τὸ τὴν ἄγκυραν φέρον "ἐπιμελήθητι" ἔφη "τῶν Ἀπολλωνίου ἑταίρων." ὁ δὲ πολλῷ θᾶττον ἢ οἱ ταχεῖς τῶν ὀρνίθων πορευθείς τε καὶ ἐπανελθὼν "ἐπιμεμέλημαι" ἔφη. θεραπεύσαντες οὖν τὰ πολλὰ τῶν ἱερῶν ἀνεπαύοντο ἐν τοῖς θάκοις, ὁ

Apollonius," he replied, "make out every kind of soul, and have countless clues to discover them. But as it is nearly noon, and we must prepare the gods' due rites, let us attend to them, and later let us discuss whatever you like. You may attend all our rites." "Well," said Apollonius, "I would certainly be wronging the Caucasus and the Indus, which I crossed to get to you, if I did not absorb all your rites." "Absorb them," said Iarchas, "and let us go."

17. So they went to a spring of water, which Damis after seeing it later compares to Dirce in Boeotia.[16] After disrobing, they then anointed their heads with an ointment like amber, which had such a warming effect on the Indians that their bodies steamed and their sweat ran in streams as when people use the hot bath. Then, after diving into the water and washing, in this state they proceeded to the temple garlanded and full of song.

There they stood around in a kind of chorus and, taking 2
their cue from Iarchas, struck the ground with their uplifted staves; and the ground, flexing like a wave, shot them two cubits into the air. They then sang a song like Sophocles's *Hymn of Praise* that is sung to Asclepius at Athens. When they had come down to earth, Iarchas called the youth carrying the anchor and said, "Take care of Apollonius's friends." The youth went and came back much faster than the swiftest bird, and said, "I have taken care of them." Then, having performed most of their rites, they

[16] River that rises near Thebes.

δὲ Ἰάρχας πρὸς τὸ μειράκιον "ἔκφερε" εἶπε "τῷ σοφῷ Ἀπολλωνίῳ τὸν Φραώτου θρόνον, ἵν᾽ ἐπ᾽ αὐτοῦ διαλέγοιτο."

18. Ὡς δὲ ἐκάθισεν "ἐρώτα," ἔφη "ὅ τι βούλει, παρ᾽ ἄνδρας γὰρ ἥκεις πάντα εἰδότας." ἤρετο οὖν ὁ Ἀπολλώνιος, εἰ καὶ αὑτοὺς ἴσασιν, οἰόμενος αὐτόν, ὥσπερ Ἕλληνες, χαλεπὸν ἡγεῖσθαι τὸ ἑαυτὸν γνῶναι, ὁ δὲ ἐπιστρέψας παρὰ τὴν τοῦ Ἀπολλωνίου δόξαν "ἡμεῖς" ἔφη "πάντα γιγνώσκομεν, ἐπειδὴ πρώτους ἑαυτοὺς γιγνώσκομεν, οὐ γὰρ ἂν προσέλθοι τις ἡμῶν τῇ φιλοσοφίᾳ ταύτῃ μὴ πρῶτον εἰδὼς ἑαυτόν." ὁ δὲ Ἀπολλώνιος ἀναμνησθεὶς ὧν τοῦ Φραώτου ἤκουσε καὶ ὅπως ὁ φιλοσοφήσειν μέλλων ἑαυτὸν βασανίσας ἐπιχειρεῖ, τούτῳ ξυνεχώρησε τῷ λόγῳ, τουτὶ γὰρ καὶ περὶ ἑαυτοῦ ἐπέπειστο. πάλιν οὖν ἤρετο, τίνας αὑτοὺς ἡγοῖντο, ὁ δὲ "θεοὺς" εἶπεν, ἐπερομένου δὲ αὐτοῦ, διὰ τί, "ὅτι" ἔφη "ἀγαθοί ἐσμεν ἄνθρωποι." τοῦτο τῷ Ἀπολλωνίῳ τοσαύτης ἔδοξεν εὐπαιδευσίας εἶναι μεστόν, ὡς εἰπεῖν αὐτὸ καὶ πρὸς Δομετιανὸν ὕστερον ἐν τοῖς ὑπὲρ ἑαυτοῦ λόγοις.

19. Ἀναλαβὼν οὖν τὴν ἐρώτησιν "περὶ ψυχῆς δὲ" εἶπε "πῶς φρονεῖτε;" "ὥς γε" εἶπε "Πυθαγόρας μὲν ὑμῖν, ἡμεῖς δὲ Αἰγυπτίοις παρεδώκαμεν." "εἴποις ἂν οὖν," ἔφη "καθάπερ ὁ Πυθαγόρας Εὔφορβον ἑαυτὸν ἀπέφηνεν, ὅτι καὶ σύ, πρὶν ἐς τοῦθ᾽ ἥκειν τὸ σῶμα, Τρώων τις ἢ Ἀχαιῶν ἦσθα ἢ ὁ δεῖνα;" ὁ δὲ Ἰνδὸς "Τροία μὲν ἀπώλετο" εἶπεν "ὑπὸ τῶν πλευσάντων Ἀχαιῶν τότε, ὑμᾶς δὲ ἀπολωλέκασιν οἱ ἐπ᾽ αὐτῇ

rested in their chairs, and Iarchas said to the boy, "Bring out the throne of Phraotes for the wise Apollonius, so that he can converse sitting in it."

18. When Apollonius had taken his seat, Iarchas said, "Ask me whatever you like, since you have come among Eminences who know everything." Apollonius therefore asked if they had self-knowledge, expecting that like the Greeks they would think self-knowledge something hard to achieve. But to Apollonius's surprise Iarchas corrected him and said, "We know everything because we begin by knowing ourselves. None of us would embark on this kind of philosophy without first knowing himself." Apollonius remembered what he had heard from Phraotes, how the man who intends to be a philosopher tests himself before making the attempt, and so he accepted this statement, having the same conviction about himself. He next proceeded to ask who they thought they were, and Iarchas replied, "Gods." "Why?" asked Apollonius. "Because we are good men." Apollonius thought this so full of good sense that he later repeated it to Domitian in his speech of self-defense.[17]

19. Resuming the interrogation, he said, "What is your belief about the soul?" "It is what Pythagoras transmitted to you Greeks," said Iarchas, "and we to the Egyptians." Apollonius replied, "Would you say, then, that before you entered this body you were some Trojan or Achaean or so-and-so, as Pythagoras revealed himself to be Euphorbus?" "Troy was destroyed," said the Indian, "by the Achaeans that sailed there at the time, and you Greeks have been de-

[17] See VIII 5.1.

λόγοι· μόνους γὰρ ἄνδρας ἡγούμενοι τοὺς ἐς Τροίαν στρατεύσαντας ἀμελεῖτε πλειόνων τε καὶ θειοτέρων ἀνδρῶν, οὓς ἥ τε ὑμετέρα γῆ καὶ ἡ Αἰγυπτίων καὶ ἡ Ἰνδῶν ἤνεγκεν. ἐπεὶ τοίνυν ἤρου με περὶ τοῦ προτέρου σώματος, εἰπέ μοι, τίνα θαυμασιώτερον ἡγῇ τῶν ἐπὶ Τροίαν τε καὶ ὑπὲρ Τροίας ἐλθόντων;"

2 "Ἐγὼ," ἔφη, "Ἀχιλλέα τὸν Πηλέως τε καὶ Θέτιδος, οὗτος γὰρ δὴ κάλλιστός τε εἶναι τῷ Ὁμήρῳ ὕμνηται, καὶ παρὰ πάντας τοὺς Ἀχαιοὺς μέγας ἔργα τε αὐτοῦ μεγάλα οἶδε. καὶ μεγάλων ἀξιοῖ τοὺς Αἴαντάς τε καὶ Νιρέας, οἳ μετ᾽ ἐκεῖνον καλοί τε αὐτῷ καὶ γενναῖοι ᾄδονται."[21] "πρὸς τοῦτον," ἔφη "Ἀπολλώνιε, καὶ τὸν πρόγονον θεώρει τὸν ἐμόν, μᾶλλον δὲ τὸ πρόγονον σῶμα, τουτὶ γὰρ καὶ Πυθαγόρας Εὔφορβον ἡγεῖτο.

20. "Ἦν τοίνυν" ἔφη "χρόνος, ὅτ᾽ Αἰθίοπες μὲν ᾤκουν ἐνταῦθα, γένος Ἰνδικόν, Αἰθιοπία δ᾽ οὔπω ἦν, ἀλλ᾽ ὑπὲρ Μερόην τε καὶ Καταδούπους ὥριστο Αἴγυπτος, αὐτὴ καὶ τὰς πηγὰς τοῦ Νείλου παρεχομένη καὶ ταῖς ἐκβολαῖς ξυναπολήγουσα. ὃν μὲν δὴ χρόνον ᾤκουν ἐνταῦθα οἱ Αἰθίοπες ὑποκείμενοι βασιλεῖ Γάγγῃ, ἥ τε γῆ αὐτοὺς ἱκανῶς ἔφερβε καὶ οἱ θεοὶ σφῶν ἐπεμελοῦντο, ἐπεὶ δὲ ἀπέκτειναν τὸν βασιλέα τοῦτον, οὔτε τοῖς ἄλλοις Ἰνδοῖς καθαροὶ ἔδοξαν, οὔτε ἡ γῆ ξυνεχώρει αὐτοῖς ἵστασθαι, τήν τε γὰρ σποράν, ἣν ἐς αὐτὴν ἐποιοῦντο, πρὶν ἐς κάλυκα ἥκειν, ἔφθειρε τούς τε τῶν γυναικῶν τόκους ἀτελεῖς ἐποίει, καὶ τὰς ἀγέλας πονήρως ἔβοσκε, πόλιν τε ὅποι βάλοιντο, ὑπεδίδου ἡ γῆ καὶ ὑπεχώρει κάτω.

stroyed by the tales about it. You think the only heroes are the sackers of Troy, and you neglect more numerous and more inspired men produced by your own country, by Egypt, and by India. But since you asked me about my former body, tell me whom you think most outstanding of the attackers or defenders of Troy."

"For myself," said Apollonius, "I think Achilles the son 2
of Peleus and Thetis, since Homer sings of him as a very handsome man and greater than all the other Greeks, and records great deeds of his. He also has a high opinion of men like Ajax and Nireus, whom he celebrates as second to Achilles in beauty and nobility." "Compare my ancestor," Iarchas replied, "with Achilles, Apollonius, or rather my ancestral body, since that is what Pythagoras considered Euphorbus.

20. "You see," he said, "there was a time when the Ethiopians lived here and were an Indian tribe. As yet Ethiopia did not exist, but Egypt had its boundary beyond Meroe and the Cataracts, and the same country contained the source of the Nile and ended at its mouth. As long as the Ethiopians lived here as subjects of king Ganges, the earth fed them plentifully and the gods protected them. But when they killed this king, the other Indians considered them polluted, and the earth no longer allowed them to stay. It destroyed the seed that they put in it before it came to the ear, it caused their wives to miscarry, and gave poor fodder to the cattle, and wherever they founded a city, the earth caved in and gave way.

---

21 ᾄδονται Kay.: ᾄδοιντο

2 "Καὶ γάρ τι καὶ φάσμα τοῦ Γάγγου προϊόντας αὐτοὺς ἤλαυνεν ἐνταραττόμενον τῷ ὁμίλῳ, ὃ οὐ πρότερον ἀνῆκε, πρίν γε δὴ τοὺς αὐθέντας καὶ τοὺς τὸ αἷμα χερσὶ[22] πράξαντας τῇ γῇ καθιερεύσαιεν.[23] ἦν δὲ ἄρα ὁ Γάγγης οὗτος δεκάπηχυς μὲν τὸ μῆκος, τὴν δὲ ὥραν οἷος οὔπω τις ἀνθρώπων, ποταμοῦ δὲ Γάγγου παῖς· τὸν δὲ πατέρα τὸν ἑαυτοῦ τὴν Ἰνδικὴν ἐπικλύζοντα αὐτὸς ἐς τὴν Ἐρυθρὰν ἔτρεψε καὶ διήλλαξεν αὐτὸν τῇ γῇ, ὅθεν ἡ γῆ ζῶντι μὲν ἄφθονα ἔφερεν, ἀποθανόντι δὲ ἐτιμώρει.

3 "'Ἐπεὶ δὲ τὸν Ἀχιλλέα Ὅμηρος ἄγει μὲν ὑπὲρ Ἑλένης ἐς Τροίαν, φησὶ δὲ αὐτὸν δώδεκα μὲν πόλεις ἐκ θαλάττης ᾑρηκέναι, πεζῇ δὲ ἕνδεκα, γυναῖκά τε ὑπὸ τοῦ βασιλέως ἀφαιρεθέντα ἐς μῆνιν ἀπενεχθῆναι, ὅτε δὴ ἀτεράμονα καὶ ὠμὸν δόξαι, σκεψώμεθα τὸν Ἰνδὸν πρὸς ταῦτα. πόλεων μὲν τοίνυν ἑξήκοντα οἰκιστὴς ἐγένετο, αἵπερ εἰσὶ δοκιμώταται τῶν τῇδε, τὸ δὲ πορθεῖν πόλεις ὅστις εὐκλεέστερον ἡγεῖται τοῦ ἀνοικίζειν οὐκ ἔστι. Σκύθας δὲ τοὺς ὑπὲρ Καύκασόν ποτε στρατεύσαντας ἐπὶ τήνδε τὴν γῆν ἀπεώσατο. τὸ δὲ ἐλευθεροῦντα τὴν ἑαυτοῦ γῆν ἄνδρα ἀγαθὸν φαίνεσθαι πολλῷ βέλτιον τοῦ δουλείαν ἐπάγειν πόλει καὶ ταῦθ' ὑπὲρ γυναικός, ἣν εἰκὸς μηδὲ ἄκουσαν ἡρπάσθαι.[24] ξυμμαχίας δὲ αὐτῷ γενομένης πρὸς τὸν ἄρχοντα τῆς χώρας, ἧς νῦν Φραώτης ἄρχει, κἀκείνου παρανομώτατά τε καὶ ἀσελγέστατα γυναῖκα ἀφελομένου αὐτόν, οὐ παρέλυσε τοὺς ὅρκους, οὕτω βεβαίως ὀμωμοκέναι φήσας, ὡς μηδὲ ὁπότε ἠδικεῖτο λυπεῖν αὐτόν.

"Moreover, the ghost of Ganges drove them on as they 2
progressed, causing terror among the mob, and gave them no peace until they had sacrificed to the earth the murderers and those that had stained their hands with blood. This Ganges was ten cubits tall, beautiful as no other man ever was, and was the son of the river Ganges. His father had flooded India, but he diverted it into the Red Sea and reconciled it with the land. In consequence the earth produced plenty for him in life, and avenged him after death.

"Now Homer makes Achilles come to Troy because of 3
Helen, and says that he had captured twelve cities by sea and eleven by land, and that he flew into a fury when the king took a woman away from him, showing himself harsh and savage. Let us consider the Indian by comparison. He founded sixty cities, the most esteemed in the country, and there is nobody who thinks sacking cities is more glorious than building them. He also repulsed the Scythians from above the Caucasus when once they made an attack on this land; and to show yourself a good man and true when defending the liberty of your own land is far better than bringing slavery on a city, especially when a woman is at stake who probably did not mind being abducted. He made an alliance with the ruler of the land now ruled by Phraotes, and when the man, in sheer lawlessness and lust, took away his wife, he did not break his oaths, saying he had sworn so solemnly that he could not injure him even when wronged.

---

22 χερσὶ Spengel (Kay.): χωρὶς

23 καθιερεύσαιεν West.: καθιέρευσαμεν

24 ἡρπάσθαι Kay.: ἀνηρπάσθαι

21. "Καὶ πλείω διῄειν ἂν τοῦ ἀνδρός, εἰ μὴ ἐς ἔπαινον ὤκνουν ἑαυτοῦ καθίστασθαι, εἰμὶ γάρ σοι ἐκεῖνος, τουτὶ δὲ ἐδήλωσα γεγονὼς ἔτη τέτταρα. ἑπτὰ γάρ ποτε ἀδαμάντινα τοῦ Γάγγου τούτου ξίφη ἐς γῆν πήξαντος ὑπὲρ τοῦ μηδὲν δεῖμα ἐμπελάζειν τῇ χώρᾳ, καὶ τῶν θεῶν θύειν μὲν κελευόντων ἥκοντας, οὗ πέπηγε ταῦτα, τὸ δὲ χωρίον οὐκ ἐξηγουμένων, ἐν ᾧ ἐπεπήγει, παῖς ἐγὼ κομιδῇ τυγχάνων ἤγαγον τοὺς ἐξηγητὰς ἐπὶ τάφρον καὶ ὀρύττειν προσέταξα ἐκεῖ φήσας κατατεθεῖσθαι αὐτά.

22. "Καὶ μήπω θαυμάσῃς τοὐμόν, εἰ ἐξ Ἰνδοῦ ἐς Ἰνδὸν διεδόθην· οὗτος γάρ," δείξας τι μειράκιον εἴκοσί που γεγονὸς ἔτη, "πέφυκε μὲν πρὸς φιλοσοφίαν ὑπὲρ πάντας ἀνθρώπους, ἔρρωται δέ, ὡς ὁρᾷς, καὶ κατεσκεύασται γενναίως τὸ σῶμα, καρτερεῖ δὲ πῦρ καὶ τομὴν πᾶσαν, καὶ τοιόσδε ὢν ἀπεχθάνεται τῇ φιλοσοφίᾳ." "τί οὖν," εἶπεν "ὦ Ἰάρχα, τὸ <τοῦ>[25] μειρακίου πάθος; δεινὸν γὰρ λέγεις, εἰ ξυντεταγμένος οὕτως ὑπὸ τῆς φύσεως μὴ ἀσπάζεται τὴν φιλοσοφίαν, μηδὲ ἐρᾷ τοῦ μανθάνειν καὶ ταῦτα ὑμῖν ξυνών."

2 "Οὐ ξύνεστιν," εἶπεν "ἀλλ' ὥσπερ οἱ λέοντες, ἄκων εἴληπται, καὶ καθεῖρκται μέν, ὑποβλέπει[26] δὲ ἡμῶν τιθασευόντων αὐτὸν καὶ καταψώντων. γέγονε μὲν οὖν τὸ μειράκιον τοῦτο Παλαμήδης ὁ ἐν Τροίᾳ, κέχρηται δὲ ἐναντιωτάτοις Ὀδυσσεῖ καὶ Ὁμήρῳ, τῷ μὲν ξυνθέντι ἐπ' αὐτὸν τέχνας, ὑφ' ὧν κατελιθώθη, τῷ δὲ οὐδὲ

21. "I could tell you more about the hero, if I was not reluctant to start praising myself, since I am he, as I proved when I was four. This Ganges once drove seven swords of adamant into the earth so that no danger could come near this land, and the gods ordered us to go to where the swords were planted and to sacrifice, but they did not reveal the place. Still just a child, I led the prophets to a ditch and told them to dig, saying that the swords were deposited there.

22. "You must not be surprised at me for passing from one Indian to another. He" (pointing to a youth about twenty years old) "has a greater innate aptitude for philosophy than any human being, and as you see his body is strong and excellently endowed, so as to be indifferent to fire and any incision, and yet with these gifts he is an enemy of philosophy." "What is wrong with the lad, Iarchas?" asked Apollonius. "It is a shame if one so equipped by nature does not embrace philosophy, and if he does not love learning even though he is your follower."

"He is not our follower," replied Iarchas, "but is like a 2
lion, a reluctant captive, a prisoner who suspects us for taming and stroking him. This boy was once Palamedes at Troy, and his two greatest enemies are Odysseus and Homer, Odysseus for devising a scheme against him by which he was stoned to death, Homer for not thinking him

---

25 <τοῦ> Jackson

26 ὑποβλέπει Morel: ἀποβλέπει

ἔπους αὐτὸν ἀξιώσαντι. καὶ ἐπειδὴ μήθ' ἡ σοφία αὐτόν τι, ἣν εἶχεν, ὤνησε, μήτε Ὁμήρου ἐπαινέτου ἔτυχεν, ὑφ' οὗ πολλοὶ καὶ τῶν μὴ πάνυ σπουδαίων ἐς ὄνομα ἤχθησαν, Ὀδυσσέως τε ἥττητο ἀδικῶν οὐδέν, διαβέβληται πρὸς φιλοσοφίαν καὶ ὀλοφύρεται τὸ ἑαυτοῦ πάθος. ἔστι δὲ οὗτος Παλαμήδης, ὃς καὶ γράφει μὴ μαθὼν γράμματα."

23. Τοιαῦτα διαλεγομένων προσελθὼν τῷ Ἰάρχᾳ ἄγγελος "ὁ βασιλεὺς" ἔφη "περὶ δείλην πρωίαν[27] ἀφίξεται ξυνεσόμενος ὑμῖν περὶ τῶν ἑαυτοῦ πραγμάτων." ὁ δὲ "ἡκέτω," εἶπε "καὶ γὰρ ἂν καὶ βελτίων ἀπέλθοι γνοὺς ἄνδρα Ἕλληνα." καὶ εἰπὼν ταῦτα πάλιν τοῦ προτέρου λόγου εἴχετο. ἤρετο οὖν τὸν Ἀπολλώνιον "σὺ δ' ἂν εἴποις" ἔφη "τὸ πρῶτον σῶμα καὶ ὅστις πρὸ τοῦ νῦν ἦσθα;" ὁ δὲ εἶπεν "ἐπειδὴ ἄδοξον ἦν μοι ἐκεῖνο, ὀλίγα αὐτοῦ μέμνημαι." ὑπολαβὼν οὖν ὁ Ἰάρχας "εἶτα ἄδοξον" ἔφη "ἡγῇ τὸ γενέσθαι κυβερνήτης Αἰγυπτίας νεώς; τουτὶ γάρ σε ὁρῶ γεγονότα."

2 "Ἀληθῆ μὲν" εἶπεν "λέγεις, ὦ Ἰάρχα, τουτὶ γὰρ ἀτεχνῶς ἐγενόμην, ἡγοῦμαι δ' αὐτὸ οὐκ ἄδοξον μόνον, ἀλλὰ καὶ καταβεβλημένον, καὶ τοσούτου μὲν ἄξιον τοῖς ἀνθρώποις, ὅσουπερ τὸ ἄρχειν καὶ τὸ στρατοῦ ἡγεῖσθαι, κακῶς δὲ ἀκοῦον ὑπὸ τῶν καθαπτομένων τῆς θαλάττης. τὸ γοῦν γενναιότατον τῶν ἐμοὶ πραχθέντων οὐδὲ ἐπαίνου τις ἠξίωσε τότε." "τί δὲ δὴ

[27] πρωίαν Cob.: πρώτην

worth a single line.[18] The wisdom he had brought him no advantage, he got no praise from Homer, who brought fame to many men of no importance at all, and he fell victim to Odysseus despite having done him no wrong. So he is an enemy of philosophy and bewails his ill-treatment. This is Palamedes, and he can write without having learned to write."

23. While they were conversing in this way, a messenger came up to Iarchas and said, "The king will arrive early this evening to consult with you all about business of his." "Let him come," said Iarchas, "since he may go away a better man after encountering a true Greek." With these words he resumed their previous conversation, and asked Apollonius, "Can you say what your first body was, and who you were before this?" Apollonius replied, "It was disreputable, and so I remember little about it." Iarchas replied, "Why, do you think it is disreputable to have been the captain of an Egyptian ship? Since that is what you were, I see."

"You are right, Iarchas," said Apollonius, "since that is 2
exactly what I was. I consider it not just disreputable but also despised. It is just as valuable to mankind as ruling and leading an army are, but has a bad name among those who take to the sea. At any rate, the noblest of my deeds no one thought praiseworthy at the time." "What is this noble

[18] Palamedes fought on the Greek side at Troy, and was remembered as the inventor of several arts, but is not mentioned in the Homeric poems. A later tradition said that Odysseus persuaded the Greeks that he was a traitor and so caused his death.

γενναῖον εἰργάσθαι φήσεις; ἢ[28] τὸ περιβεβληκέναι Μαλέαν τε καὶ Σούνιον χαλινώσας ἐκφερομένην τὴν ναῦν, καὶ τὸ κατὰ πρύμναν τε καὶ πρῷραν τῶν ἀνέμων, ὁπόθεν ἐκδοθήσονται, σαφῶς διεγνωκέναι, ἑρμάτων τε ὑπερᾶραι τὸ σκάφος ἐν Εὐβοίᾳ κοίλῃ, οὗπερ πολλὰ τῶν ἀκρωτηρίων ἀναπέπηγεν;"

24. Ὁ δὲ Ἀπολλώνιος "ἐπεί με" εἶπεν "ἐς κυβερνητικὸν ἐμβιβάζεις λόγον, ἄκουε, ὃ δοκῶ[29] μοι τότε ὑγιῶς πρᾶξαι. τὴν θάλαττάν ποτε τῶν Φοινίκων λῃσταὶ ὑπεκάθηντο, καὶ ἐφοίτων περὶ τὰς πόλεις ἀναμανθάνοντες τίς τί ἄγοι. κατιδόντες οὖν ἐμπορίαν λαμπρὰν τῆς νεὼς οἱ τῶν λῃστῶν πρόξενοι διελέγοντό μοι ἀπολαβόντες με, πόσον τι μεθέξοιμι τοῦ ναύλου, ἐγὼ δὲ χιλίων ἔφην, ἐπειδὴ τέτταρες ἐκυβέρνων τὴν ναῦν. 'οἰκία δὲ' ἔφασαν 'ἔστι σοι;' 'καλύβη πονηρὰ' ἔφην 'περὶ τὴν νῆσον τὴν Φάρον, οὗ πάλαι ποτὲ ὁ Πρωτεὺς ᾤκει.' 'βούλοιο ἂν οὖν' ἤροντό με 'γενέσθαι σοι γῆν μὲν ἀντὶ θαλάττης, οἰκίαν δὲ ἀντὶ τῆς καλύβης, τὸ δὲ ναῦλον δεκάκις τοῦτο, κακῶν τε ἐξελθεῖν μυρίων, ἃ ἀπὸ τῆς θαλάττης ἀνοιδούσης ἐγχρίπτει τοῖς κυβερνῶσιν;'

2 "Βούλεσθαι μὲν εἶπον, οὐ μὴν ἁρπαγῶν γε ἐμαυτὸν ἀξιοῦν, ὁπότε σοφώτερος ἐμαυτοῦ γέγονα καὶ στεφάνων ἠξίωμαι παρὰ τῆς τέχνης. προϊόντων δ' αὐτῶν καὶ βαλάντιά μοι δραχμῶν μυρίων δώσειν φασκόντων, εἰ γενοίμην αὐτοῖς, ὃ ἐβούλοντο, λέγειν ἤδη

[28] ἢ Jon.: ἢ [29] δοκῶ Bentl.: δοκεῖ

thing you will claim to have done? Is it to have rounded Cape Malea and Cape Sounion, restraining the ship when it was being carried away, to have clearly determined the direction from which the winds would fall on the prow or the stern, to have carried your vessel past the reefs in the Hollows of Euboea, where many a headland juts out?"[19]

24. Apollonius replied, "Since you are starting me on a discussion of piloting, I will tell you what I think my good deed was at the time. Phoenician pirates were infesting the sea, and as they went from city to city they inquired who was carrying what cargo. The pirates' agents spied the rich freight of our ship, and taking me aside began to discuss my share of the cargo. I told them it was a thousand drachmas, since there were four of us piloting the ship. 'Do you have a house?' they said. 'A wretched hut,' I said, 'on the island of Pharos, where Proteus once lived.'[20] 'Well then,' they asked me, 'would you like to have land instead of sea, a house instead of your hut, ten times as much cargo, and an escape from the endless troubles that bedevil pilots from the tossing of the sea?'

"I would like that, I said, but I did not consider myself 2
fitted for robbery since I was at the peak of my expertise, and my skill had won me prizes. However, they proceeded to promise me a purse of ten thousand drachmas if I would be their man for anything they wanted. Thereupon I en-

[19] Malea is the southeastern cape of the Peloponnese, Sounion the southern cape of Attica. The Hollows of Euboea are probably the bays on the southeast coast of the island.

[20] On Proteus, see I 4. Pharos lies off the westernmost mouth of the Nile.

παρεκελευσάμην ὡς μηδὲν ἐλλείψων τοῦ πᾶς ἀνὴρ γενέσθαι σφίσι. λέγουσι δὴ μελεδωνοὶ μὲν εἶναι λῃστῶν, δεῖσθαι δέ μου μὴ ἀφελέσθαι αὐτοὺς τὸ τὴν ναῦν ἑλεῖν, μηδὲ ἐς ἄστυ ἐκπλεῦσαι, ὁπότε ἐκεῖθεν ἄραιμι,[30] ἀλλ' ὑφορμίσασθαι τῷ ἀκρωτηρίῳ, τὰς ναῦς γὰρ τὰς λῃστρικὰς ἐν περιβολῇ ἑστάναι, καὶ ὀμνύναι μοι ἐβούλοντο μήτ' αὐτόν με ἀποκτενεῖν καὶ ἀνήσειν δὲ τὸν θάνατον οἷς ἂν ἐγὼ παραιτῶμαι.

3 "'Εγὼ δὲ νουθετεῖν μὲν αὐτοὺς οὐκ ἀσφαλὲς ἐμαυτῷ ἡγούμην, δείσας μὴ ἀπογνόντες ἐμβάλωσι μετεώρῳ τῇ νηὶ καὶ ἀπολώμεθά που τοῦ πελάγους, ὡς δὲ ὑπήκουσα[31] ἃ ἐβούλοντο [μήτ' αὐτὸν ἀποκτεῖναι],[32] ὀμνύναι ἔφην αὐτοὺς δεῖν ἦ μὴν ἀληθεύσειν ταῦτα. ὀμοσάντων τοίνυν, καὶ γὰρ ἐν ἱερῷ διελέγοντο, 'χωρεῖτε' ἔφην 'ἐπὶ τὰ τῶν λῃστῶν πλοῖα, ἡμεῖς γὰρ νύκτωρ ἀφήσομεν.' καὶ πιθανώτερος ἐδόκουν ἔτι περὶ τοῦ νομίσματος διαλεγόμενος, ὡς δόκιμον ἀπαριθμηθείη μοι καὶ μὴ πρότερον ἢ τὴν ναῦν ἕλωσιν. οἱ μὲν δὴ ἐχώρουν, ἐγὼ δὲ ἧκα ἐς τὸ πέλαγος ὑπεράρας τοῦ ἀκρωτηρίου." "ταῦτ' οὖν," εἶπεν ὁ 'Ιάρχας "'Απολλώνιε, δικαιοσύνης ἡγῇ ἔργα;" "καὶ πρός γε" ἔφη "φιλανθρωπίας, τὸ γὰρ μὴ ἀποδόσθαι ψυχὰς ἀνθρώπων, μηδ' ἀπεμπολῆσαι τὰ τῶν ἐμπόρων, χρημάτων τε κρείττω γενέσθαι ναύτην ὄντα πολλὰς ἀρετὰς οἶμαι ξυνειληφέναι."

25. Γελάσας οὖν ὁ 'Ινδὸς, "ἔοικας," ἔφη, "τὸ μὴ ἀδικεῖν δικαιοσύνην ἡγεῖσθαι, τουτὶ δὲ οἶμαι καὶ πάντας Ἕλληνας. ὡς γὰρ ἐγώ ποτε Αἰγυπτίων δεῦρο

couraged them to speak out, saying I would not fail to be their man for anything. So they said they were the agents of pirates, and they asked me not to rob them of the chance to take the ship. I was not to make for my destination after setting sail from there, but to anchor off the headland, since the pirate ships were standing within lee of it. They were ready to swear to me that they would not kill me myself, and would spare the life of anyone for whom I interceded.

"I did not think it was safe for me to rebuke them, fear- 3
ing that they might give up their plan and attack our ship at sea, and we would perish somewhere on the deep. So after agreeing to what they wanted, I said they must swear to keep faith in all this. After they had sworn (since they were holding this conversation in a sanctuary), I said, 'Go to the pirates' ships, since we will sail tonight.' I made myself even more plausible by asking about the money, saying it should be paid to me in good coin, and not until they had seized the ship. So they went on their way, while I made for the high seas after doubling the headland." "Why, Apollonius," said Iarchas, "do you consider those to be acts of justice?" "Yes, and of humanity too," was the reply, "for I think it a combination of many virtues not to sell human souls, not to barter away merchants' property, and to show yourself above money when you are a sailor."

25. With a laugh the Indian said, "You seem to think avoidance of wrong is the same as justice, as I believe all the Greeks do. I once heard from Egyptians visiting here

---

30 ἄραιμι Cob.: ἄροιμι

31 ὑπήκουσα Jon.: ὑπούργησα

32 secl. Jac. (Kay.)

ἀφικομένων ἤκουσα, φοιτῶσι μὲν ὑμῖν ἀπὸ τῆς Ῥώμης ἡγεμόνες γυμνὸν ἠρμένοι τὸν πέλεκυν ἐφ᾽ ὑμᾶς, οὔπω γιγνώσκοντες, εἰ φαύλων ἄρξουσιν, ὑμεῖς δέ, εἰ μὴ πωλοῖεν τὰς δίκας οὗτοι, φατὲ αὐτοὺς δικαίους εἶναι. τουτὶ δὲ καὶ τοὺς τῶν ἀνδραπόδων καπήλους ἀκούω ἐκεῖ πράττειν, εἰ γὰρ ἀφίκοιντο κατάγοντες ὑμῖν ἀνδράποδα Καρικὰ καὶ τὸ ἦθος αὐτῶν ἐφερμηνεύοιεν ὑμῖν, ἔπαινον ποιοῦνται τῶν ἀνδραπόδων τὸ μὴ κλέπτειν αὐτά. τοὺς μὲν δὴ ἄρχοντας, οἷς ὑποκεῖσθαί φατε, τοιούτων ἀξιοῦτε, καὶ λαμπρύνοντες αὐτοὺς ἐπαίνοις, οἷσπερ τὰ ἀνδράποδα, ζηλωτοὺς πέμπετε, ὡς οἴεσθε.

2 "Οἱ δέ γε σοφώτατοι ποιηταὶ ὑμῶν οὐδ᾽ εἰ βούλεσθε δίκαιοί τε καὶ χρηστοὶ εἶναι ξυγχωροῦσιν ὑμῖν γενέσθαι. τὸν γὰρ Μίνω τὸν ὠμότητι ὑπερβαλόμενον πάντας καὶ δουλωσάμενον ταῖς ναυσὶ τοὺς ἐπὶ θαλάττῃ τε καὶ ἐν θαλάττῃ δικαιοσύνης σκήπτρῳ τιμῶντες, ἐν Ἅιδου καθίζουσι διαιτᾶν ταῖς ψυχαῖς· τὸν δ᾽ αὖ Τάνταλον, ἐπειδὴ χρηστός τε ἦν καὶ τοῖς φίλοις τῆς ὑπαρχούσης αὐτῷ παρὰ τῶν θεῶν ἀθανασίας μετεδίδου, ποτοῦ τε εἴργουσι καὶ σίτου. εἰσὶ δὲ οἳ καὶ λίθους αὐτῷ ἐπικρεμάσαντες δεινὰ ἐφυβρίζουσι θείῳ τε καὶ ἀγαθῷ ἀνδρί, οὓς ἐβουλόμην ἂν μᾶλλον λίμνην αὐτῷ περιβλύσαι νέκταρος, ἐπειδὴ φιλανθρώπως αὐτοῦ καὶ ἀφθόνως προὔπινε."

3 Καὶ ἅμα λέγων ταῦτα ἐπεδείκνυ ἄγαλμα ἐν ἀριστερᾷ, ᾧ ἐπεγέγραπτο "Τάνταλος." τὸ μὲν δὴ ἄγαλμα τετράπηχυ ἦν, ἀνδρὶ δὲ ἐῴκει πεντηκοντούτῃ καὶ τρό-

that governors from Rome come to you regularly with naked axes raised against you.[21] While they do not yet know if their subjects will be bad, you call them just if they refuse to sell their verdicts. I also hear that slave dealers do the same over there. If they arrive with a cargo of Carian slaves, and describe their characters to you, they make it an item of praise in the slaves that they are not thieves. You set the same value on the rulers whose subjects you call yourselves, and you glorify them with the same praises as you bestow on slaves, and send them off as admirable men, so you think.

"As for the most expert of your poets, they do not allow you to be just and virtuous even if you wish. Minos had no equal for savagery, and with his ships he enslaved those on the coast and on islands, and yet the poets honor him with the scepter of justice, and set him up in Hades as the judge of souls. Tantalus, by contrast, was good, and gave his friends a share of the immortality he had received from the gods, and yet the poets deprive him of food and drink, and some of them hang stones over him and cruelly mistreat this godly and virtuous man. I would rather wish they poured a pool of nectar over him, since that was what he presented to others with kindness and generosity." 2

As he said this, he pointed to a statue on his left inscribed "Tantalus." It was four cubits high, and took the shape of a fifty-year-old man dressed in the Argive way, 3

[21] Roman provincial governors were preceded by attendants carrying axes, symbolizing their power to inflict capital punishment.

που Ἀργολικὸν ἔσταλτο, παρήλλαττε δὲ τὴν χλαμύδα, ὥσπερ οἱ Θετταλοί, φιάλην τε προὔπινεν ἀποχρῶσαν ἑνὶ διψῶντι, ἐν ᾗ στάλαγμα ἐκάχλαζεν ἀκηράτου πώματος οὐχ ὑπερβλύζον τῆς φιάλης. (ὅ τι μὲν οὖν ἡγοῦνται αὐτὸ καὶ ἐφ᾿ ὅτῳ ἀπ᾿ αὐτοῦ πίνουσι, δηλώσω αὐτίκα.) πλὴν ἀλλὰ ἡγεῖσθαι χρὴ τὸν Τάνταλον μὴ τῇ γλώττῃ ἐφέντα, κοινωνήσαντα δὲ ἀνθρώποις τοῦ νέκταρος ὑπὸ τῶν ποιητῶν ἐλαύνεσθαι, θεοῖς δὲ μὴ διαβεβλῆσθαι αὐτόν, οὐ γὰρ ἄν, εἰ θεοῖς ἀπήχθετο, κριθῆναί ποτε ὑπὸ τῶν Ἰνδῶν ἀγαθόν, θεοφιλεστάτων ὄντων καὶ μηδὲν ἔξω τοῦ θείου πραττόντων.

26. Διατρίβοντας δὲ αὐτοὺς περὶ τὸν λόγον τοῦτον θόρυβος ἐκ τῆς κώμης προσέβαλεν, ἀφῖκτο δὲ ἄρα ὁ βασιλεὺς μηδικώτερον κατεσκευασμένος καὶ ὄγκου μεστός. ἀχθεσθεὶς οὖν ὁ Ἰάρχας "εἰ δὲ Φραώτης" ἔφη "καταλύων ἐτύγχανεν, εἶδες ἂν ὥσπερ ἐν μυστηρίῳ σιωπῆς μεστὰ πάντα." ἐκ τούτου μὲν δὴ ξυνῆκεν ὁ Ἀπολλώνιος, ὡς βασιλεὺς ἐκεῖνος οὐκ ὀλίγῳ μέρει, φιλοσοφίᾳ δὲ πάσῃ τοῦ Φραώτου λείποιτο, ῥᾳθύμους δὲ ἰδὼν τοὺς σοφοὺς καὶ μηδὲν παρασκευάζοντας, ὧν δεῖ τῷ βασιλεῖ μετὰ μεσημβρίαν ἥκοντι "ποῖ" ἔφη "ὁ βασιλεὺς διαιτήσεται;" "ἐνταῦθα," ἔφασαν, "ὧν γὰρ ἕνεκα ἥκει, νύκτωρ διαλεγόμεθα, ἐπειδὴ καὶ βελτίων ὁ καιρὸς πρὸς βουλάς."

2 "Καὶ τράπεζα" ἔφη "παρακείσεται ἥκοντι;" "νὴ Δί᾿," εἶπον[33] "παχεῖά τε καὶ πάντα ἔχουσα, ὁπόσα ἐνταῦθα." "παχέως οὖν" ἔφη "διαιτᾶσθε;" "ἡμεῖς μὲν"

though he wore his cloak symmetrically as the Thessalians do,[22] and he was sipping from a goblet large enough for one thirsty man, in which a distillation of pure liquid bubbled without overflowing the goblet. (What they consider this liquid to be, and for what purpose they drink it, I will show in a moment.) Now we not must suppose that it was his loose tongue, but his giving mankind a taste of nectar, that made the poets attack Tantalus. The gods were not cross with him, for if he had been their enemy he would never have been judged a good man by the Indians, who are much favored by the gods and do nothing without divine sanction.

26. They were lingering over this topic when there came a noise from the village. The king had arrived arrayed somewhat in the Median style and full of pomp. In vexation Iarchas said, "Now if Phraotes were staying here, you would see everything plunged in silence, as in a sacred rite." From this Apollonius gathered that the king was inferior to Phraotes, not to a slight degree but in every aspect of wisdom. Seeing the wise men unconcerned and making no preparations such as the king needed for an afternoon arrival, he said, "Where will the king be lodged?" "Here," they replied, "for we discuss the business of his visit at night, since that is a better time for deliberation."

"Will a table be set for him when he comes?" asked 2
Apollonius. "Certainly," they replied, "a full one with all the local products." "So you have a heavy diet?" he said.

[22] Cut so as to hang with the so-called "Thessalian wings," rather like a swallowtail coat.

---

33 εἶπον West.: εἶπε

ἔφασαν "λεπτῶς, πλείονα γὰρ ἡμῖν ἐξὸν σιτίζεσθαι μικροῖς χαίρομεν, τῷ δὲ βασιλεῖ πολλῶν δεῖ, βούλεται γάρ. σιτήσεται δὲ ἔμψυχον μὲν οὐδέν, οὐ γὰρ θέμις ἐνταῦθα, τραγήματα δὲ καὶ ῥίζας καὶ ὡραῖα, ὁπόσα νῦν ἡ Ἰνδικὴ ἔχει ὁπόσα τε αἱ ἐς νέωτα ὧραι δώσουσιν. ἀλλ' ἰδοὺ" ἔφη "οὗτος."

27. Προῄει δὲ ἄρα ὁ βασιλεὺς ἀδελφῷ τε καὶ υἱῷ ἅμα χρυσῷ τε ἀστράπτων καὶ ψήφοις. ὑπανισταμένου δὲ τοῦ Ἀπολλωνίου, κατεῖχεν αὐτὸν ὁ Ἰάρχας ἐν τῷ θρόνῳ, μηδὲ γὰρ αὐτοῖς πάτριον εἶναι τοῦτο. τούτοις ὁ Δάμις αὐτὸς μὲν οὔ φησι παρατυχεῖν διὰ τὸ τὴν ἡμέραν ἐκείνην ἐν τῇ κώμῃ διαιτᾶσθαι, Ἀπολλωνίου δὲ ἀκηκοὼς ἐγγράψαι αὐτὰ ἐς τὸν αὐτοῦ λόγον. φησὶ τοίνυν καθημένοις μὲν αὐτοῖς τὸν βασιλέα προτείνοντα τὴν χεῖρα οἷον εὔχεσθαι τοῖς ἀνδράσι, τοὺς δὲ ἐπινεύειν, ὥσπερ ξυντιθεμένους οἷς ᾔτει, τὸν δὲ ὑπερήδεσθαι τῇ ἐπαγγελίᾳ, καθάπερ ἐς θεοῦ ἥκοντα. τὸν δὲ ἀδελφὸν τοῦ βασιλέως καὶ τὸν υἱόν, κάλλιστον μειράκιον ὄντα, μηδὲν ὁρᾶσθαι βέλτιον ἢ εἰ ἀνδράποδα τουτωνὶ τῶν ἀκολούθων ἦσαν.

2 Μετὰ ταῦτα ἐξαναστῆναι τὸν Ἰνδὸν καὶ φωνὴν ἱέντα κελεύειν αὐτὸν σίτου ἅπτεσθαι, προσδεξαμένου δ' αὐτοῦ καὶ τοῦτο μάλα ἀσμένως, τρίποδες μὲν ἐξεπορεύθησαν Πυθικοὶ τέτταρες αὐτόματοι, καθάπερ οἱ Ὁμήρειοι προϊόντες, οἰνοχόοι δ' ἐπ' αὐτοῖς χαλκοῦ μέλανος, οἷοι παρ' Ἕλλησιν οἱ Γανυμήδεις τε καὶ οἱ Πέλοπες. ἡ γῆ δὲ ὑπεστόρνυ πόας μαλακωτέρας ἢ αἱ εὐναί. τραγήματα δὲ καὶ ἄρτοι καὶ λάχανα καὶ τρωκτὰ

"We have a light one," they replied; "we could consume more, but we like to consume little. The king's needs however are greater, according to his wish. But he will not consume any animal food, since that is forbidden here, but only dried fruits, herbs, and fresh fruits, all that India produces at the moment and the seasons will bring next year. But look," he said, "here he is."

27. And indeed the king was approaching with his brother and son, and sparkled with gold and jewels. Apollonius wanted to rise, but Iarchas restrained him in his throne, saying that that was not their tradition. According to Damis, he himself was not present at all this, since he was staying in the village that day, but after hearing about it from Apollonius he included it in his own account. He says, then, that while they remained seated, the king stretched out his hand to the sages as if in prayer, and they nodded as if granting his request, at which he was overjoyed by their promise, like someone entering a god's shrine. The king's brother, and his son, a very handsome youth, were shown no higher regard than if they had been slaves of their own attendants.

After that, the Indian got up and, giving utterance, 2
invited the king to begin his meal. When he received this invitation too with great pleasure, out rolled four Pythian three-legged urns of their own accord, emerging like the ones in Homer,[23] and following them came cupbearers of dark bronze like the famous Ganymede and Pelops in Greece, while the earth was blanketed with grass softer than a bed. Dried fruits, loaves, vegetables, and seasonal

[23] Such urns (tripods) were sometimes called "Pythian" after the prophetic tripod of Delphi. In *Iliad* 18.373–79, Hephaestus makes twenty self-propelling tripods.

ὡραῖα, πάντα ἐν κόσμῳ ἐφοίτα, διακείμενα ἥδιον ἢ εἰ ὀψοποιοὶ αὐτὰ παρεσκεύαζον. τῶν δὲ τριπόδων οἱ μὲν δύο οἴνου ἐπέρρεον, τοῖν δυοῖν δὲ ὁ μὲν ὕδατος θερμοῦ κρήνην παρεῖχεν, ὁ δὲ αὖ ψυχροῦ.

3 Αἱ δ' ἐξ Ἰνδῶν φοιτῶσαι λίθοι παρ' Ἕλλησι μὲν ἐς ὅρμους τε καὶ δακτυλίους ἐμβιβάζονται διὰ σμικρότητα, παρὰ δὲ Ἰνδοῖς οἰνοχόαι τε ψυκτῆρές τε γίγνονται διὰ μέγεθος καὶ κρατῆρες ἡλίκοι ἐμπλῆσαι τέτταρας ὥρᾳ ἔτους διψῶντας. τοὺς δὲ οἰνοχόους τοὺς χαλκοῦς ἀρύεσθαι μέν φησι ξυμμέτρως τοῦ τε οἴνου καὶ τοῦ ὕδατος, περιελαύνειν δὲ τὰς κύλικας, ὥσπερ ἐν τοῖς πότοις. κατακεῖσθαι δὲ αὐτοὺς ὡς ἐν ξυσσιτίῳ μέν, οὐ μὴν πρόκριτόν γε τὸν βασιλέα, τοῦτο δὴ τὸ παρ' Ἕλλησί τε καὶ Ῥωμαίοις πολλοῦ ἄξιον, ἀλλ' ὡς ἔτυχέ γε, οὗ ἕκαστος ὥρμησεν.

28. Ἐπεὶ δὲ προῄει ὁ πότος "προπίνω σοι," ὁ Ἰάρχας εἶπεν "ὦ βασιλεῦ, ἄνδρα Ἕλληνα," τὸν Ἀπολλώνιον ὑποκεκλιμένον αὐτῷ δείξας καὶ τῇ χειρὶ προσημαίνων, ὅτι γενναῖός τε εἴη καὶ θεῖος. ὁ δὲ βασιλεὺς "ἤκουσα" ἔφη "προσήκειν Φραώτῃ τοῦτόν τε καὶ τοὺς ἐν τῇ κώμῃ καταλύοντας." "ὀρθῶς" ἔφη "καὶ ἀληθῶς ἤκουσας, ἐκεῖνος γὰρ κἀνταῦθα ξενίζει αὐτόν." "τί" ἔφη "ἐπιτηδεύοντα;" "τί δ' ἄλλο γε" εἶπεν "ἢ ἅπερ ἐκεῖνος;" "οὐδὲν" ἔφη "ξένον εἴρηκας ἀσπαζόμενον ἐπιτήδευσιν, ἣ μηδὲ ἐκείνῳ ξυνεχώρησε γενναίῳ γενέσθαι." ὁ μὲν δὴ Ἰάρχας "σωφρονέστερον," ἔφη "ὦ βασιλεῦ, περὶ φιλοσοφίας τε καὶ Φραώτου γίγνωσκε, τὸν μὲν γὰρ χρόνον, ὃν μειράκιον ἦσθα,

morsels all kept arriving, more elegantly set out than if chefs had prepared them, while two of the urns flowed with wine, and the other two gave forth, one a stream of warm water, and the other a stream of cold.

The gems that come to Greece from India are small, 3
and so are mounted in necklaces and rings, but in India they are large enough to form decanters and wine coolers because of their size, and mixing bowls big enough to satisfy four thirsty people in high summer. Damis says that the bronze cupbearers drew the wine and the water expertly, and made the cups go round as at a drinking party. The seating plan resembled a club dinner, the king not having that precedence which is so highly valued by Greeks and Romans, but each being placed according to his inclination.

28. The drinking had gone on a while when Iarchas said, "I propose the health of a notable Greek, Majesty," pointing out to him Apollonius who was reclining next to him, and indicating with a gesture that he was virtuous and godly. The king replied, "I had heard that this man and those staying in the village were connected with Phraotes." "You heard rightly and truly," said the other, "since here too he is Phraotes's guest." "What is his profession?" asked the king. "The same as Phraotes's, of course," was the reply. "What you say is nothing strange, that he should have embraced a calling which kept him too from distinction." Iarchas replied, "You should be more circumspect in your attitude to philosophy and Phraotes, Majesty. While you

ξυνεχώρει σοι ἡ νεότης τὰ τοιαῦτα, ἐπεὶ δὲ ἐς ἄνδρας ἐξαλλάττεις ἤδη, φειδώμεθα τῶν ἀνοήτων τε καὶ εὐκόλων."

2 Ὁ δὲ Ἀπολλώνιος ἑρμηνεύοντος τοῦ Ἰάρχα "σοὶ δὲ τί," ἔφη "ὦ βασιλεῦ, τὸ μὴ φιλοσοφῆσαι δέδωκεν;" "ἐμοὶ δὲ ἀρετὴν πᾶσαν καὶ τὸ εἶναί με τὸν αὐτὸν τῷ Ἡλίῳ." ὁ δὲ ἐπιστομίζων αὐτοῦ τὸν τῦφον "εἰ ἐφιλοσόφεις," εἶπεν, "οὐκ ἂν ταῦτα ᾤου." "σὺ δέ, ἐπειδὴ φιλοσοφεῖς, ὦ βέλτιστε," ἔφη, "τί περὶ σαυτοῦ οἴει;" "τό γε ἀνὴρ" ἔφη "ἀγαθὸς δοκεῖν, εἰ φιλοσοφοίην." ἀνατείνας οὖν τὴν χεῖρα ἐς τὸν οὐρανὸν "νὴ τὸν Ἥλιον," ἔφη "Φραώτου μεστὸς ἥκεις." ὁ δὲ ἕρμαιόν γε ἐποιήσατο τὸν λόγον καὶ ὑπολαβὼν "οὐ μάτην ἀποδεδήμηταί μοι," εἶπεν "εἰ Φραώτου μεστὸς γέγονα· εἰ δὲ κἀκείνῳ νῦν ἐντύχοις, πάνυ φήσεις αὐτὸν ἐμοῦ μεστὸν εἶναι, καὶ γράφειν δὲ ὑπὲρ ἐμοῦ πρὸς σὲ ἐβούλετο, ἀλλ' ἐπειδὴ ἔφασκεν ἄνδρα ἀγαθὸν εἶναί σε, παρῃτησάμην τὸν ὄχλον τῆς ἐπιστολῆς, ἐπεὶ μηδὲ ἐκείνῳ τις ὑπὲρ ἐμοῦ ἐπέστειλεν."

29. Ἡ μὲν δὴ πρώτη παροινία τοῦ βασιλέως ἐνταῦθα ἔληξεν· ἀκούσας γὰρ ἐπαινεῖσθαι αὐτὸν ὑπὸ τοῦ Φραώτου τῆς τε ὑπεροψίας[34] ἐπελάθετο, καὶ ὑφεὶς τοῦ τόνου "χαῖρε," ἔφη "ἀγαθὲ ξένε." ὁ δὲ Ἀπολλώνιος "καὶ σύ, βασιλεῦ," εἶπεν "ἔοικας γὰρ νῦν ἥκοντι." "τίς σε" ἔφη "πρὸς ἡμᾶς ἤγαγεν;" "οὗτοι" εἶπεν "οἱ θεῖοι[35] τε καὶ σοφοὶ ἄνδρες." "περὶ ἐμοῦ δέ," ἔφη "ὦ ξένε, τίς λόγος ἐν τοῖς Ἕλλησιν;" "ὅσος γε" εἶπε "καὶ περὶ Ἑλλήνων ἐνταῦθα." "οὐδὲν," ἔφη "τῶν παρ' Ἕλλησιν

were a lad, your youth allowed you such remarks, but now that you are coming to manhood, let us avoid folly and thoughtlessness."

With Iarchas as translator, Apollonius said, "What has 2
the avoidance of philosophy given you, Majesty?" "Every virtue, and my being an avatar of the Sun god." To curb his vanity, Apollonius said, "If you were a philosopher, you would not think such things." "And you, my good sir," said the king, "since you study philosophy, what do you think about yourself?" "That I am thought a good man, if I study philosophy," Apollonius replied. So the king raised his hand to heaven and said, "By the Sun, you come full of Phraotes." Apollonius thought this remark a lucky sign, and replied, "My journey was not for nothing if I have become full of Phraotes. And if you were to meet him now, you would say he was full of me. He wanted to write to you on my behalf, but because he said you were a good man I declined to bother him with a letter, since nobody wrote to him about me."

29. The king's initial rudeness now ended, since he forgot his pride when he heard that he was praised by Phraotes, and moderating his tone he said, "Welcome, good stranger." "You too, Majesty," said Apollonius, "since you seem to have just arrived." "And who brought you to us?" said the other. "These did," Apollonius replied, "these wise and godly men." "And what is my reputation among the Greeks, stranger?" said the king. "As high as that of the Greeks is here." "I do not value anything belonging to the

---

34 *ὑπεροψίας* Bentl.: *ὑποψίας*
35 *θεῖοι* West.: *θεοί*

ἔγωγε λόγου ἀξιῶ." "ἀπαγγελῶ ταῦτα," εἶπε "καὶ στεφανώσουσί σε ἐν Ὀλυμπίᾳ."

30. Καὶ προσκλιθεὶς τῷ Ἰάρχᾳ "τοῦτον μὲν" ἔφη "μεθύειν ἔα, σὺ δέ μοι εἰπὲ τοῦ χάριν τοὺς περὶ αὐτὸν τούτους ἀδελφόν, ὥς φατέ, καὶ υἱὸν ὄντας οὐκ ἀξιοῦτε κοινῆς τραπέζης, οὐδὲ ἄλλης τιμῆς οὐδεμιᾶς;" "ὅτι" ἔφη "βασιλεύσειν ποτὲ ἡγοῦνται, δεῖ δὲ αὐτοὺς ὑπερορωμένους παιδεύεσθαι τὸ μὴ ὑπερορᾶν." ὀκτωκαίδεκα δὲ ὁρῶν τοὺς σοφοὺς πάλιν τὸν Ἰάρχαν ἤρετο, τί βούλοιτο αὐτοῖς τὸ εἶναι τοσούτους, "οὔτε γὰρ τῶν τετραγώνων ὁ ἀριθμός, οὔτε τῶν εὐδοκιμούντων τε καὶ τιμωμένων, καθάπερ ὁ τῶν δέκα καὶ ὁ τῶν δώδεκα καὶ ὁ ἑκκαίδεκα καὶ ὁπόσοι τοιοίδε."

2 Ὑπολαβὼν οὖν ὁ Ἰνδὸς "οὔτε ἡμεῖς" ἔφη "ἀριθμῷ δουλεύομεν οὔτε ἀριθμὸς ἡμῖν, ἀλλ' ἀπὸ σοφίας τε καὶ ἀρετῆς προτιμώμεθα, καὶ ὁτὲ μὲν πλείους τῶν νῦν ὄντων ἐσμέν, ὁτὲ δὲ ἐλάττους. τόν τοι πάππον τὸν ἐμαυτοῦ ἀκούω καταλεχθῆναι μὲν ἐς ἑβδομήκοντα σοφοὺς ἄνδρας νεώτατον αὐτὸν ὄντα, προελθόντα δὲ ἐς τριάκοντα καὶ ἑκατὸν ἔτη καταλειφθῆναι μόνον ἐνταῦθα τῷ μήτ' ἐκείνων τινὰ λείπεσθαι ἔτι μήτε εἶναί ποι τότε τῆς Ἰνδικῆς ἢ φιλόσοφον ἢ γενναίαν φύσιν. Αἰγυπτίων τοίνυν ἐν τοῖς εὐδαιμονεστάτοις γραψάντων αὐτόν, ἐπειδὴ μόνος ἐτῶν τεττάρων ἐξηγήσατο τούτου τοῦ θρόνου, παρῄνει παύσασθαι ὀνειδίζοντας Ἰνδοῖς σοφῶν ὀλιγανδρίαν.

3 "Ἡμεῖς δέ, ὦ Ἀπολλώνιε, καὶ τὰ Ἠλείων πάτρια Αἰγυπτίων ἀκούοντες καὶ τοὺς Ἑλλανοδίκας, οἳ προ-

Greeks," said he. "I will tell them that," said Apollonius, "and they will crown you at Olympia."

30. And leaning close to Iarchas, he said, "Let us leave this person to get drunk. But you must tell me why you do not admit his companions (his brother and son, you say) to the common table or to any other mark of respect." "Because," said Iarchas, "they think they will be kings one day, and they have to learn by neglect not to be neglectful." Seeing that the Wise Men numbered eighteen, he next asked Iarchas why they were that many, since it was not the square of four, or one of the respected and honored numbers, like ten, twelve, sixteen, and so on.

In reply the Indian said, "We are not slaves of number, 2
or number of us, but our honor comes from wisdom and virtue. We are sometimes more than our present number and sometimes less. I hear that when my grandfather was enrolled, there were seventy Wise Men of which he was the youngest, but when he reached the age of a hundred and thirty he was left here alone, since none of the others was any longer alive, and nowhere in India was there either a philosopher or a virtuous nature. When the Egyptians counted him as among the happiest of men, after he had been holding this chair alone for four years, he advised them to stop reproaching the Indians for their shortage of wise men.

"We have heard from the Egyptians about the tradi- 3
tions of Elis, Apollonius, and about the Judges of the Hel-

ἵστανται τῶν Ὀλυμπίων, δέκα ὄντας, οὐκ ἐπαινοῦμεν τὸν νόμον τὸν ἐπὶ τοῖς ἀνδράσι κείμενον, κλήρῳ γὰρ ξυγχωροῦσι τὴν αἵρεσιν, ὃς προνοεῖ οὐδέν, καὶ γὰρ ἂν καὶ τῶν φαυλοτέρων τις αἱρεθείη ὑπὸ τοῦ κλήρου. εἰ δέ γε ἀριστίνδην ἢ καὶ κατὰ ψῆφον ᾑροῦντο τοὺς ἄνδρας, οὐκ ἂν ἡμάρτανον παραπλησίως· ὁ γὰρ τῶν δέκα ἀριθμὸς ἀπαραίτητος ὢν ἢ πλειόνων ὄντων ἀνδρῶν δικαίων ἀφῃρεῖτο ἂν ἐνίους τὸ ἐπὶ τούτῳ τιμᾶσθαι, ἢ οὐκ ὄντων δικαίων δέκα οὐδεὶς δόξει. ὅθεν πολλῷ σοφώτερον ἐφρόνουν ἂν Ἠλεῖοι ἀριθμῷ μὲν ἄλλοτε ἄλλοι ὄντες, δικαιότητι δὲ οἱ αὐτοί."

31. Ταῦτα σπουδάζοντας αὐτοὺς ὁ βασιλεὺς ἐκκρούειν ἐπειρᾶτο, διείργων αὐτοὺς παντὸς λόγου καὶ ἀεί τι ἔμπληκτον καὶ ἀμαθὲς λέγων. πάλιν οὖν ἤρετο ὑπὲρ τοῦ σπουδάζοιεν, ὁ δὲ Ἀπολλώνιος "διαλεγόμεθα μὲν ὑπὲρ μεγάλων καὶ τῶν παρ' Ἕλλησιν εὐδοκιμωτάτων, σὺ δ' ἂν μικρὰ ταῦτα ἡγοῖο, φῂς γὰρ διαβεβλῆσθαι πρὸς τὰ Ἑλλήνων." "διαβέβλημαι μὲν ἀληθῶς," εἶπεν "ἀκοῦσαι δ' ὅμως βούλομαι, δοκεῖτε γάρ μοι λέγειν ὑπὲρ Ἀθηναίων τῶν Ξέρξου δούλων."

2 Ὁ δὲ "ὑπὲρ ἄλλων μὲν" ἔφη "διαλεγόμεθα, ἐπεὶ δ' ἀτόπως τε καὶ ψευδῶς Ἀθηναίων ἐπεμνήσθης, ἐκεῖνό μοι εἰπέ· εἰσί σοι, βασιλεῦ, δοῦλοι;" "δισμύριοι," ἔφη "καὶ οὐδὲ ἐώνημαί γε αὐτῶν οὐδένα, ἀλλ' εἰσὶν οἰκογενεῖς πάντες." πάλιν οὖν ἤρετο ἑρμηνεύοντος τοῦ Ἰάρχα, πότερ' αὐτὸς ἀποδιδράσκοι τοὺς αὑτοῦ δούλους ἢ οἱ δοῦλοι ἐκεῖνον, ὁ δὲ ὑβρίζων αὐτὸν "τὸ μὲν ἐρώτημα" ἔφη "ἀνδραποδῶδες, ὅμως δ' οὖν ἀποκρίνο-

lenes, who preside over the Olympics to the number of ten. We do not approve of the rule governing these gentlemen, since they leave the choice to the caprice of the lot, by which some inferior person may be chosen. If they selected the gentlemen by merit or by election, they would err, but not in the same way. Keeping the number fixed at ten would either deprive some of their due honor, if there were more than ten just men, or if there were not, none of them would be considered just. The Eleians would arrange things much more wisely if their number fluctuated over time, but their justice was invariable."

31. While they were deep in this discussion, the king kept trying to distract them, by diverting them from every topic and constantly saying bizarre and ignorant things. He asked them again what their subject was, and Apollonius replied, "We are conversing about important matters, highly esteemed by the Greeks, which you would think trifling, since you say that you are ill disposed towards Greek thought." "I certainly am," he said, "but still I want to hear, since I believe you are talking about the Athenians whom Xerxes made into slaves."

"In fact we are talking about something else," said 2
Apollonius, "but since you mentioned the Athenians in such an absurd and false way, tell me this. Do you have slaves, Majesty?" "Twenty thousand," he replied, "and I did not buy a single one—all of them are house-born." So Apollonius asked again, with Iarchas as interpreter, whether he himself ran away from his own slaves, or they from him. The king mocked him by saying, "That is a slave's question, but I will answer all the same that a run-

μαι τὸν ἀποδιδράσκοντα δοῦλόν τε εἶναι καὶ ἄλλως κακόν, δεσπότην δὲ οὐκ ἂν ἀποδρᾶναι τοῦτον, ὃν ἔξεστιν αὐτῷ στρεβλοῦν τε καὶ ξαίνειν." "οὐκοῦν," ἔφη "ὦ βασιλεῦ, δοῦλος εἶναι[36] Ἀθηναίων Ξέρξης ὑπὸ σοῦ ἀποπέφανται καὶ ὡς κακὸς δοῦλος ἀποδρᾶναι αὐτούς. ἡττηθεὶς γὰρ ὑπ' αὐτῶν τῇ ναυμαχίᾳ τῇ περὶ τὰ στενὰ καὶ δείσας περὶ ταῖς ἐν Ἑλλησπόντῳ σχεδίαις ἐν μιᾷ νηὶ ἔφυγε." "καὶ μὴν καὶ ἐνέπρησεν" ἔφη "τὰς Ἀθήνας ταῖς ἑαυτοῦ χερσίν."

3 Ὁ δὲ Ἀπολλώνιος "τούτου μέν," εἶπεν "ὦ βασιλεῦ, τοῦ τολμήματος ἔδωκε δίκας, ὡς οὔπω τις ἕτερος· οὓς γὰρ ἀπολωλεκέναι ᾤετο, τούτους ἀποδρὰς ᾤχετο. ἐγὼ δὲ καὶ <τὰ>[37] Ξέρξου θεωρῶν ἐπὶ μὲν τῇ διανοίᾳ, καθ' ἣν ἐστράτευσεν, ἡγοῦμαι [ἂν][38] αὐτὸν ἀξίως δοξασθῆναι[39] ἐνίοις, ὅτι Ζεὺς εἴη, ἐπὶ δὲ τῇ φυγῇ κακοδαιμονέστατον ἀνθρώπων ὑπείληφα. εἰ γὰρ ἐν χερσὶ τῶν Ἑλλήνων ἀπέθανε, τίς μὲν ἂν λόγων λαμπροτέρων ἠξιώθη; τῷ δ' ἂν μείζω τάφον ἐπεσημήναντο Ἕλληνες; ἀγωνία δ' ἐνόπλιος καὶ ἀγωνία μουσικὴ τίς οὐκ ἂν ἐπ' αὐτῷ ἐτέθη; εἰ γὰρ Μελικέρται καὶ Παλαίμονες καὶ Πέλοψ ὁ ἐπηλύτης Λυδός, οἱ μὲν ἔτι πρὸς μαζῷ ἀποθανόντες, ὁ δὲ τὴν Ἀρκαδίαν τε καὶ τὴν Ἀργολίδα καὶ τὴν ἐντὸς Ἰσθμοῦ δουλωσάμενος, ἐς θείαν μνήμην ὑπὸ τῶν Ἑλλήνων ἤρθησαν, τί οὐκ ἂν ἐπὶ Ξέρξῃ ἐγένετο ὑπ' ἀνδρῶν ἀσπαζομένων τε ἀρετὰς φύσει καὶ ἔπαινον αὑτῶν ἡγουμένων τὸ ἐπαινεῖν οὓς νικῶσιν;"

[36] εἶναι Kay.: μὲν [37] <τὰ> Kay. [38] [ἂν] secl. Jackson

away is a slave and generally bad, and no master could ever run away from someone he has the power to torture or to whip." "Well then, Majesty," said Apollonius, "you have proved that Xerxes was the slave of the Athenians, since he ran away from them as a bad slave. When he had lost to them in the sea battle around the narrows, and feared for his rafts in the Hellespont, he ran away in a single night."

"And yet," said the other, "he burned Athens with his 3
own hands." Apollonius replied, "For that outrage he paid a penalty without parallel, Majesty. He ran scurrying away from those he thought he had destroyed. When I myself consider Xerxes in the light of the ambition with which he made his expedition, I can believe that some people were not wrong to regard him as a second Zeus, but in the light of his retreat I think him the most wretched of men. Had he died at the hands of the Greeks, who would have received more glorious orations? Whom would the Greeks have commemorated with a greater tomb? Is there a competition in arms or in the arts that would not have been instituted for him? A Melicertes, a Palaemon, and a Pelops, a stranger from Lydia, were raised to eternal glory by the Greeks, though the first two died at their mothers' breast, and the third enslaved Arcadia, the Argolid, and the land within the Isthmus.[24] What commemoration would Xerxes not have received from heroes with a natural love of the virtues, who think it their own glory to glorify those whom they defeat?"

[24] The Isthmian games were held in memory of Melicertes, and Pelops was buried at Olympia.

---

[39] δοξασθῆναι Kay.: δοξασθέντα

32. Ταῦτα τοῦ Ἀπολλωνίου λέγοντος ἐς δάκρυα ἀπήχθη ὁ βασιλεύς, καὶ "ὦ φίλτατε," εἶπεν "οἵους ἄνδρας ἑρμηνεύεις μοι τοὺς Ἕλληνας εἶναι." "πόθεν οὖν, ὦ βασιλεῦ, χαλεπῶς πρὸς αὐτοὺς εἶχες;" "διαβάλλουσιν," εἶπεν "ὦ ξένε, τὸ Ἑλλήνων γένος οἱ ἐξ Αἰγύπτου φοιτῶντες ἐνταῦθα, σφᾶς μὲν αὐτοὺς ἱερούς τε καὶ σοφοὺς ἀποφαίνοντες καὶ νομοθέτας θυσιῶν τε καὶ τελετῶν, ὁπόσας νομίζουσιν οἱ Ἕλληνες, ἐκείνους δὲ οὐδὲν ὑγιὲς εἶναι φάσκοντες, ἀλλ' ὑβριστάς τε καὶ ξυγκλύδας, καὶ ἀναρχίαν πᾶσαν, καὶ μυθολόγους, καὶ τερατολόγους, καὶ πένητας μέν, ἐνδεικνυμένους δὲ τοῦτο οὐχ ὡς σεμνόν, ἀλλ' ὑπὲρ ξυγγνώμης τοῦ κλέπτειν, σοῦ δὲ ἀκούων ταῦτα καὶ ὅπως φιλότιμοί τε καὶ χρηστοί εἰσι, σπένδομαί τε λοιπὸν τοῖς Ἕλλησι, καὶ δίδωμι αὐτοῖς ἐπαινεῖσθαί τε ὑπ' ἐμοῦ καὶ εὔχεσθαί με ὑπὲρ Ἑλλήνων ὅ τι δύναμαι, καὶ τοὺς Αἰγυπτίους ὑπ' ἐμοῦ ἀπιστεῖσθαι."

2 Ὁ δὲ Ἰάρχας "κἀγώ," ἔφη "ὦ βασιλεῦ, ἐγίγνωσκον, ὅτι σοι τὰ ὦτα διέφθορεν ὑπὸ τῶν Αἰγυπτίων τούτων, διῄειν δὲ ὑπὲρ Ἑλλήνων οὐδέν, ἔστ' ἂν ξυμβούλου τοιούτου τύχῃς. ἀλλ' ἐπεὶ βελτίων γέγονας ὑπ' ἀνδρὸς σοφοῦ, νῦν μὲν ἡμῖν ἡ Ταντάλου φιλοτησία πινέσθω καὶ καθεύδωμεν δι' ἃ χρὴ νύκτωρ σπουδάσαι, λόγων δὲ Ἑλληνικῶν, ἥδιστοι[40] δ' οὗτοι τῶν κατ' ἀνθρώπους, ἐμπλήσω σε λοιπὸν ἐγὼ χαίροντα, ὁπότε ἀφίκοιο." καὶ ἅμα ἐξῆρχε τοῖς ξυμπόταις πρῶτος ἐς τὴν φιάλην κύπτων, ἡ δὲ ἐπότιζεν ἱκανῶς πάντας, τὸ γὰρ νᾶμα ἀφθόνως ἐπεδίδου, καθάπερ δὴ

32. As Apollonius was saying this, the king burst into tears, and said, "My dear friend, what heroes you make the Greeks out to be." "How is it therefore that you were angry with them?" "Visitors here from Egypt speak ill of the Greek nation, stranger," he replied. "They claim themselves to be holy, wise, and the originators of all the sacrifices and rituals that the Greeks observe. But there is nothing good about the Greeks, they assert; they are lawbreakers, immigrants, totally ungovernable, peddlers of stories and miracles, destitutes who flaunt their poverty not as something honorable but as an excuse to steal. But after hearing all this from you, that they are honorable and good, from now on I will drink to the Greeks, and agree to praise them, to pray for the Greeks as best I can, and to mistrust the Egyptians."

"I too, Majesty," said Iarchas, "realized that your ears 2
had been corrupted by the Egyptians, but I said nothing in the Greeks' defense until you had an adviser such as this. Now that a wise man has made you better, let us drink the toast of Tantalus, and then sleep on the matters that we must discuss by night. As for the doctrines of the Greeks, which are pleasanter than those of any other people, I will fill your willing ears with them whenever you visit in future." With these words, he began the round of toasts by stooping over the bowl, which supplied enough for every thirst, while the liquid rose plentifully, as when spring

40 ἥδιστοι Radermacher: πλεῖστοι

τοῖς πηγαίοις ἀναδιδομένοις. ἔπιέ τε καὶ ὁ Ἀπολλώνιος, ὑπὲρ γὰρ φιλότητος Ἰνδοῖς τὸ ποτὸν τοῦτο εὕρηται. ποιοῦνται δὲ αὐτοῦ οἰνοχόον Τάνταλον, ἐπειδὴ φιλικώτατος ἀνθρώπων ἔδοξεν.

33. Πιόντας δὲ αὐτοὺς ἐδέξατο ἡ γῆ εὐναῖς, ἃς αὐτὴ ὑπεστόρνυ. ἐπεὶ δὲ νὺξ μέση ἐγένετο, πρῶτον μὲν ἀναστάντες τὴν ἀκτῖνα μετέωροι ὕμνησαν, ὥσπερ ἐν τῇ μεσημβρίᾳ, εἶτα τῷ βασιλεῖ ξυνεγένοντο, ὁπόσα ἐδεῖτο. παρατυχεῖν μὲν οὖν τὸν Ἀπολλώνιον οἷς ἐσπούδασεν ὁ βασιλεὺς οὔ φησιν ὁ Δάμις, οἴεσθαι δ᾿ αὐτὸν περὶ τῶν τῆς ἀρχῆς ἀπορρήτων τὴν ξυνουσίαν πεποιῆσθαι. θύσας οὖν ἅμα ἡμέρᾳ προσῆλθε τῷ Ἀπολλωνίῳ καὶ ἐκάλει ἐπὶ ξένια ἐς τὰ βασίλεια, ζηλωτὸν ἀποπέμψειν φάσκων ἐς Ἕλληνας. ὁ δὲ ἐπῄνει μὲν ταῦτα, οὐ μὴν ἐπιδώσειν γε ἑαυτὸν ἔφασκεν ἀνδρὶ μηδὲν ὁμοίῳ, καὶ ἄλλως πλείω χρόνον ἀποδημῶν τοῦ εἰκότος αἰσχύνεσθαι τοὺς οἴκοι φίλους ὑπερορᾶσθαι δοκοῦντας.

2 Ἀντιβολεῖν δὲ τοῦ βασιλέως φάσκοντος καὶ ἀνελευθέρως ἤδη προσκειμένου "βασιλεὺς" ἔφη "ταπεινότερον αὑτοῦ περὶ ὧν αἰτεῖ διαλεγόμενος ἐπιβουλεύει." προσελθὼν οὖν ὁ Ἰάρχας "ἀδικεῖς," εἶπεν "ὦ βασιλεῦ, τὸν ἱερὸν οἶκον, ἀπάγων ἐνθένδε ἄνδρα ἄκοντα. καὶ ἄλλως τῶν προγιγνωσκόντων οὗτος ὢν οἶδε τὴν ξυνουσίαν αὐτῷ τὴν πρὸς σὲ μὴ ἐπ᾿ ἀγαθῷ τῷ ἑαυτοῦ ἐσομένην, ἴσως δὲ οὐδ᾿ αὐτῷ σοι χρηστόν τι ἕξουσαν."

34. Ὁ μὲν δὴ κατῄει ἐς τὴν κώμην, ὁ γὰρ θεσμὸς

waters bubble up. Apollonius too drank, since the Indians invented this toast as a pledge of friendship, and they make Tantalus its server, as one whom they considered the friendliest of men.

33. As they drank, beneath them the earth received them on couches that it spread spontaneously. At midnight, they first stood up and lauded the sunlight, suspended in the way it had been at midday, and then spoke with the king on whatever he requested. Damis says that Apollonius was not present at the king's discussion, but he thinks that the conference concerned state secrets. After sacrificing at daybreak, the king came to Apollonius and invited him as a guest to his palace, promising to send him on his way as the envy of the Greeks. Apollonius thanked him, but said he would not impart his company to a gentleman in no way like himself. In addition, he had been absent for an unreasonably long time, and was ashamed that he seemed to be neglecting his friends at home.

The king said that he insisted, and began to press him 2
so rudely that Apollonius said, "When a king discusses his requests in a manner demeaning to himself, he is up to no good." Iarchas approached and said, "Majesty, you do wrong to our sacred house in trying to take a gentleman away against his will. Besides, he is one of those endowed with foresight, and knows that your company will not be for his benefit, and will perhaps have an unwelcome result for you too."

34. The king therefore went down to the village, since

τῶν σοφῶν οὐ ξυνεχώρει τῷ βασιλεῖ ξυνεῖναί σφισιν ὑπὲρ μίαν ἡμέραν, ὁ δὲ Ἰάρχας πρὸς τὸν ἄγγελον "καὶ Δάμιν" εἶπε "τῶν δεῦρο ἀπορρήτων ἀξιοῦμεν καὶ ἡκέτω, τῶν δὲ ἄλλων ἐπιμελοῦ ἐν τῇ κώμῃ." ὡς δὲ ἀφίκετο, ξυνιζήσαντες ὥσπερ εἰώθεσαν ξυνεχώρουν τῷ Ἀπολλωνίῳ ἐρωτᾶν,

2 Ἤρετό τε ἐκ τίνων ξυγκεῖσθαι τὸν κόσμον ἡγοῖντο, οἱ δὲ ἔφασαν "ἐκ στοιχείων." "μῶν" ἔφη "τεττάρων;" "οὐ τεττάρων," ἔφη ὁ Ἰάρχας "ἀλλὰ πέντε." "καὶ τί ἂν" ἔφη "πέμπτον γένοιτο παρὰ τὸ ὕδωρ τε καὶ τὸν ἀέρα, καὶ τὴν γῆν, καὶ τὸ πῦρ;" "ὁ αἰθήρ," εἶπεν "ὃν ἡγεῖσθαι χρὴ γένεσιν θεῶν εἶναι, τὰ μὲν γὰρ τοῦ ἀέρος ἕλκοντα θνητὰ πάντα, τὰ δὲ τοῦ αἰθέρος ἀθάνατά τε καὶ θεῖα." πάλιν ἤρετο, τί τῶν στοιχείων πρῶτον γένοιτο, ὁ δὲ Ἰάρχας "ὁμοῦ" ἔφη "πάντα, τὸ γὰρ ζῷον κατὰ μέρος οὐ τίκτεται." "ζῷον" ἔφη "ἡγῶμαι τὸν κόσμον;" "ἤν γε" ἔφη "ὑγιῶς γιγνώσκῃς, αὐτὸς γὰρ ζωογονεῖ πάντα." "θῆλυν" εἶπεν "αὐτὸν καλῶμεν, ἢ τῆς ἄρσενός τε καὶ ἀντικειμένης φύσεως;"

3 "Ἀμφοῖν," ἔφη "αὐτὸς γὰρ αὐτῷ ξυγγιγνόμενος τὰ μητρός τε καὶ πατρὸς ἐς τὴν ζωογονίαν πράττει, ἔρωτά τε ἑαυτοῦ ἴσχει θερμότερον ἢ ἕτερόν τι ἑτέρου, ὃς ἁρμόττει αὐτὸν καὶ ξυνίστησιν· ἀπεικὸς δὲ οὐδὲν ἑαυτῷ ξυμφύεσθαι. καὶ ὥσπερ χειρῶν τε καὶ ποδῶν ἔργον πεποίηται ἡ τοῦ ζῴου κίνησις καὶ ὁ ἐν[41] αὐτῷ νοῦς, ὑφ᾽ οὗ ὁρμᾷ, οὕτως ἡγώμεθα καὶ τὰ μέρη τοῦ κόσμου διὰ τὸν ἐκείνου νοῦν ἐπιτήδεια παρέχειν αὑτὰ τοῖς τικτομένοις τε καὶ κυουμένοις πᾶσι. καὶ γὰρ τὰ

the Wise Men's rule did not permit him to spend more than a day with them, but Iarchas said to the messenger, "Damis too we consider worthy of the secrets here, so tell him to come, while you look after the others in the village." When Damis had come, the Wise Men formed their usual circle and gave Apollonius permission to put questions.

So he asked what they thought the universe consisted 2
of, to which they replied, "Elements," "Four, do you think?" he said. "Not four," said Iarchas, "but five." "What could a fifth one be," said Apollonius, "besides water, air, earth, and fire?" "Ether, "said Iarchas, "which we must consider to be the origin of the gods. All that breathes air is mortal, but what breathes ether is immortal and divine." Next Apollonius asked which of the elements came into existence first. "All came together," said the other, "since a living being is not born one piece at a time." "Am I to consider the universe living?" asked Apollonius. "Yes, if you reason correctly," said Iarchas, "since itself it gives life to everything." "Should we then call it female," asked Apollonius, "or of the contrary, male sex?"

"Of both," was the answer, "since it has intercourse with 3
itself, and performs both the mother's and the father's role with respect to generation. It feels a desire for itself more intense than that of any two other beings, and this joins and unites it, and there is nothing unreasonable about its coalescence. And just as the action of the hands and feet in a living creature comes from mobility and the intelligence that causes it, so also we must suppose that, because of the intelligence of the universe, its parts accommodate themselves to everything that undergoes birth and conception.

---

41 ὁ ἐν Kay.: ὅθεν

πάθη τὰ ἐξ αὐχμῶν φοιτῶντα κατὰ τὸν ἐκείνου φοιτᾷ νοῦν, ἐπειδὰν ἐκπεσοῦσα ἡ δίκη τῶν ἀνθρώπων ἀτίμως πράττῃ, ποιμαίνεταί τε χειρὶ οὐ μιᾷ τόδε τὸ ζῷον, ἀλλὰ πολλαῖς τε καὶ ἀρρήτοις, αἷς χρῆται, ἀχαλίνωτον μὲν διὰ μέγεθος, εὐήνιον δὲ κινεῖται καὶ εὐάγωγον.

35. "Καὶ παράδειγμα μὲν οὐκ οἶδ᾽ ὅ τι ἀρκέσει τῷ λόγῳ, μεγίστῳ τε ὄντι καὶ πρόσω ἐννοίας, ὑποκείσθω δὲ ναῦς, οἵαν Αἰγύπτιοι ξυντιθέντες ἐς τὴν θάλατταν τὴν ἡμεδαπὴν ἀφιᾶσιν ἀγωγίμων Ἰνδικῶν ἀντιδιδόντες Αἰγύπτια. θεσμοῦ γὰρ παλαιοῦ περὶ τὴν Ἐρυθρὰν ὄντος, ὃν βασιλεὺς Ἐρύθρας ἐνόμισεν, ὅτε τῆς θαλάττης ἐκείνης ἦρχε, μακρῷ μὲν πλοίῳ μὴ ἐσπλεῖν ἐς αὐτὴν Αἰγυπτίους, στρογγύλῃ δ᾽ αὖ μιᾷ νηὶ χρῆσθαι, σοφίζονται πλοῖον Αἰγύπτιοι πρὸς πολλὰ τῶν παρ᾽ ἑτέροις καὶ παραπλευρώσαντες αὐτὸ ἁρμονίαις, ὁπόσαι ναῦν ξυνιστᾶσι, τοίχοις τε ὑπεράραντες καὶ ἱστῷ, καὶ πηξάμενοι πλείους οἰκίας, οἵας ἐπὶ τῶν σελμάτων,

2 "Πολλοὶ μὲν κυβερνῆται τῆς νεὼς ταύτης ὑπὸ τῷ πρεσβυτάτῳ τε καὶ σοφωτάτῳ πλέουσι, πολλοὶ δὲ κατὰ πρῷραν ἄρχοντες ἄριστοί τε καὶ δεξιοὶ ναῦται καὶ πρὸς ἱστία πηδῶντες, ἔστι δέ τι τῆς νεὼς ταύτης καὶ ὁπλιτεῦον, πρὸς γὰρ τοὺς κολπίτας βαρβάρους, οἳ ἐν δεξιᾷ τοῦ ἔσπλου κεῖνται, παρατάττεσθαι δεῖ τὴν ναῦν, ὅτε λῃίζοιντο αὐτὴν ἐπιπλέοντες. τοῦτο ἡγώμεθα καὶ περὶ τόνδε τὸν κόσμον εἶναι, θεωροῦντες αὐτὸν πρὸς τὸ τῆς ναυτιλίας σχῆμα, τὴν μὲν γὰρ δὴ πρώτην καὶ τελεωτάτην ἕδραν ἀποδοτέον θεῷ γενέτορι τοῦδε τοῦ ζῴου, τὴν δὲ ἐπ᾽ ἐκείνῃ θεοῖς, οἳ τὰ μέρη αὐτοῦ

For instance, the sufferings resulting from drought arise from the mind of the universe, when justice is banished from mankind and treated with dishonor. And this being guides itself not by one hand alone but by many unseen ones that it uses; though too large to be restrained, it moves obediently and tractably.

35. "I do not know what illustration will suffice for a doctrine of such grandeur and beyond imagination, but let us imagine a ship such as the Egyptians construct and launch on our waters, giving Egyptian exports in exchange for Indian ones. There is an old rule of the Red Sea, which king Erythras once laid down when he ruled that sea, that Egyptians may not enter it in a warship, but instead must use a single round-bottomed vessel. So the Egyptians construct a ship equivalent to many of those used by others. They seal it with all the joints that hold a ship together, and over these they build hulls and a mast, and make numerous cabins such as those over the benches.

"There are many captains of this ship, sailing under the 2
command of the eldest and most skilful among them, and many steersmen at the stern, and excellent, nimble sailors who eagerly tend the sails. This ship also carries armed men, since the barbarians of the Gulf live on the right side of its entrance, and the ship must do battle with them when they attack and try to plunder it. We may suppose that the same holds for this universe, when we consider it against our image from navigation. We should assign the first and most exalted position to the God who engendered this being, and the next one to the gods who govern the parts of it.

κυβερνῶσι, καὶ τῶν γε ποιητῶν ἀποδεχώμεθα, ἐπειδὰν πολλοὺς μὲν φάσκωσιν ἐν τῷ οὐρανῷ θεοὺς εἶναι, πολλοὺς δὲ ἐν θαλάττῃ, πολλοὺς δὲ ἐν πηγαῖς τε καὶ νάμασι, πολλοὺς δὲ περὶ γῆν, εἶναι δὲ καὶ ὑπὸ γῆν τινας. τὸν δὲ ὑπὸ γῆν τόπον, εἴπερ ἐστίν, ἐπειδὴ φρικώδη αὐτὸν καὶ φθαρτικὸν ᾄδουσιν, ἀποτάττωμεν τοῦ κόσμου."

36. Ταῦτα τοῦ Ἰνδοῦ διελθόντος ἐκπεσεῖν ὁ Δάμις ἑαυτοῦ φησιν ὑπ' ἐκπλήξεως καὶ ἀναβοῆσαι μέγα, μὴ γὰρ ἄν ποτε νομίσαι ἄνδρα Ἰνδὸν ἐς τοῦτο ἐλάσαι γλώττης Ἑλλάδος, μηδ' ἄν, εἴπερ τὴν γλῶτταν ἠπίστατο, τοσῇδε εὐροίᾳ καὶ ὥρᾳ διελθεῖν ταῦτα. ἐπαινεῖ δὲ αὐτοῦ καὶ βλέμμα καὶ μειδίαμα καὶ τὸ μὴ ἀθεεὶ δοκεῖν ἐκφέρειν τὰς δόξας. τόν τοι Ἀπολλώνιον εὐσχημόνως τε καὶ ἀψοφητὶ τοῖς λόγοις χρώμενον ὅμως ἐπιδοῦναι μετὰ τὸν Ἰνδὸν τοῦτον, καὶ ὅπου καθήμενος διαλέγοιτο, θαμὰ δὲ τοῦτο ἔπραττε, προσεοικέναι τῷ Ἰάρχᾳ.

37. Ἐπαινεσάντων δὲ τῶν ἄλλων λαμπρᾷ τῇ[42] φωνῇ τὰ εἰρημένα, πάλιν ὁ Ἀπολλώνιος ἤρετο, πότερα τὴν θάλατταν μείζω ἡγοῖντο ἢ τὴν γῆν, ὁ δὲ Ἰάρχας "εἰ μὲν πρὸς τὴν θάλατταν" ἔφη "ἡ γῆ ἐξετάζοιτο, μείζων ἔσται, τὴν γὰρ θάλατταν αὕτη ἔχει, εἰ δὲ πρὸς πᾶσαν τὴν ὑγρὰν οὐσίαν θεωροῖτο, ἥττω τὴν γῆν ἀποφαινοίμεθα ἄν, καὶ γὰρ ἐκείνην τὸ ὕδωρ φέρει."

38. Μεταξὺ δὲ τῶν λόγων τούτων ἐφίσταται τοῖς σοφοῖς ὁ ἄγγελος Ἰνδοὺς ἄγων σωτηρίας δεομένους. καὶ παρῆγε γύναιον ἱκετεῦον ὑπὲρ παιδός, ὃν ἔφασκε

Let us approve of the poets when they say that there are many gods in heaven, many in the sea, many in fountains and streams, many on the earth, and some below earth. As for the realm below earth, if it exists, the poets represent it as fearsome and destructive, so let us not count it as part of the universe."

36. When the Indian had finished this speech, Damis was beside himself with amazement, so he says, and shouted out loud, for he never would have thought an Indian would progress so far in the Greek language, or even if he knew the language would have spoken of these matters with such fluency and charm. He also praises his look, his smile, and the way he seemed to offer his views with a certain divine inspiration. But Apollonius, he says, though he used language that was proper and unpretentious, nonetheless improved after meeting this Indian, and whenever he discoursed sitting down, as he often did, he resembled Iarchas.

37. The others applauded his words with a loud voice, and Apollonius next asked whether they thought the sea or the land greater. Iarchas replied, "If you were to measure the land against the sea, it would appear greater, since it includes the sea. But if we were to consider it in relation to the whole liquid element, we would prove the land to be lesser, since water produces the sea."

38. In the middle of this conversation, the Wise Men were interrupted by the messenger bringing some Indians in need of cures. He brought forward a woman praying to

---

42 λαμπρᾷ τῇ Valck.: πρώτῃ

μὲν ἑκκαίδεκα ἔτη γεγονέναι, δαιμονᾶν δὲ δύο ἔτη, τὸ δὲ ἦθος τοῦ δαίμονος εἴρωνα εἶναι καὶ ψεύστην. ἐρομένου δέ τινος τῶν σοφῶν, ὁπόθεν λέγοι ταῦτα, "τοῦ παιδὸς τούτου" ἔφη "τὴν ὄψιν εὐπρεπεστέρου ὄντος ὁ δαίμων ἐρᾷ, καὶ οὐ ξυγχωρεῖ αὐτῷ νοῦν ἔχειν, οὐδὲ ἐς διδασκάλου βαδίσαι ἐᾷ ἢ τοξότου, οὐδὲ οἴκοι εἶναι, ἀλλ' ἐς τὰ ἔρημα τῶν χωρίων ἐκτρέπει, καὶ οὐδὲ τὴν φωνὴν ὁ παῖς τὴν ἑαυτοῦ ἔχει, ἀλλὰ βαρὺ φθέγγεται καὶ κοῖλον, ὥσπερ οἱ ἄνδρες, βλέπει δὲ ἑτέροις ὀφθαλμοῖς μᾶλλον ἢ τοῖς ἑαυτοῦ. κἀγὼ μὲν ἐπὶ τούτοις κλάω τε καὶ ἐμαυτὴν δρύπτω καὶ νουθετῶ τὸν υἱόν, ὁπόσα εἰκός, ὁ δὲ οὐκ οἶδέ με.

2 "Διανοουμένης δέ μου τὴν ἐνταῦθα ὁδόν, τουτὶ δὲ πέρυσι διενοήθην, ἐξηγόρευσεν ὁ δαίμων ἑαυτὸν ὑποκριτῇ χρώμενος τῷ παιδί, καὶ δῆτα ἔλεγεν εἶναι μὲν εἴδωλον ἀνδρός, ὃς πολέμῳ ποτὲ ἀπέθανεν, ἀποθανεῖν δὲ ἐρῶν τῆς ἑαυτοῦ γυναικός, ἐπεὶ δὲ ἡ γυνὴ περὶ τὴν εὐνὴν ὕβρισε τριταίου κειμένου γαμηθεῖσα ἑτέρῳ, μισῆσαι μὲν ἐκ τούτου τὸ γυναικῶν ἐρᾶν, μεταρρυῆναι δὲ ἐς τὸν παῖδα τοῦτον. ὑπισχνεῖτο δέ, εἰ μὴ διαβάλλοιμι αὐτὸν πρὸς ὑμᾶς, δώσειν τῷ παιδὶ πολλὰ ἐσθλὰ καὶ ἀγαθά. ἐγὼ μὲν δὴ ἔπαθόν τι πρὸς ταῦτα, ὁ δὲ διάγει με πολὺν ἤδη χρόνον, καὶ τὸν ἐμὸν οἶκον ἔχει μόνος, οὐδὲν μέτριον οὐδὲ ἀληθὲς φρονῶν."

3 Ἤρετο οὖν ὁ σοφὸς πάλιν, εἰ πλησίον εἴη ὁ παῖς, ἡ δὲ οὐκ ἔφη, πολλὰ μὲν γὰρ ὑπὲρ τοῦ ἀφικέσθαι αὐτὸν πρᾶξαι, "ὁ δ' ἀπειλεῖ κρημνοὺς καὶ βάραθρα καὶ ἀποκτενεῖν μοι τὸν υἱόν, εἰ δικαζοίμην αὐτῷ δεῦρο."

them on her son's behalf. He was sixteen years old, she said, but had been possessed by a spirit for two years, and the spirit had a sly, deceitful character. When one of the Wise Men asked on what evidence she said this, she replied, "This boy of mine is rather handsome to look at, and the spirit is in love with him. He will not allow him to be rational, or go to school or to archery lessons, or to stay at home either, but carries him off into deserted places. My boy no longer has his natural voice but speaks in deep, ringing tones as men do, and his eyes, too, are more someone else's than his own. All this makes me weep and tear my hair, and I naturally scold my son, but he does not recognize me.

"But when I decided to come here, as I did a year ago, 2
the spirit confessed who he was, using my son as a medium. He said he was the ghost of a man who formerly died in war, and died still in love with his wife; but the woman broke their marriage bond three days after his death by marrying another man, and from that time, he said, he had loathed the love of women and had transferred his affection to the boy. And he promised that if I did not accuse him before you, he would give the boy many wonderful presents. This made some impression on me, but he has kept me waiting for a long time now, and acts as sole master of my house, deaf to moderation and to truth."

The Wise Man then asked her if the boy was nearby, 3
but she said, "No: I did everything to make him come, but that spirit threatened me with 'cliffs' and 'precipices,' and with killing my son if I brought my complaint here." "Take

"θάρσει," ἔφη ὁ σοφός "οὐ γὰρ ἀποκτενεῖ αὐτὸν ἀναγνοὺς ταῦτα." καί τινα ἐπιστολὴν ἀνασπάσας τοῦ κόλπου ἔδωκε τῇ γυναικί, ἐπέσταλτο δὲ ἄρα ἡ ἐπιστολὴ πρὸς τὸ εἴδωλον ξὺν ἀπειλῇ καὶ ἐπιπλήξει.[43]

39. Καὶ μὴν καὶ χωλεύων τις ἀφίκετο γεγονὼς μὲν ἤδη τριάκοντα ἔτη, λεόντων δὲ θηρατὴς δεινός, ἐμπεπτωκότος δὲ αὐτῷ λέοντος ὠλισθήκει τὸν γλουτὸν καὶ τοῦ σκέλους ἑτέρως εἶχεν. ἀλλ' αἱ χεῖρες αὐτῷ καταψῶσαι τὸν γλουτὸν ἐς ὀρθὸν τοῦ βαδίσματος ὁ νεανίας ἦλθε. καὶ ὀφθαλμὼ δέ τις ἐρρυηκὼς ἀπῆλθε πᾶν ἔχων τὸ ἐν αὐτοῖς φῶς, καὶ ἄλλος τὴν χεῖρα ἀδρανὴς ὢν ἐγκρατὴς ᾤχετο. γυνὴ δέ τις ἑπτὰ ἤδη γαστέρας δυστοκοῦσα, δεομένου ὑπὲρ αὐτῆς τἀνδρός, ὧδε ἰάθη. τὸν ἄνδρα ἐκέλευσεν, ἐπειδὰν τίκτῃ ἡ γυνή, λαγὼν ὑπὸ κόλπῳ ζῶντα ἐσφέρεσθαι οὗ τίκτει, καὶ περιελθόντα αὐτὴν ἀφεῖναι ὁμοῦ τὸν λαγών,[44] συνεκδοθῆναι γὰρ ἂν τῷ ἐμβρύῳ τὴν μήτραν, εἰ μὴ ὁ λαγὼς αὐτίκα ἐξενεχθείη θύραζε.

40. Πατρὸς δ' αὖ τινος εἰπόντος, ὡς γένοιντο μὲν αὐτῷ παῖδες, ἀποθάνοιεν δὲ ὁμοῦ τῷ ἄρξασθαι οἶνον πίνειν, ὑπολαβὼν εἶπεν ὁ Ἰάρχας "καὶ βελτίους ἀποθανόντες ἐγένοντο, οὐ γὰρ ἂν διέφυγον τὸ μὴ μανῆναι, θερμοτέρων, ὡς φαίνεται, σπερμάτων φύντες. οἴνου μὲν οὖν ἀφεκτέον τοῖς ἐξ ὑμῶν, ὡς <δὲ>[45] μηδὲ ἐς ἐπιθυμίαν ποτὲ οἴνου κατασταῖεν, εἴ [δὲ][46] σοι πάλιν παιδίον γένοιτο, γέγονε δὲ ἑβδόμην ἡμέραν, ὡς ὁρῶ, τὴν γλαῦκα τὴν ὄρνιν χρὴ ἐπιφυλάττειν, οὗ νεοττεύει, καὶ τὰ ᾠὰ σπάσαντα δοῦναι μασᾶσθαι τῷ

courage," said the Wise Man, "he will not kill him when he has read this," and producing a letter from his pocket he gave it to the woman. It was addressed to the spirit with threats and rebuke.

39. There also came a lame man of about thirty. He had been an expert lion hunter, but when a lion had attacked him his hip had been dislocated and he was lame in one leg. But when the Wise Man massaged his hip with his hands, the young man recovered his proper gait. Someone else who had lost the use of his eyes went away with his sight fully restored, and another man with a withered arm made strong again. A woman, too, who had had seven miscarriages, was cured as follows through the pleas of her husband. The Wise Man told the husband, when his wife was giving birth, to bring a live hare under his cloak to where she was in labor, to walk around her, and immediately to release the hare: for she would eject her womb as well as the embryo if the hare was not driven from the house immediately.

40. A certain father said that he had had sons, but they had died as soon as they began to drink wine. Iarchas said in reply, "And they were better off dead, since they would not have escaped going insane, being the issue of overly hot seed, it seems. Your offspring must refrain from wine, and if you have a child again (and I see that one was born seven days ago), you must watch for where an owl is nesting, seize the eggs, and give them lightly boiled to the baby

---

43 ἐπιπλήξει Lucarini: ἐκπλήξει
44 τὸν λαγών Kay.: τῷ λαγῷ
45 <δὲ> Kay.
46 [δὲ] secl. Kay.

βρέφει συμμέτρως ἕψοντα, εἰ γὰρ βρώσεταί τι τούτων, πρὶν οἴνου γεύσεται, μῖσος αὐτῷ πρὸς τὸν οἶνον ἐμφύσεται, καὶ σωφρονέστατα διακείσεται μόνου ξυγκεκραμένος τοῦ ἐν τῇ φύσει θερμοῦ."

41. Τούτων οὖν ἐμπιπλάμενοι καὶ τοὺς ἄνδρας ἐκπληττόμενοι τῆς ἐς πάντα σοφίας παμπόλλους ὁσημέραι λόγους ἠρώτων, πολλοὺς δὲ καὶ αὐτοὶ ἠρωτῶντο. τῆς μὲν οὖν διαλεκτικῆς ξυνουσίας ἄμφω μετεῖχον, τὰς δὲ ἀπορρήτους σπουδάς, αἷς ἀστρικὴν [ἢ][47] μαντείαν κατενόουν καὶ τὴν πρόγνωσιν ἐσπούδαζον, θυσιῶν τε ἥπτοντο καὶ κλήσεων, αἷς θεοὶ χαίρουσι, μόνον φησὶν ὁ Δάμις τὸν Ἀπολλώνιον ξυμφιλοσοφεῖν τῷ Ἰάρχᾳ, καὶ ξυγγράψαι μὲν ἐκεῖθεν περὶ μαντείας ἀστέρων βίβλους τέτταρας, ὧν καὶ Μοιραγένης ἐπεμνήσθη, ξυγγράψαι δὲ περὶ θυσιῶν καὶ ὡς ἄν τις ἑκάστῳ θεῷ προσφόρως τε καὶ κεχαρισμένως θύοι.

2 Τὰ μὲν δὴ τῶν ἀστέρων καὶ τὴν τοιαύτην μαντικὴν πᾶσαν ὑπὲρ τὴν ἀνθρωπείαν ἡγοῦμαι φύσιν καὶ οὐδ' εἰ κέκτηταί τις οἶδα, τὸ δὲ περὶ θυσιῶν ἐν πολλοῖς μὲν ἱεροῖς εὗρον, ἐν πολλαῖς δὲ πόλεσι, πολλοῖς δὲ ἀνδρῶν σοφῶν οἴκοις, καὶ τί ἄν τις ἑρμηνεύοι αὐτὸ σεμνῶς ξυντεταγμένον καὶ κατὰ τὴν ἠχὼ τοῦ ἀνδρός; φησὶ δὲ ὁ Δάμις καὶ δακτυλίους ἑπτὰ τὸν Ἰάρχαν τῷ Ἀπολλωνίῳ δοῦναι τῶν ἑπτὰ ἐπωνύμους ἀστέρων, οὓς φορεῖν τὸν Ἀπολλώνιον κατὰ ἕνα πρὸς τὰ ὀνόματα τῶν ἡμερῶν.

42. Περὶ δὲ προγνώσεως λόγου αὐτοῖς ποτε ὄντος,

to munch. If it eats some of these before tasting wine, it will get a fixed hatred of wine and a very sober temperament, having only its own natural heat in its constitution."

41. Apollonius and Damis listened greedily to these speeches, and were amazed at their Eminences' unlimited wisdom. Every day they put all kinds of questions to them, and were asked many in return. But while both of them shared in the conversational exchanges, Apollonius alone, Damis says, conducted secret discussions with Iarchas in which they considered astral prophecy, discussed prediction, and treated sacrifices and the appellations pleasing to the gods. From this source, he says, Apollonius derived his four books on planetary prophecy (a work also mentioned by Moeragenes), and also what he wrote about sacrifices, and how to sacrifice to each of the gods appropriately and acceptably.[25]

I myself believe that astral and similar prophecy is be- 2
yond the scope of human nature, and I do not know if anyone owns the work. But the work *On Sacrifices* I have found in many sanctuaries, many cities, and the homes of many wise men. How could anyone characterize something so loftily composed, and so reminiscent of the Master's style? Damis also says that Iarchas gave Apollonius seven rings, named from the planets, and that he wore them in succession according to the name of each day.

42. They were once conversing about foreknowledge,

[25] The first of these works, evidently not seen by Philostratus, is completely lost, but the work *On Sacrifices* was known to Porphyry in the third century. On Moeragenes, see I 3.2.

---

[47] [ἦ] secl. Kay.

καὶ τοῦ Ἀπολλωνίου προσκειμένου τῇ σοφίᾳ ταύτῃ καὶ τὰς πλείους τῶν διαλέξεων ἐς τοῦτο ξυντείνοντος, ἐπαινῶν αὐτὸν ὁ Ἰάρχας "οἱ μαντικῇ" ἔφη "χαίροντες, ὦ χρηστὲ Ἀπολλώνιε, θεῖοί τε ὑπ' αὐτῆς γίγνονται καὶ πρὸς σωτηρίαν ἀνθρώπων πράττουσι. τὸ γάρ, ἃ χρὴ ἐς θεοῦ ἀφικόμενον εὑρέσθαι, ταῦτα αὖ, ὦ χρηστέ, ἐφ' ἑαυτοῦ προϊδέσθαι, προειπεῖν τε ἑτέροις ἃ μήπω ἴσασι, πανολβίου τινὸς ἡγοῦμαι καὶ ταὐτὸν ἰσχύοντος τῷ Ἀπόλλωνι τῷ Δελφικῷ.

2 "Ἐπεὶ δὲ ἡ τέχνη τοὺς ἐς θεοῦ φοιτῶντας ἐπὶ τῷ χρήσασθαι καθαροὺς κελεύει βαδίζοντας φοιτᾶν, ἢ 'ἔξιθι τοῦ νεὼ' πρὸς αὐτοὺς ἐρεῖ, δοκεῖ μοι καὶ τὸν προγνωσόμενον ἄνδρα ὑγιῶς ἑαυτοῦ ἔχειν, καὶ μήτε κηλῖδα προσμεμάχθαι τῇ ψυχῇ μηδεμίαν, μήτε οὐλὰς ἁμαρτημάτων ἐντετυπῶσθαι τῇ γνώμῃ, καθαρῶς δὲ αὐτὸν προφητεύειν ἑαυτοῦ καὶ τοῦ περὶ τῷ στέρνῳ τρίποδος συνιέντα. γεγωνότερον γὰρ οὕτω καὶ ἀληθέστερον τὰ λόγια ἐκδώσει· ὅθεν οὐ χρὴ θαυμάζειν εἰ καὶ σὺ τὴν ἐπιστήμην ξυνείληφας, τοσοῦτον ἐν τῇ ψυχῇ φέρων αἰθέρα."

43. Καὶ χαριεντιζόμενος ἅμα πρὸς τὸν Δάμιν "σὺ δ' οὐδὲν" ἔφη "προγιγνώσκεις, Ἀσσύριε, καὶ ταῦτα ξυνὼν ἀνδρὶ τοιούτῳ;" "νὴ Δί'," εἶπε "τά γε ἐμαυτῷ ἀναγκαῖα· ἐπειδὴ γὰρ πρώτῳ ἐνέτυχον τῷ Ἀπολλωνίῳ τούτῳ, καὶ σοφίας μοι ἔδοξε πλέως δεινότητός τε καὶ σωφροσύνης καὶ τοῦ καρτερεῖν ὀρθῶς, ἐπεὶ δὲ καὶ μνημοσύνην ἐν αὐτῷ εἶδον, πολυμαθέστατόν τε καὶ φιλομαθίας ἥττω, δαιμόνιόν τί μοι ἐγένετο. καὶ ξυγ-

since Apollonius, who was attached to this form of wisdom, led most of their discussions in this direction. Iarchas praised him by saying, "Those who love prophecy, my virtuous Apollonius, become divine under its influence, and act for the salvation of mankind. To be able to foresee in one's own person things that are ordinarily revealed by visiting a god's temple, and to predict to others things that they do not know, this, my good friend, I regard as the mark of a truly blessed person, and of one whose powers equal those of Delphic Apollo.

"Now the prophetic art requires that those who go to a 2
god in order to consult him must do so in a state of purity, since otherwise he will say to them, 'Leave my temple.' So it seems to me that the Master who wishes to foretell the future should be of a healthy disposition, with no pollution besmirching his soul, and no scars of sin traced on his mind; he prophesies in purity, understanding himself and the tripod in his heart.[26] In this way he will issue his pronouncements more resoundingly and truly. It is no wonder, then, that you have imbibed this knowledge, when you contain so much ether in your soul."

43. At the same time, teasing Damis he said to him, "And you, Assyrian, do you not have foreknowledge, though you associate with such a Master?" "Oh yes," said Damis, "about what is important for me. Why, the first time I met Apollonius here, I realized that he was full of wisdom, insight, abstinence, and the proper kind of endurance. But when I saw that he had memory too, and was extremely learned and devoted to knowledge, he seemed

[26] The priestess at Delphi sat on a tripod in order to deliver her prophecies.

γενόμενος αὐτῷ σοφὸς μὲν ᾠήθην δόξειν ἐξ ἰδιώτου τε καὶ ἀσόφου, πεπαιδευμένος δὲ ἐκ βαρβάρου, ἑπόμενος δὲ αὐτῷ καὶ ξυσπουδάζων ὄψεσθαι μὲν Ἰνδούς, ὄψεσθαι δὲ ὑμᾶς, Ἕλλησί τε ἐπιμίξειν Ἕλλην ὑπ᾽ αὐτοῦ γενόμενος. τὰ μὲν δὴ ὑμέτερα περὶ μεγάλων ὄντα Δελφοὺς ἡγεῖσθε καὶ Δωδώνην καὶ ὅ τι βούλεσθε, τἀμὰ δέ, ἐπειδὴ Δάμις μὲν ὁ προγιγνώσκων αὐτά, προγιγνώσκει δ᾽ ὑπὲρ αὑτοῦ μόνου, γραὸς ἔστω ἀγυρτρίας μαντευομένης ὑπὲρ προβατίων καὶ τῶν τοιούτων."

44. Ἐπὶ τούτοις μὲν δὴ ἐγέλασαν οἱ σοφοὶ πάντες, καταστάντος δὲ τοῦ γέλωτος ἐπανῆγεν ὁ Ἰάρχας ἐς τὸν περὶ τῆς μαντικῆς λόγον, καὶ πολλὰ μὲν αὐτὴν ἀγαθὰ ἔλεγε τοὺς ἀνθρώπους εἰργάσθαι, μέγιστον δὲ τὸ τῆς ἰατρικῆς δῶρον· οὐ γὰρ ἄν ποτε τοὺς σοφοὺς Ἀσκληπιάδας ἐς ἐπιστήμην τούτου παρελθεῖν, εἰ μὴ παῖς Ἀπόλλωνος Ἀσκληπιὸς γενόμενος, καὶ κατὰ τὰς ἐκείνου φήμας τε καὶ μαντείας ξυνθεὶς τὰ πρόσφορα ταῖς νόσοις φάρμακα, παισί τε ἑαυτοῦ παρέδωκε καὶ τοὺς ξυνόντας ἐδιδάξατο, τίνας μὲν δεῖ προσάγειν πόας ὑγροῖς ἕλκεσι, τίνας δὲ αὐχμηροῖς καὶ ξηροῖς ξυμμετρίας τε ποτίμων φαρμάκων, ὑφ᾽ ὧν ὕδεροι ἀποχετεύονται, καὶ αἷμα ἴσχεται, φθόαι τε παύονται καὶ τὰ οὕτω κοῖλα. καὶ τὰ τῶν ἰοβόλων δὲ ἄκη καὶ τὸ τοῖς ἰοβόλοις αὐτοῖς ἐς πολλὰ τῶν νοσημάτων χρῆσθαι τίς ἀφαιρήσεται τὴν μαντικήν; οὐ γάρ μοι δοκοῦσιν ἄνευ τῆς προγιγνωσκούσης σοφίας θαρσῆσαί ποτε

to me a supernatural being. As I accompanied him, so I thought, I would seem a wise man and no longer an ordinary, ignorant one, a cultured man and no longer a barbarian; as I followed him and shared his pursuits, I would see the Indians and see you, and associate with Greeks when he had made a Greek out of me. Now your predictions, being about weighty matters, you may consider to be like Delphi, Dodona, or whatever you please. But let mine, since Damis predicts them and does so only for his own benefit, be those of an old gypsy woman, whose predictions concern farm animals and the like."

44. At this all the Wise Men laughed, and when the laughter had died down Iarchas led the conversation back to prophecy, claiming that it had conferred many benefits on humankind, of which the greatest was the gift of medicine. The wise sons of Asclepius, he said, would never have attained their knowledge of this unless Asclepius had been born the son of Apollo, and by following his father's sayings and prophecies had inferred the remedies appropriate to each disease. He in turn transmitted them to his sons, and taught his followers which herbs should be applied to running wounds, and which to inflamed and dry ones, and as well how to make up medicines which reduce dropsy, staunch blood, cure consumption and similar wasting diseases. And who will deprive prophecy of cures drawn from venomous creatures and of using such creatures themselves to heal many illnesses? Without the wisdom of foresight, I do not think mankind would ever have ventured to

ἄνθρωποι τὰ πάντων ὀλεθριώτατα φαρμάκων ἐγκαταμῖξαι τοῖς σώζουσιν.

45. Ἐπεὶ δὲ καὶ ὅδε ὁ λόγος ἀναγέγραπται τῷ Δάμιδι σπουδασθεὶς ἐκεῖ περὶ τῶν ἐν Ἰνδοῖς μυθολογουμένων θηρίων τε καὶ πηγῶν καὶ ἀνθρώπων, μηδ' ἐμοὶ παραλειπέσθω, καὶ γὰρ κέρδος εἴη μήτε πιστεύειν, μήτε ἀπιστεῖν πᾶσιν. ἤρετο γὰρ δὴ ὁ Ἀπολλώνιος "ἔστι τι ζῷον ἐνταῦθα μαρτιχόρας;" ὁ δὲ Ἰάρχας "καὶ τίνα" ἔφη "φύσιν τοῦ ζῴου τούτου ἤκουσας; εἰκὸς γὰρ καὶ περὶ εἴδους αὐτοῦ ‹τι›[48] λέγεσθαι." "λέγεται" εἶπε "μεγάλα καὶ ἄπιστα, τετράπουν μὲν γὰρ εἶναι αὐτό, τὴν κεφαλὴν δὲ ἀνθρώπῳ εἰκάσθαι, λέοντι δὲ ὡμοιῶσθαι τὸ μέγεθος, τὴν δὲ οὐρὰν τοῦ θηρίου τούτου πηχυαίας ἐκφέρειν καὶ ἀκανθώδεις τὰς τρίχας, ἃς βάλλειν ὥσπερ τοξεύματα ἐς τοὺς θηρῶντας αὐτό."

2 Ἐρομένου δὲ αὐτοῦ καὶ περὶ τοῦ χρυσοῦ ὕδατος, ὅ φασιν ἐκ πηγῆς βλύζειν, καὶ περὶ τῆς ψήφου τῆς ἅπερ ἡ μαγνῆτις ποιούσης, ἀνθρώπων τε ὑπὸ γῆν οἰκούντων, καὶ πυγμαίων αὖ καὶ σκιαπόδων, ὑπολαβὼν ὁ Ἰάρχας "περὶ μὲν ζῴων ἢ φυτῶν" εἶπεν "ἢ πηγῶν, ὧν αὐτὸς ἐνταῦθα ἥκων εἶδες, τί ἄν σοι λέγοιμι; σὸν γὰρ ἤδη νῦν ἐξηγεῖσθαι αὐτὰ ἑτέροις· θηρίον δὲ τοξεῦον ἢ χρυσοῦ πηγὰς ὕδατος οὔπω ἐνταῦθα ἤκουσα.

46. "Περὶ μέντοι τῆς ψήφου τῆς ἐπισπωμένης τε καὶ ξυνδούσης ἑαυτῇ λίθους ἑτέρας οὐ χρὴ ἀπιστεῖν· ἔστι γάρ σοι καὶ ἰδεῖν τὴν λίθον καὶ θαυμάσαι τὰ ἐν αὐτῇ πάντα. γίγνεται μὲν γὰρ ἡ μεγίστη κατὰ

compound the most deadly of drugs with the healing ones.

45. Damis also wrote up the following conversation that they had on the subject of the fabulous beasts, springs, and men of India. I should not therefore leave it out, since one might do well neither to believe nor to disbelieve all the details. Anyhow, Apollonius asked, "Do you have an animal called the 'martichoras'?"[27] "What have you heard about the nature of this animal?" asked Iarchas, "since I presume there is some report of its appearance." "Great and incredible things are reported," said Apollonius, "that it is a quadruped with a head like a human's and in size resembles a lion, and that this beast has a tail with prickly hairs a cubit long, which it shoots like arrows at those hunting it."

He also asked about the liquid gold, which they say 2
issues from a spring, and about the stone with the same powers as magnetite, about the people who live underground, about pygmies and Shadow Feet.[28] To this Iarchas replied, "As for animals, plants, or fountains which you have seen while coming here, what can I tell you? It is now up to you to describe them to others. But I have never heard of an arrow-shooting animal or fountains of liquid gold in these parts.

46. "But as for the stone that attracts and binds other stones to itself, you should not disbelieve that, since you may both see the stone and admire all its properties. The largest that occurs is the size of the nail of this finger,"

[27] The tiger, so called from two Persian words meaning "man" and "eater."
[28] Fabulous people with large feet, which they used as parasols.

---

48 <τι> Kay.

ὄνυχα δακτύλου τούτου," δείξας τὸν ἑαυτοῦ ἀντίχειρα, "κυίσκεται δὲ ἐν γῇ κοίλῃ βάθος ὀργυιαὶ τέτταρες, τοσοῦτον δὲ αὐτῇ περίεστι τοῦ πνεύματος, ὡς ὑποιδεῖν τὴν γῆν καὶ κατὰ πολλὰ ῥήγνυσθαι κυισκομένης ἐν αὐτῇ τῆς λίθου. μαστεῦσαι δὲ αὐτὴν οὐδενὶ ἔξεστιν, ἀποδιδράσκει γάρ, εἰ μὴ μετὰ λόγου ἀνασπῷτο. ἀλλ' ἡμεῖς μόνοι τὰ μὲν δράσαντες, τὰ δὲ εἰπόντες ἀναιρούμεθα τὴν παντάρβην· ὄνομα γὰρ αὐτῇ τοῦτο.

2 "Νύκτωρ μὲν οὖν ἡμέραν ἀναφαίνει, καθάπερ τὸ πῦρ, ἔστι γὰρ πυρσὴ καὶ ἀκτινώδης, εἰ δὲ μεθ' ἡμέραν ὁρῷτο, βάλλει τοὺς ὀφθαλμοὺς μαρμαρυγαῖς μυρίαις. τὸ δὲ ἐν αὐτῇ φῶς πνεῦμά ἐστιν ἀρρήτου ἰσχύος, πᾶν γὰρ τὸ ἐγγὺς ἐσποιεῖ αὐτῇ. τί λέγω τὸ ἐγγύς; ἔστι σοι λίθους, ὁπόσας βούλει, καταποντῶσαί ποι ἢ τῶν ποταμῶν ἢ τῆς θαλάττης καὶ μηδὲ ἐγγὺς ἀλλήλων, ἀλλὰ σποράδας καὶ ὡς ἔτυχεν, ἡ δὲ ἐς αὐτὰς καθιμηθεῖσα ξυλλέγεται πάσας τῇ τοῦ πνεύματος διαδόσει, καὶ ὑποκείσονται αὐτῇ βοτρυδὸν αἱ λίθοι, καθάπερ σμῆνος." καὶ εἰπὼν ταῦτα ἔδειξε τὴν λίθον αὐτήν τε καὶ ὁπόσα ἐργάζεται.

47. Τοὺς δὲ πυγμαίους οἰκεῖν μὲν ὑπογείους, κεῖσθαι δὲ ὑπὲρ τὸν Γάγγην ζῶντας τρόπον, ὃς πᾶσιν εἴρηται. σκιάποδας δὲ ἀνθρώπους ἢ μακροκεφάλους ἢ ὁπόσα Σκύλακος ξυγγραφαὶ περὶ τούτων ᾄδουσιν, οὔτε ἄλλοσέ ποι βιοτεύειν τῆς γῆς οὔτε μὴν ἐν Ἰνδοῖς.

48. Ὃν δ' ὀρύττουσι χρυσὸν οἱ γρῦπες, πέτραι εἰσὶν οἷον σπινθῆρσιν ἐστιγμέναι ταῖς τοῦ χρυσοῦ ῥανίσιν, ἃς λιθοτομεῖ τὸ θηρίον τοῦτο τῇ τοῦ ῥάμφους

showing his thumb, "and it is hatched in an underground cave four fathoms deep, and has so powerful an exhalation that the earth swells and splits in many places as the stone is hatched in its interior. No one may search for it, since it runs away unless drawn up methodically. We alone, by various rites and spells, raise the 'ruby' (for such is its name).

"At night it has the effect of daylight with its glow and 2
its radiance, as fire does, and if you look at it in daylight it dazzles the eyes with its innumerable sparks. The light within it is an exhalation of mysterious power, which claims everything nearby for itself. Why do I say, 'everything nearby'? You can sink as many stones as you like somewhere in a river or in the sea, not even close together, but scattered randomly, and if you let the ruby down to them it attracts them all by diffusing its exhalation, and the stones will attach themselves to it in clusters, like a swarm of bees." So saying he showed an actual specimen and all its effects.

47. The pygmies, he said, lived underground, and they dwell across the Ganges, living in the way that everyone has described. But shadow-footed men, long-headed ones, or all the creatures that Skylax[29] celebrates in his works, these lived neither in other parts of the world nor indeed in India.

48. As for the gold that griffins dig up, there are rocks that are speckled with flakes of gold as if with sparks, and this creature quarries them by the force of its beak. These

[29] Fifth-century explorer and author, whose account of his voyage from the Indus to the Gulf of Suez was widely read in antiquity.

ἰσχύϊ. τὰ γὰρ θηρία ταῦτα εἶναί τε ἐν Ἰνδοῖς καὶ ἱεροὺς νομίζεσθαι τοῦ Ἡλίου, τέθριππά τε αὐτῶν ὑποζευγνύναι τοῖς ἀγάλμασι τοὺς τὸν Ἥλιον ἐν Ἰνδοῖς γράφοντας, μέγεθός τε καὶ ἀλκὴν εἰκάσθαι αὐτοὺς τοῖς λέουσιν, ὑπὸ δὲ πλεονεξίας τῶν πτερῶν αὐτοῖς τε ἐκείνοις ἐπιτίθεσθαι, καὶ τῶν ἐλεφάντων δὲ καὶ δρακόντων ὑπερτέρους εἶναι. πέτονται δὲ οὔπω μέγα, ἀλλ᾽ ὅσον οἱ βραχύποροι ὄρνιθες, μὴ γὰρ ἐπτιλῶσθαι σφᾶς, ὡς ὄρνισι πάτριον, ἀλλ᾽ ὑμέσι τοὺς ταρσοὺς ὑφάνθαι πυρσοῖς, ὡς εἶναι κυκλώσαντας πέτεσθαί τε καὶ ἐκ μετεώρου μάχεσθαι, τὴν τίγριν δὲ αὐτοῖς ἀνάλωτον εἶναι μόνην, ἐπειδὴ τὸ τάχος αὐτὴν ἐσποιεῖ τοῖς ἀνέμοις.

49. Καὶ τὸν φοίνικα δὲ τὸν ὄρνιν τὸν διὰ πεντακοσίων ἐτῶν ἐς Αἴγυπτον ἥκοντα πέτεσθαι μὲν ἐν τῇ Ἰνδικῇ τὸν χρόνον τοῦτον, εἶναι δὲ ἕνα ἐκδιδόμενον τῶν ἀκτίνων καὶ χρυσῷ λάμποντα, μέγεθος ἀετοῦ καὶ εἶδος, ἐς καλιάν τε ἱζάνειν τὴν ἐκ τοῦ ἀρώματος ποιουμένην αὐτῷ πρὸς ταῖς τοῦ Νείλου πηγαῖς. ἃ δὲ Αἰγύπτιοι περὶ αὐτοῦ ᾄδουσιν, ὡς ἐς Αἴγυπτον φέρεται, καὶ Ἰνδοὶ ξυμμαρτυροῦσι, προσᾴδοντες τῷ λόγῳ τὸ τὸν φοίνικα τὸν ἐν τῇ καλιᾷ τηκόμενον προπεμπτηρίους ὕμνους αὑτῷ ᾄδειν. τουτὶ δὲ καὶ τοὺς κύκνους φασὶ δρᾶν οἱ σοφώτερον αὐτῶν ἀκούοντες.

50. Τοιαίδε μὲν αἱ πρὸς τοὺς σοφοὺς ξυνουσίαι Ἀπολλωνίῳ ἐγένοντο μηνῶν τεττάρων ἐκεῖ διατρίψαντι, καὶ ξυλλαβόντι λόγους φανερούς τε καὶ ἀπορρήτους πάντας. ἐπεὶ δὲ ἐξελαύνειν ἐβούλετο, τὸν μὲν

animals do exist in India, and are considered sacred to the Sun. Indian artists who portray the Sun god show his statue drawn by four of them. In size and strength they resemble lions in size, and attack even them thanks to the advantage of their wings, and also prevail over elephants and dragons. They do not fly far, but as far as birds of short flight, since they are not feathered as birds customarily are, but have scarlet webbing on their feet. When they whirl their feet they can fly and fight from the air, and only the tigress, which its speed makes equal to the wind, can escape them.

49. He also said that the bird called the phoenix, which comes to Egypt every five hundred years, flies around India in the intervening time. There is only one, which is engendered by the sun's rays and has a golden sheen, and in size and appearance resembles an eagle. It settles on the nest that it makes from incense beside the sources of the Nile. The celebrated Egyptian account, that it migrates to Egypt, is confirmed by the Indians, who add the further embellishment that as the phoenix is consumed in its nest it sings farewell songs to itself. Swans do the same thing, according to those who hear them with special insight.

50. These then were the conversations between Apollonius and the Wise Men. He had stayed there for four months and absorbed all their doctrines, both avowed and secret. When he decided to leave, they persuaded him to

ἡγεμόνα καὶ τὰς καμήλους πείθουσιν αὐτὸν ἀποπέμψαι τῷ Φραώτῃ μετ᾽ ἐπιστολῆς, αὐτοὶ δὲ ἡγεμόνα ἕτερον καὶ καμήλους δόντες προέπεμπον αὐτόν, εὐδαιμονίζοντες αὑτούς τε κἀκεῖνον. ἀσπασάμενοι δὲ τὸν Ἀπολλώνιον καὶ θεὸν τοῖς πολλοῖς εἶναι δόξειν οὐ τεθνεῶτα μόνον, ἀλλὰ καὶ ζῶντα φήσαντες, αὐτοὶ μὲν ὑπέστρεψαν ἐς τὸ φροντιστήριον ἐπιστρεφόμενοι πρὸς τὸν ἄνδρα καὶ δηλοῦντες, ὅτι ἄκοντες αὐτοῦ ἀπαλλάττονται.

2 Ὁ δὲ Ἀπολλώνιος ἐν δεξιᾷ μὲν τὸν Γάγγην ἔχων, ἐν ἀριστερᾷ δὲ τὸν Ὕφασιν, κατῄει ἐπὶ τὴν θάλατταν ἡμερῶν δέκα ὁδὸν ἀπὸ τοῦ ἱεροῦ ὄχθου. κατιοῦσι δ᾽ αὐτοῖς πολλαὶ μὲν στρουθοὶ ἐφαίνοντο, πολλοὶ δὲ ἄγριοι βόες, πολλοὶ δὲ ὄνοι καὶ λέοντες καὶ παρδάλεις, καὶ τίγρεις, καὶ πιθήκων γένος ἕτερον παρὰ τοὺς ἐν ταῖς πεπερίσι, μέλανές τε γὰρ καὶ λάσιοι ἦσαν, καὶ τὰ εἴδη κύνειοι καὶ σμικροῖς ἀνθρώποις ἴσοι. διαλεγόμενοι δὲ περὶ τῶν ὁρωμένων, ὁποῖα εἰώθεσαν, ἀφίκοντο ἐπὶ τὴν θάλατταν, ἐν ᾗ κατεσκεύαστο ἐμπόρια μικρά, καὶ πλοῖα δὲ ἐν αὐτοῖς ὥρμει πορθμεῖα παραπλήσια τοῖς Τυρρηνοῖς. τὴν δὲ θάλατταν τὴν Ἐρυθρὰν εἶναι μὲν κυανωτάτην, ὠνομάσθαι δέ, ὡς εἶπον, ἀπὸ Ἐρύθρα βασιλέως, ὃς ἐπωνόμασεν ἑαυτὸν ἐκείνῳ τῷ πελάγει.

51. Ἐνταῦθα ἥκων τὰς μὲν καμήλους ἀπέπεμψε τῷ Ἰάρχᾳ μετ᾽ ἐπιστολῆς· "Ἀπολλώνιος Ἰάρχᾳ καὶ σοφοῖς ἑτέροις χαίρειν. ἀφικομένῳ μοι πεζῇ πρὸς ὑμᾶς δεδώκατε τὴν θάλατταν, ἀλλὰ καὶ σοφίας τῆς ἐν ὑμῖν κοινωνήσαντες δεδώκατε καὶ διὰ τοῦ οὐρανοῦ πορεύ-

return the guide and the camels to Phraotes with a letter, while they themselves gave him another guide and camels, and sent him on his way, congratulating themselves as well as him. They embraced Apollonius, saying that ordinary people would regard him as a god, in life as well as in death; and then they went back to their ashram, though looking back at the Master and showing their unwillingness to let him go.

Apollonius kept the Ganges on his right and Hyphasis 2
on his left, and after ten days' journey from the sacred hill reached the sea. As they traveled, they saw many ostriches, many wild oxen, many asses, lions, leopards, tigers, and a kind of monkey different from the ones in the pepper groves, black and hairy, like dogs in appearance and the size of small humans. As they conversed about the sights in their usual way, they reached the sea, where small trading stations had been set up, and where passenger boats like the ones in Etruria were moored. The Red Sea is apparently of the deepest blue, and gets its name, as I mentioned, from Erythras, who named that stretch of sea after himself.

51. On reaching this point, Apollonius sent the camels back to Iarchas with this letter: "Apollonius greets Iarchas and the other Wise Men. I came to you by land, and you have given me the sea; but you also shared your special wisdom with me, and showed me a path through heaven. I

εσθαι. μεμνήσομαι τούτων καὶ πρὸς Ἕλληνας κοινωνήσω τε λόγων ὡς παροῦσιν ὑμῖν, εἰ μὴ μάτην ἔπιον τοῦ Ταντάλου. ἔρρωσθε ἀγαθοὶ φιλόσοφοι."

52. Αὐτὸς δὲ ἐπιβὰς νεὼς ἐκομίζετο λείῳ καὶ εὐφόρῳ πνεύματι θαυμάζων τὸ στόμα τοῦ Ὑφάσιδος, ὡς φοβερῶς δι᾽ αὐτοῦ ἐκχεῖται· τελευτῶν γάρ, ὡς ἔφην, ἐς χωρία πετρώδη καὶ στενὰ καὶ κρημνοὺς ἐκπίπτει, δι᾽ ὧν καταρρηγνὺς ἐς τὴν θάλατταν ἑνὶ στόματι χαλεπὸς δοκεῖ τοῖς ἄγαν τῇ γῇ προσκειμένοις.

53. Καὶ μὴν καὶ τὸ τοῦ Ἰνδοῦ στόμα ἰδεῖν φασι, πόλιν δὲ ἐπ᾽ αὐτοῦ κεῖσθαι Πάταλα περίρρυτον τῷ Ἰνδῷ, ἐς ἣν τὸ ναυτικὸν τοῦ Ἀλεξάνδρου ἐλθεῖν, ᾧ ναύαρχον ἐπιτετάχθαι Νέαρχον οὐκ ἀγύμναστον τῆς θαλαττίου τάξεως. ἃ δὲ Ὀρθαγόρᾳ περὶ τῆς Ἐρυθρᾶς εἴρηται, καὶ ὅτι μήτε ἡ ἄρκτος ἐν αὐτῇ φαίνοιτο, μήτε σημαίνοιντο τὴν μεσημβρίαν οἱ πλέοντες, οἵ τε ἐπίδηλοι τῶν ἀστέρων ἐξαλλάττοιεν τῆς ἑαυτῶν τάξεως, δοκεῖ καὶ Δάμιδι, καὶ χρὴ πιστεύειν ὑγιῶς τε καὶ κατὰ τὸν ἐκεῖ οὐρανὸν εἰρῆσθαι ταῦτα. μνημονεύουσι καὶ νήσου μικρᾶς, ᾗ ὄνομα εἶναι Βίβλον, ἐν ᾗ [τὸ τοῦ κογχυλίου μέγεθος καὶ][49] οἱ μύες ὄστρεά τε καὶ τὰ τοιαῦτα δεκαπλάσια τῶν Ἑλληνικῶν τὸ μέγεθος ταῖς πέτραις προσπέφυκεν. ἁλίσκεται δὲ καὶ λίθος ἐκεῖ μαργαρὶς ἐν ὀστράκῳ λευκῷ, καρδίας τόπον ἔχουσα τῷ ὀστρέῳ.

54. Κατασχεῖν δέ φασι καὶ ἐς Πάγαλα[50] τῆς τῶν Ὠρειτῶν χώρας, οἱ δὲ Ὠρεῖται, χαλκαῖ μὲν αὐτοῖς αἱ πέτραι, χαλκῆ δὲ ἡ ψάμμος, χαλκοῦν δὲ ψῆγμα οἱ

will recall all this to the Greeks, and enjoy your conversations as if you were present, unless it was for nothing that I drank to Tantalus. Farewell, good philosophers."

52. So he boarded a ship, and sailed on a gentle, favorable breeze, marveling at the estuary of the Hyphasis and how formidably the river passes through it. As I mentioned, at its end it emerges into rocky, narrow places and precipices, and after breaking through these it pours into the sea by a single channel, and is thought dangerous to those who hug the shore.

53. They claim also to have seen the estuary of the Indus, and a city called Patala that stands there surrounded by the Indus. It was here that Alexander's fleet came under the command of Nearchus, who was very experienced in naval discipline. Orthagoras says about the Red Sea that the Pole Star is not visible from it, sailors cannot tell the south, and the visible stars do not have their natural positions, and Damis agrees, so that we must accept that all this is true and accords with the sky in these parts. They also mention a little island called Biblus where the mussels, oysters, and other such creatures clinging to the rocks are ten times the size of Greek ones. A kind of pearl found there has a white shell, and takes the place of the oyster's heart.

54. They say they also put in at Pagala in the land of the Oreitae. As for the Oreitae, their rocks are of bronze, the sand is of bronze, and rivers bring down bronze dust, and

---

49 [τὸ τοῦ κογχυλίου μέγεθος καὶ] secl. Ol.
50 Πάγαλα Ol.: Πηγάδας

ποταμοὶ ἄγουσι. χρυσῖτιν δὲ ἡγοῦνται τὴν γῆν διὰ τὴν εὐγένειαν τοῦ χαλκοῦ.

55. Φασὶ δὲ καὶ τοῖς Ἰχθυοφάγοις ἐντυχεῖν, οἷς πόλιν εἶναι Στόβηρα, διφθέρας δὲ τούτους ἐνῆφθαι μεγίστων ἰχθύων, καὶ τὰ πρόβατα τὰ ἐκείνῃ ἰχθυώδη εἶναι καὶ φαγεῖν ἄτοπα, τοὺς γὰρ ποιμένας βόσκειν αὐτὰ τοῖς ἰχθύσιν, ὥσπερ ἐν Καρίᾳ τοῖς σύκοις. Καρμανοὶ δὲ Ἰνδοὶ γένος ἥμερον εὔιχθυν οὕτω νέμονται θάλατταν, ὡς μηδ᾽ ἀποθέτους ποιεῖσθαι τοὺς ἰχθῦς, μηδέ, ὥσπερ ὁ Πόντος, ταριχεύειν, ἀλλ᾽ ὀλίγους μὲν αὐτῶν ἀποδίδοσθαι, τοὺς δὲ πολλοὺς ἀσπαίροντας ἀποδιδόναι τῇ θαλάττῃ.

56. Προσπλεῦσαί φασι καὶ Βαλάροις, ἐμπόριον δὲ εἶναι τὰ Βάλαρα μεστὸν μυρρινῶν τε καὶ φοινίκων, καὶ δάφνας ἐν αὐτῷ ἰδεῖν καὶ πηγαῖς διαρρεῖσθαι τὸ χωρίον. κῆποι δὲ ὁπόσοι τρωκτοὶ καὶ ὁπόσοι ἀνθέων κῆποι βρύειν αὐτὸ, καὶ λιμένας μεστοὺς γαλήνης ἐν αὐτῷ εἶναι. προκεῖσθαι δὲ τοῦ χωρίου τούτου νῆσον ἱεράν, ἣν καλεῖσθαι Σέληρα καὶ στάδια μὲν ἑκατὸν εἶναι τῷ πορθμῷ, νηρηίδα δὲ οἰκεῖν ἐν αὐτῇ δεινὴν δαίμονα, πολλοὺς γὰρ τῶν πλεόντων ἁρπάζειν καὶ μηδὲ ταῖς ναυσὶ ξυγχωρεῖν πεῖσμα ἐκ τῆς νήσου βάλλεσθαι.

57. Ἄξιον δὲ μηδὲ τὸν περὶ τῆς ἑτέρας μαργαρίτιδος παρελθεῖν λόγον, ἐπεὶ μηδὲ Ἀπολλωνίῳ μειρακιώδης ἔδοξεν, ἀλλὰ πλάττεται ἥδιστος καὶ τῶν ἐν τῇ θαλαττουργίᾳ θαυμασιώτατος. τὰ γὰρ τετραμμένα τῆς νήσου πρὸς τὸ πελαγός ἐστι μὲν ἄπειρος πυθμὴν

the natives consider their soil to be gold-producing, so pure is the bronze.

55. They say they also came across the Fish Eaters, whose city is Stobera. These wore clothes made from the skins of huge fish; the sheep there taste of fish and have a strange diet, being fed on fish by the herdsmen as Carian sheep are on figs. The Carmani, a friendly Indian tribe, live beside a sea so plentiful in fish that they do not even store the fish, or salt them as is done in the Pontus, but after selling a few they put most of them back into the sea still gasping.

56. They say that they also put in at Balara. Balara is a port full of myrtle and palm trees; they saw laurels there too, and the place has an abundance of springs. It is full of every kind of vegetable and flower garden, and the harbors there are extremely calm. Opposite this place is a sacred island called Selera, separated by a strait of a hundred stades, and inhabited by a mermaid who is a fearful demon. She snatches up many who sail there, and will not let a ship even throw a cable to the island.

57. It would not be right to omit the account of another kind of pearl, since even Apollonius did not think the story puerile, and it is a very charming tale and involves the most amazing kind of fishing. Where the island faces the open sea, the water is of unfathomable depth, and produces a

θαλάττης, φέρει δὲ ὄστρεον ἐν ἐλύτρῳ λευκῷ μεστὸν πιμελῆς, οὐδὲ γὰρ λίθον φύει οὐδένα. γαλήνην δὲ ἐπιφυλάξαντες καὶ τὴν θάλατταν αὐτοὶ λεάναντες, τουτὶ δὲ ἡ τοῦ ἐλαίου ἐπιρροὴ πράττει, καταδύεταί τις ἐπὶ τὴν θήραν τοῦ ὀστρέου τὰ μὲν ἄλλα κατεσκευασμένος, ὥσπερ οἱ τὰς σπογγιὰς κείροντες, ἔστι δὲ αὐτῷ καὶ πλινθὶς σιδηρᾶ καὶ ἀλάβαστρος μύρου.

2 Παριζήσας οὖν ὁ Ἰνδὸς τῷ ὀστρέῳ δέλεαρ αὐτοῦ τὸ μύρον ποιεῖται, τὸ δὲ ἀνοίγνυταί τε καὶ μεθύει ὑπ' αὐτοῦ, κέντρῳ δὲ διελαθὲν ἀποπτύει τὸν ἰχῶρα, ὁ δὲ ἐκδέχεται αὐτὸν τῇ πλινθίδι τύπους ὀρωρυγμένῃ. λιθοῦται δὲ τὸ ἐντεῦθεν καὶ ῥυθμίζεται καθάπερ ἡ φύσει μαργαρίς, κἄστιν ἡ μαργαρὶς αἷμα λευκὸν ἐξ ἐρυθρᾶς τῆς θαλάττης. ἐπιτίθεσθαι δὲ τῇ θήρᾳ ταύτῃ καὶ τοὺς Ἀραβίους φασὶν ἀντιπέρας οἰκοῦντας. τὸ δὲ ἐντεῦθεν θηριώδη μὲν τὴν θάλατταν εἶναι πᾶσαν, ἀγελάζεσθαι δὲ ἐν αὐτῇ τὰ κήτη, τὰς δὲ ναῦς ἔρυμα τούτου κωδωνοφορεῖν κατὰ πρύμναν τε καὶ πρῷραν, τὴν δὲ ἠχὼ ἐκπλήττειν τὰ θηρία, καὶ μὴ ἐᾶν ἐμπελάζειν ταῖς ναυσί.

58. Καταπλεύσαντες δὲ ἐς τὰς ἐκβολὰς τοῦ Εὐφράτου φασὶν ἐς Βαβυλῶνα δι' αὐτοῦ ἀναπλεῦσαι παρὰ τὸν Οὐαρδάνην, καὶ τυχόντες αὐτοῦ οἷου ἐγίγνωσκον, ἐπὶ τὴν Νίνον ἐλθεῖν αὖθις, καὶ τῆς Ἀντιοχείας συνήθως ὑβριζούσης καὶ μηδὲν τῶν Ἑλληνικῶν ἐσπουδακυίας, ἐπὶ θάλαττάν τε καταβῆναι τὴν ἐπὶ Σελευκείᾳ[51] νεώς τε ἐπιτυχόντες προσπλεῦσαι Κύπρῳ

white-shelled oyster that is full of fat but produces no stone at all. The natives wait for a calm, and in fact smooth the waters themselves by pouring olive oil on them. A man dives down to find the oyster, equipped in every respect like a sponge gatherer except that he has an iron plate and a flask of perfume.

2 The Indian then sits beside the oyster and tempts it with the perfume, which then causes it to open and get intoxicated. He then pries it open with a point, so that it squirts out its juice. This he catches in the plate, which is dotted with cavities, and the juice immediately petrifies in regular shapes like natural pearls, so that the pearl is the white blood of the Red Sea. They say that the Arabians who live opposite also go in for this kind of fishing. Thereafter the sea is all full of creatures, and monsters swarm in it. To keep them away, the ships carry bells fore and aft, and the sound frightens the creatures, preventing them from obstructing the ships.

58. After sailing into the estuary of the Euphrates, they say they went up it as far as Babylon to visit Vardanes, whom they found just as they had known him, and then returned to Ninos. Since Antioch was as unruly as ever, and had no interest in Greek culture, they went down to the sea at Seleuceia.[30] There they met a ship and sailed to Cyprus,

[30] Seleuceia Pieria, the port city of Antioch.

---

51 Σελευκείᾳ Kay.: Σελεύκειαν

κατὰ τὴν Πάφον, οὗ τὸ τῆς Ἀφροδίτης ἕδος, ὃ ξυμβολικῶς ἱδρυμένον θαυμάσαι τὸν Ἀπολλώνιον, καὶ πολλὰ τοὺς ἱερέας ἐς τὴν ὁσίαν τοῦ ἱεροῦ διδαξάμενον ἐς Ἰωνίαν πλεῦσαι, θαυμαζόμενον ἱκανῶς καὶ μεγάλων ἀξιούμενον παρὰ τοῖς τὴν σοφίαν τιμῶσιν.

putting in at Paphos where the idol of Aphrodite is.[31] Apollonius admired its symbolic shape, and gave the priests much advice about the rites of the sanctuary. Thence he sailed to Ionia, where he was much admired and highly esteemed by devotees of wisdom.

31 Old Paphos in southwestern Cyprus had an idol of Aphrodite in the form of a conical rock.

Δ΄

1. Ἐπεὶ δὲ εἶδον τὸν ἄνδρα ἐν Ἰωνίᾳ παρελθόντα ἐς τὴν Ἔφεσον, οὐδὲ οἱ βάναυσοι ἔτι πρὸς ταῖς ἑαυτῶν τέχναις ἦσαν, ἀλλ᾿ ἠκολούθουν ὁ μὲν σοφίας, ὁ δὲ εἴδους, ὁ δὲ διαίτης, ὁ δὲ σχήματος, οἱ δὲ πάντων ὁμοῦ θαυμασταὶ ὄντες, λόγοι τε περὶ αὐτοῦ ἐφοίτων, οἱ μὲν ἐκ τοῦ Κολοφῶνι μαντείου κοινωνὸν τῆς ἑαυτοῦ σοφίας καὶ ἀτεχνῶς σοφὸν καὶ τὰ τοιαῦτα τὸν ἄνδρα ᾄδοντες, οἱ δὲ ἐκ Διδύμων, οἱ δὲ ἐκ τοῦ περὶ τὸ Πέργαμον ἱεροῦ, πολλοὺς γὰρ τῶν ὑγιείας δεομένων ὁ θεὸς ἐκέλευσε προσφοιτᾶν τῷ Ἀπολλωνίῳ, τουτὶ γὰρ αὐτός τε βούλεσθαι καὶ δοκεῖν ταῖς Μοίραις.

2 Ἐφοίτων καὶ πρεσβεῖαι πρὸς αὐτὸν ἐκ τῶν πόλεων, ξένον τε αὐτὸν ἡγούμενοι καὶ βίου ξύμβουλον βωμῶν τε ἱδρύσεως καὶ ἀγαλμάτων, ὁ δὲ ἕκαστα τούτων τὰ μὲν ἐπιστέλλων, τὰ δὲ ἀφίξεσθαι φάσκων διωρθοῦτο. πρεσβευσαμένης δὲ καὶ τῆς Σμύρνης καὶ ὅ τι μὲν δέοιτο οὐκ εἰπούσης, ἐκλιπαρούσης δὲ ἀφικέσθαι, ἤρετο τὸν πρεσβευτήν, ὅ τι αὐτοῦ δέοιντο, ὁ δὲ "ἰδεῖν" ἔφη "καὶ ὀφθῆναι." ὁ δὲ Ἀπολλώνιος "ἀφίξομαι" εἶπε "δοίητε δέ, ὦ Μοῦσαι, καὶ ἐρασθῆναι ἀλλήλων."

BOOK IV

1. When they saw the Master as he entered Ephesus in Ionia, not even workmen stayed at their crafts, but followed him in admiration of his wisdom, his appearance, his diet, his dress, or all at once. Pronouncements about him circulated, for example from the oracle at Colophon praising the Master as a sharer in its own knowledge, perfectly wise, and so on, and also from Didyma and the sanctuary outside Pergamum.[1] There the god advised many of those seeking health to visit Apollonius, that being the god's own wish and the will of the Fates.

Embassies also came to him from the cities proclaiming 2
him their guest and their adviser about modes of life and how to set up altars and cult statues. On all these matters he set them right, either by writing letters or by promising a visit. When the Smyrneans sent an embassy and begged him to come without saying what they wanted, he asked the envoy what they wanted from him, and he replied, "To see you and to be seen by you." To which Apollonius replied, "I will come, but you, Muses, grant also that we feel affection for each other."

[1] The oracle of Colophon was at Claros, while Didyma belonged to Miletus: the "sanctuary outside Pergamum" is the Asclepieum.

2. Τὴν μὲν δὴ διάλεξιν τὴν πρώτην ἀπὸ τῆς κρηπῖδος τοῦ νεὼ πρὸς τοὺς Ἐφεσίους διελέχθη, οὐχ ὥσπερ οἱ Σωκρατικοί, ἀλλὰ τῶν μὲν ἄλλων ἀπάγων τε καὶ ἀποσπουδάζων, φιλοσοφίᾳ δὲ μόνῃ ξυμβουλεύων προσέχειν καὶ σπουδῆς ἐμπιπλάναι τὴν Ἔφεσον μᾶλλον ἢ ῥᾳθυμίας τε καὶ ἀγερωχίας, ὁπόσην εὗρεν. ὀρχηστῶν γὰρ ἡττημένοι καὶ πρὸς πυρρίχαις αὐτοὶ ὄντες αὐλῶν μὲν πάντα μεστὰ ἦν, μεστὰ δὲ ἀνδρογύνων, μεστὰ δὲ κτύπων. ὁ δὲ καίτοι μεταθεμένων τῶν Ἐφεσίων πρὸς αὐτὸν οὐκ ἠξίου περιορᾶν ταῦτα, ἀλλ' ἐξῄρει αὐτὰ καὶ διέβαλλε τοῖς πολλοῖς.

3. Τὰς δὲ ἄλλας διαλέξεις περὶ τὰ ἄλση τὰ ἐν τοῖς ξυστοῖς δρόμοις ἐποιεῖτο. διαλεγομένου δέ ποτε περὶ κοινωνίας καὶ διδάσκοντος, ὅτι χρὴ τρέφειν τε ἀλλήλους καὶ ὑπ' ἀλλήλων τρέφεσθαι, στρουθοὶ μὲν ἐκάθηντο ἐπὶ τῶν δένδρων σιωπῶντες, εἷς δὲ αὐτῶν προσπετόμενος ἐβόα, παρακελεύεσθαί τι δοκῶν τοῖς ἄλλοις, οἱ δέ, ὡς ἤκουσαν, αὐτοί τε ἀνέκραγον καὶ ἀρθέντες ἐπέτοντο ὑπὸ τῷ ἑνί. ὁ μὲν δὴ Ἀπολλώνιος εἴχετο τοῦ λόγου γιγνώσκων μέν, ἐφ' ὅ τι οἱ στρουθοὶ πέτοιντο, πρὸς δὲ τοὺς πολλοὺς οὐχ ἑρμηνεύων αὐτό, ἐπεὶ δὲ ἀνέβλεψαν ἐς αὐτοὺς πάντες καὶ ἀνοήτως ἔνιοι τερατῶδες αὐτὸ ἐνόμισαν, παραλλάξας ὁ Ἀπολλώνιος τοῦ λόγου "παῖς" εἶπεν "ὤλισθεν ἀπάγων πυροὺς ἐν σκάφῃ καὶ κακῶς αὐτοὺς ξυλλεξάμενος αὐτὸς μὲν ἀπελήλυθε, πολλοὺς δ' ἐσκεδασμένους ἀπολέλοιπεν ἐν στενωπῷ τῷ δεῖνι, ὁ δὲ στρουθὸς παρατυχὼν οὗτος

2. He gave his first discourse to the Ephesians from the steps of the temple.[2] He did not use the Socratic method, but drawing his listeners' minds and interest away from all other subjects, he advised them to study only philosophy, and to fill Ephesus with seriousness rather than idleness and arrogance, of which he found a great deal. For they were captivated by pantomimes and occupied with the pyrrhic dance, and the whole place teemed with piping, with hermaphrodites, and with castanets.[3] Though the Ephesians went over to his view, he thought it wrong to overlook such practices, and tried to abolish and to discredit them in the eyes of the people.

3. He gave his other discourses in the groves among the walkways. Once as he held forth on fellow feeling, preaching that we must nourish one another and be nourished in return, sparrows were sitting silently on the branches. But another one flew to join them and began to chirp loudly, as if it was passing some message to the others, and on hearing it they piped up and then took off flying after the first one. Apollonius pursued his argument knowing why the sparrows had flown, but not explaining it to his audience. When however everyone looked up at the birds, and some foolishly took this for an omen, Apollonius laid aside his topic and said, "A slave boy has slipped carrying wheat grains in a tray. Now he has gone off without picking them up properly, but leaving a lot of them scattered in such-and-such an alley. Since this sparrow happened to be

[2] The temple of Artemis.

[3] Mime or "pantomime" was a form of raucous ballet, while the pyrrhic, originally a war dance, had also become a kind of ballet.

πρόξενος τοῖς ἄλλοις ἥκει τοῦ ἑρμαίου καὶ ποιεῖται αὐτοὺς ξυσσίτους."

2 Οἱ μὲν δὴ πλεῖστοι τῶν ἀκροωμένων δρόμῳ ἐπὶ τοῦτο[1] ᾤχοντο, ὁ δὲ Ἀπολλώνιος πρὸς τοὺς παρόντας διῄει τὸν λόγον, ὃν περὶ τῆς κοινωνίας προὔθετο, καὶ ἐπειδὴ ἀφίκοντο βοῶντές τε καὶ μεστοὶ θαύματος "οἱ μὲν στρουθοὶ" εἶπεν "ὁρᾶτε, ὡς ἐπιμελοῦνταί τε ἀλλήλων καὶ κοινωνίᾳ χαίρουσιν, ἡμεῖς δὲ οὐκ ἀξιοῦμεν, ἀλλὰ κἂν κοινωνοῦντα ἑτέροις ἴδωμεν, ἐκεῖνο μὲν ἀσωτίαν καὶ τρυφὴν καὶ τὰ τοιαῦτα ἡγούμεθα, τοὺς δὲ ὑπ' αὐτοῦ τρεφομένους παρασίτους τε καὶ κόλακας φαμέν. καὶ τί λοιπὸν ἀλλ' ἢ ξυγκλείσαντας αὐτούς, ὥσπερ τοὺς σιτευομένους τῶν ὀρνίθων, ἐν σκότῳ γαστρίζεσθαι, μέχρις ἂν διαρραγῶμεν παχυνόμενοι;"

4. Λοιμοῦ δὲ ὑφέρποντος τὴν Ἔφεσον καὶ οὔπω ἀνοιδούσης τῆς νόσου ξυνῆκε μὲν ὁ Ἀπολλώνιος τῆς προσβολῆς, ξυνεὶς δὲ προὔλεγε. πολλαχοῦ τε τῶν διαλέξεων "ὦ γῆ, μένε ὁμοία," καὶ τοιαῦτα ἐπεφθέγγετο ξὺν ἀπειλῇ, "τούσδε σῶζε" καὶ "οὐ παρελεύσῃ ἐνταῦθα." οἱ δ' οὐ προσεῖχον καὶ τερατολογίαν τὰ τοιαῦτα ᾤοντο τοσῷδε μᾶλλον, ὅσῳ καὶ ἐς πάντα τὰ ἱερὰ φοιτῶν ἀποτρέπειν αὐτὸ ἐδόκει καὶ ἀπεύχεσθαι. ἐπεὶ δὲ ἀνοήτως εἶχον τοῦ πάθους, ἐκείνοις μὲν οὐδὲν ᾤετο δεῖν ἐπαρκεῖν ἔτι, τὴν δὲ ἄλλην Ἰωνίαν περιῄει διορθούμενος τὰ παρ' ἑκάστοις καὶ διαλεγόμενος ἀεί τι σωτήριον τοῖς παροῦσιν.

5. Ἀφικνουμένῳ δὲ αὐτῷ ἐς τὴν Σμύρναν προαπήντων[2] μὲν οἱ Ἴωνες, καὶ γὰρ ἔτυχον Πανιώνια

nearby, it has now come to invite the others to this bonanza, and makes them its dinner guests."

Most of Apollonius's listeners went running off to the place, while he continued to address his remaining audience on the subject of sharing which he had begun. When the others returned shouting and full of amazement, he said, "You see, the sparrows care for one another and love to share, but we think it to be beneath us. Even if we see someone sharing with others, we consider that to be wastefulness, luxury, and so on, while we call the objects of his hospitality parasites and flatterers. The only thing left is to cage ourselves like force-fed birds, and gorge in darkness until we are fattened to bursting." 2

4. A plague was approaching Ephesus, but before the disease broke out, Apollonius was aware of its coming, and foretold it accordingly. Often in his discourses he would say, "Earth, stay as you are" and, in threatening tones, such things as "Save these people" and "You are not to come here." But the inhabitants paid no notice, and were all the more inclined to think such things exaggeration because Apollonius visited all the sanctuaries and so appeared to be averting and exorcising the plague. Since they were indifferent to their fate, he decided that he should not help them any longer, and traveled around the rest of Ionia, improving the customs in each place and always discoursing to his audiences on subjects beneficial to them.

5. As he approached Smyrna, the Ionians came out to meet him, since they were making the Panionian sacrifice

---

1 *τοῦτο* Rsk.: *τούτῳ*

2 *προαπήντων* Rsk.: *προσαπήντων*

θύοντες, ἀναγνοὺς δὲ καὶ ψήφισμα Ἰωνικόν, ἐν ᾧ ἐδέοντο αὐτοῦ κοινωνῆσαί σφισι τοῦ ξυλλόγου, καὶ ὀνόματι προστυχὼν ἥκιστα Ἰωνικῷ, Λούκουλλος γάρ τις ἐπεγέγραπτο τῇ γνώμῃ, πέμπει ἐπιστολὴν ἐς τὸ κοινὸν αὐτῶν, ἐπίπληξιν ποιούμενος περὶ τοῦ βαρβαρισμοῦ τούτου· καὶ γὰρ δὴ καὶ Φαβρίκιον καὶ τοιούτους ἑτέρους ἐν τοῖς ἐψηφισμένοις εὗρεν. ὡς μὲν οὖν ἐρρωμένως ἐπέπληξε, δηλοῖ ἡ περὶ τούτου ἐπιστολή.

6. Παρελθὼν δὲ ἐπ' ἄλλης ἡμέρας ἐς τοὺς Ἴωνας, "τίς" ἔφη "ὁ κρατὴρ οὗτος;" οἱ δὲ ἔφασαν "Πανιώνιος." ἀρυσάμενος οὖν καὶ σπείσας, "ὦ θεοί," εἶπεν "Ἰώνων ἡγεμόνες, δοίητε τῇ καλῇ ἀποικίᾳ ταύτῃ θαλάττῃ ἀσφαλεῖ χρῆσθαι καὶ μηδὲν τῇ γῇ κακὸν ἐξ αὐτῆς προσκωμάσαι, μηδ' Αἰγαίωνα σεισίχθονα τινάξαι ποτὲ τὰς πόλεις." τοιαῦτα ἐπεθείαζε προορῶν, οἶμαι, τὰ χρόνοις ὕστερον περί τε Σμύρναν, περί τε Μίλητον, περί τε Χίον καὶ Σάμον, καὶ πολλὰς τῶν Ἰάδων ξυμβάντα.

7. Σπουδῇ δὲ ὁρῶν τοὺς Σμυρναίους ἁπάντων ἁπτομένους λόγων, ἐπερρώννυε καὶ σπουδαιοτέρους ἐποίει, φρονεῖν τε ἐκέλευεν ἐφ' ἑαυτοῖς μᾶλλον ἢ τῷ τῆς πόλεως εἴδει, καὶ γάρ, εἰ καὶ καλλίστη πόλεων, ὁπόσαι ὑπὸ ἡλίῳ εἰσί, καὶ τὸ πέλαγος οἰκειοῦται, ζεφύρου τε πηγὰς ἔχει, ἀλλ' ἀνδράσιν ἐστεφανῶσθαι αὐτὴν ἥδιον ἢ στοαῖς τε καὶ γραφαῖς καὶ χρυσῷ πλείονι τοῦ δέοντος.[3] τὰ μὲν γὰρ οἰκοδομήματα ἐπὶ ταὐτοῦ μένειν

[3] δέοντος Rsk.: ὄντος

at the time.[4] He also read a decree of the Ionians in which they asked him to join their conference. In this Apollonius came across a name that was not Ionic at all, since a certain "Lucullus" headed the motion. So he sent a letter to their assembly rebuking them for their solecism, having also found a "Fabricius" and other such people named in the resolution. His letter on the subject shows how severely he rebuked them.[5]

6. On another day he came before the Ionians and said, "What is this bowl?" "The Panionian bowl," they replied. He then drew from it, poured a libation, and said, "You gods that guide Ionia, let this beautiful colony enjoy safety from the sea. Let no disaster burst from the sea on to the land. Do not let Aegaeon[6] the Earth Shaker ever shatter the cities." This was what he pronounced, foreseeing, I suppose, what later happened to Smyrna, Miletus, Chios, Samos, and many of the Ionian cities.[7]

7. Seeing how eagerly the Smyrneans pursued every kind of knowledge, he encouraged them and added to their eagerness. They must put more pride in themselves, he told them, than in the appearance of their city; even if it was the most beautiful beneath the sun, with the sea at its command and always supplied with a west wind, still it had a pleasanter crown in its true men than in its colonnades, pictures, and excess of gold. Buildings stayed in one place,

[4] Sacrifice held by the league of Ionian cities of Asia.

[5] This letter, or one fabricated to fit this passage, survives as Letter no. 71.

[6] Poseidon.

[7] Possibly referring to an earthquake in the reign of Claudius.

οὐδαμοῦ ὁρώμενα πλὴν ἐκείνου τοῦ μέρους τῆς γῆς, ἐν ᾧ ἐστιν, ἄνδρας δὲ ἀγαθοὺς πανταχοῦ μὲν ὁρᾶσθαι, πανταχοῦ δὲ φθέγγεσθαι, τὴν δὲ πόλιν, ἧς γεγόνασιν, ἀποφαίνειν τοσαύτην, ὅσοιπερ αὐτοὶ γῆν ἐπελθεῖν δύνανται.

2 Ἔλεγε δὲ τὰς μὲν πόλεις τὰς οὕτω καλὰς ἐοικέναι τῷ τοῦ Διὸς ἀγάλματι, ὃς ἐν Ὀλυμπίᾳ τῷ Φειδίᾳ ἐκπεποίηται, καθῆσθαι γὰρ αὐτὸ οὗ τῷ[4] δημιουργῷ ἔδοξε, τοὺς δὲ ἄνδρας ἐπὶ πάντα ἥκοντας μηδὲν ἀπεοικέναι τοῦ Ὁμηρείου Διός, ὃς ἐν πολλαῖς ἰδέαις Ὁμήρῳ πεποίηται θαυμασιώτερον ξυγκείμενος τοῦ ἐλεφαντίνου· τὸν μὲν γὰρ ἐν γῇ φαίνεσθαι, τὸν δὲ ἐς πάντα ἐν τῷ οὐρανῷ ὑπονοεῖσθαι.

8. Καὶ μὴν καὶ περὶ τοῦ πῶς ἂν πόλεις ἀσφαλῶς οἰκοῖντο ξυνεφιλοσόφει τοῖς Σμυρναίοις, διαφερομένους ὁρῶν ἀλλήλοις καὶ μὴ ξυγκειμένους τὰς γνώμας. ἔλεγε γὰρ δὴ τὴν ὀρθῶς οἰκησομένην πόλιν ὁμονοίας στασιαζούσης δεῖσθαι, τούτου δὲ ἀπιθάνως τε καὶ οὐκ ἐς τὸ ἀκόλουθον εἰρῆσθαι δόξαντος, ξυνεὶς ὁ Ἀπολλώνιος ὅτι μὴ ἕπονται οἱ πολλοὶ τῷ λόγῳ, "λευκὸν μὲν" ἔφη "καὶ μέλαν οὐκ ἄν ποτε ταὐτὸν γένοιτο, οὐδ᾽ ἂν τῷ γλυκεῖ τὸ πικρὸν ὑγιῶς ξυγκραθείη, ὁμόνοια δὲ στασιάσει σωτηρίας ἕνεκα τῶν πόλεων.

2 "Ὃ δὲ λέγω, τοιοῦτον ἡγώμεθα. στάσις ἡ μὲν ἐπὶ ξίφη καὶ τὸ καταλιθοῦν ἀλλήλους ἄγουσα ἀπέστω πόλεως, ᾗ παιδοτροφίας τε δεῖ καὶ νόμων καὶ ἀνδρῶν, ἐφ᾽ οἷς λόγοι καὶ ἔργα. φιλοτιμία δὲ ἡ πρὸς ἀλλήλους ὑπὲρ τοῦ κοινοῦ καὶ πῶς ἂν ὁ μὲν γνώμης εἴποι

never seen anywhere except in the part of the world where they were, while good men were seen everywhere and spoken of everywhere, and they made the city of their origin larger in proportion to the number of them that could travel the world.

Cities as beautiful as this one, he said, were like the 2
statue of Zeus made by Phidias at Olympia. It was seated where the artist wished, whereas good men went everywhere, and were no different from Homer's Zeus, who in his many forms is a more marvelous creation of Homer than the ivory Zeus, for this Zeus was visible on earth, while the other could be sensed in every corner of the universe.

8. Moreover, he gave the Smyrneans a disquisition on the safe governance of cities, since he saw that they were quarreling with one another and had no agreed policy. He told them that to be governed rightly a city needed both unity and disunity. This remark seemed implausible and illogical, so that Apollonius, aware that most of them could not follow his meaning, said, "Black and white can never be the same, and sweet and bitter can never mix properly, but unity in disunity is the saving of cities.

"Let us understand my meaning this way. Disunity that 2
causes people to use the sword, or to stone each other, a city must avoid, since what it needs is child welfare, law, and true men capable of speech and action. But there is a kind of mutual competition for the common good, in

[4] οὗ τῷ Jackson: οὕτως τῷ

βελτίω γνώμην, ὁ δ' ἑτέρου ἄμεινον ἀρχῆς προσταίη, ὁ δὲ πρεσβεύσειεν, ὁ δ' ἐξοικοδομήσαιτο λαμπρότερον τῆς ἑτέρου ἐπιστατείας, ἔρις, οἶμαι, αὕτη ἀγαθὴ καὶ στάσις πρὸς ἀλλήλους ὑπὲρ τοῦ κοινοῦ.

3 "Τὸ δ' ἄλλον ἄλλο ἐπιτηδεύοντας ἐς τὸ τῆς πόλεως ὄφελος ξυμφέρειν Λακεδαιμονίοις μὲν εὔηθες ἐδόκει πάλαι, τὰ γὰρ πολεμικὰ ἐξεπονοῦντο καὶ ἐς τοῦτο ἔρρωντο πάντες καὶ τούτου μόνου ἥπτοντο, ἐμοὶ δ' ἄριστον δοκεῖ τὸ πράττειν ἕκαστον, ὅ τι οἶδε καὶ ὅ τι δύναται. εἰ γὰρ ὁ μὲν ἀπὸ δημαγωγίας θαυμασθήσεται, ὁ δὲ ἀπὸ σοφίας, ὁ δὲ ἀπὸ τοῦ ἐς τὸ κοινὸν πλουτεῖν, ὁ δὲ ἀπὸ τοῦ χρηστὸς εἶναι, ὁ δὲ ἀπὸ τοῦ ἐμβριθὴς καὶ μὴ ξυγγνώμων τοῖς ἁμαρτάνουσιν, ὁ δὲ ἀπὸ τοῦ μὴ διαβεβλῆσθαι τὰς χεῖρας, εὖ κείσεται ἡ πόλις, μᾶλλον δὲ ἑστήξει."

9. Καὶ ἅμα διϊὼν ταῦτα ναῦν εἶδε τῶν τριαρμένων ἐκπλέουσαν καὶ τοὺς ναύτας ἄλλον ἄλλως ἐς τὸ ἀνάγεσθαι αὐτὴν πράττοντας. ἐπιστρέφων οὖν τοὺς παρόντας "ὁρᾶτε" εἶπε "τὸν τῆς νεὼς δῆμον, ὡς οἱ μὲν τὰς ἐφολκίδας ἐμβεβήκασιν ἐρετικοὶ ὄντες, οἱ δ' ἀγκύρας ἀνιμῶσί τε καὶ ἀναρτῶσιν, οἱ δὲ ὑπέχουσι τὰ ἱστία τῷ ἀνέμῳ, οἱ δὲ ἐκ πρύμνης τε καὶ πρῴρας προορῶσιν; εἰ δὲ ἓν τούτων εἷς ἐλλείψει τι τῶν ἑαυτοῦ ἔργων ἢ ἀμαθῶς τῆς ναυτικῆς ἅψεται, πονήρως πλευσοῦνται καὶ ὁ χειμὼν αὐτοὶ δόξουσιν. εἰ δὲ φιλοτιμήσονται πρὸς ἑαυτοὺς καὶ στασιάσουσι μὴ κακίων ἕτερος ἑτέρου δόξαι, καλοὶ μὲν ὅρμοι τῇ νηὶ ταύτῃ, μεστὰ δὲ εὐδίας τε καὶ εὐπλοίας πάντα, Ποσειδῶν δὲ

which one man seeks to give better advice than another's, or to hold office better than another, or go on an embassy, or erect finer buildings than when another man was commissioner. This I hold to be beneficial strife, disunity with others for the general good.

"The idea that every man should have different pur- 3
suits and contribute them to the city's welfare long ago seemed foolish to the Spartans. They practiced warfare, and all of them trained for that and made it their only pursuit. But in my opinion it is best that everybody does what he knows and what he can. If one man is admired for persuasiveness, another for wisdom, another for spending his wealth on the general good, another for his virtue, another for his steadiness and severity with wrongdoers, another for keeping his hands free from bribes, the city will be firmly grounded, or rather exalted."

9. Just as he was making this speech, he saw a three-masted ship sailing out of harbor with each of the sailors doing different things to prepare the voyage. He called his audience's attention to it and said, "Do you see the crew of that ship? Some have manned the dinghies as expert rowers, others are hauling up and stowing anchors, some are spreading the sails to the wind, others looking out from the prow and the stern. If one of them omits one of these tasks or proves an ignorant sailor, they will have a bad voyage and prove to be their own storm. But if they compete with one another, and turn their disunity to proving themselves as good as the next man, this ship will have safe harbor, all will be calm sea and prosperous voyage, and their pru-

Ἀσφάλειος ἡ περὶ αὐτοῖς εὐβουλία δόξει."

10. Τοιούτοις μὲν δὴ λόγοις ξυνεῖχε τὴν Σμύρναν, ἐπεὶ δὲ ἡ νόσος τοῖς Ἐφεσίοις ἐνέπεσε καὶ οὐδὲν ἦν πρὸς αὐτὴν αὔταρκες, ἐπρεσβεύοντο παρὰ τὸν Ἀπολλώνιον, ἰατρὸν ποιούμενοι αὐτὸν τοῦ πάθους. ὁ δὲ οὐκ ᾤετο δεῖν ἀναβάλλεσθαι τὴν ὁδόν, ἀλλ' εἰπὼν "ἴωμεν" ἦν ἐν Ἐφέσῳ, τοῦ Πυθαγόρου, οἶμαι, ἐκεῖνο πράττων τὸ ἐν Θουρίοις ὁμοῦ καὶ Μεταποντίοις εἶναι. ξυναγαγὼν οὖν τοὺς Ἐφεσίους "θαρσεῖτε," ἔφη "τήμερον γὰρ παύσω τὴν νόσον," καὶ εἰπὼν ἦγεν ἡλικίαν πᾶσαν ἐπὶ τὸ θέατρον, οὗ τὸ τοῦ Ἀποτροπαίου ἵδρυται. πτωχεύειν δέ τις ἐνταῦθα ἐδόκει γέρων ἐπιμύων τοὺς ὀφθαλμοὺς τέχνῃ, καὶ πήραν ἔφερε καὶ ἄρτου ἐν αὐτῇ τρύφος, ῥάκεσί τε ἠμφίεστο καὶ αὐχμηρῶς εἶχε τοῦ προσώπου.

2 Περιστήσας οὖν τοὺς Ἐφεσίους αὐτῷ "βάλλετε τὸν θεοῖς ἐχθρὸν" εἶπε "ξυλλεξάμενοι τῶν λίθων ὡς πλείστους."[5] θαυμαζόντων δὲ τῶν Ἐφεσίων, ὅ τι λέγοι, καὶ δεινὸν ἡγουμένων, εἰ ξένον ἀποκτενοῦσιν ἀθλίως οὕτω πράττοντα, καὶ γὰρ ἱκέτευε καὶ πολλὰ ἐπὶ ἐλέῳ ἔλεγεν, ἐνέκειτο παρακελευόμενος τοῖς Ἐφεσίοις ἐρείδειν τε καὶ μὴ ἀνιέναι. ὡς δὲ ἀκροβολισμῷ τινες ἐπ' αὐτῷ ἐχρήσαντο, καὶ καταμύειν δοκῶν ἀνέβλεψεν ἀθρόον, πυρός τε μεστοὺς τοὺς ὀφθαλμοὺς ἔδειξε, ξυνῆκαν οἱ Ἐφέσιοι τοῦ δαίμονος καὶ κατελίθωσαν οὕτως αὐτόν, ὡς κολωνὸν λίθων περὶ αὐτὸν χώσασθαι.

3 Διαλιπὼν δὲ ὀλίγον ἐκέλευσεν ἀφελεῖν τοὺς λίθους, καὶ τὸ θηρίον, ὃ ἀπεκτόνασι, γνῶναι. γυμνωθέντος

dence will prove to be Poseidon the Bringer of Safety."

10. With speeches like this he unified Smyrna. In Ephesus, however, the plague had arrived and nothing proved effective against it, and so they sent an embassy to Apollonius, hoping to make him the physician of their misfortunes. Thinking he should not delay the journey, and merely saying, "Let us go," he was in Ephesus, imitating, I suppose, Pythagoras's famous act of being in Thurii and in Metapontum simultaneously. After calling the Ephesians together, he said, "Take heart, since I will end the plague today." So saying, he led them all, young and old, towards the theater where the statue of the Averter stands.[8] There it seemed that an old man was begging, craftily blinking his eyes. He carried a bag and a lump of bread in it, and had ragged clothing and a grizzled face.

Apollonius made the Ephesians encircle the man, and 2
said, "Stone this accursed wretch, but first collect as many stones as possible." The Ephesians were puzzled by his meaning and shocked at the thought of killing someone who was a visitor and so destitute, and who was pleading with them, and saying such pitiable things. But Apollonius was relentless, urging the Ephesians to crush him without pity. Some of them had begun to lob stones at him when, after seeming to blink, he suddenly glared and showed his eyes full of fire. The Ephesians realized it was a demon and stoned it so thoroughly as to raise a pile of stones on it.

After a while Apollonius told them to remove the stones 3
and to see what animal they had killed. When the supposed

[8] "Averter" (*apotropaios*) was a title of Heracles.

---

[5] πλείστους Rsk.: πλείους

οὖν τοῦ βεβλῆσθαι δοκοῦντος ὁ μὲν ἠφάνιστο, κύων δὲ τὸ μὲν εἶδος ὅμοιος τῷ[6] ἐκ Μολοττῶν, μέγεθος δὲ κατὰ τὸν μέγιστον λέοντα ξυντετριμμένος ὤφθη ὑπὸ τῶν λίθων καὶ παραπτύων ἀφρόν, ὥσπερ οἱ λυττῶντες. τὸ μὲν δὴ τοῦ Ἀποτροπαίου ἕδος, ἔστι δὲ Ἡρακλῆς, ἵδρυται περὶ τὸ χωρίον, ἐν ᾧ τὸ φάσμα ἐβλήθη.

11. Καθήρας δὲ τοὺς Ἐφεσίους τῆς νόσου καὶ τῶν κατὰ τὴν Ἰωνίαν ἱκανῶς ἔχων, ἐς τὴν Ἑλλάδα ὥρμητο. βαδίσας οὖν ἐς τὸ Πέργαμον, καὶ ἡσθεὶς τῷ τοῦ Ἀσκληπιοῦ ἱερῷ, τοῖς τε ἱκετεύουσι τὸν θεὸν ὑποθέμενος, ὁπόσα δρῶντες εὐξυμβόλων ὀνειράτων τεύξονται, πολλοὺς δὲ καὶ ἰασάμενος, ἦλθεν ἐς τὴν Ἰλιάδα, καὶ πάσης τῆς περὶ αὐτὴν[7] ἀρχαιολογίας ἐμφορηθεὶς ἐφοίτησεν ἐπὶ τοὺς τῶν Ἀχαιῶν τάφους, καὶ πολλὰ μὲν εἰπὼν ἐπ' αὐτοῖς, πολλὰ δὲ τῶν ἀναίμων τε καὶ καθαρῶν καθαγίσας, τοὺς μὲν ἑταίρους ἐκέλευσεν ἐπὶ τὴν ναῦν χωρεῖν, αὐτὸς δὲ ἐπὶ τοῦ κολωνοῦ τοῦ Ἀχιλλέως ἐννυχεύσειν ἔφη.

2 Δεδιττομένων οὖν τῶν ἑταίρων αὐτόν, καὶ γὰρ δὴ καὶ οἱ Διοσκορίδαι καὶ οἱ Φαίδιμοι καὶ ἡ τοιάδε ὁμιλία πᾶσα ξυνῆσαν ἤδη τῷ Ἀπολλωνίῳ, τόν τε Ἀχιλλέα φοβερὸν ἔτι φασκόντων φαίνεσθαι, τουτὶ γὰρ καὶ τοὺς ἐν τῷ Ἰλίῳ περὶ αὐτοῦ πεπεῖσθαι, "καὶ μὴν ἐγὼ" ἔφη "τὸν Ἀχιλλέα σφόδρα οἶδα ταῖς ξυνουσίαις χαίροντα, τόν τε γὰρ Νέστορα τὸν ἐκ τῆς Πύλου μάλα ἠσπάζετο, ἐπειδὴ ἀεί τι αὐτῷ διῄει χρηστόν, τόν τε Φοίνικα 'τροφέα' καὶ 'ὀπαδὸν' καὶ τὰ

target of their stones was uncovered, he had vanished, and instead there appeared a dog, like some Molossian hound in shape but the size of the largest lion, crushed by the stones and spewing foam as maniacs do. The statue of the Averter, who is Heracles, stands near the spot where the phantom was stoned.

11. After cleansing the Ephesians of the plague, and having had his fill of the sights in Ionia, he set out for Greece. Arriving in Pergamum, he was pleased by the sanctuary of Asclepius, where he made suggestions to the god's supplicants about all they should do in order to get auspicious dreams, and he cured many of them. Thence he arrived in the territory of Ilium,[9] where he imbibed all the lore about it. When visiting the tombs of the Achaeans, he made many funeral speeches, and many heroic sacrifices of a bloodless and pure kind. Then he told his companions to go to the ship, while he himself would spend the night on Achilles's mound.[10]

His companions tried to scare him (for by now men like 2
Dioscorides, Phaedimus, and all that company were following Apollonius), saying that Achilles still had a terrifying appearance, and that this was the very firm belief of the Ilians about him. "And yet I," said Apollonius, "know that Achilles is very fond of company. He greeted Nestor from Pylos warmly, as someone who always had something improving to say to him. He honored Phoenix by calling him

[9] The city that had succeeded the Homeric Troy.

[10] There are several mounds on the plain of Troy, but it is uncertain which one was believed to be Achilles's burial place.

---

[6] τῳ West.: τῷ [7] αὐτὴν Rsk.: αὐτῶν

τοιαῦτα τιμῶν ὠνόμαζεν,[8] ἐπειδὴ διῆγεν αὐτὸν ὁ Φοῖνιξ λόγοις. καὶ τὸν Πρίαμον δὲ καίτοι πολεμιώτατον αὐτῷ ὄντα πρᾳότατα εἶδεν, ἐπειδὴ διαλεγομένου ἤκουσε, καὶ Ὀδυσσεῖ δὲ ἐν διχοστασίᾳ ξυγγενόμενος οὕτω μέτριος ὤφθη, ὡς καλὸς τῷ Ὀδυσσεῖ μᾶλλον ἢ φοβερὸς δόξαι.

3 "Τὴν μὲν δὴ ἀσπίδα καὶ τὴν κόρυν τὴν δεινόν, ὥς φασι, νεύουσαν, ἐπὶ τοὺς Τρῶας οἶμαι αὐτῷ εἶναι μεμνημένῳ, ἃ ὑπ᾽ αὐτῶν ἔπαθεν ἀπιστησάντων πρὸς αὐτὸν ὑπὲρ τοῦ γάμου, ἐγὼ δὲ οὔτε μετέχω τι τοῦ Ἰλίου, διαλέξομαί τε αὐτῷ χαριέστερον ἢ οἱ τότε ἑταῖροι. κἂν ἀποκτείνῃ με, ὥς φατε, μετὰ Μέμνονος δήπου καὶ Κύκνου κείσομαι, καὶ ἴσως με ἐν καπέτῳ κοίλῃ, καθάπερ τὸν Ἕκτορα, ἡ Τροία θάψει." τοιαῦτα πρὸς τοὺς ἑταίρους ἀναμὶξ παίξας τε καὶ σπουδάσας προσέβαινε τῷ κολωνῷ μόνος, οἱ δὲ ἐβάδιζον ἐπὶ τὴν ναῦν ἑσπέρας ἤδη.

12. Ὁ δὲ Ἀπολλώνιος περὶ ὄρθρον ἥκων "ποῦ" ἔφη "Ἀντισθένης ὁ Πάριος;" ἑβδόμην δὲ οὗτος ἡμέραν ἐτύγχανεν ἤδη προσπεφοιτηκὼς αὐτῷ ἐν Ἰλίῳ. ὑπακούσαντος δὲ τοῦ Ἀντισθένους "προσήκεις τι," ἔφη "ὦ νεανία, τῇ Τροίᾳ"; "σφόδρα," εἶπεν "εἰμὶ γὰρ δὴ ἄνωθεν Τρῴς." "ἦ καὶ Πριαμίδης;" "νὴ Δί᾽," εἶπεν "ἐκ τούτου γὰρ δὴ ἀγαθός τε οἶμαι κἀξ ἀγαθῶν εἶναι." "εἰκότως οὖν" ἔφη "ὁ Ἀχιλλεὺς ἀπαγορεύει μοι μὴ

[8] ὠνόμαζεν Jackson: ἐνόμιζεν

'foster father,' 'companion,' and so on, because he entertained him with his tales. And yet when he heard the conversation of Priam, his greatest enemy, he looked very kindly on him too, and though he had been at loggerheads with Odysseus, he behaved so modestly as to seem handsome to Odysseus rather than terrifying.

As for his shield and his crest 'fearfully nodding,'[11] as 3
they call it, these I think are aimed at the Trojans in memory of his sufferings when they cheated him in the matter of the marriage.[12] I myself have no connection with Ilium, and I will talk to him more pleasantly than his companions once did. Even if he kills me, as you say he will, well, I will lie next to Memnon and Cycnus,[13] and perhaps Troy will bury me 'in hollow grave'[14] like Hector." All this he said to his companions in a mixture of jest and earnest, and then approached the mound alone, while they went to the ship, since it was now evening.

12. Joining them at dawn, Apollonius said, "Where is Antisthenes of Paros?" (This man had now been accompanying him for a week in Ilium.) When Antisthenes answered the summons, Apollonius said, "Do you have some connection with Ilium, young man?" "Certainly," he replied, "since I am a Trojan by descent." "Are you also of the line of Priam?" "Yes indeed," the other replied, "and so I believe myself a noble man of noble stock." "Achilles is right, then," said Apollonius, "to forbid me from associ-

[11] Homer, *Iliad* 3.337 and elsewhere. [12] According to a late tradition, Achilles had fallen in love with Polyxena, the daughter of Priam, and was treacherously killed during the marriage negotiations. [13] Two heroes killed by Achilles in the post-Homeric tradition. [14] Homer, *Iliad* 24.797.

ξυνεῖναί σοι, κελεύσαντος γὰρ αὐτοῦ πρεσβεῦσαί με πρὸς τοὺς Θετταλοὺς περὶ ὧν αἰτιᾶται σφᾶς, ὡς ἠρόμην, τί ἂν πρὸς τούτῳ ἕτερον πρὸς χάριν αὐτῷ πράττοιμι, τὸ μειράκιον ἔφη τὸ ἐκ Πάρου μὴ ποιούμενος ξυνέμπορον τῆς ἑαυτοῦ σοφίας, Πριαμίδης τε γὰρ ἱκανῶς ἐστι καὶ τὸν Ἕκτορα ὑμνῶν οὐ παύεται." ὁ μὲν δὴ Ἀντισθένης ἄκων ἀπῆλθεν,

13. Ἐπεὶ δὲ ἡμέρα ἐγένετο, καὶ τὸ πνεῦμα ἐκ τῆς γῆς ἐπεδίδου, περί τε ἀναγωγὴν ἡ ναῦς εἶχεν, ἐπέρρεον αὐτῇ σμικρᾷ οὔσῃ πλείους ἕτεροι βουλόμενοι τῷ Ἀπολλωνίῳ ξυμπλεῖν, καὶ γὰρ μετόπωρον ἤδη ἐτύγχανε καὶ ἡ θάλαττα ἧττον βεβαία. πάντες οὖν, καὶ χειμῶνος καὶ πυρὸς καὶ τῶν χαλεπωτάτων κρείττω τὸν ἄνδρα ἡγούμενοι, ξυνεμβαίνειν ἤθελον καὶ ἐδέοντο προσδοῦναί σφισι τῆς κοινωνίας τοῦ πλοῦ. ἐπεὶ δὲ τὸ πλήρωμα πολλαπλάσιον ἦν τῆς νεώς, ναῦν μείζω ἑτέραν ἐπισκεψάμενος, πολλαὶ δὲ περὶ τὸ Αἰάντειον ἦσαν, "ἐνταῦθα" ἔφη "ἐμβαίνωμεν, καλὸν γὰρ τὸ μετὰ πλειόνων σώζεσθαι."

2 Περιβαλὼν οὖν τὸ Τρωϊκὸν ἀκρωτήριον, ἐκέλευσε τὸν κυβερνήτην κατασχεῖν ἐς τὴν Αἰολέων, ἣ ἀντιπέρας Λέσβου κεῖται, πρὸς Μήθυμνάν τε μᾶλλον τετραμμένον ποιεῖσθαι τὸν ὅρμον. "ἐνταῦθα γάρ που τὸν Παλαμήδην φησὶν ὁ Ἀχιλλεὺς κεῖσθαι, οὗ καὶ ἄγαλμα αὐτοῦ εἶναι πηχυαῖον, ἐν πρεσβυτέρῳ, ἢ ὡς Παλαμήδης, τῷ εἴδει." καὶ ἅμα ἐξιὼν τῆς νεὼς "ἐπιμεληθῶμεν," εἶπεν "ὦ ἄνδρες Ἕλληνες, ἀγαθοῦ ἀνδρός, δι' ὃν σοφία πᾶσα, καὶ γὰρ ἂν καὶ τῶν γε

ating with you. He told me to act as his envoy to the Thessalians on a complaint he has against them, but when I asked what else I could do as a favor to him, he said, 'Do not make the young man from Paros a partner in your wisdom, for he is far too much a descendant of Priam, and never stops praising Hector.'" So Antisthenes left reluctantly.

13. When it was day, and the off shore wind was rising and the ship was preparing to launch, a good number of other people poured into it, small as it was, wanting to sail with Apollonius, since it was now already autumn and the sea was none too predictable. Thinking the Master superior to storm, fire, and the greatest obstacles, everybody wanted to go on board with him, and begged him to allow them to share the voyage. Since the passengers were far too numerous for the ship, Apollonius picked out a bigger one from the many that were moored by Aianteion,[15] saying, "Let us go on board this one, since it is honorable to arrive safely with a larger number."

After passing the headland of Troy, he told the pilot 2
to make straight for the Aeolic district that lies opposite Lesbos, and then to anchor as best he could opposite Methymna.[16] "For according to Achilles," he said, "that is where Palamedes is buried, and where there is a statue of him, a cubit tall, though it looks too old to be Palamedes." As soon as he had disembarked he said, "Nobles of Greece, let us show consideration for a noble man, the source of all

15 A harbor on the north coast of the Troad, near the reputed burial mound of Greater Ajax.

16 This part of Asia, and also Lesbos, were settled by immigrants from Aeolis in Greece speaking the Aeolic dialect.

Ἀχαιῶν βελτίους γενοίμεθα, τιμῶντες δι᾽ ἀρετήν, ὃν ἐκεῖνοι δίκῃ οὐδεμιᾷ ἀπέκτειναν."

3 Οἱ μὲν δὴ ἐξεπήδων τῆς νεώς, ὁ δὲ ἐνέτυχε τῷ τάφῳ καὶ τὸ ἄγαλμα κατορωρυγμένον πρὸς αὐτῷ εὗρεν. ἐπεγέγραπτο[9] δὲ τῇ βάσει τοῦ ἀγάλματος "θείῳ Παλαμήδει." καθιδρύσας οὖν αὐτό, ὡς κἀγὼ εἶδον, καὶ ἱερὸν περὶ αὐτὸ βαλόμενος, ὅσον οἱ τὴν Ἐνοδίαν τιμῶντες, ἔστι γὰρ ὡς δέκα ξυμπότας ἐν αὐτῷ εὐωχεῖσθαι, τοιάνδε εὐχὴν ηὔξατο· "Παλάμηδες, ἐκλάθου τῆς μήνιδος, ἣν ἐν τοῖς Ἀχαιοῖς ποτε ἐμήνισας, καὶ δίδου γίγνεσθαι πολλούς τε καὶ σοφοὺς ἄνδρας. ναὶ Παλάμηδες, δι᾽ ὃν λόγοι, δι᾽ ὃν Μοῦσαι, δι᾽ ὃν ἐγώ."

14. Παρῆλθε καὶ ἐς τὸ τοῦ Ὀρφέως ἄδυτον προσορμισάμενος τῇ Λέσβῳ. φασὶ δὲ ἐνταῦθά ποτε τὸν Ὀρφέα μαντικῇ χαίρειν, ἧς τὸν Ἀπόλλω ἐπιμεμελῆσθαι αὐτόν. ἐπειδὴ γὰρ μήτε ἐς Γρύνειον ἐφοίτων ἔτι ὑπὲρ χρησμῶν ἄνθρωποι, μήτε ἐς Κλάρον, μήτ᾽ ἔνθα ὁ τρίπους ὁ Ἀπολλώνειος, Ὀρφεὺς δὲ ἔχρα μόνος ἄρτι ἐκ Θρᾴκης ἡ κεφαλὴ ἥκουσα, ἐφίσταταί οἱ χρησμῳδοῦντι ὁ θεὸς καὶ "πέπαυσο" ἔφη "τῶν ἐμῶν, καὶ γὰρ δὴ ᾄδοντά σε ἱκανῶς ἤνεγκα."

15. Πλεόντων δὲ αὐτῶν μετὰ ταῦτα τὸ ἐπ᾽ Εὐβοίας πέλαγος, ὃ καὶ Ὁμήρῳ δοκεῖ τῶν χαλεπῶν καὶ δυσμετρήτων εἶναι, ἡ μὲν θάλαττα ὑπτία καὶ τῆς ὥρας

[9] ἐπεγέγραπτο Kay.: ὑπεγέγραπτο

wisdom. We can show ourselves better than the Achaeans if we honor for his virtue someone whom they killed with no regard for justice."

The others jumped out of the ship, while he sought out 3
the tomb and found the statue buried beside it. On the base of the statue was written, "To the divine Palamedes." He reerected it, as I myself have seen, and marked out a sanctuary around it of the size that devotees of Enodia[17] use, since it has room for about ten drinking companions to celebrate. Then he made this prayer: "Palamedes, forget the wrath which once you felt towards the Achaeans, and grant that they may have many true philosophers. Yes, Palamedes, the source of language, of the Muses, of myself."

14. He also entered the shrine of Orpheus after putting in at Lesbos. Here they say Orpheus once loved to indulge in prophecy, which was the business of Apollo himself. People were no longer going to Gryneion for oracles,[18] nor to Claros, nor to any place where the tripos of Apollo stands, but Orpheus alone was giving oracles, his head having lately arrived from Thrace.[19] So the god appeared to him as he was prophesying and said, "Stop doing my business, since I put up with you long enough when you were a singer."

15. After this they sailed the waters off Euboea, which Homer too considers harsh and difficult to cross;[20] but the sea proved calm and unusually favorable for the season. So

[17] Hecate, goddess whose many aspects included the protection of travelers.

[18] Oracle of Apollo near Pergamum.

[19] The head of Orpheus was buried at Antissa in Lesbos, west of Methymna.

[20] *Odyssey* 3.174–79.

κρείττων ἐφαίνετο, λόγοι τε ἐγίγνοντο περί τε νήσων, ἐπειδὴ πολλαῖς τε καὶ ὀνομασταῖς ἐνετύγχανον, περί τε ναυπηγίας καὶ κυβερνητικῆς πρόσφοροι τοῖς πλέουσιν. ἐπεὶ δὲ ὁ Δάμις τοὺς μὲν διέβαλλε τῶν λόγων, τοὺς δὲ ὑπετέμνετο, τοὺς δὲ οὐ ξυνεχώρει ἐρωτᾶν, ξυνῆκεν ὁ Ἀπολλώνιος, ὅτι λόγον ἕτερον σπουδάσαι βούλοιτο, καὶ "τί παθών," ἔφη "ὦ Δάμι, διασπᾷς τὰ ἐρωτώμενα; οὐ γὰρ ναυτιῶν γε ἢ ὑπὸ τοῦ πλοῦ πονήρως ἔχων ἀποστρέφῃ τοὺς λόγους, ἡ γὰρ θάλαττα, ὁρᾷς, ὡς ὑποτέθεικεν ἑαυτὴν τῇ νηὶ καὶ πέμπει. τί οὖν δυσχεραίνεις;"

2 "Ὅτι" ἔφη "λόγου μεγάλου ἐν μέσῳ ὄντος, ὃν εἰκὸς ἦν ἐρωτᾶν μᾶλλον, ἡμεῖς δὲ τοὺς ἑώλους τε καὶ ἀρχαίους ἐρωτῶμεν." "καὶ τίς" εἶπεν "ὁ λόγος οὗτος εἴη ἄν, δι' ὃν τοὺς ἄλλους ἡγῇ περιττούς;" "Ἀχιλλεῖ" ἔφη "ξυγγενόμενος, ὦ Ἀπολλώνιε, καὶ πολλὰ ἴσως διακηκοὼς μήπω ἡμῖν γιγνωσκόμενα, οὐ δίει ταῦτα, οὐδὲ τὸ εἶδος ἡμῖν τοῦ Ἀχιλλέως ἀνατυποῖς, περιπλεῖς δὲ τὰς νήσους καὶ ναυπηγεῖς τῷ λόγῳ." "εἰ μὴ ἀλαζονεύεσθαι" ἔφη "δόξω, πάντα εἰρήσεται."

16. Δεομένων δὲ καὶ τῶν ἄλλων τοῦ λόγου τούτου καὶ φιληκόως ἐχόντων αὐτοῦ "ἀλλ' οὐχὶ βόθρον" εἶπεν "Ὀδυσσέως ὀρυξάμενος, οὐδὲ ἀρνῶν αἵματι ψυχαγωγήσας ἐς διάλεξιν τοῦ Ἀχιλλέως ἦλθον, ἀλλ' εὐξάμενος, ὁπόσα τοῖς ἥρωσιν Ἰνδοί φασιν εὔχεσθαι, 'ὦ Ἀχιλλεῦ,' ἔφην 'τεθνάναι σε οἱ πολλοὶ τῶν ἀνθρώπων φασίν, ἐγὼ δὲ οὐ ξυγχωρῶ τῷ λόγῳ, οὐδὲ Πυθαγόρας σοφίας ἐμῆς πρόγονος. εἰ δὴ ἀληθεύομεν, δεῖξον ἡμῖν

they held discussions suitable for a sea voyage, on the many celebrated islands that they came across, or about shipbuilding and the pilot's craft. Damis however, criticized some of their subjects, interrupted others, and did not allow others to be raised, until Apollonius realized that he wanted to go into a different question, and said, "Why is it, Damis, that you disrupt the discussions? You are not rejecting our topics because you are seasick or made ill by our voyage, since just look how the sea yields to the ship and moves it along. What is annoying you, then?"

"There is an important subject before us," he replied, 2
"which it is more proper for us to raise, but we are raising old and tired ones." "And what," said Apollonius, "might this subject be that makes you think the other ones superfluous?" "After conversing with Achilles," he replied, "Apollonius, maybe you have heard many things quite unknown to us, yet you do not report them, you give us no idea of how Achilles looked, but your conversation is all about touring the islands and shipbuilding." "If you do not think me boastful," said Apollonius, "I will tell all."

16. The others too asked him for this account, and prepared to listen eagerly, so he said: "I did not dig Odysseus's ditch, or raise spirits with sheep's blood, in order to enter into conversation with Achilles. I made the prayers which the Indians claim to make to the heroes, and said, 'Achilles, most people say that you died, but I do not agree with this story, nor does Pythagoras from whom I inherit my wisdom. If we are right, then, reveal your own appearance

τὸ σεαυτοῦ εἶδος, καὶ γὰρ ἂν ὄναιο ἄγαν τῶν ἐμῶν ὀφθαλμῶν, εἰ μάρτυσιν αὐτοῖς τοῦ εἶναι χρήσαιο.'

2 "Ἐπὶ τούτοις σεισμὸς μὲν περὶ τὸν κολωνὸν βραχὺς ἐγένετο, πεντάπηχυς δὲ νεανίας ἀνεδόθη Θετταλικὸς τὴν χλαμύδα, τὸ δὲ εἶδος οὐκ ἀλαζών τις ἐφαίνετο, ὡς ἐνίοις ὁ Ἀχιλλεὺς δοκεῖ, δεινός τε ὁρώμενος οὐκ ἐξήλλαττε[10] τοῦ φαιδροῦ, τὸ δὲ κάλλος οὔπω μοι δοκεῖ ἐπαινέτου ἀξίου ἐπειλῆφθαι, καίτοι Ὁμήρου πολλὰ ἐπ' αὐτῷ εἰπόντος, ἀλλὰ ἄρρητον εἶναι καὶ καταλύεσθαι μᾶλλον ὑπὸ τοῦ ὑμνοῦντος ἢ παραπλησίως ἑαυτῷ ᾄδεσθαι. ὁρώμενος δέ, ὁπόσον εἶπον, μείζων ἐγίγνετο καὶ διπλάσιος καὶ ὑπὲρ τοῦτο, δωδεκάπηχυς γοῦν ἐφάνη μοι, ὅτε δὴ τελεώτατος ἑαυτοῦ ἐγένετο, καὶ τὸ κάλλος ἀεὶ ξυνεπεδίδου τῷ μήκει. τὴν μὲν δὴ κόμην οὐδὲ κείρασθαί ποτε ἔλεγεν, ἀλλὰ ἄσυλον φυλάξαι τῷ Σπερχειῷ, ποταμῶν γὰρ πρώτῳ Σπερχειῷ χρήσασθαι, τὰ γένεια δ' αὐτῷ πρώτας ἐκβολὰς εἶχε.

3 "Προσειπὼν δέ με 'ἀσμένως' εἶπεν 'ἐντετύχηκά σοι, πάλαι δεόμενος ἀνδρὸς τοιοῦδε· Θετταλοὶ γὰρ τὰ ἐναγίσματα χρόνον ἤδη πολὺν ἐκλελοίπασί μοι, καὶ μηνίειν μὲν οὔπω ἀξιῶ, μηνίσαντος γὰρ ἀπολοῦνται μᾶλλον ἢ οἱ ἐνταῦθά ποτε Ἕλληνες, ξυμβουλίᾳ δὲ ἐπιεικεῖ χρῶμαι, μὴ ὑβρίζειν σφᾶς ἐς τὰ νόμιμα, μηδὲ κακίους ἐλέγχεσθαι τουτωνὶ τῶν Τρώων, οἳ τοσούσδε ἄνδρας ὑπ' ἐμοῦ ἀφαιρεθέντες δημοσίᾳ τε θύουσί μοι καὶ ὡραίων ἀπάρχονται καὶ ἱκετηρίαν τιθέμενοι σπονδὰς αἰτοῦσιν, ἃς ἐγὼ οὐ δώσω· τὰ γὰρ ἐπιορκηθέντα

to us. You would be much obliged to my eyes if you used them to attest your existence.'

"At this there was a brief earthquake in the area of the mound, and a youth five cubits tall emerged, with his cloak in the Thessalian fashion. In appearance he did not seem the boastful sort, as Achilles is represented by some. He looked formidable and yet steadily cheerful, and his beauty seemed to me never to have found its true celebrant, despite the many things that Homer said about it, but to be beyond words, and to be diminished by its bard rather than celebrated to the extent it deserves. Though he had seemed to be as tall as I mentioned, he grew taller, twice the size or even more, in fact he seemed to me twelve cubits high when he had reached his full measure, and his beauty constantly increased with his height. He said that he had never cut his hair, but kept it sacred in honor of Spercheios,[21] since this was the first river that he had ever been familiar with, and his cheeks had their first down. 2

"Addressing me, he said, 'I am glad to have met you, having long needed a man such as you. The Thessalians have neglected their sacrifices to me for many years, and I have not so far chosen to be angry with them, since if I am they will perish more surely than the Greeks once did here. I give them some mild advice: they must not violate the rites, or show themselves inferior to the Trojans here. These lost many noble men at my hands, and yet they make public sacrifice to me, give me their first fruits, and holding olive branches they ask for a truce. I will not grant it, for 3

[21] River of southern Thessaly.

---

10 ἐξήλλαττε Kay.: ἐξηλλάττετο

τούτοις ἐπ᾽ ἐμὲ οὐκ ἐάσει τὸ Ἴλιόν ποτε τὸ ἀρχαῖον ἀναλαβεῖν εἶδος, οὐδὲ τυχεῖν ἀκμῆς, ὁπόση περὶ πολλὰς τῶν καθῃρημένων ἐγένετο, ἀλλ᾽ οἰκήσουσιν αὐτὸ βελτίους οὐδὲν ἢ εἰ χθὲς ἥλωσαν. ἵν᾽ οὖν μὴ καὶ τὰ Θετταλῶν ἀποφαίνω ὅμοια, πρέσβευε παρὰ τὸ κοινὸν αὐτῶν ὑπὲρ ὧν εἶπον.᾽

4 "'Πρεσβεύσω,' ἔφην 'ὁ γὰρ νοῦς τῆς πρεσβείας ἦν μὴ ἀπολέσθαι αὐτούς. ἀλλ᾽ ἐγώ τί σου, Ἀχιλλεῦ, δέομαι.' 'ξυνίημι,' ἔφη 'δῆλος γὰρ εἶ περὶ τῶν Τρωικῶν <ἐρωτήσων>.[11] ἐρώτα δὲ λόγους πέντε, οὓς αὐτός τε βούλει καὶ Μοῖραι ξυγχωροῦσιν.' ἠρόμην οὖν πρῶτον, εἰ κατὰ τὸν τῶν ποιητῶν λόγον ἔτυχε τάφου. 'κεῖμαι μέν,' εἶπεν 'ὡς ἔμοιγε ἥδιστον καὶ Πατρόκλῳ ἐγένετο, ξυνέβημεν γὰρ δὴ κομιδῇ νέοι, ξυνέχει δὲ ἄμφω χρυσοῦς ἀμφορεὺς κειμένους, ὡς ἕνα. Μουσῶν δὲ θρῆνοι[12] καὶ Νηρηίδων, οὓς ἐπ᾽ ἐμοὶ γενέσθαι φασί, Μοῦσαι μὲν οὐδ᾽ ἀφίκοντό ποτε ἐνταῦθα, Νηρηίδες δὲ ἔτι φοιτῶσι.' μετὰ ταῦτα δὲ ἠρόμην, εἰ ἡ Πολυξένη ἐπισφαγείη αὐτῷ, ὁ δὲ ἀληθὲς μὲν ἔφη τοῦτο εἶναι, σφαγῆναι δὲ αὐτὴν οὐχ ὑπὸ τῶν Ἀχαιῶν, ἀλλ᾽ ἑκοῦσαν ἐπὶ τὸ σῆμα ἐλθοῦσαν καὶ τὸν ἑαυτῆς τε κἀκείνου ἔρωτα μεγάλων ἀξιῶσαι προσπεσοῦσαν ξίφει ὀρθῷ.

5 "Τρίτον ἠρόμην· 'ἡ Ἑλένη, ὦ Ἀχιλλεῦ, ἐς Τροίαν ἦλθεν, ἢ Ὁμήρῳ ἔδοξεν ὑποθέσθαι ταῦτα;' 'πολὺν' ἔφη 'χρόνον ἐξηπατώμεθα πρεσβευόμενοί τε παρὰ

11 <ἐρωτήσων> Rsk. 12 θρῆνοι Kay.: θρήνων

the perjury[22] that they committed against me will never allow Ilium to recover its ancient appearance, or regain the glory that many destroyed cities have achieved. It will be no better a home for them than if it had been captured yesterday. In order that I do not reduce the Thessalians to the same state, convey what I have said to their council.'

"'I will,' I replied, 'since the purpose of the message is 4
to save them from destruction. But I have a request to make of you, Achilles.' 'I understand,' he replied; 'you are obviously going to ask about the Trojan War. So you can ask five questions, such as you wish and the Fates permit.' So first I asked if he received burial in the way the poets describe. 'I am buried,' he replied, 'in the way most pleasing to myself and to Patroclus, for we met when we were very young men, and a golden vessel holds us both as a single person. But as for the dirges which they say the Muses and the Nereids made over me, why, the Muses never once came here, though the Nereids still visit.' After that I asked if Polyxena had been slaughtered in his honor. He said that this was true, though she had not been sacrificed by the Achaeans, but had come to the tomb by her own choice, and had paid a great tribute to their mutual love by falling on an upturned sword.[23]

"Thirdly I asked, 'Did Helen come to Troy, Achilles, or 5
did Homer choose to invent all that?' 'For a long time,' he replied, 'we were fooled, sending embassies to the Trojans

[22] See 11.3 and note 12 there.

[23] The usual version was that the Greeks had sacrificed Polyxena on Achilles's tomb to appease his wrath; for Philostratus's version, see also 11.3.

τοὺς Τρῶας καὶ ποιούμενοι τὰς ὑπὲρ αὐτῆς μάχας, ὡς ἐν τῷ Ἰλίῳ οὔσης, ἡ δ' Αἴγυπτόν τε ᾤκει καὶ τὸν Πρωτέως οἶκον ἁρπασθεῖσα ὑπὸ τοῦ Πάριδος. ἐπεὶ δὲ ἐπιστεύθη τοῦτο, ὑπὲρ αὐτῆς τῆς Τροίας λοιπὸν ἐμαχόμεθα, ὡς μὴ αἰσχρῶς ἀπέλθοιμεν.' ἡψάμην καὶ τετάρτης ἐρωτήσεως καὶ θαυμάζειν ἔφην, εἰ τοσούσδε ὁμοῦ καὶ τοιούσδε ἄνδρας ἡ Ἑλλὰς ἤνεγκεν, ὁπόσους Ὅμηρος ἐπὶ τὴν Τροίαν ξυντάττει. ὁ δὲ Ἀχιλλεὺς 'οὐδὲ οἱ βάρβαροι' ἔφη 'πολὺ ἡμῶν ἐλείποντο, οὕτως ἡ γῆ πᾶσα ἀρετῆς ἤνθησε.'

6 "Πέμπτον ἠρόμην· 'τί παθὼν Ὅμηρος τὸν Παλαμήδην οὐκ οἶδεν, ἢ οἶδε μέν, ἐξαιρεῖ δὲ τοῦ περὶ ὑμῶν λόγου;' 'εἰ Παλαμήδης' εἶπεν 'ἐς Τροίαν οὐκ ἦλθεν, οὐδὲ Τροία ἐγένετο· ἐπεὶ δὲ ἀνὴρ σοφώτατός τε καὶ μαχιμώτατος ἀπέθανεν, ὡς Ὀδυσσεῖ ἔδοξεν, οὐκ ἐσάγεται αὐτὸν ἐς τὰ ποιήματα Ὅμηρος, ὡς μὴ τὰ ὀνείδη τοῦ Ὀδυσσέως ᾄδοι.' καὶ ἐπολοφυράμενος αὐτῷ ὁ Ἀχιλλεὺς ὡς μεγίστῳ τε καὶ καλλίστῳ, νεωτάτῳ τε καὶ πολεμικωτάτῳ, σωφροσύνῃ τε ὑπερβαλομένῳ πάντας, καὶ πολλὰ ξυμβαλομένῳ ταῖς Μούσαις, 'ἀλλὰ σύ,' ἔφη 'Ἀπολλώνιε, σοφοῖς γὰρ πρὸς σοφοὺς ἐπιτήδεια, τοῦ τε τάφου ἐπιμελήθητι καὶ τὸ ἄγαλμα τοῦ Παλαμήδους ἀνάλαβε φαύλως ἐρριμμένον· κεῖται δὲ ἐν τῇ Αἰολίδι κατὰ Μήθυμναν τὴν ἐν Λέσβῳ.' ταῦτα εἰπὼν καὶ ἐπὶ πᾶσι τὰ περὶ τὸν νεανίαν τὸν ἐκ Πάρου ἀπῆλθε ξὺν ἀστραπῇ μετρίᾳ, καὶ γὰρ δὴ καὶ ἀλεκτρυόνες ἤδη ᾠδῆς ἥπτοντο." τοιαῦτα μὲν τὰ ἐπὶ τῆς νεώς,

and doing battle on her account, as if she was in Ilium. In fact she was living in Egypt and the house of Proteus after Paris had carried her off.[24] Once we were convinced of this, thereafter we fought to win Troy itself, so as not to leave in disgrace.' I ventured my fourth question, and said I was surprised that Greece had produced as many and as great heroes as Homer arrays against Troy. Achilles replied, 'Nor were the barbarians much our inferiors, so much did the whole world teem with virtue.'

"My fifth question was: 'How is it that Homer does not 6
know about Palamedes, or if he does excises him from his account of you all?' 'If Palamedes did not come to Troy,' he replied, 'Troy did not exist either. But since that wisest and most warlike of heroes was killed by a ruse of Odysseus, Homer does not bring him into his poem to avoid celebrating Odysseus's crimes.' Achilles then lamented Palamedes as the greatest, handsomest, noblest, and bravest man, who surpassed all in chastity and made many contributions to the Muses. He then said, 'You, however, Apollonius, since there is an affinity of the wise with the wise, must look after his burial place, and set up the statue of Palamedes that is shamefully overthrown. He is buried in Aeolian soil opposite Methymna in Lesbos.' After saying all this, and at the end mentioning the youth from Paros, he disappeared in a slight flash, since the cocks were just then beginning to crow." So much for what happened on board.

[24] The story of the "Egyptian Helen" is first found in Herodotus (II 113–20).

17. Ἐς δὲ τὸν Πειραιᾶ ἐσπλεύσας περὶ μυστηρίων ὥραν, ὅτε Ἀθηναῖοι πολυανθρωπότατα Ἑλλήνων πράττουσιν, ἀνῄει ξυντείνας ἀπὸ τῆς νεὼς ἐς τὸ ἄστυ, προιὼν δὲ πολλοῖς τῶν φιλοσοφούντων ἐνετύγχανε Φάληράδε κατιοῦσιν, ὧν οἱ μὲν γυμνοὶ ἐθέροντο, καὶ γὰρ τὸ μετόπωρον εὐήλιον τοῖς Ἀθηναίοις, οἱ δὲ ἐκ βιβλίων ἐσπούδαζον, οἱ δ' ἀπὸ στόματος ἠσκοῦντο,[13] οἱ δὲ ἤριζον. παρῄει δὲ οὐδεὶς αὐτόν, ἀλλὰ τεκμηράμενοι πάντες, ὡς εἴη Ἀπολλώνιος, ξυνανεστρέφοντό τε καὶ ἠσπάζοντο χαίροντες, νεανίσκοι δὲ ὁμοῦ δέκα περιτυχόντες αὐτῷ "νὴ τὴν Ἀθηνᾶν ἐκείνην," ἔφασαν ἀνατείναντες τὰς χεῖρας ἐς τὴν ἀκρόπολιν, "ἡμεῖς ἄρτι ἐς Πειραιᾶ ἐβαδίζομεν πλευσόμενοι ἐς Ἰωνίαν παρὰ σέ." ὁ δὲ ἀπεδέχετο αὐτῶν καὶ ξυγχαίρειν ἔφη φιλοσοφοῦσιν.

18. Ἦν μὲν δὴ Ἐπιδαυρίων ἡμέρα. τὰ δὲ Ἐπιδαύρια μετὰ πρόρρησίν[14] τε καὶ ἱερεῖα δεῦρο μυεῖν Ἀθηναίοις πάτριον ἐπὶ θυσίᾳ δευτέρᾳ, τουτὶ δὲ ἐνόμισαν Ἀσκληπιοῦ ἕνεκα, ὅτι δὴ ἐμύησαν αὐτὸν ἥκοντα Ἐπιδαυρόθεν ὀψὲ μυστηρίων. ἀμελήσαντες δὲ οἱ πολλοὶ τοῦ μυεῖσθαι περὶ τὸν Ἀπολλώνιον εἶχον, καὶ τοῦτ' ἐσπούδαζον μᾶλλον ἢ τὸ ἀπελθεῖν τετελεσμένοι. ὁ δὲ ξυνέσεσθαι μὲν αὐτοῖς αὖθις ἔλεγεν, ἐκέλευσε δὲ πρὸς τοῖς ἱεροῖς τότε γίγνεσθαι, καὶ γὰρ αὐτὸς μυεῖσθαι. ὁ δὲ ἱεροφάντης οὐκ ἐβούλετο παρέχειν τὰ ἱερά,

[13] ἠσκοῦντο Kay.: ἤσκηντο
[14] πρόρρησιν M. Solanus (Schenkl 1893): πρόσρησιν

17. He sailed into Piraeus about the time of the Mysteries,[25] when Athens is the most crowded city of Greece, and went eagerly up from the ship to the city. As he advanced he met many students of philosophy coming down to Phalerum;[26] some had stripped to tan themselves (since late autumn is sunny in Athens), others were studying from books, others were sharpening their verbal skills, others were disputing. Not one of them passed him by, but all inferred that he was Apollonius, and joyfully gathered round to greet him. A group of ten youths fell in with him and said, "By Athena there," (stretching out their hands towards the acropolis) "we were just coming down to Piraeus planning to sail to you in Ionia." He approved of them, and congratulated them on their love of wisdom.

18. Now it was the day of the Epidauria. At the Epidauria, after an announcement and sacrifice of victims, it is customary for the Athenians even now to give induction accompanied by a secondary sacrifice.[27] This practice they instituted in honor of Asclepius, because they inducted him when he had arrived from Epidaurus too late for the Mysteries. But most people omitted their induction out of their interest in Apollonius, which excited them more than the prospect of leaving as initiates. He said that he would meet with them thereafter, but for the moment told them to attend to the rites, since he himself was receiving induction. But the hierophant did not want to make the rites

[25] The "Greater" Mysteries, held in Boedromion (September/October).

[26] Harbor just east of Piraeus.

[27] The Epidauria was held when the Greater Mysteries had already begun, for the benefit of those who had missed the first days.

μὴ γὰρ ἄν ποτε μυῆσαι γόητα, μηδὲ τὴν Ἐλευσῖνα ἀνοῖξαι ἀνθρώπῳ μὴ καθαρῷ τὰ δαιμόνια.

2 Ὁ δὲ Ἀπολλώνιος, οὐδὲν ὑπὸ τούτων ἥττων αὑτοῦ γενόμενος, "οὔπω" ἔφη "τὸ μέγιστον, ὧν ἐγὼ ἐγκληθείην ἄν, εἴρηκας, ὅτι περὶ τῆς τελετῆς πλείω ἢ σὺ γιγνώσκων ἐγὼ δὲ ὡς παρὰ σοφώτερον ἐμαυτοῦ μυησόμενος ἦλθον." ἐπαινεσάντων δὲ τῶν παρόντων, ὡς ἐρρωμένως καὶ παραπλησίως αὑτῷ ἀπεκρίνατο, ὁ μὲν ἱεροφάντης, ἐπειδὴ ἐξείργων αὐτὸν οὐ φίλα τοῖς πολλοῖς ἐδόκει πράττειν, μετέβαλε τοῦ τόνου καὶ "μυοῦ," ἔφη "σοφὸς γάρ τις ἥκειν ἔοικας," ὁ δὲ Ἀπολλώνιος "μυήσομαι" ἔφη "αὖθις, μυήσει δέ με ὁ δεῖνα," προγνώσει χρώμενος ἐς τὸν μετ᾽ ἐκεῖνον ἱεροφάντην, ὃς μετὰ τέτταρα ἔτη τοῦ ἱεροῦ προὔστη.

19. Τὰς δὲ Ἀθήνησι διατριβὰς πλείστας μὲν ὁ Δάμις γενέσθαι φησὶ τῷ ἀνδρί, γράψαι δὲ οὐ πάσας, ἀλλὰ τὰς ἀναγκαίας τε καὶ περὶ μεγάλων σπουδασθείσας. τὴν μὲν δὴ πρώτην διάλεξιν, ἐπειδὴ φιλοθύτας τοὺς Ἀθηναίους εἶδεν, ὑπὲρ ἱερῶν διελέξατο, καὶ ὡς ἄν τις ἐς τὸ ἑκάστῳ τῶν θεῶν οἰκεῖον, καὶ πηνίκα δὲ τῆς ἡμέρας τε καὶ νυκτὸς ἢ θύοι ἢ σπένδοι ἢ εὔχοιτο, καὶ βιβλίῳ Ἀπολλωνίου προστυχεῖν ἔστιν, ἐν ᾧ ταῦτα τῇ ἑαυτοῦ φωνῇ ἐκδιδάσκει. διῆλθε δὲ ταῦτα Ἀθήνησι πρῶτον μὲν ὑπὲρ σοφίας αὑτοῦ τε κἀκείνων, εἶτ᾽ ἐλέγχων τὸν ἱεροφάντην δι᾽ ἃ βλασφήμως τε καὶ ἀμαθῶς εἶπε. τίς γὰρ ἔτι ᾠήθη τὰ δαιμόνια μὴ καθαρὸν εἶναι τὸν φιλοσοφοῦντα, ὅπως οἱ θεοὶ θεραπευτέοι;

available, saying he would never induct a fraud, or open Eleusis up to a man who was impure in spiritual matters.

Apollonius did not degrade himself because of all this, 2
but said, "You have not yet mentioned the gravest charge that could be brought against me, that I know more about the rite than you do, and yet have come as if the person inducting me was wiser than I am." When those present praised him for a bold and characteristic answer, the hierophant saw that he was causing general displeasure by excluding him, and changed his tone, saying, "You may be inducted, since you seem to come as a kind of wise man." To this Apollonius replied, "I will be inducted another time, and so-and-so will induct me," using his foreknowledge of the man who took charge of the sanctuary four years later as that one's successor.[28]

19. According to Damis, the Master gave very many lectures at Athens, but he himself did not record all, but only the important ones concerning lofty subjects. Seeing that the Athenians were fond of making sacrifices, Apollonius gave his first lecture on religion, and how to make a sacrifice, libation, or prayer in the way appropriate to each god, and at which time of night or day. One may also find a book of Apollonius in which he gives these instructions in his own words.[29] He gave this lecture at Athens primarily as a tribute to his own wisdom and theirs, but also to show up the hierophant for his blasphemous and ignorant talk. Who could think after that that a man who lectured on the right way to cultivate the gods was "impure in spiritual matters"?

[28] See V 19.1.

[29] See III 41.

20. Διαλεγομένου δὲ αὐτοῦ περὶ τοῦ σπένδειν, παρέτυχε μὲν τῷ λόγῳ μειράκιον τῶν ἁβρῶν οὕτως ἀσελγὲς νομιζόμενον, ὡς γενέσθαι ποτὲ καὶ ἁμαξῶν[15] ᾆσμα, πατρὶς δὲ αὐτῷ Κέρκυρα ἦν καὶ ἐς Ἀλκίνουν ἀνέφερε τὸν ξένον τοῦ Ὀδυσσέως τὸν Φαίακα, καὶ διῄει μὲν ὁ Ἀπολλώνιος περὶ τοῦ σπένδειν, ἐκέλευε δὲ μὴ πίνειν τοῦ ποτηρίου τούτου, φυλάττειν δὲ αὐτὸ τοῖς θεοῖς ἄχραντόν τε καὶ ἄποτον. ἐπεὶ δὲ καὶ ὦτα ἐκέλευσε τῷ ποτηρίῳ ποιεῖσθαι καὶ σπένδειν κατὰ τὸ οὖς, ἀφ᾿ οὗ μέρους ἥκιστα πίνουσιν ἄνθρωποι, τὸ μειράκιον κατεσκέδασε τοῦ λόγου πλατύν τε καὶ ἀσελγῆ γέλωτα· ὁ δὲ ἀναβλέψας ἐς αὐτὸ "οὐ σὺ" ἔφη "ταῦτα ὑβρίζεις, ἀλλ᾿ ὁ δαίμων, ὃς ἐλαύνει σε οὐκ εἰδότα."

2 Ἐλελήθει δὲ ἄρα δαιμονῶν τὸ μειράκιον· ἐγέλα τε γὰρ ἐφ᾿ οἷς οὐδεὶς ἕτερος καὶ μετέβαλλεν ἐς τὸ κλάειν αἰτίαν οὐκ ἔχον, διελέγετό τε πρὸς ἑαυτὸν καὶ ᾖδε. καὶ οἱ μὲν πολλοὶ τὴν νεότητα σκιρτῶσαν ᾤοντο ἐκφέρειν αὐτὸ ἐς ταῦτα, ὁ δ᾿ ὑπεκρίνετο ἄρα τῷ δαίμονι, καὶ ἐδόκει παροινεῖν ἃ ἐπαρῳνεῖτο.[16] ὁρῶντός τε ἐς αὐτὸ τοῦ Ἀπολλωνίου, δεδοικότως τε καὶ ὀργίλως φωνὰς ἠφίει τὸ εἴδωλον, ὁπόσαι καομένων τε καὶ στρεβλουμένων εἰσίν, ἀφέξεσθαί τε τοῦ μειρακίου ὤμνυ καὶ μηδενὶ ἀνθρώπων ἐμπεσεῖσθαι. τοῦ δὲ οἷον δεσπότου πρὸς ἀνδράποδον ποικίλον πανοῦργόν τε καὶ ἀναιδὲς καὶ τὰ τοιαῦτα ξὺν ὀργῇ λέγοντος, καὶ κελεύοντος

[15] ἁμαξῶν Bentl.: ἀμαζῶν or Ἀμαζόνων
[16] ἐπαρῳνεῖτο Headlam: ἐπαρῴνει τότε

20. Once he was lecturing on the subject of libations, and there happened to be present at the talk a foppish youth with such a reputation for shamelessness that he had once been the subject of bawdy songs.[30] Corcyra was his place of origin, and he claimed descent from Alcinous, Odysseus's host on Phaeacia. Apollonius was explaining how to pour libations, and advising not to drink from this kind of cup, but to keep it for the gods, undefiled and untouched by human lips. He also advised that the cup should have handles, and that one should pour libations over the handle, the part from which humans are least likely to drink. The youth greeted his remark with a loud, licentious laugh, at which Apollonius looked up at him and said, "It is not you that are committing this outrage, but the demon who controls you without your knowledge."

In fact without knowing it the youth was possessed by 2
a demon. He laughed at things that nobody else did and went over to weeping without any reason, and he talked and sang to himself. Most people thought that the exuberance of youth produced these effects, but he was being prompted by the demon, and only seemed to be playing the tricks that were being played on him. When Apollonius looked at the spirit, it uttered sounds of fear and fury, such as people being burned alive or tortured do, and it swore to keep away from the youth and not enter into any human. But Apollonius spoke to it as an angry householder does to a slave who is wily, crafty, shameless, and so on, and told it

[30] Literally, "song of the carts," since carts were used at the Eleusinian mysteries as a place for bawdy repartee.

αὐτῷ ξὺν τεκμηρίῳ ἀπαλλάττεσθαι, "τὸν δεῖνα" ἔφη "καταβαλῶ ἀνδριάντα," δείξας τινὰ τῶν περὶ τὴν Βασίλειον στοάν, πρὸς ᾗ ταῦτα ἐπράττετο.

3 Ἐπεὶ δὲ ὁ ἀνδριὰς ὑπεκινήθη πρῶτον, εἶτα ἔπεσε, τὸν μὲν θόρυβον τὸν ἐπὶ τούτῳ, καὶ ὡς ἐκρότησαν ὑπὸ θαύματος, τί ἄν τις γράφοι; τὸ δὲ μειράκιον ὥσπερ ἀφυπνίσαν τούς τε ὀφθαλμοὺς ἔτριψε, καὶ πρὸς τὰς αὐγὰς τοῦ ἡλίου εἶδεν, αἰδῶ τε ἐπεσπάσατο πάντων ἐς αὐτὸ ἐστραμμένων, ἀσελγές τε οὐκέτι ἐφαίνετο, οὐδὲ ἄτακτον βλέπον, ἀλλ' ἐπανῆλθεν ἐς τὴν ἑαυτοῦ φύσιν μεῖον οὐδὲν ἢ εἰ φαρμακοποσίᾳ ἐκέχρητο, μεταβαλόν τε τῶν χλανιδίων καὶ ληδίων καὶ τῆς ἄλλης συβάριδος, ἐς ἔρωτα ἦλθεν αὐχμοῦ καὶ τρίβωνος καὶ ἐς τὰ τοῦ Ἀπολλωνίου ἤθη ἀπεδύσατο.

21. Ἐπιπλῆξαι δὲ λέγεται περὶ Διονυσίων Ἀθηναίοις, ἃ ποιεῖταί σφισιν ἐν ὥρᾳ τοῦ Ἀνθεστηριῶνος· ὁ μὲν γὰρ μονῳδίας ἀκροασομένους καὶ μελοποιίας παραβάσεών τε καὶ ῥυθμῶν, ὁπόσοι κωμῳδίας τε καὶ τραγῳδίας εἰσίν, ἐς τὸ θέατρον ξυμφοιτᾶν ᾤετο, ἐπεὶ δὲ ἤκουσεν ὅτι αὐλοῦ ὑποσημήναντος λυγισμοὺς ὀρχοῦνται, καὶ μεταξὺ τῆς Ὀρφέως ἐποποιίας τε καὶ θεολογίας τὰ μὲν ὡς Ὧραι, τὰ δὲ ὡς Νύμφαι, τὰ δὲ ὡς Βάκχαι πράττουσιν, ἐς ἐπίπληξιν τούτου κατέστη καὶ "παύσασθε" εἶπεν "ἐξορχούμενοι τοὺς Σαλαμινίους καὶ πολλοὺς ἑτέρους κειμένους ἀγαθοὺς ἄνδρας, εἰ μὲν γὰρ Λακωνικὴ ταῦτα ὄρχησις, εὖγε οἱ στρατιῶται, γυμνάζεσθε γὰρ πολέμῳ καὶ ξυνορχήσομαι, εἰ δὲ ἁπαλὴ καὶ ἐς τὸ θῆλυ σπεύδουσα, τί φῶ περὶ τῶν

to give a proof of its departure. It replied, "I will knock that statue over," indicating one of the statues around the Royal Colonnade,[31] where all this was taking place.

When the statue first moved slightly, then fell, the out- 3
cry at this and the way people clapped in amazement were
past description. The youth, as if waking up, rubbed his
eyes, looked at the sun's beams, and won the respect of all
the people gazing at him. From then on he no longer
seemed dissolute, or had an unsteady gaze, but returned to
his own nature no worse off than if he had taken a course of
medicine. He got rid of his capes, cloaks, and other frip-
peries, and fell in love with deprivation and the philosopher's cloak, and stripped down to Apollonius's style.

21. He is said to have rebuked the Athenians over the Dionysia, which they celebrate at the time of Anthesterion.[32] He thought that they were frequenting the theater to hear solos and lyrics, addresses to the audience, and the meters proper to tragedy and comedy. But when he heard that they were dancing sinuously to the call of the pipe, and in between the lofty verse and religious poetry of Orpheus were acting now as the Seasons, or the Nymphs, or as Bacchants,[33] he undertook to denounce all this. "Stop burlesquing the men of Salamis," he said, "and many other brave souls, now buried. If this is Spartan dancing, then I applaud you soldiers, since you are practicing for war, and I will join you. But if this is dainty dancing that leads to effeminacy, what shall I say about your trophies? They will

[31] In the northwest corner of the Agora.

[32] February/March.

[33] In cities of the imperial period, the Dionysia were an occasion for cross-dressing and general revelry.

τροπαίων; οὐ γὰρ κατὰ Μήδων ταῦτα ἢ Περσῶν, καθ' ὑμῶν δὲ ἑστήξει, τῶν ἀναθέντων αὐτὰ εἰ λίποισθε.

2 "Κροκωτοὶ δὲ ὑμῖν καὶ ἁλουργία καὶ κοκκοβαφία τοιαύτη πόθεν; οὐδὲ γὰρ αἱ Ἀχαρναί γε ὧδε ἐστέλλοντο, οὐδὲ ὁ Κολωνὸς ὧδε ἵππευε. καὶ τί λέγω ταῦτα; γυνὴ ναύαρχος ἐκ Καρίας ἐφ' ὑμᾶς ἔπλευσε μετὰ Ξέρξου, καὶ ἦν αὐτῇ γυναικεῖον οὐδέν, ἀλλ' ἀνδρὸς στολὴ καὶ ὅπλα, ὑμεῖς δὲ ἁβρότεροι τῶν Ξέρξου γυναικῶν ἐφ' ἑαυτοὺς στέλλεσθε οἱ γέροντες οἱ νέοι τὸ ἐφηβικόν, οἳ πάλαι μὲν ὤμνυσαν ἐς Ἀγραύλου φοιτῶντες ὑπὲρ τῆς πατρίδος ἀποθανεῖσθαι καὶ ὅπλα θήσεσθαι,[17] νῦν δὲ ἴσως ὀμοῦνται ὑπὲρ τῆς πατρίδος βακχεύσειν καὶ θύρσον λήψεσθαι κόρυν μὲν οὐδεμίαν φέρον, 'γυναικομίμῳ δὲ μορφώματι,' κατὰ τὸν Εὐριπίδην, αἰσχρῶς διαπρέπον.

3 "Ἀκούω δὲ ὑμᾶς καὶ ἀνέμους γίγνεσθαι καὶ λήδια ἀνασείειν λέγεσθε, ἔπιπλα μετεώρως αὐτὰ κολποῦντες. ἔδει δὲ ἀλλὰ τούτους γε αἰδεῖσθαι, ξυμμάχους ὄντας καὶ πνεύσαντας ὑπὲρ ὑμῶν μέγα, μηδὲ τὸν Βορέαν κηδεστήν γε ὄντα καὶ παρὰ πάντας τοὺς ἀνέμους ἄρσενα ποιεῖσθαι θῆλυν, οὐδὲ γὰρ τῆς Ὠρειθυίας ἐραστὴς ἄν ποτε ὁ Βορέας ἐγένετο, εἰ κἀκείνην ὀρχουμένην εἶδε."

17 θήσεσθαι Hamaker (Kay.): στήσεσθαι

commemorate not the Medes or the Persians but you, if you prove inferior to those who set them up.

"Where do these saffron clothes, such purple and crim- 2
son dyes, come from? This was not how Acharnae arrayed itself, or Colonus rode out.[34] Why mention those? A woman admiral sailed against you from Caria with Xerxes,[35] and there was nothing effeminate about her; she had a man's clothing and arms, while you, more dainty than Xerxes's harem, are setting out to defeat yourselves, old men, young men, ephebes. These used to go to the sanctuary of Agraulos[36] swearing to die and take up arms for their native city, but now perhaps they will swear to be Bacchants on their city's behalf and carry a wand, not wearing any helmet, but shamefully resplendent in 'woman-like' disguise, as Euripides says.[37]

"I hear also that you turn into winds, and they say that 3
you lift your dresses, making them billow high in the air.[38] At least you should show respect for the winds, since they were your allies and blew hard in your cause, and you should not turn Boreas, your relative and the most manly of all the winds, into a woman. Boreas would not have been Oreithyia's lover long ago if he had seen her dancing too."[39]

[34] Two demes of Attica famous for their warriors.

[35] Artemisia, ally of Xerxes against the Greeks.

[36] Athenian heroine worshiped on the Acropolis; the ephebes took an annual oath in her sanctuary.

[37] *Bacchae* 980.

[38] The Greek of this phrase is obscure.

[39] According to legend, Boreas (the north wind) fell in love with the Attic heroine Oreithyia. Consequently, the Athenians invoked Boreas as their relative to help them against the Persians in 480 (Herodotus VII 189).

22. Διωρθοῦτο δὲ κἀκεῖνο Ἀθήνησιν· οἱ Ἀθηναῖοι ξυνιόντες ἐς θέατρον τὸ ὑπὸ τῇ ἀκροπόλει προσεῖχον σφαγαῖς ἀνθρώπων, καὶ ἐσπουδάζετο ταῦτα ἐκεῖ μᾶλλον ἢ ἐν Κορίνθῳ νῦν, χρημάτων τε μεγάλων ἐωνημένοι ἤγοντο μοιχοί, καὶ πόρνοι, καὶ τοιχωρύχοι, καὶ βαλαντιοτόμοι, καὶ ἀνδραποδισταί, καὶ τὰ τοιαῦτα ἔθνη, οἱ δ᾽ ὥπλιζον αὐτοὺς καὶ ἐκέλευον ξυμπίπτειν. ἐλάβετο δὲ καὶ τούτων ὁ Ἀπολλώνιος, καὶ καλούντων αὐτὸν ἐς ἐκκλησίαν Ἀθηναίων οὐκ ἂν ἔφη παρελθεῖν ἐς χωρίον ἀκάθαρτον καὶ λύθρου μεστόν.

2 Ἔλεγε δὲ ταῦτα ἐν ἐπιστολῇ, καὶ θαυμάζειν ἔλεγεν "ὅπως ἡ θεὸς οὐ καὶ τὴν ἀκρόπολιν ἤδη ἐκλείπει τοιοῦτον αἷμα ὑμῶν ἐκχεόντων αὐτῇ. δοκεῖτε γάρ μοι προϊόντες, ἐπειδὰν τὰ Παναθήναια πέμπητε, μηδὲ βοῦς ἔτι, ἀλλ᾽ ἑκατόμβας ἀνθρώπων καταθύσειν τῇ θεῷ. σὺ δέ, Διόνυσε, μετὰ τοιοῦτον αἷμα ἐς τὸ θέατρον φοιτᾷς; κἀκεῖ σοι σπένδουσιν οἱ σοφοὶ Ἀθηναῖοι; μετάστηθι καὶ σύ, Διόνυσε· Κιθαιρὼν καθαρώτερος." τοιάδε εὗρον τὰ σπουδαιότατα τῶν φιλοσοφηθέντων Ἀθήνησιν αὐτῷ τότε.

23. Ἐπρέσβευσε δὲ καὶ παρὰ τοὺς Θετταλοὺς ὑπὲρ τοῦ Ἀχιλλέως κατὰ τοὺς ἐν Πυλαίᾳ ξυλλόγους, ἐν οἷς οἱ Θετταλοὶ τὰ Ἀμφικτυονικὰ πράττουσιν, οἱ δὲ δείσαντες ἐψηφίσαντο ἀναλαβεῖν τὰ προσήκοντα τῷ τάφῳ. καὶ τὸ Λεωνίδου σῆμα τοῦ Σπαρτιάτου μονονοὺ

---

40 Gladiatorial games were especially popular in the Roman colony of Corinth.

22. He also corrected the following practice at Athens. The Athenians used to assemble in the theater below the acropolis and watch human slaughter, so that it was more popular there than it now is in Corinth.[40] Paying large sums of money, they assembled adulterers, pimps, burglars, cutpurses, slave dealers, and types like that, and then armed them and told them to enter combat. This too Apollonius denounced, and when the Athenians summoned him to the assembly, he said he would not enter a place that was impure and full of gore.[41]

This he said in a letter, and added: "I am surprised that 2
the goddess has not already left the acropolis when you pour out blood of this kind for her. At this rate, it seems to me, you will no longer sacrifice oxen when you celebrate the Panathenaea, but human hecatombs in the goddess's honor. And you, Dionysus, do you frequent the theater after so much blood? And do the wise Athenians pour libations to you here? You too must leave, Dionysus: Cithaeron is purer."[42] These are the most earnest of his disquisitions at Athens on that occasion that I have discovered.

23. He also went as Achilles's emissary to the Thessalians at the time of the meetings in Pylaea, at which the Thessalians do business with the Amphictyony,[43] and he frightened them into voting to resume the due rites for the tomb. He practically embraced the tomb of Leonidas the

[41] Popular assemblies were often held in theaters.

[42] Mountain sacred to Dionysus between Attica and the Megarid.

[43] The Amphictyony, the sacred council of Delphi, regularly met at Thermopylae, also known as "Pylaea."

περιέβαλεν ἀγασθεὶς τὸν ἄνδρα. ἐπὶ δὲ τὸν κολωνὸν βαδίζων, ἐφ᾽ οὗ λέγονται Λακεδαιμόνιοι περιχωσθῆναι τοῖς τοξεύμασιν, ἤκουσε τῶν ὁμιλητῶν διαφερομένων ἀλλήλοις, ὅ τι εἴη τὸ ὑψηλότατον τῆς Ἑλλάδος, παρεῖχε δὲ ἄρα τὸν λόγον ἡ Οἴτη τὸ ὄρος ἐν ὀφθαλμοῖς οὖσα, καὶ ἀνελθὼν ἐπὶ τὸν λόφον, "ἐγὼ" ἔφη "τὸ ὑψηλότατον τοῦτο ἡγοῦμαι, οἱ γὰρ ἐνταῦθα ὑπὲρ ἐλευθερίας ἀποθανόντες ἀντανήγαγον αὐτὸ τῇ Οἴτῃ καὶ ὑπὲρ πολλοὺς Ὀλύμπους ἦραν. ἐγὼ δὲ ἄγαμαι μὲν καὶ τούσδε τοὺς ἄνδρας, τὸν δὲ Ἀκαρνᾶνα Μεγιστίαν καὶ πρὸ τούτων, ἃ γὰρ πεισομένους ἐγίγνωσκε, τούτων ἐπεθύμησε κοινωνῆσαι τοῖς ἀνδράσιν, οὐ τὸ ἀποθανεῖν δείσας, ἀλλὰ τὸ μετὰ τοιῶνδε μὴ τεθνάναι."

24. Ἐπεφοίτησε δὲ καὶ τοῖς Ἑλληνικοῖς ἱεροῖς πᾶσι, τῷ τε Δωδωναίῳ καὶ τῷ Πυθικῷ καὶ τῷ ἐν Ἀβαῖς, ἐς Ἀμφιάρεώ τε καὶ Τροφωνίου ἐβάδισε, καὶ ἐς τὸ Μουσεῖον τὸ ἐν Ἑλικῶνι ἀνέβη. φοιτῶντι δὲ ἐς τὰ ἱερὰ καὶ διορθουμένῳ αὐτὰ ξυνεφοίτων μὲν οἱ ἱερεῖς, ἠκολούθουν δὲ οἱ γνώριμοι, λόγων τε κρατῆρες ἵσταντο καὶ ἠρύοντο αὐτῶν οἱ διψῶντες. ὄντων δὲ καὶ Ὀλυμπίων καὶ καλούντων αὐτὸν Ἠλείων ἐπὶ κοινωνίαν τοῦ ἀγῶνος, "δοκεῖτέ μοι" ἔφη "διαβάλλειν τὴν τῶν Ὀλυμπίων δόξαν, πρεσβειῶν δεόμενοι πρὸς τοὺς αὐτόθεν[18] ἥξοντας."

2 Γενόμενος δὲ κατὰ τὸν Ἰσθμόν, μυκησαμένης τῆς περὶ τὸ Λέχαιον θαλάττης, "οὗτος" εἶπεν "ὁ αὐχὴν τῆς

[18] αὐτόθεν Rsk.: αὐτόθι

Spartiate in his admiration for the hero. When he came to the hill where they say the Spartans were buried under the arrows, he heard his companions arguing among themselves as to the highest point in Greece (the subject had apparently been supplied by Mount Oeta which was in view). Climbing the hillock, Apollonius said, "I myself think this the highest point, since those who died for liberty here made it the equal of Oeta, and raised it above many an Olympus. And while I admire these heroes, I admire the Acarnanian Megistias even more, for although he knew what they were going to suffer, he wanted to share it with the heroes, not fearing death, but a death apart from men such as this."[44]

24. He also visited all the Greek sanctuaries, at Dodona, Delphi, and Abae, and walked to those of Amphiaraus and Trophonius,[45] and climbed up to the shrine of the Muses on Helicon. As he visited the holy sites and made improvements, he was accompanied by the priests, and followed by his pupils; there were veritable punch bowls of discourse, from which the thirsty drew. It was the time of the Olympics, and the Eleians invited him to participate in the festival, but he said: "You seem to me to degrade the repute of the Olympics if you need embassies to those coming by their own choice."

And when he was at the Isthmus, and a roar arose from 2
the sea off Lechaeum, he said, "This neck of land will be

[44] Megistias the seer, though foreseeing the Greek defeat of the Greeks at Thermopylae, refused to desert.

[45] Abae: city of Phocis. Sanctuaries of Amphiaraus and Trophonius: Oropus and Lebadea.

γῆς τετμήσεται, μᾶλλον δὲ οὔ." εἶχε δὲ αὐτῷ καὶ τοῦτο πρόρρησιν τῆς μικρὸν ὕστερον περὶ τὸν Ἰσθμὸν τομῆς, ἣν μετὰ ἔτη ἑπτὰ Νέρων διενοήθη· τὰ γὰρ βασίλεια ἐκλιπὼν ἐς τὴν Ἑλλάδα ἀφίκετο κηρύγμασιν ὑποθήσων ἑαυτὸν Ὀλυμπικοῖς τε καὶ Πυθικοῖς, ἐνίκα δὲ καὶ Ἰσθμοῖ· αἱ δὲ νῖκαι ἦσαν κιθαρῳδοὶ[19] καὶ κήρυκες, ἐνίκα δὲ καὶ τραγῳδοὺς ἐν Ὀλυμπίᾳ. τότε λέγεται καὶ τῆς περὶ τὸν Ἰσθμὸν καινοτομίας ἅψασθαι, περίπλουν αὐτὸν ἐργαζόμενος καὶ τὸν Αἰγαῖον τῷ Ἀδρίᾳ ξυμβάλλων, ὡς μὴ πᾶσα ναῦς ὑπὲρ Μαλέαν πλέοι, κομίζοιντό τε αἱ πολλαὶ διὰ τοῦ ῥήγματος ξυντέμνουσαι τὰς περιβολὰς τοῦ πλοῦ.

3 Πῇ δὲ ἀπέβη τὸ τοῦ Ἀπολλωνίου λόγιον; ἡ ὀρυχὴ τὴν ἀρχὴν ἀπὸ Λεχαίου λαβοῦσα στάδια προὔβη ἴσως τέτταρα ξυνεχῶς ὀρυττόντων, σχεῖν δὲ λέγεται Νέρων τὴν τομὴν οἱ μὲν Αἰγυπτίων φιλοσοφησάντων αὐτῷ τὰς θαλάττας καὶ τὸ ὑπὲρ Λεχαίου πέλαγος ὑπερχυθὲν ἀφανιεῖν εἰπόντων τὴν Αἴγιναν, οἱ δὲ νεώτερα περὶ τῇ ἀρχῇ δείσαντα. τοιοῦτον μὲν δὴ τοῦ Ἀπολλωνίου τὸ τὸν Ἰσθμὸν τετμήσεσθαι καὶ οὐ τετμήσεσθαι.

25. Ἐν Κορίνθῳ δὲ φιλοσοφῶν ἐτύγχανε τότε Δημήτριος ἀνὴρ ξυνειληφὼς ἅπαν τὸ ἐν Κυνικῇ κράτος, οὗ Φαβωρῖνος ὕστερον ἐν πολλοῖς τῶν ἑαυτοῦ λόγων

[19] κιθαρῳδοὶ Rsk.: κιθαρῳδίαι

cut, or rather not cut." This in fact was his prophecy of the cutting of the Isthmus not long after. Nero conceived the idea seven years later, when he left his capital and arrived in Greece, intending to subject himself to the rules of the Olympic and Pythian games, though he also won at the Isthmia. His victories were in the lyre-playing and heraldic divisions, and even in tragedy at the Olympics.[46] They say he also started on his excavation project at the Isthmus at that time, in order to make it navigable and to join the Aegean to the Adriatic. In that way, not all ships would have to sail around Malea, but most could travel through the canal, lessening the circuitousness of the journey.

What was the fulfillment of Apollonius's prophecy? 3
The digging started from Lechaeum[47] and went some four stades with continuous excavation. But Nero halted the procedure, it is said either because Egyptians who studied the two seas for him said that the sea at Lechaeum would flood and overwhelm Aegina, or because he was afraid of an uprising against his rule. That then was the meaning of Apollonius's saying that the Isthmus would be cut and not cut.

25. At that time, Demetrius was lecturing in Corinth, a man who incorporated all the strength of Cynic philosophy, and later was mentioned with considerable respect by

[46] Nero toured Greece from late 66 to early 68, and took part in the four major contests. He also began to cut a canal through the Isthmus, but left it unfinished because of rebellion in the West.

[47] Port of Corinth on the Corinthian Gulf.

οὐκ ἀγεννῶς ἐπεμνήσθη. παθὼν δὲ πρὸς τὸν Ἀπολλώνιον, ὅπερ φασὶ τὸν Ἀντισθένην πρὸς τὴν τοῦ Σωκράτους σοφίαν παθεῖν, εἵπετο αὐτῷ μαθητιῶν καὶ προσκείμενος τοῖς λόγοις, καὶ τῶν αὐτῷ γνωρίμων τοὺς εὐδοκιμωτέρους ἐπὶ τὸν Ἀπολλώνιον ἔτρεπεν, ὧν καὶ Μένιππος ἦν ὁ Λύκιος ἔτη μὲν γεγονὼς πέντε καὶ εἴκοσι, γνώμης δὲ ἱκανῶς ἔχων καὶ τὸ σῶμα εὖ κατεσκευασμένος, ἐῴκει γοῦν ἀθλητῇ καλῷ καὶ ἐλευθερίῳ τὸ εἶδος.

2 Ἐρᾶσθαι δὲ τὸν Μένιππον οἱ πολλοὶ ᾤοντο ὑπὸ γυναίου ξένου, τὸ δὲ γύναιον καλή τε ἐφαίνετο καὶ ἱκανῶς ἁβρὰ καὶ πλουτεῖν ἔφασκεν, οὐδὲν δὲ τούτων ἄρα ἀτεχνῶς ἦν, ἀλλὰ ἐδόκει πάντα. κατὰ γὰρ τὴν ὁδὸν τὴν ἐπὶ Κεγχρεὰς βαδίζοντι αὐτῷ μόνῳ φάσμα ἐντυχὸν γυνή τε ἐγένετο καὶ χεῖρα ξυνῆψεν ἐρᾶν αὐτοῦ πάλαι φάσκουσα, Φοίνισσα δὲ εἶναι καὶ οἰκεῖν ἐν προαστείῳ τῆς Κορίνθου, τὸ δεῖνα εἰποῦσα προάστειον, "ἐς ὃ ἑσπέρας" ἔφη "ἀφικομένῳ σοι ᾠδή τε ὑπάρξει ἐμοῦ ᾀδούσης καὶ οἶνος, οἷον οὔπω ἔπιες, καὶ οὐδὲ ἀντεραστὴς ἐνοχλήσει σε, βιώσομαι δὲ καλὴ ξὺν καλῷ."

3 Τούτοις ὑπαχθεὶς ὁ νεανίας, τὴν μὲν γὰρ ἄλλην φιλοσοφίαν ἔρρωτο, τῶν δὲ ἐρωτικῶν ἥττητο, ἐφοίτησε περὶ ἑσπέραν αὐτῇ καὶ τὸν λοιπὸν χρόνον ἐθάμιζεν, ὥσπερ παιδικοῖς, οὔπω ξυνεὶς τοῦ φάσματος. ὁ δὲ Ἀπολλώνιος ἀνδριαντοποιοῦ δίκην ἐς τὸν Μένιππον βλέπων ἐζωγράφει τὸν νεανίαν καὶ ἐθεώρει, κατα-

Favorinus in many of his discourses.[48] Apollonius had the same effect on him as they say the wisdom of Socrates had on Antisthenes:[49] he followed him, eager to learn and devoted to his lectures, and sent the more outstanding of his own pupils to Apollonius. Among these was Menippus of Lycia, twenty-five years old, well endowed with intelligence and physically well built, since his appearance suggested a handsome and well bred athlete.

It was generally believed that Menippus was the lover 2
of a foreign woman. This woman appeared to be beautiful and very refined, and claimed to be rich, but in fact she was none of these things at all: it was all a delusion. He had been walking alone along the road to Cenchreae[50] when a phantom met him in the shape of a woman. Taking his hand, she claimed to have been in love with him for a long time; she was Phoenician, and lived in a suburb of Corinth. Naming one of the suburbs, she said, "Come there this evening, and you will have a song sung by me, and wine such as you have never tasted. There will be no rival in your way, but we will live as a beautiful couple."

The youth was seduced by this, since despite his firm- 3
ness in other areas of philosophy, he had a weakness for love. He went to her house in the evening, and visited her often thereafter as if she was his boyfriend, not yet realizing she was a phantom. Apollonius looked over Menippus as a sculptor does, getting an impression and a view of him.

[48] Demetrius: Cynic prominent under Nero and Vespasian. Favorinus: sophist, philosopher, and prolific author of the second century.

[49] Ascetic follower of Socrates, sometimes regarded as the founder of Cynicism.

[50] Port on the Saronic Gulf.

γνοὺς δὲ αὐτὸν "σὺ μέντοι" εἶπεν "ὁ καλός τε καὶ ὑπὸ τῶν καλῶν γυναικῶν θηρευόμενος, ὄφιν θάλπεις καὶ σὲ ὄφις." θαυμάσαντος δὲ τοῦ Μενίππου "ὅτι γυνή σοι" ἔφη "ἐστὶν οὐ γαμετή. τί δέ; ἡγῇ ὑπ' αὐτῆς ἐρᾶσθαι;" "νὴ Δί'," εἶπεν "ἐπειδὴ διάκειται πρός με ὡς ἐρῶσα." "καὶ γήμαις δ' ἂν αὐτήν;" ἔφη. "χαρίεν γὰρ ἂν εἴη τὸ ἀγαπῶσαν γῆμαι." ἤρετο οὖν "πηνίκα οἱ γάμοι;" "θερμοὶ" ἔφη "καὶ ἴσως αὔριον."

4 Ἐπιφυλάξας οὖν τὸν τοῦ συμποσίου καιρὸν ὁ Ἀπολλώνιος καὶ ἐπιστὰς τοῖς δαιτυμόσιν ἄρτι ἥκουσι, "ποῦ" ἔφη "ἡ ἁβρά, δι' ἣν ἥκετε;" "ἐνταῦθα" εἶπεν ὁ Μένιππος καὶ ἅμα ὑπανίστατο ἐρυθριῶν. "ὁ δὲ ἄργυρος καὶ ὁ χρυσὸς καὶ τὰ λοιπά, οἷς ὁ ἀνδρὼν κεκόσμηται, ποτέρου ὑμῶν;" "τῆς γυναικός," ἔφη "τἀμὰ γὰρ τοσαῦτα" δείξας τὸν ἑαυτοῦ τρίβωνα. ὁ δὲ Ἀπολλώνιος "τοὺς Ταντάλου κήπους" ἔφη "οἴδατε,[20] ὡς ὄντες οὐκ εἰσί;" "παρ' Ὁμήρῳ γε," ἔφασαν "οὐ γὰρ ἐς Αἵδου γε καταβάντες." "τοῦτ'" ἔφη "καὶ τουτονὶ τὸν κόσμον ἡγεῖσθε, οὐ γὰρ ὕλη ἐστίν, ἀλλὰ ὕλης δόξα. ὡς δὲ γιγνώσκοιτε, ὃ λέγω, ἡ χρηστὴ νύμφη μία τῶν ἐμπουσῶν ἐστιν, ἃς λαμίας τε καὶ μορμολυκεῖα[21] οἱ πολλοὶ ἡγοῦνται. ἐρῶσι δ' αὗται καὶ ἀφροδισίων μέν, σαρκῶν δὲ μάλιστα ἀνθρωπείων ἐρῶσι καὶ παλεύουσι[22] τοῖς ἀφροδισίοις, οὓς ἂν ἐθέλωσι δαίσασθαι."

20 οἴδατε Rsk.: εἴδετε

21 μορμολυκεῖα Rsk.: μορμολυκίας

22 παλεύουσι Lobeck (Kay.): πάλλουσι

Then, sizing him up, he said, "Now, you are the beautiful boy that beautiful women chase. You are nursing a snake, and a snake is nursing you." Menippus was bewildered, and Apollonius said, "You have a woman who is not your wife. Well, do you think she is in love with you?" "Certainly," was the reply, "since she treats me as a woman in love would." "Would you marry her?" said Apollonius. "Yes, it would be a joy to marry a woman that loved you." So Apollonius asked, "When is the wedding?" "It is imminent," the boy replied, "tomorrow perhaps."

So Apollonius waited for the time of the wedding feast, 4
and joining the guests when they had just arrived, he asked "Where is the fine lady in whose honor you have come?" "Here," said Menippus, at the same time rising with a blush. "And the silver, the gold, and the other decorations of the banqueting hall, to which of you do they belong?" "To my wife," he replied, "since all I have is this," pointing to his philosopher's cloak. "Do you all know," asked Apollonius, "about Tantalus's gardens, which exist and yet do not exist?" "Yes," they said, "from Homer, not having been down to Hades."[51] "That," said Apollonius, "is how to regard this display. It is not material, but the appearance of matter. To prove to you what I mean, this excellent bride is one of the vampires, though most people think vampires are the same as sirens[52] and werewolves. Vampires also feel love, but they love human intercourse and human flesh above all, and use intercourse to catch those they want to devour."

[51] Homer, *Odyssey* 11.582–92.

[52] The Greek word is *lamia*, whence the title of Keats's poem.

5 Ἡ δὲ "εὐφήμει" ἔλεγε "καὶ ἄπαγε," καὶ μυσάττεσθαι ἐδόκει, ἃ ἤκουε, καί που καὶ ἀπέσκωπτε τοὺς φιλοσόφους, ὡς ἀεὶ ληροῦντας. ἐπεὶ μέντοι τὰ ἐκπώματα τὰ χρυσᾶ καὶ ὁ δοκῶν ἄργυρος ἀνεμιαῖα ἠλέγχθη, καὶ διέπτη τῶν ὀφθαλμῶν ἅπαντα, οἰνοχόοι τε καὶ ὀψοποιοὶ καὶ ἡ τοιαύτη θεραπεία πᾶσα ἠφανίσθησαν, ἐλεγχόμενοι ὑπὸ τοῦ Ἀπολλωνίου, δακρύοντι ἐῴκει τὸ φάσμα καὶ ἐδεῖτο μὴ βασανίζειν αὐτό, μηδὲ ἀναγκάζειν ὁμολογεῖν, ὅ τι εἴη, ἐπικειμένου δὲ καὶ μὴ ἀνιέντος ἔμπουσά τε εἶναι ἔφη καὶ πιαίνειν ἡδοναῖς τὸν Μένιππον ἐς βρῶσιν τοῦ σώματος, τὰ γὰρ καλὰ τῶν σωμάτων καὶ νέα σιτεῖσθαι ἐνόμιζεν, ἐπειδὴ ἀκραιφνὲς αὐτοῖς τὸ αἷμα.

6 Τοῦτον τὸν λόγον γνωριμώτατον τῶν Ἀπολλωνίου τυγχάνοντα ἐξ ἀνάγκης ἐμήκυνα, γιγνώσκουσι μὲν γὰρ πλείους αὐτόν, ἅτε καθ' Ἑλλάδα μέσην πραχθέντα, ξυλλήβδην δὲ αὐτὸν παρειλήφασιν, ὅτι ἕλοι ποτὲ ἐν Κορίνθῳ λάμιαν, ὅ τι μέντοι πράττουσαν καὶ ὅτι ὑπὲρ Μενίππου, οὔπω γιγνώσκουσιν, ἀλλὰ Δάμιδί τε καὶ ἐκ τῶν ἐκείνου λόγων ἐμοὶ εἴρηται.

26. Τότε καὶ πρὸς Βάσσον διηνέχθη τὸν ἐκ τῆς Κορίνθου, πατραλοίας γὰρ οὗτος καὶ ἐδόκει καὶ ἐπεπίστευτο, σοφίαν δὲ ἑαυτοῦ κατεψεύδετο καὶ χαλινὸς οὐκ ἦν ἐπὶ τῇ γλώττῃ. λοιδορούμενον δὲ αὐτὸν ἐπέσχεν ὁ Ἀπολλώνιος οἷς τε ἐπέστειλεν οἷς τε διελέχθη κατ' αὐτοῦ. πᾶν γάρ, ὅπερ ὡς ἐς πατραλοίαν ἔλεγεν, ἀληθὲς ἐδόκει, μὴ γὰρ ἄν ποτε τοιόνδε ἄνδρα ἐς λοιδορίαν ἐκπεσεῖν, μηδ' ἂν εἰπεῖν τὸ μὴ ὄν.

“Watch your language, and be off with you,” the woman 5
said, pretending to find what he said repulsive, and also making fun of philosophers as perpetual talkers of nonsense. But then the golden cups and the apparent silver proved illusory, and all faded from sight, and the cupbearers, cooks, and all such servants vanished under Apollonius’s scrutiny. Whereupon the phantom pretended to weep, begging him not to interrogate it or force it to confess its true nature. But Apollonius insisted relentlessly, until it confessed it was a vampire, fattening Menippus with pleasures in order to feed on his body, since it was its custom to devour beautiful young bodies because their blood was fresh.

This is the most famous of the stories about Apollonius, 6
but I have been obliged to dwell on it, since most people know of it as something that happened in the middle of Greece, and yet they have only heard a general account, that he once unmasked a siren in Corinth; they do not know at all how it behaved and that he acted to save Menippus. Damis, however, has told the tale, and so have I from his account.

26. That was also when he quarreled with Bassus of Corinth, who both seemed and was believed to be a parricide, though he falsely claimed wisdom and had an unbridled tongue. Abusive as he was, Apollonius stopped him, both by the letters and by the lectures he directed against him. For everything that he said of him as a parricide seemed true, since it was impossible that such a Master should descend to abuse, or say something false.[53]

[53] Enemy of Apollonius, mentioned only here in the *Life*, though several of the letters are written to or about him.

27. Τὰ δὲ ἐν Ὀλυμπίᾳ τοῦ ἀνδρὸς τοιαῦτα. ἀνιόντι τῷ Ἀπολλωνίῳ ἐς Ὀλυμπίαν ἐνέτυχον Λακεδαιμονίων πρέσβεις ὑπὲρ ξυνουσίας, Λακωνικὸν δὲ οὐδὲν περὶ αὐτοὺς ἐφαίνετο, ἀλλ' ἁβρότερον Λυδῶν[23] εἶχον καὶ συβάριδος μεστοὶ ἦσαν. ἰδὼν δὲ ἄνδρας λείους τὰ σκέλη, λιπαροὺς τὰς κόμας, καὶ μηδὲ γενείοις χρωμένους, ἀλλὰ καὶ τὴν ἐσθῆτα μαλακούς, τοιαῦτα πρὸς τοὺς ἐφόρους ἐπέστειλεν, ὡς ἐκείνους κήρυγμα ποιήσασθαι δημοσίᾳ τήν τε πίτταν τῶν βαλανείων ἐξαιροῦντας, καὶ τὰς παρατιλτρίας ἐξελαύνοντας, ἐς τὸ ἀρχαῖόν τε καθισταμένους πάντα, ὅθεν παλαῖστραί τε ἀνήβησαν καὶ σπουδαὶ καὶ τὰ φιλίτια ἐπανῆλθε, καὶ ἐγένετο ἡ Λακεδαίμων ἑαυτῇ ὁμοία. μαθὼν δὲ αὐτοὺς τὰ οἴκοι διορθουμένους ἔπεμψεν ἐπιστολὴν ἀπ' Ὀλυμπίας βραχυτέραν τῆς Λακωνικῆς σκυτάλης. ἔστι δὲ ἥδε· "Ἀπολλώνιος ἐφόροις χαίρειν. Ἀνδρῶν μὲν τὸ μὴ ἁμαρτάνειν, γενναίων δὲ τὸ καὶ ἁμαρτάνοντας αἰσθέσθαι."

28. Ἰδὼν δὲ ἐς τὸ ἕδος τὸ ἐν Ὀλυμπίᾳ "χαῖρε," εἶπεν "ἀγαθὲ Ζεῦ, σὺ γὰρ οὕτω τι ἀγαθός, ὡς καὶ σαυτοῦ κοινωνῆσαι τοῖς ἀνθρώποις." ἐξηγήσατο δὲ καὶ τὸν χαλκοῦν Μίλωνα καὶ τὸν λόγον τοῦ περὶ αὐτὸν σχήματος. ὁ γὰρ Μίλων ἑστάναι μὲν ἐπὶ δίσκου δοκεῖ τὼ πόδε ἄμφω συμβεβηκώς, ῥόαν δὲ ξυνέχει τῇ ἀριστερᾷ, ἡ δεξιὰ δέ, ὀρθοὶ τῆς χειρὸς ἐκείνης οἱ δάκτυλοι καὶ οἷον διείροντος. οἱ μὲν δὴ κατ' Ὀλυμ-

[23] Λυδῶν Valck.: αὐτῶν

27. The Master's actions in Olympia were the following. As Apollonius was going up to Olympia he was met by Spartan ambassadors inviting him to visit, but there was nothing Spartan about their appearance; they were daintier than Lydians and full of foppery. Seeing men with smooth legs and well oiled hair, not even wearing beards, with soft clothing, he sent such a letter to the ephors that they issued a public edict in which they forbade the use of pitch in bathhouses, expelled female depilators, and returned everything to the ancient standard. This led to a regeneration of the wrestling places and of serious pursuits, the common meals came back, and Sparta looked like itself. When Apollonius heard that they were correcting their local habits, he wrote them a letter from Olympia which was briefer than a Spartan telegram, and ran as follows: "Apollonius to the Spartans, greetings. It is the mark of true men not to err, but of noble ones also to realize their errors."[54]

28. Looking towards the cult statue in Olympia, he said, "Hail, kindly Zeus, since you so are so kind as even to make yourself available to humans." He also explained the bronze statue of Milo and the reason for its pose.[55] Milo can be seen standing on a discus with both his feet together, grasping a pomegranate in his left hand, while he holds the fingers of his right one straight as if he were jabbing with them. The scholars at Olympia and in Arcadia

[54] Also preserved as Letter 42a.

[55] Milo of Croton, sixth-century wrestler and the most famous of Greek athletes. Cf. Pausanias, *Description of Greece* 6.14.5–8.

πίαν τε καὶ Ἀρκαδίαν λόγιοι[24] τὸν ἀθλητὴν ἱστοροῦσι τοῦτον ἄτρεπτον γενέσθαι καὶ μὴ ἐκβιβασθῆναί ποτε τοῦ χώρου, ἐν ᾧ ἔστη, δηλοῦσθαι δὲ τὸ μὲν ἀπρὶξ τῶν δακτύλων ἐν τῇ ξυνοχῇ τῆς ῥόας, τὸ δὲ μηδ᾽ ἂν σχισθῆναί ποτ᾽ ἀπ᾽ ἀλλήλων αὐτούς, εἴ τις πρὸς ἕνα αὐτῶν ἁμιλλῷτο, τῷ τὰς διαφυὰς ἐν ὀρθοῖς τοῖς δακτύλοις εὖ ξυνηρμόσθαι, τὴν ταινίαν δέ, ἣν ἀναδεῖται, σωφροσύνης ἡγοῦνται ξύμβολον.

2 Ὁ δὲ Ἀπολλώνιος σοφῶς μὲν εἶπεν ἐπινενοῆσθαι ταῦτα, σοφώτερα δὲ εἶναι τὰ ἀληθέστερα. "ὡς δὲ γιγνώσκοιτε τὸν νοῦν τοῦ Μίλωνος, Κροτωνιᾶται τὸν ἀθλητὴν τοῦτον ἱερέα ἐστήσαντο τῆς Ἥρας. τὴν μὲν δὴ μίτραν ὅ τι χρὴ νοεῖν, τί ἂν ἐξηγοίμην ἔτι, μνημονεύσας ἱερέως ἀνδρός; ἡ ῥόα δὲ μόνη φυτῶν τῇ Ἥρᾳ φύεται, ὁ δὲ ὑπὸ τοῖς ποσὶ δίσκος, ἐπὶ ἀσπιδίου βεβηκὼς ὁ ἱερεὺς τῇ Ἥρᾳ εὔχεται, τουτὶ δὲ καὶ ἡ δεξιὰ σημαίνει, τὸ δὲ ἔργον τῶν δακτύλων καὶ τὸ μήπω διεστὼς τῇ ἀρχαίᾳ ἀγαλματοποιίᾳ προσκείσθω."

29. Παρατυγχάνων δὲ τοῖς δρωμένοις ἀπεδέχετο τῶν Ἠλείων, ὡς ἐπεμελοῦντό τε αὐτῶν καὶ ξὺν κόσμῳ ἔδρων, μεῖόν τε οὐδὲν ἢ οἱ ἀγωνιούμενοι τῶν ἀθλητῶν κρίνεσθαι ᾤοντο, καὶ μήθ᾽ ἑκόντες τι μήτ᾽ ἄκοντες ἁμαρτάνειν προὐνοοῦντο. ἐρομένων δ᾽ αὐτὸν τῶν ἑταίρων, τίνας Ἠλείους περὶ τὴν διάθεσιν τῶν Ὀλυμπίων ἡγοῖτο, "εἰ μὲν σοφούς," ἔφη "οὐκ οἶδα, σοφιστὰς μέντοι."

relate that this athlete was invincible, and never gave up the ground on which he stood. His grasp of the pomegranate symbolized the strength of his fingers; and the impossibility of prying them apart, even if one were to tug at a single one of them, was conveyed by the fact that the spaces between the fingers fit tightly when the fingers are straight; and the ribbon which he wears they explain as a symbol of his self-control.

Apollonius however said that this was a clever conceit, 2
but the truer version was cleverer still. "If you want to know the explanation for Milo's statue, the Crotoniates appointed this athlete priest of Hera. Why should I go on to explain the symbolism of the ribbon, when I have mentioned one who was a priest? The pomegranate is the only fruit sacred to Hera, while the discus is beneath his feet because the priest prays to Hera standing on a small shield, and prayer also is the meaning of the right hand. The attitude of the fingers, and the fact that they are joined together, we should ascribe to the technique of ancient sculptors."

29. Apollonius took part in the rites, and approved the Eleians for taking care of them and performing them with propriety, and because they considered themselves to be on trial no less than the competing athletes, and made sure to commit no errors either voluntary or accidental. When his companions asked him what he thought of the Eleians in their running of the Olympics, he replied, "I do not know if they are wise, but they certainly pretend to wisdom."

---

24 λόγιοι Rsk.: λόγοι

30. Ὡς δὲ καὶ διεβέβλητο πρὸς τοὺς οἰομένους ξυγγράφειν καὶ ἀμαθεῖς ἡγεῖτο τοὺς ἁπτομένους λόγου μείζονος, ὑπάρχει μαθεῖν ἐκ τῶνδε. μειράκιον γὰρ δοκησίσοφον ἐντυχὸν αὐτῷ περὶ τὸ ἱερὸν "συμπροθυμήθητί μοι" ἔφη "αὔριον, ἀναγνώσομαι γάρ τι." τοῦ δὲ Ἀπολλωνίου ἐρομένου, ὅ τι ἀναγνώσοιτο, "λόγος" εἶπε "ξυντέτακταί μοι ἐς τὸν Δία." καὶ ἅμα ὑπὸ τῷ ἱματίῳ ἐπεδείκνυ αὐτὸν σεμνυνόμενος τῇ παχύτητι τοῦ βιβλίου. "τί οὖν" ἔφη "ἐπαινέσῃ τοῦ Διός; ἦ[25] τὸν Δία τὸν ἐνταῦθα καὶ τὸ μηδὲν εἶναι τῶν ἐν τῇ γῇ ὅμοιον;" "καὶ τοῦτο μέν," ἔφη "πολλὰ δὲ πρὸ τούτου καὶ ἐπὶ τούτῳ ἕτερα, καὶ γὰρ αἱ ὧραι καὶ τὰ ἐν τῇ γῇ καὶ τὰ ὑπὲρ τὴν γῆν, καὶ ἀνέμους εἶναι καὶ ἄστρα Διὸς πάντα."

2 Ὁ δὲ Ἀπολλώνιος "δοκεῖς μοι" εἶπεν "ἐγκωμιαστικός τις εἶναι σφόδρα." "διὰ τοῦτο" ἔφη "καὶ ποδάγρας ἐγκώμιόν τί μοι ξυντέτακται καὶ τοῦ τυφλόν τινα ἢ κωφὸν εἶναι." "ἀλλὰ μηδὲ τοὺς ὑδέρους" εἶπε "μηδὲ τοὺς κατάρρους ἀποκήρυττε τῆς ἑαυτοῦ σοφίας, εἰ βούλοιο ἐπαινεῖν τὰ τοιαῦτα, βελτίων δὲ ἔσῃ καὶ τοῖς ἀποθνήσκουσιν ἑπόμενος καὶ διιὼν ἐπαίνους τῶν νοσημάτων, ὑφ᾽ ὧν ἀπέθανον, ἧττον γὰρ ἐπ᾽ αὐτοῖς ἀνιάσονται πατέρες τε καὶ παῖδες καὶ οἱ ἀγχοῦ τῶν ἀποθανόντων." κεχαλινωμένον δὲ ἰδὼν τὸ μειράκιον ὑπὸ τοῦ λόγου "ὁ ἐγκωμιάζων," εἶπεν "ὦ ξυγγραφεῦ, πότερον ἃ οἶδεν ἐπαινέσεται ἄμεινον ἢ ἃ οὐκ οἶδεν;" "ἃ οἶδεν," ἔφη "πῶς γὰρ ἄν τις ἐπαινοῖ, ἃ οὐκ οἶδε;"

3 "Τὸν πατέρα οὖν ἤδη ποτὲ τὸν σαυτοῦ ἐπῄνεσας;"

30. How little esteem he had for self-proclaimed authors, and how ignorant he thought those who undertook subjects beyond their powers, is evident from the following. A superficially clever youth met him in the sanctuary and said, "Lend me your support tomorrow, since I am going to recite something." Apollonius asked what he was going to recite. "I have written a treatise on Zeus," the youth replied, at the same time pointing to it under his tunic, and priding himself on the thickness of the manuscript. "Which aspect of Zeus will you praise?" said Apollonius. "Will you praise the Zeus here, and the fact that that there is nothing equal to it on earth?" "Well, that too," was the reply, "but many things before that and others after it. You see, the seasons and everything on the earth and above it, the winds and the stars are all in Zeus's power."

"You seem to me very adept at speeches of praise," said 2
Apollonius. "Yes," the youth replied, "and so I have composed a *Praise of Gout* and a *Praise of Being Blind or Deaf*." "In that case," said Apollonius, "do not withhold your genius from dropsy or catarrh, if you want to praise such things as that. It would also do you good to follow the dead and recite praises of the diseases that killed them. That way parents and children and those close to the dead will feel less grief." Seeing the youth silenced by his words, he said, "When someone writes a speech of praise, my literary friend, will he be better at praising what he knows, or what he does not?" "What he knows," was the answer, "since how could one praise what he does not know?"

"Well then, have you written a *Praise of Father* yet?" "I 3

25 ἦ Jon.: ἣ

"ἐβουλήθην," εἶπεν "ἀλλ' ἐπεὶ μέγας τε μοι δοκεῖ καὶ γενναῖος, ἀνθρώπων τε ὧν οἶδα κάλλιστος, οἶκόν τε ἱκανὸς οἰκῆσαι καὶ σοφίᾳ ἐς πάντα χρῆσθαι, παρῆκα τὸν ἐς αὐτὸν ἔπαινον, ὡς μὴ αἰσχύνοιμι τὸν πατέρα λόγῳ ἥττονι." δυσχεράνας οὖν ὁ Ἀπολλώνιος, τουτὶ δὲ πρὸς τοὺς φορτικοὺς τῶν ἀνθρώπων ἔπασχεν, "εἶτα," ἔφη "ὦ κάθαρμα, τὸν μὲν πατέρα τὸν σεαυτοῦ, ὃν ἴσα καὶ σεαυτὸν γιγνώσκεις, οὐκ ἄρ'[26] οἴει πότ' ἂν ἱκανῶς ἐπαινέσαι, τὸν δ' ἀνθρώπων καὶ θεῶν πατέρα καὶ δημιουργὸν τῶν ὅλων, ὅσα περὶ ἡμᾶς καὶ ὑπὲρ ἡμᾶς ἐστιν, εὐκόλως οὕτως ἐγκωμιάζων οὔθ', ὃν ἐπαινεῖς, δέδιας, οὔτε ξυνίης ἐς λόγον καθιστάμενος μείζονα ἀνθρώπου;"

31. Αἱ δὲ ἐν Ὀλυμπίᾳ διαλέξεις τῷ Ἀπολλωνίῳ περὶ τῶν χρησιμωτάτων ἐγίγνοντο, περὶ σοφίας τε καὶ ἀνδρείας καὶ σωφροσύνης καὶ καθάπαξ, ὁπόσαι ἀρεταί εἰσι· περὶ τούτων ἀπὸ τῆς κρηπῖδος τοῦ νεὼ διελέγετο πάντας ἐκπλήττων οὐ ταῖς διανοίαις μόνον, ἀλλὰ καὶ ταῖς ἰδέαις τοῦ λόγου. περιστάντες δὲ αὐτὸν οἱ Λακεδαιμόνιοι ξένον τε παρὰ τῷ Διὶ ἐποιοῦντο καὶ τῶν οἴκοι νέων πατέρα, βίου τε νομοθέτην καὶ γερόντων γέρας. ἐρομένου δὲ Κορινθίου τινὸς κατὰ ἀχθηδόνα, εἰ καὶ θεοφάνια αὐτῷ ἄξουσι, "ναὶ[27] τὼ Σιώ," ἔφη, "ἕτοιμά γε." ὁ δὲ Ἀπολλώνιος ἀπήγαγεν αὐτοὺς τῶν τοιούτων, ὡς μὴ φθονοῖτο.

2 Ἐπεὶ δὲ ὑπερβὰς τὸ Ταΰγετον εἶδεν ἐνεργὸν Λακεδαίμονα καὶ τὰ τοῦ Λυκούργου πάτρια εὖ πράττοντα, οὐκ ἀηδὲς ἐνόμισε τὸ καὶ τοῖς τέλεσι τῶν

wanted to," the youth replied, "but I think him great and noble, the handsomest man I know, skillful in managing a household and in applying his wisdom to everything, so I gave up trying to praise him, not wanting to dishonor my father with an inadequate speech." Apollonius grew angry, as he did with pretentious people, and said, "Why, you good-for-nothing, you do not think you could praise your father properly in a speech, when you know him as well as you do yourself. And yet when you so lightly praise the father of gods and men, the architect of the universe that is around us and above us, do you not feel afraid of him who is your theme? Do you not realize that you are taking on a subject beyond human power?"

31. Apollonius's lectures in Olympia were on very useful subjects, wisdom, courage, chastity, in short every virtue that there is, and on these he lectured from the steps of the temple, amazing everyone not just by his ideas but also by the way he expressed his thoughts. The Spartans surrounded him and made him a guest in the sanctuary of Zeus, a father of the local youths, a legislator of their way of life, and a glory of their senior citizens. A Corinthian asked them malevolently whether they were also going to celebrate a divine epiphany for him, and they replied, "By tha Guids, wee're riddy." But Apollonius discouraged them from such ideas in order to avoid envy.

After crossing Taygetus, however, and seeing Sparta in 2
action, and the customs of Lycurgus in good train, he took no small pleasure in meeting with the Spartan magistrates

---

26 ἄρ᾽ Kay.: ἂν
27 ναὶ Cob.: νὴ

Λακεδαιμονίων ξυγγενέσθαι περὶ ὧν ἐρωτᾶν ἐβούλοντο. ἤροντο οὖν ἀφικόμενον, πῶς θεοὶ θεραπευτέοι, ὁ δὲ εἶπεν "ὡς δεσπόται." πάλιν ἤροντο, πῶς ἥρωες· "ὡς πατέρες." τρίτον δὲ ἐρομένων, πῶς δὲ ἄνθρωποι· "οὐ Λακωνικὸν" ἔφη "τὸ ἐρώτημα." ἤροντο καὶ ὅ τι ἡγοῖτο τοὺς παρ᾽ αὐτοῖς νόμους, ὁ δὲ εἶπεν "ἀρίστους διδασκάλους, οἱ διδάσκαλοι δὲ εὐδοκιμήσουσιν, ἢν οἱ μαθηταὶ μὴ ῥᾳθυμῶσιν." ἐρομένων δ᾽ αὐτῶν, τί περὶ ἀνδρείας ξυμβουλεύοι, "καὶ τί" ἔφη "τῇ ἀνδρείᾳ χρήσεσθε;"

32. Ἐτύγχανε δὲ περὶ τὸν χρόνον τοῦτον νεανίας Λακεδαιμόνιος αἰτίαν ἔχων παρ᾽ αὐτοῖς, ὡς ἀδικῶν περὶ τὰ ἤθη. Καλλικρατίδα μὲν γὰρ τοῦ περὶ Ἀργινούσας ναυαρχήσαντος ἦν ἔκγονος, ναυκληρίας δὲ ἤρα καὶ οὐ προσεῖχε τοῖς κοινοῖς, ἀλλ᾽ ἐς Καρχηδόνα ἐξέπλει καὶ Σικελίαν ναῦς πεποιημένος. ἀκούσας οὖν κρίνεσθαι αὐτὸν ἐπὶ τούτῳ, δεινὸν ᾠήθη περιϊδεῖν τὸν νεανίαν ὑπαχθέντα ἐς δίκην, καὶ "ὦ λῷστε," ἔφη "τί πεφροντικὼς περίει[28] καὶ μεστὸς ἐννοίας;" "ἀγὼν" εἶπεν "ἐπήγγελταί μοι δημόσιος, ἐπειδὴ πρὸς ναυκληρίαις εἰμὶ καὶ τὰ κοινὰ οὐ πράττω." "πατὴρ δέ σοι ναύκληρος ἐγένετο ἢ πάππος;" "ἄπαγε," εἶπε "γυμνασίαρχοι τε καὶ ἔφοροι καὶ πατρονόμοι πάντες, Καλλικρατίδας δὲ ὁ πρόγονος καὶ τῶν ναυαρχησάντων ἐγένετο." "μῶν" ἔφη "τὸν ἐν Ἀργινούσαις λέγεις;" "ἐκεῖνον" εἶπε "τὸν ἐν τῇ ναυαρχίᾳ ἀποθανόντα." "εἶτ᾽

[28] περίει Cob.: περίεις

on the questions they wanted to put to him. So when they asked him on his arrival how the gods should be worshiped, he replied, "As masters." They next asked, "And the heroes?" "As fathers." And when thirdly they asked, "And humans?" he said, "That is not a question for Spartans." They also asked him his opinion about their laws, and he said, "They are excellent teachers, but the teachers will be well spoken of if their pupils shun idleness." And when they asked him what advice he gave about courage, he said, "Well, what use will you have for courage?"

32. It so happened about this time that a young Spartan was formally accused there of an offense against custom. He was a descendant of Callicratidas, the admiral at Arginusae,[56] and had a passion for seafaring. He paid no attention to public affairs but sailed off to Carthage and Sicily in the ships he had built. Hearing that he was on trial for this, Apollonius thought it intolerable to allow the youth to be condemned, and said to him, "My good friend, why do you go around anxious and completely preoccupied?" The youth replied, "A civil charge has been brought against me, because I am engaged in seafaring and avoid public affairs." "Was your father or your grandfather a ship's captain?" "Quite the opposite," he replied, "they were all gymnasiarchs, ephors, and patronomoi, and my ancestor Callicratidas was actually an admiral." "You mean the Callicratidas of Arginusae?" said Apollonius. "Yes," said the other, "the one who died in the sea battle." "So

[56] Battle of 406 in which the Athenians marred their victory by failing to pick up survivors.

οὐ διέβαλέ σοι" εἶπε "τὴν θάλατταν ἡ τελευτὴ τοῦ προγόνου;" "μὰ Δί'," εἶπεν "οὐ γὰρ ναυμαχήσων γε πλέω."

2 "Ἀλλ' ἐμπόρων τε καὶ ναυκλήρων κακοδαιμονέστερόν τί ἐρεῖς ἔθνος; πρῶτον μὲν περινοστοῦσι, ζητοῦντες ἀγορὰν κακῶς πράττουσαν, εἶτα προξένοις καὶ καπήλοις ἀναμιχθέντες πωλοῦσί τε καὶ ὠνοῦνται,[29] καὶ τόκοις ἀνοσίοις τὰς αὑτῶν κεφαλὰς ὑποτιθέντες ἐς τὸ ἀρχαῖον σπεύδουσι, κἂν μὲν εὖ πράττωσιν, εὐπλοεῖ ἡ ναῦς καὶ πολὺν ποιοῦνται λόγον τοῦ μήτε ἑκόντες ἀνατρέψαι μήτε ἄκοντες, εἰ δὲ ἡ ἐμπορία πρὸς τὰ χρέα μὴ ἀναφέροιτο, μεταβάντες ἐς τὰ ἐφόλκια προσαράττουσι τὰς ναῦς καὶ τὸν ἑτέρων [ναῦται][30] βίον, θεοῦ ἀνάγκην εἰπόντες, ἀθεώτατα καὶ οὐδὲ ἄκοντες αὐτοὶ ἀφείλοντο.

3 "Εἰ δὲ καὶ μὴ τοιοῦτον ἦν τὸ θαλαττουργόν τε καὶ ναυτικὸν ἔθνος, ἀλλὰ τό γε Σπαρτιάτην ὄντα καὶ πατέρων γεγονότα, οἳ μέσην ποτὲ τὴν Σπάρτην ᾤκησαν, 'ἐν κοίλῃ νηὶ' κεῖσθαι, λήθην μὲν ἴσχοντα Λυκούργου τε καὶ Ἰφίτου, φόρτου δὲ μνήμονα καὶ ναυτικῆς ἀκριβολογίας, τίνος αἰσχύνης ἄπεστιν; εἰ γὰρ καὶ μηδὲν ἄλλο, τὴν γοῦν Σπάρτην αὐτὴν ἔδει ἐνθυμεῖσθαι, ὡς ὁπότε μὲν τῆς γῆς εἴχετο οὐρανομήκη δόξασαν, ἐπεὶ δὲ θαλάττης ἐπεθύμησε, βυθισθεῖσάν τε καὶ ἀφανισθεῖσαν οὐκ ἐν τῇ θαλάττῃ μόνον, ἀλλὰ καὶ ἐν τῇ γῇ."

4 Τούτοις τὸν νεανίαν οὕτω τι ἐχειρώσατο[31] τοῖς

your ancestor's death," said Apollonius, "did not turn you against the sea?" "Certainly not," said the youth, "since I do not sail as an admiral."

"But what more godforsaken class can you name than merchants and ship's captains? First of all, they sail around looking for a depressed market; they mingle with agents and retailers; they buy and sell, submitting their own persons to unholy rates of interest, and striving after their capital. If they prosper, the ship has a safe voyage, and they make a great thing of not having capsized it either deliberately or accidentally. But if their profit does not answer their investment, they climb into their lifeboats, wreck the ships, and pleading 'divine intervention' they personally deprive others of their lives, doing so with no regard for the god but on purpose. 2

"Even if the breed of seafarers and sailors were not of this kind, the idea that a Spartiate, the offspring of ancestors who once lived in the center of Sparta, should lie 'in a hollow ship' oblivious of Lycurgus and Iphitus,[57] and mindful only of his cargo and nautical expertise, all this is the depth of disgrace. For if nothing else, one should think of Sparta itself, and how when it clung to the land it seemed to rise as high as heaven, but when it became ambitious for the sea, it sank and disappeared not only on sea but on land too." 3

With such arguments he so won the youth over that he 4

[57] Lycurgus: legendary Spartan lawgiver. Iphitus: king of Elis, believed a contemporary of Lycurgus.

---

29 ὠνοῦνται Cob.: πωλοῦνται　　30 [ναῦται] secl. Kay.
31 τι ἐχειρώσατο West.: διεχειρώσατο

λόγοις, ὡς νεύσαντα αὐτὸν ἐς τὴν γῆν κλαίειν, ἐπεὶ τοσοῦτον ἤκουσεν ἀπολελεῖφθαι τῶν πατέρων, ἀποδόσθαι τε τὰς ναῦς, ἐν αἷς ἔζη. καθεστῶτα δὲ αὐτὸν ἰδὼν ὁ Ἀπολλώνιος καὶ τὴν γῆν ἀσπαζόμενον κατήγαγε παρὰ τοὺς ἐφόρους καὶ παρῃτήσατο τῆς δίκης.

33. Κἀκεῖνο τῶν ἐν Λακεδαίμονι· ἐπιστολὴ ἐκ βασιλέως Λακεδαιμονίοις ἧκεν ἐπίπληξιν ἐς τὸ κοινὸν αὐτῶν φέρουσα, ὡς ὑπὲρ τὴν ἐλευθερίαν ὑβριζόντων, ἐκ διαβολῶν δὲ τοῦ τῆς Ἑλλάδος ἄρχοντος ἐπέσταλτο αὐτοῖς ταῦτα. οἱ μὲν δὴ Λακεδαιμόνιοι ἀπορίᾳ εἴχοντο καὶ ἡ Σπάρτη πρὸς ἑαυτὴν ἤριζεν, εἴτε χρὴ παραιτουμένους τὴν ὀργὴν τοῦ βασιλέως εἴτε ὑπερφρονοῦντας ἐπιστέλλειν. πρὸς ταῦτα ξύμβουλον ἐποιοῦντο τὸν Ἀπολλώνιον τοῦ τῆς ἐπιστολῆς ἤθους, ὁ δέ, ὡς εἶδε διεστηκότας, παρῆλθέ τε ἐς τὸ κοινὸν αὐτῶν καὶ ὧδε ἐβραχυλόγησε· "Παλαμήδης εὗρε γράμματα οὐχ ὑπὲρ τοῦ γράφειν μόνον, ἀλλὰ καὶ ὑπὲρ τοῦ γιγνώσκειν, ἃ δεῖ μὴ γράφειν." οὕτω μὲν δὴ Λακεδαιμονίους ἀπῆγε τοῦ μήτε θρασεῖς μήτε δειλοὺς ὀφθῆναι.

34. Διατρίψας δ' ἐν τῇ Σπάρτῃ μετὰ τὴν Ὀλυμπίαν χρόνον, ὡς ἐτελεύτα ὁ χειμών, ἐπὶ Μαλέαν ἦλθεν ἀρχομένου ἦρος, ὡς ἐς τὴν Ῥώμην ἀφήσων. διανοουμένῳ δ' αὐτῷ ταῦτα ἐγένετο ὄναρ τοιόνδε· ἐδόκει γυναῖκα μεγίστην τε καὶ πρεσβυτάτην περιβάλλειν αὐτὸν καὶ δεῖσθαί οἱ ξυγγενέσθαι, πρὶν ἐς Ἰταλοὺς πλεῦσαι, Διὸς δὲ εἶναι ἡ τροφὸς ἔλεγε καὶ ἦν αὐτῇ στέφανος πάντ' ἔχων τὰ ἐκ γῆς καὶ θαλάττης. λογισμὸν δὲ αὐτῷ διδοὺς τῆς ὄψεως ξυνῆκεν, ὅτι πλευ-

hung his head and wept at having fallen so far short of his ancestors, and then sold the ships by which he had made his living. When Apollonius saw that he had settled down and embraced a life on land, he brought him before the ephors and obtained his acquittal from the charge.

33. Another incident in Sparta involved a letter that came from the emperor to the Spartans, rebuking their state for unruliness incompatible with their freedom. Now the slanders of the governor of Greece had caused this letter to be sent to them. The Spartans were in a quandary, and Sparta was divided within itself as to whether it should write placating the emperor's anger or despising it. They therefore called on Apollonius to advise them about the tone of their letter. When he saw their division, he came into their assembly and made this brief speech: "Palamedes discovered writing, not only so that we should write, but also so that we should know what not to write." In this way he saved the Spartans from appearing either rash or cowardly.

34. After staying in Sparta for a while after the Olympics, now that the winter was at an end, he came to Malea in early spring, intending to set sail for Rome. He was pondering this when he had the following dream. He dreamt that a very tall and venerable woman embraced him, and asked him to stay with her before sailing to Italy. She said she was the nurse of Zeus, and she wore a crown containing every product of land and sea. He thought the vision

στέα εἴη ἐς Κρήτην πρότερον, ἣν τροφὸν ἡγούμεθα τοῦ Διός, ἐπειδὴ ἐν ταύτῃ ἐμαιεύθη, ὁ δὲ στέφανος καὶ ἄλλην ἴσως δηλῶσαι[32] νῆσον.

2 Οὐσῶν δὲ ἐν Μαλέᾳ νεῶν πλειόνων, αἳ ἐς Κρήτην ἀφήσειν ἔμελλον, ἐνέβη ναῦν ἀποχρῶσαν τῷ κοινῷ· κοινὸν δὲ ἐκάλει τούς τε ἑταίρους καὶ τοὺς τῶν ἑταίρων δούλους, οὐδὲ γὰρ ἐκείνους παρεώρα. προσπλεύσας δὲ Κυδωνίᾳ καὶ παραπλεύσας ἐς Κνωσσὸν τὸν μὲν Λαβύρινθον ὃς ἐκεῖ δείκνυται (ξυνεῖχε δέ, οἶμαί, ποτε τὸν Μινώταυρον) βουλομένων ἰδεῖν τῶν ἑταίρων, ἐκείνοις μὲν ξυνεχώρει τοῦτο, αὐτὸς δὲ οὐκ ἂν ἔφη θεατὴς γενέσθαι τῆς ἀδικίας τοῦ Μίνω. προῄει δὲ ἐπὶ Γόρτυναν πόθῳ τῆς Ἴδης.

3 Ἀνελθὼν οὖν καὶ τοῖς θεολογουμένοις ἐντυχὼν ἐπορεύθη καὶ ἐς τὸ ἱερὸν τὸ Λεβηναῖον. ἔστι δὲ Ἀσκληπιοῦ καὶ ὥσπερ ἡ Ἀσία ἐς τὸ Πέργαμον, οὕτως ἐς τὸ ἱερὸν τοῦτο ξυνεφοίτα ἡ Κρήτη, πολλοὶ δὲ καὶ Λιβύων ἐς αὐτὸ περαιοῦνται· καὶ γὰρ τέτραπται πρὸς τὸ Λιβυκὸν πέλαγος κατὰ γοῦν τὴν Φαιστόν, ἔνθα τὴν πολλὴν ἀνείργει θάλατταν ὁ μικρὸς λίθος. Λεβηναῖον δὲ τὸ ἱερὸν ὠνομάσθαι φασίν, ἐπειδὴ ἀκρωτήριον ἐξ αὐτοῦ κατατείνει λέοντι εἰκασμένον, οἷα πολλὰ αἱ ξυντυχίαι τῶν πετρῶν ἀποφαίνουσι, μῦθόν τε ἐπὶ τῷ ἀκρωτηρίῳ ᾄδουσιν, ὡς λέων εἷς οὗτος γένοιτο τῶν ὑποζυγέντων[33] ποτὲ τῇ Ῥέᾳ.

4 Ἐνταῦθα διαλεγομένου ποτὲ τοῦ Ἀπολλωνίου περὶ μεσημβρίαν, διελέγετο δὲ πολλοῖς ἀνδράσιν, ὑφ᾽ ὧν τὸ ἱερὸν ἐθεραπεύετο, σεισμὸς ἀθρόως τῇ Κρήτῃ

over, and realized that he must sail first to Crete, which we consider the nurse of Zeus, since he was brought to birth there, but that the crown perhaps indicated another island.

There were several ships at Malea about to sail for Crete, and so he embarked on one large enough for his group. "Group" was what he called his companions and his companions' slaves, since he did not overlook these either. After putting in at Cydonia and sailing on to Cnossus, his companions wanted to see the labyrinth that is one of the sights there (I believe it once contained the Minotaur). But Apollonius said that he would not be a witness of Minos's injustice, and went on to Gortyn, eager to visit Ida. 2

After climbing it and visiting the sites of sacred history, he also traveled to the sanctuary of Leben. This is devoted to Asclepius, and just as the Asians flock to Pergamum, so the Cretans used to flock to this sanctuary. Many Africans cross over to it as well, since it faces the African sea in the region of Phaestus, where a small rock keeps back the mighty surge. They say that the sanctuary of Leben gets its name from the fact that a headland extends out from it in the shape of a lion.[58] Many such rock formations occur by chance, and a story is told about this headland that it was one of the lions once harnessed to Rhea's chariot. 3

Apollonius was lecturing here once about noontime, and doing so to many men worshipping in the sanctuary, when an earthquake suddenly struck Crete, thunder was 4

[58] The name "Leben" appears to derive from Phoenician *labi*, "lion." The headland is still called *Lionta*.

---

[32] δηλῶσαι Kay.: δηλώσει
[33] ὑποζυγέντων Cob.: ὑποζυγίων

προσέβαλε, βροντὴ δὲ οὐκ ἐκ νεφῶν ἀλλ᾽ ἐκ τῆς γῆς ὑπήχησεν, ἡ θάλαττα δὲ ὑπενόστησε στάδια ἴσως ἑπτά. καὶ οἱ μὲν πολλοὶ ἔδεισαν μὴ τὸ πέλαγος ὑποχωρῆσαν ἐπισπάσηται τὸ ἱερὸν καὶ ἀπενεχθῶσιν, ὁ δὲ Ἀπολλώνιος "θαρσεῖτε," ἔφη "ἡ γὰρ θάλαττα γῆν ἔτεκε." καὶ οἱ μὲν ᾤοντο αὐτὸν τὴν ὁμόνοιαν τῶν στοιχείων λέγειν, καὶ ὅτι μηδὲν ἂν ἡ θάλαττα νεώτερον ἐς τὴν γῆν ἐργάσαιτο, μετὰ δὲ ἡμέρας ὀλίγας ἀφικόμενοί τινες ἐκ τῆς Κυδωνιάτιδος ἤγγειλαν, ὅτι κατὰ τὴν ἡμέραν τε καὶ μεσημβρίαν, ἣν ἐγένετο ἡ διοσημία, νῆσος ἐκ τῆς θαλάττης ἀνεδόθη περὶ τὸν πορθμὸν τὸν διαρρέοντα Θήραν τε καὶ Κρήτην. ἐάσαντες οὖν λόγων μῆκος ἔλθωμεν καὶ ἐπὶ τὰς ἐν Ῥώμῃ σπουδάς, αἳ ἐγένοντο αὐτῷ μετὰ τὰ ἐν Κρήτῃ.

35. Νέρων οὐ ξυνεχώρει φιλοσοφεῖν, ἀλλὰ περίεργον αὐτῷ χρῆμα οἱ φιλοσοφοῦντες ἐφαίνοντο καὶ μαντικὴν συσκιάζοντες, καὶ ἤχθη ποτὲ ὁ τρίβων ἐς δικαστήριον, ὡς μαντικῆς σχῆμα. ἐῶ τοὺς ἄλλους, ἀλλὰ Μουσώνιος ὁ Βαβυλώνιος, ἀνὴρ Ἀπολλωνίου μόνου δεύτερος, ἐδέθη ἐπὶ σοφίᾳ καὶ ἐκεῖ μένων ἐκινδύνευσεν, ἀπέθανε δ᾽ ἂν τὸ ἐπὶ τῷ δήσαντι, εἰ μὴ σφόδρα ἔρρωτο.

36. Ἐν τοιαύτῃ καταστάσει φιλοσοφίας οὔσης ἔτυχε προσιὼν τῇ Ῥώμῃ, στάδια δὲ εἴκοσι καὶ ἑκατὸν ἀπέχων ἐνέτυχε Φιλολάῳ τῷ Κιτιεῖ περὶ τὸ νέμος τὸ ἐν τῇ Ἀρικίᾳ. ἦν δὲ ὁ Φιλόλαος τὴν μὲν γλῶτταν ξυγκείμενος, μαλακώτερος δὲ καρτερῆσαί τι. οὗτος

heard not from the clouds but from the earth, and the sea retreated for about seven stades. Most people were terrified, in case the sea as it retreated might carry off the sanctuary and sweep them away, but Apollonius said, "Take courage; the sea has given birth to land." They thought he meant the harmony of the elements, and that the sea would do nothing to change the face of the land. After a few days people arriving from the region of Cydonia reported that, at the very day and noontime when the portent had occurred, an island had risen from the sea in the strait that separates Thera and Crete. Well, let us not go into a long explanation, but come to the activities that occupied him in Rome after his stay in Crete.

35. Nero did not tolerate philosophy. Its practitioners he considered inquisitive creatures who concealed their practice of divination, and the philosopher's cloak was once brought to court as cover for divination. To mention only one man, Musonius of Babylon,[59] a man second only to Apollonius, was put into chains because of his wisdom, and while kept there was in danger of his life. His jailor would have let him die, if he had not been extremely resolute.

36. This was the situation of philosophy at the time when Apollonius was approaching Rome. When he was a hundred and twenty stades away from it, he met Philolaus of Citium near the grove of Aricia.[60] Philolaus, a practised speaker but too cowardly to endure any danger, was on

[59] Philosopher from Etruria, imprisoned by Nero (cf. V 19.2). "Of Babylon" is a mistake due either to Philostratus or to a scribe.

[60] Philolaus of Citium (Cyprus): unknown. Aricia, near Rome, had a famous grove of Diana.

ἀναλύων ἀπὸ τῆς Ῥώμης αὐτός τε ἐῴκει φεύγοντι, καὶ ὅτῳ ἐντύχοι φιλοσοφοῦντι παρεκελεύετο τὸ αὐτὸ πράττειν. προσειπὼν οὖν τὸν Ἀπολλώνιον ἐκέλευεν ἐκστῆναι τῷ καιρῷ, μηδὲ ἐπιφοιτᾶν τῇ Ῥώμῃ διαβεβλημένου τοῦ φιλοσοφεῖν, καὶ διηγεῖτο τὰ ἐκεῖ πραττόμενα θαμὰ ἐπιστρεφόμενος, μὴ ἐπακροῷτό τις αὐτοῦ κατόπιν. "σὺ δὲ καὶ χορὸν φιλοσόφων ἀναψάμενος" εἶπε "βαδίζεις φθόνου μεστός, οὐκ εἰδὼς τοὺς ἐπιτεταγμένους ταῖς πύλαις ὑπὸ Νέρωνος, οἳ ξυλλήψονταί σέ τε καὶ τούτους, πρὶν ἔσω γενέσθαι."

2 "Τί δ'," εἶπεν "ὦ Φιλόλαε, τὸν αὐτοκράτορα σπουδάζειν φασίν;" "ἡνιοχεῖ" ἔφη "δημοσίᾳ, καὶ ᾄδει παριὼν ἐς τὰ Ῥωμαίων θέατρα, καὶ μετὰ τῶν μονομαχούντων ζῇ, μονομαχεῖ δὲ καὶ αὐτὸς καὶ ἀποσφάττει." ὑπολαβὼν οὖν ὁ Ἀπολλώνιος "εἶτα", ἔφη "ὦ βέλτιστε, μεῖζόν τι ἡγῇ θέαμα ἀνδράσι πεπαιδευμένοις ἢ βασιλέα ἰδεῖν ἀσχημονοῦντα; θεοῦ μὲν γὰρ παίγνιον ἄνθρωπος" εἶπε "κατὰ τὴν Πλάτωνος δόξαν, βασιλεὺς δὲ ἀνθρώπου παίγνιον γιγνόμενος, καὶ χαριζόμενος τοῖς ὄχλοις τὴν ἑαυτοῦ αἰσχύνην, τίνας οὐκ ἂν παράσχοι λόγους τοῖς φιλοσοφοῦσι;"

3 "Νὴ Δί'," εἶπεν ὁ Φιλόλαος "εἴγε μετὰ τοῦ ἀκινδύνου γίγνοιτο. εἰ δὲ ἀπόλοιο ἀναχθεὶς καὶ Νέρων σε ὠμὸν φάγοι μηδὲν ἰδόντα ὧν πράττει, ἐπὶ πολλῷ ἔσται σοι τὸ ἐντυχεῖν αὐτῷ καὶ ἐπὶ πλείονι ἢ τῷ Ὀδυσσεῖ ἐγένετο, ὁπότε παρὰ τὸν Κύκλωπα ἦλθεν. ἀπώλεσε γὰρ πολλοὺς τῶν ἑταίρων ποθήσας ἰδεῖν αὐτὸν καὶ ἡττηθεὶς ἀτόπου καὶ ὠμοῦ θεάματος." ὁ δὲ

his way from Rome. He looked like a man running away, and urged every philosopher he met to do the same. Addressing Apollonius, he advised him to yield to circumstances and not visit Rome when philosophy was under an indictment; and as he described events there, he kept turning around in case someone was listening behind his back. "But you," he said, "have a whole string of philosophers attached to you, and are coming under especial disfavor. You do not know about the men that Nero has posted at the gates. They will arrest you and the others here before you get inside."

"What are the emperor's interests said to be, Philo- 2
laus?" asked Apollonius. "He races in public," was the reply, "he enters the Roman theaters as a singer, he lives with gladiators, and is a gladiator and a murderer himself." "Well, my friend," replied Apollonius, "what more profitable spectacle do you think educated men could have than to see an emperor who disgraces himself? Man is the plaything of god, as Plato taught us,[61] but if an emperor becomes the plaything of man, and degrades himself to please the masses, what reflections might he not prompt in lovers of wisdom?"

"Certainly," said Philolaus, "if it could be done without 3
danger, but suppose you die after your arrest, and Nero eats you raw before you have seen any of his acts? That will be a high price for meeting him, a higher price than Odysseus paid when he visited the Cyclops. He lost many of his comrades because he longed to see him and could not resist the monstrous, savage sight." Apollonius however

[61] *Laws* VII 803 C.

Ἀπολλώνιος "οἴει γὰρ" ἔφη "τοῦτον ἧττον ἐκτετυφλώσεσθαι[34] τοῦ Κύκλωπος, εἰ τοιαῦτα ἐργάζεται;" καὶ ὁ Φιλόλαος "πραττέτω μέν," εἶπεν "ὅ τι βούλεται, σὺ δὲ ἀλλὰ τούτους σῶζε."

37. Φωνῇ δὲ ταῦτα μείζονι ἔλεγε καὶ ἐῴκει κλᾴοντι. ἐνταῦθα δείσας ὁ Δάμις περὶ τοῖς νέοις, μὴ χείρους αὐτῶν γένοιντο ὑπὸ τῆς τοῦ Φιλολάου πτοίας, ἀπολαβὼν τὸν Ἀπολλώνιον "ἀπολεῖ" ἔφη "τοὺς νέους ὁ λαγὼς οὗτος, τρόμων καὶ ἀθυμίας ἀναπιμπλὰς πάντα." ὁ δὲ Ἀπολλώνιος "καὶ μὴν πολλῶν" ἔφη "ἀγαθῶν ὄντων, ἃ μηδ' εὐξαμένῳ μοι πολλάκις παρὰ τῶν θεῶν γέγονε, μέγιστον ἂν ἔγωγε φαίην ἀπολελαυκέναι τὸ νυνὶ τοῦτο. παραπέπτωκε γὰρ βάσανος τῶν νέων, ἣ σφόδρα ἐλέγξει τοὺς φιλοσοφοῦντάς τε αὐτῶν καὶ τοὺς ἕτερόν τι μᾶλλον ἢ τοῦτο πράττοντας."

2 Καὶ ἠλέγχθησαν αὐτίκα οἱ μὴ ἐρρωμένοι σφῶν, ὑπὸ γὰρ τῶν τοῦ Φιλολάου λόγων ἀπαχθέντες οἱ μὲν ἔφασαν νοσεῖν, οἱ δ' οὐκ εἶναι αὐτοῖς ἐφόδια, οἱ δὲ τῶν οἴκοι ἐρᾶν, οἱ δὲ ὑπὸ ὀνειράτων ἐκπεπλῆχθαι, καὶ περιῆλθεν ἐς ὀκτὼ ὁμιλητὰς ὁ Ἀπολλώνιος ἐκ τεττάρων καὶ τριάκοντα, οἳ ξυνεφοίτων αὐτῷ ἐς τὴν Ῥώμην. οἱ δ' ἄλλοι Νέρωνά τε καὶ φιλοσοφίαν ἀποδράντες φυγῇ ᾤχοντο.

38. Ξυναγαγὼν οὖν τοὺς περιλειφθέντας, ὧν καὶ Μένιππος ἦν ὁ ξυναλλάξας τῇ ἐμπούσῃ καὶ Διοσκορίδης ὁ Αἰγύπτιος καὶ Δάμις, "οὐ λοιδορήσομαι" ἔφη "τοῖς ἀπολελοιπόσιν ἡμᾶς, ἀλλ' ὑμᾶς ἐπαινέσομαι μᾶλλον, ὅτι ἄνδρες ἐστὲ ἐμοὶ ὅμοιοι, οὐδ', εἴ τις

said, "Do you think that this man is less likely to be blinded than the Cyclops was, if he does such things?" Philolaus replied, "He can do what he pleases, but you must at least preserve these people here."

37. As he said this, he raised his voice and seemed to shed tears. At this Damis feared for the young men, in case they were undone by Philolaus's panic. Taking Apollonius aside he said, "This hare will ruin the young men, infecting everything with his terror and despondency." Apollonius replied, "There are many blessings that the gods have sent me often without my even asking, but I would say that the greatest benefit is the present one. There has come to me a touchstone for the young men, and it will clearly distinguish which of them pursue philosophy, and which of them are interested in anything but that."

Immediately those of them who were irresolute were 2
shown up. Dismayed by Philolaus's words, some pleaded illness, others lack of provisions, others homesickness, others terrifying dreams, until Apollonius was reduced from thirty-four disciples to eight, who followed him to Rome, while the others ran as fast as they could away from Nero and philosophy.

38. Calling together those that remained, who included Menippus the vampire's betrothed, Dioscorides of Egypt, and Damis, Apollonius said, "I will not scold those who deserted us, but instead praise you for being true men of my own kind. And I will not think a man a coward for leaving in

---

34 ἐκτετυφλώσεσθαι Rsk.: ἐκτετυφλῶσθαι

Νέρωνα δείσας ἀπῆλθε, δειλὸν ἡγήσομαι τοῦτον, ἀλλ' εἴ τις τοῦ δέους τούτου κρείττων γίγνεται, φιλόσοφος ὑπ' ἐμοῦ προσειρήσεται, καὶ διδάξομαι αὐτόν, ὁπόσα οἶδα. δοκεῖ δή μοι πρῶτον μὲν εὔξασθαι τοῖς θεοῖς, δι' οὓς ταῦτα ἐπὶ νοῦν ἦλθεν ὑμῖν τε κἀκείνοις, ἔπειθ' ἡγεμόνας αὐτοὺς ποιεῖσθαι, θεῶν[35] γὰρ χωρὶς οὐδ' ἐν ἀλλοτρίᾳ[36] ἐσμέν.

2 "Παριτητέα ἐς πόλιν, ἣ τοσούτων τῆς οἰκουμένης μερῶν ἄρχει. πῶς οὖν ἂν παρέλθοι τις, εἰ μὴ ἐκεῖνοι ἡγοῖντο; καὶ ταῦτα τυραννίδος ἐν αὐτῇ καθεστηκυίας οὕτω χαλεπῆς, ὡς μὴ ἐξεῖναι σοφοῖς εἶναι. ἀνόητόν τε μηδενὶ δοκείτω τὸ θαρσεῖν ὁδόν, ἣν πολλοὶ τῶν φιλοσόφων φεύγουσιν, ἐγὼ γὰρ πρῶτον μὲν οὐδὲν ἂν ἡγοῦμαι φοβερὸν οὕτω γενέσθαι τῶν κατ' ἀνθρώπους, ὡς ἐκπλαγῆναί ποτε ὑπ' αὐτοῦ τὸν σοφόν, εἶτ' οὐδ' ἂν προθείην[37] ἀνδρείας[38] μελέτας, ἐὰν μὴ μετὰ κινδύνων γίγνοιντο.

3 "Καὶ ἄλλως ἐπελθὼν γῆν, ὅσην οὔπω τις ἀνθρώπων, θηρία μὲν Ἀράβιά τε καὶ Ἰνδικὰ πάμπολλα εἶδον, τὸ δὲ θηρίον τοῦτο, ὃ καλοῦσιν οἱ πολλοὶ τύραννον, οὔτε ὁπόσαι κεφαλαὶ αὐτῷ οἶδα, οὔτε εἰ γαμψώνυχόν τε καὶ καρχαρόδουν ἐστί. καίτοι πολιτικὸν μὲν εἶναι τὸ θηρίον τοῦτο λέγεται καὶ τὰ μέσα τῶν πόλεων οἰκεῖν, τοσούτῳ δὲ ἀγριώτερον διάκειται τῶν ὀρεινῶν τε καὶ ὑλαίων, ὅσῳ λέοντες μὲν καὶ παρδάλεις ἐνίοτε κολακευόμενοι ἡμεροῦνται καὶ μεταβάλλουσι τοῦ ἤθους, τουτὶ δὲ ὑπὸ τῶν καταψηχόντων

fear of Nero, but rather give the title of philosopher to anyone who shows himself superior to such fear, and I will teach him all I know. In my opinion, we should first thank the gods who caused you and the others to adopt this plan. Secondly, we should make them our guides, since even in a strange land we are not separated from the gods.

2 "We must approach a city that rules so many parts of the earth, and how could one enter it without the gods' guidance? All the more since it has so oppressive a tyranny established inside it that wisdom is forbidden. Let no one think it folly to go cheerfully on a path that many philosophers are shunning. For one thing, I myself do not think that anything on earth could prove so terrifying as ever to dismay a wise man, and besides I would not set up tests of courage that did not involve danger.

3 "Furthermore, I have traveled through more lands than any human ever did, and seen a multitude of beasts in Arabia and India, but as for this beast generally called a tyrant, I have no idea how many heads it has, or whether it has crooked talons and jagged teeth. This beast is said to be urban, and to live in the middle of cities, but its nature is wilder than beasts of mountains or forests in that lions and leopards are sometimes tamed by flattery, and change their ways, whereas this beast is incited by those who

---

35 *θεῶν* Jac.: *ὧν*
36 *οὐδ' ἐν ἀλλοτρίᾳ* Jon.: *οὐδ' ἐν ἄλλῳ* or *οὐδὲν ἄλλο*
37 *προθείην* Rsk.: *προσθείην*
38 *ἀνδρείας* Kay.: *ἀνδρὶ τὰς*

ἐπαιρόμενον ἀγριώτερον αὑτοῦ γίγνεται καὶ λαφύσσει πάντα. περὶ μέν γε θηρίων οὐκ ἂν εἴποις, ὅτι τὰς μητέρας ποτὲ τὰς αὑτῶν ἐδαίσαντο, Νέρων δὲ ἐμπεφόρηται τῆς βορᾶς ταύτης. εἰ δὲ καὶ ταῦτα γέγονεν ἐπ' Ὀρέστῃ καὶ Ἀλκμαίωνι, ἀλλ' ἐκείνοις σχῆμα τοῦ ἔργου πατέρες ἦσαν ὁ μὲν ἀποθανὼν ὑπὸ τῆς ἑαυτοῦ γυναικός, ὁ δὲ ὅρμου πραθείς,

4 "Οὑτοσὶ δὲ καὶ ἐσποιηθεὶς ὑπὸ τῆς μητρὸς γέροντι βασιλεῖ καὶ κληρονομήσας τὸ ἄρχειν ναυαγίῳ τὴν μητέρα ἀπέκτεινε πλοῖον ἐπ' αὐτῇ ξυνθείς, ὑφ' οὗ ἀπώλετο πρὸς τῇ γῇ. εἰ δὲ ἐκ τούτων φοβερόν τις ἡγεῖται Νέρωνα καὶ διὰ τοῦτο ἀποπηδᾷ φιλοσοφίας, οὐκ ἀσφαλὲς αὐτῷ νομίζων τὸ ἀπὸ θυμοῦ τι αὐτῷ πράττειν, ἴστω τὸ μὲν φοβερὸν ἐκείνοις ὑπάρχον, ὅσοιπερ ἂν σωφροσύνης τε καὶ σοφίας ἅπτωνται, τούτοις γὰρ καὶ τὰ παρὰ τῶν θεῶν εὖ ἔχει, τὰ δὲ τῶν ὑβριζόντων ὕθλον ἡγείσθω, καθὰ καὶ τὰ τῶν μεμεθυσμένων, καὶ γὰρ δὴ κἀκείνους γε ἠλιθίους μὲν ἡγούμεθα, φοβεροὺς δὲ οὔ.

5 "'Ἴωμεν οὖν ἐς τὴν Ῥώμην, εἴγε ἐρρώμεθα, πρὸς γὰρ τὰ Νέρωνος κηρύγματα, δι' ὧν ἐξείργει φιλοσοφίαν, ἔστιν ἡμῖν τὸ τοῦ Σοφοκλέους λέγειν[39] 'οὐ γάρ τί μοι Ζεὺς ἦν ὁ κηρύξας τάδε,' οὐδὲ Μοῦσαι καὶ Ἀπόλλων λόγιος. εἰκὸς δὲ καὶ αὐτὸν Νέρωνα γιγνώσκειν τὰ ἰαμβεῖα ταῦτα, τραγῳδίᾳ, ὥς φασι, χαίροντα." ἐνταῦθά τις τὸ Ὁμήρου ἐνθυμηθείς, ὡς, ἐπειδὰν ὁ

[39] λέγειν E. Miller (Kay.): ἐλεγεῖον

stroke it, becomes even more savage than it was before, and devours everything. You could not say of animals that they ever devoured their mothers, whereas Nero has gorged himself on that kind of flesh. It is true the same happened with Orestes and Alcmaeon, but their deeds have an excuse in their fathers, of whom one was killed by his own wife, and the other was bartered for a trinket.[62]

"This man, however, even though his mother caused 4
him to be adopted by a senile emperor, and he inherited the throne, yet he killed his mother by shipwreck, devising a ship for her in which she perished close to land.[63] All this may make some people think Nero terrifying, and that may scare them from philosophy because they think it unsafe to practice something that displeases him. But they should recall that the advantage of terror lies with those who follow moderation and wisdom, since such men are on good terms with the gods, and they should also consider the acts of ruffians insignificant, like the acts of drunkards, since those too we consider foolish rather than menacing.

"So let us proceed to Rome, if we are resolute, and 5
against the pronouncements of Nero banishing philosophy we can say with Sophocles, 'Indeed it was not Zeus that gave this order,'[64] or the Muses or Apollo the Prophet. I suppose Nero himself knows this verse, since they say he is fond of tragedy." At that moment recalling Homer's lines

[62] Orestes killed Clytemnestra to avenge her murder of Agamemnon; Alcmaeon killed his mother Eriphyle when she connived at the death of her husband Amphiaraus in return for a necklace. [63] In fact, Agrippina escaped the shipwreck, but was killed on land that same night. [64] *Antigone* 450.

λόγος ἁρμόσῃ πολεμικοὺς ἄνδρας, μία μὲν κόρυς γίγνονται, μία δὲ ἀσπίς, εὑρεῖν ἄν μοι δοκεῖ αὐτὸ τοῦτο καὶ περὶ τούσδε τοὺς ἄνδρας γενόμενον· ὑπὸ γὰρ τῶν τοῦ Ἀπολλωνίου λόγων ξυγκροτηθέντες ἀποθνήσκειν τε ὑπὲρ φιλοσοφίας ἔρρωντο καὶ βελτίους τῶν ἀποδράντων φαίνεσθαι.

39. Προσῄεσαν μὲν οὖν ταῖς πύλαις, οἱ δὲ ἐφεστῶτες οὐδὲν ἠρώτων, ἀλλὰ περιήθρουν τὸ σχῆμα καὶ ἐθαύμαζον· ὁ γὰρ τρόπος ἱερὸς ἐδόκει καὶ οὐδὲν ἐοικὼς τοῖς ἀγείρουσι. καταλύουσι δ' αὐτοῖς ἐν πανδοχείῳ περὶ τὰς πύλας καὶ δεῖπνον αἱρουμένοις, ἐπειδὴ καιρὸς ἑσπέρας ἤδη ἐτύγχανεν, ἐπὶ κῶμον ἔρχεται μεθύων ἄνθρωπος οὐκ ἀγλευκῶς τῆς φωνῆς ἔχων, περιῄει δὲ ἄρα κύκλῳ τὴν Ῥώμην ᾄδων τὰ τοῦ Νέρωνος μέλη καὶ μεμισθωμένος τοῦτο, τὸν δὲ ἀμελῶς ἀκούσαντα, ἢ μὴ καταβαλόντα μισθὸν τῆς ἀκροάσεως, ξυνεκεχώρητο αὐτῷ καὶ ἀπάγειν ὡς ἀσεβοῦντα. ἦν δὲ αὐτῷ καὶ κιθάρα καὶ ἡ πρόσφορος τῷ κιθαρίζειν σκευὴ πᾶσα, καί τινα καὶ νευρὰν τῶν ἐφαψαμένων τε καὶ προεντεταμένων ἀποκειμένην ἐν κοιτίδι εἶχεν, ἣν ἔφασκεν ἐκ τῆς Νέρωνος ἐωνῆσθαι κιθάρας δυοῖν μναῖν, καὶ ἀποδώσεσθαι αὐτὴν οὐδενί, ἣν μὴ κιθαρῳδὸς ᾖ τῶν ἀρίστων τε καὶ ἀγωνιουμένων Πυθοῖ.

2 Ἀναβαλόμενος οὖν, ὅπως εἰώθει, καὶ βραχὺν διεξελθὼν ὕμνον τοῦ Νέρωνος ἐπῆγε μέλη τὰ μὲν ἐξ Ὀρεστείας, τὰ δὲ ἐξ Ἀντιγόνης, τὰ δ' ὁποθενοῦν[40] τῶν τραγῳδουμένων αὐτῷ, καὶ ᾠδὰς ἔκαμπτεν, ὁπόσας

to the effect that when a speech unites heroes of war, they become "one helmet and one shield,"[65] you might find the same thing happening with these heroes. Welded together by Apollonius's words, they had the resolution to die for philosophy and to show their superiority to the fugitives.

39. When they approached the gates, the guards asked them no question, but simply inspected their clothes in amazement, because their manner was that of holy men and not at all like that of beggars. They had put up at an inn near the gates and were choosing dinner, since it was by now evening, when a drunken man came in merrymaking. He had quite a pleasant voice, and went around Rome singing Nero's songs for pay and making a business out of it. If anybody listened without attention, or refused to pay for the performance, the man was privileged to arrest him for treason. He also had a lyre and all the paraphernalia appropriate for lyre-players. In addition, he kept stored in a box a lyre string that was already strung, which he claimed was from Nero's lyre. He had bought it for two minae, he said, and would not sell it to anybody unless they were first-class lyre players and planning to compete at the Pythian games.

So he struck up in his usual way, and after completing 2
a short hymn in praise of Nero started on solos, some from the *Oresteia*,[66] some from the *Antigone*, and similarly from other plays in which the emperor had performed; and the

[65] *Iliad* 13.131.

[66] Perhaps one of the plays of Sophocles or Euripides concerned with Orestes, rather than the trilogy of Aeschylus.

---

[40] ὁποθενοῦν Cob.: ὅποθεν γοῦν

Νέρων ἐλύγιζέ τε καὶ κακῶς ἔστρεφεν. ἀργότερον δὲ ἀκροωμένων ὁ μὲν ἀσεβεῖσθαι Νέρωνα ὑπ᾽ αὐτῶν ἔφασκε καὶ πολεμίους τῆς θείας φωνῆς εἶναι, οἱ δὲ οὐ προσεῖχον. ἐρομένου δὲ τοῦ Μενίππου τὸν Ἀπολλώνιον, πῶς ἀκούοι λέγοντος ταῦτα, "πῶς" ἔφη "ἢ ὡς ὅτε ᾖδεν; ἡμεῖς μέντοι, ὦ Μένιππε, μὴ παροξυνώμεθα πρὸς ταῦτα, ἀλλὰ τὸν μισθὸν τῆς ἐπιδείξεως δόντες ἐάσωμεν αὐτὸν θύειν ταῖς Νέρωνος Μούσαις."

40. Τοῦτο μὲν δὴ ἐπὶ τοσοῦτον ἐπαρῳνήθη. ἅμα δὲ τῇ ἡμέρᾳ Τελεσῖνος ὁ ἕτερος τῶν ὑπάτων καλέσας τὸν Ἀπολλώνιον "τί" ἔφη "τὸ σχῆμα;" ὁ δὲ "καθαρὸν" εἶπε "καὶ ἀπ᾽ οὐδενὸς θνητοῦ." "τίς δὲ ἡ σοφία;" "θειασμὸς" ἔφη "καὶ ὡς ἄν τις θεοῖς εὔχοιτο καὶ θύοι." "ἔστι δέ τις, ὦ φιλόσοφε, ὃς ἀγνοεῖ ταῦτα;" "πολλοί," εἶπεν "εἰ δὲ καὶ ὀρθῶς τις ἐπίσταται ταῦτα, πολλῷ γένοιτ᾽ ἂν αὑτοῦ βελτίων ἀκούσας σοφωτέρου ἀνδρὸς ὅτι, ἃ οἶδεν, εὖ οἶδεν."

2 Ταῦτα ἀκούοντα τὸν Τελεσῖνον, καὶ γὰρ ἐτύγχανεν ὑποθεραπεύων τὸ θεῖον, ἐσῆλθεν ὁ ἀνὴρ δι᾽ ἃ πάλαι περὶ αὐτοῦ ἤκουε καὶ τὸ μὲν ὄνομα οὐκ ᾤετο δεῖν ἐς τὸ φανερὸν ἐρωτᾶν, μή τιν᾽ ἔτι λανθάνειν βούλοιτο, ἐπανῆγε δὲ αὐτὸν πάλιν ἐς τὸν λόγον τὸν περὶ τοῦ θείου, καὶ γὰρ πρὸς διάλεξιν ἐπιτηδείως εἶχε, καὶ ὡς σοφῷ γε εἶπε "τί εὔχῃ προσιὼν τοῖς βωμοῖς;" "ἔγωγε" ἔφη "δικαιοσύνην εἶναι, νόμους μὴ καταλύεσθαι, πένεσθαι τοὺς σοφούς, τοὺς δὲ ἄλλους πλουτεῖν μέν, ἀδόλως δέ." "εἶτα" εἶπε "τοσαῦτα αἰτῶν οἴει τεύ-

man played all the tortuous melodies that Nero warbled in his ugly coloratura. When the group listened with only half an ear, he claimed that they were showing impiety towards Nero and were enemies of the Divine Voice, but they paid no attention. Menippus asked Apollonius how he could listen to the man saying all this, and Apollonius replied, "Just as I listened to his singing. But let us not get annoyed at all this, Menippus, but pay him for his exhibition, and let him sacrifice to Nero's Muses."

40. That was the end of that outrage. Early the next day Telesinus, one of the two consuls,[67] summoned Apollonius and said, "What is this clothing?" "Pure," said Apollonius, "and made of nothing subject to mortality." "What kind of philosophy do you practice?" "Theology, and how to pray and sacrifice to the gods." "My good philosopher, is there anyone who does not know that?" "Many do not," said Apollonius, "and anybody that does have a proper understanding of these things might be greatly improved if a wiser master told him that what he knows he truly knows."

Telesinus was rather given to cultivating the higher 2
powers, and when he heard this, he recognized the Master from what he had long since heard about him. He thought it better not to ask his name openly, in case Apollonius wished somebody not to know it yet, and so brought him back to the subject of the gods, as he was well trained in discussion. Treating Apollonius as a wise man, he said, "What do you pray when approaching the altars?" "I," said Apollonius, "pray that justice may be done, that laws be not broken, that wise men may be poor and all others may enjoy wealth, but honestly." "Do you think you will

[67] C. Luccius Telesinus, consul for the year 66.

ξεσθαι;" "νὴ Δί'," εἶπε "ξυνείρω γὰρ τὰ πάντα ἐς εὐχὴν μίαν καὶ προσιὼν τοῖς βωμοῖς ὧδε εὔχομαι· 'ὦ θεοί, δοίητέ μοι τὰ ὀφειλόμενα.' εἰ μὲν δὴ τῶν χρηστῶν εἰμι ἀνθρώπων, τεύξομαι πλειόνων ἢ εἶπον, εἰ δὲ ἐν τοῖς φαύλοις με οἱ θεοὶ τάττουσι, τἀναντία μοι παρ' αὐτῶν ἥξει, καὶ οὐ μέμψομαι τοὺς θεοὺς εἰ κακῶν ἀξιοῦμαι μὴ χρηστὸς ὤν."

3 Ἐξεπέπληκτο μὲν δὴ ὁ Τελεσῖνος ὑπὸ τῶν λόγων τούτων, βουλόμενος δὲ αὐτῷ χαρίζεσθαι "φοίτα" ἔφη "ἐς τὰ ἱερὰ πάντα, καὶ γεγράψεται παρ' ἐμοῦ πρὸς τοὺς ἱερωμένους δέχεσθαί σε καὶ διορθουμένῳ εἴκειν." "ἢν δὲ μὴ γράψῃς," ἔφη "οὐ δέξονταί με;" "μὰ Δί'," εἶπεν "ἐμὴ γὰρ [ἔφη][41] αὕτη ἀρχή." "χαίρω," ἔφη "ὅτι γενναῖος ὢν μεγάλου ἄρχεις, βουλοίμην δ' ἄν σε κἀκεῖνο περὶ ἐμοῦ εἰδέναι· ἐγὼ τῶν ἱερῶν τὰ μὴ βεβαίως κλειστὰ χαίρω οἰκῶν καὶ παραιτεῖταί με οὐδεὶς τῶν θεῶν, ἀλλὰ ποιοῦνται κοινωνὸν στέγης. ἀνείσθω δέ μοι καὶ τοῦτο, καὶ γὰρ οἱ βάρβαροι ξυνεχώρουν αὐτό." καὶ ὁ Τελεσῖνος "μέγα" ἔφη "Ῥωμαίων ἐγκώμιον οἱ βάρβαροι προὔλαβον, τουτὶ γὰρ ἐβουλόμην ἂν καὶ περὶ ἡμῶν λέγεσθαι."

4 Ὤικει μὲν δὴ ἐν τοῖς ἱεροῖς, ἐναλλάττων αὐτὰ καὶ μεθιστάμενος ἐξ ἄλλου ἐς ἄλλο, αἰτίαν δὲ ἐπὶ τούτῳ ἔχων "οὐδὲ οἱ θεοὶ" ἔφη "πάντα τὸν χρόνον ἐν τῷ οὐρανῷ οἰκοῦσιν, ἀλλὰ πορεύονται μὲν ἐς Αἰθιοπίαν, πορεύονται δὲ ἐς Ὄλυμπόν τε καὶ Ἄθω, καὶ οἶμαι ἄτοπον τοὺς μὲν θεοὺς τὰ τῶν ἀνθρώπων ἔθνη περινοστεῖν πάντα, τοὺς δὲ ἀνθρώπους μὴ τοῖς θεοῖς

be granted so many prayers, then?" asked Telesinus. "Of course," replied Apollonius, "because I include them all in one prayer, and when I approach the altars asking for this, this is my prayer: 'Gods, give me my deserts.' If I am a good person, I will get more than what I mentioned, but if the gods count me among the wicked, they will give me the opposite. I will not blame the gods for thinking me to deserve evil, if in fact I am not good."

Telesinus was struck by these doctrines, and to do Apollonius a favor said, "You may visit any shrine, and I will write to the priests, telling them to welcome you and to accede to your improvements." "And if you do not write," said Apollonius, "will they not welcome me?" "Certainly not," he replied, "that is for my office to determine." "I am glad," said Apollonius, "that as a virtuous man you have an important office, but there is something else about me I would have you know. I like to live in any sanctuary that is not completely closed, and none of the gods refuses me, but they let me share their roof. Please grant me this too, since even the barbarians granted it." Telesinus replied, "The barbarians have anticipated the Romans in a very praiseworthy deed, for I would like the same to be said of us too." 3

Apollonius therefore lived in the sanctuaries, moving and changing from one to another. When criticized for this, he said, "Even the gods do not spend all their time dwelling in heaven, but travel to Ethiopia, to Olympus, and to Athos. I think it absurd that the gods circulate among all the haunts of mankind, while men do not visit all the 4

---

41 [ἔφη] secl. West.

ἐπιφοιτᾶν πᾶσι. καίτοι δεσπόται μὲν ὑπερορῶντες δούλων οὔπω αἰτίαν ἕξουσιν, ἴσως γὰρ ἂν καταφρονοῖεν αὐτῶν, ὡς μὴ σπουδαίων, δοῦλοι δὲ μὴ πάντως τοὺς αὐτῶν δεσπότας θεραπεύοντες ἀπόλοιντο ἂν ὑπ᾽ αὐτῶν ὡς κατάρατοί τε καὶ θεοῖς ἐχθρὰ ἀνδράποδα."

41. Διαλεγομένου δὲ αὐτοῦ περὶ τὰ ἱερὰ οἱ θεοὶ ἐθεραπεύοντο μᾶλλον καὶ ξυνῄεσαν οἱ ἄνθρωποι ἐς ταῦτα, ὡς τὰ ἀγαθὰ πλείω παρὰ τῶν θεῶν ἕξοντες, καὶ οὔπω διεβάλλοντο αἱ ξυνουσίαι τοῦ ἀνδρὸς διὰ τὸ σπουδάζεσθαί τε δημοσίᾳ λέγεσθαί τε ἐς πάντας. οὐδὲ γὰρ θύραις ἐπεπόλαζεν, οὐδὲ ἐτρίβετο περὶ τοὺς δυνατούς, ἀλλ᾽ ἠσπάζετο μὲν ἐπιφοιτῶντας, διελέγετο δὲ αὐτοῖς ὁπόσα καὶ τῷ δήμῳ.

42. Ἐπεὶ δὲ ὁ Δημήτριος διατεθεὶς πρὸς αὐτόν, ὡς ἐν τοῖς Κορινθιακοῖς λόγοις εἴρηκα, παραγενόμενος ἐς τὴν Ῥώμην ὕστερον ἐθεράπευε μὲν τὸν Ἀπολλώνιον, ἐπηφίει δ᾽ αὐτὸν τῷ Νέρωνι, τέχνη ταῦτα ὑπωπτεύθη τοῦ ἀνδρός, καὶ τὸν Δημήτριον αὐτὸς ἐδόκει καθεικέναι ἐς αὐτά, καὶ πολὺ μᾶλλον, ὁπότε γυμνάσιον μὲν ἐξεποιήθη τῷ Νέρωνι θαυμασιώτατον τῶν ἐκεῖ, λευκὴν δ᾽ ἔθυον ἐν αὐτῷ ἡμέραν Νέρων τε αὐτὸς καὶ ἡ βουλὴ ἡ μεγάλη καὶ τὸ ἱππεῦον τῆς Ῥώμης, παρελθὼν δὲ ὁ Δημήτριος ἐς αὐτὸ τὸ γυμνάσιον διεξῆλθε λόγον κατὰ τῶν λουμένων, ὡς ἐκλελυμένων τε καὶ αὑτοὺς χραινόντων, καὶ ἐδείκνυεν, ὅτι περιττὸν ἀνάλωμα εἴη τὰ τοιαῦτα. ἐφ᾽ οἷς ξυνήρατο μὲν αὐτῷ μὴ ἀποθανεῖν αὐτίκα τὸ τὸν Νέρωνα εὐφωνότατα ἑαυτοῦ κατὰ τὴν ἡμέραν ἐκείνην ᾄδειν,

gods. Moreover, masters who neglect their slaves are not blamed, since perhaps they neglect them for being no good, but servants that did not show all due respect to their masters would be killed by them as accursed and as damned chattels."

41. When he discoursed in the sanctuaries, the gods received more worship, and people came to these places thinking to receive more blessings from the gods. The Master's conversations were not yet suspect, because they were conducted openly and held with everybody. He did not hang about other men's doors, or spend time with the powerful, but greeted them if they visited him, and conversed with them as he did with ordinary people.

42. When however Demetrius, whose attitude towards him I have mentioned in my account of Corinth, arrived in Rome later, he cultivated Apollonius but attacked Nero. This was believed to be a ruse of the Master, who was thought to be inciting Demetrius to this course deliberately. This got worse when Nero completed a gymnasium that was the most amazing there.[68] Nero himself with the Great Council and the knights of Rome was sacrificing there during a holiday, when Demetrius came right into the gymnasium and declaimed a speech against bathers, saying that they were effeminates who defiled themselves. Such things he tried to show were a useless extravagance. After that, he was saved from summary execution by the fact that Nero was in his best singing voice that day. He

[68] This building burned down in 62 (Tacitus, *Annals* 15.22), whereas the present incident is supposed to have taken place in 66. It may, however, have been rebuilt after the Great Fire of 64.

ᾖδε δὲ ἐν καπηλείῳ πεποιημένῳ ἐς τὸ γυμνάσιον διάζωμα ἔχων γυμνός, ὥσπερ τῶν καπήλων οἱ ἀσελγέστατοι.

2 Οὐ μὴν διέφυγεν ὁ Δημήτριος τὸ ἐφ᾽ οἷς εἶπε κινδυνεῦσαι, Τιγελλῖνος γάρ, ὑφ᾽ ᾧ τὸ ξίφος ἦν τοῦ Νέρωνος, ἀπήλαυνεν αὐτὸν τῆς Ῥώμης, ὡς τὸ βαλανεῖον κατασκάψαντα οἷς εἶπε, τὸν δ᾽ Ἀπολλώνιον ἀφανῶς ἀνίχνευεν, ὁπότε καὶ αὐτὸς ἐπιλήψιμόν τι καὶ παραβεβλημένον εἴποι.

43. Ὁ δ᾽ οὔτε καταγελῶν φανερὸς ἦν οὔτ᾽ αὖ πεφροντικώς, ὥσπερ οἱ φυλαττόμενοί τινα κίνδυνον, ἀλλ᾽ ἀποχρώντως περὶ τῶν προκειμένων διελέγετο, ξυμφιλοσοφοῦντος αὐτῷ τοῦ Τελεσίνου καὶ ἑτέρων ἀνδρῶν, οἳ καίτοι φιλοσοφίας ἐπικινδύνως πραττούσης οὐκ ἂν ᾤοντο κινδυνεῦσαι ξὺν ἐκείνῳ σπουδάζοντες. ὑπωπτεύετο δέ, ὡς ἔφην, καὶ πολὺ μᾶλλον ἐφ᾽ οἷς καὶ περὶ τῆς διοσημίας εἶπε· γενομένης γάρ ποτε ἐκλείψεως ἡλίου καὶ βροντῆς ἐκδοθείσης, ὅπερ ἥκιστα ἐν ἐκλείψει δοκεῖ ξυμβαίνειν, ἀναβλέψας ἐς τὸν οὐρανὸν "ἔσται τι" ἔφη "μέγα, καὶ οὐκ ἔσται."

2 Ξυμβαλεῖν μὲν δὴ τὸ εἰρημένον οὔπω εἶχον οἱ παρατυχόντες τῷ λόγῳ, τρίτῃ δ᾽ ἀπὸ τῆς ἐκλείψεως ἡμέρᾳ ξυνῆκαν τοῦ λόγου πάντες. σιτουμένου γὰρ τοῦ Νέρωνος, ἐμπεσὼν τῇ τραπέζῃ σκηπτὸς διήλασε τῆς κύλικος ἐν χεροῖν οὔσης καὶ οὐ πολὺ ἀπεχούσης τοῦ στόματος. τὸ δὴ παρὰ τοσοῦτον ἐλθεῖν τοῦ βληθῆναι αὐτὸν πεπράξεσθαί τι εἶπε καὶ μὴ πεπράξεσθαι. ἀκούσας δὲ Τιγελλῖνος τὸν λόγον τοῦτον ἐς δέος ἀφίκετο

sang in a tavern built next to the gymnasium, naked except for a loincloth, like the most shameless publican.

Even so Demetrius did not escape danger for his speech, since Tigellinus, who had the command of Nero's sword,[69] expelled him from Rome for ruining the bathhouse with his speech. He also had Apollonius secretly followed, expecting that he too might say something criminal and careless. 2

43. But Apollonius was not to be seen either making light of this or worried, like a man guarding against some danger, but fully discussed the subject at hand with Telesinus and others as his participants. These thought that, even if philosophy was in a dangerous position, they would run no risk studying with Apollonius. But he incurred suspicion, as I said, and much more so after saying something about an omen. An eclipse of the sun occurred together with a clap of thunder, something considered very unusual in an eclipse. Apollonius looked up at the sky and said, "Something momentous is going to happen and not to happen."

Those present when he said this could not immediately interpret his words, but three days after the eclipse they all understood the meaning. When Nero was at dinner, a thunderbolt hit the table, splitting a cup that he had in his hands not far from his lips. It was his coming close to being struck that Apollonius meant as something that would happen and not happen. When Tigellinus heard this story, he 2

[69] Ofonius Tigellinus, much feared prefect of the Praetorian Guard from 62 to 68.

τοῦ ἀνδρός, ὡς σοφοῦ τὰ δαιμόνια, καὶ ἐς ἐγκλήματα μὲν φανερὰ καθίστασθαι πρὸς αὐτὸν οὐκ ᾤετο δεῖν, ὡς μὴ κακόν τι ἀφανὲς ὑπ' αὐτοῦ λάβοι, διαλεγόμενον δὲ καὶ σιωπῶντα, καὶ καθήμενον καὶ βαδίζοντα, καὶ ὅ τι φάγοι καὶ παρ' ὅτῳ,[42] καὶ εἰ ἔθυσεν ἢ μὴ ἔθυσε, περιήθρει πᾶσιν ὀφθαλμοῖς, ὁπόσοις ἡ ἀρχὴ βλέπει.

44. Ἐμπεσόντος δὲ ἐν Ῥώμῃ νοσήματος, ὃ κατάρρουν οἱ ἰατροὶ ὀνομάζουσιν, ἀνίστανται δὲ ἄρα ὑπ' αὐτοῦ βῆχες καὶ ἡ φωνὴ τοῖς λαλοῦσι πονήρως ἔχει, τὰ μὲν ἱερὰ πλέα ἦν ἱκετευόντων τοὺς θεούς, ἐπεὶ διῳδήκει τὴν φάρυγγα Νέρων καὶ μελαίνῃ τῇ φωνῇ ἐχρῆτο. ὁ δὲ Ἀπολλώνιος ἐρρήγνυτο μὲν πρὸς τὴν τῶν πολλῶν ἄνοιαν, ἐπέπληττε δὲ οὐδενί, ἀλλὰ καὶ τὸν Μένιππον παροξυνόμενον ὑπὸ τῶν τοιούτων ἐσωφρόνιζέ τε καὶ κατεῖχε, ξυγγιγνώσκειν κελεύων τοῖς θεοῖς εἰ μίμοις γελοίων χαίρουσιν. ἀπαγγελθέντος δὲ τῷ Τιγελλίνῳ τοῦ λόγου τούτου, πέμπει τοὺς ἄξοντας αὐτὸν ἐς τὸ δικαστήριον, ὡς ἀπολογήσαιτο μὴ ἀσεβεῖν ἐς Νέρωνα,

2 Παρεσκεύαστο δὲ καὶ κατήγορος ἐπ' αὐτὸν πολλοὺς ἀπολωλεκὼς ἤδη καὶ τοιούτων Ὀλυμπιάδων μεστός, καί τι καὶ γραμματεῖον εἶχεν ἐν ταῖν χεροῖν γεγραμμένον τὸ ἔγκλημα, καὶ τοῦτο ὥσπερ ξίφος ἀνασείων ἐπὶ τὸν ἄνδρα ἠκονῆσθαί τε αὐτὸ ἔλεγε καὶ ἀπολεῖν αὐτόν. ἐπεὶ δὲ ἀνελίττων Τιγελλῖνος τὸ γραμματεῖον γραμμῆς μὲν ἴχνος ἐν αὐτῷ οὐχ εὗρεν, ἀσήμῳ δέ τινι βιβλίῳ ἐνέτυχεν, ἐς ἔννοιαν ἀπηνέχθη δαίμονος. (τουτὶ δὲ καὶ Δομετιανὸς ὕστερον πρὸς αὐτὸν

began to fear the Master as an expert in supernatural matters. He did not think he should bring charges against him in case he did him some invisible harm. But as Apollonius conversed, spoke or was silent, as he sat or walked, whatever he ate and with whom, when he sacrificed or did not sacrifice, Tigellinus was spying with all the eyes by which his office sees.

44. Rome had an attack of the illness called by doctors catarrh. It causes a cough and talking makes the voice hoarse. The sanctuaries were full of people praying to the gods, since Nero's throat was swollen and his voice was thick. Apollonius fumed at the general madness, but criticized nobody, and in fact when Menippus expressed outrage at these events, he restrained and checked him, advising him to pardon the gods for enjoying the capers of buffoons. This remark was reported to Tigellinus, who sent men to bring Apollonius to court so as to answer a charge of impiety towards Nero.

Prepared against him was an accuser who had already 2
caused the deaths of many, and had a pile of such trophies. This man had a paper in his hands with the charge written on it, and he brandished it at the Master like a sword, saying that it had been sharpened and would finish him off. But on unrolling the paper Tigellinus found no trace of writing on it, and instead was confronted by a blank sheet, so that he suspected a demon. (Apollonius is later said to

42 ὅτῳ Rsk.: ὅτου

λέγεται παθεῖν.) ἀπολαβὼν οὖν τὸν Ἀπολλώνιον ἤνεγκεν ἐς τὸ ἀπόρρητον δικαστήριον, ἐν ᾧ περὶ τῶν μεγίστων ἡ ἀρχὴ αὕτη ἀφανῶς δικάζει, καὶ μεταστησάμενος πάντας ἐνέκειτο ἐρωτῶν, ὅστις εἴη, ὁ δὲ Ἀπολλώνιος πατρός τε ἐμέμνητο καὶ πατρίδος, καὶ ἐφ' ὅ τι τῇ σοφίᾳ χρῷτο, ἔφασκέ τε αὐτῇ χρῆσθαι ἐπί τε τὸ[43] θεοὺς γιγνώσκειν ἐπί τε τὸ ἀνθρώπων[44] ξυνιέναι, τοῦ γὰρ ἑαυτὸν γνῶναι χαλεπώτερον εἶναι τὸ ἄλλον γνῶναι.

3 "Τοὺς <δὲ>[45] δαίμονας," εἶπεν "ὦ Ἀπολλώνιε, καὶ τὰς τῶν εἰδώλων φαντασίας πῶς ἐλέγχεις;" "ὥς γε" ἔφη "τοὺς μιαιφόνους τε καὶ ἀσεβεῖς ἀνθρώπους." ταυτὶ δὲ πρὸς τὸν Τιγελλῖνον ἀποσκοπῶν[46] ἔλεγεν, ἐπειδὴ πάσης ὠμότητός τε καὶ ἀσελγείας διδάσκαλος ἦν τῷ Νέρωνι. "μαντεύσαιο δ' ἂν" ἔφη "δεηθέντι μοι;" "πῶς" εἶπεν "ὅ γε μὴ μάντις ὤν;" "καὶ μὴν σὲ" ἔφη "φασὶν εἶναι τὸν εἰπόντα ἔσεσθαί τι μέγα καὶ οὐκ ἔσεσθαι." "ἀληθῶς" εἶπεν "ἤκουσας, τοῦτο δὲ μὴ μαντικῇ προστίθει, σοφίᾳ δὲ μᾶλλον, ἣν θεὸς φαίνει σοφοῖς ἀνδράσιν." "Νέρωνα δὲ" ἔφη "διὰ τί οὐ δέδοικας;" "ὅτι" εἶπεν "ὁ θεὸς ὁ παρέχων ἐκείνῳ φοβερῷ δοκεῖν κἀμοὶ δέδωκεν ἀφόβῳ εἶναι."

4 "Φρονεῖς δὲ πῶς" εἶπε "περὶ Νέρωνος;" ὁ δὲ Ἀπολλώνιος "βέλτιον" εἶπεν "ἢ ὑμεῖς· ὑμεῖς γὰρ ἡγεῖσθε αὐτὸν ἄξιον τοῦ ᾄδειν, ἐγὼ δὲ ἄξιον τοῦ σιωπᾶν." ἐκπλαγεὶς οὖν ὁ Τιγελλῖνος "ἄπιθι" ἔφη "καταστήσας ἐγγυητὰς τοῦ σώματος." ὁ δὲ Ἀπολλώνιος "καὶ τίς" εἶπεν "ἐγγυήσεται σῶμα, ὃ μηδεὶς δήσει;" ἔδοξε τῷ

have had the same effect on Domitian.) So he took him off to his closed court, where the holders of this office judge matters of state in private. Dismissing everyone, he pressed Apollonius with questions about himself. Apollonius named his father, his city, and his purpose in studying wisdom. He practiced it, he said, in order to know the gods and to understand humanity, since knowing oneself was less difficult than knowing someone else.

"But demons and ghostly phantoms, Apollonius," asked 3
Tigellinus, "how do you unmask them?" "The way I unmask murderous and impious humans," he replied with a hint at Tigellinus, who was Nero's instructor in every kind of cruelty and profligacy. "Would you give me a prophecy," he said, "if I asked you?" "How can I," replied Apollonius, "not being a prophet?" "Yet they say," he replied, "that you are the one who said that something momentous would happen and not happen." "What you have heard is true, but do not ascribe it to prophecy, but rather to the wisdom which god reveals to wise men." "And why is it that you do not fear Nero?" he said. "Because god," replied Apollonius, "who granted him a fearful appearance has also granted me immunity from fear."

"And what is your attitude to Nero?" asked Tigellinus. 4
"Better than yours," was the reply. "You people think he deserves to sing, but I think he deserves to keep quiet." In amazement Tigellinus said, "You may leave, but give bondsmen for your person." "Who will go bond," asked Apollonius, "for a person that no one can imprison?" Tigel-

---

43 τὸ (bis) Kay.: τῷ 44 ἀνθρώπων Kay.: ἀνδρῶν

45 <δὲ> Jon.

46 ἀποσκοπῶν Kay.: ἀποσκώπτων

Τιγελλίνῳ ταῦτα δαιμόνιά τε εἶναι καὶ πρόσω ἀνθρώπου, καὶ ὥσπερ θεομαχεῖν φυλαττόμενος, "χώρει", ἔφη "οἷ βούλει, σὺ γὰρ κρείττων ἢ ὑπ' ἐμοῦ ἄρχεσθαι."

45. Κἀκεῖνο Ἀπολλωνίου θαῦμα· κόρη ἐν ὥρᾳ γάμου τεθνάναι ἐδόκει καὶ ὁ νυμφίος ἠκολούθει τῇ κλίνῃ βοῶν ὁπόσα ἐπ' ἀτελεῖ γάμῳ, ξυνωλοφύρετο δὲ καὶ ἡ Ῥώμη, καὶ γὰρ ἐτύγχανεν οἰκίας ἡ κόρη τελούσης ἐς ὑπάτους. παρατυχὼν οὖν ὁ Ἀπολλώνιος τῷ πάθει "κατάθεσθε" ἔφη "τὴν κλίνην, ἐγὼ γὰρ ὑμᾶς τῶν ἐπὶ τῇ κόρῃ δακρύων παύσω." καὶ ἅμα ἤρετο, ὅ τι ὄνομα αὐτῇ εἴη. οἱ μὲν δὴ πολλοὶ ᾤοντο λόγον ἀγορεύσειν αὐτόν, οἷοι τῶν λόγων οἱ ἐπικήδειοί τε καὶ τὰς ὀλοφύρσεις ἐγείροντες, ὁ δὲ οὐδὲν ἀλλ' ἢ προσαψάμενος αὐτῆς καί τι ἀφανῶς ἐπειπὼν ἀφύπνισε τὴν κόρην τοῦ δοκοῦντος θανάτου, καὶ φωνήν τε ἡ παῖς ἀφῆκεν, ἐπανῆλθέ τε ἐς τὴν οἰκίαν τοῦ πατρός ὥσπερ ἡ Ἄλκηστις ὑπὸ τοῦ Ἡρακλέους ἀναβιωθεῖσα.

2 Δωρουμένων δὲ αὐτῷ τῶν ξυγγενῶν τῆς κόρης μυριάδας δεκαπέντε, φερνὴν ἔφη ἐπιδιδόναι αὐτὰς τῇ παιδί. καὶ εἴτε σπινθῆρα τῆς ψυχῆς εὗρεν ἐν αὐτῇ, ὃς ἐλελήθει τοὺς θεραπεύοντας (λέγεται γὰρ ὡς ψεκάζοι μὲν ὁ Ζεύς, ἡ δὲ ἀτμίζοι ἀπὸ τοῦ προσώπου), εἴτ' ἀπεσβηκυῖαν τὴν ψυχὴν ἀνέθαλψέ τε καὶ ἀνέλαβεν, ἄρρητος ἡ κατάληψις τούτου γέγονεν οὐκ ἐμοὶ μόνῳ, ἀλλὰ καὶ τοῖς παρατυχοῦσιν.

46. Ἐτύγχανε δὲ περὶ τὸν χρόνον τοῦτον καὶ Μου-

linus decided that these words were supernatural and superhuman, and as if reluctant to fight a god he said, "Go where you like, for you are too powerful to be ruled by me."

45. Apollonius performed another miracle. There was a girl who appeared to have died just at the time of her wedding. The betrothed followed the bier, with all the lamentations of an unconsummated marriage, and Rome mourned with him, since the girl belonged to a consular family.[70] Meeting with this scene of sorrow, Apollonius said, "Put the bier down, for I will end your crying over the girl." At the same time he asked her name, which made most people think he was going to declaim a speech of the kind delivered at funerals to raise lamentation. But Apollonius, after merely touching her and saying something secretly, woke the bride from her apparent death. The girl spoke, and went back to her father's house like Alcestis revived by Heracles.[71]

Her kinsmen wanted to give Apollonius a hundred and 2
fifty thousand drachmas, but he said he gave it as an extra dowry for the girl. He may have seen a spark of life in her which the doctors had not noticed, since apparently the sky was drizzling and steam was coming from her face, or he may have revived and restored her life when it was extinguished, but the explanation of this has proved unfathomable, not just to me but to the bystanders.

46. It was at that time that Musonius was confined in

[70] I.e. with a consul in her immediate family. Compare the similar story about Jesus and a young girl, Mark 5.35–43.

[71] Alcestis, wife of the Thessalian king Admetus, was rescued from the underworld by Heracles.

σώνιος κατειλημμένος ἐν τοῖς δεσμωτηρίοις τοῦ Νέρωνος, ὅν φασι τελεώτατα ἀνθρώπων φιλοσοφῆσαι, καὶ φανερῶς μὲν οὐ διελέγοντο ἀλλήλοις, παραιτησαμένου τοῦ Μουσωνίου τοῦτο, ὡς μὴ ἄμφω κινδυνεύσειαν, ἐπιστολιμαίους δὲ τὰς ξυνουσίας ἐποιοῦντο φοιτῶντος ἐς τὸ δεσμωτήριον τοῦ Μενίππου καὶ τοῦ Δάμιδος. τὰς δὲ οὐχ ὑπὲρ μεγάλων ἐπιστολὰς ἐάσαντες τὰς ἀναγκαίας παραθησόμεθα κἀξ ὧν ὑπάρχει κατιδεῖν τι μέγα.

2 "Ἀπολλώνιος Μουσωνίῳ φιλοσόφῳ χαίρειν. βούλομαι παρὰ σὲ ἀφικόμενος κοινωνῆσαί σοι λόγου καὶ στέγης, ὥς τι ὀνήσαιμί σε. εἴ γε μὴ ἀπιστεῖς, ὡς Ἡρακλῆς ποτε Θησέα ἐξ Ἅιδου ἔλυσε, γράφε, τί βούλει. ἔρρωσο."

3 "Μουσώνιος Ἀπολλωνίῳ φιλοσόφῳ χαίρειν. ὧν μὲν ἐνενοήθης, ἀποκείσεταί σοι ἔπαινος, ἀνὴρ δὲ ὁ ὑπομείνας ἀπολογίαν καὶ ὡς οὐδὲν ἀδικεῖ δείξας ἑαυτὸν λύει. ἔρρωσο."

4 "Ἀπολλώνιος Μουσωνίῳ φιλοσόφῳ χαίρειν. Σωκράτης Ἀθηναῖος ὑπὸ τῶν ἑαυτοῦ φίλων λυθῆναι μὴ βουληθεὶς παρῆλθε μὲν ἐς δικαστήριον, ἀπέθανε δέ. ἔρρωσο."

5 "Μουσώνιος Ἀπολλωνίῳ φιλοσόφῳ χαίρειν. Σωκράτης ἀπέθανεν, ἐπεὶ μὴ παρεσκεύασεν ἐς ἀπολογίαν ἑαυτόν, ἐγὼ δὲ ἀπολογήσομαι. ἔρρωσο."

47. Ἐξελαύνοντος δὲ ἐς τὴν Ἑλλάδα τοῦ Νέρωνος καὶ προκηρύξαντος δημοσίᾳ μηδένα ἐμφιλοσοφεῖν τῇ Ῥώμῃ, τρέπεται ὁ Ἀπολλώνιος ἐπὶ τὰ ἑσπέρια τῆς

Nero's prisons. He is reputed to have been the truest philosopher that ever was. The two of them did not converse openly, since Musonius was opposed to that in case it endangered them both. They conversed by letter through visits of Menippus and Damis to the prison. The letters that concern unimportant subjects I will omit, and transcribe the essential ones and those that allow something essential to appear.[72]

"Apollonius greets Musonius the philosopher. I wish to 2
come to you and share your conversation and your roof so as to help you, at least if you admit that Heracles once liberated Theseus from Hades. Write and tell me your wish. Goodbye."

"Musonius greets Apollonius the philosopher. Praise 3
awaits you for your intentions. But a true man who undertakes his defense and proves his innocence is his own liberator. Goodbye."

"Apollonius greets Musonius the philosopher. Socrates 4
of Athens preferred not to be liberated by his friends, and so came to trial, but died. Goodbye."

"Musonius greets Apollonius the philosopher. Socrates 5
died because he was not prepared to defend himself, but I will defend myself. Goodbye."

47. Nero was departing for Greece, and had issued a general edict that no one was to teach philosophy in Rome. Apollonius therefore turned his thoughts towards

[72] These letters are preserved independently as nos. 42b–e of the *Letters*.

γῆς, ἅ φασιν ὁρίζεσθαι ταῖς Στήλαις, τὰς ἀμπώτεις τοῦ Ὠκεανοῦ ἐποψόμενος καὶ τὰ Γάδειρα. καὶ γάρ τι καὶ περὶ φιλοσοφίας τῶν ἐκείνῃ ἀνθρώπων ἤκουεν, ὡς ἐς πολὺ τοῦ θείου προηκόντων, ἠκολούθησαν δὲ αὐτῷ οἱ γνώριμοι πάντες, ἐπαινοῦντες καὶ τὴν ἀποδημίαν καὶ τὸν ἄνδρα.

the western part of the world, of which they say the Pillars are the limit. He planned to see the Ocean tides and Gadeira, and he had also heard something about the love of wisdom of the people there and their high degree of sanctity. All his pupils followed him, praising the expedition as well as the Master.